THE · URBAN · WORLD

FIFTH EDITION

J. JOHN PALEN
Virginia Commonwealth University

The McGraw-Hill Companies, Inc.
New York   St. Louis   San Francisco   Auckland   Bogotá   Caracas
Lisbon   London   Madrid   Mexico City   Milan   Montreal   New Delhi
San Juan   Singapore   Sydney   Tokyo   Toronto

For Madeleine and Jack
who will grow up in an urban world

McGraw-Hill

A Division of The McGraw·Hill Companies

The Urban World

Copyright © 1997, 1992, 1987, 1981, 1975 by The McGraw-Hill Companies, Inc. All rights reserved. Printed in the United States of America. Except as permitted under the United States Copyright Act of 1976, no part of this publication may be reproduced or distributed in any form, or by any means, or stored in a data base or retrieval system, without the prior written permission of the publisher.

This book is printed on acid-free paper.

2 3 4 5 6 7 8 9 0 DOC DOC 9 0 9 8 7

ISBN 0-07-048168-7

This book was set in Times Roman by Graphic World, Inc.
The editor was Jill S. Gordon;
the production supervisor was Denise L. Puryear.
The design manager was Charles A. Carson.
The cover was designed by Lisa Cicchetti.
The photo editor was Inge King.
Project supervision was done by The Total Book.
R. R. Donnelley & Sons Company was printer and binder.

Credit for Part Opening Photograph/Atlanta Convention and Visitors Bureau.

Library of Congress Cataloging-in-Publication Data

Palen, J. John.
   The urban world / J. John Palen.—5th ed.
      p.   cm.
   ISBN 0-07-048168-7
   1. Cities and towns.   2. Cities and towns—United States.
3. Urbanization—Developing countries.   I. Title.
HT151P283 1997
307.76—dc20

CONTENTS

Part Four: Problems, Housing, and Planning 295

Part Five: Worldwide Urbanization 371

LIST OF SPECIAL SECTIONS

ABOUT THE AUTHOR

J. John Palen is Professor of Sociology at Virginia Commonwealth University, where in 1994 he received the College's Distinguished Scholar Award. His primary research interests are patterns of suburbanization and gentrification in the United States, and comparative urbanization in Southeast Asia. One of his recent books, *The Suburbs,* was published by The McGraw-Hill Companies in 1995. Palen is a Civil War buff who enjoys hiking in Virginia's Blue Ridge Mountains and observing the street life and social organization of any large city.

PREFACE

The fifth edition of *The Urban World* represents an extensive and detailed revision of this widely used text. The fifth edition brings the range of urban changes up to the new century. Of course, selectivity is both inevitable and necessary. The topics included here and the emphasis they receive reflect the state of social science knowledge, my own interests, and a conscious effort to provide for the needs of students with different backgrounds and interests. There has also been a conscious attempt to explore emerging developments. A textbook should reflect contemporary developments rather than simply rehash stale issues of decades past. There is a substantially new chapter on suburbs titled, "Changing Suburbanization Patterns," which reflects new developments. A new chapter also has been added discussing the changing roles of women in urban and suburban places, titled "Women in Metropolitan Life." This chapter has been written by colleagues Christine Wright-Isak and Sylvia Fava.

The fifth edition contains revised chapters on "Urban Political Economy," "Metropolitan and Edge-City Growth," and "Housing and the Community." The first of these was especially written for this book by colleagues David Smith and Michael Timberlake. In order to provide students greater theoretical insight, the chapter on "Urban Political Economy" directly follows the discussion of ecological models.

Every chapter has been rewritten to reflect new research findings and recent demographic and social changes. More than half the pages contain updates or new research. Examples of changes are new discussions of suburban economic and demographic dominance, the growth of Hispanic populations during the next decade to become the nation's largest minority population, and the effective end of federally sponsored public housing. Throughout the text, the latest available figures have been used. Additionally, a half dozen maps have been included to increase reader understanding. Hopefully, the overall result is a volume that has organizational continuity with earlier editions while containing substantially new and updated material.

The goal of this new edition is to convey to students the excitement I feel when studying our changing urban environment. The goal is to give a student having little formal exposure to urban sociology and urban studies a coherent overview of the urban scene, while providing the most up-to-date information on urbanization and the nature of urban life as the century turns.

I find that reviewers play an important role in the development of a manuscript. This fifth edition benefited from the comments of Robert L. Boyd, SUNY at Buffalo; William M. Cross, Illinois College; Susan A. Farrell, Kingsborough Community College; Geoffry Grant, South Dakota State University; Jan C. Lin, University of Houston; Patrick McNamara, University of New Mexico; and Dale R. Spady, Northern Michigan University. Contributions to earlier editions were made by James Bessers, Ed Borgatta, Harvey Choldin, Thomas Drabek, Gary Crester, William Cross, William Engelman, Scott Greer, George Hesslink, Christen Jonassen, Michael Lang, Bruce London, William Michelson, Ephraim Mizruchi, Alex Muntean, Leo Schnore, Daphne Spain, John Stahura, and Ralph Tonlinson.

Finally, special thanks go to Phillip Butcher as publisher, Jill Gordon as sponsoring editor, Kate Scheinman as project supervisor, and Inge King as photo editor. It was my good fortune to again be able to work with such fine professionals. Invariably even the most carefully edited work contains errors of omission or commission. Hopefully, these are minimal, but in any instance they are solely my responsibility.

J. John Palen

PART ONE

FOCUS AND
DEVELOPMENT

CHAPTER

1

THE URBAN WORLD

A city is a collective body of persons sufficient in themselves for all purposes of life.

Aristotle, *Politics*

INTRODUCTION: THE PROCESS OF URBANIZATION

This book is about urban places, the cities and suburbs where most of us live. We tend to take the existing situation for granted, but in reality metropolitan areas aren't museums; they are constantly undergoing change. And to understand where we are going, it is necessary to have an understanding of how we arrived at our current state. Jumping right into a discussion of contemporary urban life might be more interesting to some, but with a bit of background contemporary occurrences make far more sense.

Cities themselves are a relatively new idea. The human species has been on this globe several millions of years, according to archeologists. However, for the overwhelming number of these millennia humans have lived in a world without cities. Cities and urban places, in spite of our acceptance of them as an inevitable consequence of human life, are in the eyes of history a comparatively recent social invention, having existed a scant 7,000 to 9,000 years. Their period of social, economic, and cultural dominance is even shorter. Nonetheless, the era of cities encompasses the totality of the period we label "civilization." The saga of wars, architecture, and art—almost the whole of what we know of human triumphs and tragedies—is encompassed within that period. The story of human social and cultural development—and regression—is in major part the tale of the cities that have been built and the lives that have been lived within them. The very terms "civilization" and "civilized" come from the Latin *civis,* which refers to a citizen living in a city. In Roman times *civitas* was concerned with the political and moral nature of community, while the term *urbs,* from which we get urban, referred more to the built form of the city.

The vital and occasionally magnificent cities of the past, however, existed as islands in an overwhelmingly rural sea. Less than 200 years ago, in the year 1800, the population of the world was still 97 percent rural.[1] By the beginning of the twentieth century, the world was still 86 percent rural. In the year 1900, the proportion of the world's population in cities of 100,000 or more had increased to 5.5 percent, and 13.6 percent lived in places of 5,000 or more. While cities were growing very rapidly, most people still lived in the countryside or small villages.

Today this has changed radically. We now are on the threshold of living in a world that will be numerically more urban than rural. Slightly after the turn of the twenty-first century the globe will for the first time in history be an urban world (Figure 1-1).[2]

The rapidity of the change from rural to urban life is as important as the degree of urbanization. As of 1850, not a single country was as urban as the world is today. During the nineteenth century and the first half of the twentieth century, the fastest urban growth took place in European countries and in countries largely settled by Europeans, such as the United States. These were the places that first developed modern agricultural and transportation technologies. Thus England, the

---

[1] As of 1800, only 1.7 percent of the world's population resided in places of 100,000 or more, 2.4 percent in places of 20,000 or more, and 3 percent in communities of 5,000 or larger. Philip Hauser and Leo Schnore (eds.), *The Study of Urbanization,* Wiley, New York, 1965, p. 7.

[2] Philip Hauser and Robert Gardner, "Urban Future: Trends and Prospects," in Philip Hauser et al., *Population and the Urban Future,* U.N. Fund for Population Activities, SUNY Press, Albany, N.Y., 1982, pp. 10–11.

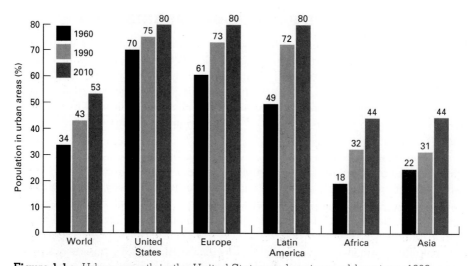

Figure 1-1. Urban growth in the United States and major world regions, 1960, 1990, and 2010.
Source: UN, *World Urbanization Prospects: The 1992 Revision,* New York: UN, 1993.

first country to enter the industrial age, was also the first country to undergo the urban transformation. A century ago England was the world's only predominately urban country.[3] Not until 1920 did the United States have half its population residing in urban places. The rapid growth of cities during the nineteenth and particularly the twentieth centuries is referred to as the *urban revolution*. Figure 1-2 documents the extent and rapidity of this change.

Because we live in an urban world where the mega-metropolises Tokyo-Yokohama and greater Mexico City have populations of over 20 million and greater New York has over 16 million, and because almost all of us have spent at least part of our lives in central cities or their surrounding suburbs, it is difficult for us to conceive of a world without large cities. The rapidity and extent of the urban revolution can perhaps be understood if one reflects that if metropolitan Indianapolis, Indiana, with a 1990 population of 1.3 million, had the same population two centuries ago, it would have been the largest urban agglomeration that had ever existed in the world at any time.[4] By contrast, the World Bank estimates that at the turn of the new century there are 391 cities of over a million inhabitants. More than a third of these cities first reached the million mark in the 1990s.

Most people are not aware that the *overwhelming majority* of urban growth in the world today (over 90 percent) is taking place in economically less-developed countries (LDCs). This has profound consequences, for twenty-first century world urbanization patterns will be quite different from those of the twentieth century. Currently, developed western nations are experiencing little city growth. According

[3] Adna Ferrin Weber, *The Growth of Cities in the Nineteenth Century,* Cornell University Press, Ithaca, N.Y., 1899, table 3.
[4] The best source of data for cities in earlier eras is Tertius Chandler and Gerald Fox, *3000 Years of Urban Growth,* Academic Press, New York, 1974.

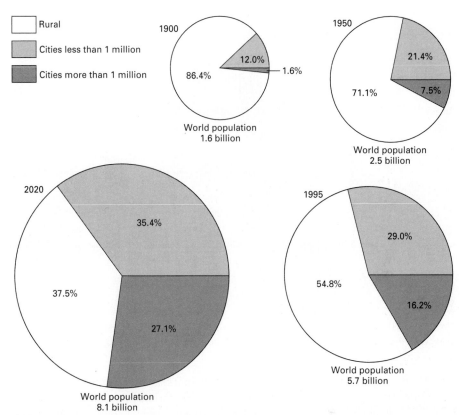

Figure 1-2. Patterns of urbanization, 1900–2020.
Source: Kingsley Davis, *International Technical Cooperation Centre Review*, 1972;
World Facts and Figures, 1985; United Nations Population Division, 1985, and
Population Reference Bureau, 1995.

to the United Nations, as of the turn of the twenty-first century there will be 391 cities of over a million inhabitants, and 284 of these cities will be in less-developed countries. Few of us could name more than a couple of dozen of such million-plus LDC cities. Equally important, by the turn of the century there also will be 26 mega-cities with more than 10 million residents. Of these 26 mega-cities, 21 are found in less-developed countries. Bombay, for example, is adding half a million new city residents each year. It is difficult for us to keep up either intellectually or emotionally with these changes.

Since 1950 there has been over a fifteenfold increase in the population living in such cities. By the year 2000, the United Nations projects a population of 26.3 million for the mega-city of Mexico City; 24 million for Sao Paulo, Brazil; 16.6 million for Calcutta; and 16.3 million for greater Cairo.

Some of our difficulty in understanding or coping with urban patterns and problems can be attributed to the recency of the emergence of this contemporary urban

Overloaded buses and trucks carrying two or three times their rated load are a common sight in rapidly urbanizing countries. (UN/DPI Photo 151865.)

world with its huge mega-cities. Living as we do in urban-oriented places, it is easy for us to forget two important facts: (1) Over half the world's population is still rural-based, and (2) even in the industrialized west, massive urbanization is a very recent phenomenon. This rapid transformation from a basically rural to a heavily urbanized world and the development of urbanism as a way of life has been far more dramatic and spectacular than the much better known population explosion. The bulk of the world's population growth is occurring in the cities of the third world. The population explosion is in reality an urban explosion.

THE HISTORY OF URBAN EXPLOSION

Today, the number of people living in cities outnumbers the entire population of the world only 100 years ago. Urban growth accelerated cumulatively during the nineteenth and twentieth centuries. By 1800 the population of London had reached almost 1 million, Paris exceeded 500,000, and Vienna and St. Petersburg had each reached 200,000. As the twentieth century began, ten cities had reached or exceeded 1 million: London, Paris, Vienna, Moscow, St. Petersburg (Leningrad), Calcutta, Tokyo, New York, Chicago, and Philadelphia. This urban explosion, which will be discussed in greater detail later, initially began over 200 years ago in the more-developed nations of Europe, especially England. Among the more important reasons for this spurt in European population were (1) declining death rates, (2) the beginning of scientific management of agriculture, (3) improved transportation and communication systems, (4) stable political governments, and (5) the development of the industrial revolution. While details differ from country to country, the pattern for western nations is similar. Improvements in agriculture raised the food surplus above previous subsistence levels. Then, in rather short order, this extra margin was transferred by entrepreneurs, and later by governments, into the manufacturing sector.[5] The result was urban expansion and growth fed by a demand by the burgeoning manufacturing, commercial, and service sectors for a concentrated labor force.

Heavy urbanization in third world countries is largely a post–World War II phenomenon (as we will see in the next chapter, Emergence of Cities, and in Part Five, Worldwide Urbanization) and the pace of urbanization in developing countries has been far more rapid than that found during the nineteenth century in Europe or North America. Whichever stereotypes we embrace regarding the dramatic growth of urban places, whether we are delighted by the variety and excitement of urban life or horrified by the cities' anonymity and occasional brutality, population concentration—that is, urbanization—is increasingly becoming the way of life in developing as well as developed nations. Attempts to return to a supposedly simpler rural past must be viewed as futile escapism. Longings for a pastoral utopia where all exist in rural bliss have no chance of becoming reality. We live in an urban world; and for all our complaints about it, few would reverse the clock.

DEFINING URBAN AREAS

Before proceeding further, it is necessary to define some of the terms we will be using. This is not altogether as simple as it might seem, since countries differ in what they mean when they call a place "urban." About thirty definitions of "urban population" are currently in use, none of them totally satisfactory.[6]

Urban settlements have been defined on the basis of an urban culture (a cultural definition), administrative functions (a political definition), the percentage of people in nonagricultural occupations (an economic definition), and the size of the population (a demographic definition). In the United States, we define places as "urban" by using population criteria along with some geographical and political elements. In actual practice the various criteria tend to overlap and be reinforcing.

Let us look briefly at some of the criteria that can be used. In terms of cultural criteria, a city is "a state of mind, a body of customs and traditions."[7] The city thus is the place, as sociologists put it, where relations are "gesellschaft" (larger-scale "societal" or formal role relationships) rather than "gemeinschaft" (more-intimate-scale "community" or primary relationships) and where forms of social organization are organic rather than mechanical (see page 17). In short, the city is large, culturally

---

[5] *Urbanization in the Second United Nations Development Decade,* United Nations, New York, 1970, p. 6.
[6] Milos Macura, "The Influence of the Definition of Urban Place on the Size of Urban Population," in Jack Gibbs (ed.), *Urban Research Methods,* Van Nostrand, New York, 1961, pp. 21–31.
[7] Robert E. Park, "The City: Suggestions for the Investigation of Human Behavior in the Urban Environment," in Robert E. Park, E. W. Burgess, and Roderick D. McKenzie (eds.), *The City,* University of Chicago Press, Chicago, 1925.

heterogeneous, and socially diverse. It is the antithesis of "folk society." The problem with the cultural definitions of an urban place is the difficulty of measurement; for example, if a city is a state of mind, who can ever say where the boundaries of the urban area lie?

Economic standards have also been used in defining what is urban. In terms of economic criteria, a country has sometimes been described as urban if less than half its workers are engaged in agriculture. Here "urban" and "nonagricultural" are taken to be synonymous. This distinction, of course, tells us nothing about the degree of urbanization or its pattern of spatial distribution within the country. A distinction has also been made between the town as the center for processing and service functions and the countryside as the area for producing raw materials.[8] However, while in the past these distinctions may have had utility, it is becoming increasingly difficult to distinguish among areas by means of such criteria. How far out do the producing and service functions of a New York or a Los Angeles extend?

Politically, a national government may define its urban areas as such in terms of administrative functions. The difficulty is that there is no agreement internationally on what the political or administrative criteria shall be. In many countries small administrative centers are recognized as urban regardless of their population or economic significance. Kenya, for example, has a number of "urban" administrative centers with populations under 2,000, and the same is true of many other countries such as Thailand. Until the 1990s South Africa combined political and population criteria by defining an area as urban if it had 500 white persons.

Finally, size of population is used frequently as a criterion in deciding what is urban and what is not. Demographically, a place is defined as being urban because a certain number of people live in it, a certain density of people live in it, or both. Measurement and comparison of rural and urban populations within a country are relatively simple when demographic criteria are used, although the problem of making comparisons among nations still remains. Only 250 persons are necessary to qualify an area as urban in Denmark, while 10,000 are needed in Greece.

According to the definition adopted by the United States Bureau of the Census for the 1990 census, the urban population of the United States comprises all persons living in urbanized areas and all persons outside of urbanized areas who live in places of 2,500 or more. For practical purposes the urban population of the United States therefore includes anyone in a place having 2,500 or more inhabitants. By this definition, three-quarters of the United States population is urban.

The United Nations has attempted to bring some order out of the various national definitions by setting up its own classifications scheme, which it uses for publishing its international data. The definitions of the United Nations are as follows:

> A *"big city"* is a locality with 500,000 or more inhabitants.
> A *"city"* is a locality with 100,000 or more inhabitants.
> An *"urban locality"* is a locality with 20,000 or more inhabitants.
> A *"rural locality"* is a locality with less than 20,000 inhabitants.[9]

---

[8] Amos H. Hawley, *Human Ecology: A Theory of Community Structure*, Ronald Press, New York, 1950, p. 245.
[9] *Demographic Handbook for Africa*. United Nations Economic Commission for Africa. Addis Ababa, 1968, p. 38.

This is a reasonable classification scheme for less-developed countries since it is rare that places under 20,000 have urban characteristics. The major limitation of the United Nations definition is not logical but practical: Most of the more urbanized countries, such as the United States, simply do not use them, preferring to keep their own national definitions.[10] To make a complicated situation as simple as possible, this book will use the definitions established by the United States when presenting data for the United States and the definitions established by the United Nations when presenting international data. The reader can thus assume that outside the United States, "urban" refers to places with 20,000 or more inhabitants.

According to the United Nations, the percentage of the population living in urban places varies from 2 percent in Burundi to 100 percent in the city-state of Singapore.

URBANIZATION AND URBANISM

In this work we will distinguish between "urbanization," which is the number of people in urban places, and "urbanism," which is the sociocultural consequences of living in urban places, the human side of urbanization. As we will see in Part Five, Worldwide Urbanization, cities in the developing world are among the largest and the fastest growing in the world. Nevertheless, it must be kept in mind that the growth of cities and a high level of national urbanization are not the same thing. In the western world the two things happened at the same time, but it is possible to find extremely large cities in overwhelmingly rural countries. Some of the world's largest cities—for example, Shanghai, Bombay, and Cairo—exist in nations that are still largely rural. A number of extremely large cities does not necessarily indicate an urban nation.

Urbanization

"Urbanization" refers to the changes in the proportion of the population of a nation living in urban places—that is, the process of people moving to cities or other densely settled areas. The term "urbanization" is also used to describe the changes in social organization that occur as a consequence of population concentration. Urbanization is thus a process—the process by which rural areas become transformed into urban areas. In demographic terms, urbanization is an increase in population concentration (numbers and density); organizationally, it is an alteration in structure and patterns of organization. Demographically, urbanization involves two elements: the multiplication of points of concentration and the increase in the size of individual concentrations.[11]

Urbanization, described demographically as the percentage of a nation's total population living in urban areas, is a process that clearly has a beginning and an

---

[10] A team working under Kingsley Davis during the 1950s defined "metropolitan areas" for 720 of the then 1,046 areas in the world having at least 100,000 persons in their metropolitan areas and at least 50,000 in the central city (International Urban Research, *The World's Metropolitan Areas,* University of California Press, Berkeley, 1959). This system will not be used in this text, since the United Nations system is far more widely accepted and provides more current data.

[11] Hope Tisdale Eldridge, "The Process of Urbanization," in J. J. Spengler and O. D. Duncan (eds.), *Demographic Analysis,* Free Press, Glencoe, Ill., 1956, pp. 338–343.

end. For instance, three-quarters of the United States population of 265 million is now urban; the maximum level of urbanization is probably somewhere around 90 percent. (Nations that comprise only one city, such as Singapore, can be 100 percent urban.) However, even after a nation achieves a high level of urbanization, its cities and metropolitan areas can continue to grow. This is clearly the case in North America and western Europe. While there is a limit to the percentage of urbanization possible, it is not yet known what the practical limit is on the size of cities or metropolitan areas.

Urbanism

While "urbanization" has to do with metropolitan growth, "urbanism" refers to the social patterns and behaviors associated with living in cities.[12] Urbanism, with its changes in the values, mores, customs, and behaviors of a population, is often seen as one of the consequences of urbanization.[13] Urbanism is a social and behavioral response to living in certain places.

Under the conceptual label "urbanism" is found research concerning the social-psychological aspects of urban life, urban personality patterns, and the behavioral adaptations required by city life. Urbanism as a way of life receives detailed treatment in Chapters 7, 8, and 9, City Life-Styles, Social Environment of the City, and Changing Suburbanization Patterns, as well as in later chapters, particularly those on developing areas.

It should be noted, though, that it is possible to live in an area with a high degree of urbanization (population concentration) and a low level of urbanism (urban behaviors) or—less commonly—a low level of urbanization and a high level of urbanism. Examples of the former can be found in the large cities of the developing world, where the city is filled with immigrants who now reside in an urban place but remain basically rural in outlook. Cairo, for example, is typical of developing cities in that over one-third of its residents were born outside the city. Many of these newcomers are urban in residence but remain rural in outlook and behavior.[14] On the other hand, if the urbanization process in the United States becomes one of population decentralization, the United States might in the future have some decline in levels of urbanization, while urban life-styles become even more universal.[15]

The explicit belief in most older sociological writings—and an implicit premise in much of what is written about cities today—is that cities produce a characteristic way of life known as "urbanism." Moreover, urbanism as a way of life, while often successful economically, is said to produce personal alienation, social disorganization, and the whole range of ills falling under the cliché "the crisis of the cities."

---

[12] Paul Meadows and Ephraim Mizurchi (eds.), *Urbanism, Urbanization, and Change: Comparative Perspectives,* Addison-Wesley, Reading, Mass., 1969, p. 4.

[13] Leo Schnore, "Urbanization and Economic Development, the Demographic Contribution," *American Journal of Economics and Sociology,* **23**:37–48, 1964.

[14] See, for example, Janet Abu-Lughod, "Migrant Adjustment to City Life: The Egyptian Case," *American Journal of Sociology,* **67**:22–32, July, 1961.

[15] Brian J. L. Berry, "The Counterurbanization Process: Urban America since 1970," in *Urbanization and Counterurbanization,* Vol. II: *Urban Affairs Annual Reviews,* Sage Publications, Beverly Hills, Calif., 1976, pp. 17–39.

Traffic gridlock is often worse in developing nations than in developed nations because the number of vehicles expands far faster than the road networks. This traffic jam is in Cairo. (John Isaac/UN/DPI Photo 152221.)

A classic statement of the effects of urbanization on urban behavior patterns is Louis Wirth's article "Urbanism as a Way of Life."[16] According to Wirth, "For sociological purposes a city may be defined as a relatively large, dense, permanent settlement of socially heterogeneous individuals."[17] Wirth further suggested that these components of urbanization—size, density, and heterogeneity—are the independent variables that create a distinct way of life called "urbanism." Urbanism, with its emphasis on competition, achievement, specialization, superficiality, anonymity, independence, and tangential relationships, is often compared—at least implicitly—with a simpler and less competitive idealized rural past. (The adequacy of this approach is addressed in detail in Chapter 7, City Life-Styles.)

Today urbanism as a way of life is virtually universal in nations with high levels of urbanization such as the United States, with their elaborate media and communications networks. The attitudes, behaviors, and cultural patterns of rural areas in the United States are dominated by urban values and life-styles. Rural wheat farmers, cattle ranchers, and dairy farmers, with their accountants, professional lobbies, and government subsidies, are all part of a complex and highly integrated agribusiness enterprise. They are hardly innocent country bumpkins, preyed upon by city slickers. By comparison, urban consumers often appear naive regarding contemporary rural life.

[16] Louis Wirth, "Urbanism as a Way of Life," *American Journal of Sociology,* **44**:1–24, July, 1938.
[17] Ibid., p. 8.

The degree to which even two score years ago urbanism already had permeated every aspect of American culture was documented in Vidich and Bensman's study of an upstate New York hamlet with a population of 1,700. Their book, which they titled *Small Town in Mass Society,* presented a detailed and careful picture of how industrialization and bureaucratization totally permeated the rural village.[18] Everything—from 4-H Clubs and Boy Scout and Girl Scout troops, through the American Legion and national churches, to university agriculture agents, the Social Security Administration, and marketing organizations to raise the price supports for milk—influenced how the village residents thought, acted, and lived. The town was totally dependent on outside political and economic institutions for its survival.

The small-towners, though, had an entirely different conception of themselves and their hamlet. They saw themselves as rugged individualists living in a town that, in contrast to outside city life, prided itself on friendliness, neighborliness, grass roots democracy, and independence. Their town was small, self-reliant, and friendly, while the city was large, coldly impersonal, and full of welfare loafers. In spite of the absence of a viable local culture, and the clear division of the town by socioeconomic-class differences, the myth of a unique rural life-style and social equality persisted. Small-town America is totally enmeshed in an urban economic and social system despite its pride in its independence of the city and cosmopolitan ways. The small town even relies on the mass media to help reaffirm its own fading self-image.[19] Communication developments such as CNN International and satellite dishes shrink distance and difference even further. You can view American news in small towns in Indonesia. The Internet provides an international information superhighway. Today, young people in both rural and urban areas follow the same TV and rock concert stars. With the exception of separatist religious groups such as the Amish, there is no unique rural culture independent of urban influence.

ORGANIZING THE STUDY OF URBAN LIFE

Over the years cities have been studied by scholars in many different ways. Academics and others have concerned themselves with a wide variety of questions such as why cities are located at particular places and not others, what the growth patterns of cities are, who lives in cities, how different ethnic and racial groups arrange themselves therein, how living in cities affects social relationships, and whether city living produces social problems.

If these and numerous other questions addressed in this book are to have meaning for the student, the questions have to be more than an ad hoc list of interesting topics. The material has to be related and organized in some general fashion in order to provide a common understanding and body of knowledge.

[18] Arthur J. Vidich and Joseph Bensman, *Small Town in Mass Society,* Princeton University Press, Princeton, N.J., 1958.
[19] Maurice R. Stein, *The Eclipse of Community,* Princeton University Press, Princeton, N.J., 1961.

The material that follows can be organized—with an occasional bit of squeezing—under the previously mentioned headings of "urbanization" and "urbanism." Under the more abstract heading of urbanization are included those questions and issues dealing with the city as a spatial, economic, and political entity. This traditionally was referred to by sociologists as the "human ecological" approach since it is broadly concerned with the interrelationship and interdependence of organisms and their environment. Such macro-level approaches are heavily used in Part One, Focus and Development, and Part Two, American Urbanization. The urbanization, ecological, or political economy focus is generally on the big picture. It tends to use cities—or, at its most micro level, neighborhoods—as its unit of analysis. A human ecologist, for example, might research the possibility of a predictable pattern of neighborhood change over time.

"Political economy," an alternative theoretical approach to understanding urbanization, also falls under urbanization. Urban scholars with a neo-Marxist or conflict orientation also focus on the aggregate or macro level. They, however, are most likely to be interested in how economic forces shape urban patterns. Research, for example, might be done on how property values are manipulated to encourage gentrification.[20] (Neo-Marxist and other conflict approaches are discussed in detail in Chapter 5, Political Economy and the City.)

Urbanism as a way of life, on the other hand, is far more micro-level-oriented. It focuses on small groups or individuals. This "sociocultural," "social-psychological," or "psychosocial approach" focuses on how the experience of living in cities affects people's social relationships and personalities. The concern of this approach is primarily with the psychological, cultural, and social ramifications of city life. For example, one of the questions regarding the social-psychological impact of city life that we will examine in some detail is whether living in a city, suburb, or rural area produces differences in personalities, socialization patterns, or even levels of pathology. To put it in oversimplified form, are city dwellers different? While human ecology focuses on how social and spatial patterns are maintained, and political economy focuses on economic systems, the social-psychological approach is concerned with human effects.

Historically, urbanization scholars and urban social psychologists have gone their own way, while largely ignoring their opposite numbers. Textbooks also sometimes perpetuate the division by all but ignoring alternative approaches. This is unfortunate, for the perspectives complement each other in the same way that the social science disciplines of political science, economics, and sociology provide alternative focuses and approaches. This book, while written by one trained in the urban ecology tradition, and sympathetic to much of the political economy model, makes a conscious effort to understand better the patterns of metropolitan areas and of the lives of those of us living within them. For this it is necessary to have some understanding both of urbanization and of urbanism as a way of life, or if you prefer the alternate terminology, urban ecology and social psychology.

---

[20] See, for example, Neil Smith and Michele LeFaivre, "A Class Analysis of Gentrification," in J. John Palen and Bruce London (eds.), *Gentrification, Displacement and Neighborhood Revitalization,* SUNY Press, Albany, N.Y., 1984.

CONCEPTS OF THE CITY

Urban Change and Confusion

The scientific study of urbanism and urbanization is a relative newcomer to the academic scene. Systematic empirical examination of cities and city life only began somewhat over half a century ago during a period in which American cities were experiencing considerable transformation in terms of both industrialization and a massive influx of immigrants from the rural areas of Europe and the American south. To many observers of the time, the city, with its emphasis on efficiency, technology, and division of labor, was undermining simpler rural forms of social organization. The social consequences were disorganization, depersonalization, and the breakdown of traditional norms and values. Novels such as Upton Sinclair's *The Jungle* (1906) and Theodore Dreiser's *Sister Carrie* (1900) reflect this breakdown. An anonymous poem of 1916, called "While the City Sleeps," mirrors this negative view of urban life:

> Stand in your window and scan the sights,
> On Broadway with its bright white lights.
> Its dashing cabs and cabarets,
> Its painted women and fast cafes.
> That's when you really see New York.
> Vulgar of manner, overfed,
> Overdressed and underbred.
> Heartless and Godless, Hell's delight,
> Rude by day and lewd by night.

Rural Simplicity versus Urban Complexity

In the usual description of the transition from simple to complex forms of social organization, there is, at least implicitly, a time frame in which rural areas represent the past and traditional values, and the city represents the future with its emphasis on technology, division of labor, and emergence of new values. Such a picture of fast-paced, alienating, stimulating, and anonymous city life along with the contrasting romanticized picture of the warm, personal, and well-adjusted rural life is, of course, a stereotype. Such stereotypes affect not only social behavior, but also social policy—even if they are poor reflectors of reality. For example, in spite of the emphasis on the isolation, anonymity, and mental stress of the city, there are some indications that city residents are actually happier and better adjusted than their rural cousins.

With the exception of the largest cities, Fischer found, for example, that on a worldwide scale there is greater evidence of rural as opposed to urban dissatisfaction, unhappiness, despair, and melancholy.[21] Also, research by Palen and Johnson on the relationship between urbanization and health status in nineteenth- and twentieth-century American cities found that inhabitants of large cities were con-

---

[21] Claude S. Fischer, "Urban Malaise," *Social Forces,* **52**(2):221, December, 1973.

Physical and social changes often proceed at different paces. In Quito, Ecuador, shoeless Indians still carry heavy goods. (Bernard Pierre Wolff/Photo Researchers.)

sistently healthier than inhabitants of rural areas or small towns.[22] Contrary to the stereotype, mental health is also probably superior in the city, and possibly is improving from what it was a generation ago in Manhattan.[23]

Early Social Theories and Urban Change

The cleavage between the city and the countryside is, of course, not a uniquely American idea. The great European social theorists of the nineteenth century described the social changes that were then taking place in terms of a shift from a warm, supportive community based on kinship in which common aims are shared to a larger, more impersonal society in which ties are based not on kinship but on interlocking economic, political, and other interests. These views had, and continue to have, profound impact on sociological thought.[24]

European Theorists. Many of the core ideas of the classical (so-called) Chicago school writings of the 1920s and 1930s were based implicitly on the thoughts of late nineteenth- and early twentieth-century European social theorists. Of these, the most influential were the Germans Ferdinand Tönnies (1855–1936), Karl Marx (1818–1883), Max Weber (1864–1920), and Georg Simmel (1858–1918) and the Frenchman Emile Durkheim (1858–1917).

---

[22] J. John Palen and Daniel Johnson, "Urbanization and Health Status," in Ann Greer and Scott Greer (eds.), *Cities and Sickness,* Sage Publications, Beverly Hills, Calif., 1983, pp. 25–34.

[23] Leo Srole, "Mental Health in New York," *The Sciences,* **20**:16–29, 1980.

[24] Michael P. Smith, *The City and Social Theory,* St. Martin's Press, New York, 1979.

These theorists sought to explain the twin changes of industrialization and urbanization that were undermining the small-scale, traditional, rural-based communities of Europe. All about, they saw the crumbling of old economic patterns, social customs, and family organization. The growth of urbanization was bringing in its wake new urban ways of life. They sought to theoretically explain these changes.

Commonly, the changes were presented by the theorists in terms of dichotomous typologies of logical constructs, which sociologists refer to as "ideal types." The term "ideal type" doesn't mean "perfect"; rather, an ideal type is a *model.* One of these ideal types was a model of rural society; its opposite number was urban society.

The most important nineteenth-century European social theorist was Karl Marx, who was born in 1818 in Trier into an agrarian Germany that had yet to undergo the industrial revolution. Yet Marx spent most of his adult life in an industrializing London where factories, and exploitation of the new class of wage workers, were part of daily life. In the booming cities, a few industrialists enjoyed a level of wealth and comfort more luxurious than that of kings of old, while workers slaved twelve hours a day, six days a week, for subsistence wages and lived in unspeakable tenements and slums (see "Engels on Industrial Slums," pp. 58–59).

Not surprisingly, Marx saw economic structure as the infrastructural foundation of society. It therefore follows that change in society is through conflict over resources and the means of production. Ultimately, the final struggle of mature industrial capitalism would be between the capitalists, who owned factories and the means of production, and the proletariat, who provided the underpaid labor. However, for Marx, before this could occur, there first had to be a shift from agrarian feudal society to the new, urban, property-owning bourgeoisie. (Since a "bourg," or "burg," is a town, a "bourgeois" is by definition a town dweller.) According to Marx:

> The greatest division of material and mental labour is the separation of town and country. The antagonism between town and country begins with the transition from barbarism to civilization, from tribe to State, from locality to nation, and runs through the whole history of civilization to the present day. . . . Here first became the division of the population into two great classes, which is directly based on the division of labour and on the instruments of production.[25]

In early urban sociology Ferdinand Tönnies had great impact with his elaborate discussions of the shift from "gemeinschaft"—a smaller community based on ties of blood (family) and kinship—to "gesellschaft"—a larger, more complex society or association based on economic, political, or other interests.[26] In rural gemeinschaft, people were bound together by common values and by family and kinship ties, and they worked together for the common good. At the gesellschaft pole of the typology, on the other hand, personal relationships count for little, with money and contract replacing sentiment. For Tönnies this change arose as a consequence of the growth

---

[25] Karl Marx and Friedrich Engels, *The German Ideology,* R. Pascal (trans.), International Publishers, New York, 1947, pp. 68–69.

[26] Ferdinand Tönnies, *Community and Society,* Charles P. Loomis (trans.), Harper & Row, New York, 1963.

of money-based capitalism. Further, he saw this evolutionary change as inevitable, but not desirable. Tönnies mourned the increasing loss of community.

Others were more positive regarding urban life. The great French sociologist Emile Durkheim similarly saw societies moving from a commonality of tasks and outlook to a complex division of labor. Societies based on shared sentiments and tasks were said to possess "mechanical solidarity," while those based on integrating different but complementary economic and social functions were said to possess "organic solidarity."[27] In Durkheim's view, the collective conscience of rural society is replaced by a complex division of labor in urban society. The latter is far more productive economically. Some of the same concepts can be found in the distinction made by the German sociologist Max Weber. Weber's distinction was between "traditional society" based upon ascription and "rational society" based on the "technical superiority" of formalized and impersonal bureaucracy.[28]

More psychologically oriented than these theorists was Georg Simmel, whose famous essay "The Metropolis and Mental Life" concentrated on how urbanization increases individuals' alienation and mental isolation.[29] Simmel saw the city as a place of intense stimuli that stimulated freedom but forced the city dweller to become blasé and calculating in order to survive. Simmel's ideas are discussed further in Part Three, Urban Life.

Finally, a twentieth-century version of the dichotomy between rural and urban places is the distinction made by the anthropologist Robert Redfield between what he characterized as "folk" and "urban" societies. Folk peasant societies were described as being:

> . . . small, isolated, non-literate, and homogeneous, with a strong sense of group solidarity. The ways of living are conventionalized into that coherent system which we call "a culture." Behavior is traditional, spontaneous, uncritical, and personal; there is no legislation, or habit of experiment and reflection for intellectual ends. Kinship, its relationships and institutions, are the type categories of experience and the familial group is the unit of action. The sacred prevails over the secular; the economy is one of status rather than market.[30]

Interestingly, Redfield never did fully define "urban life," simply saying that it was the opposite of folk society.

Assumptions. The theoretical frameworks described above contain three general assumptions: (1) The evolutionary movement from simple rural to complex urban is unilinear (that is, it goes only in one direction), (2) modern urban life stresses achievement over ascription, and (3) the supposed characteristics of city life apply to urban areas as a whole. As you read through this text, note whether these assumptions are supported or rejected. These models have at least an implicit evolutionary

---

[27] Emile Durkheim, *The Division of Labor in Society,* George Simpson (trans.), Free Press, Glencoe, Ill., 1960.

[28] H. H. Gerth and C. Wright Mills (trans. and ed.), *Max Weber, Essays in Sociology,* Oxford University Press, New York, 1966.

[29] Georg Simmel, "The Metropolis and Mental Life," *The Sociology of Georg Simmel,* Kurt Wolff (trans.), Free Press, New York, 1964.

[30] Robert Redfield, "The Folk Society," *American Journal of Sociology,* **52**:53–73, 1947.

framework: Societies follow a unilinear path of development from simple rural to complex urban. Rural areas and ways of life typify the past, while the city is the mirror to the future. This change is assumed to be both inevitable and irreversible.

A subset of the belief that the city fosters more formal secondary-group relationships—rather than face-to-face primary-group relationships—is the unspoken but often implicit value judgment that the old ways were better, or at least more humane. The city is presented as more efficient, but the inevitable price of efficiency is the breakdown of meaningful social relationships. The countryside exemplifies stable rules, roles, and relationships, while the city is characterized by innovation, experimentation, flexibility, and disorganization. In cultural terms the small town represents continuity, conformity, and stability, while the big city stands for heterogeneity, variety, and originality. In terms of personality, country folk are supposed to be neighborly people who help one another—they lack the sophistication of city slickers but also lack the city dweller's guile. In short, country folk are "real," while city people are artificial and impersonal.

Fortunately, the newly emerging discipline of urban sociology did not calcify into explaining differences between the rural and the urban, but rather began to examine the urban scene empirically and systematically. Eventually the original rural-urban dichotomy was abandoned, and hypotheses began to be developed on the basis of empirical research. This emphasis on the importance of actual studies and research data is one of the characteristics of urban sociology.

The Chicago School. Early urban research is largely associated with a remarkable group of scholars connected with the University of Chicago during the 1920s and 1930s. The "Chicago school" found sociology a loose collection of untested theories, interesting facts, social work, and social reform. It converted sociology into an established academic discipline and an emerging science.[31]

Foremost among the Chicago school pioneers was Robert Park (1864–1944), who emphasized not moral preachments about the sins of the city, but detailed empirical observation. Park, who had been a newspaper reporter among other things, remained constantly fascinated by the city, and passed his enthusiasm on to several generations of graduate students. He was also most interested in how the supposed chaos of the city actually was underlaid by a pattern of systematic social and spatial organization.[32]

Early empirical sociologists, studying under Park, described the effects of urbanization on immigrant and rural newcomers to the city, and the emergence of "urbanization as a way of life." Works such as *The Polish Peasant in Europe and America, The Ghetto, The Jack Roller,* and *The Gold Coast and the Slum* are minor classics describing the effects of urbanization.[33]

---

[31] For an evaluation of the Chicago legacy, see Lyn H. Lofland, "Understanding Urban Life: The Chicago Legacy," *Urban Life,* **11**:491–511, 1983.

[32] Park, "The City: Suggestions for the Investigation of Human Behavior in the Urban Environment."

[33] William I. Thomas and Florian Znaniecki, *The Polish Peasant in Europe and America,* 5 vols., University of Chicago Press, Chicago, 1918–1920; Louis Wirth, *The Ghetto,* University of Chicago Press, Chicago, 1928; Clifford R. Shaw, *The Jack Roller,* University of Chicago Press, Chicago, 1930; and Harvey W. Zorbaugh, *The Gold Coast and the Slum,* University of Chicago Press, Chicago, 1929.

Robert Park (1864–1944) guided
scores of urban students and
developed the idea of using the
city as a natural laboratory.
(Courtesy of the American
Sociological Association.)

Louis Wirth (1897–1952)
researched urban communities
and wrote a classic article on
urbanism as a way of life. He was
among the first to push the
concept of social planning.
(Joseph Regenstein Library,
University of Chicago.)

However, it remained for Louis Wirth (1897–1952), a student of Park, to consolidate and expressly formulate how the size, density, and heterogeneous nature of cities produce a unique urban way of life. Wirth's essay "Urbanism as a Way of Life," although much challenged, remains the most influential essay in urban studies.[34] Wirth suggested that large cities inevitably produce a host of changes that, although economically productive, are destructive of family life and close social interaction. Wirth's ideas are examined in detail in Chapter 7, City Life-Styles.

For now, however, let us temporarily put aside the questions of the social psychology of city living and focus our primary attention on the spatial and social patterning of urban places. We will begin our discussion of the urbanization process by examining how and why cities have come into existence.

[34]Wirth, "Urbanism as a Way of Life."

2

EMERGENCE OF CITIES

Men come together in cities for security; they stay together for the good life.

Aristotle

INTRODUCTION

This chapter outlines the dramatic growth of urban life from the first tentative agricultural villages to the massive industrial cities of the nineteenth century. In brief, what is being discussed is the rise of civilization. Our goal is not to memorize a series of dates and places, but rather to develop some understanding of the process of urban development; that is how and why cities developed. Archeological, anthropological, and historical material is included, not because there is anything sacred about beginnings as such, but because having some understanding of the origin and function of cities helps us to better understand contemporary cities and how and why they got to be what they are today.

THE ECOLOGICAL COMPLEX

In this chapter we shall mostly be using an ecosystem framework. This is an urbanization model or a paradigm used to explain urban change. An "ecosystem" is defined as a natural unit in which there is an interaction of an environmental and a biotic system—that is, a community together with its habitat. At the upper extreme, the whole earth is a world ecosystem.[1]

Urban ecologists study urban spatial and social growth patterns in terms of changes in the system, using a set of categories known as the "ecological complex." In basic terms, the ecological complex identifies the relationship between four concepts or classes of variables: population, organization, environment, and technology. (Some add a fifth category of "social.") These variables are frequently referred to by the acronym "POET."

"Population" refers not only to the number of people but also to growth or decrease through either migration or natural increase. An example of the first is the growth of Houston from 1975 to the turn of the century through immigration from frost belt cities. "Population" also refers to the composition of the population by variables such as age, sex, and race.

"Organization," or social structure, is the way urban populations are organized according to social stratification, the political system, and the economic system. For example, one might want to examine the effect of Houston's political system and related tax system in encouraging population growth through immigration.

"Environment" refers to the natural environment (e.g., Houston's absence of snow) and the built environment. The latter includes streets and parks as well as buildings.

"Technology" refers to tools, inventions, ideas, and techniques that directly impact on urban growth and form. Examples in Houston's case are the private automobile and air-conditioning. Air-conditioning has made the sun belt not only prosperous but possible. Without air-conditioning the two fast-growing states of Florida and Texas would still be the relative economic backwaters they were fifty

---

[1] See Lee Raymond Dice, *Man's Nature and Nature's Man: The Ecology of Human Communities,* University of Michigan Press, Ann Arbor, 1955, pp. 2–3.

Preventable ecological disasters aren't only the province of the third world. The city of Butte, Montana, is being devoured by an open-pit copper mine. (George W. Gardner/The Image Works.)

years ago. Humid Houston, the control center for the world's gas and oil industry, would be unthinkable without air-conditioning. Similarly, Dallas would never have emerged as a business center, and Austin's rise as a computer technology center would have been impossible. (Microchip manufacturing requires a constant 72 degrees and 35 percent humidity.) It should be kept in mind that how technology is used, and who has access to it, has social and political ramifications.

The ecological complex thus reminds one of the interrelated properties of life in urban settings, and how each class of variables is related to and has implications for the others. Each of the four variables is causally interdependent; depending on the way a problem is stated, each may serve as either an independent (or thing-explaining) or a dependent (thing-to-be-explained) variable. In sociological research, organization is commonly viewed as the "dependent variable" to be influenced by the other three "independent variables," but a more sophisticated view of organization sees it as reciprocally related to the other elements of the ecological complex.

In Otis Dudley Duncan's words: "These categories: population, organization, environment, and technology (P.O.E.T.), provide a somewhat arbitrary simplified way of identifying systems of relationships in a preliminary description of ecosystem process."[2] For example, if we are looking at the destruction of the Brazilian rain forests, we can view rapid population growth and availability of modern technology as "causing" massive environmental degradation and destruction of the earth's ozone layer. On the other hand, one could view the environmental variable as "causing" the social organizational response of the international environmental movement.

Strengths

A major advantage of the ecological complex as a conceptual scheme is its simplicity, since economy of explanation is a basic scientific goal. If our interest is in social organization as the dependent variable—the thing to be explained—our focus is on how population, technology, and environment operate singly and jointly in the modification of urban social organization. For instance, using the example of smog in Los Angeles, one can see that as transportation technology changed, the environment, organization, and population of the city also changed.[3] In Los Angeles a favorable natural environment led to large-scale increases in population, which resulted in organizational problems (civic and governmental) and technological changes (freeways and factories). These in turn led to environmental changes (smog), which resulted in organizational changes (new pollution laws), which in turn resulted in technological changes (antipollution devices on automobiles). Los Angeles has also now built a subway, although it is limited in length.

This example illustrates how sociologists can use the conceptual scheme of the ecological complex to clarify significant sets of variables when studying urban growth patterns. This can be of considerable help in enlightening policy options. Note, for example, the dominant importance of environmental factors in the first cities and how this in time is modified by technological and social inventions. The role of technology becomes increasingly important in the nineteenth century (railroads, telephones, elevators, and high-rise buildings).

Limitations

A problem with the ecological complex is that the categories themselves are somewhat arbitrary, and so the boundaries between them are not always precise. The ecological complex, however, is simply a tool to help us better understand the interaction patterns within urban systems. It is not intended to be a fully developed theory of urbanization. Perhaps the greatest limitation of the original ecological complex is that it subsumes cultural values under the variable of organization, while a very strong case can be made that culture should be a separate reference

[2] Otis Dudley Duncan, "From Social System to Ecosystem," *Sociological Inquiry,* **31**:145, 1961.
[3] Ibid., pp. 140–149.

variable in its own right. Thus, as previously noted, some would add an "S" for "social" to make the acronym POETS. Another limitation is that the ecological complex as such does not explain how, when, to what degree, and under what circumstances the categories of variables interact.

The ecological approach has been criticized, particularly by neo-Marxists and others taking a political economic approach.[4] Finally, it doesn't explain why the variables interact in the particular fashion they do. Nonetheless, the ecological complex remains a useful explanatory tool for organizing material and showing relationships. The ecological complex is useful in organizing large bodies of information at a high level of abstraction. It is less useful when addressing specific questions requiring conceptual precision.

POLITICAL ECONOMIC MODELS

Since the 1970s the ecological model has been increasingly challenged by the emergence of a variety of critical political economic models. These paradigms or models, which during the 1980s were described as the "new urban sociology," are based on conflict models, originally largely of a neo-Marxist nature. More recently political economic models have, for the most part, abandoned Marxism, and the models are undergoing considerable change.[5] (Political economic conflict theories will be discussed in detail in Chapter 5.)

Political economic models differ in specifics, but they all stress that urban growth is largely a consequence of capitalist economic systems of capital accumulation, conflict between classes, and economic exploitation of the powerless by the rich and powerful. The capitalist mode of production and capital accumulation are seen as being manipulated by real estate speculators and business elites for their private profit. The assumption is that "societal interaction is dominated by antagonistic social relationships," "social development is unstable in societies with antagonistic owner relationships," and "power inequality is a basic element in societal relationships."[6]

Conflict theorists criticize ecological models as being ahistorical and mechanistic, and stress that social conflict is an inevitable consequence of capitalistic political economies. Thus, they discount the ecological model's reliance on transportation and communication technologies in explaining urban-suburban development. Rather they place greater emphasis on the deliberate and conscious conspiracy and manipulation by real estate and government interests in order to promote growth and profits. Suburbanization, for example, would not be viewed as resulting from individual choices made possible by access to outer land through streetcar and automobile, but rather as the deliberate decision of economic elites to disinvest in the city and to manipulate suburban real estate markets.[7] The strength of political economic models is their attention to the in-

---

[4] Manuel Castells, *The Urban Question: A Marxist Approach,* Alan Sheridan (trans.), M.I.T. Press, Cambridge, Mass., 1977.
[5] See the discussion by John Logan, Robert Beauregard, and Herbert Gans in *Community and Urban Sociology,* Section Newsletter, American Sociological Association, Summer, 1995, pp. 6–7.
[6] Mark Gottdiener and Joe Feagan, "The Paradigm Shift in Urban Sociology," *Urban Affairs Quarterly,* **24**, 174, 1988.
[7] Joe Feagan and Robert Parker, *Building American Cities: The Real Estate Game,* Prentice-Hall, Englewood Cliffs, N.J., 1990.

Men doing laundry by hand, with Bombay high-rises in the background. The traditional job of laundryman is being threatened because the middle-class is now able to purchase washing machines. Before the free-market reforms of the early 1990's, no washing machines were manufactured in India, nor were they allowed to be imported. (Peter Menzel/Stock, Boston.)

fluence of economic elites on political decision making and the role played by real estate speculators. The weakness is the assumption that local government acts largely at the bidding of economic elites, and thus citizens' wishes have little impact on growth patterns or local government.

FIRST SETTLEMENTS

Our knowledge of the origin and development of the first human settlements and our understanding of the goals, hopes, and fears of those who lived within them must forever remain tentative. Because the first towns emerged before the invention of writing about 3,500 B.C., we must depend for our knowledge on the research of archeologists. Understandably, historians, sociologists, and other scholars sometimes differ in their interpretations of the limited archeological and historical data. Lewis Mumford has stated the problem aptly:

> Five thousand years of urban history and perhaps as many of proto-urban history are spread over a few score of only partly exposed sites. The great urban landmarks Ur, Nippur, Uruk, Thebes, Helopolis, Assur, Nineveh, Babylon, cover a span of three thousand years whose vast emptiness we cannot hope to fill with a handful of monuments and a few hundred pages of written records.[8]

[8] Lewis Mumford, *The City in History, Its Origins, Its Transformations and Its Prospects,* Harcourt, Brace, and World, New York, 1961, p. 55.

   This chapter, which outlines the growth of urban settlements, must necessarily be based in part on scholarly speculation about what happened before the historical era. Fortunately, though, our interest is not so much in an exact chronology of historical events as in the patterns and process of development.

Agricultural Revolution

Hunting-and-Gathering Societies. It is generally believed that before the urban revolution could take place, an agricultural revolution was necessary.[9] Before the invention of the city, nomadic hunting-and-gathering bands could not accumulate, store, and transport more goods than could be carried with them. Hunting-and-gathering groups were small, ranging from twenty-five to at most fifty persons. Hunting-and-gathering societies were equalitarian, lacked private property, and had no fixed leadership. The nuclear family of parents and their children was the norm. Since the group was mobile, there was little in goods parents could pass on to their children. Each generation started with equal resources. Settled agriculture changed everything by allowing population growth, limited economic specialization, and a more complex social organization.

Settled Agriculture. Eventually, some groups gained enough knowledge of the relationship between the seasons and the cycle of growth to forsake constant nomadism in favor of permanent settlement in one location. The Neolithic period is characterized by this change from gathering food to producing it. There is fairly clear evidence that about 8,000 B.C. in the middle east there was a transformation from a specialized food-collecting culture to a culture where grains were cultivated.

   Herd animals such as oxen, sheep, donkeys, and finally horses were first used during this period, allowing the available supply of food to be substantially increased and the first solid steps toward permanent settlement of a single site to be made. Animals such as the horse and the donkey could also serve, in addition to humans, as beasts of burden and a source of pulling power. In all likelihood there were decreases in the very high mortality rates, and increases in population, at this same time.

   Only when the agricultural system became capable of producing a surplus was it possible to withdraw labor from food production and apply it to the production of other goods.[10] The size of the urban population was thus directly related to the efficiency of agricultural workers, and agriculture remained primitive for millennia.

   However, while a food surplus was essential to the emergence of towns, it was not essential that the surplus come from agriculture. Perhaps as early as 15,000 years ago, during the Mesolithic period, there were hamlets from India to the Baltic

[9] Not everyone agrees with an implicit evolutionary typology such as the one used in this chapter. Bruce Trigger, for instance, strongly argues against an evolutionary approach in explaining the emergence and growth of cities, and states that "what seems to be required is a more piecemeal and institutional approach to complex societies." [Bruce Trigger, "Determinants of Urban Growth in Pre-industrial Societies," in Peter Ucko, Ruth Tringham, and G. W. Dimbleby (eds.), *Man, Settlement, and Urbanism*, Schenkman, Cambridge, Mass., 1972, p. 576.]

[10] Jane Jacobs reverses the order presented here, suggesting that intensive agriculture was the result rather than the cause of cities. This theory suggests that population growth forced agricultural improvements. See Jane Jacobs, *The Economy of Cities*, Random House, New York, 1969.

area that based their culture on the use of shellfish and fish.[11] Within these Mesolithic hamlets possibly were seen the earliest domestic animals, such as pigs, ducks, geese, and our oldest companion, the dog. Mumford suggests that the practice of reproducing food plants through plant cuttings—as with the date palm, the olive, the fig, and the grape—probably derives from Mesolithic culture. Small towns and villages could manage by food gathering if their ecological site was especially bountiful. Services and natural resources could also be exchanged for food.

Nor did the absence of settled agriculture necessarily mean the absence of rudimentary division of labor and hierarchical social order. Jericho—which some argue was the first "city," with some 600 people around 8,000 B.C.—had a fairly complex architectural construction.[12] The inhabitants, for example, had sufficient civic organization and division of labor to build defensive walls and towers in a period when they had barely begun to domesticate grains. They also built round houses of sun-dried bricks.

Population Expansion

The first population explosion, by increasing a tribe to the point where hunting and gathering could no longer provide adequate food, further encouraged fixed settlements. This was most likely to occur in fertile locations where land, water, and climate favored intensive cultivation of food. Archeologists suggest that population growth in fact forced the invention of agriculture.[13] Hunting, gathering, and primitive horticulture simply could not support the growing population. Large-scale agrarian societies did not emerge until the technological invention of the animal-drawn plow.

Since the plow did not yet exist—it was not invented until sometime in the fourth century B.C.—farmers of this period used a form of slash-and-burn agriculture.[14] This meant cutting down what you could and burning off the rest before planting—an inefficient form of farming but one with a long history. It was even used by the American pioneers who first crossed the Appalachian Mountains into the new lands of Kentucky and Ohio. It was still being used in isolated areas of the Appalachians in the first decades of the twentieth century. The first horticulturalists in ancient times soon discovered that slash-and-burn farming quickly depleted the soil, and so they were forced to migrate—thus probably spreading their knowledge by means of cultural diffusion.

The consequences of these developments were momentous; with cultivation a surplus could be accumulated, and people could plan for the future. One of the earliest permanent Neolithic farming communities so far excavated, Jarmo, in the Kurdistan area of Iraq, was inhabited between 7,000 and 6,500 B.C. It has been calculated that approximately 150 people lived in Jarmo, and archeological evidence indicates a population density of 27 people per square mile (this is about the

[11] Mumford, *The City in History*, p. 10.
[12] Kathleen Mary Kenyon, *Archeology in the Holy Land*, 3d ed., Praeger, New York, 1970; 4th ed., Methuen, London, 1985.
[13] Kent J. Flannery, "The Origins of Agriculture," *Annual Review of Anthropology*, **2**:271–310, 1973.
[14] E. Cecil Curwen and Gudmund Hatt, *Plough and Pasture: The Early History of Farming*, Collier Books, New York, 1961, p. 64.

same as the population density today in that area).[15] Soil erosion, deforestation, and 10,000 years of human habitation and warfare have offset the technological advantages of the intervening centuries.

The early inhabitants of Jarmo had learned to domesticate dogs, goats, and possibly sheep. The farmers living in Jarmo raised an early form of domesticated barley and wheat but still had to hunt and collect much of their food. Since the earliest farmers lacked plows to break the tight grassland sod, they worked the hillsides where grass was scarce and trees broke the earth. Similarly, America's tightly packed western prairie soil remained untamed until the steel plow was invented in the nineteenth century.

Village farming communities like Jarmo had stabilized by about 5,500 B.C., and over the next 1,500 years such settlements gradually spread from the flanks of hills into the alluvial plains of river valleys like that of the Tigris-Euphrates. A similar process took place in the great river valleys of the Nile, the Indus, and the Hwang Ho. The invention of agriculture was quite possibly an independent development in China and was certainly independent in the new world.[16] The civilizations of Mesoamerica were physically isolated from those of the middle east and Asia and thus had to invent independently, since they were unable to borrow. (See Figure 2-1.)

[15] Robert Braidwood, "The Agricultural Revolution," *Scientific American,* September, 1960, p. 7.
[16] Ibid., p. 3.

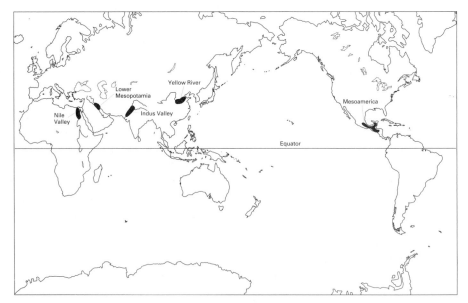

Figure 2-1. The earliest cities first evolved from villages in lower Mesopotamia and the Nile Valley. Cities also arose in alluvial valleys along the Indus and Yellow Rivers. Mesoamerican settlements were a separate development.
Source: Gideon Sjoberg, "The Origin and Evolution of Cities." Copyright (c) 1965 by Scientific American, Inc. All rights reserved.

Particularly environmentally blessed were those settlements of Mesopotamia and the Nile River valley which could exploit the rich soil of the alluvial riverbeds. The very name Mesopotamia, which refers to the land between the Tigris and Euphrates rivers in what is now Iraq, means "land between rivers." Egypt was among the first to adopt sedimentary agriculture. By the middle of the fourth millennium B.C. the economy of the Nile valley in Egypt had shifted once and for all from a combination of farming and food gathering to a major reliance on agriculture.[17] In the great river valley two and sometimes three crops a year were possible because the annual floods brought rich silt to replace the exhausted soil. (The Aswan Dam now blocks the annual floods.) To the dependable crops of wheat and barley was added the cultivation of the date palm. This was a great improvement. In Mesopotamia the palm provided more than simple food; from it were obtained wood, roofing, matting, wine, and fiber for rope.

INTERACTIONS OF POPULATION, ORGANIZATION, ENVIRONMENT, AND TECHNOLOGY (POET)

The relationships between population, organization, environment, and technology are clearer in their consequences than in their timing. The immediate result of the agricultural revolution was a spurt in population size, since a larger population could be maintained on a permanent basis. Stable yields meant that larger numbers of people could be sustained in a relatively compact space. The creation of an agricultural surplus made permanent settlements possible. Agricultural villages could support up to twenty-five persons per square mile; this was a dramatic improvement over the maximum of three to ten persons per square mile found in hunting-and-gathering societies.[18] Technology had spurred population growth.

The establishment of sedentary agricultural villages with growing populations increased the pressure for more intensive agriculture and complex patterns of organization. Agriculture in the river valleys required at least small-scale irrigation systems, something not necessary in the highlands. Rudimentary social organization and specialization began to develop; the periodic flooding made it necessary for the village farmers to band together to create a system of irrigation canals and repair the damage done by the floods. The existence of irrigation systems also led to the development of systems of control and the emergence of more detailed social stratification within the permanent settlements.

Relatively permanent settlements in one place also allowed the structure of the family itself to change. In a hunting-and-gathering society, the only legacy parents could pass on to their progeny was their physical strength and knowledge of rudimentary skills. Agriculturalists, though, can also pass land on to their children, and all land is not equal. Over generations social stratification emerged, with some children born into prosperity and others into poverty.

[17] Robert William July, *A History of the African People,* Scribner, New York, 1970, p. 14.
[18] Gerhard E. Lenski, *Human Societies: A Macrolevel Introduction to Sociology,* McGraw-Hill, New York, 1970, p. 164.

Extended family forms can also more easily emerge under sedentary conditions—for example, a patriarchal society where polygyny is practiced. Such extended family systems only become possible when settled agriculture exists. Patriarchal family systems such as those found in the Bible can have major economic as well as sexual advantages for those in charge, since extra wives mean extra hands to tend the animals and cultivate the fields. More important, many wives mean many sons—sons to work the fields, help protect what one has from the raiding of others, provide for one in old age, make offerings to the gods at one's grave, and carry one's lineage forward. The last was particularly important in many societies. For example, in the Old Testament the greatest gift God could bestow on Abraham was not wealth or fame or everlasting life, but descendants—descendants that would number more than the stars in the sky and grains of sand. In China today, sons still are valued because they are responsible for caring for aged parents.

Environmentally, those located on rivers had advantages not only of soil fertility, but also of transportation and trade. The city served as a "central place" where goods and services could be exchanged. The use of rivers for transportation further encouraged the aggregation of population, for now it was relatively easy to gather food at a few centers. Thus in the valleys of the Nile, the Tigris-Euphrates, and the Indus there first developed a population surplus, which in turn permitted the rise of the first cities. By the third century B.C. Egyptian peasants from the fertile river flood plain could produce approximately three times the food they needed.[19] The result was the first cities.

CITY POPULATIONS

By contemporary standards, the largest cities were little more than small towns. However, in their own day they must have been looked upon with the same awe with which nineteenth-century immigrants viewed New York, for these first cities were ten times the size of the Neolithic villages that had previously been the largest settlements. Babylon, with its hanging gardens, one of the wonders of the ancient world, embraced a physical area of only roughly 3.2 square miles.[20] The city of Ur, located at the confluence of the Tigris and Euphrates rivers, was the largest city in Mesopotamia. With all its canals, temples, and harbors, it occupied only 220 acres.[21] Ur was estimated to have contained 24,000 persons; other towns ranged in population from 2,000 to 20,000 inhabitants.[22] Such cities remained urban islands in the midst of rural seas.

Hawley estimates that although these cities were large for their time, they probably represented no more than 3 or 4 percent of all the people within the various localities.[23] Even Athens at its peak had only 612 acres within its

---

[19] July, *A History of the African People*, p. 14.
[20] Kingsley Davis, "The Origin and Growth of Urbanization in the World," *American Journal of Sociology*, **60**:430, March, 1955.
[21] V. Gordon Childe, *What Happened in History*, rev. ed., Penguin Books, New York, 1964, p. 87.
[22] Ibid., p. 86.
[23] Amos H. Hawley, *Urban Society*, Ronald Press, New York, 1981, pp. 32–33 .

The ancient city of Babylon at the time of
Nebuchadnezzar (604–561 B.C.). (Bettmann Archive.)

walls—an area less than 1 square mile. Ancient Antioch was roughly half this
size; Carthage at its peak was 712 acres. Of all the ancient cities, only imperial
Rome exceeded an area of 5 square miles. Kingsley Davis estimates that even
the biggest places before the Roman period could scarcely have exceeded
200,000 inhabitants, since from fifty to ninety farmers were required to support
one person in a city.[24] In an agricultural world, the size of cities was limited by
how much surplus could be produced and what technology was available to
transport it.

EVOLUTION IN SOCIAL ORGANIZATION

These cities were important not because they were a certain size, but because they
frequently not only tolerated but actively encouraged innovations in social organization. Even though small in number, the urban elite was the principal carrier of the

[24] Davis, "The Origin and Growth of Urbanization in the World," p. 430.

all-important cultural and intellectual values of the civilization. Needless to say, the city also held economic and political sway over the more numerous country dwellers. The Arab philosopher-sociologist Ibn Khaldun, writing in the fourteenth century, pointed out that the concentration of economic power and the proceeds of taxation in the cities led to a profound difference between the economic pattern of the city and that of the country. The concentration of governmental and educational functions in the city also stimulated new demands that affected the patterns of production and supply.

Division of Labor

A surplus in the food supply not only allowed populations to grow; it also allowed the emergence of some nonagricultural specialists. The city's greater population density, along with its sedentary way of life, made possible the development of an urban culture emphasizing trade, manufacturing, and services. However, early cities were at least as important as administrative and religious centers. Cities were as much symbolic places for the worship of the sacred as practical places for secular concerns. The earliest cities began to evolve a social organization immensely more complex than that found in the Neolithic village. The slight surplus of food permitted the emergence of a rudimentary division of labor. No longer did each person have to do everything for himself or herself. The city thus differed from a large village not only because it had a larger number of people, but because it had a larger and more extensive division of labor. The consequence was hierarchy and stratification. Surplus permitted inequality.[25]

Archeological records indicate that the earliest public buildings were temples, suggesting that specialized priests were the first to be released from direct subsistence functions. Early Sumerian cities were basically theocracies, that is, ruled by priests. That the priests also assumed the role of economic administrators is indicated by ration or wage lists found in places where temples were located.[26] In Egypt the temples were also used as granaries for the community surplus. This surplus could be used to carry a community through a period of famine. The technology of food storage was a major achievement of the city. The biblical story of Joseph, who was sold by his jealous brothers into slavery in Egypt, only to become advisor to the Pharaoh and predict seven good years of harvest followed by seven lean years of famine, points out the vulnerability of the nomadic Israelites to their physical environment, and the relative control of the more advanced Egyptians over their environment. Even if the nomadic Jews had received Joseph's warning, they would have been unable to profit from it. They lacked the transportation and storage technology of the more urban Egyptians. The Egyptians had learned how to move a surplus through time as well as through space. Long-term planning—whether to avoid famines, build pyramids, or construct temples—was possible only where a surplus was assured and storage was available.

[25] Gerhard E. Lenski and Jean Lenski, *Human Society: An Introduction to Macrosociology*, McGraw-Hill, New York, 1987.
[26] Robert M. Adams, "The Origins of Cities," *Scientific American,* September, 1960, p. 7.

Kingship and Social Class

For a long time the temples were the largest and most complex institutions that existed; kingship and dynastic political regimes developed later. Apparently, warrior-leaders were originally selected by all other males and served only during times of external threat. Eventually, those chosen as short-term leaders during periods of war came to be retained even during periods of peace. As the process evolved in China in the fifth century B.C.:

> Perhaps whole settlements sometimes found it was easier to set up as warriors, and let the people around them work for them, than to labor in the fields. The chiefs and their groups of warriors, no doubt, provided the farmers with "protection" whether they wanted it or not, and in return for that service they took a share of the peasant's crop.[27]

It is hardly necessary to add that the size of the warrior's share of the peasant's crop was fixed by the warrior, not the peasant. The growth of military establishments did contribute, though, to technological innovations—metallurgy for weapons, chariots for battle, and more efficient ships.

It was but a step from a warrior class to kingship and the founding of dynasties with permanent hereditary royalty. The gradual shifting of the central focus from temple to palace was accompanied by the growth of social and economic stratification. Artists working in precious metals became a regular attachment of palace life. Records of sales of land indicate that even among the agriculturalists there were considerable inequalities in the ownership of productive land. As a result, social differences grew. Some few members of each new generation were born with marked hereditary social and economic advantages over the others. If they couldn't afford the luxuries of palace life, they nonetheless lived in considerable comfort. Archeologically, the emergence of social classes can be seen clearly in the increasing disparity in the richness of grave offerings.[28] The tombs of royalty are richly furnished with ornaments and weapons of gold and precious metals; those of others, with copper vessels; while the majority have only pottery vessels or nothing at all. The building of burial pyramids was the ultimate case of monumental graves. In China a social evolution led to the replacement of hereditary feudal lords with centrally appointed mandarins selected by examination. This bureaucratic system survived over 3,000 years until its abolishment in 1905.

TECHNOLOGICAL AND SOCIAL EVOLUTION

We are just discovering the elaborate water collection and distribution systems of the ancient Mayan culture of Central America. The system allowed the Mayan elite to develop large cities in areas that had long dry spells. The failure to maintain the water system may have led to the civilization's collapse about 900 A.D.[29]

---

[27] Herrlee Glessner Creel, *The Birth of China: A Study of the Formative Period of Chinese Civilization,* Reynal and Hitchcock, New York, 1937, p. 279.
[28] Adams, "The Origins of Cities," p. 9.
[29] "Did Maya Tap Water for Power?" *Washington Post,* Feb. 18, 1991, p. A3.

In early cities technology was spurred on by the existence of the palace elite. The military required armor, weapons, and chariots, and the court demanded ever-more ornaments and other luxuries. A constant market was created for nonagricultural commodities, and the result was the establishment of a class of full-time artisans and craft workers. The near-isolation of earlier periods was now replaced with trade over long distances, which brought not only new goods but also new ideas.

The first city was far more than an enlarged village—it was a clear break with the past, a whole new social system. It was a social revolution involving the evolution of a whole new set of social institutions. Unlike the agricultural revolution that preceded it, this urban revolution was far more than a basic change in subsistence. It was "pre-eminently a social process, an expression more of change in man's interaction with his fellows than in his interaction with his environment."[30]

Once begun, the urban revolution created its own environment. Inventions that have made large settlements possible have been due to the city itself—for example, writing, accounting, bronze, the solar calendar, bureaucracy, and the beginning of science. Ever since Mesopotamia, the city as a social institution has been shaping human life.[31]

URBAN REVOLUTION

A number of years ago V. Gordon Childe listed ten features that, he said, define the "urban revolution," that is, features that set cities apart from earlier forms of human settlement. The features are:

1. Permanent settlement in dense aggregations
2. Nonagriculturalists engaging in specialized functions
3. Taxation and capital accumulation
4. Monumental public buildings
5. A ruling class
6. The technique of writing
7. The acquisition of predictive sciences—arithmetic, geometry, and astronomy
8. Artistic expression
9. Trade for vital materials
10. The replacement of kinship by residence as the basis for membership in the community[32]

Whether all ten are necessary is debatable. For example, monumental urban places did not develop in Mesoamerica until the first century B.C., but even at that comparatively late date, these cities lacked some of the technical advances found

---

[30] Creel, *The Birth of China,* p. 279.
[31] Adams, "The Origin of Cities," p. 9.
[32] V. Gordon Childe, "The Urban Revolution," *Town Planning Review,* **21**:4–7, 1950.

in cities of the middle east, the Indus River area, and China at that time. Central American cities existed without the wheel, the raising of animals, the plow, or the use of metals. (Actually, Mayan civilization did have the wheel, but for some reason the Mayans used it only on child's toys.) They did, however, have compensatory advantages; the most significant probably was the knowledge of how to cultivate large surpluses of domesticated maize (corn). The Mayans also had made major advances in mathematics, including the invention of the concept of zero. They were accurate astronomers and had an exact calendar. Both of the latter were for religious purposes but had secular consequences (e.g., indicating when to plant). Social organizations, culture, and technology were interrelated.

Lists such as the above are most useful in indicating what we have come to accept as the general characteristics of cities. What is important for our purposes is that cities possessing these characteristics did emerge in Mesopotamia and the Nile valley.

SURVIVAL OF THE CITY

Finally, it should be noted that the stable location of the city was not an unmixed blessing. It was not simply for the sake of convenience that gardens and pasturelands were found within the city walls. Cities had to be equipped to withstand a siege, since the earliest cities were vulnerable not only to conquest by other peoples but also to periodic attacks by nomadic raiders. For the numerous cities built on the banks of rivers, floods were also a recurrent problem.

Mesopotamian cities were perpetually under attack by nomadic tribes.[33] The Bible, for instance, devotes considerable attention to the successes of the nomadic Israelites in taking and pillaging the cities of their more advanced enemies. The description of the fall of the Canaanite city of Jericho tells us that:

> The People went out into the city, every man straight before him, and they took the city. And they utterly destroyed all that was in the city, both man and woman, young and old, and ox and sheep and ass, with the edge of the sword—and they burnt the city with fire and all that was therein (Joshua **2:**20–24).

That "Joshua fit the battle of Jericho . . . and the walls came tumbling down" is known to all those who have heard the stirring spiritual, even if they have not read the Old Testament. While the walls Joshua is believed to have miraculously brought down with trumpet blasts about 1,500 B.C. have not been located with certainty, the remains of other walls dating back to 8,000 B.C. have been excavated. As with some other long-inhabited ancient sites, the walls had been breached many times—sometimes by invaders, sometimes by earthquakes. Actually destroying everything and everyone in the city was remarkably shortsighted. By Solomon's time a more complex social organization had evolved where subjugated peoples were taxed yearly rather than destroyed.

---

[33] Stuart Piggot, "The Role of the City in Ancient Civilization," in Robert Moor Fisher (ed.), *The Metropolis in Modern Life,* Russel and Russel, New York, 1955.

The Agora, or marketplace, of Athens also was the place where the council of citizens met to decide civic business. (Culver Pictures.)

There also were threats to the inhabitants within the city walls, the most dangerous being fires and epidemic diseases. City life was more exciting, but it was not necessarily more secure or healthful than the countryside.

THE HELLENIC CITY

As we have noted, environmental factors played a decisive role in early cities. The history of the city can be considered the story of human attempts, through the use of technology and social organization, to lessen the impact of environmental factors. An example is Athens, widely regarded as the apex of ancient western urbanism. Not only was the Greek soil thin and rocky and of marginal fertility, but the mountainous hinterland made inland transportation and communication almost impossible. Aside from the sacred ways to Delphi and Eleusis, the roads were mere paths, suitable only for pack animals or porters. It is estimated that the cost of transporting goods 10 miles from Athens was more than 40 percent of the value of the goods.[34]

But Greece was blessed with fine harbors. Consequently, Athens turned to the sea. A Greek ship could carry 7,000 pounds of grain 65 nautical miles a day, and do it at one-tenth the cost of land transportation. (Storms at sea and pirates, however,

---

[34] Gustave Glotz, *Ancient Greece at Work: An Economic History of Greece from the Homeric Period to the Roman Conquest,* M. R. Dobie (trans.), Norton, New York, 1967, pp. 291-293.

often made this an ideal rather than a reality.) There were also technological contributions to Greek prosperity: the use of the lodestone as a basic nautical compass and the development of more seaworthy ships.

Social Invention

The greatest achievement of the Greeks was not in the area of technology but in that of social organization. The social invention of the "polis," or "city-state," enabled families, phratries (groups of clans), and tribes to organize for mutual aid and protection as citizens of a common state. Because they acknowledged a common mythical ancestry among the gods, different families were able to come together in larger bodies. Gradually the principle of common worship was extended to the entire community. Citizenship within the state and the right to worship at civic shrines were two sides of the same coin.

Citizens were those who could trace their ancestry back to the god or gods responsible for the city and thus could participate in public religious worship. An Athenian citizen was one who had the right to worship at the temple of Athena, the protector of the city-state of Athens. Thus religion had strong social consequences since it conferred citizenship. The ancient city was a religious community, and citizenship was at its basis a religious status.[35] Socrates's questioning the existence of the gods was considered a grave offense because, by threatening established religion, he was undermining the very basis of citizenship in the city-state. His crime was not heresy but treason. As punishment for such a subversive act, he was forced to take poison hemlock. Unfortunately, the Greeks never devised a system for extending citizenship to political units larger than the city-state. This was to be the great achievement of the Romans.

Being a citizen of the city was of supreme importance to the Greeks. When Aristotle wished to characterize humans as social animals, he said that "man is by nature a citizen of the city." To the Greeks, being ostracized, or forbidden to enter into the city, was a severe punishment. To be placed beyond the city walls was to be cast out of civilized life. The terms "pagan" and "heathen" originally referred to those beyond the city walls; our adjective "urban" and our nouns "citizen" and "politics" are derived from the Latin terms for the city. As previously noted, the English terms "city" and "civilization" are both derived from the Latin *civis*.

Physical Design and Planning

Physically, the Greek cities were of fairly similar design, a phenomenon that is not surprising given the amount of social borrowing that took place among the various city-states and the fact that the cities were built with military defense in mind. The major city walls were built around a fortified hill called an "acropolis." Major temples were also placed upon the acropolis. The nearby "agora" served as both a meeting place and, in time, a marketplace. All major buildings were located within

---

[35] Numa Denis Fustel de Coulanges, *The Ancient City: A Study on the Religion, Laws and Institutions of Greece and Rome,* Doubleday, Garden City, N.Y., 1956 (first published 1865), p. 134.

the city walls. Housing, except for the most privileged, was outside the walls but huddled as close to the protective shelter of the walls as was possible.

In describing the Greek polis, there is a strong tendency to focus on the image of the Athenian Acropolis harmoniously crowned by the perfectly proportioned Parthenon. Separated by seas and centuries, it is perhaps natural for us to accept Pericles's own praise of his fellow Athenians as "lovers of beauty without extravagance and lovers of wisdom without unmanliness."

Yet below the inner order and harmony of the Parthenon was a sprawling, jumbled town in which streets were no more than dirty, winding, narrow lanes and unburied refuse rotted in the sun. Housing for the masses was squalid and cramped. Today it is easy to forget that the white stone of the Parthenon was once painted garish colors. Traces of red paint can still be seen. While Hippodamus designed a grid street pattern for Piraeus, the port city of Athens, Athens itself had no such ordered arrangement. Athens was the center of an empire, but little of its genius was given to urban design or municipal management.

Population

Athens had considerable population problems—partially due to the scarcity of productive land in Greece, which resulted in heavy migration from rural areas to the cities. During its peak the city achieved a population of only between 120,000 and 180,000. The major limit on population growth was the limited technological base. The city was still dependent on the surplus of agricultural activities. Much of the land within Athens itself was given over to gardening. The great sociologist Max Weber put the Greek city-states in perspective when he wrote, "The full urbanite of antiquity was a semi-peasant."[36]

Expansion of Greek cities was also limited by preference and policy. The ancient Greeks preferred fairly small cities. Both Plato and Aristotle firmly believed that good government was directly related to the size of the city. Plato specified that in the ideal republic there should be exactly 5,040 citizens, since that number had 59 divisors and would "furnish numbers for war and peace, and for all contracts and dealings, including taxes and divisions of the land."[37] Why Plato chose the number 5,040 isn't known, since his totalitarian state would be governed not by citizen vote but by a small group of guardians presided over by a philosopher-king. Lewis Mumford suggested two possible reasons for the limited size: A larger population would be more difficult to control strictly, and there may have been a desire to keep the population low enough to live off the local food supply.[38] He also notes that when noncitizens such as children, slaves, and foreigners are added into the calculation, the total population of the city-state is approximately 30,000, or about the size chosen later by Leonardo da Vinci and Ebenezer Howard for their ideal cities. (Slaves constituted perhaps a third of the population.)

[36] Max Weber, *The City*, Don Martindale and Gertrud Neuwirth (trans.), Free Press, New York, 1958.
[37] Plato, *The Laws*, Book V, p. 437, B. Jowett (trans.), 1926 ed.
[38] Mumford, *The City in History*, p. 180.

Aristotle informs us that the town planner Hippodamus envisioned a city of 10,000 citizens divided into three parts: one of artisans, one of farmers, and one of warriors. The land was likewise to be divided in three parts: one to support the gods, one public to support the warriors defending the state, and one private to support the farm owners.[39] This illustrates the classic Greek interest in balance.

Aristotle's views on the ideal size of the city are less specific, although he recognized that increasing the number of inhabitants beyond a certain point changes the character of a city. In his view, the city-state had to be large enough to defend itself and to be economically self-sufficient, but not so large as to prevent the citizens from knowing each other's character. In other words, justice should not be blind. As he stated it:

> A state then only begins to exist when it has attained a population sufficient for a good life in the political community; it may somewhat exceed this number, but as I was saying there must be a limit. What should be the limit will be easily ascertained by experience. —If the citizens of a state are to judge and distribute offices according to merit, then they must know each other's characters: where they do not possess this knowledge, both the election to offices and the decisions of lawsuits will go wrong—Clearly then the best limit of the population of a state is the largest number which suffices for the purposes of life and can be taken at a single view.[40]

Diffusion of People and Ideas

City-states were also restrained from growing overly large by the policy of creating colonies. When a city began growing overly large, a colony city was established. Between 479 and 431 B.C., over 10,000 families migrated from established cities to newer Greek colonial settlements. Colonization both met the needs of empire and provided a safety valve for a chronic population problem. This diffusion of population led in turn to a diffusion of Greek culture and ideas of government far beyond the Peloponnesus. The military campaigns of Alexander the Great (356–323 B.C.) also spread Greek culture and led to the establishment of new cities to control conquered territory (e.g., Alexandria in Egypt).

ROME

If Greece represented philosophy and the arts, Rome represented power and technology. The city as a physical entity reached a high point under the Roman caesars. Not until the nineteenth century was Europe again to see cities as large as those found within the Roman Empire. Rome itself may have contained 1 million inhabitants at its peak, although an analysis of density figures would make an estimate two-thirds that number seem more reasonable; scholarly estimates vary from a low of 250,000 to a high of 1.6 million. These wide variations are a result of different interpretations of inadequate data. The number given in the total Roman census, for

---

[39] Aristotle, *Politics,* Book VII, ii, p. 8, B. Jowett, (trans.), 1932 ed.
[40] Aristotle, *Politics,* Book VII, iv, pp. 7–8.

example, jumped from 900,000 in 69 B.C. to over 4 million in 28 B.C. No one is quite sure what this increase indicates—perhaps an extension of citizenship, perhaps the counting of women and children, perhaps something else.[41]

Readers should remind themselves that all figures on the size of cities before the nineteenth century should be taken as estimates rather than empirical census counts. At their most accurate, such figures are formed by multiplying the supposed number of dwelling units in a city at a given period and then by estimating average family size.

Size and Number of Cities

Expertise in the areas of technology and social organization enabled the Romans to organize, administer, and govern an empire containing several cities of more than 200,000 inhabitants. The population of the Roman Empire exceeded that of all but the largest twentieth-century superpowers. According to the historian Edward Gibbon, "We are informed that when the emperor Claudius [reigned A.D. 41–54] exercised the office of censor, he took account of six million nine hundred and forty-five thousand Roman citizens, who with women and children, must have amounted to about twenty million souls." He concludes that there were "about twice as many provincials as there were citizens, of either sex and of every age; and that the slaves were at least equal in number to the free inhabitants of the Roman world. The total amount of this imperfect calculation would rise to about one hundred and twenty millions."[42] The total world population at this time was roughly 250 million so Rome controlled half the world's population.

Gibbon further states that ancient Italy was said to contain 1,197 cities—however defined; and Spain, according to Pliny, had 360 cities.[43] North Africa had hundreds of cities, and north of the Alps major cities rose from Vienna to Bordeaux. Even in far-off Britain there were major cities at York, Bath, and London. What made all this possible for hundreds of years was a technology of considerable sophistication and—most important—Roman social organization. Wherever the legions conquered, they also brought Roman law and Roman concepts of government. Rome's domination resulted in an urban imperialism.

Housing and Planning

"Rome, Goddess of the earth and of its people, without a peer or a second" remains the wonder of the ancient world. Yet despite the emperor Augustus's proud claim that he found a city of brick and left one of marble, much of the city centuries later was still composed of buildings with wood frames and wood roofs on narrow crowded alleys. Fire was a constant worry, and the disastrous fires of A.D. 64 that some say Nero started left only four of the city's fourteen districts intact.

Wealthy Romans lived on the Palatine Hill, where the imperial palaces overlooked the Forum with its temples and public buildings and the Colosseum. How-

---

[41] William Petersen, *Population,* Macmillan, New York, 1969, p. 369.
[42] Edward Gibbon, *The Decline and Fall of the Roman Empire,* Dell, New York, 1979 (first published 1776), p. 53.
[43] Ibid., pp. 54–55.

ever, as was the case in Athens, Roman municipal planning was definitely limited in scope. Magnificent though it was, it did not extend beyond the center of the municipality. Once one branched off the main thoroughfare leading to the city gates, only a maze of narrow, crooked lanes wound through the squalid tenements that housed the great bulk of the population. The masses crowded in the poor quarters were offered periodic "bread and circuses" to keep their minds off revolt. Magnificent public squares and public baths were built with public taxes for the more affluent Romans, not for the masses. As the city grew, the old city walls were torn down and rebuilt to include buildings that had been constructed on the outer fringe. In time even the Forum became crowded and congested, as the ruins still standing amply testify.

The city was supplied with fresh water through an extensive system of aqueducts. The most important of these, which brought water from the Sabine Hills, was completed in 144 B.C. Parts of aqueducts still stand—testament to the excellence of their engineering and the skill of their builders. (However, use of lead pipes in homes gradually poisoned the wealthy, who could afford piped running water.) Rome even had an elaborate sewer system—at least in the better residential areas. It is an unfortunate comment on progress to note that present-day Rome still dumps untreated sewage in the Tiber River.

In many ways provincial Roman cities such as Paris, Vienna, Cologne, Mainz, and London exhibited greater civic planning than Rome itself. These cities grew out of semipermanent military encampments and thus took the gridiron shape of the standard Roman camp. (The pattern can be seen today on football fields and also is the origin of the square city block.) The encampments and later the cities were laid out on a rectangular grid pattern with a gate on each side. The center was reserved for the forum, the coliseum, and municipal buildings such as public baths. Markets were also generally found in the forum.

Elsewhere in the empire, the major distinction was between preexisting cities and new provincial towns and cities. In the east there were Hellenic and other cities which the Romans simply took over and expanded under Roman jurisdiction. In the west (western Europe and Britain), on the other hand, there was no preexisting system of cities; here the Romans created a wholly new system of Roman rather than Hellenic cities. The differences between the older eastern and newer western segments of the empire were never fully resolved, with the empire eventually splitting into eastern and western sections. Eastern cities differed from each other physically as well as politically; because of their commonality of origin, the western European provincial Roman cities were all remarkably similar in design (for more detail on Hellenic and Roman planning, see Chapter 14, Planning in the United States and Elsewhere).

Transportation

Rome was an exporter of ideas—such as Roman law, government, and engineering—which enabled it to control the hinterland. It was an importer of necessary goods and therefore depended on the hinterland not only for tribute and slaves but for its very life. The city of Rome could feed its population and also import vast quantities of goods other than food because of an unrivaled road network and peaceful routes of sea trade. (The roads were built and the galleys powered largely by slaves.) Some 52,000 miles of well-maintained roads facilitated rapid movement of goods and people. Parts of some of the original roads are still in use today, and the quality of their construction surpasses that of even the most rigorous contemporary federal standards.

With the elimination of Carthage as a rival, the Mediterranean truly became *"Mare Nostrum,"* or a Roman lake. Foodstuffs for both the civilian population and the legions could be transported easily and inexpensively from the commercial farming areas of Iberia and north Africa. When the African grain-producing areas were lost to the Vandals, and the barbarians in Germany, Gaul, and England pressed the empire, disrupting vital transportation routes, the decline of Rome was inevitable. Rome lived off its hinterland.

Life and Leisure

The prosperity of the Roman Empire during its peak and the leisure it afforded the residents of the capital were imperial indeed. By the second century after Christ, between a third and a half of the population was on the dole, and even those who worked (including the third of the population who were slaves) rarely spent more than six hours at their jobs. Moreover, by that period, religious and other holidays had been multiplied by the emperors until the ratio of holidays to workdays was one to one.[44]

To amuse the population and keep their mind off uprisings against the emperor, chariot races and gladiatorial combats were staged. The scene of the races was the colossal Circus Maximus, which seated 260,000 persons, and gladiatorial fights were staged at the Colosseum. When the emperor Titus inaugurated the Colosseum in A.D. 80, he imported 5,000 lions, elephants, deer, and other animals to be slaughtered in a single day to excite the spectators. The role Christians came to play in these amusements is well known. Our contemporary beliefs about proper civic amusements were not necessarily shared by earlier eras of urbanites.

EUROPEAN URBANIZATION UNTIL THE INDUSTRIAL CITY

The dissolution of the Roman Empire in the fifth century after Christ marked the effective decay of cities in western Europe for a period of 600 years. This is not the place to detail why Rome fell; it is sufficient to note that under the combined impact of the barbarian invasion and internal decay, the empire disintegrated and commerce shrank to a bare minimum. Once-proud Roman provincial centers disappeared or declined to the point of insignificance. By the end of the sixth century,

---

[44] Jerome Carcopino, *Daily Life in Ancient Rome: The People and the City at the Height of the Empire,* E. O. Lorimer (trans.), Yale University Press, New Haven, Conn., 1940.

war, devastation, plague, and starvation had destroyed the glory that was Rome. From the status of megalopolis, the city was reduced to its early medieval character of a collection of separate villages whose population had taken shelter in the ruins of ancient grandeur, and had dug wells to replace the aqueducts. The small population was supported by the pope, rather than by the emperor, from the produce of the papal territory.[45]

Nonetheless, while the social and physical city withered and decayed into poverty and ruins, the idea and myth of Rome and a Roman Empire remained alive even in the darkest medieval periods, and led eventually in the Renaissance to a new burst of urban activity. The throttling of Mediterranean trade by the advance of Islam in the seventh century and the pillaging raids of the Norsemen in the ninth century did further damage to what remained of European commercial life. In the east, however, cities continued to prosper. Constantinople, built by the emperor Constantine between 324 and 330, survived as the capital of the Byzantine Empire until its conquest by the Turks in 1453.

The Medieval Feudal System

The preceding pages discussed the development of the city through the Roman period. Here emphasis is placed on the reemergence of European urban places after the decline of Rome and on how such cities laid the basis for the western industrial city with which we are all so familiar.

The fall of Rome meant that each locality was isolated from every other and thus had to become self-sufficient in order to survive. Local lords offered peasants in the region protection from outside raiders in return for the virtual slavery—called "serfdom"—of the peasants. Removed from outside influences, local social structures congealed into hereditary hierarchies, with the local lord at the top of the pyramid of social stratification and the serfs at the bottom.[46] It is important to note that the economic and political base of the feudal system, unlike that of the Roman period, was *rural,* not urban. Its center was not a city but the rural manor or castle from which the local peasantry could be controlled. Trade all but vanished. The economy was a subsistence agriculture based solely on what was produced in the local area; transportation of goods from one area to another was extremely difficult. Lack of communication, the virtual absence of a commonly accepted currency, and the land-tenure system that bound serfs to the soil all contributed to a narrow inward-looking localism.

However, not all former provincial cities were totally abandoned; a few managed to survive with greatly reduced populations. These were generally under the secular control of the residing bishop. The Catholic church had based its diocesan boundaries on those of the old Roman cities, and as the empire faded and then collapsed, the bishops sometimes came to exercise secular as well as religious power.

[45] Mason Hammond, *The City in the Ancient World,* Harvard University Press, Cambridge, Mass., 1972, p. 324.
[46] Henri Pirenne, *Medieval Cities: Their Origins and the Revival of Trade,* Frank D. Halsey (trans.), Princeton University Press, Princeton, N.J., 1939, particularly pp. 84–85. For an excellent discussion of the Byzantine Empire, Islam, India, Japan, and southeast Asia, see S. N. Eisenstadt and A. Shachar, *Society, Culture, and Urbanization,* Sage, Newbury Park, Calif., 1987.

By the ninth century, *civitas* had come to be synonymous with these "episcopal cities."[47]

According to Henri Pirenne, the "episcopal cities" were cities in name only, for they more clearly resembled medieval fortresses than true cities. They had a maximum of 2,000 or 3,000 persons and were frequently even smaller. But they were to play a crucial historical role as "stepping stones."[48] By the time of Charlemagne (ninth century) the cities—or towns—had lost most of their urban functions:

> The Carolingians used the ancient cities as places of habitation, as fortified settlements from which to dominate the surrounding countryside. The surviving physical apparatus of the old town, the walls, and buildings, served because it already existed, a convenient legacy of an earlier age.[49]

Town Revival

Cities began to revive, very slowly, in the eleventh century. According to Pirenne, most of these new towns were not continuations of ancient cities but new social entities. Originally they were formed as a byproduct of the merchant caravans that stopped to trade outside the walls of the medieval episcopal cities such as Amiens, Tours, and Cologne. Under the influence of trade, the old Roman cities took on new life and became repopulated, while new towns were also being established. Mercantile groups formed around the military burgs, along seacoasts, on riverbanks, and at the confluences and junctions of the natural routes of trade and communication.[50]

Over time the seasonal fairs that were held outside the town gates came to take on a more permanent year-round character. Since at this time the merchants were not allowed inside the town walls, they settled in the outside shadow of the walls and in some cases built their own walls, which attached to those of the town. These *faubourgs,* or medieval suburbs, came to be incorporated into the town proper, and by the thirteenth century merchants had an accepted and important role in the growing medieval towns. Revitalized city life was most prominent in Italy when city-states such as Venice established extensive commercial ties with the Byzantine and even the Arab empires. Trade with Constantinople enabled the Venetians to prosper and in time create a mini-empire of their own based upon the skills of their sea captains and the size of their fleets.

Two external factors during the Middle Ages also greatly contributed to the growth of towns elsewhere in Europe: the Crusaders and the overall population growth. A great impetus for the revival of trade came from the medieval religious crusades. The Crusaders returned from the urban Byzantine Empire with newly developed tastes for the consumer goods and luxuries of the east. The crusading

[47] Weber, *The City,* p. 49.
[48] Pirenne, *Medieval Cities: Their Origins and the Revival of Trade,* p. 76.
[49] Howard Saalman, *Medieval Cities,* Braziller, New York, 1968, p. 15.
[50] Fritz Rörig, *The Medieval Town,* University of California Press, Berkeley, 1967, p. 15.

movement provided an excellent opportunity for the town entrepreneurs to put their commercial instincts into practice.[51] Sociologically, the marketplace made merchants negotiators responding to market conditions.

Trading activities greatly accelerated despite the pillaging that traders suffered from highwaymen and the endless feudal taxes and dues the traders were forced to pay to local lords as they transported goods through their territories. Still, the social system was definitely more stable than that of the early Middle Ages, with their marauding raiders and internal warfare. The increasing stability led to a more constant food supply, which in turn resulted in lower death rates and improvement in the rate of natural increase of the population.

Technological innovations also contributed to population growth. The moldboard plow, which had been used in Roman times, was rediscovered. This heavier plow could turn the tight soils of northern Europe, and it came to be commonly used during the tenth century. The substitution of three-field rotation for the two-field system permitted three plantings a year rather than two, while at the same time raising the productivity of each planting by 16 percent. The effect was to double production and permit stable growth.

England in the time of William the Conqueror (1066) had a population of approximately 1.8 million. Three hundred years later the population had increased to roughly 2.7 million. Some of this increased population migrated to the small but growing towns. Without such increases, the growth of towns would hardly have been possible.

While the feudal order was basically rural, certain elements of the medieval legal and social system indirectly encouraged the growth of towns. Feudal lords were forbidden by custom to sell their lands, but lords badly in need of new funds could sell charters for new towns within their lands. Also, by encouraging the growth of older towns such lords could increase their annual rents. Towns were frequently able to purchase or bargain for various rights, such as the right to hold a regular market, the right to coin money and establish weights and measures, the right of citizens to be tried in their own courts, and—most important—the right to bear arms.[52] Over time cities became more or less autonomous and self-governing. City charters, in fact, bestowed the right of citizenship upon those living within the urban walls. As a result, medieval cities attracted the more skilled and the more ambitious of the rural population. In a sense the towns did not grow out of the feudal social order, but in opposition to it.

Characteristics of Towns

Medieval cities were quite small by contemporary standards, having hardly more inhabitants than present-day towns or villages (Table 2-1). Even during the Renaissance, cities of considerable prominence often had only 10,000 to 30,000 inhabitants.[53] Only Paris, Florence, Venice, and Milan are thought to have possibly

---

[51] For a superb analysis of the importance of trade to the development of Europe, see Fernand Braudel, *The Mediterranean and the Mediterranean World in the Age of Philip II*, Sian Reynolds (trans.), Harper & Row, New York, 1973.

[52] Mumford, *The City in History*, p. 263.

[53] Frederick Hiorns, *Town Building in History*, Han-ap, London, 1956, p. 110.

TABLE 2-1
Estimated Populations and Areas of Selected
Medieval Cities

City	Year	Population	Land area, acres
Venice	1363	77,700	810
Paris	1192	59,200	945
Florence	1381	54,747	268
Milan	1300	52,000	415
Genoa	1500	37,788	732
Rome	1198	35,000	3,450
London	1377	34,971	720
Bologna	1371	32,000	507
Barcelona	1359	27,056	650
Naples	1278	22,000	300
Hamburg	1250	22,000	510
Brussels	1496	19,058	650
Siena	1385	16,700	412
Antwerp	1437	13,760	880
Pisa	1228	13,000	285
Frankfort	1410	9,844	320
Liège	1470	8,000	200
Amsterdam	1470	7,476	195
Zurich	1357	7,399	175
Berlin	1450	6,000	218
Geneva	1404	4,204	75
Vienna	1391	3,836	90
Dresden	1396	3,745	140
Leipzig	1474	2,076	106

Source: J. C. Russell, *Late Ancient and Medieval Population*, American Philosophical Society, Philadelphia, 1958, pp. 60–62.

reached populations of 100,000.[54] These figures are of course scholarly estimates of past size, rather than counts taken at the time. (For a discussion of the larger and more socially developed Arab cities of this period, see Chapter 17.)

Thick walls enclosed the medieval city; watchtowers and sometimes even external moats added to its military defense. The main thoroughfares led directly from the outer gates to the source of protection and power—the cathedral or the feudal castle. The religious cathedral dominated the medieval skyline as the skyscraper dominates the contemporary urban skyline. Outside the medieval burgs, land was reserved for expansion, so that when the population increased, the older fortifications could be torn down and new city walls built farther out. The magnificent ringlike boulevards of Vienna and Paris are reminders of the medieval origins of these cities. When the walls were finally demolished in the later part of the nineteenth century, the resulting open space was used to construct the now-famous boulevards.

[54] Henri Pirenne, *Economic and Social History of Medieval Europe*, I. E. Clegg (trans.), Harcourt, New York, 1956, p. 173.

Within the medieval towns or burgs could be found a new social class of arti-sans, weavers, innkeepers, money changers, and metalsmiths known as the "bour-geoisie." This new class of merchants was in many ways the antithesis of the feu-dal nobility. The merchants were organized into guilds, and their way of life was characterized by trade and functionally specialized production, not by the owner-ship of land. The rise of the medieval bourgeoisie undermined the traditional sys-tem and prepared the way for further changes, for, as a German phrase put it, *"Stadtluft machtfrei"* ("City air makes one free").[55]

What eventually developed was a distinct form, a full urban community. Such communities, as defined by the German sociologist Max Weber, were economically based on trading and commercial relations. They exhibited the following features: (1) a fortification, (2) a market, a court of its own, and at least partial autonomous law, (3) a related form of association, and (4) at least partial political autonomy and self-governance.[56] Weber argues convincingly that such a totally self-governing urban community could emerge only in the west, where cities had political autonomy and urban residents shared common patterns of association and social statuses.

By the fourteenth century it was clear that the growth of town-based com-merce was turning Europe away from the earlier manorial self-sufficiency toward an urban-centered, profit-oriented economy. The more ambitious cities were start-ing to flex their economic muscles. The Italian port cities grew wealthy on trade and began to expand their influence over the surrounding hinterland. Economic com-petition among the Italian city-states was augmented by warfare. Florence elimi-nated the competition of Pisa and Siena by conquering them militarily. The cities to the north were equally active in carving out a hinterland under their economic domination. Rouen was the economic center for 35 villages, Metz controlled 168, and Lijbeck claimed 240 dependent villages within its territory.[57]

Plague

Urban development, however, received a major blow in the fourteenth century by the outbreak of the plague. The plague was spread from the east by fleas that lived on rats found on ships. But even the devastation of the plague could not reverse the long-term growth of cities, although in the short run it wrought havoc to a degree that is difficult to exaggerate. In its first three years, from 1348 through 1350, the plague, or "black death," wiped out at least a fourth of the population of Europe. One scholar of the plague simply says that "it undoubtedly was the worst disaster that has ever befallen mankind."[58] Before the year 1400, mortality due to the plague rose to more than a third of the population of Europe. Cities with their congestion were especially vulnerable. Over half the population of most cities was wiped out;

[55] In its precise sense, the phrase refers to the medieval practice of recognizing the freedom of any serf who could manage to remain within the walls of the city for a year and a day.

[56] Weber, *The City,* p. 81.

[57] John H. Mundy and Peter Riesenberg, *The Medieval Town,* Van Nostrand, New York, 1958, p. 35.

[58] William L. Langer, "The Black Death," in Kingsley Davis, *Cities, Their Origin, Growth, and Human Impact: Readings from Scientific American,* Freeman, San Francisco, 1973, p. 106.

The great plague of 1348–1350 claimed as victims at least one-third of all European city dwellers. (Bettmann Archive.)

few cities escaped with losses of less than a third. Florence went from 90,000 to 45,000 inhabitants and Siena from 42,000 to 15,000, and Hamburg lost almost two-thirds of its inhabitants.[59] As put by the traditional nursery rhyme:

> Ring around a rosie,
> Pocket full of posies.
> Ashes, ashes we all fall down.

(Rosies were the pox marks on a victim, and posies were supposed to ward off the plague.)

The path of the black death, which began in India and spread to the middle east and then Europe, followed the major trade routes. Thus, the effects were most pronounced in seaports and caravan centers.[60] The greatest losses occurred at the emerging centers of development and change. While the blow to the cities was severe, the effect of the plague on the rural manorial system was fatal. The feudal social structure never really recovered. Those peasants who were not killed by the plague fled to the towns, thus depriving the manors of their essential labor force. Serfs fleeing the plague often found that labor shortages had turned them into con-

[59] Ibid., pp. 106–107.
[60] Andre Siegfried, *Routes of Contagion,* Harcourt, Brace and World, New York, 1965.

tract laborers or even town artisans. Population declines changed the economic structure.

The structure of basic social institutions such as the Catholic church was also dramatically altered by the black death. Many of the senior and most learned clergy perished; those who survived were often more concerned with taking care of themselves than their flocks. New priests were trained hastily, if at all. While some clergy did far more than their duties, others deserted their parishes when plague threatened. Their participation in the general loose living and immorality of the time contributed to the religious upheavals that swept Europe for the next two centuries and culminated in the Protestant Reformation.

Since the plagues were considered to be a consequence of the wrath and vengeance of God, some people became fanatically religious, while the majority embraced the philosophy of "live, drink, and be merry, for tomorrow we may die." In the words of one scholar, "Charity grew cold, workers grew arrogant, revenues of Church and State dropped, people everywhere were more self-indulgent and frivolous than ever."[61] Chroniclers stress the lawlessness, depravity, and dissolute behavior of the time. In London, "In one house you might hear them roaring under the pangs of death, in the next tippling, whoring and belching out blasphemies against God."[62] The plague had given the rural-based feudal system a blow from which it never recovered. From this point onward the history of western civilization was again to be the history of cities and city inhabitants.

Renaissance Cities

By the sixteenth century numerous cities, and particularly the Italian city-states, had developed a wealthy patrician class which had the interest, resources, and time to devote to the development and beautification of their cities. Renaissance cities such as Florence embarked on major building programs. The revival of interest in the classical style, and in classical symmetry, perspective, and proportion, had a profound effect on the design of both public and private structures. The artistic talents even of artists such as Michelangelo and Leonardo da Vinci were used to beautify the cities; Leonardo also developed proposals for urban planning. Rather than simply building at random, the more prosperous city-states hired architects to make planned changes. The classical effect can be seen in the use of straight streets and regular squares, and particularly in the use of perspective. The early medieval city with its semirural nature had aptly symbolized that age. A sixteenth- and seventeenth-century Renaissance city, such as Florence, symbolized the humanistic ideology of its age and proudly proclaimed its secular urban culture.[63]

The sixteenth-century city gained ever-greater economic and cultural domination over rural areas, but it also marked the beginning of the end of the city as a self-governing unit independent of the larger nation-state. During the medieval

[61] George Deauz, *The Black Death,* Weybright and Talley, New York, 1969, p. 145.
[62] Langer, "The Black Death," p. 109.
[63] For an excellent discussion of European urbanization, see Jan de Vries, *European Urbanization 1500–1800,* Harvard University Press, Cambridge, Mass., 1984; and Paul M. Hohenberg and Lynn Hollen Lees, *The Making of Urban Europe 1000–1950,* Harvard University Press, Cambridge, Mass., 1985.

Preindustrial and Industrial Cities: A Comparison

A comparison of the social structures of preindustrial and industrial cities helps us understand how the cities we live in differ from preindustrial cities and from the cities of the developing nations of the "third world." The industrial and preindustrial cities here described are "ideal types"—that is, they do not exist in reality but are rather abstractions or constructs obtained by carrying certain characteristics of each type of city to their logical extremes. Such ideal types can never exist in reality, but they are most useful in accentuating characteristics for the purposes of comparative historical research.

In his much-quoted article "Urbanism as a Way of Life," Louis Wirth gives a number of characteristics that he suggests are common to cities, and in particular to industrial cities.* For Wirth, a city is a permanent settlement possessing the following characteristics: (1) size, (2) density, and (3) heterogeneity. The city is the place where large numbers of persons are crowded together in a limited space—persons who have different skills, interests, and cultural backgrounds. The result is the independence, anonymity, and cultural heterogeneity of city dwellers.

Modern industrial cities, he says, are characterized by (1) extensive division of labor, (2) emphasis on innovation and achievement, (3) lack of primary ties to a localized neighborhood, (4) breakdown of primary groups, leading to social disorganization, (5) reliance on secondary forms of social control, such as the police, (6) interaction with others as players of specific roles rather than as total personalities, (7) destruction of close family life and a transfer of its functions to specialized agencies outside the home, (8) a diversity permitted in values and religious beliefs, (9) encouragement of social mobility and working one's way up, and (10) universal rules applicable to all, such as the same legal system, standardized weights and measures, and common prices. The industrial city thus is achievement-oriented and prizes a rationally oriented economic system. It is predominantly a middle-class city. In brief, urbanism as a way of life prizes rationality, secularism, diversity, innovation, and progress. It is change-oriented. According to Wirth, "The larger, the more densely populated,

---

* Louis Wirth, "Urbanism as a Way of Life," *American Journal of Sociology,* **44:**1–24, July, 1938.

the more heterogeneous the community, the more accentuated the characteristics associated with urbanism will be."* (Wirth's views are discussed in detail in Chapter 7, City Life-Styles.)

Gideon Sjoberg paints a different picture for preindustrial cities.† He suggests that a number of factors we associate with cities are probably generic only to industrial cities. In contrast to Wirth, he suggests that preindustrial cities serve primarily as governmental or religious centers and only secondarily as commercial hubs. Specialization of work is limited, and the production of goods depends on animate (human or animal) power. There is little division of labor; the artisan participates in every phase of manufacture. Home and workplace are not separate as in the industrial city; an artisan or merchant lives in back of or above the workplace. Justice is based not on what you do but on who you are. Standardization is not of major importance. Different people pay different prices for the same goods, and there is no universal system of weights and measures. In brief, the preindustrial city stresses particularism over universalism. Class and kinship systems are relatively inflexible; education is the prerogative of the rich. A small elite maintains a privileged status over the disadvantaged masses.

The continuity with rural values is obvious. Emphasis is on traditional ways of doing things; the guild system discourages innovation. Ascription rather than achievement is the norm; a worker is expected to do the job he or she was born into. A person lives and works in a particular quarter of the city and rarely moves beyond this area. Social control is the responsibility of the primary group rather than secondary groups; persons are known to one another and are subject to strict kinship control. Formal police forces are unnecessary. Family influence is strong, with the traditional extended family accepted as the ideal. Within all classes, children, and especially sons, are valued. There is great similarity in values, and little diversity in religion is tolerated. Opportunity for social mobility is severely restricted by a caste system or rigid class system. There is little or no middle class, which is the backbone of the industrial city; one is either rich or poor.

The preindustrial city lacks what the great French sociologist Emile Durkheim called "moral density," or what we today call "social integration." By contemporary standards the preindustrial city is neither socially nor economically integrated. The walled quarters of the preindustrial city are

* Ibid., p. 9
† Gideon Sjoberg, *The Preindustrial City: Past and Present*, Free Press, New York, 1960.

largely independent units; their physical proximity to one another does not lead to social interaction. The city as a whole may possess heterogeneity, but actual social contacts rarely extend beyond one's own group.

No real city of course conforms exactly either to the industrial model or to the preindustrial model. (Note in Chapter 3, The Rise of Urban America, that the preindustrial model does not appear to fit American colonial cities, although these were clearly preindustrial.) Models are best used as aids that sharpen our comparative understanding of differences; they should never be mistaken for actual places.

period, kings and city dwellers had been natural allies, since both wished to subdue the power of the local nobility. In order to cast off the last fetters of feudal restraint, the city burghers supplied the monarch with men and—most important—money to fight wars; the monarch in turn granted ever-larger charter powers to the towns.

Once the monarchs had subdued the rural lords, however, they turned their attention to the prosperous towns. Gradually the independent powers of the cities were reduced as they became part of nations in fact as well as in name. The structure of social organization in Europe was changing to the larger geographical unit: the nation-state. The loss of political independence, however, was compensated for by the economic advantages of being part of a nation-state rather than a collection of semi-independent feudal states and chartered cities. National government usually meant better and safer roads and therefore easier and cheaper transport of goods and a larger potential market area. Merchants also had the advantages of reasonably unified laws, a common coinage, and standardized measures of weight and volume—all things that today we take for granted. Emergent business classes prospered from the certainty and stability provided by the king's national government. The capitalist city was coming into existence.

Influences of Technology. The technological development of gunpowder and the cannon also contributed to changing the nature of the walled city. The traditional defenses of rampart, bastion, and moat were of limited utility in stopping cannon fire. Cities that hoped to resist the armies of a king had to shift their attention from interior architecture and urban planning to the engineering of fortifications. Only elaborate defensive outworks could stop cannon fire, and so the city unwittingly became the captive of its own horizontal defenses. While one can question the urbanologist Lewis Mumford's view that the decline of the city as a place of comfortable habitation began with the end of the Middle Ages, it is certainly true that the city of the seventeenth century was changing.

Unable to grow outward, cities began to expand vertically and fill in open spaces within the city walls. The increased crowding that resulted had a bad effect on both the quality and the length of life. For example, extending the second floor of houses over the street decreased sunlight below. This led to vitamin D deficiency, which caused rickets in children. Filthy living conditions, combined with minimal sanitation and an absence of any knowledge of public health practices, resulted in the rapid spread of contagious diseases and consequently high death rates. As John Graut's pioneer research in the seventeenth century on the London Bills of Mortality demonstrated, London actually recorded more deaths than births. Only heavy migration from the countryside allowed the city to grow in population rather than decline as would otherwise have been the case with such a high mortality rate. As late as 1790 the city of London had three deaths for every two births.[64] A century later mortality rates in the city still exceeded those in rural districts.[65] The possibilities of jobs and excitement in the city continued to attract ruralites.

---

[64] Mary Dorothy George, *London Life in the Eighteenth Century,* Harper Torchbooks, New York, 1964, p. 25.
[65] Eric Lampara, "The Urbanizing World," in H. J. Dyds and Michael Wolfe (eds.), *The Victorian World,* Routledge & Kegan Paul, London, 1976.

Hogarth's eighteenth-century print of people drinking on Beer Street in London shows how streets served as more than transportation arteries. (Bettmann Archive.)

Demographic Transition. Urban growth was closely tied to the growth of the population as a whole, and until about the middle of the seventeenth century, the population of the world had been growing at a very slow rate: 0.4 percent a year. As a result, by the beginning of the eighteenth century the world population was roughly 500 million, or double that at the time of Christ. Then momentous changes occurred that resulted in what we call the "demographic transition" or the demographic revolution. Population growth suddenly spurted in the latter part of the eighteenth century, not through increases in the birthrate—it was already high—but through declines in the death rate. Population increases continued to the nineteenth and twentieth centuries. The term "demographic transition" refers to this transition from a time of high birthrates matched by almost equally high death rates, through a period of declining death rates, to a period where birthrates also begin to decline, and eventually to a period where population stability is reestablished—this time through low birthrates matched by equally low death rates.

Changes in Agriculture. Much of the decline in the death rates can be attributed to technological changes in agriculture that assured both a better and a more reliable food supply. Without such increases in food supply, cities could not grow and expand. As late as the beginning of the nineteenth century, the produce of nine farms was still required to support one urban family. (Today each American farmer supports over a hundred other persons.)

At the beginning of the eighteenth century, English agriculture was still primitive. One-quarter of the farmland was left fallow and thus unproductive each year. Pasturelands and water rights were held in common, as were the woods that provided hunting and firewood. Then, within the period of half a century, English agriculture was revolutionized. Jethro Tull published the results of thirty years of research on his estates, and the new ideas were quickly adopted by much of the landed aristocracy. Tull advocated planting certain crops, such as clover, on fallow land to restore nutrients to the earth, thus radically increasing the usable acreage. (Today, we still use the expression "being in clover" to indicate prosperity.) He also recommended deep plowing and a system for foddering animals through the winter. Seeds were now planted in rows rather than through broadcasting into the air.

At the same time it was being discovered that selective breeding of animals was far superior to letting nature take its course. Before it had been believed that animals could only grow larger by eating more. Striking changes can be seen by comparing the weight of animals at the Smithfield Fair in 1710 and 1795; the average weight of oxen went from 370 pounds to 800 pounds, that of calves from 50 to 150 pounds, and that of sheep from 38 to 80 pounds. Larger animals also meant more fertilizer for the fields.

Accompanying these agricultural improvements in England were the notorious Enclosure Acts, which took the village commons from joint ownership and gave them to the lord enjoying ancient title to the land. While disastrous for the local yeoman, the larger enclosures could be worked more efficiently by the lords who were using the new agricultural knowledge. The result was an increase in both the quality and the quantity of the food supply. While it is extremely hazardous to generalize about living conditions, there apparently was an improvement over earlier centuries. Death rates began to go down, and populations expanded rapidly.

The abandonment of traditional subsistence agriculture and the orientation to a market economy meant that rationality was replacing tradition, and contract was taking the place of custom. The calculation implicit in the land enclosure acts destroyed small peasant landholders but made it possible for London and other cities to be assured of foodstuffs and thus to grow as manufacturing and commercial centers. The movement of agriculture surpluses was facilitated greatly by the construction of new toll roads, which were built in great numbers after 1745.

INDUSTRIAL CITIES

Technological Improvements and the Industrial Revolution

Roughly at the same time that agricultural improvements were both increasing yields and releasing workers, inventions were being made that would allow for the growth of new industries. Eighteenth-century inventions in the manufacture of

Industrialization brought terrible abuses. These young boys were chained to their mules as coal mine drivers. The photo was taken in Gary, Indiana, in 1908. (Bettmann Archive.)

cloth, such as the flying shuttle and the spinning jenny, were capped in 1767 by Watt's invention of a usable steam engine. The steam engine provided a new and bountiful inanimate source of energy. The cotton industry boomed, and it was soon followed by other industries. The machines, rather than eliminating the need for workers, rapidly increased the demand for an urban work force. A factory system began to emerge based on specialization and mechanization. As a consequence, new forms of occupational structure and a more complex stratification system began to develop. In the mechanized, capital-intensive industries urban bondage replaced rural bondage for poor laborers.

The Second Urban Revolution

The second urban revolution was not the emergence of cities but rather the changes that for the first time made it possible for more than 10 percent of the population to live in urban places. This new urban revolution started in Europe. Without population growth and the release of workers from the land, it is hard to see how the early industrial cities could have grown at all, for as noted earlier, unhealthful living conditions in cities meant that they were not able to maintain, much less increase, their population without in-migration from rural areas.

Rapid expansion of population (Figure 2-2) and national economic expansion did not, however, translate into healthful living conditions in the bulging European towns that were turning into cities. Eighteenth-century London was a model of

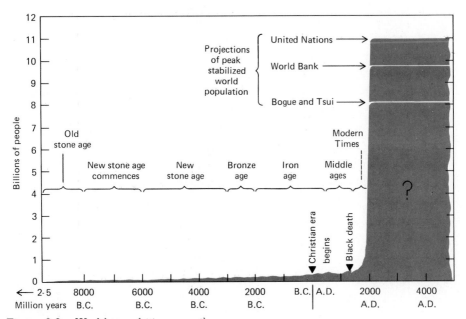

Figure 2-2. World population growth.
Source: From Population Reference Bureau.

filth, crowding, and disease. The early stages of industrialism hardly did much to improve the situation. While rural mortality decreased, urban mortality was kept high by unbelievably poor sanitary conditions. The novels of Charles Dickens, such as *Oliver Twist* (1838), give an accurate portrayal of life in such cities. Cholera and other epidemics were common until the middle of the nineteenth century, and until the 1840s many of London's sewers emptied into the Thames just a few feet above the ducts that drew drinking water from the river. It was fortunate that the fascination and opportunities of the city continued to attract rural migrants, since without migration the cities would not have grown but died. Until the latter part of the nineteenth century, the Old English observation "The city is the graveyard of countrymen" was all too accurate.

Engels on Industrial Slums

Friedrich Engels (1820–1895), Karl Marx's close associate and collaborator, was an acute observer of the social horrors of nineteenth-century urban industrialization. He likewise was a fine writer with a mastery of detail and mood rivaling Dickens's. Note his description of life in the industrial slums of Manchester.[*]

The view from this bridge—mercifully concealed from smaller mortals by a parapet as high as a man—is quite characteristic of the entire district. At the bottom the Irk flows, or rather stagnates. It is a narrow, coal-black stinking river full of filth and garbage which it deposits on the lower-lying bank. In dry weather, an extended series of the most revolting blackish green pools of slime remain standing on this bank, out of whose depths bubbles of miasmatic gases constantly rise and give forth a stench that is unbearable even on the bridge forty or fifty feet above the level of the water. . . . Above Ducie Bridge there are tall tannery buildings, and further up are dye-works, bone mills, and gasworks. The total entirety of the liquid wastes and solid offscourings of these works finds its way into the River Irk, which receives as well the contents of the adjacent sewers and privies. One can therefore imagine what kind of residues the stream deposits. Below Ducie Bridge, on the left, one looks into piles of rubbish, the refuse, filth and decaying matter of the courts on the steep left bank of the river. Here one house is packed very closely upon another, and because of the steep pitch of the bank a part of every house is visible. All of them are blackened with smoke, crumbling, old, with broken window panes and window frames. The background is formed by old factory buildings, which resemble barracks. On the right, low-lying bank stands a long row of houses and factories. The second house is a roofless ruin, filled with rubble, and the third stands in such a low situation that the ground floor is uninhabitable and is as a result without windows and doors. The background here is formed by the paupers' cemetery and the stations of the railways to Liverpool and Leeds. Behind these is the workhouse, Manchester's "Poor Law Bastille." It is built on a hill, like a citadel, and from behind its high walls and battlements looks down threateningly upon the working-class quarter that lies below. . . .

Passing along a rough path on the river bank, in between posts and washing fines, one penetrates into this chaos of little one-storied, one-roomed huts. Most of them have earth floors, cooking, living and sleeping all take place in one room. In such a hole, barely six feet long and five feet wide, I saw two beds—and what beds and bedding—that filled the room, except for the doorstep and fireplace in several others I found absolutely nothing, although the door was wide open and the inhabitants were leaning against it. Everywhere in front of the doors were rubbish and refuse, it was impossible to see whether any sort of pavement lay

---

[*] Friedrich Engels, *The Condition of the Working Class in England in 1844* (first published in 1845), Publishers Moscow, 1973.

under this, but here and there I felt it out with my feet. This whole pile of cattle-sheds inhabited by human beings was surrounded on two sides by houses and a factory and on a third side by the river. . . . [A] narrow gateway led out of it into an almost equally miserably-built and miserably-kept labyrinth of dwellings.

PART TWO

AMERICAN
URBANIZATION

3

THE RISE OF URBAN AMERICA

Cities force growth and make men talkative and entertaining, but they also make them artificial.

Ralph Waldo Emerson

INTRODUCTION

In this chapter we cross the ocean to the wilderness of North America and trace the coming of age of the American city. As you read through the following pages, note the major role played by environmental factors during the colonial period. (All the major early cities were seaports.) During the nineteenth century, by contrast, changing technology, particularly advances in transportation such as the railroad, came to have a far more important—if not dominant—impact. Dramatic population growth through immigration and changes in urban governance and organization also came to play a major role in the growth and development of cities. This chapter, then, takes us from Jamestown up to the contemporary era following World War II.

COLONISTS AS TOWN BUILDERS

We are rather new at being an urban continent. The first European colonists to arrive in North America found a land without indigenous cities, although the Indians of the northwest coast, with their reliable food supply from the sea, had established well-built settled villages with an elaborate social structure. Also at Mesa Verde in southwest Colorado the "ancient ones" had built cliff dwellings. By and large though, the North American Indian population was nomadic or lived in agricultural villages such as Taos in the southwest. Cahokia, located in the Mississippi River valley of southern Illinois, was the most populous pre-Columbian settlement north of Mexico, thriving from about A.D. 900 to A.D. 1400 as a farming and trade center. Unlike the Spanish colonists, the first English settlers found no existing urban civilizations. The Native American population of North America may have numbered less than 1 million at the time of the Jamestown settlement (1607).[1]

From the first, the town-building orientation of the colonists contrasted with Indian ways. The North American Indians lived in nature rather than building upon it. They viewed themselves as part of the ecology, part of the physical world. Their goal was not to master nature but to identify their niche and their relationship with the world around them. The Europeans came, on the contrary, not to adjust to the environment but to dominate and reshape it. The Puritans, for example, believed themselves to be God's chosen people. Moreover, the Europeans brought a land-tenure system based on private ownership of land—something quite alien to the Native American way of life.[2]

The colonists' emphasis was on conquering nature, and unfortunately for the Indians, the colonists tended to view Native Americans as a part of the environment. They were treated as just another environmental problem that had to be encountered and mastered before civilization could be introduced. The implication for the future was clear. There was no niche for the Indian in the town-oriented civilization of the colonists.

---

[1] Some estimates range as high as 10 million Native Americans, but in any case, smallpox, cholera, and other European-introduced diseases destroyed most of the indigenous population.

[2] Marshall Dees Harris, *The Origin of the Land Tenure System in the United States,* Iowa State University, Ames, 1953.

What has just been said is, of course, an overgeneralization, but from our urban perspective the important point is that the concept of the city, and all the good and evil it represents, came to North America with the first European colonist. This concept, with all the special technology, social organizations, and attitudes it entailed, was an importation from post-Renaissance Europe. This meant, among other things, that North American cities had no feudal period.[3]

The plans of the various companies that settled the English colonies in North America called for the establishment of tight little villages and commercial centers. The first successful settlements at Jamestown and Plymouth Colony were in fact small towns. Thus, early English settlers were not primarily agriculturists but rather town dwellers coming with town expectations. In fact, the initially limited number of farmers was a problem. Jamestown nearly perished from an excess of adventurers and a dearth of skilled artisans and farmers. As John Smith wrote back to the English sponsors of the Jamestown colony,

> When you send againe I intreat you rather send but thirty Carpenters, husbandmen, gardners, fisher men, blacksmiths, masons, and diggers up of trees, roots, well provided; then a tousand of such as we haus: for except we be able both to loge them, and feed them the most will consume with what of necessaries before they can be made good for anything.[4]

The wilderness of the new world appeared strange and hostile, and the early colonists sorely missed their towns. William Bradford movingly describes the world of the Pilgrims of 1620:

> They had now no friends to wellcome them nor inns to entertaine or refresh their weatherbeaten bodys, no houses or much less townes to repaire too, to seeke for succoure. . . . Besids, what could they see but a hidious and desolate wilderness, full of wild beasts and wild men? and what multituds ther might be of them they knew not.[5]

MAJOR SETTLEMENTS

The following pages note the role played by population, organization, environment, and technology in shaping the cities of North America. Five seaport communities spearheaded the urbanization of the seventeenth-century English colonies. The northernmost was Boston on New England's "stern and rockbound coast"; the southernmost was the newer and much smaller settlement of Charles Town in South Carolina.[6] Barely making an indentation in the 1,100 miles of wilderness separating these two were Newport, in the Providence Plantations of Rhode Island; New Amsterdam, which in 1664 became New York; and William Penn's Philadelphia on the Delaware River at the mouth of the Schuylkill River.

Environment played a heavy role in the early development of these first five cities. All five were seaports, either on the Atlantic or—as in the case of Philadel-

---

[3] Lewis Mumford would not agree with this statement. Mumford saw New England villages and towns as the last flickering of the medieval order. See, for example, Lewis Mumford, *Sticks and Stones: A Study of American Architecture and Civilization*, Liveright, New York, 1924.

[4] John Smith, *The General Historie of Virginia, New England, and the Summer Isles*, University Microfilms, Ann Arbor, Mich., 1966 (first published in London, 1624), p. 72.

[5] *Bradford's History of Plymouh Plantation*, William T. Davis (ed.), Scribner, New York, 1908, p. 96.

[6] Constance McLaughlin Green, *The Rise of Urban America*, Harper & Row, New York, 1965, p. 2.

phia—with access to the sea. Later towns such as Baltimore had similar environmental advantages. As seaports they became commercial centers funneling trade between Europe and the colonies. In terms of social structure all were Protestant, and against the established church, except for the ruling class of Charleston and (partially) New York. As Bridenbaugh points out, the social structure of these towns was fashioned by a background of relatively common political institutions; and the economic and cultural roots, whether English or Dutch, lay for the most part in the rising middle class of the old world.[7]

The five important urban settlements had certain similar characteristics. First, all had favorable sites. As noted above, all were coastal seaports or, like Philadelphia, were on a navigable river. Second, all were commercial cities emphasizing trade and commerce. Third, all had hinterlands or back country to develop, although Newport would find its hinterland increasingly cut off by Boston in the eighteenth century. Finally, all these cities were fundamentally British. Even New York, which was more cosmopolitan than many European cities, was controlled by a British upper stratum.

New England

The story of early New England is the story of its towns, for New England from the very beginning was town-oriented. The Puritan religious dissenters who originally settled New England came heavily from the more populous centers of old England. They numbered in their midst many tradespeople, mechanics, and artisans. In the new world these religious dissenters sought to create tight urban communal utopias rather than spreading themselves widely over the landscape. Massachusetts Bay, according to John Winthrop, was to be "as a City upon a Hill." In that colony there existed a social system of a nature unknown outside New England. The cordial union between the clergy, the bench, the bar, and respectable society formed a tight, self-reinforcing social elite.

Boston early outstripped its rivals in both population size and economic influence and kept its lead for a century in spite of Indian wars that twice threatened its existence. Boston had barely 300 residents in the 1630s, but by 1650 there were over 2,000 residents, and a visitor could report—with some exaggeration, perhaps—that it was a sumptuous "city" and "Center Towne and Metropolis of this Wildernesse."[8]

By 1742, Boston had a population of 16,000. The barrenness of Boston's hinterland inclined Bostonians to look to the sea, and the town grew to prosperity on trade and shipbuilding. Before Boston was a generation old, it had "begun to extend its control into the back country, and to develop a metropolitan form of economy that was essentially modern."[9]

Newport, the second New England city down the coast, was founded in 1639 by victims of religious bigotry in Massachusetts. Newport's growth was steady but

[7] Carl Bridenbaugh, *Cities in the Wilderness,* Capricorn Books, New York, 1964.
[8] Quoted in Kenneth T. Jackson and Stanley K. Schutty (eds.), *Cities in American History: The First Century of Urban Life in America, 1625–1742,* Knopf, New York, 1972.
[9] Carl Bridenbaugh, quoted in Charles N. Glaab and A. Theodore Brown, *A History of Urban America,* 2 ed., Macmillan, New York, 1976, p. 12.

far from spectacular; in a hundred years the population grew from 96 to 6,200. However, although Newport remained small, its growing commerce and well-ordered community life gave it a significant place in emerging urban America. In Newport, as in Boston, education was encouraged; in addition, Newport, due to the influence of religious leaders such as Anne Hutchinson, had religious toleration.

The Middle Colonies

Manhattan from the beginning had the most cosmopolitan population of the colonial cities, a fact reflected in the diversity of languages spoken there. Father Isaac Jogues recorded that as early as 1643 there were already "men of 18 different languages." Partially because of this mixture of national and religious backgrounds (Dutch Calvinists, Anglicans, Quakers, Baptists, Huguenots, Lutherans, Presbyterians, and even a sprinkling of Jews, Congregation Shearith Israel being organized in 1706), New York was by far the liveliest of the towns, a position many people maintain it still holds. Interestingly enough, as of 1720 a third of New York's population was black.[10] With the gradual abandonment of slavery in the north—largely for economic reasons—the proportion of blacks declined substantially over the next century. New York was already an American melting pot, although the stew would still be a bit lumpy three centuries later.

New York also had decisive environmental advantages that contributed heavily to its eventual emergence as "the American city." First, Manhattan had a magnificent deepwater natural harbor. Second, New York was blessed with a fertile soil. Third, the city had easy access to the interior hinterland by way of the Hudson River. The New England towns, by contrast, found their economic growth greatly hindered by the lack of an accessible, fertile hinterland.

Philadelphia, William Penn's "City of Brotherly Love," laid out in 1692, was the youngest of the colonial cities. This was in many ways an advantage, for by the time the city was organized, the Indians had departed and the land was already being settled. A policy of religious toleration and an extremely rich and fertile hinterland allowed rapid growth. By the time Philadelphia was six years old it had 4,000 inhabitants; by 1720 the number had risen to 10,000.[11] Accounts of the day noted the regularity of the town's gridiron pattern with its central square, and most frequently the substantial nature of its buildings.

> A City, and Towns. were raised then,
> Wherein we might abide.
> Planters also, and Husband-men,
> Had Land enough beside.
> The best of Houses then was known,
> To be of Wood and Clay,
> But now we build of Brick and Stone,
> Which is a better way.[12]

[10] Green, *The Rise of Urban America*, p. 22.
[11] Ibid., p. 27.
[12] Richard Frame, "A Short Description of Pennsylvania in 1692," in Albert Cook Myers (ed.), *Narratives of Early Pennsylvania, West New Jersey, and Delaware,* Scribner, New York, 1912; reprinted in Ruth E. Sutter, *The Next Place You Come: A Historical Introduction to Communities in North America,* Prentice-Hall, Englewood Cliffs, N.J., 1973, p. 90.

The South

The southernmost of the colonial cities was Charles Town (Charleston), founded in 1680 on a spit of land between the mouths of the Ashley and Cooper rivers. The town grew slowly; two decades after its founding it had only 1,100 inhabitants and had "not yet produced any Commodities fit for ye markett or Europe, but a few skins—and a little cedar."[13] For decades rice, indigo, and skins formed the basis of its commerce. Far more than northern cities, Charleston retained a negative trade balance with Great Britain.

Charleston's social organization and structure was unique among the major cities. The major difference was that by the 1740s over half of Charleston's inhabitants were slaves. The middle-class artisans and shopkeepers who were the backbone of the northern cities were caught in Charleston between the aristocratic pretensions of the large landowners and the increasing skills of the trained slaves. The result was civic atrophy, the major local event being the opening of the horse-racing season. Charleston had few municipal services and could not claim even a single tax-supported school.

COLONIAL URBAN INFLUENCE

The relatively small populations by contemporary standards of the cities and towns of colonial America should not distract us from their seminal importance. Politically, economically, and socially these five towns dominated early colonial life. Because of their access to the sea they served as entrepôts, exchanging the produce of the hinterland for the finished products of Europe. In addition to their commercial function they also served as the places where new ideas and forms of social organization could be developed.

Because the colonial cities had to meet uniquely urban problems, such as paving streets, removing garbage, and caring for the poor, collective efforts developed. In the words of one historian:

> In these problems of town living which affected the entire community lay one of the vast differences between town and country society, and out of the collective efforts to solve these urban problems arose a sense of community responsibility and power that was to further differentiate the two ways of life.[14]

As a result of the town-based settlement pattern, by 1690 almost 10 percent of the colonial population was urban, a higher percentage than that found in England itself at the same time. With the subduing of the Indians and the opening up of the hinterland for cultivation, the percentage (not, of course, the actual number) of urban dwellers decreased between 1690 and 1790. The opening up of frontier hinterlands permitted greater population dispersal than had previously been possible. Not until 1830 was the urban percentage of the total population as high as it had been at the close of the seventeenth century.[15]

---

[13] Constance M. Green, *The Rise of Urban America*, Harper and Row, New York, 1965, p. 21. For further information on Charleston, see David A. Smith, "Dependent Urbanization in Colonial America: The Case of Charleston, South Carolina," *Social Forces*, **66**:1–28, September, 1987.

[14] Charles N. Glaab (ed.), *The American City: A Documentary History*, Dorsey, Homewood, Ill., 1963, p. 3.

[15] Glaab and Brown, *A History of Urban America*, p. 21.

TABLE 3-1
Great Cities of America, 1790, 1870 (Post-Civil War), 1990*

1790	1870	1990
New York, N.Y.	New York, N.Y.	New York, N.Y.
Philadelphia, Pa.	Philadelphia, Pa.	Los Angeles, Calif.
Boston, Mass.	Brooklyn, N.Y.	Chicago, Ill.
Charleston, S.C.	St. Louis, Mo.	Houston, Tex.
Baltimore, Md.	Chicago, Ill.	Philadelphia, Pa.
Salem, Mass.	Baltimore, Md.	Detroit, Mich.
Newport, R.I.	Boston, Mass.	San Diego, Calif.
Providence, R.I.	Cincinnati, Ohio	Dallas, Tex.
Gloucester, Mass.	New Orleans, La.	Phoenix, Ariz.
Newburyport, Mass.	San Francisco, Calif.	San Antonio, Tex.

* City population only, not total metropolitan area population.
Source: U.S. Bureau of the Census.

Politically, the cities were dominant. With the exception of Virginia, where the landed aristocracy did not live in cities but nonetheless followed the latest London fashions and maintained a strong commerce with Europe, the cities set the political as well as the social tone. And the merchant classes became increasingly dissatisfied with British policy. The crown's tax measures had a bad effect on business. Boston was called "the metropolis of sedition"; and as Lord Howe, commander of the British forces at the time of the Revolution, noted, "Almost all of the People of Parts and Spirit were in the Rebellion."[16] This was not surprising, since Britain's revenue policy had struck deep at urban prosperity. Business and commercial leaders were determined to resist the crown rather than suffer financial reverses. This helps to explain the middle-class and upper-class nature of much of the support for the American Revolution. Urban-based merchants, rather than farmers, were the most upset by "taxation without representation."

THE GROWING NEW REPUBLIC: 1790–1860

After the Revolutionary War the cities continued their growth, although the first United States Census, taken in 1790, revealed that only 5 percent of the new nation's 4 million people lived in places of 2,500 or more. Numerically, America was overwhelmingly rural, but this demographic dominance was not reflected in the distribution of power or the composition of the leadership groups. The urban population had an influence on government, finance, and society as a whole far out of proportion to its size. The Federalist Party, which elected John Adams as the second president, was largely an urban-based party representing commercial and banking rather than agrarian interests.

Although three-quarters of the national population still lived within 50 miles of the Atlantic Ocean, there were already clear and widening differences between

[16] Green, *The Rise of Urban America*, p. 51.

New York's Wall Street in 1790. The two men in the foreground are Governor Phillip Schuyler and Alexander Hamilton. Walking toward them are Aaron Burr and his daughter, Theodosia. (Museum of the City of New York.)

townspeople and rural dwellers. The farmers' orientation was toward the expanding western frontier, while the townspeople were still oriented toward Europe. Because of their status as ocean ports, the American coastal cities frequently had more in common with the old world, and certainly better communication with it, than with their own hinterlands. Traveling from Washington to New York took eight days by horse or coach in 1790.

The census of 1790 showed that the largest city in the young nation was New York, with 33,000 inhabitants. Philadelphia was the second-largest city, with a population of 28,000 (see Table 3-1). Twenty years later New York had over 100,000 persons. In 1790, only 5 percent of the population lived west of the Allegheny Mountains.

Such rapid growth of the cities after the Revolutionary War was not only the result of foreign and rural immigration; an exceptionally high rate of natural replacement also played a large part. Precise data are lacking, but the birthrate is estimated to have been at least 55 per 1,000, or near the physiological upper limit. Each married woman in 1790 bore an average of almost eight children. One result of the high birthrate and the immigration from Europe of young adults was a national median age of only sixteen years. (By comparison, the median age for the white population today is thirty-five years.) Between 1790 and 1860 the population would increase dramatically, doubling every twenty-three years—a rate equivalent to that in some developing countries today.

TABLE 3-2
Percent of Urban Population, United States, 1790–1990

Year	Percent	Year	Percent
1790	5.1	1900	39.7
1800	6.1	1910	45.7
1810	7.3	1920	51.2
1820	7.2	1930	56.2
1830	8.8	1940	56.5
1840	10.8	1950 (old def.)	59.0
1850	15.3	1950 (new def.)	64.0
1860	19.8	1960	69.9
1870	25.7	1970	73.5
1880	28.2	1980	73.7
1890	35.1	1990	73.9

Source: U.S. Bureau of the Census.

The sheer abundance of land and the almost unlimited possibilities for fee-simple tenure meant freedom from Europe's lingering feudal constraints.[17] As put by a European visitor: "It does not seem difficult to find out the reasons why people multiply faster here than in Europe. . . . There is such an amount of good land yet uncultivated that a newly married man can get a spot of ground where he may comfortably subsist with his wife and children."[18]

As Table 3-2 indicates, the percentage of the population that is urban has grown every decade except 1810–1820. The decline in that decade was chiefly due to the destruction of American commerce resulting from the Embargo Acts and the War of 1812. That war came close to destroying the coastal cities; and partially as a result of isolation from English manufactures and products, the American cities began developing manufacturing interests. Even Thomas Jefferson, an ardent opponent of cities, was forced to concede:

> He, therefore, who is now against domestic manufacture, must be for reducing us either to dependence on that foreign nation or to be clothed in skins and to live like wild beasts in dens and caverns. I am not one of them; experience has taught me that manufacturers are now as necessary to our independence as to our comfort.[19]

Founding and Expansion of Cities

The period before the Civil War saw a rapid expansion of existing cities and the founding of many new ones. The invention of the railroad played a major role in this growth. During the period from 1820 to 1860, cities grew at a more rapid rate than at any other time before or since in American history.[20] It is noteworthy that of the fifty largest cities in America, only seven were incorporated before 1816, thirty-

[17] Sam Bass Warner, Jr., *The Urban Wilderness: A History of the American City,* Harper & Row, New York, 1972, p. 16.
[18] Quoted in James H. Cassedy, *Demography in Early America: Beginnings of the Statistical Mind,* Harvard University Press, Cambridge, Mass., 1969, pp. 154–155.
[19] P. L. Ford, *The Works of Thomas Jefferson,* Putnam, New York, 1904, pp. 503–504.
[20] Glaab, *The American City,* p. 65.

nine were incorporated between 1816 and 1876, and only four have been incorporated since 1876. Cincinnati, Pittsburgh, Memphis, Louisville, Detroit, Chicago, Denver, Portland, and Seattle are all early and mid-nineteenth-century cities. In the far west, the discovery of gold and then silver did much to spur town building. Some later became ghost towns, but San Francisco prospered as *the* major city of the west.

The influence of environmental factors on the growth of nineteenth-century cities can be seen from the fact that of the nine cities which by 1860 had passed the 100,000 mark, eight were ports. The one exception really wasn't an exception; it was the then independent city of Brooklyn, which shared the benefits of the country's greatest harbor.[21]

By the eve of the Civil War the first city of the nation was clearly New York. It had both a magnificent harbor and a large hinterland to sustain growth, and it had relatively flat terrain westward from the Hudson River. Nonetheless, what assured New York its dominance was the willingness to speculate on the technologies of first the Erie Canal and then the railroad. Mayor DeWitt Clinton prophesied that the canal would "create the greatest inland trade ever witnessed" and allow New York to "become the granary of the world, the emporium of commerce, the seat of manufactures, the focus of moneyed operations." He was right.

The completion of the canal in 1825 greatly stimulated New York City's trade and gave it an economic supremacy that has yet to be surpassed. Thus, the original environmental advantage stimulated a technological advance—the Erie Canal—which in turn led to population growth and changes in the social organization of business and government. New York's quick acceptance of railroads as a technological breakthrough, and the possibilities thus presented, further solidified the city's dominant position. Not only was New York the most important American city; it also had become a major world metropolis by the time of the Civil War. New York grew from just over 60,000 in 1800 to over 1 million in 1860. Of the world's cities only London and Paris were larger. By 1860, in addition to serving as the nation's financial center, New York also handled a third of the country's exports and a full two-thirds of the imports. New York's increase in size was matched by the increasing heterogeneity of its inhabitants, with their different tastes, aspirations, and needs—all of which could be best satisfied only in the large city.

Land speculation spurred the growth of cities. Fueled by a stream of immigrants and a greed for profits, cities went through periods of wild land speculation and building—only to be followed eventually by economic collapse and depression. Cincinnati, the "Queen City of the West," for example, experienced a boom during the 1820s, and during that decade its population expanded rapidly as a result of the development and use of steamboats. In other cities the technology of the railroad played a similar role in spurring growth.

Only in the deep south, where cotton was king, did the building of cities languish. In the plantation owners' view, cotton fields came before manufacturing and

[21] Blake McKelvey, *The Urbanization of America, 1860–1915,* Rutgers University Press, New Brunswick, N.J., 1963, p. 4.
See Howard P. Chudacoff, *The Evolution of American Urban Society,* Prentice-Hall, Englewood Cliffs, N.J., 1975, chap. 9.

commerce. The dominance of agriculture can be seen in the development—or, more correctly, the lack of development—of Charleston. At the beginning of the nineteenth century Charleston was the fifth-largest American city; by 1860 it had slipped to twenty-sixth place.[22] As a consequence of the Civil War, a devastating earthquake, and economic stagnation, Charleston was not numbered among even the fifty largest cities in 1900. The city had lost its economic reason for existing. The post–Civil War stagnation of Charleston is reflected in the saying that Charleston was "too poor to paint and too proud to whitewash."

Marketplace Centers

Before the Civil War (1861–1864), American cities, while undergoing tremendous growth, retained many preindustrial characteristics. The urban economy was still in a commercial rather than an industrial stage. Businesspeople were primarily merchants who intermittently took on subsidiary functions such as manufacturing, banking, and speculating. In 1850, 85 percent of the population was still classified as rural; 64 percent was engaged in agriculture.

Physically, the city prior to the Civil War was a walking city with a radius extending not over 3 miles. The separation of workplace and residence so common in contemporary American cities was limited. Local transportation by omnibus was slow, uncomfortable, and relatively expensive. Residences, businesses, and public buildings were intermixed with little specialization by area: "The first floor was given over to commerce, the second and third reserved for the family and clerks, and the fourth perhaps for storage. People lived and worked in the same house or at least in the same neighborhood."[23]

The separation that did occur was the obverse of the pattern of wealthy in the suburbs and poor in the city that we have come to accept as the American norm. (See Chapters 4 and 5 for discussion of theories of contemporary urban growth.) In early American cities, the well-to-do tended to live not on the periphery but near the center. In an era of slow, uncomfortable, and inadequate transportation, the poor were more often relegated to the less accessible areas on the periphery.[24]

THE INDUSTRIAL CITY: 1860–1950

The Civil War accelerated the shift from a mercantile or trade to an industrial economy. Aided by the new protective tariffs and the inflated profits, stimulated by the war, northern industrialists began producing steel, coal, and woolen goods, most of which had previously been imported. The closing of the Mississippi was a boon to Chicago and the east-west railroads.

A century after its founding (1880), the American nation had grown to 50 million and stretched from coast to coast. The lands of the Louisiana Purchase and

[22] "Nelson M. Blake, *A History of American Life and Thought,* McGraw-Hill, New York, 1963, p. 156.

[23] Christopher Tunnard and Henry Hope Reed, *American Skyline: The Growth and Form of Our Cities and Towns,* New American Library, New York, 1956, p. 59.

[24] Sam Bass Warner, Jr., *The Private City: Philadelphia in Three Periods of Its Growth,* University of Pennsylvania Press, Philadelphia, 1968, p. 13.

the Northwest Cession were already settled, while the western prairie was being peopled and plowed. However, in retrospect, this was the end, not the beginning, of the age of agriculture. The census of 1880 for the first time indicated that less than half the employable population worked in agriculture. Meanwhile, foreign immigration was swelling the cities, and urban areas held 28 percent of the population. A century ago (1890), the census counted 63 million persons. Today, we have over four times as many people. In 1890, New York was the nation's largest city with 1.5 million persons (Brooklyn, then separate, had 800,000 more people.)[25] The other cities with over a million persons were Chicago and Philadelphia.

During the last quarter of the nineteenth century, urbanism for the first time became a controlling factor in national life. This was a period of economic expansion for the nation. Capital-intensive industrialism was changing the nature of the economic system, rapidly changing America from a rural to an urban continent. The extent of this change can be seen in Table 3-3.

While the frontier captured the attention of writers and the imagination of the populace, the bulk of the nation's growth during the nineteenth century took place in cities. (The classic statement on the significance of the west was Frederick J. Turner's famous 1893 paper, "The Frontier in American History." A major urban response did not come until almost half a century later, with Arthur M. Schlesinger's "The City in American History.")[26] By the turn of the twentieth century, 38 cities had populations of over 100,000; the most notable of these new cities was the prairie metropolis of Chicago, which had bet heavily on the technology of the railroad. Chicago mushroomed from 4,100 at the time of its incorporation in 1833 to 1 million in 1890. Between 1850 and 1890 Chicago doubled its population every decade; in 1910 it passed 2 million. Nationally, in 100 years between 1790 and 1890 the total population grew 16-fold, while the urban population grew 139-fold.

[25] Bryant Robey, "Two Hundred Years and Counting: The 1990 Census," *Population Bulletin,* **44**:1, April, 1989, p. 7.
[26] Arthur M. Schlesinger, "The City in American History," *Mississippi Valley Historical Review,* **27**:43–66, June, 1940.

TABLE 3-3
Number of Urban Places by Population Size: Selected Years, 1850-1990

Size of place	1850	1900	1950	1990
1,000,000 or more	—	3	5	8
500,000 to 1,000,000	1	3	13	15
250,000 to 500,000	—	9	23	41
100,000 to 250,000	5	23	65	131
50,000 to 100,000	4	40	126	309
25,000 to 50,000	16	82	252	567
10,000 to 25,000	36	280	778	1,290

Source: U.S. Bureau of the Census, *U.S. Census of Population,* 1950, vol II; 1980, vol. I, table 23, and *Statistical Abstract of the United States,* 1994.

This Currier & Ives engraving shows the railroad bringing both prosperity and settlements with public schools. It is entitled "Westward the course of empire takes its way." (Bettmann, Archive.)

Technological Developments

As Richard Wade aptly phrased it, "The towns were the spearhead of the frontier." Technology was used to overcome the environment. This was particularly true west of the Mississippi, where the technological breakthrough of the railroad had reversed earlier patterns of settlement. Josiah Strong, writing in 1885, noted:

> In the Middle States the farms were the first taken, then the town sprang up to supply its wants, and at length the railway connected it with the world, but in the West the order is reversed—first the railroad, then the towns, then the farms. Settlement is, consequently, much more rapid, and the city stamps the country, instead of the country stamping the city. It is the cities and towns which will frame state constitutions, make laws, create public opinion, establish social usages, and fix standards of morals in the West.[27]

Strong may have exaggerated his case somewhat, but the railroad was crucial in the development of the west. During the second half of the nineteenth century, the railroads expanded from 9,000 to 193,000 miles—much of it built with federal loans and land grants.[28] The railroads literally opened the west.

At the same time, changes in farming technology were converting the self-sufficient yeoman into an entrepreneur raising cash crops for market. Horse-drawn

---

[27] Josiah Strong, *Our Country: Its Possible Future and Its Present Crisis,* Baker and Taylor, New York, 1885, p. 206.
[28] William Petersen, *Population,* Macmillan, New York, 1961, p. 34.

mechanical reapers, steel plows, and threshers heralded the shift from self-sufficient to commercial farming.

Spatial Concentration in Cities

The great cities of the east and midwest, with their hordes of immigrants, frantic
pace, municipal corruption, and industrial productivity, built much of their present
physical plant in the era of steam stretching from the 1880s to the depression of the
1930s. It is important to remember that the late-nineteenth-century city was a city
of concentration and centralization accentuated by industrialization. Initial industrialization encouraged centripetal rather than centrifugal forces. Since steam is
most cheaply generated in large quantities and must be used close to where it is produced, steam power thus fostered a compact city. Steam power encouraged the
proximity of factory and power supply. It fostered the concentration of manufacturing processes in a core area that surrounded the central business district and had
access to rail and often water transportation. This in turn tended to concentrate
managerial and wholesale distributing activities and, above all, population near the
factory.

The limited transportation technology meant that workers had to live near the
factories; this gave rise to row upon row of densely packed tenements. The distant
separation of residence and place of work was a luxury only the very wealthy in
commuting suburbs could afford. Surrounding the factories, slumlords built jaw-to-
jaw tenements on every available open space. These tenements were then packed
to unbelievable densities with immigrant workers—first Irish, then German, Jewish, Italian, and Polish—who could afford no other housing on the pitiful wages
they made working twelve hours a day, six days a week. Slums provided the immigrant laborers with housing close to the factories, but at a horrendous price in
terms of health and quality of life.

In the brief twelve-year period between 1877 and 1889, inventions such as
steel-frame buildings, the light bulb, electric power lines, electric streetcars, electric elevators, the telephone, subways, and the internal combustion engine were introduced.[29] Such inventions spurred the growth of cities.

The compact trade and commerce-oriented central business districts of northern industrial and commercial cities reflected the needs of the nineteenth century.
Before the widespread use of the automobile and telephone, it was necessary that
business offices be close to one another so that information could be transmitted by
means of messengers. High central-city land values were an inevitable result of the
common business demand for a central location. Nineteenth-century inventions
such as a practical steam elevator and steel-girdered buildings further enabled the
core area to become even more densely inhabited. Steel-girdered buildings no
longer had to be supported by massive outer walls, and offices and businesses could
be stacked vertically upon one another as high as foundations, local ordinances, and
economics would allow.

---

[29] Janice Perlman, "Mega Cities and New Technologies," paper presented at XI World Congress of Sociology, New Delhi,
India, July, 1986.

Note the congestion of downtown Philadelphia of a hundred years ago (1897) with pedestrians, carriages, electric streetcar, and wagons. (National Archives.)

The fact that New York, Chicago, Philadelphia, and St. Louis, to name only a few, are essentially cities built before the twentieth century, and before the automobile, is a problem we have to cope with today. Any attempt to deal with present-day transportation or pollution problems has to take into account the fact that most American cities were planned and built in the nineteenth century. We still live largely in cities designed, at best, for the age of steam and the horse-drawn streetcar.

As a side note, a quick way of determining the earlier boundaries of a city is to note the location of older cemeteries. Since cemeteries were traditionally placed on the outskirts, large cemeteries within present city boundaries effectively show earlier high-water marks of urban growth.

A Note on Urban Pollution

It is revealing, if depressing, to recognize that the problems of pollution and environmental destruction did not begin in the twentieth century. Until late in the nineteenth century most American cities, such as Baltimore and New Orleans, still relied on open trenches for sewage. The only municipal garbage collection provided by most cities until after the Civil War was that provided by scavenging hogs and dogs and other carrion eaters. Colonial Charleston even passed an ordinance protecting vultures because they performed a public service by cleaning the carcasses of dead animals.* In 1666 a Boston municipal ordinance ordered the inhabitants to bury all filth, while "all garbage, beasts, entralls &c," were to be thrown from the drawbridge into Mill Creek.† Colonial Boston's system of burying what you can and throwing the rest into the nearest river was used by many cities well into the modern era.

A description of Pittsburgh dating from the late nineteenth century details its air pollution in these terms:

> Pittsburgh is a smoky, dismal city, at her best. At her worst, nothing darker, dingier or more dispiriting can be imagined. The city is in the heart of the soft coal region; and the smoke from her dwellings, stores, factories, foundries, and steamboats, uniting settles in a cloud over the narrow valley in which she is built, until the very sun looks coppery through the sooty haze. According to a circular of the Pittsburgh Board of Trade, about twenty per cent, or one-fifth of all the coal used in the factories and dwellings of the city escapes into the air in the form of smoke. . . . But her inhabitants do not seem to mind it; and the doctors hold that this smoke from the carbon sulphur, and iodine contained in it, is highly favorable to the lung and cutaneous diseases, and is the sure death of malaria and its attendant fevers.‡

Public waterworks were luxuries found in few communities until well after the Civil War. Some medium-sized cities such as Providence, Rochester, and Milwaukee relied entirely on private wells and water carriers. Sanitation fared little better. Boston, which had attained a level few communities could equal, had under 10,000 water closets for its residents.§ Until the twentieth century, facilities were all but nonexistent in the congested tenements of the slums.

---

* Charles N. Glaab (ed.), *The American City: A Documentary History*, Dorsey, Homewood, Ill., p. 115.
† Carl Bridenbaugh, *Cities in the Wilderness*, Capricorn Books, New York, 1964, p. 18.
‡ Willard Glazier, *Peculiarities of American Cities*, Hubbard, Philadelphia, 1884, pp. 322–333.
§ Blake McKelvey, *The Urbanization of America, 1860–1915*, Rutgers University Press, New Brunswick, N.J., 1963, p. 13.

Twentieth-Century Dispersion

Contemporary metropolitan areas reflect dispersion rather than concentration. Three technological inventions contributed to this change: the telephone, the electric streetcar, and, most important, the automobile. The telephone meant that city business could be conducted other than by face-to-face contact or messenger. It enabled businesses to locate their factories separate from their offices.

Before the electric streetcar, separation of places of living from places of work was a luxury restricted to the affluent or well-to-do. Nineteenth-century suburbs developed along commuter railroad lines and were the private preserves of those who had both the time and the money to commute. The North Shore suburbs of Chicago are an example. Common people, however, walked or rode the horse streetcars to work. At the beginning of the twentieth century, the average New Yorker lived a quarter of a mile, or roughly two blocks, from his or her place of work. Chicago at that time contained 1,690,000 inhabitants, half of them living within 3.2 miles of the city center.[30]

The electric streetcar changed all this. Perfected in 1888 in Richmond, Virginia, the streetcar moved twice as fast as the horse-drawn car and had over three times the carrying capacity. The new system of urban transportation was almost immediately adopted everywhere. By the turn of the century horsecar lines, which had accounted for two-thirds of all street railways a decade earlier, had all but vanished. Electric trolleys accounted for 97 percent of all mileage in 1902, with 2 percent still operated by cable car lines and only 1 percent by horsecars.[31]

The result was the rapid development of outer areas of the city and the proliferation of middle-class streetcar suburbs.[32] With one's home somewhere along the streetcar line, it was possible to live as far as 12 miles from the central business district and commute relatively rapidly and inexpensively. This led to an outward expansion of the city and the establishment of residential suburbs in strips along the right-of-way of the streetcar line. Those high in the electric traction industry and corrupt politicians with influence made fortunes when streetcar lines were built to outlying areas where they just happened to own all the vacant lots.

The above should also help us keep in mind that technology is not a neutral force. The benefits of the streetcar–and later the automobile– technology especially assisted the middle classes in establishing ethnically and racially exclusive suburban neighborhoods. (For elaboration see Chapter 9, Changing Suburbanization Patterns.)

Land lying between the "spokes" formed by the streetcar lines remained undeveloped. The cities thus came to have a rather pronounced star-shaped configuration, with the points of the star being the linear rail lines.[33] This is a shape cities would hold until the era of the automobile.

---

[30] Paul F. Cressey, "Population Succession in Chicago: 1898–1930," *American Journal of Sociology,* **44**:59, 1938.

[31] Glaab and Brown, *A History of Urban America,* 2 ed., p. 144.

[32] For an excellent account of this phenomenon, see Sam Bass Warner, Jr., *Streetcar Suburbs: The Process of Growth in Boston, 1870–1900,* Atheneum, New York, 1970. Also see Kenneth T. Jackson, Crabgrass Frontier, Oxford University Press, New York, 1985; and J. John Palen, *The Suburbs,* McGraw-Hill, New York, 1995.

[33] Richard Hurd, *Principles of City Land Values,* The Record and Guide, New York, 1924.

Where street rail lines intersected, natural breaks in transit took place and secondary business and commercial districts began to develop. These regional shopping areas were the equivalent of the peripheral shopping centers of today. With the coming of the automobile, the city areas between the streetcar lines filled in, and by the 1920s most of our major cities had completed the bulk of their building. The depression of the 1930s effectively stopped downtown building; thus, many central business districts remained basically unchanged until building resumed again in the early 1960s.[34] Outlying areas similarly saw little change until the post–World War II suburbanization boom (Chapter 7).

POLITICAL LIFE

Corruption and Urban Services

In 1853 New York was described in *Putnam's Monthly* as possessing "Filthy streets, the farce of a half-fledged and inefficient police, and the miserably bad government, generally, of an unprincipled common council, in the composition of which ignorance, selfishness, impudence and greediness seem to have an equal share." Over the following score of years the situation deteriorated. Virtually everywhere venality and urban politics became synonymous. As Arthur Schlesinger charitably put it, "This lusty urban growth created problems that taxed human resourcefulness to the utmost."[35] A particularly high price was paid in the area of municipal governance. Political institutions that were adequate under simplified rural conditions but inadequate to the task of governing a complicated system of ever-expanding public services and utilities presented an acute problem. The contemporary observer Andrew White was more direct, "With very few exceptions the city governments of the United States are the worst in Christendom . . . the most expensive, the most inefficient, and the most corrupt."[36] Or as the noted British scholar James Bryce put it, "There is no denying that the government of cities is the one conspicuous failure of the United States."[37]

Boss Tweed of New York, who plundered the city of between $60 million and $200 million, was even more explicit: "The population is too helplessly split into races and factions to govern it under universal suffrage, except by bribery or patronage or corruption."[38] The political machines were renowned for graft and voting fraud. Immigrants were encouraged to "vote early and often" for the machine candidates.

On the other hand, although the political bosses emptied the public treasury, they also provided poorer citizens with urban services, jobs, and help in solving problems. The bosses were buffers between slum dwellers and the often hostile

---

[34] For more on central business districts, see Chapter 12, The Question of Urban Crisis.
[35] Schlesinger, "The City in American History," pp. 35–44.
[36] Quoted in James Bryce, *Forum,* **X,** 1890, p. 25.
[37] James Bryce, *The American Commonwealth,* vol. 1, Macmillan, London, 1891, p. 608. Reprinted by Putnam, New York, 1959.
[38] Quoted in Arthur M. Schlesinger, *Paths to the Present,* Macmillan, New York, 1949, p. 60.

Boss Tweed, head of New York's Tammany Hall political machine, as portrayed by the political cartoonist Thomas Nast. Tweed plundered the city of between $60 million and $200 million. (Culver Pictures.)

official bureaucracy. In return for the immigrants' vote, the boss provided not abstract ideals but practical services and benefits. The boss was the one to come to when you needed a job, when your child was picked up for delinquency, or when you drank a bit too much and were arrested for drunkenness. The boss would arrange something with the police at the stationhouse or even "go your bail" if the offense was serious. The boss was certain to attend every wedding and wake in the neighborhood, and often provided cash to get the newlyweds going or cover funeral expenses for a widow. The boss produced. As a Boston ward heeler, Martin Lomasney, straightforwardly expressed it, "There's got to be in every ward somebody that any bloke can come to—no matter what he's done—to get help. Help, you understand; none of your law and justice, but help."[39]

[39] Quoted in Lincoln Steffens, *The Autobiography of Lincoln Steffens,* Literary Guild, New York, 1931, p. 618.

In managing the city the bosses distinguished between dishonest graft and honest graft, or "boodie." The former would include shakedowns, payoffs, and protection money for illegal gambling, liquor, and prostitution. "Boodie," on the other hand, involved using your control over contracts for municipal services and tax assessments to maximize your advantage. The boss George Washington Plunkitt in a famous passage explained how it worked.

> Just let me explain by examples. My party's in power in the city, and it's going to undertake a lot of public improvements. Well, I'm tipped off, say, that they're going to lay out a new park at a certain place. I see my opportunity and I take it. I go to that place and I buy up all the land I can in the neighborhood. Then the board of this or that makes its plan public, and there is a rush to get my land, which nobody cared particular for before. Ain't it perfectly honest to charge a good price and make a profit on my investment and foresight? Of course it is. Well, that's honest graft.[40]

In an urban environment committed to the principle of free enterprise, politicians saw no reason for all the profits to go to businesspeople rather than politicians.

While the "better classes" viewed all machine bosses as rogues and thieves, the bosses were apparently far more personable and friendly than the elite captains of industry in the business community. A study of twenty city bosses described them as warm and often sentimental men who had come from poor immigrant families. All were naive urbanites, and most were noted for loyalty to their families.[41] The political machine provided a route for social mobility for bright and alert young immigrants. Police departments were also an avenue of upward mobility for first- and second-generation European immigrants. Without the aid of the ward bosses, the new immigrants would have had an even rougher time than they did. For the immigrants, boss rule was clearly functional. As expressed by the sociologist Robert Merton, "The functional deficiencies of the official structure generate an alternative (unofficial) structure to fulfill existing needs somewhat more effectively."[42]

Immigrants' Problems

The role of immigrants is treated in detail in Chapter 10, Ethnic Diversity: Ethnics, African Americans, Hispanics, Asians, and Native Americans. Suffice it to say here that the dimensions of the European immigrant flood are hard to overemphasize— perhaps some 40 million persons between 1800 and 1925. From the 1840s onward, waves of immigrants landed in the major northeastern ports. The first of the mass ethnic immigrations was that of the Irish, who were driven from home in the late 1840s by the ravages of the potato blight. Later, Germans and Scandinavians poured into the middle west, particularly after the development of steamships and the opening of the railroads to Chicago.

---

[40] Howard P. Chudacoff, *The Evolution of American Urban Society*, Prentice Hall, Englewood Cliffs, N.J., 1975, pp. 131–132.

[41] Harold Zink, *City Bosses in the United States: A Study of Twenty Municipal Bosses*, Duke University Press, Durham, N.C., 1930, p. 350. For a study of the role of a twentieth-century boss, see Andrew Theodore Brown and Lyle W. Dorset, *K.C.: A History of Kansas City, Missouri*, Pruett Publishing, Boulder, Colo., 1978.

[42] Robert K. Merton, *Social Theory and Social Structure*, Free Press, Glencoe, Ill., 1957, p. 73.

Immigration accelerated after the Civil War, spurred on by the need for industrialization. This was a period of industrial and continental expansion. Between 1860 and 1870, twenty-five of the thirty-eight states took official action to stimulate immigration, offering not only voting rights but also sometimes land and bonuses.

By 1890 New York had half as many Italians as Naples, as many Germans as Hamburg, twice as many Irish as Dublin, and two-and-a-half times the number of Jews in Warsaw.[43] The traditions, customs, religion, and sheer numbers of these immigrants made fast assimilation impossible. Between 1901 and 1910 alone, over 9 million immigrants were counted by immigration officials. These newcomers came largely from peasant backgrounds. They were packed into teeming slums and delegated to the lowest-paying and most menial jobs. Native-born Protestant Americans suddenly became aware of the fact that 40 percent of the 1910 population was of foreign stock—that is, immigrants or the offspring of immigrants.[44] The percentage was considerably higher in the large northern industrial cities, where over half the population was invariably of foreign stock.

To WASP (white Anglo-Saxon Protestant) writers around the turn of the century, the sins of the city were frequently translated into the sins of the new immigrant groups pouring into the ghettos of the central core. Slum housing, poor health conditions, and high crime rates were all blamed on the newcomers. Those on the city's periphery and in the emerging upper-class and upper-middle-class suburbs associated political corruption with the central city. Native-born Americans tended to view city problems as being the fault of the frequently Catholic, or Jewish, immigrants who inhabited the central-city ghettos.

Even sympathetic reformers such as Jacob Riis portrayed central-city slums as anthills teeming with illiterate immigrants. The masses in the ghettos were a threat to democracy.[45]

Reform Movements

The writings of "muckrakers" like Lincoln Steffens, who in his articles on "the shame of the cities" exposed municipal corruption, gave considerable publicity to the grosser excesses of municipal corruption, such as the deals with utility franchises. To destroy the power of the bosses and their immigrant supporters, reforms were pushed in city after city. Reformers of the period had a distinctly middle-class orientation. Social reformers such as Jane Addams, who founded Hull House to teach immigrants "Americanism" and job skills, and Margaret Sanger, who in 1916 opened the first birth control clinic for immigrants in Brooklyn (today Planned Parenthood), were upper-class or middle-class. To the general public the problems of the city were viewed then, as today, as problems of and by the poor in the central core. While the bosses represented personalized politics, reform represented abstract WASP goals such as good citizenship, efficient administration, and proper ac-

---

[43] Glaab and Brown, *A History of Urban America*, p. 125.
[44] Donald Bogue, *The Population of the United States*, Free Press, Glencoe, Ill., 1969, p. 178.
[45] Jacob Riis, *How the Other Half Lives: Studies among the Tenements of New York*, Scribner, New York, 1890; republished by Corner House, Williamstown, Mass., 1972.

Tenements such as these on the Lower East Side of
New York housed exceptionally high population
densities when this photo was taken in 1922.
(Culver Pictures.)

counting. The progressive movement at the turn of the century, at least in its urban
manifestation, was in many respects an attempt by the upper middle class to reform
the inner city. This, of course, meant white, Protestant, middle-class groups regain-
ing political power. Political reformers joined with businesspeople in organized
groups such as the National Municipal League to "reform" city government.

The National Municipal League provided model charters and moral impetus.
By 1912 some 210 communities had dropped the mayor and city-council system
and adopted the commission form of government. In 1913 Dayton adopted the first
city-manager system, and during the following year forty-four other cities followed
suit. Under the city-manager system, a nonpolitical manager is appointed to run the
city in a businesslike manner. However, in the largest cities the political machines,
while they lost a few battles, managed to weather the storm. The coming of World
War I directed crusading energies into new channels, and the Roaring Twenties was
not a decade noted for municipal reform. While there were exceptions, such as
William Hoan, the reform socialist mayor of Milwaukee, many cities during the

1920s had a colorful and corrupt mayor like James ("Gentleman Jimmy") Walker in New York or Big Bill ("The Builder") Thompson in Chicago. Today, urban corruption still occasionally surfaces.

URBAN IMAGERY

Ambivalence

America has never been neutral regarding its great cities; they have been either exalted as the centers of vitality, enterprise, and excitement or denounced as sinks of crime, pollution, and depravity. Our present ambivalence toward our cities is nothing new; even the founding fathers had great reservations about the moral worth of cities. The city was frequently equated by writers such as Thomas Jefferson with all the evils and corruption of the old world, while an idealized picture of the yeoman farmer represented the virtue of the new world. Thomas Jefferson expressed the sentiments of many of his fellow citizens when he stated in 1787 in a letter to James Madison,

> I think our governments will remain virtuous as long as they are chiefly agricultural; and this will be as long as there shall be vacant land in any part of America. When they get piled upon one another in large cities, as in Europe, they will become corrupt as in Europe.[46]

In a famous letter to Benjamin Rush, written in 1800, Jefferson even saw some virtue in the yellow fever epidemics that periodically ravaged seaboard cities. Philadelphia, for example, lost over 4,000 persons, almost 10 percent of its population, in the epidemic of 1793. Jefferson wrote to Rush:

> When great evils happen I am in the habit of looking out for what good may arise from them as consolations to us, and Providence has in fact, so established the order of things, as that most evils are the means of producing some good. The yellow fever will discourage the growth of great cities in our nation, and I view great cities as pestilential to the morals, the health, and the liberties of man.[47]

This, however, is not the entire picture, for in spite of these sentiments Jefferson proposed a model town plan for Washington, D.C., and after the War of 1812 came to support urban manufacturing. Also, although in his writings Jefferson advised against sending Americans to Europe for education lest they be contaminated by urban customs, he himself enjoyed visiting Paris and was a social success there. Other Americans were similarly inconsistent.

Benjamin Franklin, never one to be far from the stimulation, pleasures, and excitement of the city, went so far as to say that agriculture was "the only honest way to acquire wealth . . . as a reward for innocent life and virtuous industry." Ben Franklin was many things during his long, productive life, but never a farmer; and

---

[46] Quoted in Glaab, *The American City,* p. 38.
[47] Andrew A. Lipscomb and Albert E. Bergh (eds.), *The Writings of Thomas Jefferson,* vol. X, The Thomas Jefferson Memorial Association, Washington, D.C., 1904, p. 173.

his own way of life indicates that he never considered an innocent life or conventional virtue to be much of a reward. Writers as diverse as de Tocqueville, Emerson, Melville, Hawthorne, and Poe all had strong reservations about the city.[48]
According to de Tocqueville:

> I look upon the size of certain American cities, and especially on the nature of their population, as a real danger which threatens the future security of the democratic republics of the New World; and I venture to predict they will perish from this circumstance, unless the Government succeeds in creating an armed force which while it remains under the control of the majority of the nation, will be independent of town population, and able to repress its excess.[49]

Cowley's line "God the first garden made, and the first city Cain" expressed an attitude toward cities shared by many Americans. Thoreau sitting in rural solitude, watching a sunset, is an acceptable image. Thoreau sitting on a front stoop in Boston, watching the evening rush hour, creates an entirely different image. In the twentieth century the famous architect Frank Lloyd Wright carried on the anti-urban ideology, referring to cities as "a persistent form of social disease."

Americans, even while pouring into the cities, have traditionally idealized the country. A 1989 Gallup poll indicates that, given the choice, almost half of American adults would move to towns with less than 10,000 inhabitants or to rural areas.[50] The clearing of the wilderness by the pioneers, and the taming (eradication) of savages—human and animal—was considered a highly laudable enterprise. By contrast, the building of cities by the sweat and muscle of immigrants was ignored. It is as if we consider the history of the immigrants somewhat discreditable and thus best forgotten.

Vigorous attacks on the city came from writers such as Josiah Strong, who condemned it as the source of the evils of "rum, romanism, and rebellion." Strong's book *Our Country* sold a phenomenal—for that date—175,000 copies. He effectively mirrored the fears of small-town Protestant America that urban technology and the growth of foreign immigrant groups were in the process of undermining the existing social order and introducing undesirable changes such as political machines, slums, and low church attendance. Several excerpts give the general tone of his "rum, romanism, and rebellion" argument:

> The city has become a serious menace to our civilization. . . . It has a particular fascination for the immigrant. Our principal cities in 1880 contained 39.3 percent of our entire German population, and 45.8 percent of the Irish. Our ten larger cities at that time contained only nine percent of the entire population, but 23 percent of the foreign. . . .
> Because our cities are so largely foreign, Romanism finds in them its chief strength. For the same reason the saloon together with the intemperance and liquor power which it represents, is multiplied. . . .
> Socialism centers in the city, and the materials of its growth are multiplied with the growth of the city. Here is heaped the social dynamite; here roughs, gamblers, thieves,

[48] Morton White and Lucia White, *The Intellectual versus the City,* Harvard and M.I.T. Presses, Cambridge, Mass., 1962.
[49] Alexis de Tocqueville, *Democracy in America,* Henry Reeve (trans.), New York, 1839, p. 289.
[50] Gallup poll, *New York Times News Service,* Oct. 8, 1989.

robbers, lawless and desperate men of all sorts congregate; men who are ready on any pretext to raise riots for the purpose of disruption and plunder; here gather the foreigners and wage-workers who are especially susceptible to socialist arguments; here skepticism and irreligion abound; here inequality is the greatest and most obvious, and the contrast between opulence and penury the most striking; there the suffering is the sorest.[51]

An extremely influential lecture by Frederick Jackson Turner at the turn of the century, "The Winning of the West," also struck a responsive chord: It glorified the pioneer and the virtues of the west. Needless to say, such homage was not paid to tenement dwellers working under oppressive conditions, who were simply trying to raise decent families. Today, television perpetuates the same myth when it gives us drama after drama concerning life in the nineteenth-century American west, but nothing about the nineteenth-century American city dweller. The cowboy, not the factory hand, is the American hero.

Criticism of the city contained some contradictory premises, although these were generally not noticed: While it was being castigated for not exhibiting rural or agrarian values, it was also being taken to task for failing to be truly urban and reach the highest ideals of an urban society. In short, the city was at the same time supposed to be both more rural and more urban.

Distrust and dislike of the city simmered during the latter part of the nineteenth century and finally crystallized around the issue of the free coinage of silver, with silver representing the agrarian west and gold the commercial and industrial east. William Jennings Bryan's campaign for the presidency in 1896 was a major attempt by the agricultural antiurbanites to gain national political power. As Bryan put it in his famous "cross of gold" speech: "Burn down your cities and leave our farms, and your cities will spring up again as if by magic; but destroy our farms, and the grass will grow in the streets of every city in the country."[52] But by the end of the nineteenth century Bryan's day had passed, and although agricultural fundamentalism still had some strength, it was no longer a commanding ideology. The city, not the farm, represented the future.

Myth of Rural Virtue

The myth of agrarian virtue continues to live in politics. As Hofstadter has amusingly noted, one of President Calvin Coolidge's campaign photographs in 1924 showed him posing as a simple farmer haying in Vermont. However, the photograph said more than was intended, for the President's overalls are obviously fresh, his shoes are highly polished, and if one looks carefully, one can see his expensive Pierce Arrow, with Secret Service men waiting to rush him back to the city once the picture-taking was completed.[53] Within more recent times President Carter wasn't averse to having himself pictured as a small-town "good ole boy." President Reagan similarly posed for publicity photos of himself cutting wood on his "ranch,"

[51] Strong, *Our Country*, chap. 11.
[52] Glaab and Brown, *The American City*, p. 59.
[53] Richard Hofstadter, *The Age of Reform: From Bryan to FDR*, Knopf, New York, 1955, p. 31.

while George Bush, the archetypal easterner, billed himself as a "Texan," and Bill Clinton in 1992 ran as being a small-town boy from Hope, Arkansas.

Numerically, for two-thirds of a century America has been a nation of urban dwellers, and with every census the percentage of urban dwellers climbs higher. Only 1.9 percent of the nation's population resides on farms.[54] Even the quarter of the population that does not live in urban places is clearly tied to an urban way of life. As noted in Chapter 1, the profits of wheat farmers, cattle ranchers, dairy farmers, and other agribusiness people are tied more to government price-support systems than to weather or other natural factors.

Today our picture of how rural life is lived and the nature of the basic rural virtues is the creation of mass media based in and directed from cities. Television shows written in New York and produced in Hollywood try to create an image of small towns, filled with friendly folk, with "down-home" wisdom, rather like a Norman Rockwell painting. Urban advertising also hits hard at the same bogus theme—commercials often depend heavily on nostalgia, with old cars, fields of wheat, the old farmhouse, and the front porch swing.

What all this reflects is a deep ambivalence regarding cities and city life. A 1989 Gallup poll indicated that only 19 percent consider city life to be the ideal. Suburbs (24 percent), small towns (34 percent), and farms (22 percent) are all rated higher.[55] As a people, we glorify rural life but live in urban areas. North America is the most urbanized of the continents (excluding Australia), but our attitude toward cities is frequently unrealistic. Ours is an urban continent, but we treat our major cities as though we don't trust them and wish they would fade away and stop causing problems.

---

[54] U.S. Census of Population, "Residents of Farms and Rural Areas: 1990," *Current Population Reports,* series P-20, no. 457, 1992, p. 2.
[55] Gallup Organization. "Your Kind of Town," *Richmond Times Dispatch,* Oct. 8, 1989, p. K1.

Carl Sandburg's Chicago

Probably the most quoted image of the raw vitality, strength, and brutality of the early twentieth-century American city is Sandburg's poem "Chicago."* An excerpt follows:

> Hog Butcher for the World,
> Tool Maker, Stacker of Wheat,
> Player with Railroads and the Nation's Freight Handler;
> Stormy, husky, brawling,
> City of the Big Shoulders:
>
> They tell me you are wicked and I believe them, for I have seen
> your painted women under the gas lamps luring the farm boys.
> And they tell me you are crooked and I answer: Yes, it is true
> I have seen the gunman kill and go free to kill again,
> And they tell me you are brutal and my reply is: On the faces of
> women and children I have seen the marks of wanton hunger. And
> having answered so I turn once more to those who sneer at
> this my city, and I give them back the sneer and say to
> them:
> Come and show me another city with lifted head singing so proud
> to be alive and coarse and strong and cunning.
> Flinging magnetic curses amid the toil of piling job on job, here
> is a tall bold slugger set vivid against the little soft
> cities;
> Fierce as a dog with tongue lapping for action, cunning as a
> savage pitted against the wilderness,
> Bareheaded,
> Shoveling,
> Wrecking,
> Planning,
> Building, breaking, rebuilding,
> Under the smoke, dust all over his mouth, laughing with white
> teeth,
> Under the terrible burden of destiny laughing as a young man
> laughs,
> Laughing even as an ignorant fighter laughs who has never lost a
> battle.
>
> Bragging and laughing that under his wrist is the pulse, and
> under his ribs the heart of the people,
> Laughing!
> Laughing the stormy, husky, brawling laughter of Youth,
> half-naked, sweating, proud to be Hog Butcher, Tool Maker, Stacker of
> Wheat, Player with Railroads and Freight Handler to the Nation.

* Carl Sandburg, *Chicago Poems*, Holt, New York, 1916.

4

STRUCTURE AND ORGANIZATION OF AMERICAN CITIES

We shape our buildings, and afterwards our buildings shape us.

Winston Churchill

INTRODUCTION

Much has been written of the American city: its internal structure, its forms of social organization, its peoples and life-styles, and its problems. The sociologist Louis Wirth suggested that these various topics could be viewed empirically from three interrelated perspectives: (1) as a physical structure comprising a population base, a technology, and an ecological order, (2) as a system of social organization involving a characteristic social structure, a series of social institutions, and a typical pattern of social relationships, and (3) as a set of attitudes and ideas and a constellation of personalities engaging in typical forms of collective behavior, subject to characteristic mechanisms of social control.[1] In this chapter we shall be concerned with the first two of these perspectives: the spatial and social ecology of the city and how it affects and is affected by the city as a system of social organization. Urbanism as a system of life-styles and values is discussed in Chapter 7, City Life-Styles. Alternative political economy and neo-Marxist analyses of urban change are detailed in Chapter 5, Urban Political Economy.

ECOLOGICAL MODEL

The ecological model developed out of a concern with the development of the form and structure of the community. "Ecology" in its broadest sense is the study of the relationships among organisms within an environment. The sum total of these many relationships among organisms in a habitat is called a "biotic community," and the community together with its physical habitat forms an "ecosystem."

The ecological school and the term "human ecology" originated with the sociologists Park and Burgess at the University of Chicago in 1921, and represented an attempt to systematically apply the basic theoretical scheme of plant and animal ecology to the study of human communities. Ecological reasoning, which traces its theoretical underpinnings to Charles Darwin's research on evolution, was first applied to the study of plants in the latter part of the nineteenth century. Animal ecology emerged in the early twentieth century, and human ecology soon followed.

Contemporary human ecology is concerned with examining the independence and interdependence of specialized roles and functions (recurrent patterns of behavior) within the society. In examining the relationship between people and their environment and people within their environment, the level of analysis focuses on the aggregate level. The issue is the properties of populations rather than the properties of the individuals who constitute them. Thus, human ecology is based on the study of groups rather than individuals—and this focus on the group or aggregate is basic to sociology, as opposed to disciplines such as psychology in which the focus is on the individual. The focus here is on the structure of organized activity. Human ecology does not—and cannot—explain the beliefs, values, and attitudes of individuals while they are performing certain activities.[2]

---

[1] Louis Wirth, "Urbanism as a Way of Life," *American Journal of Sociology,* **44**:18–19, July, 1938.
[2] Members of the sociocultural school of human ecology would dispute this statement.

EARLY HUMAN ECOLOGY

Classical human ecology came into its own during the 1920s at the University of Chicago. Chicago was undergoing rapid social and physical changes, and there developed a strong interest in scientifically studying these changes. This had never been done in a systematic fashion for any city. Led by researchers such as Robert Park and Ernest Burgess, the so-called Chicago school of sociology produced a prodigious number of studies. The interest of the Chicago sociologists was not simply in mapping where groups and institutions were located, but rather in discovering how the sociological, psychological, and moral experiences of city life were reflected in spatial relationships. One member of the Chicago school said that human ecology "deals with the spatial aspects of symbiotic relationships of human beings and human institutions."[3]

Park was interested in how changes in the physical and spatial structure shaped social behavior. He felt that "most if not all cultural changes in society will be correlated with changes in its territorial organization, and every change in the territorial and occupational distribution of the population will effect changes in the existing culture."[4] This postulate of "an intimate congruity between the social and physical space, between social and physical distance, and between social equality and residential proximity is the crucial hypothetical framework supporting urban ecological theories."[5]

Classical ecological theories of the human community were analogous to evolutionary theories explaining plant and animal development. A person driving from the desert into the mountains finds that different soil, water, and temperature affect the bands of growth of the plants; by analogy, in a drive from a city's business district to its outlying suburbs, there are differing zones of development. In all these theories, competition—the Darwinian struggle for existence—played a core role. In the city, as a consequence of economic competition for prime space, there emerged distinct spatial and social zones. The internal structure of the city thus evolved not as a consequence of direct planning but through competition, which changed areas through the ecological processes of invasion, succession, and segregation of new groups (e.g., immigrants) and land uses (e.g., commercial use displacing residential use). Note that in contrast to this ecological model which places emphasis on competition and changing technology, political economy and neo-Marxist models emphasize the deliberate planned actions of government officials and economic elites in shaping urban patterns. Both ecological and political economy models stress that change occurs through conflict.

Chicago ecologically oriented sociologists were careful to stress the social as well as the economic aspects of competition for urban space. For example, in their study of ethnic and racial neighborhoods they examined the relationship between residential proximity and social equality. They found that in the large city, where one's social position would not be widely known to everyone, spatial distance was

[3] Roderick Duncan McKenzie, *The Metropolitan Community*, McGraw-Hill, New York, 1933.
[4] Robert Park, *Human Communities: The City and Human Ecology*, Free Press, New York, 1952, p. 14.
[5] Ralph Thomlinson, *Urban Structure: The Social and Spatial Character of Cities*, Random House, New York, 1969, p. 9.

often substituted for social distance—thus the importance of a fashionable address in the "right" neighborhood.

Invasion and Succession

Change in community areas comes about through intrusion of a new land use into an area of another land use, and the history of the American city is the story of the invasion of one land use by another. The end result when one group or function finally takes the place of another is called "succession."[6] None of the patterns of land use within a city are permanently fixed, although some zoning laws attempt to fix them. As cities have grown, areas that were once characterized by single-family houses have been converted to apartment, commercial, or industrial use—this is succession. All too frequently such processes are given overlays of values or morals. But the city, if it is viable, is always in the process of changing. Ecological patterns are dynamic rather than static. Cities that do not change become historical tourist attractions or stagnant backwaters.

Today one of the most spectacular instances of invasion and eventual succession is found in urban ethnic changes. Particularly on the West Coast, the new ethnic group "invading" an area is often Hispanic or Asian. Another instance of population invasion is the flow of limited numbers of affluent young whites to inner sections of the central city. This in-migration is not to areas of new housing, but rather to older neighborhoods in a state of some decline. This rehabilitation, or "gentrification," of the central-city neighborhoods is discussed in Chapter 12, The Question of Urban Crisis.

The process of economic succession, while less dramatic than population changes, can be of equally great long-term importance. Examples are the moving out of industry, the transition in neighborhoods from single-family to multiple-family dwelling units, and the change from residential to commercial land use. Students will note that the last two of these invasion-succession patterns can commonly be found in residential areas abutting growing colleges and universities. Such changes are frequently viewed in moral terms—for example, as the decline of family neighborhoods. Remember, though, that a city, if it is viable, is always in a process of change.

The early sociologists of the Chicago school were particularly interested in the segregated areas resulting from the process of selective competition. The Chicago sociologists called these areas "natural areas," since they were supposedly the results of ecological processes rather than of planning or conscious creation by any government unit. When zoning laws were established, the regulations generally recognized such natural areas of apartment houses, single-family neighborhoods, commercial areas, warehouse districts, etc., so as to maintain existing land-use patterns. A number of minor sociological classics, such as Wirth's book *The Ghetto* and Zorbaugh's book *The Gold Coast and the Slum,* deal with so-called natural

---

[6] The term "function," as used by ecologists—not by most other sociologists—means recurrent patterns of activities that depend on other activities. "Structure," to the ecologist, is the orderly arrangements of the parts that make up the whole, the loci within which the functions or activities are performed.

areas.[7] Today, only a limited number of urban neighborhoods possess sufficient social solidarity and identification to be considered natural communities. (The so-called defended neighborhoods discussed in Chapter 7, City Life-Styles, might be considered a contemporary version of natural areas.)

Criticisms

As will be seen in the next chapter, the heavy emphasis on competition in traditional human ecology, plus the nonsocial nature of some of the variables, disturbs some neo-Marxist critics. They argue that spatial patterns are the result of deliberate actions taken by capitalists, or the outcome of the contradictions in capitalist development.[8] Those taking a political economy approach see the city shaped more by deliberate political decisions than do ecologists who emphasize economic competition more.

An earlier, and now dismissed, criticism of ecology was that it borrowed concepts from other disciplines. As one critic put it, "As the ecologists have admitted, practically all their basic hypotheses have been derived from natural science sources—and the influence of certain geographers and economists is apparent."[9] To such critics the multidisciplinary base of human ecology was a weakness rather than a source of strength. Today, ecological analysis is recognized as integral to sociology, for, as expressed by Leo Schnore, "the central role given to organization—both as dependent or independent variable—places ecology clearly within the sphere of activities in which sociologists claim distinctive competence, i.e., analysis of social organization."[10]

A modification of urban ecology was the "sociocultural" school of ecology, which placed renewed emphasis on cultural and motivational factors in explaining urban land-use patterns. Scholars of the sociocultural school tend to feel that early human ecology overemphasized economic factors while ignoring social-psychological variables. Milla Alihan, in a broadly based critique of ecological studies, attacked both the theory and the application of early human ecology.[11] Another critic, Walter Firey, demonstrated in a study of land use in central Boston that many acres of valuable land in the central business district had been allowed to remain in uneconomic use, such as, for example, parks and cemeteries.[12] He suggested that "sentiment" and "symbolism" play an important part in determining spatial distributions, pointing out that the 48-acre common in the part of downtown Boston had never been developed commercially and that Beacon Hill had largely remained an upper-class residential area in spite of its proximity to the central business district. (In this respect, the area has some characteristics of the preindustrial

[7] Louis Wirth, *The Ghetto,* University of Chicago Press, Chicago, 1928; and Harvey W. Zorbaugh, *The Gold Coast and the Slum,* University of Chicago Press, Chicago, 1929.

[8] Mark Gottdiener, *The Social Production of Urban Space,* University of Texas, Austin, 1985.

[9] Warner E. Gettys, "Human Ecology and Social Theory," in George A. Theodorson (ed.), *Studies in Human Ecology,* Harper & Row, New York, 1961, p. 99.

[10] Leo Schnore, "The Myth of Human Ecology," *Sociological Inquiry,* **31**:139, 1961.

[11] Milla A. Alihan, *Social Ecology,* Columbia University Press, New York, 1938.

[12] Walter Firey, "Sentiment and Symbolism as Ecological Variables," *American Sociological Review,* **10**:140–148, 1945.

model discussed by Sjoberg on pages 50–52) Unfortunately, mass data such as census data fail to deal with such social-psychological variables.

Contemporary "neo-orthodox" ecologists see limitations in the early classical studies but also see much of value. While recognizing the importance of social-psychological variables, the members of the neo-orthodox school are more inclined toward the use of mass data such as censuses, and favor interpretation on the macrosociological level. Unlike traditional human ecology, which emphasized competition, the neo-orthodox school emphasizes interdependence, as, for example, in the use of the ecological complex (POET).

Finally, in a reversal of the social-cultural criticisms, William Michelson has taken human ecology to task for giving *too much* attention to social variables and not enough to the effect of the physical environment on behavior.[13] According to Michelson, "space has been utilized as a *medium* in most human ecology rather than as a *variable* with a potential effect of its own."[14] The wheel has thus come close to full turn. Just as cities change, so do social theories to explain change. What is taken as truth in one decade may be recast in those that follow to produce new syntheses.

BURGESS'S GROWTH HYPOTHESIS

The most famous early product of the spatial-organizational concerns of the Chicago school was Burgess's concentric-zone hypothesis, first presented in 1924. This was an attempt, largely using economic market factors, to explain why cities grow the ways they do.[15] Generations of sociology students have been exposed to the concentric-zone hypothesis—all too frequently in a form that makes it a static picture of city structure. This is unfortunate, for what Burgess was positing was the nonrandom spatial patterns that result from urban *growth*. This is in contrast to Gideon Sjoberg's model of a simpler, more static preindustrial city. We discuss the Burgess hypothesis today because it provides a good model of American urban growth up until roughly 1970. Burgess was concerned with how cities change over time from the simpler preindustrial model, in which there is no clear segregation of city land for specific functional purposes, to the more complex industrial city pattern of segregated land usages (e.g., central business district, manufacturing, and residential zones). His hypothesis is a model, and only a model, of how industrial cities evolve spatially as a result of competition for prime space. (See Figure 4-1.)

Burgess noted that in industrial cities the factories, homes, and retail shops were not randomly distributed within the urban area. Rather, there was a process of sorting by economic and social factors that resulted in concentration of similar populations and land uses. Competition for space meant that persons, organizations, and institutions were distributed within urban space in a nonrandom fashion.

---

[13] William H. Michelson, *Man and His Urban Environment: A Sociological Approach*, Addison-Wesley, Reading, Mass., 1970, pp. 3–32.

[14] Ibid., p. 17.

[15] Ernest W. Burgess, "The Growth of the City: An Introduction to a Research Project," *Publications of the American Sociological Society*, **18**:85-97, 1924.

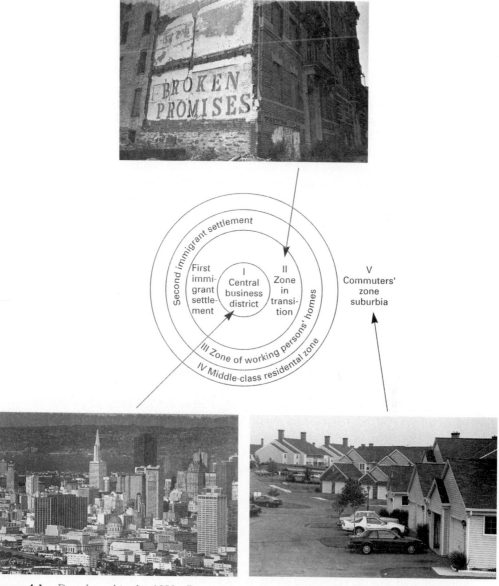

Figure 4-1. Developed in the 1920s, Burgess's zonal hypothesis provided a model of how American cities grow. (Spencer Grant/Photo Researchers.) (Barbara Alper/Stock, Boston.) (George Chan/Photo Researchers.)

Source: Ernest W. Burgess, "The Growth of the City: An Introduction to a Research Project," 1924.

The result is the ecological pattern of American cities. That all this may seem obvious to us today is in part a reflection of the acceptance of the Chicago school's work. The hypotheses of the sociologists at the University of Chicago also have had strong practical consequences. For example, while few real estate agents realize it, the filter-down housing model they use to predict housing values is based on Burgess's model.

Burgess in his model or "ideal type" suggested that cities grow radially in a series of concentric zones or rings, from the most valuable land of the central business district (CBD), through a zone of transition, zone of workingmen's homes, zone of better residences, to the commuter's zone. Competition for land means that the most valuable property goes to those functions that can use space intensively and are willing to pay the costs. Thus land values are highest in the center and decrease as one moves toward the periphery. An economic model of land use developed by William Alonso points out that only those who can pay the most can occupy CBD land.[16] Costs include not only purchase price but also taxes and nuisance factors (congestion, noise, pollution, etc.) from other nearby land users. In the industrial city of the first half of the twentieth century, centrally located land was taken by economic units, such as department stores, which could effectively use space and required heavy pedestrian traffic. Consumption-oriented commercial activities still tend to be the most centrally located; production-oriented activities are in the next ring out; and residences are the least centralized. The most strategic land tends to go to those who can afford to pay for it through intensive usages. Thus the ecologist would expect the land located at the center of the transportation network to be occupied by intensive space users such as department stores, major business headquarters, and financial institutions.

Residential users tend to be pushed out of areas desired for commercial purposes, since residential users cannot pay the high cost of central location and do not want the pollution, noise, and congestion of trucks rumbling down the street and a factory next door. If housing is to be centrally located, it must use the land intensively. As a result, the two types of housing one finds in central areas are high-income, high-rise luxury apartments and tenement and slum properties. High-rise apartments escape the pollution and noise of the city not by moving outward but by moving upward. A twentieth-floor apartment not only is quiet and convenient but also has a beautiful view. Slums are likewise intensive users of space. Even when the rent per room is low (and often it is not), the rent *per acre* is high.

Consequently, there is a tendency toward an inverse relationship between the value of land and the economic status of those who occupy it. Where people live spatially reflects their position socially. In inner areas higher land costs are compensated for by density of use. Through crowding, a slumlord can compensate for higher costs by density of use. Since land in outer areas is less valuable, less intensive use, such as single-family houses on large lots, becomes economically feasible. Thus, as you move out from the center of the city toward the periphery, land

---

[16] William Alonso, "A Theory of Urban Land Market," in Larry Bourne (ed.), *Internal Structure of the City: Readings on Space and the Environment,* Oxford University Press, New York, 1971, pp. 154–159.

values and rental per acre tend to grade downward, while the rental per housing unit grades upward.

Concentric Zones

Burgess's zones are presented here essentially as they existed during the first half of the twentieth century so they can serve as a baseline from which to examine more recent patterns of change.

Zone 1 was the central business district: the economic and (usually) the geographical center of the city. The heart of the zone was the retail shopping district, with its major department stores, theaters, hotels, banks, and central offices of economic, political, legal, and civic leaders. Consumption-oriented commercial activities tended to locate at the very core of the CBD, while the outer fringes, with lower rents, contained the wholesale business district: markets, warehouses, and storage buildings. Here also were found the wholesale markets for fresh fruits and vegetables, the markets often looking as if they had been in disrepair for a century—as they sometimes had. Today commercial and retail functions in CBDs have lost importance, while the function of providing office space and convention centers is increasing.[17]

American cities have poured millions of dollars into CBDs during the past twenty years with the hope of maintaining them or changing them back into what they once were. These efforts have largely been unsuccessful. Numerous cities such as Baltimore, Detroit, and Omaha lack even a single downtown department store.[18]

Zone 2—the zone in transition—until the 1970s contained both older factory complexes, many from the last century, and an outer ring of deteriorating neighborhoods of tenements. The zone in transition was known as an area of high crime rates and social disorganization. The zone in transition was the area where immigrants received their first view of the city. It was the point of entry. Immigrants settled here in the cheap housing near the factories because they could not compete economically for more desirable residential locations.

As the immigrants moved up in socioeconomic status, they moved out spatially and were in turn replaced by newer immigrants. Thus, a nonrandom spatial structure or pattern emerged, with groups of lower socioeconomic status most centrally located. In Burgess's day, land in the zone of transition was being held for speculation by landlords, who provided only minimum maintenance, in the expectation that the CBD would eventually expand into the area. It didn't happen that way, and today many of the slums remain—others having been destroyed by urban renewal. Chapter 7, City Life-Styles, discusses patterns of life in zones 2 and 3 in greater detail.

Zone 3 was the zone of "working people's homes." This was the area settled by second-generation families, the children of the immigrants; it was the place where one moved when one could get out of the inner core. Physically it was (at

---

[17] For a detailed analysis of CBD changes in Baltimore and in Hamburg, Germany, see Jurgen Friedrichs and Allen C. Goodman, *The Changing Downtown: A Comparative Study of Baltimore and Hamburg,* Walter de Gruyter, New York, 1987.

[18] J. John Palen, *The Suburbs,* McGraw-Hill, New York, 1995, p. 182.

Red-Light Districts and Combat Zones

In Burgess's day, at one edge of the CBD was located a sleazy but highly profitable area specializing in those activities and enterprises of a disreputable nature which needed accessibility but could not for social reasons be located in the heart of the downtown area. Here were found cheap bars specializing in women hustling drinks, pornographic movie houses, strip joints, pinball arcades, and bookshops that sold magazines you couldn't buy in the suburbs. Today these areas are dying, partially because urban renewal has encroached on their territory and partially because technology has made the "adult" movie theater obsolete. It is no longer necessary to go to a movie house to see pornographic movies; they can be rented in neighborhood video stores for viewing on home screens.

Until the period before World War I, every major city in the United States also had a clearly marked "red-light district" just off the central business district which devoted itself to servicing needs that were not met elsewhere. Among the most famous were Storyville in New Orleans, the Tenderloin in San Francisco, and the Levee in Chicago. A turn-of-the-century social reform tract, *If Christ Came to Chicago*, provided a detailed map of every brothel, gambling place, and saloon in the downtown area of that city. The intent was to document the amount of vice, but the map also probably proved a useful guide to many visitors.

The term "red-light district" comes from the red lights that prostitutes put in their front windows to indicate that they were open for business. Numerous European cities such as Amsterdam and Hamburg still have clearly defined red-light districts—lights and all. These areas become quite congested during the evening and during lunch hours. American red-light districts were shut down by local societies for the suppression of vice, and as a result, displaced prostitutes set up business in apartments throughout the city. The technology of the telephone and automobile meant that the call girl replaced the brothel. With service only a telephone call away, public visibility was a disadvantage rather than an asset.

During the 1970s, a number of cities reintroduced a section of the city devoted to commercial vice, known officially as "adult entertainment districts" but commonly called "combat zones." Combat zones were established in response to citizens' outcries over adult bookstores, pornographic movie houses, massage parlors, and open gay pickup bars in residential areas. The Supreme Court ruled in 1976 that it is legal to "zone out" as well as "zone in" certain activities to a specialized zone. The approval hinged in part on the fact that the law only affected new businesses. New York in 1994 passed a zoning-out plan that would close the existing adult entertainment establishments in Times Square after a fixed period of years. Whether such zoning out of existing usages is legal is currently being fought in the courts.

least in Chicago, Burgess's model) a neighborhood of basic two-family houses rather than tenements, apartments, or single-family houses. Typically, the father of the family had a blue-collar job in the city. The children, however, planned to marry and move out of the old neighborhood, perhaps to live in the suburbs (see Chapter 9, Changing Suburbanization Patterns).

Zone 4 was called the "zone of the better residences." This was the zone of the great middle class—small-business people, professional people, sales workers, and those holding white-collar jobs. However, even in the 1920s this zone was in the process of changing from a community of single-family houses to one of apartment buildings and residential hotels (that is, there was an invasion of new land-use patterns).

The final zone, zone 5, was the "commuter zone." In the early 1920s the commuter zone, thanks to the commuter railroads and the automobile, comprised the upper-middle-class and upper-class dormitory suburbs. Here were found the classic suburban life patterns—the husband leaving in the morning for the city and returning in the evening, the wife remaining there to raise the children, maintain the house, and participate in civic affairs. Chapter 9 deals in detail with this outer zone, which today we call "suburbia."

We study the Burgess hypothesis today because it provided a long-accepted model of how American cities, and by implication, cities elsewhere, would change. This hypothesis has held real policy implications. As previously noted, the belief in the filter-down housing model based on the Burgess hypothesis dominated American real estate for decades. The filter-down model suggested that housing and neighborhoods would inevitably filter from higher-status to lower-status populations. Thus, inner-city neighborhoods were seen as going from middle to lower class (or from white to black) but never the reverse. As Chapter 12 details, this led to policies of disinvestment in the central city. Urban gentrification during the 1980s and 1990s turns Burgess's pattern inside out. In many cities central commercial property and warehouses are now being converted to residential usages.

The Zonal Hypothesis: Criticism and Evaluation

Over the years there has been considerable debate about the adequacy of the zonal hypothesis in analyzing community spatial organization and growth. In the decades since its formation, Burgess's hypothesis has come under severe criticism on both theoretical and empirical grounds. As Alihan pointed out, Burgess's zonal boundaries "do not serve as demarcations in respect to the ecological or social phenomena they circumscribe, but are arbitrary divisions."[19] This is an overstatement, but it is clear that Burgess's zones are not totally homogeneous units. When evaluating Burgess's hypothesis, we have to keep in mind that he was proposing a model or ideal type of what American cities would look like if other factors did not

---

[19] Alihan, *Social Ecology,* p. 225.

intervene—but, of course, other factors do intervene. Burgess's own statements make it clear that he recognized the effects of distorting factors. He said:

> If radial extension were the only factor affecting the growth of American cities, every city in this country would exhibit a perfect exemplification of these five urban zones. But since other factors affect urban development (including) situation, site, natural and artificial barriers, survival of an earlier use of a district, prevailing city plan and its system of transportation, many distortions and modifications of this pattern are actually found. Nevertheless, so universal and powerful is the force of expansion outward from the city's core that in every city these zones can be more or less clearly delimited.[20]

The question, then, is not whether the zonal pattern is an exact description, for it obviously is not. The question is whether the growth patterns of American cities were best described by Burgess's or other models. To date, empirical tests have both supported and failed to support Burgess's hypothesis.[21] Haggerty, for example, looked at changes in educational levels from 1940 to 1960 in census tracts in eight large cities, using the statistical technique of Markov analysis. He reported that there was a definite trend through time toward a direct association between an area's social status and its distance from the city center. This tendency toward higher status on the periphery held even in cities whose original or present pattern was for higher-status groups to be more centrally located. Thus, whatever the original pattern, over time there appears to be a movement toward a concentric-zone system.[22]

Schwirian and Matre, on the other hand, found a more mixed pattern in their study of Canada's eleven largest cities.[23] A major study carried out by Schnore for 200 urbanized areas in the United States showed that especially for the oldest and largest cities, there is the predicted pattern of higher socioeconomic status being found in peripheral suburban rather than central-city locations.[24] A follow-up study by Palen and Schnore found that for the black population, Burgess's pattern holds in the north and west but not the south.[25] (In older southern cities, black families often lived in smaller alley houses behind the larger, white-occupied homes on the main streets. Also, in the south, blacks have traditionally lived in marginal peripheral semirural "suburban" locations.)

Research shows that a rough version of Burgess's model does appear to have held, at least for larger and older American cities, up until the suburban era of the last thirty years or so. As later chapters will demonstrate, for the more recent decades population growth, job growth, and office growth have concentrated heavily in the suburbs.

[20] Ernest W. Burgess, "Residential Segregation in American Cities," *Annals of the American Academy of Political and Social Science,* **140:**108, November, 1928.

[21] Leo F. Schnore and Joy K. O. Jones, "The Evolution of City-Suburban Types in the Course of a Decade," *Urban Affairs Quarterly,* **4:**421–422, June, 1969; Joel Smith, "Another Look at Socioeconomic Status Distributions in Urbanized Areas," *Urban Affairs Quarterly,* **5:**423–453, June, 1970; and Lee J. Haggerty, "Another Look at the Burgess Hypothesis: Time as an Important Variable," *American Journal of Sociology,* **76:**1084–1093, May, 1971.

[22] Haggerty, "Another Look at the Burgess Hypothesis," pp. 1084–1093.

[23] Kent P. Schwirian and Marc D. Matre, "The Ecological Structure of Canadian Cities," in Kent P. Schwirian (ed.), *Comparative Urban Structure,* Heath, Lexington, Mass., 1974.

[24] Leo F. Schnore, "The Socioeconomic Status of Cities and Suburbs," *American Sociological Review,* **28:**76–85, February, 1963.

[25] J. John Palen and Leo F. Schnore, "Color Composition and City-Suburban Status Differences," *Land Economics,* **41:**87–91, February, 1965.

ALTERNATIVE THEORIES

Two major ecological model alternatives to Burgess's hypothesis have been proposed. One is the sector theory. The other is the multiple-nuclei theory.

Sector Theory

Homer Hoyt proposed what has become known as the "sector theory."[26] Hoyt suggested that rather than growth through rings, growth took place in homogeneous pie-shaped sectors that extended radially from the center toward the periphery of the city. His research indicated that residential areas extended rapidly along establish lines of travel where economic resistance was least. A pattern of land use was said to develop in which each use—industrial, commercial, high-income residential, or low-income residential—tended to push out from the city core in specific sectors or wedges that cut across concentric zones.

Thus, high-income housing could radiate from the core in one wedge, a racial ghetto in a second, industrial firms in a third, and working-class residences in a fourth. The sector theory focuses attention on the role of transportation arteries, and on the choices. Although originally developed to explain city patterns, the sector theory easily accommodates to explaining development out along interstate and other major highways. Thus it is a particularly useful modification of the Burgess hypothesis when discussing the postwar development of suburbs.

Multiple-Nuclei Theory

A third theory of spatial growth rejects the idea of a unicentered city altogether and instead holds that differing land uses have different centers. This "multiple-nuclei" theory was suggested by Chauncy Harris and Edward Ullman.[27] They argued that land-use patterns developed around what were originally independent nuclei. Four factors were said to account for the rise of the different nuclei:

1. Certain activities require specialized facilities. Retailing, for example, requires a high degree of accessibility, while manufacturing needs ample land and railroad service.
2. Like activities group together for mutual advantages, as in the case of the central business district.
3. Some unlike activities are mutually detrimental or incompatible with one another. For example, it is unlikely that high-income or high-status residential areas will locate close to heavy industry.
4. Some users, such as storage and warehousing facilities, which have a relatively lower competitive capacity to purchase good locations, are able to afford only low-rental areas.[28]

In many respects the multiple-nuclei hypothesis better describes the entire metropolitan area than it does the central city. The multinucleated pattern does in

---

[26] Homer Hoyt, "The Structure and Growth of Residential Neighborhoods in American Cities," U.S. Federal Housing Administration, Washington, D.C., 1939.
[27] Chauncy Harris and Edward Ullman, "The Nature of Cities," *The Annals of the American Academy of Political and Social Science*, **252**:7–17, 1945.
[28] Ibid.

The opening of the Rock and Roll Hall of Fame has contributed in a major way to the revitalization of downtown Cleveland. (Piet van Lier/Courtesy of the Rock and Roll Hall of Fame.)

fact describe contemporary suburbia with its mixture of outlying shopping malls, office and industrial parks, and residential areas.

Hawley has suggested the importance of the transportation net in a multi-nucleated theory of growth.[29] He notes that within metropolitan areas there is not one retail business district, but a hierarchical, multinucleated system of districts. Second- and third-rank business districts particularly develop at transportation intersections where traffic converges from four directions. Greater specialization of both services and products is found at the CBD, while outlying centers offer more standardized services and items. We will explore this further in Chapter 6, Metropolitan and Edge City Growth.

URBAN GROWTH OUTSIDE NORTH AMERICA

The Burgess concentric-zone pattern of urban growth, which says that there is an increasing status gradient as one goes from city core to periphery, has never been very useful in describing patterns of ecological growth outside North America.[30] The zonal pattern has not been the typical pattern of growth in the nonindustrial cities of Asia, Africa, and Latin America.

In cities with a preindustrial heritage, there appears to be an inverse zonal hypothesis. That is, instead of the poor in the inner core and the elite farther out, the central core is occupied by the elite whereas the disadvantaged fan out toward the

[29] Amos H. Hawley, *Urban Society: An Ecological Approach,* Wiley, New York, 1981.
[30] Bruce London and William G. Flanagan, "Comparative Urban Ecology: A Summary of the Field," in John Walton and Louis H. Masotti (eds.), *The City in Comparative Perspective: Cross National Research and New Directions in Theory,* Sage, Beverly Hills, Calif., 1979, pp. 41–66.

periphery.[31] In such cities, it is common to find a pattern in which upper-class and upper-middle-class groups occupy the city proper and poor in-migrants settle on the "suburban" periphery in squatter shantytowns. These *favelas, barriadas, gecekondulas, or bustees* can be found on the periphery of almost every major city in Latin America, Africa, and Asia.

As Part Five, Worldwide Urbanization, details, cities in the third world differ from North American cities in a number of respects. First, American cities have a commercial-industrial base not found in cities that grew primarily as administrative centers. Second, the American city is based upon a highly developed transportation technology that allows relatively rapid movement between central-city offices and suburban residences. Where rapid inexpensive transportation is lacking, central-city location may be more desirable. Finally, there is the inertia to change created by preexisting locational patterns and preferences. Without draconian measures, cities cannot rapidly change their physical characteristics.

Cultural differences also have to be taken into account. For example, as Chapter 16, Asian Urban Patterns, demonstrates, cities in India such as New Delhi and Calcutta are organized in a way that is both socially and spatially different from American cities. The city of Jerusalem, to use another example, is in practice two separate cultural worlds, one Jewish and the other Muslim.

There is also reason to question just how applicable Burgess's theory is to older European cities. Certainly the major cities of Europe that were established before the industrial revolution have an internal distribution of social and economic classes that does not easily fit Burgess's model.[32] In the older cities the elites preempted the prestigious central locations and the poor were forced to live in more peripheral locations. Manufacturing and commerce, when located within the city, were restricted to specific areas. Thus, the East End of London was, before the bombing of World War II, composed of small factories, workshops, and poor homes surrounding the dock area. On the other hand, the central and western districts of Westminster, Marylebone, and Kensington have continued to retain their upper-class airs for two centuries in spite of their central location. Moscow, before the Russian Revolution, clearly had the urban structure of a preindustrial city with its inverse zonal pattern.[33]

Within European cities with central land already filled, heavy industry was confined to "suburban" areas where there was sufficient land for the growing factories. Thus, Paris has a concentration of automobile and aircraft factories to the south and east of the city, and the population of such suburban areas is heavily working-class. The continuation of a preindustrial ecological pattern results in social-class distribution and political voting patterns that are quite different from those found in American cities. Some suburban areas of Paris, the so-called red

[31] Gideon Sjoberg, *The Preindustrial City,* Free Press, New York, 1960, pp. 97–98.

[32] Francis L. Hauser, "Ecological Patterns of European Cities," in Sylvia Fleis Fava (ed.), *Urbanism in World Perspective: A Reader,* Crowell, New York, 1968; and London and Flanagan, "Comparative Urban Ecology," p. 56.

[33] Walter F. Abbott, "Moscow in 1897 as a Preindustrial City: A Test of the Inverse Burgess Zonal Hypothesis," *American Sociological Review,* **39:**542–550, August, 1974.

ring to the north and east, for decades provided the major political support for the Communist Party. By contrast, the inner-city middle-class districts vote for the more conservative candidates—exactly the opposite of the American stereotype. For major leftist political protests, protesters are bused into Paris from the suburbs.

Gideon Sjoberg sees this pattern of identification of high-status groups with central-city location as a persistence of a "feudal tradition" that is not present in American cities. In his view, "In many European cities, including those in the U.S.S.R., the persistence of the feudal tradition has inhibited suburbanization because high status has attached to residence in the central city."[34]

One can question whether a preference for central-city locations is today "feudalistic" or part of a "feudal tradition." Manhattan doesn't have a feudal tradition, but it still has a pattern of the well-to-do locating in certain areas of the central city. Cosmopolites, whether in London, Paris, or New York, simply prefer to live where they can easily get to work, where they can find a full cultural life, and where they can easily get a drink or a sandwich at 2 a.m. It can be argued that, particularly in Europe, upper-status urban populations live in the city because they feel it is an exciting and attractive place to live.

It is possible that the differences in land use between North American industrialized cities and nonindustrial cities elsewhere, particularly in the developing world, may be part of an evolutionary pattern.

---

[34] Gideon Sjoberg, "Cities in Developing and in Industrial Societies: A Cross-Cultural Analysis," in Philip Hauser and Leo F. Schnore, *The Study of Urbanization,* Wiley, New York, 1965, p. 230.

Cafe patrons on the Champs Elysees in Paris enjoy an urban life-style. (Mark Antman/The Image Works.)

A NOTE ON ECOLOGICAL METHODOLOGY

Ecologists, by and large, collect their data in the same manner as other sociologists. What distinguishes them is their preference for operating on the systems level rather than the individual level. The human ecologist's interest is in the characteristics and behavior of groups rather than the attitudes, motivations, and personalities of the individual members of groups. As a result, ecologists usually use quantitative rather than qualitative data. They are most interested in how groups or aggregates behave. Probably the most-used source of data is the United States Census, which provides a wealth of information on the social and economic characteristics of groups, their housing patterns, and even their family patterns. In the United States the decennial census is supplemented by the monthly Current Population Survey of households across the nation, which yields far more detailed information. The Current Population Survey provides up-to-date information on social and economic questions—detailed information no single researcher or group of researchers could afford to gather.

Ecologists' use of nonsocial variables such as distance, transportation, and physical environment means that ecologists sometimes have more in common with economists than with sociologists doing behavioral studies in the social psychology of small groups. For example, in a study of occupational stratification and residential location, the Duncans empirically demonstrated the relationship between what one does and where one lives.[35] Spatial distances between occupational groups are closely related to their social distances, whether measured in terms of the conventional indicators of socioeconomic status (income, education, occupation) or in terms of differences in occupational origins. In accordance with accepted ecological theory, they found that the occupational groups most segregated physically were those at the very bottom and very top of the occupational scale.

Likewise, residence in low-rent areas and residence near the center of the city were inversely related to socioeconomic status. However, near the middle of the socioeconomic scale, where blue-collar and white-collar clerical occupations meet, the pattern is less clear. Although white-collar clerical workers on the average have considerably lower income than blue-collar craft workers and line supervisors, they have a pattern of residential distribution more in common with other white-collar groups. It appears that social status, or prestige, is more important to clerical groups, although their relatively lower income level vis à vis other white-collar groups does set up cross-pressures, as is indicated by a high rent-to-income ratio for clerical workers. A replication by Albert Simkus indicated that occupational segregation remains high.[36] Nonwhites in the highest occupational categories are becoming less segregated from whites, while those in the lowest occupational categories are becoming more segregated.

---

[35] Otis Dudley Duncan and Beverly Duncan, "Residential Distribution and Occupational Stratification," *American Journal of Sociology,* **60:**493–503, March, 1955.
[36] Albert A. Simkus, "Residential Segregation by Occupation and Race in Ten Urbanized Areas, 1950–1970," *American Sociological Review,* **43:**81–93, February, 1978.

A Note on Urbanization and Environment

Our discussion of the ecology of the city would be incomplete without the mention of the effect of cities on the physical environment and vice versa. The actual physical shape of cities has been modified by human design. Much of contemporary Boston, for instance, was under water at the time of the Revolution. One of the former underwater zones is known today as Back Bay. Chicago in similar fashion created an Outer Drive and lakefront park system out of filled land, as did New Orleans. In other cases the pumping out of subsurface groundwater and other fluids has led, as in parts of Houston and in Long Beach, California, to subsidence. In the latter case, from 1937 through 1962 some 913 million barrels of oil, 482 million barrels of water, and 832 billion cubic feet of gas were extracted, causing parts of this heavily urbanized area to sink as much as 27 feet.[*]

Cities also create atmospheric changes. Buildings and paved streets retain heat, and urban areas become heat islands, as anyone who has spent a hot summer day in the central city knows. What is less well known is that the condensation nuclei produced by activity in cities increase cloudiness and precipitation over cities.[†]

Also by covering the ground with buildings, paved roads, and parking lots, urban development in effect waterproofs the land surface. Rainfall cannot be normally absorbed into the soil; instead, storm runoff must be handled by massive systems of storm sewers. The paving over of city and suburban areas, by preventing water absorption, actually increases the risk of severe flooding.[‡] The relationship between urban residents and their physical environment is much closer than most city dwellers or suburbanites recognize. Those living in coastal areas subject to hurricanes, or in localities that flood, or on earthquake-prone fault lines, are particularly sensitive to the extent to which we are subject to the laws of nature and the environment. During the 1990s both San Francisco and Los Angeles suffered earthquake damage.

---

[*] Donald Eachman and Melvin Marcus, "The Geologic and Topographic Setting of Cities," in Thomas Detwyler and Melvin Marcus (eds.), *Urbanization and Environment: The Physical Geography of the City,* Duxbury Press, Belmont, Calif., 1972, p. 46.
[†] Rid Bryson and John Ross, in Detwyler and Marcus, *Urbanization and Environment,* p. 63.
[‡] Robert Kates, Ian Burton, and Gilbert F. White, *The Environment as Hazard,* Oxford University Press, New York, 1978; and Stanley A. Changon et al., *Summary of Metromex,* Vol. 1: *Weather Anomalies and Impacts,* Illinois State Water Survey, Urbana, 1977.

Cities, of course, are notorious for their effect on air pollution. One of the worst cases occurred London in 1952 when a disastrous temperature inversion kept a deadly smog over the city for a week, and some 4,000 Londoners died of smog-related causes before the smog lifted. Today London has strict air pollution controls; the air is actually getting cleaner, and the city's sooty fogs are a thing of the past.

In the United States, a nationwide study tracking the health histories of 552,138 adults in 151 metropolitan areas was released in 1995.[*] The good news is that due to the Clean Air Act air quality has improved dramatically since 1982. The bad news is that after factoring in each subject's age, sex, occupational exposure to pollution, obesity, and alcohol use, living in a city having high sulfate and fine-particle levels raised the risk of premature death by 15 and 17 percent, respectively. Living in high-pollution cities such as Los Angeles, Denver, or Salt Lake City can substantially shorten life.

Los Angeles is perhaps most notorious for its polluted air. Its well-known smog is a consequence of an environmental location that encourages thermal inversions that trap pollutants, a population that has been increasing, and a transportation technology based on automobiles. California now has passed laws mandating the use of some zero-pollution vehicles (i.e., electric vehicles) by the beginning of the new century in order to attempt to clean its air. However, by far the most serious air and other pollution now occurs in the cities of the developing world. The air in Bangkok is often so dirty it can be seen, and just breathing the air in Mexico City is equivalent to smoking two packages of cigarettes a day.

[*] Curt Suplee, "Dirty Air Can Shorten Your Life, Study Says: Death Rate Much Higher in Worst Cities," *Washington Post*, Mar. 10, 1995, pp. A1 and A15.

5

URBAN POLITICAL ECONOMY

David A. Smith
Michael F. Timberlake

Woe to them that join house to house.
Woe to them that lay field to field till there be no place.

Isaiah 5:8

The purpose of this chapter is to describe a theoretical approach that has emerged in the last twenty-five years in reaction to the urban ecology model. In contrast to the urban ecology model, this alternative pays more attention to social inequality and social conflict and less attention to the role of technology as a driving force defining city living and changing urban patterns. Urban political economy draws on diverse strands of theory and research including Marxism and neo-Marxism, critical theory, conflict theory, various types of political economy theories, and world-system theories.

Some authors refer to this alternative approach as "the new urban sociology" and emphasize it as a "challenger" to the ecological paradigm. But this is a little misleading since the key arguments are not very new (dating back to the early 1970s). Furthermore, many urban sociologists argue that a basic paradigm shift has occurred and this theoretical perspective is now the *dominant* one among researchers[1] (though sometimes still slighted in urban textbooks).[2] Acknowledging some diversity of views under this label, we will focus on common features of the urban political economy approach.

Urban political economy theory interprets social change, and particularly urban change, in terms of the ways societal processes and structures produce advantages for some groups and disadvantages for others. It frequently examines aspects of modern city life such as urban poverty, residential class and race segregation, "deindustrialization," urban fiscal crisis, inequality in the distribution of city services, "overurbanization" in the world's poorer countries, and the emergence of global cities in the richest nations. In an analysis of such issues, the focus is on factors such as the interest and actions of economic and political elites, influential urban institutions and organizations, incentives and disincentives that are built into the "system" (or systems) in which cities are situated, and relationships between cities and global forces.

Like urban ecology, urban political economy is concerned with systems of dominance and subordination operating across spatial boundaries. But unlike urban ecology, these systems are seen as driven by the actions (or inactions) of social groups pursuing their particular interests, sometimes with a vengeance. The focus is on how various political-economic systems usually operate, which groups tend to hold more power, and who tends to benefit and who is likely to lose from "the way things are" in cities. For example, both ecological and urban political economy approaches can be used to interpret the spatial differentiation of American cities: the separation of areas that contain factories and offices from areas of residence, and the concentration of housing among people of similar income and ethnicity.

Urban ecologists interpret these facts by stressing, among other factors, the causal importance of technology embodied in predominant modes of transportation. As automobiles became more widely used, for example, North American cities

[1] Mark Gottdiener and Joe Feagin, "The Paradigm Shift in Urban Sociology," *Urban Affairs Quarterly,* **24** (2):163–187, 1988; John Walton, "Urban Sociology: The Contributions and Limits of Political Economy," *Annual Review of Sociology,* pp. 301–319, 1993; David A. Smith, "The New Urban Sociology Meets the Old: Rereading Some Classical Human Ecology," *Urban Affairs Review,* **30**(3):432–457, 1995.

[2] For a discussion see Ray Hutchinson, "The Crisis in Urban Sociology," in Ray Hutchinson (ed.), *Research in Urban Sociology,* JAI Press, Greenwich, Conn., 1993, pp. 3–26.

became more decentralized with respect to the location of workplaces and homes, and higher-income groups were increasingly more likely to take up suburban residence, outside city limits. Urban political economy agrees that the rise of the automobile was critically important, but asks, Why did the automobile become so widely used? How was it allowed to become such a dominant form of transportation (especially given its costs and disadvantages)?

The answers that urban ecologists give to these questions link technological development with the individual economic decisions of U.S. families. Urban political economy, on the other hand, moves away from explanations of consumer preferences, in favor of an approach that examines the role of powerful corporate actors and political institutions. Political economists point to the key role of automobile manufacturers, rubber tire companies, and the oil industry in influencing public policy favoring the development of elaborate highway systems at the expense of rail and other mass transit systems. Further, this approach focuses on the conflicts between working-class people and minorities, on the one hand, and affluent professionals and managerial classes, on the other, in contributing to suburbanization and "exurbanization."

Additionally, political economy analyses of changes in North American cities in the late twentieth century increasingly emphasize how spatial and material segregation and inequalities are linked to globalization and worldwide economic restructuring.

THE RISE OF URBAN POLITICAL ECONOMY THEORY

Beginning over two decades ago, some urban sociologists began to develop a theoretical perspective that questioned many of the assumptions of the urban ecology approach. Drawing on scholarship of social science disciplines and history, this approach pays more attention to how cities change in response to the actions of individuals and groups who are pursuing their own, often narrow, interests. Urban political economy research demonstrates how city-building actions usually serve the economic or political interests of some groups at the expense of others. Urban political economy focuses attention on the exercise of social power and the frequency of social conflict in pursuit of economic, political, and cultural resources. This is not generally true of studies following the urban ecology tradition.

While the ecological tradition's initial impetus was efforts by the Chicago school of urban researchers to understand cities in the United States and other advanced industrial countries, and was later applied to cities in less-developed countries, the urban political economy perspective has emerged from research on urbanization both in the United States and throughout the world. For urban political economy theorists, studies of both advanced industrial cities and third world urbanization seriously undermine major assumptions of the urban ecology approach.

The urban political economy approach received its initial boost from two books written in the early 1970s. In the first, Harvey argued that severe urban problems and social inequality in Baltimore were the direct, predictable results of the operation of capitalist markets in land and real estate.[3] In the second, Castells offered a sweeping critique of the existing field of urban sociology and suggested that it be supplanted by a more consistent, theoretically focused Marxist approach to cities and urban life.[4] Thus, in contrast to an urban ecology analysis of cities, which largely takes "the system" for granted, urban political economy attaches great importance to the ways that urban patterns are linked to a socioeconomic system of competitive capitalism.

Also during the 1970s, in addition to agreeing on the paramount importance of linking city growth to capitalism, there was growing agreement that capitalism itself involves *global* political-economic relations. In other words, the setting in which particular cities grow larger or smaller, prosper or decline, is the whole world.

Urban political economy theory rejects images of cities as abstractions. Instead, it sees cities as complex places in which activities like production, consumption, and control are carried out. It is largely in real urban areas like New York City, Seoul, and Nairobi, where men and women work to meet their needs and the needs of others, that the fruits of human labor are used, and it is usually in those areas that the various institutions that facilitate, regulate, and control aspects of daily life are located. The interrelations (or "articulation") between these locally based activities and organizations and other social systems (like the national political system or the international economy) are a central concern to urban political economy theory and research.[5]

WORLD SYSTEM

This global urban political economy approach is usually tied to the more generic world-system theoretical perspective. It is important, therefore, to briefly describe this approach. World-system theory suggests that the development of capitalism has been a long historical process in which increasingly more areas of the globe are incorporated into an overarching geopolitical and economic system.[6] But different areas gain membership in this world system on different terms. Some countries constitute the "core" of the world system. These are the more economically developed countries, like the United States, Japan, and many European nations. They are home to the advanced capitalist institutions, like large transnational corporations, and this creates opportunities for people who live in the major cities of these societies to be involved in high-level jobs and decision-making processes that are usually not available to people living in countries outside of the core. Many of these other countries are said to constitute the "periphery." Examples include many African, Asian, and Latin American societies—the relatively poor, less-developed countries. There is also a group of nations intermediate between the core and the

[3] David Harvey, *Social Justice and the City,* Arnold, London, 1973.
[4] Manuel Castells, *The Urban Question: A Marxist Approach,* M.I.T. Press, Cambridge, Mass., 1977.
[5] Michael Smith and Joe Feagin (eds.), *The Capitalist City: Global Restructuring and Community Politics,* Blackwell, New York, 1987.
[6] For a good introduction to world-system analysis, see essays by Immanuel Wallerstein, *The Capitalist World-Economy,* Cambridge University Press, New York, 1979.

The movement of third world peasants to the cities represents one of the largest migrations in human history. The photo shows movement of people and goods into Kampot, Kampuchea (Cambodia). (P.S. Sudhakaran/UN/DPI Photo 159468.)

periphery—countries that have qualities of both development and underdevelopment, which could conceivably move into the core, or which possibly have been in the core in earlier times. These constitute the "semiperiphery," and they include places like South Korea, Argentina, and Poland.

The core, periphery, and semiperiphery are united into a hierarchical and global "division of labor" such that core "development" and peripheral "underdevelopment" reinforce each other. The core's transnational business firms, like Nike, the athletic apparel firm, provide relatively well-paid design and research opportunities in the cities of the core, but their shoes are assembled by workers paid as little as 15 cents an hour in countries like China and Indonesia.[7] The workers in such third world factories are likely to be sons and daughters of peasants or former peasants—people

---

[7] See Miguel Korzeniewicz, "Commodity Chains and Marketing Strategies: Nike and the Global Athletic Footwear Industry," in Gary Gereffi and Miguel Korzeniewicz (eds.), *Commodity Chains and Global Capitalism,* Greenwood Press, Westport, Conn., 1994, or R. Barff and K. Austen, "'It's gotta be da shoes': Domestic Manufacturing, International Subcontracting, and the Production of Athletic Footwear," *Environment and Planning,* **A25**:1103–1114, 1993.

These young women working in a garment factory in Ho Chi Minh City earn about $2 per day. (David Smith.)

who may have once lived in self-sufficient communities, producing many of their own daily necessities. Pushed from rural areas by limited supplies of land, overpopulation, and war or social unrest or pulled to urban areas by the lure of a "modern" life-style, such former peasant family members migrate to cities, seeking the opportunity to sell the only valuable thing they own—their labor—for a wage. They hope to earn money not only to feed, clothe, and shelter themselves, but also to purchase modern goods that are becoming increasingly available in the places where they live.

This example illustrates two important processes that are fundamental to the world system and shape the historical development of cities. One is the long-run trend for more and more of what we use and consume to be goods and services that we buy in markets. This process is called "commodification." The other process is "proletarianization": the long-run trend for a larger and larger proportion of the world's adult population to depend on earning paid wages for work. In case of third world manufacturing, former peasants become proletarians, and they must buy what they consume (e.g., food, clothing, shelter) rather than produce it for themselves.

Thinking about the third world village peasant who migrates to the city and becomes a wage worker (proletariat) producing athletic shoes sold to teenagers in Los Angeles or Kansas City reminds us that "development" and urban change are based on the global interdependency of human communities. In fact, we can think of the world's cities as constituting key interlinked nodes in this world system. The cities of the world represent a global network of places interlinked through the flow of commodities, people, technology, and ideas. Though countries are doubtlessly key political units of the global system, urban places and the connections between cities are extremely important. As critical nodes in the larger system, cities are in nearly constant direct contact with one another through various city-to-city flows (airline flights, telephone calls, shipped goods, electronically transmitted cash and investment, etc.). Global intercity relationships help shape the world system, and their involvement in the world system shapes individual cities.

How a city fits into the world system's city system is important to know if we are to truly understand the forces affecting the quality of human life in that city (i.e., its class structure, standard of living, and economic base). Though the basic structure of the world system is relatively stable over time, there is constant shifting among its constituent parts. In other words, there is some upward and downward mobility for particular countries and regions as some regions prosper while others decline. Cities are a part of these changes, and their growth and stagnation is linked to the role they play in the global network and the position they occupy in worldwide hierarchies.

World cities like London or New York rose to the apex of the global urban hierarchy when each was the financial capital of the nation that dominated the world economy. But it is also true for less prominent cities, too, whose booms and/or busts are inexorably linked to their global roles. Feagin's comparative research on Houston, Texas, and Aberdeen, Scotland, is illustrative.[8] Both of these "oil capitals" experienced tremendous economic and employment growth in the 1970s and 1980s due to a worldwide rise in oil prices and rapid expansion of petroleum-related industries. But global conditions changed. New emphasis on energy conservation, the substitution of non-oil-based fuels, and rapid increases in oil production in other parts of the world led to significant declines in oil prices—and full-fledged recession in Houston and Aberdeen.

What this shows is that when the world system as a whole changes, whether in terms of long-term historical shifts of power toward certain dominant countries or in terms of relatively short-term cycles of economic growth and recession, intercity relations are altered, and the consequences become evident in particular cities and regions. Similarly, when regions of the world redefine their relationship to the world system, then the cities within those areas are changed dramatically. Finally, when cities occupy new roles in the world-city hierarchy, then the lives of the people who live in those cities are changed as well. A global political economy perspective reminds us that the lives of urban residents are constrained by larger "structural" forces, some of which reach all the way down from the heights of the world economy.

ASSUMPTIONS OF THE URBAN POLITICAL ECONOMY PERSPECTIVE

Before proceeding to applications of the urban political economy perspective to particular empirical cases, we need to review the major elements of the approach.

---

[8] Joe Feagin, "Extractive Regions in Developed Countries: A Comparative Analysis of the 'Oil Capitals,' Houston and Aberdeen," *Urban Affairs Quarterly,* **25**(4):591–619.

The following five assumptions are taken largely from Feagin,[9] though we have modified them somewhat.

1. *Cities are situated in a hierarchical global system, and global linkages among cities help define the structure of this world system.* Cities and urban life in both developed and less-developed countries are shaped, to a significant degree, by their specific location and involvement in the world system. Groups in some areas, both historically and in the present day, "exploit" groups and resources in other regions. As a result, major social differences (e.g., patterns of urbanization) across the globe have much to do with how a region fits into this international division of labor and with how local systems of class, racial/ethnic, and gender relations have developed in connection with the operation of the world system.

2. *The world system is one of competitive capitalism.* This world system is driven, to a significant degree, by the logic of capitalism, and is, therefore, competitive. Locally based actors (e.g., local politicians and business people) attempt to outbid one another for access to capital, cheap labor, and resources. This process transmits the aspects of competitive capitalism to geographical space (e.g., land), and it involves the creation and destruction of the land and built environments we term "cities." Moreover, it leads to the concentration and locational shifts of human populations *within* the urban landscape (resulting in suburbs, neighborhoods, slums, etc.).

3. *Capital is easily moved; locations of cities are fixed.* Gain and loss are usually calculated within corporations. Owners and managers of companies act to maximize the profitability and ensure the survival of their firms. These actions often include moving capital (in the form of factories and production facilities, corporate offices, etc.) from one spatial location to another in attempting to improve the "bottom line." Investment and disinvestment often have profound effects on the locales in question, many of which are large cities. For instance, this can lead to "capital drain" and "deindustrialization" in these places.[10]

4. *Politics and government matter.* "The state in modern capitalist societies is linked, in historically shaped and fluctuating ways," to the economic processes that form cities.[11] Both local and national-level government and "politics" play critical roles in setting the rules and "greasing the skids" for business profitability. Contrary to the assumption that the driving force behind capitalist economies is the free market, states are fundamental elements that help determine the flow of capital over the face of the globe, including from one city or region to another. The policies of different political jurisdictions—on corporate taxes, road building, the regulation of workers, etc.—help define local business climates, which in turn strongly influence patterns of urban growth and decline.

5. *People and circumstances differ according to time and place, and these differences matter.* "Specific economic and state forms do not develop inevitably.

[9] Joe Feagin, *The Free Enterprise City,* Rutgers, New Brunswick, N.J., 1988, chap. 2.
[10] See Barry Bluestone and Bennett Harrison, *The Deindustrialization of America,* Basic Books, New York, 1982.
[11] Feagin, *The Free Enterprise City,* p. 24.

They develop as the result of conscious actions taken by members of various classes, acting singly or in concert, under particular historical and structural circumstances."[12] In other words, cities are shaped by real flesh-and-blood people making decisions in particular situations. This may seem pretty obvious—but it often gets lost in abstract social science explanations focusing on "variables" and "social forces." People may cooperate with each other in opposition to or support of the existing system, or in opposition to or support of alternatives.

USING THE URBAN POLITICAL ECONOMY APPROACH: RESEARCH FINDINGS

Now that we have identified the major characteristics of the new urban sociology in contrast to conventional urban ecology, we need to show how it helps us understand cities and urbanization in the real world.

American Cities and "Urban Growth Machines"

Some of the early urban political economy studies focused on U.S. cities and were primarily concerned with urban growth and decline. For example, Feagin and Parker argue that in U.S. cities the powerful elites are usually composed of "the industrial executives, developers, bankers, and their political allies."[13] Similarly, Soja identifies "business interests and the state" as the driving forces behind the restructuring of Los Angeles,[14] Glasberg focuses on the power of banks in making urban policy in Cleveland after the city went into default,[15] and Gottdeiner emphasizes the role that land investors and speculators played in the suburbanization of New York's Long Island.[16]

Perhaps the most systematic attempt to use urban political economy theory to address the issue of who are the central decision makers and what are their motivations is by Logan and Molotch, who argue that a place is valuable in two ways: as an object of exchange (to be bought and sold) and as something that is valuable when it is used (as a place to live or do business).[17] In the latter sense, particular pieces of land take on a "preciousness" to their residents associated with neighborhoods and neighbors, schools, jobs, and all the psychological and symbolic values that are tied to the notion of one's "hometown" or "community."

However, the people making up "urban growth coalitions" are primarily interested in real estate as a commodity that can be bought and sold. Unlike residents who see their cities and towns as places to live, work, and build supportive social

---

[12] Ibid.

[13] Joe Feagin and Robert Parker, *Building American Cities: The Real Estate Game,* Prentice-Hall, Englewood Cliffs, N.J., 1990.

[14] Edward Soja, "Restructuring and the Internationalization of the Los Angeles Region," in Smith and Feagin (eds.), *The Capitalist City,* Blackwell, pp. 178–198.

[15] Davita Glasberg, *The Power of Collective Purse Strings: The Effects of Bank Hegemony on Corporations and the State,* University of California Press, Berkeley, 1989.

[16] Mark Gottdeiner, *Planned Sprawl: Private and Public Interests in Suburbia,* Sage, Beverly Hills, Calif., 1977.

[17] John Logan and Harvey Molotch, *Urban Fortunes: The Political Economy of Place,* University of California Press, Berkeley, 1987.

networks, the individuals and organizations that are part of the "growth machine" are primarily interested in increasing the market value of land, stimulating in-migration of new residents, and smoothing the way for continued investment and development of the area.

Thus, they push municipal governments to create a "good business climate" and advocate various types of civic boosterism (from promoting the local sports teams to touting the museums or orchestras), in the hope that new people and dollars will flow into their locale instead of elsewhere.[18] Logan and Molotch go so far as to claim that "cities become organized as enterprises devoted to the increase of aggregate rent levels through the intensification of land use."[19]

Clearly, the main backers of this urban growth machine are those who can benefit from increasing "rents." These are primarily large corporate and individual property owners and the various institutions that provide financial and legal services to them. Comparing modern suburbia to feudal Europe, Logan and Molotch note, "North Americans do not pay tribute to barons and bishops; instead they pay banks and savings institutions, real estate brokers, and landlords."[20]

The local political scene is almost invariably dominated by elites drawn from these powerful constituencies. Because of this, municipal government today (and through most of U.S. history) is oriented toward "growth" and is competing with other places for it. Unfortunately, this often is *not* in the interests of local residents. While civic leaders trumpet the enormous benefits of intensive development (more jobs, a bigger tax base, etc.), in fact, rapid growth creates many problems (environmental degradation, traffic congestion, escalating housing costs, etc.):

> In many cases, probably in most, additional growth under current arrangements is a transfer of wealth and life chances from the general public to the rentier groups and their associates. Use values of a majority are sacrificed for the exchange values of a few.[21]

Although these authors generally see local politics as captive to the interests of a wealthy but powerful minority, they are not fatalistic about the prospects of changing this situation and, in effect, derailing the growth machine.

If local residents, whose interests in protecting the use values of their communities make them natural proponents of slow growth, were to organize and participate in local politics, then resistance to pro-development elite-backed politics would emerge.[22] Localities that have effectively fought back against versions of the growth machine often do so around environmental concerns.

Unfortunately, another dimension of North American cities in the late twentieth century makes effective political action at the local level increasingly difficult. Logan and Molotch argue that cities in the United States are directly affected by recent changes in the world system. A "new international division of labor" emerged in the past twenty years which has triggered the flight of industrial capital from the United States and has established new roles for American cities (see the discussion

[18] Ibid., chap. 3.
[19] Ibid., p. 13
[20] Ibid., p. 26.
[21] Ibid., p. 98.
[22] Ibid., chap. 6.

of New York City, below). While this new global economy creates tremendous profit opportunities for major corporations, the deindustrialization of North America hurts the working class and poor in our society and further heightens social inequality in our cities. Organizing effective opposition to changes that are tied to global restructuring is much more difficult than opposing the policies of local growth elites.

Feagin's historical case study of Houston emphasizes the critical role *politics* plays in urban growth. Feagin portrays the growth of Houston, from sparsely populated swampland to one of the largest cities in the United States, as a process that relied heavily on the ability of the region's economic elites to mobilize the resources of the local government, the state of Texas, and the national government in their own interests.[23] His research documents how leaders of the timber industry, then cotton producers, and finally rich and influential oil men came together in efforts (which were usually successful) to manipulate "the state" (as these different levels of government institutions are generally referred to) in support of their economic interests. Such support has come in the form of government subsidies to transportation infrastructure (e.g., building highways and airports, dredging the harbor), policies setting the prices of commodities (like oil), and laws giving employers power over workers (for example, making union organizing difficult).

Moreover, some urban problems facing the city today, such as severe air and water pollution, notorious traffic congestion, and poor public-service delivery, are attributable, in part, to elites promoting an ideology of free enterprise while actually pursuing policies tantamount to "socialism for the rich." Feagin's analysis provides a particularly compelling illustration of the inadequacy of ecological images of city growth as a "natural" product of new technologies and efficient markets. He even suggests that conventional urban ecology itself plays an ideological role: By ignoring the critical role that the narrow interests of powerful people (like politicians, industrialists, and major landowners) play in shaping cities, the ecologists deflect criticism away from elites and legitimate the status quo.

Global Cities

A theme emerging in urban political economy approaches to U.S. urbanization is the critical link between city growth and changes in the world economy. If we agree that there is a world-city system, then describing how particular urban places fit into the hierarchy in terms of rank order, or the role that they play, becomes an issue. Presumably, urban political economists should also be able to show how a city's place in the world urban hierarchy impacts various patterns of growth *within* that city.

Recent research on global cities attempts to describe the urban areas at the very top of the hierarchy—and highlights the paradoxical finding that these "command and control" centers of the world economy are also cities characterized by high levels of social inequality, with *both* great wealth and vast poverty. Sassen's book, *The Global City: New York, Tokyo, and London,* represents the most systematic combination of theoretical analysis and empirical research in this area.[24] She describes how

---

[23] Feagin, *The Free Enterprise City,* chap. 2.
[24] Saskia Sassen, *The Global City: New York, Tokyo, and London,* Princeton University Press, Princeton, N.J., 1991.

recent changes in the international division of labor have led to a situation where manufacturing is increasingly dispersed to remote locations around the globe (often driven by a search for lower labor costs), but various functions associated with the command and control of this far-flung world production system are concentrated in a few global cities. The distinguishing characteristics of these places are clear:

> These cities now function in four new ways: first, as highly concentrated command posts in the organization of the world economy; second, as key locations for finance and specialized service firms, which have replaced manufacturing as the leading economic sectors; third, as sites of production, including the production of innovations, in these leading industries; and fourth, as markets for the products and innovations produced.[25]

Sassen's identification of the three cities New York, Tokyo, and London as members of a special category at the top of the world-city hierarchy is widely accepted. Other classifications, including the qualitative assessment of Friedmann,[26] and our own empirical network analysis of intercity air-travel linkages,[27] generally support Sassen's conclusion (although our research suggests that Paris may also fit with the other three). The polarized socioeconomic structure within global cities is the most surprising and interesting outcome of this research. For instance, Sassen finds that to some extent each of her global cities were experiencing fiscal crises, growing poverty and unemployment, increasing class inequality, and residential segregation.

At the bottom socioeconomic layers of all three cities (including Tokyo) is a growing low-wage labor force engaged in sweatshop and homework manufacturing, staffed by isolated and politically marginalized immigrants and racial and ethnic minorities.[28] King's detailed description of growing social inequality in the global city of London reinforces this argument.[29]

New York City

New York is this country's leading global city. It is the quintessential American city, atop the U.S. urban system in terms of population, power, and prestige, but also plagued by all of the prototypical urban problems: crime, poverty, racism, drugs, etc. Social inequality in the nation's largest city seems to have grown much worse in the past two decades.

Mainstream urban social scientists attribute New York's escalating urban problems to economic changes that occurred in the mid-1970s and resulted in many fewer jobs in manufacturing, construction, wholesale and retail trade, and transportation.[30] Others have shown that many of the last jobs, though blue collar, were relatively well-paying, unionized ones with fairly substantial health and retirement benefits. Although there is now more work in some areas, notably services, overall

[25] Ibid., pp. 3–4.
[26] John Friedmann, "Where We Stand: A Decade of World City Research," in Paul Knox and Peter Taylor (eds.), World Cities in a World-System, Cambridge University Press, New York, 1995, pp. 21–47.
[27] David Smith and Michael Timberlake, "Conceptualizing and Mapping the World-Systems City System," Urban Studies, 32(2):287–302, 1995.
[28] Sassen, The Global City, chaps. 8 and 9.
[29] Anthony King, Global Cities: Post-Imperialism and the Internationalization of London, Routledge, London, 1990.
[30] George Sternlieb and James Hughes, "New York City," in Matteri Dogan and John Kasarda (eds.), The Metropolis Era, Vol. 2: Mega-Cities, Sage, Beverly Hills, Calif., 1987, pp. 27–55.

fewer jobs are available. Consequently, average income in the city has dropped, welfare participation has risen, and total population has declined. The areas of employment growth are in industries that require skilled workers, especially in terms of formal education, at the same time the work force is becoming increasingly low-skilled and minority. Jobs for this group are stagnant. Thus, there is a demographic-employment mismatch: New York City is becoming increasingly populated by unskilled, poor, working-class people, many of whom are members of racial and ethnic minorities, while the employment trends in the city are linked to its function as an international corporate headquarters and information and financial center.

An urban political economy approach provides a more compelling interpretation for current trends in New York City.[31] First, it highlights New York's role as a node in a globally competitive capitalist economy. In order for firms to survive and profit, costs associated with their operation must be kept as low as possible so that these companies can sell their products at competitive prices. One important cost factor is wages, and so businesses want to operate in areas where workers are willing (or, for that matter, forced) to work for lower wages. Therefore, other things being equal, it is perfectly rational for firms to move factories from high-wage places like New York City to low-wage localities in Tennessee, or even Taiwan or Thailand. Thus, the urban political economy approach explains the decline of manufacturing, and the rise of low-wage service jobs, in New York City (and other large U.S. urban areas) as a normal and predictable outcome of international capitalism. Ross and Trachte[32] stress the "globalization of production" and the corresponding flight of capital away from high-wage, unionized labor pools historically in existence in New York City. They highlight a less-well-recognized aspect of the employment situation: the increasing prevalence of low-wage sweatshops and service industries, including the rise of a poorly regulated, semi-legal "informal sector." The third world comes home.[33]

Another set of forces at work which some political economy sociologists emphasize is the continuing centrality of race, ethnicity, and gender to urban change. Williams points out that "racial aversion" is an important factor in decisions to locate and relocate manufacturing firms away from metropolitan areas with substantial populations of African Americans and other subordinated races and ethnic groups.[34] (Ecology explanations tend to downplay racial motivations in favor of

---

[31] Saskia Sassen-Koob, "Capital Mobility and Labor Migration: Their Expression in Core Cities," in Michael Timberlake (ed.), *Urbanization in the World-Economy*, Academic Press, New York, 1985; Saskia Sassen-Koob, "Growth and Informalization at the Core: A Preliminary Report on New York City," in Smith and Feagin (eds.), *The Capitalist City*, pp. 138–154; Robert Ross and Kent Trachte, *Global Capitalism: The New Leviathan*, State University of New York, Albany, 1990.

[32] Ross and Trachte, *Global Capitalism*, chap. 8.

[33] Another particularly graphic example of "the third world coming home" to the United States came to light in the summer of 1995 in Los Angeles, our nation's second-ranked global city. A garment factory employing seventy undocumented immigrants from Thailand under virtual slave conditions was discovered in suburban El Monte. Workers were not allowed to leave the guarded compound which was surrounded by barbed-wire fences; they were expected to work up to 22 hours a day, at pay as low as 59 cents an hour. Investigators discovered that the clothing they produced was being marketed by major U.S. brand names and retailers including Disney, J. C. Penney, and Bloomingdale's.

The *Los Angeles Times* provided detailed coverage of this story. Two particularly useful articles were "It's Blood, Sweatshops, and Tears" by Vicki Torres and Donna Walters on August 23, 1995, and "Sweatshop Goods Destined for Major Retailers, Labor Department Says" by Patrick McDonnell on August 26, 1995.

[34] Bruce Williams, *Black Workers in an Industrial Suburb: The Struggle against Discrimination*, Rutgers, New Brunswick, N.J., 1987.

economic explanations, such as the need for cheaper land and lower tax rates.) This pattern of racial aversion contributes directly to rising black and other minority unemployment and underemployment in the urban informal economy. Moreover, Wilson's research indicates that this factor also undermines the stability of healthy black institutions, including the local community and family.[35] Thus, he attributes the increasing number of female-run households among the urban "underclass" to the declining pool of men with incomes sufficient to contribute to family well-being and to the breakdown of normatively stable inner-city neighborhoods, as middle-class and professional African Americans choose suburban residence. This accounts for the increasing proportion of women and female-headed households living in poverty (termed the "feminization of poverty").[36]

Ironically, at the same time that changes have been disorganizing labor in general, and marginalizing and pauperizing some of the most disadvantaged workers, New York City has become a global control center where transnational corporations do "planning, marketing, internal administration and distribution control over a wide variety of types of information, and other activities that entail centralization of management, control, and highly specialized services."[37] Among those headquartered in the Big Apple are several banks whose influence is international and numerous manufacturing firms that have worldwide operations. But there also is a need for low-skilled workers to provide services to the relatively affluent professionals, managers, lawyers, and accountants who now live and work in this global control center. "Dog walkers, restaurant workers, housekeepers, and hand launderers are some of the jobs reflecting the underside of 'gentrification'"[38] (see Chapter 12, The Question of Urban Crisis).

Despite the precipitous drop in some types of manufacturing, the city's economy still fuels specialized industries—customized manufacturing (like fashion clothes) which requires proximity to designers and developers but which can utilize the poorly paid sweatshop labor of undocumented immigrant workers. Many of these workers operate in an underground economy in which benefits such as health insurance and unemployment compensation are unknown. Workers in New York and other cities who work for minimum wage in the fast-food industry are only marginally better off. And this is one of the fastest-growing types of employment in the United States today. This does not bode well for solving the growing problems associated with the underclass in America's cities.

Dependent/Peripheral Urbanization in the Third World

In contrast to core cities like New York that rank near the top of the global system of cities, many urban areas in the third world are lower in this hierarchy. There is a large literature that interprets urbanization in less-developed countries from the perspective of urban political economy. These analyses link the subordinate role

[35] William J. Wilson, *The Truly Disadvantaged,* University of Chicago, Chicago, 1987.
[36] I. Garfinkel and S. McLanahan, "The Feminization of Poverty, Nature, Causes and a Partial Cure," *Institute for Poverty Discussion,* Paper No. 776-85, University of Wisconsin, Madison, 1985.
[37] Sassen-Koob, "Capital Mobility and Labor Migration," pp. 231–265 (quote on p. 238).
[38] Ibid., p. 262.

that third world countries play in the world political and economic system to their patterns of city growth.

Analytically, we can distinguish three types of urban "unevenness."[39] First, demographic and economic imbalances occur between the urban and rural sectors; these problems are usually referred to as "overurbanization" or "urban bias." Second, skewed patterns of population distribution are characterized by rapid concentrations of people and resources in the largest places, leading to debates over "optimal city size" and "urban primacy." Finally, great material disparities within cities are reflected in dualistic patterns of housing, consumption, and access to political participation, generating slums, squatter settlements, urban poverty, and the "informal sector."

Both quantitative cross-national research and historical case studies demonstrate that "dependent cities" outside the core of the world system are characterized by urban unevenness of all three types. The penetration of the world economy into peripheral areas leads to a pattern of development with relatively few large cities, which are control centers in a web of exploitation. The result is a process of urbanization which leads to urban primacy, regional inequalities, centralization of political and economic power within huge cities, and intraurban segregation and inequality.[40] The role of the dependent city in the world system is explained this way: "Peripheral primate cities are nodes on the conduit which transmits surplus value to the core and domination to the periphery, while primate cities in the core receive surplus value and transmit domination."[41] This suggests that, contrary to the historical experiences of the western nations, there is no natural link between urbanization, on the one hand, and industrialization and economic growth, on the other. In fact, rapid, uneven city growth and relative economic stagnation are likely to occur together in third world countries, since both are associated with high levels of international economic dependence.[42]

An important and comprehensive example of comparative historical research on urbanization and development is Roberts's *Cities of Peasants: The Political Economy of Peasants in the Third World*. The book's topic is dependent urbanization in Latin America. While Roberts insists that city growth is closely intermeshed with a society's role in the world system, his major emphasis is on "the internal structure of class relationships which work to the economic advantage of the metropolis and to the progressive underdevelopment of the periphery."[43] Patterns of urbanization, migration, and urban economic and social structure are affected by

[39] Joseph Gugler and William Flanagan, "On the Political Economy of Urbanization in the Third World: The Case of West Africa," *International Journal of Urban and Regional Research*, 1(2):272–292, 1977.

[40] See Timberlake, *Urbanization in the World Economy*; John Walton, "The International Economy and Peripheral Urbanization," in N. Fainstein and S. Fainstein (eds.), *Urban Policy under Capitalism*, Sage, Beverly Hills, Calif., 1982, pp. 119–135. For the most recent comprehensive treatment of these issues, see David A. Smith, *Third World Cities in Global Perspective: The Political Economy of Uneven Urbanization*, Westview Press, Boulder, Colo., 1995.

[41] Christopher Chase-Dunn, "Urbanization in the World-System: New Directions for Research," in Michael P. Smith (ed.), *Cities in Transformation*, Sage, Beverly Hills, Calif., 1984, pp. 111–120.

[42] David Smith, "Overurbanization Reconceptualized: A Political Economy of the World-System Approach," *Urban Affairs Quarterly*, 23(2):270–294, 1987; Bruce London and David Smith, "Urban Bias Dependence and Economic Stagnation in Non-Core Nations," *American Sociological Review*, 53:454–463, 1988.

[43] Bryan Roberts, *Cities of Peasants: The Political Economy of Peasants in the Third World*, Sage, Beverly Hills, Calif., 1978.

This street market in Ho Chi Minh City is typical of the small-scale or bazaar economy that constitutes the large urban informal sector in most peripheral cities. (David Smith.)

the changing contexts of industrialization, elite power, and state centralization in Latin American countries. Different countries and cities experienced colonialism and (later) recolonialism differently. Therefore, their patterns of urban growth and development are not identical. Nevertheless, Roberts does claim that the *mechanisms* stimulating urbanization have been similar across the region. And despite some variations, in all of Latin America the contexts of urban and economic growth have been basically the same: underdevelopment directed by (and in the benefit of) foreign powers and businesses.

An important topic that Roberts discusses in his book is the prevalence of a "small-scale" or "bazaar" economy in third world cities. This economic sector includes people who are food vendors, rickshaw pullers, homemade beer brewers, repairmen, etc. The conventional developmentalist theorists argued that this sector was a "traditional" aspect of urbanization in the less-developed countries which would disappear with the rise of industrialization and "modernity." However, studies provide empirical evidence that this is not the case—in fact, this so-called informal sector seems to be growing in size and importance over time.[44]

[44] Chris Birkbeck, "Garbage, Industry, and the 'Vultures' of Cali, Colombia," in R. Bromley and C. Gerry (eds.), *Casual Work and Third World Cities,* Wiley, New York, 1978, pp. 161–183; Christopher Gerry, "Petty Production and Capitalist Production in Dakar," *World Development,* **6**(9/10):1147–1160, 1978; T. G. McGee, *The Southeast Asian City,* Praeger, New York, 1969; T. G. McGee, "Peasants in the Cities: A Paradox, a Paradox, a Most Ingenious Paradox," *Human Organization,* **32**(2):135–142, 1973; S. Sethuraman, "The Urban Informal Sector in Africa," *International Labor Review,* **116**(3):434–452, 1977; G. Williams and E. Tumusiime-Muteble, "Capitalist and Petty Commodity Production in Nigeria: A Note," *World Development,* **6**:1103–1104, 1978.

How are we to understand this apparent paradox? The key lies in understanding the function of the informal sector and its connections to the formal "firm-centered" economy. On the one hand, the bazaar economy is "basically a symptom of underdevelopment" which absorbs the excess labor of urban masses in cities where unemployment is very high.[45] Going beyond this, social scientists recognize that the workers in the formal sector perform socially useful, but very inexpensive, work—which eventually benefits the formal economy. Portes pointed to two key attributes of informal-sector enterprises: "First, they are labor intensive. Second, they avoid formal state supervision and regulations."[46] As a result, because laborers work long hours, utilize friends and family, and escape all tax, wage, and social security regulation, the cost of labor in the informal sector is much less than wages paid by formally regulated businesses. Lower wages mean that goods and services produced in this informal economy can be purchased by formal-sector workers and firms for less. This, in turn, lowers labor and material costs for those formal businesses, allowing the manufacturing done in the underdeveloped country to be highly competitive in the world market.

China provides an exception that may well "prove the rule" concerning political economy interpretations of third world urbanization. Since the Chinese revolution in 1949, China's urban patterns have contrasted sharply with those in most other less-developed countries. Levels and rates of urbanization were much lower, the nonagricultural labor force was more evenly distributed between manufacturing and service jobs, the informal sector was exceptionally small, and there was no evidence of urban primacy.[47] For decades China's strong state insulated its socio-economic system from the capitalist world economy. But since the late 1980s, this has begun to change, particularly in coastal regions. The government is allowing market relations to develop in these areas and now actively seeks foreign investment. In other words, large parts of China are now becoming integrated (actually, reintegrated) into the world system. Rapidly growing new industries in the coastal cities, producing manufactured products for export, are creating relatively attractive jobs that are drawing migrants from the countryside and smaller towns. However, the supply of jobs does not match the large numbers who come to seek them—leading to the development of a large "floating population" of "urban transients" in Chinese cities.[48] Consistent with urban political economy theory, we not only are seeing the predictable trends toward more and more commodification and proletarianization, but also are observing changing cumulative patterns of urbanization, with coastal Chinese cities like Shanghai and Guangzhou beginning to look like other third world cities in terms of rates of population growth, the emergence of a large informal economy, growing slums, shantytowns, homelessness, and sky-

---

[45] Terry G. McGee, "Catalysts or Cancers? The Role of Cities in Asian Societies," in L. Jacobson and V. Prakash (eds.), *Urbanization and National Development,* Sage, Beverly Hills, Calif., 1971, p. 165.

[46] Alejandro Portes, "The Informal Sector and the World-Economy," in Timberlake (ed.), *Urbanization in the World Economy,* p. 57.

[47] For a discussion of China's divergent pattern of urbanization, see Martin Whyte and William Parish, *Urban Life in Contemporary China,* University of Chicago Press, Chicago, 1995; also see the discussion in David Smith, *Third World Cities in Global Perspective,* chap. 6.

[48] Dorothy Solinger, "China's Urban Transients in the Transition from Socialism and the Collapse of the 'Urban Public Goods Regime,'" *Comparative Politics,* **27**(2):127–146, 1993.

rocketing unemployment and poverty. At the same time, a newly wealthy class of industrial entrepreneurs is emerging in these Chinese cities.

Thus, while manifestations of urban unevenness may create misery for most residents in cities in the less-developed countries, the skewed patterns of urbanization may fit the needs of the privileged classes and large corporations in these societies. We encounter an overriding global political economy theme: The mundane circumstances of everyday social inequality in particular cities are linked to the overarching structure of the capitalist world system.

FUTURE DIRECTIONS FOR URBAN POLITICAL ECONOMY

As this chapter indicates, urban political economy includes a diverse set of studies and scholars. They do not really share a tightly argued "theory" of "the city." But they do agree on a series of assumptions, elaborated above, as the starting point for serious research on cities and social change.

Figure 5-1 schematically represents some of the key elements of the urban political economy perspective. It shows a sequence of macrostructures, beginning with the global system itself, which set progressively narrower parameters for urban outcomes. In directly linking infrastructure to urbanization, the proximate causal effect of transportation and communication networks is acknowledged, as are other aspects of the built environment, on the evolution of cities and urban systems. For this causal link, it is appropriate to credit the urban ecology perspective. But infrastructure provision itself is a product of political-economic processes emanating from the state and class structure.

At this point, political struggles come in. In turn, the basic political-economic conditions within a society are constrained by the nation's (or a city's) role in the international system. And this role is limited by the phase of world-system development: Certain international niches are more likely during periods of expansion, contraction, or reorganization of the global system; particular economic specializa-

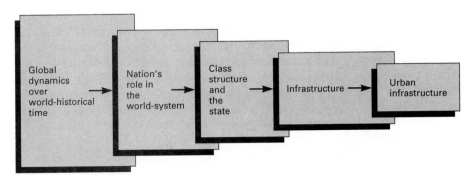

Figure 5-1. Urbanization in the world system: Model of how macrostructures set the parameters for urban development. The image of smaller "windows" of possible variability, instead of deterministic causal arrows, is chosen because this figure is intended to provide a general theoretical orientation for research (i.e., point to the key elements), rather than pretend to provide a verifiable model for testing.

tions arise in response to the historical needs of the system as a whole. By depicting an image of *"vertically integrated processes* passing through a network from the international level to the urban hinterland," this figure begins to capture the complexity of the global perspective on urbanization developed by the urban political economy.[49] Of course, it is overly "infrastructural": Actually all the systems and structures are made up of living people whose decisions and actions shape the process at each step.

The emphasis that urban political economy places on political struggles, historical context, and the contingencies of individual and group action suggests a dramatic reorientation of research strategy in urban sociology. While conventional sociological studies of urbanization often focus on statistical analysis of contemporary data from many cities to derive general trends, a better understanding of cities may come from grounded historical case studies of particular places.

Theoretically, urban political economy faces two major challenges. The first is a paradoxical one: Urban political economy faces "the threat of its own success." As Walton points out, while the urban political economy approach has largely replaced urban ecology as the dominant paradigm, today there is some sense of complacency, where replication replaces innovative research, and studies "confirm" theory instead of posing new questions.[50] Walton calls for a reinvigorated urban political economy that avoids an overemphasis on narrowly economic explanations, and revives "a genuine sense of puzzlement"[51] about the dynamics and complexities of cities and urbanization.

The second challenge to urban political economy is one shared by all useful social change paradigms: How can the perspective keep up with astonishingly rapid changes in the global system in the closing decade of the twentieth century? A central concern here is how an approach that owes much to neo-Marxism can accommodate itself to a world in which so many self-proclaimed "socialist" regimes have collapsed and/or "reformed," and the very nature of world capitalism is rapidly restructuring itself.

Our view is that understanding global political economy remains crucial—but changing times require theory building that keeps pace. While it has been less U.S.-centered than the old urban ecology paradigm, there still is a need to be more comparative. Is there, for instance, a "semiperipheral" pattern of city growth that occurs in various societies around the world? More research comparing Asia's newly industrialized countries to one another, or to southern Europe, might provide an answer. What about urbanization in societies that call themselves "socialist" (or did until recently)? The events of 1989–1990 in eastern Europe forcefully reminded scholars that even self-proclaimed socialist states remain part of the modern world system (and research suggests that urban patterns there are the result of the regions' long historical *integration* into that system).[52] This suggests a serious investigation

[49] John Walton, "From Cities to Systems: Recent Research in Latin American Urbanization," *Latin American Research Review,* **14**(1):164, 1979.

[50] John Walton, "Urban Sociology: The Contributions and Limits of Political Economy," *Annual Review of Sociology,* **19**:301–320, 1993.

[51] Ibid., p. 318

[52] Michael Kennedy and David Smith, "East Central European Urbanization: A Political Economy of the World System Perspective," *International Journal of Urban and Regional Research,* **13**(4):597–624, 1989.

of the degree to which urbanization in places like eastern Europe, the ex-Soviet Union, China, or Cuba might relate to the role these nations play in the overarching global system. What about cities in "societies in transition" that are moving toward "market reform" (like contemporary China or Vietnam)? Finally, a growing literature on the nature of the new international division of labor, on global restructuring, and on the rise of new increasingly "flexible" forms of corporate organization has enormous implications for the structure of urban and regional development and the future of cities throughout the world. Current political economy research addressing these changes should provide insight into fundamental changes in urbanization in the twenty-first century that are linked to basic global transformations that we are only becoming dimly aware of today.

6

METROPOLITAN AND EDGE-CITY GROWTH

A city is a perfect and absolute assembly or communion of many towns or streets in one.

Aristotle, *Politics*

INTRODUCTION

Urbanization patterns in the United States have undergone several profound changes in recent decades. In this chapter, three major transformations are emphasized. The first is the metropolitan area replacing the city as the major urban unit. Nine-tenths of the nation's growth (89 percent) now occurs in metropolitan areas. The second is the emergence of outer or edge cities as the major locus of metropolitan growth. The third transformation we will discuss is the continued shift from frost belt to sun belt growth.

METROPOLITAN URBAN GROWTH

Let us begin by looking at the metropolitan area. The twentieth century was a period of dramatic metropolitan development and ascendancy. By the beginning of the century, the era of the frontier was closed, and it was clear that future national growth would have an urban nexus. The ecological and demographic pattern was one of population shifting into ever-larger metropolitan areas. Rural counties were being depopulated, while population in the central cities was becoming denser. The census of 1910 recognized this centripetal population movement by establishing forty-four ad hoc "metropolitan districts" whose boundaries extended beyond those of the central city. At that time, roughly one-third of the nation's population resided in metropolitan areas.

Today the dominance of metropolitan areas is demographic as well as economic and social. Half (51 percent) of all Americans live in the thirty-seven largest Metropolitan Statistical Areas with a population of 1 million or more. These large metropolitan areas have 125 million residents. Moreover, the dominance of metropolitan areas is increasing. One state, New Jersey, is entirely covered by metropolitan areas, while seven other states—California, Maryland, Connecticut, Rhode Island, Florida, Massachusetts, and New York—have over 90 percent of their populations in metropolitan areas. Idaho, at the other extreme, has only 20 percent of its population in metropolitan areas.

If changes in the definition of "metropolitan areas" are taken into account, *all* population growth during this century in the contiguous United States has occurred in metropolitan areas. The only exception was a brief revival of nonmetropolitan growth during the 1970s, which some predicted (mistakenly it turned out) would be the pattern of the future.[1] However, by the 1980s and 1990s, the pattern of higher metropolitan growth had returned. Moreover, beyond the metropolitan area there exists a daily commuting field that further extends metropolitan influence to virtually the entire population.

Metropolitan dominance had been foreseen by scholars as far back as the 1920s. The awareness that cities had become part of a larger urban complex was re-

---

[1] Calvin L. Beale and Glen V. Fuguitt, "The New Pattern of Non-metropolitan Population Change," Center for Demography and Ecology, University of Wisconsin, Madison, Center Paper 75–22, 1975; James Zuiches, "Residential Preference and Rural Population Growth," paper prepared for Farmers Home Administration, U.S. Department of Agriculture, Washington, D.C., 1980; and William H. Frey, "Migration and Metropolitan Decline in Developed Countries," *Population and Development Review,* **14:**595–628, December, 1988.

TABLE 6-1
Population of the Twenty-Five Largest Metropolitan Areas, 1992

Metropolitan area (CMSA or MSA)	Population in 1992
New York–Northern N.J.–Long Island CMSA	19,670,175
Los Angeles–Anaheim–Riverside CMSA	15,047,772
Chicago–Gary–Lake County CMSA	8,410,402
Washington–Baltimore CMSA	6,919,572
San Francisco–Oakland–San Jose CMSA	6,409,891
Philadelphia–Wilmington–Alantic City CMSA	5,938,528
Boston–Worcester–Lawrence CMSA	5,438,815
Detroit–Ann Arbor–Flint CMSA	5,245,906
Dallas–Fort Worth CMSA	4,214,532
Houston–Galveston–Brazoria CMSA	3,962,365
Miami–Fort Lauderdale CMSA	3,309,246
Atlanta MSA	3,142,857
Seattle–Tacoma–Bremereton CMSA	3,131,392
Cleveland–Akron CMSA	2,890,402
Minneapolis–St. Paul MSA	2,617,973
San Diego MSA	2,601,055
St. Louis MSA	2,518,528
Pittsburgh MSA	2,406,452
Phoenix–Mesa MSA	2,330,353
Tampa–St. Petersburg–Clearwater MSA	2,107,271
Denver–Boulder–Greeley CMSA	2,089,321
Portland–Salem CMSA	1,896,895
Cincinnati–Hamilton CMSA	1,865,002
Milwaukee–Racine CMSA	1,629,420
Kansas City MSA	1,616,930

Source: U.S. Bureau of the Census, Areas defined by OMB as of June 30, 1993.

flected in the pioneering works of perceptive writers such as Gras and McKenzie.[2] They foresaw that the city per se was yielding its influence to a larger unit: the metropolitan area.

Movement of twentieth-century population toward the largest urban concentrations (city and suburb) both depopulated rural counties and magnified urban problems.[3] The magnitude of the rural out-migration is reflected in Bureau of the Census figures (see Table 6-1 and Figure 6-1). In 1920, 30 percent of the American population still lived on farms; by the 1990s this figure had shrunk to under 2 percent.[4] In the half century from 1920 to 1970, the net out-migration from farms to cities was 29 million.[5] Under one person in fifty lives on a farm today. For the overwhelming majority of Americans, the family farm is simply history.

[2] Norman Scott Brien Gras, *Introduction to Economic History,* Harper, New York, 1922; and Roderick McKenzie, *The Metropolitan Community,* McGraw-Hill, New York, 1933.
[3] Amos H. Hawley, "Urbanization as Process," in David Street (ed.), *Handbook of Contemporary Urban Life,* Jossey-Bass, San Francisco, 1978, p. 7.
[4] U.S. Bureau of the Census, "Residences of Farms and Rural Areas: 1990," *Current Population Reports,* series P-20, no. 457, 1992, p. 2.
[5] U.S. Bureau of the Census, U.S. Department of Commerce, "Population Profile of the United States: 1981," *Current Population Reports,* series P-20, no. 394, Washington, D.C., September, 1982, p. 7.

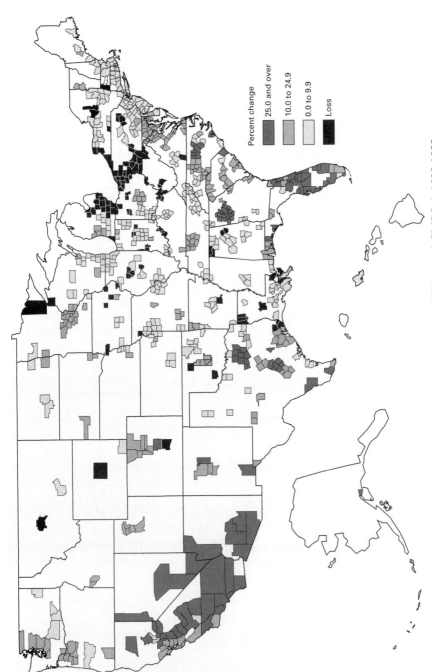

Figure 6-1. Population growth and decline in metropolitan areas (MSAs and CMSAs), 1980-1990.
Source: Population Reference Bureau, *U.S. Metro Data Sheet,* 2/e, 1990.

For the first half of this century the central city, and particularly its downtown, was dominant. While the central city increasingly found its *physical* expansion contained by surrounding suburbs, the *influence* of the central city expanded. Once independent, outlying towns, villages, and crossroad markets found themselves engulfed in an urban network. The local bank became a branch of a large city bank; local papers were replaced by metropolitan dailies; and local dairies and breweries went under, unable to compete with metropolitan-based firms. Where once such places were moderately self-sufficient, they now either declined in significance or began to perform specialized functions for the larger metropolitan area. Some previously independent communities became satellite towns, while others specialized as bedroom suburbs.[6] The consequence was the emergence during the first half of the century of the era of the city-dominated metropolitan unit.

DECENTRALIZATION OF POPULATION WITHIN METROPOLITAN AREAS

The twentieth century witnessed a massive population implosion or in-gathering of population into urban concentrations. However, *within* metropolitan areas the movement has been the other way, from the center toward the periphery. Throughout the twentieth century, again with annexation taken into account, the population of outer "suburban" areas has grown faster than that of central cities.[7] Almost all metropolitan growth during the twentieth century occurred in the suburban ring beyond the central city. The redistribution of population began in the larger and older metropolitan areas and then became general for cities of all sizes except the very newest. (This suburban decentralization is further treated in Chapter 9, Changing Suburbanization Patterns.) Moreover, the highest rate of growth in nonmetropolitan counties has occurred in counties having growing metropolitan characteristics, experiencing overspill, or both. The areas of overspill, commonly referred to as "exurbs," simply confirmed the patterns of metropolitan dominance.

Over time the edges of metropolitan areas were increasingly converted from less-intensive to more-intensive uses, such as housing and manufacturing. Less-intensive land uses such as grain production and cattle grazing have been pushed outward; near the city even agriculture is intensive—truck farms, greenhouses, chicken farms, etc. Fertility of the soil is less important than nearness of the city: Consider, for example, the intensive use of relatively poor farmland near New England cities.

Out-Movement: 1950 to the End of the Century

Downtown, until the 1960s, was where all the major department stores and retail outlets were located. For major shopping one went downtown, usually by public transit. However, not since the 1970s have downtowns accounted for over half the nation's sales. Retail trade, service establishments, and manufacturing firms have

[6] Leo F. Schnore, "Satellites and Suburbs," *Social Forces,* **36:**121–127, December, 1957.
[7] J. John Palen, *The Suburbs,* McGraw-Hill, New York, 1995.

increasingly followed the population to suburban areas. For example, suburban shopping malls—virtually nonexistent thirty years ago—now number 40,000. With over three-quarters of employed suburbanites working in the suburbs, old commutation patterns (residents of suburbs commuting to the central city) have also broken down. The average commute since 1980 has not been from suburb to city, but suburb to suburb. (The major role of the federal government in subsidizing suburbanization is discussed in Chapter 9, Changing Suburbanization Patterns, and Chapter 13, Housing Policies and Change.)

Likewise, in the American city of fifty years ago, industry was concentrated in an inner belt or zone located between the central business district and the better residential areas. As the factories prospered, the original space became more and more crowded. However, central-city expansion was both difficult and expensive. Assembly lines or other factory operations had to be fitted into existing buildings, and even moving goods from floor to floor was a serious problem. At the same time, external expansion was limited by the cost, in both land and taxes. Surrounding land was already occupied, which meant that whatever was on the land had to be bought and torn down before the factory could expand. Transportation also was an increasing problem. Trucks had to move down busy city streets before lining up to wait to get into inadequate loading docks. Parking space for workers' cars developed into another major headache. Nonetheless, factories stayed in the city because they needed access to rail lines to ship their goods, and most workers did not use private cars, but rather came to work on public transportation.

Technological Advances and the Metropolitan Area

What made the outward flow of urban population in the twentieth century possible were a number of technological breakthroughs in the areas of electrification, transportation, and communication. The nineteenth-century city based on steam power was transformed into one dependent on petroleum and electricity. Widespread use of automobiles, trucks, telephones, and electric power increased the movement of persons, goods, and ideas.

Research shows that the factor most closely related to a city's growth during the first half of the twentieth century was its transportation network with other cities.[8] Within metropolitan areas, transportation was also critical to growth. The automobile provided mobility to the average urban dweller and allowed—and even encouraged—rapid settlement of previously inaccessible areas on the periphery of the central city. Henry Ford's Model T changed the automobile from a toy of the rich to a middle-class necessity. Automobile registration in the United States increased from 2.5 million in 1915 to 9 million in 1920 and 26 million in 1930. Following World War II, car ownership became common in working-class as well as middle-class families. Currently, there is more than one auto for every two persons in the United States.

[8] Mark LaGory and James Nelson, "An Ecological Analysis of Growth between 1900 and 1940," *Sociological Quarterly,* **19:**590–603, 1978.

Defining Metropolitan Areas

The term "metropolitan area" is a popular term rather than one
defined by the Bureau of the Census. It commonly refers to a
large concentration of 100,000 or more inhabitants that contains
as its core a legal city with 50,000 or more inhabitants and is
surrounded by suburban areas. The Bureau of the Census has
two ways of defining metropolitan areas: as urbanized areas
and as Metropolitan Statistical Areas.

Urbanized Areas. According to the Bureau of the Census, an
urbanized area consists of a central city, or cities, of 50,000
people or more and the surrounding closely settled territory,
whether incorporated or unincorporated. The term, thus, refers
to the actual urban population of an area regardless of political
boundaries such as county or state lines. All those in the
urbanized area are considered urban, but the population is
also divided into those in the central city and those in the
remainder of the area, or "urban fringe."

Because it is based on density (at least 1,000 persons per
square mile), the urbanized area has no fixed boundaries, and
thus changes from census to census to reflect actual population
changes. This potential strength can, however, become a
weakness when one is doing longitudinal research, since the
urbanized area of any city covered different land areas in the
1970, 1980, and 1990 censuses. The proportion of a state's
population living in urbanized areas in 1990 varied from 85
percent in New Jersey to 15 percent in Vermont.

Metropolitan Statistical Area. Metropolitan Statistical Areas
(MSAs) are officially designated by the U.S. Office of
Management and Budget, and are based on territory rather
than population. (Before 1983 MSAs were known as SMSAs, or
Standard Metropolitan Statistical Areas.) A Metropolitan
Statistical Area is a *county* or *group* of counties having a
central city of 50,000 or more, or twin cities with a combined
population of 50,000 or more. The MSA includes the county in
which the central city is located plus any adjacent counties that
are judged by the Bureau of the Census to be metropolitan in
character and socially and economically integrated with the
central city. In New England, where there are no counties,
MSAs consist of townships and cities instead. As of the 1990
census 283 areas were designated as MSAs. The seventy-one
largest of these were designated Primary Metropolitan
Statistical Areas (PMSAs).

Consolidated Metropolitan Statistical Areas. In order to distinguish the very largest concentrations of metropolitan populations, Consolidated Metropolitan Statistical Areas (CMSAs) have been designated. A CMSA must have at least a million persons and is composed of a number of PMSAs. As of 1990 there were twenty Consolidated Metropolitan Statistical Areas.

All the variously defined metropolitan areas can cross state lines. The New York CMSA, for example, includes portions of New Jersey and Connecticut. The Philadelphia CMSA includes, in addition to the section in Pennsylvania, portions of New Jersey, Maryland, and Delaware.

In 1990, the term "metropolitan area" (MA) became the overall umbrella term covering MSAs, PMSAs, and CMSAs.

Spatially the auto now dominates American cities. One-quarter of all city land is devoted to the movement or storage of vehicles. Roads, garages, car dealerships, parking lots, and truck facilities define urban areas.

With the coming of the automobile, the maximum distance that workers could live from their place of employment and commute within an hour increased from a dozen miles to perhaps 25 miles or so. (Theoretically, the automobile more than doubled the commuting radius, but the practical realities of poor roads and traffic congestion set lower limits.) As of 1920 a Chicago study indicated that the average distance from home to workplace was 1.5 miles.[9] (By the 1980s the distance had increased to 9.2 miles.) Just at the time when Burgess was expounding his theory of growth from the center through intermediate zones (detailed in Chapter 4, Structure and Organization of American Cities), the automobile and the truck were partially outdating his work. (See Figure 6-2.)

What the automobile did for people, the truck did for goods. Prior to the 1920s there really was no alternative to the railroad for moving intercity goods. Beyond city lines no national road system existed. Following World War I the army sent a convoy of trucks coast to coast to demonstrate the need for a national road. It took

[9] Beverly Duncan, "Factors in Work-Residence Separation: Wages and Salary Workers, 1951," *American Sociological Review,* **21:**48–56, 1956.

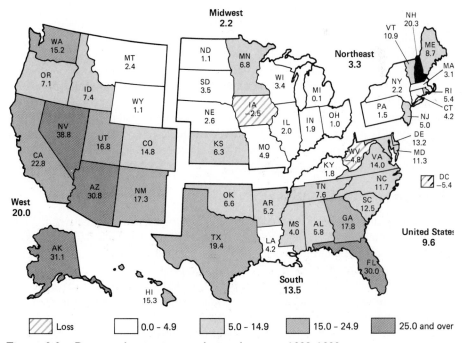

Figure 6-2. Percent change in population, by state, 1980–1989.
Source: U.S. Bureau of the Census, "Special Studies," *Current Population Reports,* series P-23, no 164, January, 1990, p. 2.

the army convoy sixty-two difficult days to cross the country. One of the officers in the 1919 Washington–to–San Francisco convoy was Captain Dwight Eisenhower. During the 1950s, as president, he signed the bill creating the present interstate highway system.

Trucks, which during the 1920s saw their registration triple from 1 million to 3.5 million, were incomparably more flexible than railroads for short hauls. Trucks were free of fixed routes and fixed schedules, needed no elaborate terminal facilities on expensive inner-city land, and could make door-to-door pickups and deliveries. No longer was it necessary for the factory to be on the rail line. For all but the longest hauls, the speed of motor trucks was also superior. However, during the 1920s and 1930s, the major advantage of motor transport was its lower cost per mile within the first 250 miles of the city.[10] Not only were equipment and maintenance costs far lower, but in truck cartage the cost per mile was lowest for the shortest distances. In train transport, on the other hand, the lowest cost per mile was for the longest trips. The motor truck, then, was by far the superior competitor for the short haul—an advantage that was increased considerably by the public building of new roads. The interstate expressway system, begun during the late 1950s, extended the trucks' longer-haul advantage. Where goods are needed more rapidly, they are increasingly shipped by air.

What the motor vehicle did for transportation, the telephone did for communication. Not until 1920 did over half of all residences have telephones. By the 1920s the telephone had become a common adjunct of local business, and long-distance telephone communication was a practical—if expensive—reality.

Rural electrification, sponsored by federal legislation during the depression of the 1930s, brought the possibility of modern appliances to rural households. Today technology goes anywhere. There is more than a little truth in the claim that the West Virginia state flower is the satellite dish. Air transportation and the use of computers for information transfer have further weakened the need for a central-city business location. The use of fax, e-mail, and mobile telephones means a central location is no longer a requirement for adequate telecommuting. Business as well as residential sprawl is possible. Once inaccessible locations now have addresses on the information superhighway.

Changing Central Cities

The changes noted above have radically altered the relationship between central cities and their suburbs. In the quarter century between 1970 and 1995, for example, the overall population of central cities remained about the same. Losses in northern cities were offset by growth and annexations in southern and western sun belt cities. However, during that same period, suburbs grew so that there are now over three suburbanites for every two central-city residents. More important, the cities have been losing blue-collar jobs. This includes both well-paying union jobs and the entry-level jobs through which poor city dwellers traditionally entered the

[10] National Resources Committee, *Technological Trends and National Policy,* U.S. Government Printing Office, Washington, D.C., 1937.

labor market. Already by 1980 there were almost twice as many persons employed in manufacturing in the suburbs (10.9 million) as in the cities (5.9 million).

Within metropolitan areas, decentralization has been specific as regards both industrial movement and population movement. The greatest decentralization has occurred in the larger, older cities of the northeast and middle west.[11] Decentralization of business and industry to fringe locations has also been somewhat selective. Operations that require large plants and large amounts of ground space per worker, that have a high "nuisance factor" (that is, create noise, pollution, odor, and waste), and that need little contact with local buyers tend to be drawn increasingly toward the periphery. Obsolete central-city plants cannot compete economically with new, specifically designed single-story facilities. Automobile plants, chemical firms, steel mills, and petroleum refineries also require large areas of fringe land for their newer operations. The American auto plants of the last decade have been built not in Detroit but in locations such as rural Tennessee, South Carolina, and Alabama. Generally, production and distribution have decentralized; and as markets have decentralized, wholesaling has too, since it needs space as well as access to markets. The use of trucks and air rather than railroads for transportation also argues for the more flexible outer locations. By locating businesses outside the congested city core and near the interstate expressways, owners could reduce transportation costs. Rapid transportation provides a form of storage in route. Over 5,000 suburban industrial parks have been formed since 1960.

On the other hand, finance, advertising, legal services, management, educational institutions, medical centers, and government have shown far less inclination to decentralize. While manufacturing, retail trade, and wholesaling typically have large space-per-employee requirements, most managerial, clerical, professional, and business functions are highly space-intensive.[12] They can be stacked, layer upon layer, in high-rise office buildings.

While downtowns have clearly lost much of their retailing function, CBDs have been experiencing new business construction for decades. From the mid-1960s to the 1970s alone there was over a 50 percent *increase* in office space in older cities such as New York and Chicago, while Houston doubled its office space.[13] This growth continued into the 1990s. Management, finance, government, and law still remain at the center of the city because they do not require great amounts of space per worker and they need access to one another; a downtown location makes far more sense when services are oriented not to individuals but to other organizations. In the CBD, communications are easy and informal—business may be conducted over lunch, for example—and there are many services and economies available outside the firm itself. Outside specialists are readily accessible to cover areas such as advertising, legal services, accounting, tax information, and mailing. Firms located on the periphery must provide all sorts of services often not required of those in the center, such as parking lots, cafeterias, and medical

[11] Brian J. L. Berry and John D. Kasarda, *Contemporary Urban Ecology*, Macmillan, New York, 1977, p. 234.
[12] William Parker Frisbie and John D. Kasarda, "Spatial Processes," in Neil Smelser (ed.), Handbook of Modern Sociology, Sage, Beverly Hills, Calif., 1988, p. 636.
[13] Gerald Manners, "The Office in the Metropolis: An Opportunity for Shaping Metropolitan America," *Economic Geography,* **50**:93–110, 1974.

services. Top management may also remain in the city so that it does not become isolated from the informal information networks about competitors, government policy, and buying patterns that are always found when a number of firms in the same sort of business are located in the same spatial area. Even in an era of computer-based information systems, face-to-face contact remains important.

Also downtowns have become major convention sites, based on new downtown hotels and convention centers. In twenty years the thirty-eight largest urban areas have added more than 300 downtown hotels, and more than a hundred cities have built convention centers.[14]

Overall, however, the growth of office white-collar employment has not been able to compensate fully for blue-collar and retail trade losses. For example, between 1970 and 1986 the city of Chicago lost 211,000 jobs that did not require a high school diploma. During the same period the city gained 112,000 jobs requiring a college degree.[15] As of the mid-1990s central cities were holding their own, but at a reduced level of employment. In spite of population losses, cities as of 1995 were in their best financial shape in years.[16]

Physically, newer cities are more "suburban" and spread out than older preautomobile cities.[17] Research by Guterbock indicates that the density pattern of cities throughout the country has changed.[18] Although older metropolitan areas have seen sharp decreases in density in their central cores, newer post–World War II cities never had high-density neighborhoods of apartments in their central cities. The result is a national pattern of moderate to low-level density throughout the metropolitan area—in effect, the suburbanization of the central cities.

Metropolitan Economic Dispersion and Edge Cities

The move of manufacturing and industry out of the central city was greatly accelerated by the postwar out-movement of population and by the building of interstate superhighways. The interstate expressway system built in the 1950s, 1960s, and 1970s gave industry genuine alternatives to central-city locations. Goods now could cheaply and rapidly be moved by truck rather than rail. Suburban land was cheap, and suburban taxes were low. Importantly, the plant could be designed from the inside out. A common pattern was to lay out an assembly line all on one level and then simply build walls around the work space. The size and shape of the building could be determined by the needs of the factory rather than by the size and shape of a lot or an existing plant.

The postwar suburban housing boom (discussed in Chapter 9, Changing Suburbanization Patterns) provided a middle- and working-class suburban workforce,

---

[14] Bernard Frieden and Lynne B. Sagalyn, *Downtown Inc: How America Rebuilds Cities,* M.I.T. Press, Cambridge, Mass., 1989.

[15] John D. Kasarda, quoted in "Social Scientists Examine Common Challenges Facing Industrial Cities," *Chronicle of Higher Education,* July 11, 1990, p. A6.

[16] Steven Holmes, "Budget Woes Ease for Cities in U.S., Analysts Report," *New York Times,* Jan. 8, 1995, p. 1.

[17] Rob Kling, Spencer Olin, and Mark Poster (eds.), *Posturban California: The Transformation of Orange County since World War II,* University of California Press, Berkeley, 1991.

[18] Thomas A. Guterbock, "Suburbanization of American Cities of the Twentieth Century: A New Index and Another Look," paper presented at the meeting of the American Sociological Association, Toronto, 1982.

a workforce that now commuted to work by auto. The location of factories in suburbs in turn encouraged workers to move to new suburban tract-type housing developments that were sprouting in the cornfields near the factories. Before long, shopping centers followed; and more and more mixed industrial-residential suburbs were born.

Thus in the decades following World War II industry increasingly leapfrogged over intermediate-city residential areas and moved directly from the inner city to suburban industrial parks. When a firm was serving only local markets, a central-city location, with its ease of access to all parts of a city, made sense. Such a location was reasonable even if the major transport between cities was done by rail. Today, however, firms with national markets usually seek a location on or near an interstate expressway.

Today the industrial park has supplanted the city factory, with twice as many manufacturing jobs now located in suburbs as in central cities. Not only manufacturing but also white-collar jobs have suburbanized. Places of employment of all sorts now are most likely to have a suburban Zip Code. Outer Dallas, for example, has three times the office space as does the central business district, while suburban Atlanta has twice the office space of the center city. Even in the New York metropolitan area, northern New Jersey now has more office space than Manhattan. Nor are suburban offices simply back-office operations seeking low rentals; the executive suite has come to the suburbs. For example, Plano, Texas, north of Dallas, was a bedroom suburb two decades ago. Today it is the national headquarters for five major corporations: Frito-Lay, Electronic Data Systems, Murata Business Systems, Southland Life Insurance, and J. C. Penney. J. C. Penney moved its headquarters to Plano from New York City.[19] The suburban economy is substantially service-oriented, often with its marketplace patterns being nationally or internationally rather than locally oriented.[20]

Sears shows a similar pattern. Somewhat over two decades ago Sears consolidated its operations in the world's tallest building, the new 110-story Sears Tower in downtown Chicago. However, as Sears was placing its head in the clouds, its urban-based stores increasingly lost touch with suburban customers. In 1992 Sears moved all of its 5,000 merchandise-group employees from Sears Tower to suburban Hoffman Estates 35 miles northwest of Chicago. The new Sears headquarters, named Prairie Stone, occupies a former soybean field and boasts 200 acres of reconstructed prairie and wetlands. The tallest building is six stories high.

As suburbs have gone from being primarily residential areas to being the major location of shopping, manufacturing, and office space, the old Burgess hypothesis of economic growth out from the CBD through a series of zones has lost its force. As suburbs have become the new commercial and economic cores, metropolitan areas have gone from core-periphery modes to a multinucleated or multicentered pattern.[21]

---

[19] Palen, *The Suburbs,* 1995, p. 186.

[20] Mark Schneider and Fabio Fernandez, "The Emerging Service Economy; Changing Patterns of Employment," *Urban Affairs Quarterly,* **24:**537–555, 1989.

[21] Peter Muller, *Contemporary Suburban America,* Prentice-Hall, Englewood Cliffs, N.J., 1981, p. 8.

Sears has moved its headquarters from Sears Tower, the world's tallest building, to suburban Prairie Stone. (The Image Works Archives.) (Courtesy of Sears.)

Malling of the Land

If the dominant urban symbol for the beginning of the twentieth century was the skyscraper, the dominant symbol for the beginning of the twenty-first century is the suburban shopping mall. As expressed by one academic, "More than locations for consumption, malls have become the signature structure of the age."[22] You may love the malls or believe they represent all that is wrong with the country, but it is impossible to discuss contemporary metropolitan life without discussing the role of the shopping mall. As downtown retail outlets have closed, the malls have become social as well as retail centers. They have become America's town centers and main streets. As of 1992 the National Research Bureau counted some 38,966 shopping malls of which 1,835 had more than 400,000 square feet of retail space. Shopping centers from convenience centers to massive malls accounted for 54 percent of the nation's nonautomotive retail sales as of 1987.

Shopping centers are actually a rather new development. The first shopping center, as we understand the term, was Country Club Plaza developed in 1923 in Kansas City. At the end of World War II there were only eight shopping centers in all of North America.[23] The first modern mall surrounded by parking places was Northgate, which opened on the edge of Seattle in 1950. The first enclosed mall, Southgate Center, designed by the architect Victor Gruen, did not open until 1956 outside Minneapolis. The age of the malls really began with the 1960s. Things we take for granted, such as the ubiquitous food court, was first introduced by the Rouse Company in the early 1970s.

Today the nation's 40,000 shopping malls are an integral part of the suburban landscape, and range in size from small strip malls to the West Edmonton mega-mall, which is the size of 115 football fields and has 800 shops, 19 movie theaters, 110 places to eat, a 355-room hotel, the world's largest indoor amusement park, a 5-acre lake with the world's largest wave machine, and parking for over 200,000 cars. Malls sometimes almost become cities unto themselves. San Jose has an en-closed air-conditioned center that includes 130 stores, 27 restaurants, and 9,000 parking spaces. Houston's "Galleria," modeled after a nineteenth-century gallery in Milan, Italy, set the pattern for the multi-use malls to follow; it has three levels which in addition to the usual department stores, restaurants, and shops also in-cludes an athletic club with ten air-conditioned tennis courts and a jogging track. (Many college athletic departments would gladly exchange their facilities for those of this shopping mall.) It is connected to two high-rise office buildings and a 404-room hotel. Malls, with their fountains, film festivals, and wine-tasting contests, have come a long way from the mercantile stores of the last century. The shopping mall is replacing Main Street as the core of the community. Increasingly, the malls serve social as well as commercial functions. (Reflecting this, a shopping mall in the author's city changed its name from Chesterfield Mall to Chesterfield Town Center.) Malls with their "mall rats" and "mall bunnies" provide a place for young

[22] William S. Kowinski, *The Malling of America,* Murrow, New York, 1985, p. 22.

[23] Kenneth T. Jackson, *Crabgrass Frontier,* Oxford, New York, 1985, p. 259. For a discussion of surburban changes within urbanized New Jersey, see Judith J. Friedman, "Suburban Variations within Highly Urbanized Regions: The Case of New Jersey," Research in Community Sociology, **4:**97–132, 1994.

adolescents to socialize. At the other end of the age spectrum, the mall also provides a safe and weather-free place for seniors to gather, walk, and socialize.[24] As downtowns have faded as the center of retail trade, and during evenings even as a place of safety, the mall has become the contemporary version of the ancient Greek agoras.

Malls and "Street Safety"

Successful malls exude an image of a comfortable, safe, and secure place. In good part this is done by excluding from the mall any persons or activities that might seem disruptive or disturbing. The strength of traditional downtowns was their ability to produce surprise and excitement, of not knowing what was around the next corner. Malls, by contrast, emphasize total predictability. No street musicians, no Hari Krishnas, and no activities that might in any way disturb or offend any customers. Malls for all their open courtyards and talk of "town centers" are private rather than public places. Thus they can ban from the property teenagers who are disruptive, panhandlers, and poorly dressed bag ladies. No one has a right to walk through a mall just because he or she feels like walking.

Enforcing the image of the mall as a secure place into which outside problems don't intrude are the mall police. They walk inside beats, and they patrol parking lots in highly visible vehicles with revolving flashing lights. However, while the mall police may wear the uniforms, badges, and even weapons of police, they usually are private security officers dressed up to look like police officers. Their role is basically public relations. In most states, security guards lack police powers to arrest. Similarly, the stop signs on mall roads, while looking official, are only advisory since they are not located on municipal or state roads. To maintain the image of safety, malls that have problems with robbery, car theft, or even rape work hard to ensure that most offenses are not reported in local advertiser-supported media. To acknowledge that malls have crimes other than shoplifting would damage the illusion that both mall operators and their patrons seek to maintain.

Private Edge Cities

Suburban outer or edge cities are difficult to define since they don't look the way we think cities should look, nor are they organized like cities are organized.[25] For starters they often lack any clearly definable borders. Unlike legally defined cities, or suburbs, there are no signposts to tell you when you are entering or leaving. They lack municipal boundaries because they are not actually legal entities. Legally they often are nonplace places—having names but not legal status. Tysons Corner in Virginia outside of Washington, D.C., is one of the nation's largest edge cities, having more office space than Tucson and more major retailing than Washington, but

[24] Dawn Graham, "Going to the Mall: A Leisure Activity for Urban Elderly People," *Canadian Journal of Aging,* **10:**345–358, 1991.

[25] For a discussion of the emergence of outer cities, see Joel Garreau, *Edge City: Life on the New Frontier,* Doubleday, New York, 1991.

it doesn't appear on Virginia state maps. Legally Tysons Corner is just another part of Fairfax County.

Not being legal municipalities, outer cities have another strange characteristic for a city: They have no elected government. Within edge cities there is no real civic order. Being private places, they are not governed by municipal legislation, codes, or ordinances. They are private property governed not by elected representatives, but by executives appointed by corporate boards. Tysons Corner, Dallas's Las Colinas, Los Angeles's Marina Del-Ray, and Boston's Burlington Mall are in effect *private cities* unto themselves.

What makes these places a sharp break with the past is not that they are planned, newer, shinier, or air-conditioned, or have more glass and marble. What makes them different is that they are *private* domains rather than incorporated legally defined areas. The old downtowns, whether planned or unplanned, are public spaces open to all. The rules that govern public dress and behavior are ordinances passed by elected officials. Outer cities, for all their open courtyards and fountains, and their calling themselves town centers, are fundamentally different. Basic questions about who can be in an outer-city office park or shopping mall, and what they can or cannot do while there, are determined not by civic ordinance but by private corporate policy. The new outer cities are administered by decree. They may be safe, but they are not democratic. They are privately managed city-states controlled by an oligarchy.

Remarkably, this shift of the new edge cities from public to private control has taken place almost completely without public notice, discussion, or debate. The

The West Edmonton Mall is the largest in the world. In the foreground can be seen part of its indoor lagoon with the four submarines in which visitors can ride. (Chris Schwarz/Canapress.)

The Ultimate Malls

The goliath of shopping malls is the West Edmonton Mall in Edmonton, Alberta.* Edmonton is a city of 790,000 persons, but the mall alone during the after-Christmas sales draws as many as a quarter of a million people a day to the cold and inhospitable Canadian prairie. The mall attracts 20 million people a year in a country that has 26 million people. What they come to see is a shopper's fantasyland. As noted in the text, there are some 800 stores, 110 restaurants, 19 movie theaters, and even a Caesar's Palace Bingo Parlor. Beyond this, there is the world's largest indoor amusement park, with 24 rides including two 13-story-plus roller coasters. There is, additionally, an 18-hole miniature par-46 golf course, an NHL-size ice rink, and a dolphin lagoon. And set in a balmy 86-degree atmosphere, the world's largest indoor wave pool boasts a sand beach, palm trees, and 22 water slides. At a lower level, the mall also houses an aquarium.

The most spectacular feature, however, is the mall's 200-foot artificial lake. At one end of the lake, a replica of Christopher Columbus's ship, the *Santa Maria*, rests on a coral reef, illuminated by a giant skylight. At the other end of the lake, children and parents line up to cruise the 20-foot-deep lake in one of four 25-person submarines. The mall actually has more submarines than the Canadian navy. In essence, the West Edmonton Mall moves the activity of shopping to the level of a total experience and way of life.

In 1992 the Ghermezian brothers opened a United States version of the above in Bloomington, Minnesota, outside of Minneapolis. Only slightly smaller than the Canadian version, the Mall of America covers 4.2 million square feet and has 350 stores, 14 movie screens, and 46 places to eat. Its Knott's Berry Farm Camp Snoopy has 7 acres of indoor amusement rides including a half-mile-long rubber-wheeled roller coaster, a log flume ride, and a Hormell cookout area named Spamland. The Mall of America has 400 live trees, 300,000 plants, and a 4-story waterfall. It also has its own zip code, police, doctors, dentists, and a public school for the children of the mall's 10,000 employees.

Where all this will end is a matter of professional dispute. Some see this as a new model, while others believe that the mega-mall, like the brontosaurus, is the final gasp of a concept that has been pushed to excess. So far the idea that "build it and they will come" seems to be working.

* Based on material in J. John Palen, *The Suburbs*, McGraw-Hill, New York, 1995, pp. 199–201.

once public city has been privatized. Residential areas within edge cities are sometimes even walled off and "gated," with private security guards restricting entrance. The new edge cities are private rather than public places.

NONMETROPOLITAN GROWTH

Historically, metropolitan areas in the United States have grown faster than nonmetropolitan areas. The classical ecological model assumed centripetal movement of population from rural hinterland to metropolitan area. This was the case for the first seventy years of this century, when the metropolitan sector—core or fringe—was growing while rural areas consistently lost population. However, during the 1970s, for the first time, rural counties not only stopped declining but increased in population. The fastest-growing counties from 1970 to 1980 were rural in character. As a result, some academics said the pattern of increasing population concentration in metropolitan areas had come to a close.[26] The pattern of metropolitan dominance was said to be challenged by an emerging pattern of increased dispersion and deconcentration. However, by the 1980s talk of a "rural renaissance" had been followed by a decade of farm depression, with metropolitan areas again growing considerably faster than nonmetropolitan areas.[27] The 1990s have seen some rural rebound. By the mid-1990s, two-thirds (64 percent) of rural counties were growing again. The greatest rural rebound is occurring in areas offering retirement and recreation opportunities.[28]

Diffuse Growth

What is causing rural growth? Is the growth of the nonmetropolitan population a sign of a return to older and simpler rural ways? Are we about to experience a rural renaissance?

No. We are experiencing a transformation in special settlement patterns, but this does not represent a rebirth of rural ways of life. Rather what we are witnessing is the out-movement of population into a new form of community that is more diffuse.[29] These are "metropolitan" nonmetropolitan areas that can't be sharply defined as suburbs, small towns, or rural countryside. Catchy phrases like "rural renaissance" tend to trap us in our own rhetoric. As previously noted, both the proportion and the absolute number of persons engaged in agriculture continue to decrease. Farm population dropped about a quarter during the last decade, and under 2 percent of the U.S. population lives on farms. Clearly, any rural renaissance does not mean a renaissance of the family farm or a return to agricultural pursuits.

Few people are moving to truly rural areas. Rural growth is now often related to recreational opportunities for metropolitan residents. Employment-oriented nonmetropolitan growth can be best seen as not something totally separate from urban

---

[26] Beale and Fuguitt, "The New Pattern of Non-metropolitan Population Change."
[27] Larry Long and Diana DeAre, "US Population Redistribution: A Perspective on the Nonmetropolitan Turnaround," *Population and Development Review,* **14**:433–450, 1988.
[28] Sharon O'Malley, "The Rural Rebound," *American Demographics,* May, 1994, pp. 24–29.
[29] John Herbers, *The New Heartland; America's Flight beyond the Suburbs and How It Is Changing Our Future,* Times Books, New York, 1986.

areas, but rather as an extension of the metropolitan area's influence beyond the commuting range. Over fifty years ago, Louis Wirth noted that urbanism—that is, urban behavior patterns—had become the American way of life. Now, urbanization, or living in urban-defined places, has also become ubiquitous. As we continue to expand into a national metropolitan society, distinctions between metropolitan and nonmetropolitan will become even more blurred. With the number of MSAs and CMSAs over 300 and the boundaries of existing metropolitan areas progressively expanding, it becomes increasingly difficult to distinguish between metropolitan and developing nonmetropolitan areas.

National Society?

We are rapidly moving toward a national urban system where old differences no longer make any difference. The pattern of discrete metropolitan concentrations is being challenged by an emerging pattern of increased dispersion and deconcentration. Metropolitan areas are no longer even semi-independent. Communication and transportation advances such as fax machines, the Internet, and commuter air shuttles have further reduced the friction of space. While at the turn of the century the commuter railroad and streetcar made it possible for a vanguard of businesspeople to move their residences from the city, commuter air travel now puts a premium on accessibility to an airport. In an era of air travel, the significant factor is no longer distance. Distance is increasingly being measured not in miles or kilometers, but by time. Even with terrestrial travel, the question "How far is it?" commonly anticipates a temporal rather than spatial response: how long it takes to get there. Increased mobility of goods, persons, and ideas suggests that a new urban phase—a national urban unit—is in a formative stage.

Local weather reports now commonly also give the weather in "commuter cities." Cable TV provides a national weather channel. Numerous air shuttles tie cities together: A commuter between New York and Chicago or Los Angeles and San Francisco is able to catch a flight in either direction almost every half hour from dawn to dusk. Shuttle flights linking San Diego, Los Angeles, and San Francisco make it easier (and faster) to move between these cities than around Los Angeles. It is one of the peculiarities of modern life that the air shuttles from city to city offer better, more frequent, and even faster transportation than that often available within some metropolitan area. More and more, we don't even physically commute but rather telecommute. Physical distance is losing importance.

The emerging pattern of a national urban society forces us to rethink traditional assumptions. In the 1950s, Otis Dudley Duncan suggested that the concept of a "rural-urban continuum," while perhaps having heuristic value, has little empirical validity.[30] Emerging nonmetropolitan growth patterns strongly suggest that the concept of a rural-urban continuum has now lost even heuristic utility. The demographic and economic growth of counties several counties removed from MSAs

---

[30] Otis Dudley Duncan, "Community Size and the Rural-Urban Continuum," in Paul K. Hatt and Albert J. Reiss (eds.), *Cities and Society,* Free Press, New York, 1957, pp. 35–45.

increasingly suggests that any rural-urban division has lost the shards of meaning it may still have possessed even a score of years ago. New patterns also contradict the theory that the social and economic conditions of urbanization are a consequence of the distance from the point of population concentration. This change has yet to be fully reflected in policy or research.[31] As rural-urban divisions have lost meaning, so contemporary distinctions between metropolitan and nonmetropolitan are becoming more blurred with each passing decade. In the contemporary information society, it is increasingly difficult to distinguish metropolitan and nonmetropolitan residents on the basis of occupations, consumer habits, and degree of sophistication.[32] In many respects the rural-urban differences are differences that have ceased to make a difference. Whether we live in a metropolitan area or not, we are all part of a metropolitan society.

THE RISE OF THE SUN BELT

Population Shifts

One of the most dramatic urban changes since 1975—at least in terms of attention paid by the media—has been the historic shift of population and power from the old industrial heartland of the northeast and north central regions to the metropolises of first the west and then the south (see Figure 6-2). The rise of Houston from a steamy Texas town of little interest to the oil capital of the world "typifies the pattern."[33] Houston is now the nation's fourth-largest city, exceeded in size only by New York, Los Angeles, and Chicago.

During the 1980s the older economic areas of the midwest (both metropolitan and nonmetropolitan) continued to lose population. The midwest and northeast lost about 2.5 million persons through emigration between 1980 and 1990, while the south and west gained more than 7 million immigrants. This pattern of sun belt growth has continued into the 1990s (see Table 6-2). Half the national population growth during the past decade occurred in the three sun belt states of California, Florida, and Texas. While the northeast grew less than 3 percent during the 1980s and the midwest only 1.5 percent, the south gained 16 percent and the west 21 percent.[34]

Among large metropolitan areas of a million or more, Phoenix was the fastest growing during the period up to the 1990 census, increasing 30 percent. Dallas–Fort Worth was second at 27 percent. Greater Los Angeles, in terms of economic activity and cultural influence, is now second only to New York. It is argued that Los

[31] The Department of Agriculture, for example, divides nonmetropolitan counties into six types, which "describe a dimension of urban influence in which each succeeding group is affected to a lesser degree by the social and economic conditions of urban areas. This includes the influence of urban areas at a distance as well as within counties themselves," U.S. Department of Agriculture, PA-1, U.S. Government Printing Office, Washington, D.C., 1974.

[32] Frisbie and Kasarda, "Spatial Processes," p. 636.

[33] Joe R. Feagin, *Free Enterprise City: Houston in Political-Economic Perspective,* Rutgers University Press, New Brunswick, N.J., 1989.

[34] Signe Wetrogen, "Projections of the Population of States by Age, Sex and Race, 1988 to 2010," *Current Population Reports,* p. 25, October, 1988.

TABLE 6-2
Ten Fastest-Growing Metropolitan Areas: 1960 to 1970,
1970 to 1980, and 1980 to 1990

Rank	SMSA, 1960 to 1970*	Percent increase
1	Las Vegas, Nev.	115
2	Anaheim–Santa Ana–Garden Grove, Calif.	102
3	Oxnard–Ventura, Calif.	89
4	Fort Lauderdale–Hollywood, Fla.	86
5	San Jose, Calif.	66
6	Colorado Springs, Colo.	64
7	Santa Barbara, Calif.	56
8	West Palm Beach, Fla.	53
9	Huntsville, Ala.	48
10	Nashua, N.H.	48

Rank	MSA and CMSA, 1970 to 1980†	Percent increase
1	Fort Myers, Fla.	95
2	Fort Pierce, Fla.	91
3	Ocala, Fla.	77
4	Las Vegas, Nev.	70
5	Sarasota, Fla.	68
6	Fort Collins–Loveland, Colo.	66
7	West Palm Beach–Boca Raton–Delray Beach, Fla.	65
8	Olympia, Wash.	62
9	Bryan–College Station, Tex.	61
10	Reno, Nev.	60

Rank	MSA and CMSA, 1980 to 1990	Percent increase
1	Naples, Fla.	49
2	Ocala, Fla.	48
3	Fort Myers–Cape Coral, Fla.	44
4	Fort Pierce, Fla.	43
5	Austin, Tex.	38
6	Melbourne–Titusville–Palm Bay, Fla.	37
7	West Palm Beach–Boca Raton–Delray Beach, Fla.	37
8	Las Cruces, N.M.	34
9	McAllen–Edinburg–Mission, Tex.	34
10	Orlando, Fla.	34

* Definitions as of later census.
† 1983 definitions.
Source: U.S. Bureau of the Census.

Angeles might be the leading western hemisphere city in the early twenty-first century.[35] The sun belt, long a virtual dependent colony of the industrial northeast, has undergone an economic transformation.[36] The regional landscape has been transformed by the opening of a new urban frontier. Older northern frost belt cities have seen population and industry depart for the "boom" areas of the south and southwest. Businesses are supposedly attracted to such areas by a good business climate consisting of lower wages, lower taxes, a lower rate of unionization, and higher-productive efficiency.

The result of interregional population shifts has been dramatic. The south, which historically always had migratory outflows of population, now is the fastest-growing region in the nation. Since the mid-1960s the south has also replaced the west as the major locus of new employment growth. During this same period, economically powerful industrial cities of the north have experienced decline in both population and economic influence. For example, after several decades of central-city population losses, the central city of St. Louis now has only as many people as it did in 1890; Cleveland now has as many as during World War I; and Detroit now has no more than in 1920.[37] In large frost belt metropolitan areas such as Pittsburgh, Philadelphia, Chicago, Boston, and New York, inner suburbs have also been losing population albeit at a rate somewhat slower than their central cities. The sun belt as an energy-producing area also enjoys a cost advantage, particularly when oil costs are high. Also, the milder climate requires less energy for heat (this is only partially offset by higher air-conditioning costs). The racial climate has also improved markedly.

Population is flowing southward and west, attracted by new jobs, the mild climate, a lower cost of living, and a life-style stressing outdoor living, year-round golf and tennis, and informal entertaining. Newer cities, because of the office-at-home phenomenon, also require far less office space. Greater New York has some 27 feet of office space per person. In Greater Los Angeles by comparison, the figure is a mere 15 square feet per person. The consultant subculture often works at home.

Economic Shifts

The impression is sometimes given that most sun belt growth is a consequence of runaway smokestack industries that are abandoning the industrial heartland to build low-wage nonunion plants in the south. This view is largely inaccurate.[38] Steel mills and other heavy industry are not moving south when they close down in older industrial areas. Rather than attracting smokestack industries, the sun belt states are

---

[35] Charles Lockwood and Christopher Lemberger, "Los Angeles Comes of Age," *The Atlantic,* January, 1988, pp. 31–56.
[36] For details on the change and its meaning, see David C. Perry and Alfred J. Watkins (eds.), *The Rise of the Sunbelt Cities,* Sage, Beverly Hills, Calif., 1977; and Larry Sawers and William K. Tabb (eds.), *Sunbelt/Snowbelt: Urban Development and Regional Restructuring,* Oxford University Press, New York, 1984.
[37] Larry Long, "Population Redistribution in the U.S.," *Population Reference Bureau,* Washington, D.C., 1983, p. 10.
[38] Perry and Watkins, *The Rise of the Sunbelt Cities.*

developing new economic activities. As summed up by Kirkpatrick Sale, the writer who first focused national attention on the changing nature of the southern rim:

> In broad terms there has been a shift from the traditional heavy manufacturing long associated with the industrial belt of the Northeast to the new technological industries that have grown up in the Southern Rim—aerospace, defense, electronics.[39]

While the north and midwest still have more corporate headquarters, there has been movement toward the south and the west.[40] The fastest-growing sun belt industries are service industries such as real estate and tourism plus the newer, highly skilled industries such as electronics, energy, and aircraft. These often have a preference for a location in the southwest, particularly suburbs of major cities. Federal-level political decisions, such as locating the space agency in Houston and the national center for silicon research in Austin, have strongly reinforced growth trends. Even after base cutbacks, military budgets disproportionately directed monies and employment to areas with substantial military basing, i.e., the south.

Some even suggest that the advantage of the sun belt is largely political in origin. Mollenkopf argues that the advantage comes not from lower wages or nonunionized work forces but from the comparative political advantages of sun belt cities' being able to push business-oriented growth policies: These cities' governments have less need to placate the poor or nonwhite groups, who wield less influence than they do in northern cities.[41] As the Congressional elections of 1994 demonstrated, sun belt populations are also much less likely to support liberal political candidates.

Although the population shift to the south and southwest was long in coming, the consequences and implications for urban areas of the old industrial heartland were not immediately recognized. The northeast had been long accustomed to viewing the south as an economic backwater and a cultural desert. Now those in the sun belt view the old industrial cities as unsafe places fighting inevitable decline. For almost two decades, California, Florida, and Texas have led the nation in building construction. Not only people but the tax base as well has been flowing southward. As a consequence of regional shifts, northern urban areas that have been the nation's centers of population and power for a century or more are finding themselves on the defensive. In national politics the sun belt is clearly gaining influence and power.

Sun Belt Problems

However, the sun belt is not all sunshine. The rise of the sun belt has also produced problems for the expanding population. The depletion of groundwater reserves in the southwest is already producing serious problems. Breakneck growth has brought massive urban sprawl, overtaxed water and sewer systems, rising air pol-

[39] Kirkpatrick Sale, *Power Shift: The Rise of the Southern Rim and Its Challenge to the Eastern Establishment,* Random House, New York, 1975, p. 5.

[40] Sally K. Ward, "Trends in the Location of Corporate Headquarters, 1969–1989," *Urban Affairs Quarterly,* **29:**468–478, 1994.

[41] John H. Mollenkopf, *The Contested City,* Princeton University Press, Princeton, N.J., 1983.

lution, environmental degradation, and traffic congestion. Pollution of air and water, auto congestion, adequate water supplies, and sewage disposal problems are growing ever-more severe in cities such as Houston.[42]

Sun belt cities such as Miami, Houston, Dallas, San Antonio, Albuquerque, Phoenix, and San Diego have all had to cope with phenomenal growth, and the responses have not all been similar.[43] Sun belt cities are being pressured to expand educational opportunities, housing stock, and social services. At the same time, citizen groups are lobbying for limits on taxes. City officials are caught by contradictory expectations of northern-level services and southern-level taxes. How a state spends its resources helps determine the future of its cities. In the mid-1990s, for example, Texas decided to devote resources to building new prisons rather than new schools. However, it is doubtful whether having the world's highest prison population is going to help attract new businesses to the state.

It should also be remembered that sun belt cities are not necessarily immune to the population declines that affected frost belt cities. While during the last decade population was lost by 86 percent of the U.S. central cities in the northeast and 66 percent of those in the industrial north central region, this was also true of 26 percent of the south's cities and 12 percent of the west's. A sun belt location does not prevent people from moving out. After outpacing the rest of the nation's rate of economic growth for three decades, some long-term problems are emerging. Low wages once gave the sun belt a competitive advantage. However, not only have sun belt wages gone up, but in a global economy firms that once moved to Alabama or the Carolinas can now move to Central America or southeast Asia. There is no guarantee that the collapse of property values that hit Houston in the late 1980s and southern California in the early 1990s will not repeat itself.

Finally, in the application of a high-technology economy, some of the south still has a major liability: an academic system that needs upgrading at the primary and secondary school levels. In competing for the expanding high-technology and service-sector jobs, a mismatch is developing between the available jobs and the skill level required for these jobs. As a region, the south has not been as willing to invest the necessary tax money in developing its human capital. Unless it does so, the south may again see itself outshone by the north and particularly by the west, with its much better educational systems at the primary and secondary levels.

With the initial southern advantages of lower wage scales, a nonunion industrial climate, and cheaper energy losing force, there is nothing necessarily permanent about the sun belt boom. Increasingly, economic success will depend on the training and quality of the labor force.

---

[42] Joe R. Feagin, "Tallying the Social Costs of Urban Growth under Capitalism: The Case of Houston," in Scott Cummings (ed.), *Business Elites and Urban Development,* SUNY Press, Albany, N.Y., 1989, pp. 205–234.

[43] For a comparison of what has occurred in various cities, see Richard M. Bernard and Bradley R. Rice (eds.), *Sunbelt Cities: Politics and Growth since World War II,* University of Texas Press, Austin, 1983.

PART THREE

URBAN AND
SUBURBAN LIFE

CHAPTER

7

CITY LIFE-STYLES

What is the city but the people?

Shakespeare, *Coriolanus*

INTRODUCTION

Now we turn from the spatial and macro-level construction of the city to a consideration of the city as a unique social-organizational form and social-psychological milieu. Here we ask questions such as: What are the characteristics of urban dwellers? Do urbanites differ from ruralites or small-town residents? Do cities produce a unique way of life or psychological outlook?

Certainly life in the city is different. Cities differ from towns and rural areas not only in their size and patterns of economic activities, but also in their tone, texture, and pace. Heterogeneity, variety, and change are assumed, as is a potpourri of different occupations, social classes, cultural backgrounds, and interests. As expressed in the major reference work of over half a century ago:

> The city has more wealth than the country, more skill, more erudition within its bounds, more initiative, more philanthropy, more science, more divorces, more aliens, more births and deaths, more accidents, more rich, more poor, more wise men and more fools.[1]

As noted in Chapter 3, The Rise of Urban America, Americans have a history of ambivalence in how cities and city life are viewed. On one hand the city is praised as the height of civilization—the new Athens—and the center of progress, energy, and enterprise. But more frequently the city is characterized as the source of crime, corruption, and social disorganization—the repository of all the problems of the society. Kenneth Boulding dramatically contrasts these views in western society:

> The city is not only Zion, the city of God; it is Babylon, the scarlet woman. On the one hand, we have the opposition of urbane splendor and culture with rural cloddishness and savagery; on the other hand, we have the opposition of urban vice, corruption and cruelty, as against rural virtue and purity. The Bible, to take but one instance, furnishes us with innumerable examples of this deep ambivalence towards the city. It is at once the house of God and the house of inequity. Amos, the herdsman, denounces it; Jeremiah weeps over it; Christ is crucified for it. One of the great threads through the Bible is the destruction and rebuilding of the city—a pattern which is wholly characteristic of the age of civilization.[2]

The contrast between urban and rural ways of life was a basic part of urban studies and writings before World War II. The terms used to define the dichotomy sometimes differed, but the underlying content remained remarkably similar; the country represented simplicity; the city complexity. Rural areas were typified by stable rules, roles, and relationships, while the city was characterized by innovation, change, and disorganization. The city was the center of variety, heterogeneity, and social novelty, while the countryside or small town represented tradition, social continuity, and cultural conformity. The stereotype also included a view of city people as possessing greater sophistication but less real warmth and feeling.

Implicit and sometimes explicit in this viewpoint was that modern mass society was destroying close attachments to kin and community. In their place were

[1] William B. Munro, "City," in *Encyclopedia of the Social Sciences,* Macmillan, New York, 1930, p. 474.
[2] Kenneth E. Boulding, "The Death of the City: A Frightened Look at Postcivilization," in Gino Germani (ed.), *Modernization, Urbanization, and the Urban Crisis,* Little, Brown, Boston, 1973, p. 265.

Isolation in the modern city is a recurrent (and probably overworked) theme in contemporary literature. (M. Dwyer/Stock, Boston.)

being substituted uprooted, isolated, and alienated individuals who were free of traditional bonds but alone in the big city. An excellent portrayal of this view is Charlie Chaplin's classic film *Modern Times,* in which the helpless worker is literally chewed up and spit out by the faceless factory.

Here we won't debate the inherent biases that occur when emotionally loaded terms such as "warmth," "friendliness," and "community" are associated with small places, while terms such as "anonymity," "alienation," and "isolation" appear to be reserved for large cities. What is important for our purposes is to understand the influence such beliefs have had on traditional and contemporary views of urban life.

CHARACTERISTICS OF URBAN POPULATIONS

Age

Everywhere urban populations are younger than their rural counterparts. This is particularly true of cities in less-developed countries (LDCs), but it is also true of North America. (This subject is discussed further in Chapter 16, Asian Urban Patterns; Chapter 17, African and Middle Eastern Urbanization; and Chapter 18 , Urbanization in Latin America.) City populations are younger not because they have higher birthrates and thus more children; that is not the case. Rather, cities attract immigrants, and such immigrants tend to be young adults. This in turn means that, overall, cities have a smaller proportion of children and elderly. (An exception is poor inner-city neighborhoods which have a high proportion of children, but few elderly.) A consequence is that cities have more young adults and as a consequence more of the activities in which young adults engage. This means more bars (single and otherwise), more places of entertainment (even movies are an activity primarily of the young), more crime (young people commit most crime), and more social change (younger populations are less bound by tradition). The terms "yuppie" (young urban professional) and "dink" (dual income no kids) both refer to twenty-something to forty-something urban populations. Both terms now have derogatory connotations, but they reflect one facet of urban life.

Gender

The pattern of urban-rural sex ratios differs for developed countries and LDCs. Less-developed countries have a higher proportion of urban males because young men come to the city and leave the women behind to care for the farms. In African cities, for instance, there are often three males for every two females. This pattern of women staying at home to care for the farm while men migrate to the cities is particularly prevalent where women marry early. Unmarried men tend to be less socially integrated than are husbands, and to have weaker social commitments to the community. Young males also engage in higher rates of socially disruptive behavior such as drunkenness, gambling, prostitution, and crime. (This was the history of the American west before the arrival of settlers with families. Frontier towns were rowdier before churches and the school marm arrived.)

In developed countries, on the other hand, there is a somewhat greater likelihood that single women will leave rural areas for city jobs. Upon graduating from high school, young women from farm-based areas have little option but to go elsewhere for jobs, training, or further schooling. Often the only option at home is to get married. The result is greater numbers of women leave for urban places. The sex ratio may be particularly unbalanced in heavily administration-oriented cities, such as state capitals.

Race, Ethnicity, and Religion

Cities are more racially, ethnically, and religiously heterogeneous than the countryside. Small towns may be largely all one race or ethnic group, but cities are far more mixed. Even groups that are proportionately only a small part of the urban population can band with enough similar groups to constitute a minority group. This ethnic, racial, and religious mosaic led Louis Wirth to describe heterogeneity (along with size and density) as one of the basic characteristics of the city.[3]

---

[3] Louis Wirth, "Urbanism as a Way of Life," *American Journal of Sociology,* **44**(10):8, July, 1938.

Ethnic and racial heterogeneity also raises the potential of intergroup cleavages, competition, and conflict. Greater religious and ethnic heterogeneity can lead to greater tolerance, but it does not have to do so. Tolerance is greater when race, ethnicity, and religion lose force as the primary way of identifying persons. In areas of centuries-old ethnic strife such as Bosnia, religion defines one's group membership.

As well, cleavage is most likely to occur when racial, ethnic, and religious boundaries also represent socioeconomic-status boundaries. An example would be when most of the poor are also of one ethnic or racial background.

Claude Fischer argues that urban places actually foster heterogeneity beyond race, ethnicity, and religion since only with urban concentrations can smaller groups achieve a "critical" mass and thus become active subcultures in their own right.[4] Thus only in the city can you find subcultures devoted to classic viola music, model railroads, or S&M. Urban places thus not only tolerate diversity, they create it.

Socioeconomic Status

As the discussion at the opening of this chapter indicates, the city is a place of extremes, a site of both extreme wealth and poverty. Occupation and education show a similar spread. United States cities have been losing middle-class residents for decades, and thus increasingly house the affluent and the poor. Once-solid-working-class neighborhoods have declined, reflecting the 20 percent decline in the income of blue-collar males from the 1970s to the 1990s. Within metropolitan areas suburbs have become richer while central cities as a whole have fallen farther behind. However, overall city averages tend to hide sharp individual and neighborhood variations in socioeconomic status. What is clear is that, in urban areas, socioeconomic-status criteria such as income, education, and occupation tend to supplant family, ethnicity, religion, and the other more traditional ways of ordering people used in rural areas and small towns. This matter is explored further later in this chapter and in Chapter 10, Ethnic Diversity: Ethnics, African Americans, Hispanics, Asians, and Native Americans.

SOCIAL PSYCHOLOGY OF URBAN LIFE

Earlier Formulations

As noted in Chapter 1, The Urban World, the specter of the city as the source of isolation and alienation for the individual, and social problems and collapse for the society, is far from new. It is not a consequence of the riots or rebellions of the 1960s, the city financial crises of the 1970s, or the divisions of the 1990s. Classical social theorists such as Ferdinand Tönnies, Karl Marx, Emile Durkheim, Max Weber, and Georg Simmel all discussed the decline of local attachments and the rise of mass urban society. The changes were frequently presented in terms of log-

---

[4] Claude Fischer, *The Urban Experience*, Harcourt Brace Jovanovich, San Diego, 1984, pp. 36–37.

ical constructs or models, which sociologists refer to as "ideal types." Among the most noteworthy of these dichotomies, in terms of its impact upon later urban research, was Tönnies's elaborate description of the shift from gemeinschaft—a community where ties were based upon kinship (that is, personal ties and relationships)—to *gesellschaft*—a society based on common economic, political, and other interests. Gemeinschaft communities tend to be smaller places where people know one another, and where people react to one another as members of the group, rather than as someone playing a specific role such as merchant or banker. Gesellschaft societies on the other hand are far more goal-oriented and impersonal, with money and contractual relationships dominating. Thus in contractually based societies we expect to have a leaking roof repaired by the roofer offering the best price, not by cousins who automatically do it for free because they are relations.

The German social theorist Max Weber made similar distinctions between "traditional society" and "rational society"—that is, the substitution in modern society of formal rules and procedures for earlier, more spontaneous patterns. The prime ideal type of rational behavior was institutionalized bureaucracy since bureaucracies have formal job descriptions and rules for appointment and promotion. Bureaucracy, in its best sense, thus promotes predictability and uniformity of action.

The French theorist Emile Durkheim distinguished between societies based on "mechanical solidarity" and those based on "organic solidarity." For Durkheim, the old mechanical social order was one in which all had similar interests and carried out similar tasks. In rural areas all the peasants led similar lives. They got up at the same time, planted the same way, and followed the same seasonal patterns. Organic solidarity of urban places was by contrast based not on everyone doing the same things but on a division of labor. The analogy was to the body where different organs perform different functions and thus by specializing create a more efficient organic system.

Karl Marx also discussed the dichotomy between the urban and the rural. For Marx, the emergence of urban-based capitalism meant destruction of the older agrarian-based social order. Market-based relations replaced feudal relationships, and industrial capitalism encouraged the exploitation and alienation of urban workers. Eventually this would result in the workers' developing a class consciousness and uniting to overthrow their capitalist oppressors. The workers' new unity was based, though, on common interest rather than being a commonality based on residing in similar areas.

While there were significant differences among the frameworks, all the comparisons had an implicit time frame in which rural areas represented the past—sometimes in a glorified form (the "good old days")—and the city represented the future, with its technology and division of labor.

The Chicago School

American urban scholars were influenced at least implicitly by the previously mentioned European theorists, as well as by the changes they saw occurring in the cities where they lived. Members of the so-called Chicago school of sociology assembled during the 1920s at the University of Chicago and were concerned with change induced by urbanization. They focused particularly on the way urban life disrupted traditional ties to kin and community. Some of their writings on such diverse phenomena as juvenile delinquency, organized vice, ethnic community ghettos, and the nature of the city's ecological growth have become sociological classics. Writings such as *The Ghetto* (Wirth), *The Gold Coast and the Slum* (Zorbaugh), and *The Polish Peasant in Europe and America* (Thomas and Znaniecki) are descriptive gems giving insights into this unique period in the urbanization of the United States.[5]

Writers of the Chicago school such as Wirth were especially influenced by Georg Simmel's earlier vision of the social-psychological consequences of city life—a life-style where as a result of city size, calculated sophistication would replace close and meaningful relationships.[6] Simmel suggested that the pace of city life and the overwhelming number of stimuli in the city result in a state of mental overstimulation and excitement.

Simmel said that there is a constant nervous stimulation produced by shifting internal and external situations and that city dwellers have difficulty in maintaining an integrated personality in a social situation where the reference points are constantly changing: As a result they seek to protect themselves by anonymity and sophistication. Calculating expediency takes the place of affective feelings and personal relationships. One is forced to become blasé in the urban environment in order to protect one's psyche from overstimulation.

> If so many inner reactions were responses to the continuous external contacts with innumerable people as are those in the small town, where one knows almost everybody one meets and where one has a positive relation to almost everyone, one would be completely atomized internally and come to an unimaginable psychic state.[7]

Reformulations of Simmel's belief that the city produces "nervous stimulation" among its inhabitants, and of the socially disorganizing and disruptive effects of urbanism as a way of life, were found in Alvin Toffler's popular and much overrated book *Future Shock* and in Stanley Milgram's use of the concept of "psychic overload."[8] The term "overload" comes from systems analysis, where an overload is said to occur when a system cannot process inputs because they are coming too fast or because there are too many of them. Under such circumstances, adaptations are said to occur. This is essentially Simmel's argument restated using a contemporary analogy.

A comparative testing of the consequences of urban life has been done by Robert Levine, who compared the pace of life in thirty-six American cities.[9] What he discovered was that cities differ. Northeasterners in larger cities generally walk

---

[5] Louis Wirth, *The Ghetto*, University of Chicago Press, Chicago, 1928; Harvey W. Zorbaugh, *The Gold Coast and the Slum: A Sociological Study of Chicago's Near North Side*, University of Chicago Press, Chicago, 1929; William I. Thomas and Florian Znaniecki, *The Polish Peasant in Europe and America*, 5 vols., University of Chicago Press, Chicago, 1918–1920.

[6] Georg Simmel, "The Metropolis and Mental Life," *The Sociology of Georg Simmel*, Kurt H. Wolff (trans.), Free Press, Glencoe, Ill., 1950.

[7] Ibid., p. 415.

[8] Alvin Toffler, *Future Shock*, Random House, New York, 1970; Stanley Milgram, "The Experience of Living in Cities," *Science*, **167**:1461–1468, Mar. 13, 1970.

[9] Robert Levine, "The Pace of Life," *Psychology Today*, October, 1989, pp. 42–46.

faster, talk faster, and check their watches more than those on the slower-paced west coast. He also found that fast-paced cities have higher rates of coronary heart disease. Thus, there does seem to be some support for Simmel's views. The faster pace of city life literally affects our lives.

"Urbanism as a Way of Life"

The classic formulation of how urbanization fosters innovation, specialization, diversity, and anonymity is Louis Wirth's essay "Urbanism as a Way of Life."[10] Wirth, using Simmel's ideas as a foundation, argued that the city created a distinct way of life—called "urbanism"—which is reflected in how people dress and speak, what they believe about the social world, what they consider worth achieving, what they do for a living, where they live, whom they associate with, and why they interact with other people.

Wirth further suggested that urbanization and its components—size, density, and heterogeneity—are the independent variables that determine urbanism, that is, urban behavior and life-styles. Moreover, the relationship is linear: The larger, denser, and more heterogeneous the city, the more prevalent is urbanism as a way of life.

As a way of life, urbanism was viewed by Wirth (and others) as economically successful but socially destructive:

> The distinctive features of the urban mode of life have often been described sociologically as consisting of the substitution of secondary for primary contacts, the weakening of bonds of kinship, the declining social significance of the family, the disappearance of the neighborhood, and the undermining of the traditional basis of social solidarity. All of these phenomena can be substantially verified through objective indices.[11]

Some characteristics of the urban way of life as described by Wirth are:

1. An extensive and complex division of labor replacing the artisan who participated in every phase of manufacture.
2. Emphasis on success, achievement, and social mobility as morally praiseworthy. Behavior becomes more rational, utilitarian, and goal-oriented.
3. Decline of the family (increased divorce) and weakening bonds of kinship, with previous family functions transferred to specialized outside agencies (schools, health and welfare agencies, commercial recreation).
4. Breakdown of primary groups and ties (neighborhood) and substitution of large formal secondary-group control mechanisms (police, courts). Traditional bases of social solidarity and organization are undermined, leading to social disorganization.
5. Relation to others as players of segmented roles (bus driver, shop clerk) rather than as whole persons; i.e., there is a high degree of role specialization. Utilitarian rather than affective relationships with others. Superficial sophistication as a substitute for meaningful relationships leading to alienation.

---

[10] Wirth, "Urbanism as a Way of Life," p. 8.
[11] Ibid., p. 21.

6. Decline of cultural homogeneity, and an increasing diversity of values, views, and opinions. The emergence of subcultures (ethnic, criminal, sexual) that are at variance with the larger society. Greater freedom and tolerance, but also decline in the sense of common community.

7. Spatial segregation into disparate sections on the basis of income, status, race, ethnicity, religion, and so on.[12]

Not surprisingly, many of the above read like a catalog of contemporary social changes. Wirthian social disorganization theory is sometimes referred to as a "determinist" approach.

REEVALUATION OF URBANISM AND SOCIAL DISORGANIZATION

Given the momentous changes taking place in the growing, immigrant-crowded industrializing cities of the first part of this century, it is not surprising that writers on the city tended to emphasize the negative rather than the positive aspects of urban change. The alienation, atomization, and social isolation of the city were stressed in studies dealing with juvenile delinquency, suicide, mental illness, and divorce; and a whole subfield was developed in sociology under the value-loaded title "social disorganization."

We now know that the sociologists of Wirth's day (the 1930s), in their fascination with the socially disorganizing aspects of urban life, underplayed the role of the city as a social integrator and underestimated the strength of traditional ways of life. William F. Whyte's excellent study of street life in an Italian slum of Boston just before World War II was one of the few to stress the sociocultural continuity and the vitality of traditional culture.[13] Over fifty years later, we are still predicting the imminent disappearance of these same traditional life-styles. For example, the ethnic affiliations that were supposed to have vanished long ago, and are continually being pronounced dead, seem somehow to be constantly reviving.

Wirth's essay "Urbanism as a Way of Life" has influenced both professional and popular thought about cities for over half a century. Today, however, it is easier to see how the essay suffers from not fully recognizing the degree to which Wirth's generalizations were limited both by historical time and by the differing composition and variety of urban areas. Herbert Gans questions Wirth's diagnosis of the city as producing anomic, goal-oriented, segmented role relationships on three grounds. First, Gans says, "Since the theory argues that all of society is now urban, *his analysis does not distinguish ways of life in the city from those in other settlements within modern society.*"[14] He suggests that Wirth's "urbanite" is a depersonalized and atomized member of a mass society, a representative of urban-industrial society rather than of the city itself. In other words, Wirth tended to con-

[12] For a discussion of Wirth's and others' views on community, see Dennis E. Poplin, *Communities,* 2d ed., Macmillan, New York, 1979, pp. 27–47.

[13] William F. Whyte, *Street Corner Society,* University of Chicago Press, Chicago, 1943.

[14] Herbert J. Gans, "Urbanism and Suburbanism as Ways of Life: A Re-evaluation of Definitions," in J. John Palen and Karl Flaming (eds.), *Urban America,* Holt, Rinehart and Winston, New York, 1972, p. 185.

fuse urbanization with general modernization of the society. Second, Gans believed there was not enough evidence either to prove or to deny the posited relationship among size, density, heterogeneity, and social disorganization. Newer data, however, support Wirth's contention that urbanism per se affects social behavior. Urbanism, for example, does increase tolerance for unpopular ideas and interests.[15]

Third, even if the causal relationship exists, many city dwellers are effectively isolated from it. For example, research from San Francisco demonstrated that, for many citizens, family and kinship bonds were far from dead, and relatives continued to be a significant source of socializing and support.[16] Also, recent research on inner-city neighborhoods by Anderson show they have their own moral codes and rules of behavior (especially for young men),[17] codes that may differ radically from those of the larger city. Mental health also appears to be better in urban than in rural areas.[18] The claim that urbanism impairs mental health is unfounded.[19] Moreover, urban residents have relations with others that are as full and meaningful as the relationships of those in small towns.[20] The conventional wisdom is simply wrong in painting city people as being more alienated and isolated. Knowing fewer persons in a community does not necessarily lead to atomization or isolation.[21]

Compositional Theory

An alternative to Wirthian determinist theory is compositional theory. Gans suggests that Wirth's characterization of the disorganizing aspects of urban life applies only to some inner-city residents, while other city dwellers—such as cosmopolites and suburbanites—pursue a different way of life. Thus it is the composition of the group that is important. For example, residents of the outer city have a life-style that resembles the life-style of suburbanites far more than the behavior patterns of inner-city residents. These outer-city neighborhoods, and even most inner-city populations, consist "mainly of relatively homogeneous groups, with social and cultural moorings that shield [them] fairly effectively from the suggested consequences of number, density, and heterogeneity."[22] In other words, there is not just one urban way of life but many urban life-styles.

Gans thus argues that urbanization itself does *not* cause a particular way of life to emerge. More important to the individual than the size, density, or heterogeneity of the larger population is the nature of his or her local community and primary

[15] Thomas C. Wilson, "Urbanism and Tolerance: A Test of Some Hypotheses Drawn from Wirth and Stouffer," *American Sociological Review,* **50**(1):117–123, 1985.

[16] Wendell Bell, "The City, the Suburb, and a Theory of Social Choice," in Scott Greer et al. (eds.), *The New Urbanization,* St. Martin's Press, New York, 1968, pp. 137–143; Thomas Drabek et al., "The Impact of Disaster on Kin Relationships," *Journal of Marriage and Family,* **37**(3):481–484, August, 1975; and Thomas Drabek and William Key, *Conquering Disaster: Family Recovery and Long Term Consequences,* Irvington Publishers, New York, 1984.

[17] Elija Anderson, *Streetwise: Race, Class, and Change in an Urban Community,* University of Chicago Press, Chicago, 1990.

[18] See Leo Srole's comments in Tim Hacker, "The Big City Has No Corner on Mental Illness," *New York Times Magazine,* Dec. 16, 1979, p. 136.

[19] Claude Fischer, *To Dwell among Friends: Personal Networks in Town and City,* University of Chicago Press, Chicago, 1982, p. 52.

[20] Ibid., pp. 59–60.

[21] William R. Freudenburg, "The Density of Acquaintanceship: An Overlooked Variable in Community Research?" *American Journal of Sociology,* **92**:27–63, July, 1986.

[22] Gans, "Urbanism and Suburbanism as Ways of Life," p. 186.

groups. Rather than living in the city per se, people actually live in what the early Chicago school called a "mosaic of social worlds." Some of these local social worlds, far from producing alienation, act to protect their members from negative outside influences. The differences in behavior are said to be a consequence not of place of residence, but rather of the social and economic characteristics of the group. In this view, urbanization itself has no effects; the behaviors that occur are the result of the composition of the group. Middle-class city dwellers are seen as virtually identical to middle-class suburbanites.

Subcultural Theory

A third perspective, known as "subculture theory," has become the most dominant in recent years. It is especially identified with Claude Fischer. He suggests that the urban area does indeed shape social life. However, Fischer suggests that urbanism does not destroy social groups, as posited by Wirth, but rather strengthens and intensifies subcultural groups.[23] This occurs because large cities contain enough people to allow subcultures to emerge. Urban life in fact creates new social worlds or subcultures. Only in the city can one find a subculture of model train enthusiasts or tuba players. However, sometimes conflict arises between what are considered by the mainstream to be deviant urban cultures (e.g., delinquents or gays) and the mainstream culture itself. Adherents of subculture theory argue that this occurs not because social worlds are being broken down, but because subcultures remain strong. Thus they argue that the city doesn't produce alienation and normlessness. Rather, it promotes new subcultures. The gay subculture is an example of a subculture that thrives in larger urban centers.[24] The effect of the city is greatest for the smallest groups, who would not find enough members other than in large cities.

DIVERSE LIFE-STYLES

While cities generally have the highest rates of social problems, this clearly is not the same as saying that all central-city populations or areas have high rates of alienation and disorganization. Some groups thrive in central-city locations. Inner-city working-class ethnic groups, for instance, live lives that, far from being disorganized, are probably more organized and integrated than those of other city dwellers. Characteristics of depersonalization, isolation, and social disorganization simply do not fit.

Ethnic Villagers

Far from being characterized by depersonalization, isolation, and social disorganization, working-class neighborhoods, particularly when they are dominated by a single ethnic group, often exhibit a high degree of social interaction among residents. Those living in such organized inner-city neighborhoods have been referred

[23] Claude Fischer, "Toward a Subcultural Theory of Urbanism," *American Journal of Sociology,* **80:**1319-1341, 1975.
[24] John D'Emilio, *Sexual Politics, Sexual Communities: The Making of a Homosexual Minority in the United States, 1940–1970,* University of Chicago Press, Chicago, 1983.

to as "urban villagers" or "urban provincials."[25] Such names are used to suggest that they are in, but not of, the city; they are urban in their residential patterns but not in their thought processes. These inner-city neighborhoods, whatever their predominant group, embody more of the family and peer orientation of a homogeneous small town than the attitudes of an impersonal large city.

Ethnic villagers, although they live in the city, try to isolate themselves from what they consider to be the harmful effects of urban life, preferring to live in their own tight-knit ethnic neighborhoods. Whether they are Irish in South Boston, Italian in South Philadelphia, or Mexican in East Los Angeles, they resist the encroachment of other ethnic or racial groups. Such primarily working-class neighborhoods place heavy emphasis on kinship and primary-group relationships and resent the secondary formal control mechanisms of the larger city. Some of these Italian, Puerto Rican, Mexican, Asian, or eastern European enclaves are no larger than a census tract, but some are quite extensive. Chicago and Detroit both claim the largest Polish population outside Warsaw; Cleveland's Hungarian population is said to be second only to that of Budapest. Miami has major Cuban influences, and Los Angeles's Mexican population is third behind that of Mexico City. Los Angeles's Asian population is rapidly expanding.

Several decades ago it was thought that tight ethnic urban neighborhoods were only anachronistic survivals from earlier times and were not representative

[25] See Herbert J. Gans, *The Urban Villagers,* Free Press, Glencoe, Ill., 1962.

Street festivals have become a common scene in American cities. (Akos Szilvasi/ Stock, Boston.)

The disappearance of ethnic neighborhoods has been predicted for three-quarters of a century, yet they continue to show vitality. (Kathy Sloane/Photo Researchers.)

of contemporary urban life. To some people, urban villagers represent only "by-passed preindustrial locals" who have been left behind by modern society. As put by Melvin Webber, "Here in the Harlems and South Sides of the nation are some of the last viable remnants of preindustrial societies. . . ."[26] He was wrong. New ethnic areas are bringing new vitality to American cities.

Outsiders sometimes mislabel such areas as "slums" because the buildings are old and may not appear from the exterior to be in good condition. Often the area is in better condition than it appears when viewed from the window of a passing automobile on the suburban-bound expressway, but even when an area is physically deteriorated, its social fabric may still be strong.[27] (Later in the chapter we will discuss disorganized urban neighborhoods.) Urban villagers remain in older neighborhoods in spite of the obvious physical limitations and conditions of the housing because moving to the suburbs would mean leaving the tight-knit social neighbor-

---

[26] Melvin M. Webber, "The Post-City Age," in J. John Palen (ed.), *City Scenes,* Little, Brown, Boston, 1977, p. 314.

[27] See, for example, William F. Whyte, *Street Corner Society*; and Gerald D. Suttles, *The Social Order of the Slum: Ethnicity and Territory in the Inner City,* University of Chicago Press, Chicago, 1968.

hood. If they could take neighbors and social atmosphere with them, they would happily become suburbanites.

The mother of six children living in the Near West Side of Chicago clearly expressed the affection urban villagers have for their neighborhoods:

> I got everybody on this block that would do something for me. If one of my children were sick, I wouldn't feel any compunction of waking up the man across the street to take me to the hospital. He expects this. He would expect me to do this for him.
>
> One night I took my daughter to the hospital at eleven o'clock at night. Next morning, at least eight people on my way to work asked me how my daughter was. When I got home it was worse than that. It took me an hour to get home. Because everybody wanted to know about Christine. Did the doctors do anything? Did I need anything? I get a cheery hello from everybody. Old ladies, when I get dressed to go out or to work: "Oh, how nice you look." Old and young blend together here. I have friends who live in the suburbs, they wouldn't dare be out in the dark.
>
> I know friends of ours, who've moved away from here, who bitterly lament their predicament now. They've got beautiful homes—I guess the city planners would say they've done better for themselves. Their plumbing works, their electricity is good, their environment is better—supposedly. If you're a type of person who considers a mink stole and a fountain in your living room and big bay windows, front lawn beautifully kept, all these things mean something to you, well . . . to me, we're more concerned about people.[28]

The next pages will focus on settled working-class neighborhoods and their norms. Use this material to compare the type of neighborhood described with neighborhoods with which you are personally familiar.

Neighborhood Characteristics.

Territoriality. Inner-city neighborhoods generally have a strong sense of territory. Studies of inner-city working-class areas often find that the residents, although living near the center of a large metropolis, still manage to remain physically, socially, and psychologically isolated from the rest of the urban area. Those living in inner-city areas, especially minorities, often have very restricted mental maps of even their own neighborhoods.[29] The city outside the neighborhood is viewed as a foreign land—and a potentially hostile one—into which one ventures only when necessary. Even in cosmopolitan New York there are people living in the Bronx who have never been to Manhattan—and have no real desire ever to go there.

Ordered segmentation. Ecologically settled ethnic areas are usually characterized by ordered segmentation. That is, each ethnic group carefully and specifically defines its territory. Boundaries between different ethnic groups, while invisible to the outsider, are well known and respected by the local residents. Gerald Suttles, in his study of the Taylor Street area of Chicago, points out that the Italian, Mexican, Puerto Rican, and black groups living in the area have their own provincial enclaves and conduct their daily lives within these known borders.[30] Within

---

[28] Quoted in Studs Terkel, *Division Street: America,* Pantheon Books (Avon ed.), New York, 1967, p. 198.

[29] Mark LaGory and John Pipkin, *Urban Social Space,* Wadsworth, Belmont, Calif., 1981.

[30] Suttles, *The Social Order of the Slum.*

these territorial units, one is safe and comfortable. Outsiders are made to feel unwelcome unless they are there as guests. The use of community facilities such as churches and parks is exclusively for one group. The movement of one ethnic or racial group into what is known as the social area of another is likely to lead to violence or the threat of violence.

Awareness and concern over territory are not limited to public or semipublic facilities. Business establishments—particularly bars, but even grocery stores—are viewed by local inhabitants as being the exclusive property of a single minority group. In the words of Suttles:

> When someone from outside the area or from another ethnic group enters, the proprietor and regular customers view them with great suspicion and, in some cases, use *ad hoc* measures to insure their safety. Sometimes they will simply wait for the intruder to get his bearings and leave. If that fails the proprietor may eventually get around to asking what he wants. In the meantime, everyone in the store stops and stares. The treatment of regular customers, of course, is exactly the opposite. Commercial relations with these people are intimate and all economic transactions are buried in the guise of friendship and sentiment. In large part this is the reason they cannot tolerate the presence of strangers from another ethnic group. Among themselves the customers set aside their public face and disclose much of their private life to one another.[31]

Private information is too intimate to be revealed to potentially hostile strangers. In establishments such as small snack shops that may be near the boundary line between different ethnic groups, the problem of privacy may be solved by taking turns. One group of teenagers will not enter while another is inside. Rather, they will wait until the other ethnic group leaves.

Peer-Group Orientation. The primary integrative mechanism of stable inner-city ethnic neighborhoods is the peer group—that is, a group made up of members of the same age and sex who are at the same stage of the life cycle. As Gans says, "The peer group society continues long past adolescence, and indeed, dominates the life of the West Ender [Boston] from birth to death."[32] The peer group, be it a gang of adolescents or a clique of married friends and relatives of the same sex, provides a vital buffer between the individual and the larger society.

Gans has described the relationship of the peer-group society to the larger world as follows:

> The life of the West Ender takes place within three interrelated sectors: the primary group refers to that combination of family and peer relationships which I shall call the *peer group society*. The secondary group refers to the small array of Italian institutions, voluntary organizations, and other social bodies which function to support the workings of the peer group society. This I shall call the community. . . . The outgroup, which I shall describe as the *outside world*, covers a variety of non-Italian institutions in the West End, in Boston, and in America that impinge on his life—often unhappily to the West Ender's way of thinking.[33]

---

[31] Ibid., pp. 48–49.
[32] Gans, *The Urban Villagers*, p. 37.
[33] Ibid., pp. 36–37.

The peer group sets standards for behavior and acts as a filter through which one can obtain information. It provides psychological support in that it serves as a sounding board against which one can bounce ideas and receive confirmation of values. It reduces anonymity and tells the individual that he or she belongs. Frequently, in-group membership is signified by a distinctive way of dressing and locally distinctive speech patterns. Whyte's classic treatment of a peer-group society, *Street Corner Society*,[34] deals extensively with the conflict in values between locally oriented "corner boys" and neighborhood adolescents who were success- and object-oriented, the "college boys." Peer groups of corner boys discouraged striving and emphasized personal relationships. If someone got a job and made some money (this was during the late depression), he was expected to share his good fortune with his friends. Being a good guy was socially rewarded, while putting on airs of social striving was negatively sanctioned. On the other hand, the college boys were oriented toward the achievement values of the outside world, saved rather than shared their money, and constantly sought to "better themselves." Studies of working-class populations in Boston's West End and the Addams area also indicated the priority of personal relationships over goal-oriented relationships. The absence of material wealth and luxurious consumer goods is rationalized: These goods are associated with the outside world and a cold, impersonal, friendless way of life.

Family Norms. Family life in middle-class families is child-oriented, but in settled ethnic working-class areas it is generally adult-oriented. Once out of infancy, children are expected to accommodate and adjust themselves to a world run by adults. The child is not the center of the family as in many middle-class and upper-middle-class families, where everything is adjusted to avoid conflict with the child's needs, schedule, and general "development." The role of children is to stay out of the way and behave, at least around the home, like miniature adults. Girls are expected to start helping their mothers around the home, frequently by caring for younger siblings. Boys are given a great deal more freedom to roam the streets. Children soon pick up the notion that the home is the preserve of the mother. Leisure activities for males often focus on the local tavern, which is the major neighborhood institution for many blue-collar workers.[35] The British comic strip "Andy Capp" illustrates this working-class pattern.

Unlike middle-class professionals, sociability for adults does not revolve around occupation or involve a search for new or different friends. The basis for gathering with others is not occupation but kinship or long-standing friendship and association. Parties in the middle-class sense—gatherings for which specific invitations are issued and at which you expect to meet some people you do not know—are not part of the local life-style. As one West Ender put it: "I don't want to meet any new people. I get out quite a bit all over Boston to see my brothers and sisters, and when they come over, we have others in, like neighbors. You can't do that in the

---

[34] Whyte, *Street Corner Society*.
[35] E. E. LeMasters, *Blue Collar Aristocrats*, University of Wisconsin Press, Madison, 1975; and William Kornblum, *Blue Collar Community*, University of Chicago Press, Chicago, 1974, p. 80.

suburbs."[36] Usually the same people come the same days of the week. There are no formal invitations; these are used only for major family events such as a christening, graduation, or wedding. Husband and wife are not expected to be as close or to communicate as extensively as in the middle-class family model. Bott's description of this phenomenon among English families applies equally well to American cities:

> Husband and wife have a clear differentiation of tasks and a considerable number of separate interests and activities. They have a clearly defined division of labor into male tasks and female tasks. They expect to have different leisure pursuits, and the husband has his friends . . . the wife hers.[37]

To date, the women's movement has not seriously altered this pattern.

One difference between American and English studies is that in the United States interaction is primarily with relatives of the same generation. In England, the interaction may focus on the family matriarch, "Mum." Mum is the one who settles family quarrels, lends money, and looks after the grandchildren. It is at her house that the family gathers, and if a married daughter does not live in the same building, she will be within a short distance.[38] Family ties in the United States are more likely to be horizontal as well as vertical, with greater importance given to cousins and other relatives of the same age.

Housing. Housing often does not have the same meaning in established ethnic working-class neighborhoods that it has in suburban middle-class areas. For the middle class, how one decorates one's home is viewed as an extension of one's personality. The home is a reflection of one's tastes and style of life. The working-class home, on the other hand, is not primarily viewed as a status symbol. Homes are old but quite comfortable. Rents are usually well below the average for the city.

Exteriors of buildings are not always in the best repair. However, inside the apartments everything is clean and in good order. To emphasize consumer goods is perceived as trying to be "better than you are," "snooty," or "stuck-up." Social closeness among neighbors is encouraged by the tendency of local landlords to rent apartments to their married children, relatives, and friends. The goal is a "respectable" neighborhood in which neighbors are of the same general ethnic, religious, and economic background. For the upwardly mobile members of the working class hopeful of moving into the middle class, the home frequently is a symbol of one's respectability. Cleanliness and order are emphasized. The furniture may be carefully protected by plastic seat covers and the carpeting by runners.

Imagery and Vulnerability. Blue-collar ethnic neighborhoods, although physically a central part of the city, manage to maintain a psychological distance between themselves and other areas. Their negative images of major urban institutions are remarkably similar to those of small-town dwellers, who also feel powerless in the face of the large urban institutions and organizations that control

[36] Gans, *The Urban Villagers*, p. 75.

[37] Elizabeth Bott, *Family and Social Network*, Tavistock Publications, London, 1957, p. 53.

[38] Michael Young and Peter Willmott, *Family and Kinship in East London*, rev. ed., Penguin Books, Baltimore, 1962.

much of their lives. The urban provincials may be city dwellers, but they think of the city as something removed from themselves and their neighborhood. Their area is perceived as being different from the big city outside. Thus the neighborhood is considered friendly, but the city is cold and hostile.

The peer-group orientation of working-class urban neighborhoods leaves them vulnerable to change induced from the outside. The emphasis within the community on personal relations makes residents ill-equipped to participate in large-scale formal organizations or communitywide activities. One learns from the peer group how to get along with others, but not how to organize or deal effectively with an outside bureaucracy.

This means that the community as a whole is rarely able to respond effectively as a unit to threats to its existence. In the past, the threat might be urban renewal or an urban expressway that cuts it apart. Today, it is more likely to be plans for displacing the residents so the area can be gentrified by the middle class, or it may be the threat of invasion by drug dealers. A traditional distrust of politicians and a lack of knowledge about how to lobby on the level of city government further handicap the working-class neighborhood. Suburban upper-middle-class groups are by training and inclination well equipped to organize ad hoc committees for any purpose under the sun. Working-class people are used to working within an environment of limited size, oriented toward persons more than organizations. Except in cases where a powerful communitywide ethnic church exists, there is no large-scale organization that has the power both to organize and to speak for the neighborhood in its dealings with the larger city. A peer-group society based on ethnicity, age grading, dominance of a single sex, and limited territoriality is at a considerable disadvantage when it necessarily comes into contact and confrontation with large-scale, complex, bureaucratic, middle-class organized society.

Urban provincials do not turn to outside bureaucratic structures in time of trouble. They distrust the city hall bureaucracy and that of the courts. They don't understand the system and feel that whatever happens they are going to lose. They are right, and their lack of knowledge of how to fight the system makes it all the easier for city hall and other outside interests to have their way. Urban provincials lack the bureaucratic skills to be part of the conventional political pressure-group system.

Slums of Despair

For the 15 to 20 percent of the overall population who are the bottom in terms of social status (unskilled manual workers, people with unstable and erratic work histories, the homeless, and people on welfare, particularly if they are members of minority groups), the slum has the character more of an urban jungle than an urban village. Such areas have high rates of residential instability, with the population sharing little but the physical area. They are there because they have no alternative. Poverty, crime, and welfare dependance result in an area suffering from "hyperghettoization."[39]

---

[39] Loïc J. D. Wacquant and William J. Wilson, "The Cost of Racial and Class Exclusion in the Inner City," *Annals of the American Academy of Political and Social Science,* **501**:8–25, 1989.

An excellent description and analysis of such ghetto life is provided by Elijah Anderson in his fourteen-year study of two Philadelphia neighborhoods.[40] He discusses the effect of drugs on the communities, and how the communities develop their own norms and behaviors regarding sexual activity and family life. A lack of jobs as well as pervasive racism keeps young males on the streets. The sex codes by which many inner-city young men operate makes sexual conquests a game youths play to gain respect from their male peers. Having a number of girlfriends and offspring gives males street status. Babies in this system become the "consolation prizes" for the unwed mothers who have been promised marriage and settling down.

Young males to survive learn how to be "streetwise," adopting a code of street behavior aimed at getting and keeping respect. In order to successfully move on the streets, males have to learn the "street wisdom" of how, through words, body language, and facial expressions, to signal their intentions to others. Such knowledge is essential in an atmosphere where every encounter is viewed as a test of respect, respect for which one is willing to fight to the death. Violence under such as system becomes normative. A lack of jobs to provide an alternative life-style virtually ensures that the cycle of illegitimacy, drugs, crime, and violence will continue.

Unstable slums thus differ not just because they house the very poor. Residents are not simply poorer, although that is also the case—they are in many ways excluded from the social system that includes both the rich and the blue-collar workers of stable slums. Unstable slums are the slums of despair, for most of their residents are for all practical purposes excluded from the economic and social life of the larger society. Drug dealing is often the sole route of economic mobility. Life in such an environment is not an attempt to maximize advantages but rather an attempt, frequently unsuccessful, to minimize the harsh negative realities of everyday life. Residents are surrounded by others who are out to exploit them whenever possible. They are considered fair game by everyone from landlords to hustlers to drug dealers.

Survival Strategies. For those locked into lower-class status, it often appears unrealistic to sacrifice for long-range goals. Success is measured in terms of developing strategies for day-to-day survival, not in terms of long-range goals. Even those with jobs usually are not on a track that will lead to a better job. For example, a dishwasher in a restaurant, even if he or she works hard, isn't going to become a restaurant manager.[41] For a welfare mother with children living in a high-rise public housing project, the concern is not whether there will be enough money in ten years to send a child to college, but whether the family can scrape together enough money to pay current bills and expenses. There is also a constant threat of violence. The extremely high rates of drug usage, assault, mugging, robbery, and rape in unstable slums further isolate people. Their situation does not encourage openness and easy interaction with others in the area. Rather, it fosters wariness, anonymity, noninvolvement, and impersonality. Protection from hostile others has to take first

---

[40] Elijah Anderson, *Streetwise: Race, Class, and Change in an Urban Community,* University of Chicago Press, Chicago, 1990.
[41] Elliot Liebow, *Talley's Corner,* Little, Brown, Boston, 1967.

priority. They try, often unsuccessfully, to isolate themselves from the violence of their world.

Housing Problems. The middle class may view housing as an extension of one's personality, and the working class may see the house as a place of comfort, but for the urban underclass the house is a place of refuge. Housing for the poor living in unstable slums is not a matter of self-realization or self-expression; it is a matter of providing a place of security from the physical and emotional dangers of the outside.

Urban poor, particularly those stored in public housing projects, have to be constantly on guard against violence against themselves and their possessions. Assaults, robberies, and muggings are a constant danger in stairwells, corridors, laundry rooms, and even apartments. In addition to physical violence, symbolic violence on the part of building supervisors, social workers, and others who perform caretaker services for the lower classes is also endemic in slums and public housing.

To the extent that the world is seen as consisting of dangerous others, the very act of making friends involves risks for the lower-class person. Lower-class persons are constantly being exploited, and thus it is not surprising that many view the world as threatening. In the words of a researcher, "To lower class people the major causes stem from the nature of their own peers. Thus a great deal of blaming goes on and reinforces the process of isolation, suspiciousness, and touchiness both blaming and shaming."[42] Such patterns of distrust and recrimination make it difficult to establish any type of organization for cooperation in solving problems.

As of the 1990s one out of every seven Americans remains below the poverty level.[43] Nor is poverty evenly distributed. One-third of all African Americans are below the poverty level compared with one-tenth of whites. Forty percent of those in poverty are children younger than eighteen. Half (53 percent) of all poor families are headed by women, and seven out of ten poor black families are female headed. Not surprisingly, poverty and joblessness are tightly related. Only 8.2 percent of poor female householders have year-round full-time jobs.[44]

Those with economic strength or potential having fled unstable slums, the isolation of those who are left behind locked into poverty increases.[45] It can result in the "hyperghettoization" noted above. Thus decreases in discrimination *heighten* the isolation between the very poor and other strata of blacks. Poverty and economic instability lock the urban underclass at the bottom as effectively as discrimination once did. Certainly the feeling of being ignored and bypassed while all around others rise can lead to explosions of frustration—or worse, despair and violence—not only against oneself but also against one's children. The bondage of unstable slums is made doubly oppressive by the relative prosperity of those outside their boundaries.

---

[42] Lee Rainwater, "Fear and the House-as-Haven in the Lower Class," in J. John Palen and Karl H. Flaming (eds), *Urban America*, Holt, Rinehart, and Winston, New York, 1972, p. 319.

[43] U.S. Bureau of the Census, "Income, Poverty, and Wealth in the United States: A Chart Book," *Current Population Reports*, series P-60, no. 179, 1992, p. 13.

[44] Ibid., p.18.

[45] William Julius Wilson, *The Truly Disadvantaged: The Inner City, the Underclass, and Public Policy*, University of Chicago Press, Chicago, 1987.

There, however, are within unstable slum areas populations of decent, caring, and responsible adult males. Perhaps the most important of these is the population of poor working-class adult men. Virtually invisible in most discussions of inner-city ghettos, responsible working adult males continue to espouse and practice traditional values of responsibility and hard work.[46] Although the group of working adult males is smaller in number than in the past, and often not given moral authority by younger males, stable working-class males continue to provide a moral authority, and serve within the community as role models of decency and respectability.

URBAN LIFE-STYLES

Urbanism as a way of life thus is remarkably diverse. It includes gentrifying communities of yuppies, tightly organized ethnic neighborhoods, and disorganized slums. There is no single urban life-style per se. It is important to distinguish between the different urban life-styles, and not just speak of "the city" as if it were all of one pattern.

---

[46] Mitchell Duneier, *Slim's Table: Race, Respectability, and Masculinity,* University of Chicago Press, Chicago, 1992.

CHAPTER

8

SOCIAL ENVIRONMENT OF THE CITY
Strangers, Neighbors, Crowding, Crime, and Homelessness

Hark, hark, the dogs do bark
Beggars are coming to town
Some in rags and some in tags
And some in velvet gowns.

Traditional nursery rhyme

INTRODUCTION

In the last chapter we saw how Simmel, Wirth, and the classical Chicago school emphasized the disruptive and socially disorganizing aspects of the size, density, and heterogeneity of cities. Simmel in particular stresses the degree to which one can become alienated in a city of strangers. Although we saw that this was an over-statement, a question still remains: How do people outside their own defended neighborhood, or "turf," cope with large numbers of other people whom they do not know? How do we learn to operate in what Lyn Lofland refers to as "a world of strangers"?[1]—an urban world made even more uncertain and dangerous in recent years by drug-related violent crime.

DEALING WITH STRANGERS

Lofland suggests that we cope by identifying strangers on the basis of their ap-pearance and their spatial location in the city. Our clothing, jewelry, and hair styles are all external symbols of who we are and what our social position is. In earlier eras, legal codes and custom often decreed what one could or could not wear. Vel-vet gowns, for example, were reserved for those of rank, while commoners were re-stricted to common cloth, as attested to by the nursery rhyme that began this chap-ter. In ancient Rome the white toga was a sign of Roman citizenship.[2] Colors also have historically been used to signify position. Royalty in Europe wore the royal purple; in China the emperor wore yellow. Professions also had their unique garb, such as the academic robes of the professor.

Today professorial robes are worn only on ceremonial occasions such as con-vocations, but that does not mean we no longer wear distinctive clothing. Not only priests, nurses, bus drivers, and soldiers wear uniforms or have dress codes. We still wear a "uniform," but the signs may be more subtle, such as a designer's symbol on one's shirt. Clothing also indicates social rank. Business executives wear dark blue Brooks Brothers suits; male professors wear tweed jackets with a loose tie or, sometimes, no tie; and students wear jeans. There are preppy uniforms, grunge uni-forms, and subculture uniforms. Even on supposedly homogeneous college cam-puses, business students dress differently from art students, jocks differently from fraternity brothers, and blacks often differently from whites. These dress codes help us identify strangers as being similar to or dissimilar from ourselves.

Where we see people in the city also helps us identify strangers. Young people on a college campus are assumed to be students, and conservatively dressed middle-aged persons in an office district are assumed to be businesspeople. Passengers in airports are assumed to be of higher status than passengers in the city bus station; suburbanites are assumed to be of higher status than those in slum neighborhoods.

Of course, errors are made because location and dress are not certain signs of a stranger's position. Initial conversation with a stranger is often an attempt to iden-

---

[1] Lyn Lofland, *A World of Strangers*, Basic Books, New York, 1973.
[2] Ibid., p. 45.

In London, social custom dictates that people formally queue up when waiting for the bus. In the United States, it is done informally. (Julia Green Brody/Stock, Boston.)

tify socioeconomic status. One asks the social-class question "What do you do for a living?" or "What's your line of work?" The college-age student's version of this is "Where do you go to school?" What conversation follows, if any, depends on the answer received.

CODES OF BEHAVIOR

The late Erving Goffman pointed out that even supposedly random activity is not without a system. Even such urban activity as walking down a street has a whole set of social rules.[3] People do not just walk down the street at random; rather, there is an intricate code of pedestrian behavior. For example, pedestrian traffic sorts itself into two clear streams. In North America, pedestrians, as well as drivers, keep to the right, and they "watch their step" by avoiding obstacles such as lightposts and other people on the sidewalk. Pedestrians also adjust their speed to avoid collisions; faster traffic moves to the outside lane. Pedestrians expect others to follow the "rules of the road" and negatively sanction those who break the rules by bumping into someone (a nasty look or a "Why don't you watch where you're going"), and apologize for their own infractions ("Oh, sorry").

Rules differ by culture. Where auto traffic stays to the left (e.g., England, Japan), local pedestrian traffic does likewise. (Tourists from the United States and Europe often try to move to the right, causing general confusion.) In Great Britain one queues up for a bus; in the United States one waits in an informal line. People

[3] Erving Goffman, *Relations in Public,* Basic Books, New York, 1971.

keep mental track of who has waited longest. Those pushing ahead get a dirty look or comment. A western man is traditionally expected not to shove ahead of a woman. In Israel, Singapore, Korea, and China, on the other hand, there is no queuing of any sort. In Great Britain those on escalators leave the left lane open for those who are in a hurry and wish to pass. Not to do so is considered rude. In North America, on the other hand, people stand side by side on escalators and to push past is considered rude. Thus, even pedestrian behavior follows generally internalized rules. Coping in the city is made easier by a whole series of informal rules of which we are not normally conscious.

Neighboring

We have seen that city life per se does not automatically destroy close personal relationships. However, neighboring studies do suggest that, on the whole, large-city dwellers know fewer of their neighbors than do residents of smaller places.[4] Most of us, after all, do not live in tight-knit ethnic urban enclaves. Studies of vital urban neighborhoods raise two questions: First, what characteristics distinguish the city dweller who is likely to neighbor? Second, what social conditions tend to turn people who live near each other into real neighbors?

Claude Fischer suggests several hypotheses on both these questions.[5] He suggests that persons who neighbor are, first, likely to be raising a family. Children engage parents in neighboring activities (e.g., PTA, Girl Scouts); children meeting other neighborhood children also facilitates their parents meeting, and having children increases the likelihood that a parent will be home during the day to neighbor. Second, and related to this, neighborly people are likely to be home during the day, perhaps retired or caring for children. Third, they tend to be older and more settled. Fourth, neighboring folk tend to be homogeneous, to share common ethnicity, occupations, interests, and life-styles. Working-class persons tend to rely more on neighbors than do members of the middle class. Further research, however, has questioned whether having children and having someone home during the day are good predictors of neighboring, particularly in central cities.[6] In cities, as opposed to suburbs, neighboring was seen as helping out in a crisis rather than as friendship and regular interaction.

Finally, research indicates that the longer one has been a neighborhood resident, the greater the likelihood of neighborhood involvement.[7] Since urbanites are more mobile than those living in other places, and are more likely to be working during the day and to be living in heterogeneous neighborhoods, it is understandable that city dwellers on the whole are less likely to be involved with their neighbors.

[4] Claude S. Fischer, *The Urban Experience,* 2d ed., Harcourt Brace Jovanovich, New York, 1984.
[5] Ibid., pp. 130–131.
[6] Carol J. Silverman, "Neighboring and Urbanism: Commonality versus Friendship," *Urban Affairs Quarterly,* **22:**312–328, December, 1986.
[7] John D. Kasarda and Morris Janowitz, "Community Attachment in Mass Society," *American Sociological Review,* **39:**328–339, June, 1974.

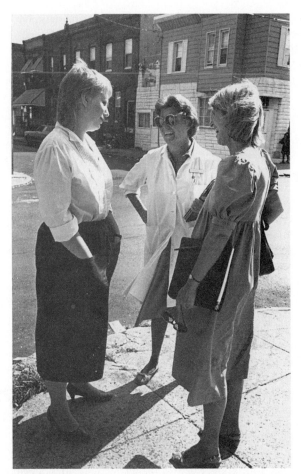

Neighborhood sidewalks are used for socialization as well as for movement. (Glassman/The Image Works.)

Neighbors and Just Neighbors

Fischer, drawing on the existing research, suggests that the social, as opposed to personal, conditions that turn "just neighbors" into "real neighbors" tend to be found less commonly in cities. Three conditions encourage "real" neighboring.[8] The first is functional interdependence. In rural America this involved mutual help with barn raising, harvesting, or meeting joint local needs. A suburban activity that generates social cooperation today is a neighborhood crime watch patrol. A second condition encouraging involvement is the preexistence of other relationships and bonds. Relatives and people who work together, who share the same

[8] Fischer, *The Urban Experience*, p. 132.

ethnicity, and who worship together have already existing bonds that being neighbors simply strengthens. Third, Fischer suggests some people neighbor because they have fewer other alternatives. The elderly and mothers with small children may have reduced mobility and thus form close relationships with those nearby. Since large-city dwellers are less likely to have such functional interdependence and do have other alternatives available to them, old-fashioned neighboring is less common for them.

DEFINING COMMUNITY

The term "community" has been used for many years but has not really been defined. Unfortunately, there is no single or even most common usage.[9] Anthropologists dealing with localized semi-isolated populations generally find the concept of community more useful than do sociologists researching contemporary urban areas, where the boundaries between distinct groups or patterns of activities become blurred. Today the term "community" has lost much of its descriptive preciseness and efficiency. It is applied arbitrarily to everything from one block in a neighborhood to those who use the Internet to the international community.

Contemporary urbanites can have "community without propinquity" (nearness). On the other hand, community, as used by ecologists, can be defined as a territorially localized population that is interdependent with regard to daily needs. Thus, this usage implies a territorial unit, as opposed to other uses of the term such as "community of scholars" or "religious community." Community as used by most sociologists refers to a spatial or territorial unit.[10] Communities provide a link between the family and primary group and the larger society. Communities edit reality on the local level so it seems manageable to community members.[11]

In the writings of the Chicago school, the term "community" was often a synonym for urban neighborhood. However, two of the most important pre–World War II community studies focused on small cities as the unit of analysis. Robert and Helen Lynd's *Middletown* and *Middletown in Transition* focused on the transformation of life in Middletown (Muncie, Indiana) as a result of absorption into an industrially oriented community.[12] The Lynds documented the decline of control by the community over its own destiny. However, in spite of the economic shocks of the depression, Middletown residents did not become radicalized, but retained complacency and belief in traditional values. A major restudy of Middletown in the

---

[9] Some ninety definitions of community are listed by G. A. Hillery, "Definitions of Community: Areas of Agreement," *Rural Sociology,* **20:**111–123, 1955. See also Joseph R. Gusfield, *Community: A Critical Response,* Harper & Row, New York, 1975.

[10] For a discussion of contemporary use of community, see Suzanne Keller, "The American Dream of Community: An Unfinished Agenda," *Sociological Forum,* **3:**167–183, Spring, 1988.

[11] Kai Erikson, *Everything in Its Path: Destruction of Community in the Buffalo Creek Flood,* Simon and Schuster, New York, 1976, p. 280.

[12] Robert S. Lynd and Helen Merrell Lynd, *Middletown,* Harcourt, Brace, New York, 1929; and *Middletown in Transition,* Harcourt Brace, New York, 1937.

late 1970s indicates that while the city is no longer economically in control of its destiny and is heavily beholden to the federal government, the traditional values and normative structure still persist. To a remarkable degree, Middletown still thinks of itself as it did half a century ago.[13]

The second major study, W. Lloyd Warner's *Yankee City* (Newburyport, Massachusetts), dealt with the degree to which the movement from craft work by individuals to mass industrial production led to a breakdown of a sense of community.[14] Local power and control, Warner suggested, had gone from ownership and control by local family-owned firms to large outside corporations. Accompanying this, he also suggested the rigidification of the social structure and decreased social mobility among workers. The historical accuracy of the latter points, however, has been strongly challenged.[15]

There is currently no consensus on the significance of community in modern social life. Some, such as Suzanne Keller and Claude Fischer, suggest that urbanites engage in activities on the basis of interests rather than propinquity, and that today neighborhood serves only minimal functions.[16] One might borrow eggs or a cup of sugar from neighbors or call on them in an emergency, but for everyday life, local attachments are seen as being quite limited. Those taking this view would agree with Roland Warren that the strengthening ties of community units to extracommunity systems orient them in important and clearly definable ways toward larger systems outside the community, making the model of a spatially delineated, relatively independent, and self-sufficient community less and less relevant to the modern scene.[17] Larger networks for some have made the spatial unit of the neighborhood no longer important.[18] Others see urban neighborhoods continuing to play a sometimes significant if changing role.[19]

CATEGORIES OF LOCAL COMMUNITIES

A number of types of local communities have been defined in the professional literature, among which are:

1. The defended neighborhood
2. The community of limited liability

[13] Theodore Caplow, Howard Bahr, Bruce Chadwick, Reuben Hill, and Margaret Holmes Williamson, *Middletown Families: Fifty Years of Change and Continuity,* University of Minnesota Press, Minneapolis, 1982.
[14] W. Lloyd Warner, *Yankee City,* Yale University Press, New Haven, Conn., 1963.
[15] Stephen Thernstrom, "Yankee City Revisited: The Perils of Historical Naivete," *American Sociological Review,* **30:**234–242, April, 1965.
[16] Suzanne Keller, *The Urban Neighborhood,* Random House, New York, 1968; and Claude S. Fischer, *The Urban Experience,* Harcourt, Brace, Jovanovich, New York, 1976.
[17] Roland L. Warren, *New Perspectives on the American Community,* Rand McNally, Chicago, 1977.
[18] Barry Wellman, "The Community Question: The Intimate Networks of East Yorkers," *American Sociological Review,* **84:**1201–1231, 1979.
[19] Albert J. Hunter, *Symbiotic Communities: Persistence and Change in Chicago's Local Communities,* University of Chicago Press, Chicago, 1974.

3. The expanded community of limited liability
4. The contrived or conscious community[20]

The defended neighborhood is an area that residents feel is their turf.[21] "Functionally, the defended neighborhood can be conceived of as the smallest spatial unit within which coresidents assume a relative degree of security on the streets as compared to adjacent areas."[22] The defended neighborhood thus is the place where people feel safe and secure. As such, it may or may not have a name or be recognized by government. Those within the defended neighborhood assume a common residential identification and identity.

The community of limited liability was first described by Morris Janowitz and later elaborated on by Scott Greer.[23] The concept of the community of limited liability emphasizes the voluntary and limited involvement of residents in the local community. The amount of emotional investment in the area, or investment of time or resources, is dependent on the degree to which the community meets the needs of individuals. If the needs are not met, the individual might withdraw psychologically and socially, if not physically. Voluntary organizations play important roles in defining and defending issues common to communities of limited liability. Communities of limited liability usually have names and boundaries that are recognized by local planning agencies and government. Local organizations and particularly the local community press have a vested interest in maintaining the identity and boundaries of the area. The community of limited liability thus is defined by commercial interests and government agencies rather than by internal community awareness, as with the defended neighborhood.

The expanded community of limited liability is more fragmented and diffuse than the community of limited liability. Expanded communities are larger areas composed of multiple communities. The boundaries of such areas usually are defined by external or government institutions. The expanded community may take in whole sections of the city such as the east side or the north side. As such, it has little real cohesion as an actual unit.

Contrived or conscious communities are areas—new or developing—in which builders, financiers, public agencies, and residents alike set out consciously to create a community image. Boundaries are clearly laid out, and the housing in the area may even be identical—e.g., all apartments or all townhouses or all public housing. The name of the area is usually given by the builder rather than emerging from the community. Conscious communities tend to be more homogeneous than other communities. Residents in the development may all be young singles, families with children, or elderly. Ethnic and racial conformity and similarity of social class are also common in both urban and suburban conscious communities. Some conscious communities are even gated.

---

[20] For information and discussion of types of communities, see Dennis E. Poplin, *Communities,* 2d ed., Macmillan, New York, 1979.

[21] See, for example, Elijah Anderson, *Streetwise, Race, Class, and Change in an Urban Community,* University of Chicago, Chicago, 1990.

[22] Gerald Suttles, *The Social Construction of Communities,* University of Chicago Press, Chicago, 1972, p. 57.

[23] Morris Janowitz, *The Community Press in an Urban Setting,* University of Chicago, Chicago, 1952; and Scott A. Greer, *The Emerging City: Myth and Reality,* Free Press, New York, 1962.

DENSITY AND CROWDING

The Chicago school saw high urban rates of density as a social problem. In fact, urban crowding and high density have long been seen as the cause of social pathology. Historically, high density (the number of people per acre, block, or other geographical unit) and crowding (the number of people per room, usually in housing) have been cited as a cause of epidemics, contagion, crime, and moral degradation.[24] The engravings of Hogarth, the novels of Dickens, and primitive health statistics all tell the same unfortunate tale—high density means disorganization and disease. As graphically expressed by Charles Dickens:

> They walked on, for some time, through the most crowded and densely inhabited part of the town; and then, striking down a narrow street more dirty and miserable than any they had yet passed through, paused to look for the house which was the object of their search. The houses on either side were high and large, but very old, and tenanted by people of the poorest class: as their neglected appearance would have sufficiently denoted, without the concurrent testimony afforded by the squalid looks of the men and women who, with folded arms and bodies half doubled, occasionally skulked along. A great many of the tenements had shopfronts; but these were fast closed, and mouldering away; only the upper rooms being inhabited. Some houses which had become insecure from age and decay, were prevented from falling into the street, by huge beams of wood reared against the walls, and firmly planted in the road; but even these crazy dens seemed to have been selected as the nightly haunts of some houseless wretches, for many of the rough boards which supplied the place of door and window, were wrenched from their positions, to afford an aperture wide enough for the passage of a human body. The kennel was stagnant and filthy. The very rats, which here and there lay putrefying in its rottenness, were hideous with famine.[25]

More recently almost every social evil—air pollution, the loss of community, the lack of response of neighbors to cries for help—has been attributed to urban density and overcrowding.[26]

Crowding Research

Experimental animal studies tend to support the view that high density and crowding produce a long list of physical and behavioral pathologies. At present we probably know more about the behavior of rats under conditions of crowding than we do about that of city dwellers. John Calhoun's now-famous article "Population Density and Social Pathology" indicates that in experiments with Norway rats, pathological states develop under conditions of crowding even when there is an abundance of food and freedom from disease and predators.[27] In Calhoun's experiment, a behavioral sink developed in which infant mortality increased, females didn't build proper nests or carry infants to term, and homosexuality and even

---

[24] See A. D. Biderman, M. Louisa, and J. Bacchus, *Historical Incidents of Extreme Overcrowding,* Bureau of Social Science Research, Washington, D.C., 1963.

[25] Excerpt from Charles Dickens, *The Adventures of Oliver Twist,* Chapman & Hall, London, 1868, pp. 42–43.

[26] See James Q. Wilson, "The Urban Unease," *The Public Interest,* **12:**25–39, 1968; James A. Swan, "Public Responses to Air Pollution," in Joachim F. Wohlwill and Daniel H. Carson, *Environment and the Social Sciences,* American Psychological Association, Washington, D.C., 1972, pp. 66–74; Robert Buckout, "Pollution and the Psychologist: A Call to Action," in Joachim F. Wohlwill and Daniel H. Carson, *Environment and the Social Sciences,* pp. 75–81; and B. Latane and J. M. Darley, *The Unresponsive Bystander: Why Doesn't He Help?* Appleton-Century-Crofts, New York, 1970.

[27] John B. Calhoun, "Population Density and Social Pathology," *Scientific American,* **206:**139–148, February, 1960.

cannibalism occurred. When the experiment was terminated, the rat population was well on the way to extinction.

Unfortunately, there is a tendency to try to transfer findings from animal studies, where they apply, to human populations, where they do not. Sometimes there is even an assumption that what holds for Norway rats automatically applies to humans. For example, one writer suggests:

> The implications of animal and human studies are clearcut. Just as the offspring of frustrated mother rats, part of whose pregnancy was spent trapped in problem boxes with no exits, carried an emotional disturbance throughout their own lives, so too many children of frustrated human mothers, trapped by urban slums, show behavioral manifestations of emotional disturbance.[28]

This analogy repeats the "commonsense" view of the effects of density and crowding.

The problem is that the commonsense view is both simplistic and inaccurate. A considerable body of sociological and psychological research on density indicates that it does *not* have any clear and definite association with human pathology.[29] Density research is a classic case: What everyone "knows to be true" is simply not being supported by the data.

What is clear is that one's social background and experience play a major role in how "high density" is defined. Upper-middle-class populations, for example, have been socialized to view crowding as a problem, and space and separation as natural and necessary. Community studies of working-class populations indicate, on the other hand, that residents of city neighborhoods often view high density as a positive sign of community vitality rather than an indication of social disorganization.[30] Contact with others is viewed positively, as a sign of belonging, rather than negatively, as a sign of crowding. Inner-city youngsters from such areas are more comfortable being with others than being alone. Gans reports how social workers in the West End of Boston were forced to abandon a summer program that gave inner-city boys a chance to spend a vacation exploring nature at Cape Cod.[31] The boys could not understand why anyone would want to visit, much less live in, such a lonely spot. They were accustomed to, and thrived on, crowded and noisy street life. The boys wanted to be where the action was, and were emotionally uncomfortable with wide vistas and open, unused space.

Similarly, much of the population of crowded and noisy Hong Kong and Singapore may want larger apartments, but they do not want to be isolated or set apart from the crowd. (While living in Singapore, I found myself craving empty, quiet spaces. By contrast, a student of mine from Singapore found it very

[28] Shirley Foster Hartley, *Population Quantity vs. Quality,* Prentice-Hall, Englewood Cliffs, N.J., 1972, p. 76.

[29] For an overview of available research, see Claude Fischer, Mark Baldassare, and Richard Ofshe, "Crowding Studies and Urban Life: A Critical Review," *Journal of the American Institute of Planners,* **41**:406–418, November, 1975; and Jonathan Freedman, *Crowding and Behavior,* Viking, New York, 1975. Also see Harvey M. Choldin and Dennis Roncek, "Density, Population Potential, and Pathology: A Block Level Analysis," *Public Data Use,* **4**:19–30, July, 1976.

[30] Herbert J. Gans, *The Urban Villagers,* Free Press, Glencoe, Ill., 1962; Gerald Suttles, *The Social Order of the Slum,* University of Chicago Press, Chicago, 1968; and Michael Young and Peter Willmott, *Family and Kinship in East London,* Penguin Books, Baltimore, 1962.

[31] Gans, *The Urban Villagers.*

Bicycle congestion reflects the high population density of Delhi, India. (Rameshwar Das/Monkmeyer.)

difficult to adjust to the nonurban University of Virginia. She found open space disorienting, and longed for high buildings, concrete, and urban noise.) In North America, some people choose a camping vacation of backpacking into the wilderness, miles from anyone, while others prefer to settle for weeks in commercial campgrounds where the density is higher than in the city. Middle-class and working-class populations may also vary in orienting themselves to a common spatial feature, such as streets. For working-class and lower-class urban groups, much daily activity takes place in the streets; streets are seen as living space, a place to congregate and gather with others in the neighborhood. Streets serve a vital social function. Upper-middle-class groups, on the other hand, are far less likely to see streets as performing a social function. In their view streets are corridors to be used to travel from place to place, and they think people should be kept off the streets, lest they interfere with rapid movement. These, however, are fairly minor differences.

The effects of interior household crowding on social relationships and mental health also are very limited.[32] Moreover, since household crowding has been sharply decreasing in recent years—with 97 percent of all housing units having less than one person per room—this should considerably lessen any causal effect housing crowding as a variable might possess.

[32] O. R. Galle and Walter R. Grove, "Crowding and Behavior in Chicago, 1940–1970," in J. R. Aiello and A. Blaum (eds.), *Residential Crowding and Design,* Plenum, New York, 1979, pp. 23–40.

Thus, contrary to the common assumption, density or crowding does not necessarily have either a negative or a positive impact on urban life. It all depends on how the level of crowding is socially defined. Urban densities, for example, have been decreasing for seventy-five years, but there has been no corresponding decrease in urban social problems. Freedman suggests that the effect of density and crowding is to "intensify the individual's typical reactions to the situation."[33] Thus, being crowded with friends may produce positive reactions, although the same degree of crowding with those one dislikes may produce negative reactions. People do not respond to density or crowding in a uniform way.

Practical Implications

For twenty-five years William H. Whyte has been examining with telephoto camera and tape recorder what makes some urban spaces "work." Why are some areas socially popular while other planned places go unused?[34] What he has discovered is that what attracts people most is other people. Rather than trying to escape crowds, people move toward areas of highest per-person density. Observing from hidden perches, researchers mapped locations and duration of conversations. Whyte discovered that most take place "right smack in the middle of the pedestrian traffic stream."[35] Moreover, people who begin conversations on the fringe drift into the traffic flow, not out of it.

A practical consequence of this is that street musicians and sidewalk vendors—those whom merchants, police, and city hall work so hard to remove—actually contribute to the social and economic vitality of a streetscape. So-called incentive zoning, which allowed developers to add extra stories to skyscrapers if they provided ground-level setbacks with parks or plazas, often resulted simply in the creation of dull zones. Sunken plazas turned out to be particularly little used.

Whyte's research led to New York City's making three important changes in its commercial zoning which has helped restore lively (and safe) street life. First, every new building must, on the street level, have retail shops (no blank walls and huge, dull lobbies). Second, there must be access to the street-level shops from the street (no turning your back on the street). Third, street-level windows must be transparent (to avoid the blank-wall-facing-the-street effect).[36] These relatively minor changes have made the newest buildings more livable than those built in the 1960s and 1970s and the streets friendlier than they were.

Finally, Whyte argues against city planners' or architects' "ideal" streetscapes. As he pronounces, "It's all in such goddam good taste! You need a touch of glitz. You need something like Trump Tower."[37] We have learned that urban sociologists can discover what makes cities livable, but sometimes the answers are counter to the sterile views that officials might see as an ideal or model cityscape.

---

[33] Freedman, *Crowding and Behavior,* p. 90.
[34] William H. Whyte, *City: Rediscovering Its Center,* Doubleday, New York, 1989.
[35] Stephen S. Hall, "Standing on Those Corners, Watching All the Folks Go By," *Smithsonian,* February, 1989, p. 123.
[36] Ibid.
[37] Ibid.

URBAN CRIME

Increases or Decreases?

It is impossible to discuss the contemporary urban environment without some discussion of crime. Crime remains perhaps the most serious problem for urban residents in general and inner-city residents in particular. People are afraid of both the increasing levels of urban violence and the increasing unpredictability of such violence. Approximately 70 people die each day as the result of a homicide, or about 25,500 deaths a year.

Official statistics don't always agree with people's perceptions. The Uniform Crime Report (UCR)—the data for which are collected by the FBI and which reports crimes known to the police—indicates, for example, that violent and property crime decreased significantly in 1994 and 1995.[38] It should also be noted that Uniform Crime Reports are far from uniform in coverage since only crimes known to the police are reported, which means that almost all homicides are reported but many burglaries and larcenies are not. Central-city residents, in particular, may feel that it is futile to fill out the reports. At best only half of actual crime is reported. For example, the Justice Department's victimization survey, which includes crimes that are never reported, indicates that during 1993 violent crimes such as assaults and robberies actually increased 5.6 percent, or three times as fast as crimes overall.[39] The public clamor for a crackdown on crime is fueled in part by fear over increasing numbers of gun murders. According to FBI figures there were 16,189 firearm homicides in 1993, which was a huge 73 percent increase over the figures for just four years earlier.[40] There are now over 200 million guns in America.

Such high rates of urban violence have not always been the case. Urban populations don't necessarily have high rates of violence. For example, during the 1940s and 1950s New York City, where the murder rate reached almost 2,000 a year in 1993, had a murder rate that fluctuated around 50 a year. In 1994 New York had more murders of cabbies than its total of all murders in the city in 1944. Today the United States rate is 17 times that of equally urban Japan, and 10 times that of France or heavily urban Germany. Cities in less-developed countries commonly have murder rates more like those of New York in the 1940s.

According to FBI statistics, nationally reported violent crimes grew from 161 per 100,000 in 1960 to 758 per 100,000 in 1992, a jump of 371 percent. An increasing concern is the relationship between guns and the drug market. The police chief of Washington, D.C., has noted that drugs constitute the biggest single source of complaints to his office, and illegal drugs are "eroding the quality of life in the City."[41] In large cities well over half of all burglaries, larcenies, and robberies are drug-related. And juveniles who have been recruited into the drug markets increasingly are heavily armed. Under such circumstances it is not surprising that in some

---

[38] Fox Butterfield, "Many Cities in U.S. Show Sharp Drop in Homicide Rate," *New York Times,* Aug. 13, 1995, p. 1.
[39] "Violent Crime Increases 5.6% Last Year, Victim Survey Finds," *Washington Post,* Oct. 31, 1994, p. A4.
[40] "93 Slaying Rate," p. A11.
[41] *Washington Post,* Nov. 15, 1984, p. C7.

cities there is a paralyzing fear and siege mentality, particularly among vulnerable groups such as the aged.

Crime and Male Youth

Crime is an activity of the young. Forty-five percent of all crimes except murder are committed by people under eighteen, and three-quarters are committed by those under twenty-five. The most likely age for being arrested is sixteen; fifteen, seventeen, and eighteen are the next most likely ages. (White-collar crimes and crimes that require training or skill such as embezzlement, fraud, and counterfeiting are most likely to be committed by older persons.) Crime is also still largely a male activity, with about 80 percent of all arrests and 90 percent of arrests for violent crimes being males. What once resulted in fistfights now leads to gunfire. Teenage homicide rates jumped 151 percent between 1985 and 1991, with the highest homicide rate among males twenty to twenty-four.[42] In spite of increasing police and penalties it is likely that crime rates will increase in the near future since there will be a 23 percent increase in the teenage population during the next decade.

Black-on-Black Crime

Blacks are more fearful of crime than are whites. According to a Gallup poll, blacks feel less secure than whites, both walking the streets and in their homes. And they have reason for their fears. Blacks, even in suburbs, are more exposed to property and especially violent crime.[43] Most urban street crime in large cities is black-on-black crime. Over 85 percent of crimes committed by blacks are against black victims. Robbery is the only largely interracial crime, with 45 percent involving a black offender (almost always a young male) and a white victim (usually a middle-aged white male). Blacks are over five times as likely to be homicide victims as are whites. Since 1989 there have been more black homicide victims than white victims. African Americans are 12 percent of the population, but they are just over half the homicide victims, and 56 percent of the offenders. Data from the National Center for Health Statistics show black-against-black homicide as of 1995 to be the leading cause of death among black men, ages sixteen to thirty-four. The rate of death by homicide for black males is six times that of white males and sixteen times that of white females.[44] One in every twenty-one young blacks is murdered. The already high homicide rates for African-American boys aged fifteen to nineteen tripled between 1985 and 1991.[45] As of 1994, black males aged fifteen to nineteen were just 1 percent of the population, but they were 14 percent of the murder victims and 19 percent of those charged with murder.

African-American males as well as having the highest victim rate also have the highest probability of being an offender. Black males account for half of those

---

[42] "Teen Homicides Increase by 154%," *Richmond Times-Dispatch*, Oct. 14, 1994, p. A20.

[43] Richard Alba, John Logan, and Paul Bellair, "Living with Crime: The Implications of Racial/Ethnic Differences in Suburban Location," *Social Forces*, **73**, 395–434, 1994.

[44] A. D. Whitman and J. Thornton, "A Nation Apart," *U.S. News & World Report*, Mar. 17, 1986, pp. 18–24.

[45] Machiko Yanagishita and F. Landis MacKellar, "Homicide in the U.S.: Who's at Risk?" *Population Today*, **23**:2, 1995.

arrested for violent crimes, just over half of those arrested for murder and nonneg-ligent manslaughter, and more than half of those arrested for forcible rape.[46] Almost two-thirds of those arrested for robbery are black males. More young black men are serving criminal sentences than are going to college. There is a clear crisis when one-third of young black males aged twenty to twenty-nine are in prison, on pro-bation, or on parole.[47] The extreme is Washington, D.C., where it is estimated that 42 percent of black men aged eighteen to thirty-five are in jail, on probation, out on bond, or being sought by the police.[48]

Urban crime doesn't just affect the poor. Jesse Jackson lives in a good neigh-borhood in Washington, D.C., but his home was burglarized in 1991, his wife saw a man murdered while she was taking out the garbage eight months later, and she witnessed a triple drug-related murder on their street in 1993. As he sadly says: "There is nothing more painful for me at this stage of my life than to walk down the street and hear footsteps and start to think about robbery and then look around and see its somebody white and feel relieved. How humiliating"[49]

Given their high victimization rate, it is not surprising that middle-class blacks traditionally have been "hard line" against street crime. During the 1980s, calls for "law and order" were often code words for racial prejudice, but today the call is coming from within the African-American community to fight black-on-black crime. Jesse Jackson has been especially strong in his statements to "Stop the Vio-lence, Save Our Children."

The problem of urban crime is not simply that rates are increasing. It is that entire inner-city neighborhoods already have much of their internal economies dominated by, and dependent on, drugs, prostitution, burglary, and robbery. Sur-veys of inner-city males indicate that they report approximately one-quarter of their income coming from criminal activities.[50] The social fabric of their urban neigh-borhoods is being stretched to the breaking point.

Blacks have low arrest rates for white-collar crime such as tax evasion, fraud, and embezzlement. This reflects occupational discrimination, which has kept blacks out of policymaking white-collar jobs. A reasonable hypothesis would be that as blacks' incomes improve and their occupational levels rise, street crime by blacks will decline and white-collar crime will increase.

Variations within the City

American crime rates show that there is more crime in larger cities, and that crime rates within urban areas generally reflect the Burgess hypothesis insofar as crime rates are highest in inner-city neighborhoods and decrease as one moves toward the periphery. Research done three-quarters of a century ago also demonstrated a high concentration of criminal activity in the central city—a phenomenon attributed to

[46] William Julius Wilson, *The Truly Disadvantaged: The Inner City, the Underclass, and Public Policy,* University of Chicago Press, Chicago, 1987.

[47] "Number of Black Offenders up Sharply, Study Says," *Washington Post,* Oct. 5, 1995.

[48] "Cracked: A City Runs Scared," *Washington Post,* June 18, 1995.

[49] "A New Civil Rights Frontier," *U.S. News & World Report,* Jan. 17, 1994, p. 38.

[50] "Whitman and Thornton, "A Nation Apart," pp. 18–24.

the "social disorganization" of such areas, as typified by high poverty and welfare rates, low levels of education, broken homes, and other social ills.[51] Since that time, the concept of social disorganization has largely been superseded by other explanations, but the pattern of decreasing crime rates as one moves toward the urban periphery has been confirmed. White-collar crime, on the other hand, is more concentrated in suburban populations.

Interestingly, the pattern of higher crime rates in central areas has held, while the occupants, and even the physical characteristics, of the area have changed completely. This consistency does not mean that these neighborhoods or their locations somehow create crime. Rather, it suggests that the inhabitants of these areas—whether European immigrants at the turn of the century, blacks after World War II, or Mexicans and other Latinos today—have been subject to the same pressures. An excellent contemporary study of gangs shows that they still occupy territorial boundaries and provide an organizational framework for their members.[52]

As Chapter 7, City Life-Styles, pointed out, not all central-city neighborhoods have gone through the cycle of invasion and reinvasion by new groups—a process that can hinder the development of social control by family, peers, and neighbors. Inner-city areas that have not been successively invaded by disadvantaged newcomers are often among the most stable areas in the city.

Suburban Crime

One of the more common explanations for suburban growth is urban crime. The assumption is that suburbs are relatively crime-free, but this assumption is no longer entirely true. As newspaper stories document, crime rates in the suburbs are increasing. Still suburban crime rates are about 28 percent of those of the nation's fifty-two largest cities.[53] Violent urban crime jumped 33 percent during the 1980s, while the suburban increase was 14 percent.

Suburban crime tends to be less violent than city crime. Someone living in the city is more likely to be murdered and more likely to be robbed than a suburban resident. The most frequently reported single crime in suburbs is bicycle theft—a problem if it's your expensive trail bike that is stolen, but not equivalent to being mugged or shot.

Moreover, within the suburbs, crime is not randomly distributed, but rather concentrated in those low-income suburbs whose character most closely approximates the central city. Older inner-ring suburbs generally have higher rates than outlying areas. Around Chicago ten suburbs accounting for 15 percent of the suburban population account for 40 percent of the murder and a majority of the armed robberies, assaults, and rapes. These suburbs have burglary rates three times as high as the richest ten suburbs of Chicago, indicating that "them that hasn't gets taken." High-crime suburbs tend to have low-income or minority residents.

[51] Clifford R. Shaw and Henry D. McKay, *Juvenile Delinquency in Urban Areas,* University of Chicago Press, Chicago, 1942.
[52] Martin Sanchez Jankowski, *Islands in the Street: Gangs and American Urban Society,* University of California Press, Berkeley, 1991.
[53] Federal Bureau of Investigation, *Uniform Crime Statistics,* Washington, D.C., 1990.

Higher crime rates are also found in suburbs with facilities that attract crime such as large shopping centers and business parks. Automobile theft is the most common crime at malls, but robbery and even rape also occur. It is hard to imagine a better location for an auto thief to operate than a large parking lot.

Affluent suburbs keep crime rates down by restricting certain economic activities and populations (fewer minority, poor, and unemployed). They thus, in effect, deflect crime to lower-status areas. Upper-income residential areas are particularly able to control violent crime by restricting the influx of outsiders.[54] As noted before, some communities are even gated.

HOMELESSNESS IN THE CITY

Each year as colder weather approaches, the media feature stories on the most disadvantaged of all urban populations, the homeless. Estimates of the number of homeless range from 250,000 to 2.2 million.[55] There have even been extreme estimates of as high as 18 million homeless just after the turn of the century.[56] What is generally agreed upon is that today's shelters do not have enough beds to accommodate more than a quarter of those in need and that life on the street can be truly life threatening.

Data about the homeless are subject to dispute, basically for two reasons. First, the homeless are a transient demographic population on which data are both difficult to obtain and often unreliable. Second, homelessness is a highly politicized issue. For example, the Washington-based Community for Creative Non-Violence, an advocacy group for the homeless, has estimated that there are at least 2 million homeless people nationwide. This figure is widely quoted in the media but is based on estimates by advocates, not on research. Another widely quoted, and far lower, set of figures is the Department of Housing and Urban Development 1984 estimates that the homeless at that date numbered only 250,000 to 350,000 persons. These figures initially came under intense criticism as being more political than empirically based. However, later studies have tended to give them more credence as a rough benchmark as of that date. On the other hand, a 1994 Clinton Administration report on homelessness said the problem was "far larger than commonly thought," and said as many as 7 million Americans were homeless for some period in the late 1980s.[57] Looking at a large number of studies, Jencks estimates the number of homeless at approximately 400,000.[58] Rossi, in perhaps the best empirically grounded study, estimates the number of homeless on a given night at roughly half a million persons.[59] Thus most scholars place the number of homeless in the

[54] John M. Stahura and John J. Sloane III, "Urban Stratification of Places, Routine Activities and Suburban Crime Rates," *Social Forces,* **66**(4):1102–1118, 1988.

[55] Jon Erickson and Charles Wilhelm (eds.), *Housing the Homeless,* Center for Urban Policy Research, Rutgers, New Brunswick, N.J., 1986, p. xix.

[56] "18 Million Homeless Seen by 2003," *Washington Post,* June 3, 1987, p. A8.

[57] Jason DeParle, "Draft Administration Report Sees Homelessness as a Vast Problem," *New York Times,* Feb. 17, 1994, p. A1.

[58] Christopher Jencks, *The Homeless,* Harvard University Press, Cambridge, Mass., 1994, p. 16.

[59] Peter H. Rossi, *Down and Out in America: The Origins of Homelessness,* University of Chicago, 1989. James D. Wright, *Address Unknown: The Homeless in America,* Aidine de Gruyter, Hawthorne, N.Y., 1989.

300,000 to 500,000 range.[60] Another 4 to 7 million are so poor they could be pushed into the ranks of the homeless by an economic downturn.

Twenty-five years ago, the homeless population was heavily made up of older, possibly alcoholic, skid row men with acute personal problems.[61] In the 1970s, the stereotype of the skid row wino was supplanted by that of the bag lady who had been deinstitutionalized from a psychiatric hospital and left to pick through refuse bins.[62]

Now a more complete picture is emerging. According to a study by the United States Conference of Mayors, over a quarter (28 percent) of the homeless consist of parents with children, 12 percent are single women, and 60 percent are single men.[63] Families on the street are predominately headed by black females, while most of the males on the street are white. Various studies commonly report roughly one-third of the homeless as being mentally ill. Involuntary commitment of the mentally ill has been virtually abolished, but no alternative housing for those needing assistance has been provided. The average age of a homeless man living on the street is approximately forty, and four out of ten street people admit to having spent time in jail. Substance abuse is also admitted to by roughly half of the street people. In both cases, actual figures are assumed to be substantially higher.

What the above picture indicates is a high level of social disabilities among the homeless. More than four out of five homeless report poor health, have been in a mental hospital or detoxification unit, have been convicted by the courts, or receive clinically high scores on the psychotic-thinking scale.[64] Social isolation is also endemic among the homeless, with six in ten never having married and most of the remainder being separated or divorced. Strained or minimal relations with family and relatives are the usual pattern.

Why is homelessness increasing? Most researchers who specialize in homeless issues point first to the decrease in available affordable housing. Additionally the homeless suffer from extreme poverty and from a multitude of personal and sometimes mental problems. In the past many of the economically marginal who were not in family units lived in single-room-occupancy (SRO) residential hotels. However, the number of SRO units has decreased over the last two decades by 80 percent or more. Moreover, at the same time that private SRO units were disappearing, federal funding for low-cost housing was being severely decreased. During the Reagan years (1980–1988), federally subsidized programs were cut by 70 percent.[65]

---

[60] For an example of the diversity of local area findings, see Jamshid A. Momenti (ed.), *Homelessness in the United States,* Vol. I: *State Surveys,* Greenwood Press, New York, 1989. See particularly the Introduction by Howard M. Bahr, pp. vi–xxv, and Chap. 11, "Homelessness in Tennessee," by Barrett A. Lee, pp. 181–203.

[61] Donald J. Bogue, *Skid Row in American Cities,* University of Chicago, Community and Family Study Center, Chicago, 1963; Carl I. Cohen and Jay Sokolovsky, *Old Men of the Bowery: Strategies for Survival among the Homeless,* Guilford Press, New York, 1989.

[62] For an examination of deinstitutionalization and its consequences, see Michael J. Dear and Jennifer R. Wolch, *Landscapes of Despair: From Deinstitutionalization to Homelessness,* Polity Press, Oxford, 1987.

[63] "Counting the Uncountable Homeless," *Population Today* vol. 14, no. 10, October, 1986, p. 8.

[64] Peter H. Rossi and James D. Wright, "The Urban Homeless: A Portrait of Urban Dislocation," *The Annals,* **501**:137, January, 1989.

[65] Some researchers deny that the severe housing subsidy cutbacks had any substantial impact on the number of homeless. See, for example, Christopher Jencks, *The Homeless.*

As an experiment, fiberglass domes have replaced shacks and shanties next to Los Angeles Harbor Freeway. The hope is that the more stable temporary homes will help homeless people get their lives in order. (Michael Tweed/NYT Pictures.)

The growing number of very low income persons is also an important contributing factor. Economics, however, is only one factor since homelessness increased throughout the 1980s and 1990s during periods of both economic recession and economic growth. Of special concern is the number of females on the street who are users of crack cocaine and IV drugs. The combination of IV drug use and unsafe sex makes AIDS infection a major health concern, since three-quarters of female AIDS infection comes from IV drug usage. Sexual AIDs infection is also a major problem since for street women using drugs, prostitution is the major source of money. Child abuse or child abandonment is a serious and growing problem in this population.

Men and women who end up on the streets also typically have multiple personal problems. Most grew up in problem families or in foster care. Many have serious learning and physical health problems. Some are mentally ill. Few have had success with marriage or other personal relationships.[66] Nonetheless some homeless not only have survived on the street, but have created their own alternative social communities.[67]

Public attitudes toward, and tolerance of, homeless, and especially of homeless panhandlers, considerably hardened during the 1990s. Increasingly, the homeless are viewed by most citizens not with pity but as a threat to public order. Even homeless

[66] Ibid.
[67] David Wagner, *Checkerboard Square: Culture and Resistance in a Homeless Community,* Westview Press, Boulder, Colo., 1993.

shelters have had to develop strict policies to deal with major behavior problems of drug usage and fighting in shelters. Crack use is a particular problem for shelters since it makes users aggressive and violent. Those who violate shelter policies are expelled from the shelters. Tough antivagrancy measures also have been taken in some of the previously most tolerant cities. New York has gotten tough with aggressive subway panhandlers, once-liberal Seattle has made it illegal to sit on downtown public sidewalks during business hours, and tolerant San Francisco now arrests homeless people sleeping on public property or urinating in public.[68]

These policies are being implemented by cities not out of mean-spiritedness, but as a means by which communities can reclaim their public spaces such as parks, subways, and plazas. Such spaces often had been made unusable for ordinary citizens by their being taken over by sometimes aggressive and occasionally dangerous panhandlers. In New York, as a means of taking back public spaces, private-public business improvement districts (BIDs) supplement city cleaning and policing efforts.[69]

It is becoming clearer that while homelessness is primarily due to absence of SRO housing, it also frequently involves a whole series of pathologies such as alcoholism, drug addiction, and mental illness. Thus, there has developed a new realism about the possibility of quick-fix answers. To the extent that most homelessness is the result of a web of problems, there may not be "a solution" to homelessness any more than there is "a cause." The primary need is for more low-cost SRO housing, but in addition there is a need for education, job training, medical care, substance-abuse treatment, and counseling. There is little chance of any such comprehensive programs being developed in today's political and social climate. Thus homelessness will remain an American disgrace.

[68] Melinda Henneberger, "Where the Beggars Meet the Begged," *New York Times,* Jan. 16, 1994, p. 6E.
[69] Fred Siegel, "Reclaiming Our Public Spaces," *City Journal,* Spring, 1992, pp. 35–45.

9

CHANGING
SUBURBANIZATION
PATTERNS

The country life is to be preferred, for there we see the works of God, but in the cities little else but the works of men.

William Penn, *Reflections and Maxims*

INTRODUCTION

For over a quarter of a century America has been a nation of suburbanites rather than one of city dwellers.[1] Suburbs have gone from being the fringe from which commuters go to the city to being the modal areas where people work, live, shop, and recreate. The suburban revolution has changed suburbs from being residential places on the periphery to being the economic and commercial centers of a new metropolitan form. The 1990 census confirms that most of us live in the suburbs, with there now being half again as many suburbanites as city dwellers (115 million in suburbs, 78 million in cities, and 56 million in smaller nonmetropolitan places). Perhaps more significant, suburbanites now constitute over half the nation's voters. Moreover, if the polls are to be believed, substantial numbers of those still living in large cities would prefer not to be. Polls indicate that 60 percent of those living in New York, half (48 percent) of those in Los Angeles, and 43 percent of those in Boston would move out of the city if they could.[2]

THE NEW SUBURBAN DOMINANCE

That the suburban shopping mall has replaced downtown as a shopping site is commonly recognized. What is less known is that factory employment now also has a noncenter zip code, with twice as many manufacturing jobs being located in suburbs as in the central city. The city factory has been supplanted by the suburban industrial park.

White-collar office jobs also have suburbanized. Outer Dallas has three times the office space of the central business district. Downtown Atlanta has a skyline of new office buildings, but suburban Atlanta has twice the office space. Even in the New York metropolitan area, northern New Jersey has more office space than does Manhattan. The movement of Sears provides an example of the changes taking place. As noted earlier, during the 1970s and 1980s Sears headquarters were in the Chicago's Sears Tower, the world's tallest building at 110 stories. In 1992 Sears moved its 5,000 merchandise-group employees out to suburban Hoffman Estates, 35 miles to the northwest beyond O'Hare Airport. The new location, named Prairie Stone, occupies a former soybean field. It boasts more than 200 acres of reconstructed prairie and wetlands, and no building is more than six stories high. Similarly J. C. Penney has recently moved its headquarters from Manhattan to an office development named Legacy Park in Plano, Texas, a growing outlying suburb north of Dallas.

Such out-movement of offices, manufacturing, and shopping is turning the Burgess zonal thesis inside out, and has created a multinucleated pattern of outer suburban centers. In a generation, suburbs have been transformed from being outlying residential areas to the nation's new economic and commercial cores. The suburbs are no longer "sub." Suburbs increasingly find themselves sandwiched between demographically and economically stressed central cities and economically

---

[1] For greater detail on suburban change, see J. John Palen, *The Suburbs,* McGraw-Hill, New York, 1995. Some of the material in this chapter is derived from that work.

[2] William Schneider, "The Suburban Century Begins," *Atlantic Monthly,* July, 1992, p. 33.

marginal rural areas. While it may twist the language a bit, the suburbs are now the demographic and economic centers.

How did this major change occur? Writing at the end of the nineteenth century, Adna Weber concluded that the most hopeful sign in American urbanization was the "tendency . . . toward the development of suburban towns," for "such a new distribution of population combines at once the open air and spaciousness of the country with the sanitary improvements, comforts, and associated life of the city,"[3] This image of the suburb as a green or pleasant oasis with its single-family homes, neighbors, children, dogs, and trail bikes—all within commuting range of the city—is one that still has force. Suburbs have been called "bourgeois utopias."[4] Intellectuals may scorn suburbia, but scorned or not, suburbs have transformed the landscape demographically, organizationally, and in life-style.

We have been a nation of suburbanites since 1970 when the census showed that for the first time suburban areas of Metropolitan Statistical Areas exceeded their central cities in population size and growth rate. Suburbs actually have been growing faster than central cities all century.[5] (Remember, though, that "suburban" as defined by the Bureau of the Census means that territory inside the MSA which is outside the central city. Some of this area and population might not ordinarily be considered suburban.) Virtually the entire metropolitan area increase of 15.7 million between 1970 and 1990 occurred in suburbs.[6] Central-city population increase was less than 100,000 for all the nation's central cities put together. Population growth in metropolitan areas is now all but synonymous with suburban growth. For the last fifty years virtually *all* population growth in metropolitan areas has occurred in the suburban rings.

The data document the recency and magnitude of the exodus to the suburbs. In 1920 only 15 percent of all Americans were suburbanites. The percentage was only 19 percent by 1930 and only 20 percent by 1940. The percentage increased to 24 in 1950, and then shot up to 33 percent in 1960, 37 percent in 1970, 40 percent in 1980, and half by the late 1990s.

The following sections begin by discussing the emergence of suburbs, next discuss their organizational and demographic aspects, then spend some pages on the question of suburbia as a way of life, and, finally, discuss the increasing role of minorities in suburbs.

EMERGENCE OF SUBURBS

The Nineteenth Century

As was noted in Chapter 3, The Rise of Urban America, the American city of the nineteenth century was compact, had high density, and could rather quickly be

---

[3] Adna Ferrin Weber, *The Growth of Cities in the Nineteenth Century,* Macmillan, New York, 1899, pp. 458–459.

[4] Robert Fishman, *Bourgeois Utopias: The Rise and Fall of Suburbia,* Basic Books, New York, 1987.

[5] John D. Kasarda and George Redfearn, "Differential Patterns of Urban and Suburban Growth in the United States," *Journal of Urban History,* **2:**43–66, November, 1975.

[6] U.S. Bureau of the Census, "Patterns of Metropolitan Area and County Population Growth," *Current Population Reports,* series P-25, no. 976, Washington, D.C., Sept. 24, 1989.

walked. Serious suburbanization was not possible prior to the transportation advances of the latter nineteenth century that permitted population dispersal. The first to move out were the wealthy, who built "suburban" communities out along the railroad lines from the city.[7] Initially, some of the homes were weekend villas, but it was not long before women and children lived away from the city and businessmen commuted daily by train. These expensive railroad commuter suburbs were to provide an idealized rural refuge from the clamor of the city.[8] As advertised by a promotional piece of a century ago:

> The controversy which is sometimes brought, as to which offers the greater advantage, the country or the city, finds a happy answer in the suburban idea which says, both—the combination of the two—the city brought to the country. The city has its advantages and conveniences, the country has its charm and health; the union of the two (a modern result of the railway), gives to man all he could ask in this respect. The great cities that are building now, all have their suburban windows at which nature may be seen in her main expressions—and these spots attract to them cultured people, with their elaborate and costly adornments.[9]

As this quotation suggests, the first suburbs were generally upper-class villages of substantial country homes. The quotation also notes the importance of the railroad. In the absence of a reliable transportation technology, one could venture no farther from the railway station than one could conveniently walk, or at least be taken by one's driver. Suburbs were thus strung out along the rail lines like beads on a string. Chestnut Hill on Philadelphia's Main Line was an early example of this pattern. Chicago's North Shore was another. Only those who could afford both the time and money could combine an urban occupation with a rural residence. This would lead to increasing social-class polarization between city and suburb.

Electric Streetcar Era: 1890–1920

As discussed in Chapter 3, The Rise of Urban America, the rapid adoption of the electric streetcar during the 1890s allowed the middle class to move out to the new suburban developments springing up along the streetcar corridors. Boston, for example, as of 1850 was a walking city extending out a maximum of 2.5 miles from city hall. The coming of the electric streetcar at the close of the last century changed the spatial configuration of Boston and other American urban areas from that of a compact city to that of a star-shaped urban area. The compact American walking city of the mid-nineteenth century was replaced by 1900 by a streetcar city in which one could live as far as 12 miles from the central business district. Moreover, one could ride the entire line for a 5-cent fare. Using the streetcars, middle-class people could separate where they worked from where they lived, just like the wealthy

---

[7] For an excellent history of American suburbanization, see Kenneth T. Jackson, *Crabgrass Frontier: The Suburbanization of the United States,* Oxford, New York, 1985. The book is strongest in its descriptions of suburbanization before 1950.

[8] In preindustrial cities such as the American cities prior to the Civil War, respectable people lived downtown. The peripheries of urban centers were disreputable shantytowns for the lower classes and those on the margins of society. Until the nineteenth century, in the terms of the *Oxford English Dictionary,* a suburb was "a place of inferior, debased, and especially licentious habits of life." In Tudor London, houses of prostitution moved to the outskirts, and so a whore was named a "suburb sinner," and it was an insult to call a person a "suburbanite." See Fishman, *Bourgeois Utopias,* pp. 6–7.

[9] "North Chicago: Its Advantages, Resources, and Probable Future," reprinted in Charles N. Glaab, *The American City,* Dorsey, Homewood, Ill., 1963, pp. 233–234.

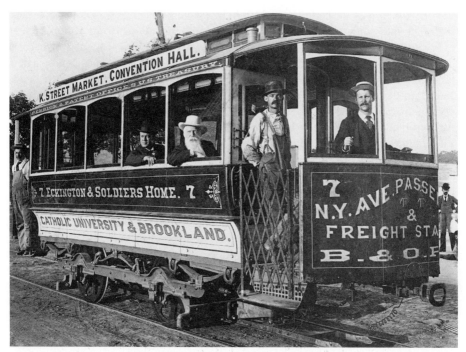

This early streetcar in Washington, D.C, (ca. 1895) used a skate at the front of the car to make contact with a surface power system. (Library of Congress.)

had been able to do for decades using the railroads. Development, both residential and commercial, occurred along the fingers of the electric streetcar tracks, while the interstices remained empty and undeveloped. The influence of early street railways on Dorchester, Roxbury, and West Roxbury as the first streetcar suburbs of Boston has been detailed by Sam Bass Warner.[10]

Annexation

New suburban housing developments on the edges of the cities, such as Hyde Park and Kenwood in southside Chicago, began as separate legal areas but were later annexed to the central city. Before the twentieth century, areas on the periphery of central cities often fought to get into the central city rather than stay out of it. Suburbs sought to be annexed by the city in order to benefit from its superior fire protection, schools, and roads; gain access to its water supply; and pay its lower taxes. Annexation was the major means of urban growth during the last part of the nineteenth century.[11] For example, in 1889 Chicago added some 133 square miles to its south side.

---

[10] Sam B. Warner, Jr., *Streetcar Suburbs,* Harvard and M.I.T. Presses, Cambridge, Mass., 1962.
[11] Peter O. Muller, *Contemporary Suburban America,* Prentice-Hall, Englewood Cliffs, N.J., 1981, p. 36.

By the turn of the century the pattern had generally reversed: Suburbs increasingly actively sought "home rule" and opposed annexation. Home rule was seen as a way of remaining free of the corruption, graft, and political bosses of the central city. Suburban autonomy meant WASPs kept control over land use and particularly taxes. Suburbanites also could exclude the immigrant Irish, Italian, Polish, and Jewish of the central cities from their suburban schools. In the twenty-five metropolitan districts defined by the census of 1910, the pattern for the future was emerging. A full quarter of the metropolitan population already lived outside the core city. The fragmentation of governmental units within the metropolitan area thus became part of the American system. Also set by the time of World War I was the pattern of ethnic working-class populations residing in the central city near employing industries, while the more affluent commuted. To move out was to move up.

The distinction between city and suburbs is, of course, basically legal rather than sociological. While local municipal boundaries are significant in many ways—including financing, taxing, and provision of public services and schools—other social, organizational, ecological, and demographic criteria could be used, such as population density, the proportion of single-family dwellings, and distance from the center of the city. However, none of these alternative schemes have gained anywhere near the acceptance of the traditional city-suburb division. The city line is commonly viewed as a social, economic, and racial boundary.

Impact of the Automobile: 1920–1950

The widespread adoption of the automobile greatly accelerated the pattern of suburbanization. Car registrations, which had been 2.5 million in 1915, took a jump to 9 million in 1920 and then skyrocketed to 26.5 million in 1930. Registration is over 150 million today. The car was no longer a plaything of the rich. Henry Ford's assembly lines were doing more than producing cars; they were bringing a revolution that was changing the face of the nation. Ford had produced 16 million Model T's by the time production switched to the Model A in 1927. At that time one of every two vehicles on the road was a Ford. Automobile usage meant that previously inaccessible land was open for suburban development. No longer was it necessary to be located along a railroad or streetcar line; commuters who were willing to pay the costs in money and time could drive their own cars to work and live where they pleased. The result was a middle-class suburban housing boom.

Ironically, the automobile was initially praised as solving the serious pollution problem caused by horses. Each horse produced an average of 26 pounds of manure and several gallons of urine a day. In New York at the beginning of the twentieth century, this meant 2.5 million pounds of horse manure and 60,000 gallons of urine each day. The manure littered the streets and provided a breeding ground for disease-carrying flies. Some 41 horses a day also died in the street. Thus, the automobile was viewed as a far less-polluting form of transportation.

Suburbs built during the 1920s were sharply distinguished according to income, occupation, religion, and ethnicity. Zoning laws, which had come to be widely used following the pioneering New York City Zoning Resolution of 1916, were often used by the developing suburbs to exclude inexpensive homes on small lots. Certainly the suburban homes of this era were well built.

Popular upper-middle-class and affluent suburbs of this era—the Grosse Pointes, Shaker Heights, and Winnetkas—established an image of suburbs as places of substantial single-family houses surrounded by lawns free of crabgrass, populated mainly by white Anglo-Saxon Protestants of upper-middle-class income and educational levels. Voting Republican was frequently included in this image.

Pre–World War II suburbs had the advantage of appealing to the long-standing antiurbanism of Americans—suburbs were supposedly closer to nature and thus better places to live, while at the same time close enough to the city to have all the advantages of the urban life that the suburbanite didn't really want to abandon. Many suburban houses built during this period reflect the romanticism of their owners. Styles were widely eclectic; houses half-timbered in the grand English Tudor style were built next to pillared Georgian colonial houses and Spanish-Moorish villas. To their owners, these homes were far more than mere housing; they represented the romantic idealization of an earlier nonurban era. "A man's home was his castle," where he could live, if not as a lord, at least as a latter-day country gentleman—and all without being isolated from the advantages of twentieth-century city life such as electricity, indoor plumbing, and central heating. Actually most of the suburban homes built during the 1920s were not grand estates but rather more utilitarian and moderately priced bungalows. Such homes were small but efficiently laid out and could be managed without servants. Bungalow homes suggested not wealth but solid middle-class comfort.

To real estate developers, the adoption of automobiles was a boon, for it meant that unbuilt land lying between the rail and streetcar axes was now open for residential development. The ideal was that every family should have a single-family home (and mortgage). The mostly middle- and upper-middle-class character of this development meant that American cities were assuming a spatial configuration in which movement out was increasingly being associated with movement up. By the 1920s the social distinction between cities and suburbs was set.[12]

Mass Suburbanization: 1950–1990s

The pent-up demand for housing that had been frustrated first by the depression of the 1930s and then by World War II burst in a suburban flow after World War II— a momentum that has carried to the present day. Following the war, the exodus of whites from the city included not only the rich and well-to-do but also large numbers of middle-class families and even blue-collar families. Across the country, once largely rural areas such as Los Angeles County saw massive conversion of rural tracts and orchards to suburban subdivisions. New families flowed to the suburbs seeking detached single-family houses in homogeneous residential areas.

This was made possible by liberalized lending policies of the Federal Housing Authority (FHA) and the new Veterans Administration (VA) loans. Often no down payment was required for purchasing a new home in a suburban subdivision. The

---

[12] The existence of another type of prewar suburb—the industrial suburb—was conveniently overlooked.

The Rancher in Levittown

$59 A MONTH
No Down Payment for Veterans!

▶ The famous Rancher of Levittown is now being built in two more sections of Levittown. When these are sold there will be no more Ranchers; we haven't any more room for them.

▶ It's a beauty of a house that's priced unbelievably low at $8990. Carrying charges are only $59 monthly, and veterans need absolutely no down payment. Non-veterans need only a total of $450 down. Can you think of anything much easier than that?

▶ The house at $8990 comes with two bedrooms, but you can have a third bedroom for only $250 more. If you're a veteran you still don't need any money down, and a non-veteran needs only $100 more. We think that's a bargain, don't you?

▶ Of course, you're not buying just a house. You own the ground—60 x 100—beautifully landscaped. You have ac- cess to the community-owned swimming pools, recreational areas, etc.

▶ Your house itself is charming, cheerful, and convenient. Such things as a four-foot medicine chest completely mirrored, picture windows from floor to ceiling, an outside garden storage room, a Bendix washer, an oil-fired radiant heating system, complete rock-wool insulation—all add to your comfort and enjoyment.

▶ Get your application in as soon as possible. Occupancy may be any time from January thru May. You pick the month. You'll need a good-faith deposit of $100, but you'll get it back at settlement if you're a veteran; credited against your down payment if you're a non-veteran.

▶ O, yes, we almost forgot! Total settlement charges are just $10! See you soon, folks!

Furnished Exhibit Homes open every day until 9 P. M.

TO LEVITTOWN

By car from Philadelphia: Drive out Roosevelt Boulevard continuing on Route 1 for about 5 miles. Turn right at Levittown sign to Route 13. Turn left on Route 13 about 4 miles to the Exhibit Center.

By bus from Philadelphia: Take Levittown Express Bus at Bridge Street station or Elevated direct to Exhibit Center.

By car from Camden: Drive out Route 130—Burlington Pike—to Burlington. Turn left and cross bridge to Bristol. Turn right on Route 13 four miles to Exhibit Center.

By car from Trenton: Cross the bridge into Pennsylvania, turn left to Route 13—Bristol Pike—Continue on Route 13 four miles past Morrisville.

Levitt and Sons
INCORPORATED

U.S. ROUTE 13 • LEVITTOWN, PA. • Telephone WINDSOR 6-1100

Philadelphia Inquirer—November 14, 1954   Camden Courier-Post—November 12, 1954
Philadelphia Bulletin—November 12, 1954   Trenton Times—November 12, 1954

Note the no down payment for veterans, $10 closing costs, and low monthly payments touted in this 1954 advertisement for suburban Levittown outside Philadelphia. (Courtesy of Levitt Homes.)

consequence, as is discussed later in this chapter, was a de facto national housing policy of subsidizing movement to suburbia. (More recently, higher interest rates, and the relative cutback of federal housing programs such as VA loans, have excluded many lower-middle-income wage earners from purchasing a house. See Chapter 13, Housing Policies and Change.)

As noted in Chapter 6, Metropolitan and Edge-City Growth, suburbanizing families were rapidly followed by retailers who discovered that retail shopping centers were more lucrative in suburban locations than in the declining central business districts. Industry was similarly leapfrogging to the suburbs in order to benefit from newer plants, increased space, lower taxes, and access to freeways.

The rapidity with which farmers' fields were converted to single-family housing developments is well known. Using mass production techniques, builders of tract developments of the Levittown type transformed huge areas of rural land into instant suburbia. Homes in the original Levittown on Long Island, New York, cost $6,900 in 1948, which even then was a real bargain. Levitt adopted a version of assembly-line type techniques to mass-produce some 17,500 houses. On the West Coast, Lakewood Village, south of Los Angeles, housed over 100,000 persons in 16 square miles. Most developments were, of course, far smaller.

The aesthetic vapidness of many of these tracts of "little boxes" has been justly condemned. On the other hand, it should be kept in mind that the city neighborhoods from which many middle-class and lower-middle-class people migrated were far from being architectural gems and that look-alike uniformity was not a suburban invention. For most families, a move to a suburban subdivision meant a move to a better house.

The titles of many suburban subdevelopments built after World War II—Rolling Meadows, Apple Orchard Valley, Oak Forest Estates—are really epitaphs for what was destroyed by the housing developments that carry on the names. I once lived for two years in a suburban apartment complex of several hundred units named Seven Oaks Farm. The farm had been plowed under by the housing project, and there were only three oaks—mere saplings hardly 3 feet tall. Country names are used to suggest an openness and rural nature which—if they ever existed—vanish as soon as the subdivision is built. But, of course, suburban developments called Congested Acres Estates or Flood Plains Hollow, while perhaps more accurately named, wouldn't have the same sales appeal.

CAUSES OF SUBURBANIZATION

The "cause" of expansion of the suburbs is frequently equated in the popular press with the decline of cities. Elements in this decline are claimed to be the deterioration of central-city services, poorer-quality schools, higher crime rates, and, of course, the influx of minorities, especially blacks, into city neighborhoods. Whatever the force of such factors today—and they tend to be overrated—it is clear that they are inadequate to explain the massive suburbanization that occurred before the 1960s, when these explanations first became fashionable. This is not to say that urban decay, poor schools, race, and crime aren't important current reasons for suburbanizing. However, "commonsense" explanations such as "white flight" had little impact on the massive postwar suburbanization prior to the late 1960s. The fact is that the cities were doing reasonably well in terms of taxes, schooling, and crime during the 1940s, 1950s, and much of the 1960s. For example, today we associate cities with high crime rates, but in New York City in 1942 there were only 44 murders in the entire city including gangland hits and family fights. White flight also was not a factor because virtually all city housing was racially segregated. Prior to the Fair Housing Act of 1968 housing was segregated by law in the south, and equally rigidly by custom in the north. Since whites already lived in segregated all-white neighborhoods, the idea of white flight from minorities made no sense prior to open housing. Blacks and whites were in separate housing pools, and publicly sanctioned racial segregation kept blacks within specific racially segregated neighborhoods. This postwar suburban growth represents more a movement *toward* values associated with suburbanization—privacy, space, cleanliness, and other amenities—than a movement fleeing from perceived central-urban ills.[13]

Why then the postwar exodus? Six factors largely account for the postwar suburban boom. First, in the eastern and northern sections of the country, almost all of the land within the legal boundaries of the city had already been developed by the 1950s. This is both the most obvious and the most overlooked factor in most explanations. Without annexation, additional growth of the urban area would, by definition, *have* to be suburban growth. The depression years of the 1930s saw little building, and during the 1940s there was a war. Thus by the 1950s there was a tremendous pent-up demand for new metropolitan housing, and most of the available open land was, by definition, suburban.

Second, and most important, government policies—whether by intent or not—acted to directly subsidize suburban growth. New VA loan guarantees made mortgage loans available to veterans at rates below those for conventional mortgages. A similar FHA program which made loans to nonveterans had made some 11 million new home loans by 1972. (FHA loans are discussed in Chapter 13, Housing Policies and Change.) Both programs required that communities be "homogeneous areas," thus reinforcing racial segregation. VA loans could be obtained with no money down and a twenty-five-year repayment schedule. Prior to this time, mortgages commonly required 50 percent down and could only be obtained for five years with a balloon payment at the end. However, with the government guaranteeing the loans, banks suddenly were competing to make loans to middle-class and lower-middle-class families that they otherwise would have ignored. As a consequence, young families flocked to the suburbs. Moreover, getting a loan was easy to do; developers such as the Levitt brothers streamlined the whole process so all the paperwork could be completed during a Sunday drive to see the development.

Third, beginning in the 1950s the federal government further subsidized outmovement by financing the construction of a system of metropolitan expressways. The resulting national interstate freeway system has been described by a secretary of commerce as "the greatest public works program in the history of the world."[14]

---

[13] Amos H. Hawley and Basil Zimmer, *The Metropolitan Community: Its People and Government,* Sage, Beverly Hills, Calif., 1970, pp. 31–33.

[14] Mark Reutter, "The Lost Promise of the American Railroad," *Wilson Quarterly,* Winter, 1994, p. 28.

Without the publicly funded freeways, many of the new suburban developments would have been impossible to reach.

Fourth, overall suburban costs were initially lower than costs in central cities. To buy older homes in the city required larger down payments. To new families just becoming economically established, this was a major consideration. They went to the suburbs not because they thought it would enhance "togetherness" or because they wanted to escape the city, but because new houses in suburban subdevelopments were frequently cheaper than housing in the city. In an era in which closing costs commonly run thousands of dollars, it is useful to note that the *total* 1954 closing cost for a Levitt-built home was $10. Of course, most suburban developers did not include "extras" such as sewers, sidewalks, street lighting, parks, and, of course, schools. Thus, in the early years at least, taxes in the suburbs were generally lower than in the central city. Therefore, the initial front-end costs of housing were frequently lower and easier to finance in the newer "package" suburbs than in the central city.

Fifth, suburbanization was "caused" by demographic changes. Prosperity and the return of veterans created a "marriage boom" that was quickly followed by a "baby boom." In the decade after the war, some 10 million new households were created. Housing in cities was simply not adequate to absorb large numbers of additional families and children. New city housing had not been built since before the war, existing housing was badly overcrowded, and landlords were not inclined to be tolerant of young children. Thus, young couples with children were, to a degree, forced toward the suburbs, since they were not welcome as renters in city apartments and could not afford to purchase city houses. The suburban baby-boom children (born between 1947 and 1964, the baby-boom years) created a need for new housing—a need that suburban developers delighted to fill.

Finally, survey data show decisively that most Americans prefer the type of newer single-family house on its own lot that is most commonly found in the suburbs. Even those who deplore suburban sprawl as a result of decisions made by powerful capitalists acknowledge that people want suburban single-family homes.[15] Planners and architects may feel that such housing defiles the landscape, but despite such views, the public overwhelmingly prefers suburban sprawl to high-rise luxury apartments or even townhouses. This is true even of those without children. Given a choice, North Americans would rather live in single-family housing outside the city. Most families residing in apartment buildings view their tenancy as a temporary step before moving to a single-family house.[16] If a suburban single-family home is too expensive, a suburban townhouse or even a garden apartment complex may substitute.

Among other things, this means that people are getting pretty much what they want in housing design. Suburban subdevelopments succeed while urban developments seek tenants, because even when alternatives are open, most people prefer suburban locations. The fact that many professional urbanologists and architects

[15] Joe R. Feagan and Robert Parker, *Building American Cities,* Prentice-Hall, Englewood Cliffs, N.J., 1990, p. 215.
[16] William Michelson, *Environmental Choice, Human Behavior, and Residential Satisfaction,* Oxford University Press, New York, 1977.

deplore the "little boxes all in a row" has had little impact on the mass of the population. Residents perceive individuality and differences even in the largest look-alike subdevelopments.[17]

CONTEMPORARY SUBURBIA

Employment Centers

Suburbia today is remarkably diverse. Affluent commuter suburbs have been joined by working-class suburbs, suburbs of condominiums, and industrial-park suburbs. Historically, suburbs were considered "sub" because they were not economically self-supporting but rather were appendages of the central city, serving as dormitories. Suburban residents had to commute to the central city in order to earn their livelihood. That no longer holds: Today suburbs are the major centers of employment. Even two decades ago, in the New York area, the legendary citadel of the commuter, only 22 percent of the suburban workers actually commuted into New York City. Our image of the suburbs, obviously, has not caught up with reality. Today's suburban commuter is more likely to commute to another suburb than to the central city. Two-thirds (68 percent) of all suburbanites who work now work in the suburbs. Today, one is twice as likely to commute between suburbs than to commute from suburb to city.[18]

There are now more large corporate headquarters in areas surrounding New York City than in the city itself. In terms of number of Fortune 500 corporations, Fairfield County, Connecticut, alone is second nationally only to New York City itself. As noted earlier, Plano, Texas, is now headquarters to five Fortune 500 corporations. In general, corporate headquarters are moving south and suburban.[19] As a result of suburban employment opportunities, reverse commuting is becoming more common. One may now live in Dallas, Los Angeles, New York, or Chicago while working beyond the city limits. Moreover, suburbs are increasing their lead as places of employment. Washington, D.C., as the nation's capital enjoys an employment advantage over most older cities. While other cities were losing jobs, Washington added 78,000 jobs between 1980 and 1990. Yet the District, which had held half (48 percent) of all metropolitan jobs in 1970, employed only 29 percent of metropolitan area workers by 1990.[20] Some 71 percent of all Washington-area workers were employed in the Virginia or Maryland suburbs.

Although figures such as these don't necessarily signal the death of the city, they definitely do indicate the increasingly diversified notion of suburbia. The image of the suburb as an exclusive area of single-family homes has to undergo revision. Even putting aside the questions of commercial and industrial construction and examining only residential building, it is clear that suburbs are building up as

[17] Herbert J. Gans, *The Levittowners*, Vintage Books, New York, 1967.
[18] Christopher Leinberger and Charles Lockwood, "How Business Is Shaping America," *Atlantic Monthly*, October, 1986, pp. 43–52.
[19] Sally Ward, "Trends in the Location of Corporate Headquarters, 1969–1989," *Urban Affairs Quarterly*, **23**:468–478, 1994.
[20] Stephan Fehr, "N. Va. Replaces DC as Area Job Center," *Washington Post*, Dec. 22, 1992, p. A14.

well as out. High-rises and apartment units—whether rental or condominiums—for young singles and the elderly have become increasingly commonplace. Suburban apartment complexes are now accepted as a part of suburbia.

In spite of rising suburban housing costs and central-city "gentrification" (see Chapter 12, The Question of Urban Crisis), research by Edmonston and Guterbock has found no real decline in the movement to the suburban periphery.[21] The out-movement of shopping malls, industrial parks, and suburban office complexes has, in fact, meant that moving "closer to the action" often means moving out rather than in.

CATEGORIES OF SUBURBS

Suburban growth is not as chaotic as it might seem. While suburbs may vary in many respects, there is a predictable pattern to the variation. There are persistent systematic differences that contribute to predicting the evolutionary development of suburban areas. Suburbs can be differentiated in many ways: old versus new, rich versus poor, incorporated versus unincorporated, ethnic versus WASP (white Anglo-Saxon Protestant), growing versus stagnant. Suburban settlements are so diverse that no single typology can adequately encompass them all.

Suburbs also differ systematically with regard to housing characteristics. Residential suburbs have the highest proportion of new housing, the highest percentage of owner-occupied units, and the highest percentage of single-family units; the employment suburbs are lowest on these measures. Older typologies that distinguished between those suburbs that function essentially as dormitories—"residential" suburbs—and those that are basically manufacturing or industrial areas—"employment" suburbs—no longer fit the polycentered nature of contemporary suburbia.

It has been suggested that suburbs be distinguished on the basis of life-style, separately from legal definition as a suburb.[22] Old industrial suburbs, all-black suburbs, and ethnic suburbs, for example, don't fit the conventional image of suburban life-style, yet they are legally suburbs. On the other hand, a place such as River Oaks, inside Houston, is very suburban in life-style but is legally within the city. Similarly, Buckhead in Atlanta fits our image of a suburb far more than that of a city district.

Persistence of Characteristics?

Since the 1920s most neighborhoods within central cities have undergone profound changes in terms of the characteristics of the residents and often even the physical structures. We take it for granted that city neighborhoods will change in socioeconomic status over time. One-time prosperous neighborhoods are expected to

---

[21] Barry Edmonston and Thomas Guterbock, "Is Suburbanization Slowing Down? Recent Trends in Population Deconcentration in U.S. Metropolitan Areas," *Social Forces,* **66**:905–925, 1984.

[22] Robert L. Lineberry, "Suburbia and Metropolitan Turf," *The Annals of the American Academy of Political and Social Science,* **442**:1–9, November, 1975.

Case Study: Levittown

Probably the most thorough case study of a suburban community is Herbert Gans's study of the social organization of Levittown, New Jersey, during the first two years of its existence.* The various Levittowns were prototypes of the postwar "package suburbs" that can now be found near all of the country's larger cities. Levitt and Sons, Inc., originally built for a lower-middle-class market, but over the years the size of their houses and their prices increased considerably. The New Jersey Levittown later changed its name to Willingboro to escape the Levittown stereotype.

Gans's findings were based on interviews with two sets of Levittowners and on his own observations, made while he lived in Levittown for two years. Gans suggests that the sociability found within the community is a direct result of the compatibility or homogeneity of the backgrounds of the residents. Homogeneity was most evident in terms of age and income. But diversity in regional backgrounds, membership in ethnic groups, and religious beliefs provided variety for the community. Even the similarity in income did not indicate as much homogeneity as the statistics indicated, for one family might be headed by a skilled worker at the peak of earning power, another by a white-collar worker with some hope of advancement, and a third by a young executive or professional just at the start of a career. Active sociability emerged only when neighboring residents shared common tastes and values, were similar with regard to race and class, and shared similar beliefs regarding child-raising practices. Family togetherness was seen by the residents as a positive attribute of the community. Parents and children all felt that because of the move they spent more time together as a family. Even commuting did not have the often-alleged negative effect on family activities. Most Levittowners did not really mind commuting unless it involved a trip of over forty minutes.

Gans's research indicated that residents of the mass look-alike suburb were generally content with their housing, life-style, and general environment. Although the popular literature is rather heavy with criticism of suburban anomie (normlessness) and malaise, boredom was not a serious problem in Levittown. Depression and loneliness appeared if anything to be less common than in the city. Almost all the emotional difficulties were concentrated among working-class women who were for the first time cut off from their parents,

* Herbert J. Gans, The Levittowners, Vintage Books, New York, 1967.

and among wives with husbands whose jobs kept them on the road and away from the family. Those most likely to find the community lacking were upper-middle-class people who had tried Levittown's organizational life and found it wanting.

Adolescents also had a hard time. The community was particularly deadly for teenagers owing to the lack of recreational facilities and even places to go. It was designed for families with young children, not adolescents. Thus, bedrooms were small and lacked the privacy or soundproofing necessary to allow teenagers to have their friends visit.

Gans found that suburbanites differed little from similar city dwellers. He said:

> The distinction between urban and suburban ways of living postulated by the critics (and by some sociologists as well) is more imaginary than real. Few changes can be traced to the suburban qualities of Levittown, and the sources that did cause change, like the house, the population mix, and newness, are not distinctively suburban. Moreover, when one looks at similar populations in city and suburb, their ways of life are remarkably alike.*

Overall, Gans's description of Levittown shows a community that was not overly exciting but that generally met the needs of its residents. The worst thing that could be said about the community is that for anyone with cosmopolitan tastes, it was rather dull. But, then, Levittowns weren't built for cosmopolites.

More recently, Popenoe, examining another Levittown across the Delaware River from Philadelphia, came to similar conclusions.[†] Residents spend their leisure time in doing locally based informal activities with friends and in watching television, and rarely in going into downtown Philadelphia. Life is comfortable, family-based, and not overly exciting. As in Gans's study, Popenoe suggests that teenagers found the residential environment most wanting. While Levittown does have recreational facilities such as pools and parks, it, like many similar suburbs in the United States, has few places just to hang out and see and be seen.

Today the original Levittown on Long Island is facing hard choices of social and economic change that are affecting older working-class suburbs. The manufacturing jobs that fueled postwar expansion are gone, and problems of welfare and crime are increasing.[‡] Older suburbs are struggling with problems they never expected to reach their door.

* Ibid., p. 288.
† David Popenoe, *The Suburban Environment: Sweden and the United States*, University of Chicago, Chicago, 1977.
‡ Diana Jean Schemo, "Facing Big-City Problems, L.I. Suburbs Try to Adapt," *New York Times*, Mar. 16, 1994, pp. A1 and B4.

decline and possibly be rebuilt or gentrified. This model of local community status change is basically a life-cycle model and is consistent with the earlier Burgess concentric-zone theory that posited neighborhood change due to competition for land and the outgoing movement of affluent populations.[23]

However, when our focus shifts to suburbs, the assumption of status change is replaced by the assumption of status consistency. Suburbs are seen as changing less than cities. It is as if suburbs are not subject to the same laws of aging and change. This status-persistence model suggests that early in a suburb's history its socioeconomic status tends to fix its position in the metropolitan area's ecological structure. Research done by Reynolds Farley and by Avery Guest indicates that there is considerable persistence in characteristics over time in the suburbs.[24] Farley's research on 137 suburbs of 24 central cities suggests that although we tend to see the suburbs as experiencing a rapid rate of change, there is considerable consistency at least among older established suburbs. The socioeconomic status of individual suburbs was generally the same as it had been twenty or forty years earlier. In fact, a sound prediction of the educational level of a suburb can be made if one knows the school attendance rate of the high-school-age population of forty years earlier. Guest's later research indicates that suburban persistence was most pronounced in the 1950–1970 period. Population growth of high-status suburbs enhanced their high position.

Individual suburbs thus were said to have changed far less than the central cities. For example, Wilmette, on Chicago's North Shore, and Chevy Chase, just outside Washington, occupy positions of social status remarkably similar to the positions they occupied in 1920. Farley suggests that suburban persistency may result because a suburb originally establishes a distinct composition, so that the people who tend to move to it have socioeconomic characteristics similar to those of people already there.

This view of suburban persistence has been challenged by research by Choldin, Hanson, and Bohrer, who found that suburbs do have a neighborhood life cycle, generally moving downward in status over time.[25] Logan and Schneider, on the other hand, found that suburban employment improved the relative income level of poorer suburbs, and that there were wide regional variations in suburban persistence.[26] John Stahura found that as suburban growth rates slowed in the 1970s, there was a tendency toward crystallization of the differences between suburbs.[27] Thus, unless circumstances dramatically change, it does not appear that there will be major changes in the status ranking of suburbs.

It does, however, appear that wealthy suburbs are relatively immune to downward changes in status. One way they are able to maintain their position is by us-

[23] Ernest Burgess, "The Growth of the City," in Robert Park, Ernest Burgess, and Roderick McKenzie (eds.), *The City,* University of Chicago Press, Chicago, 1925, pp. 47–62.

[24] Reynolds Farley, "Suburban Persistence," *American Sociological Review,* **29:**38–47, 1964; and Avery M. Guest, "Suburban Social Status: Persistence or Evolution," *American Sociological Review,* **43:**251–264, 1978.

[25] Harvey Choldin, Claudine Hanson, and Robert Bohrer, "Suburban Status Instability," *American Sociological Review,* **45:**972–983, 1980.

[26] John R. Logan and Mark Schneider, "Stratification of Metropolitan Suburbs, 1960–1970," *American Sociological Review,* **46:**175–186, 1981.

[27] John M. Stahura, "Suburban Socioeconomic Status Change: A Comparison of Models, 1950–1980," *American Sociological Review,* **52:**268–277, 1987.

ing their considerable resources to control who can move into the suburb.[28] This can be done through high tax rates or through zoning regulations that mandate certain-size homes and/or large lot sizes. These practices have the effect of excluding the nonwealthy. Such suburbs are also able to employ their social prestige of being ex-clusive areas to attract prestigious residents. This is how an elite suburb such as Lake Forest, north of Chicago, has maintained its position for a century. Upper-income suburbs thus use their political knowledge and power to protect and en-hance the value of their investment.

The political power model is usually associated with scholars taking a conflict perspective, while the status-persistence model is usually associated with those holding an ecological model. However, in this instance both approaches seem to re-inforce rather than contradict each other. Older and more affluent suburbs have had the greatest success in maintaining their favored position. There also appears to be regional variation. Specifically, in the north and midwest involuntary annexation of suburbs had ceased by the beginning of the twentieth century, while in some parts of the southwest, and especially in Texas, annexation is still possible. Thus one would expect to find the greatest number of affluent suburbs practicing exclusion-ary zoning in the north and midwest.

However, even more important than keeping undesirables out is attracting new high-status residents. Here a self-fulfilling prophesy seems to occur for affluent sub-urbs. A suburb having an established reputation as a high-status area employs its so-cial prestige to attract new high-status residents. Realtors also play a major part by steering high-income newcomers toward what are perceived as being the more pres-tigious areas. Reputation creates a reality which in turn reinforces reputation.

Ethnic and Religious Variation

Within the metropolitan area different ethnic, religious, and racial groups often sub-urbanized in specific directions. In Atlanta, for instance, blacks went south and whites went north. Ethnic groups also followed specific patterns. In Chicago over the past century Polish-heritage populations have moved from the near north side to the northwest side and into northwest suburbs such as Niles. The Jewish hous-ing pattern was roughly similar, with upper-middle-class Jews moving into north-west suburbs such as Skokie and wealthy Jews moving north to Glencoe and High-land Park. Italian-heritage populations, on the other hand, moved progressively west, and in time into western suburbs such as Melrose Park. WASPs by contrast moved up the North Shore to Evanston, Wilmette, and Winnetka. Thus, the pattern of ethnic inner-city neighborhoods was in modified form carried to the suburbs.

High-Income Suburbs

The nineteenth century saw the first examples of exclusive suburbs designed as refuges for the wealthy. Then and now, upper-status suburbs usually feature large, imposing homes built on extensive properties that are screened off from casual

---

[28] John R. Logan, "Growth, Politics, and the Stratification of Places," *American Journal of Sociology,* **84**:404–415, 1978.

external observation by shrubbery and trees. Generally such suburbs have been located at the outer suburban edges, but there are some clear exceptions such as centrally located Grosse Pointe, which is bordered by Detroit, and Beverly Hills, which is surrounded by Los Angeles.

However, what gives most upper-status suburbs their character is not so much their housing style as the style of life and patterns of social interaction among the residents. Demographically, high-income suburbs tend to have an older-median-age population and a low proportion of women employed in the labor force. Particularly in the east and midwest, the older elite suburbs were, and in many cases still are, socially closed WASP communities. Older elite suburbs have never been believers in multiculturalism. Wealth is required for entry, but nouveau riche outsiders are not considered suitable for membership in either the country clubs or the community. Traditionally racial minorities and those whites having southern or eastern European ethnic heritage were also automatically disqualified for residency, as were Jews and Catholics. When the Kennedy family bought a large home in Hyannis Port, Massachusetts, several neighbors moved out on the grounds that the community was surely going downhill. Opposition remained even after John Kennedy became president of the United States. Similarly the richest suburb in the country, Kenilworth on Chicago's North Shore, has had a reputation for discouraging Catholics and Jews as residents. Catholics and Jews who were excluded responded by founding their own exclusive suburbs and country clubs. For example, wealthy Jewish families responded by developing Glencoe and Highland Park as North Shore Jewish suburbs.

In newer upper-income growth suburbs, ethnicity and religion tend to have lesser relevance so long as one has sufficient cash. Similarly, in the rich suburbs of Texas and southern California, background is even less important. One's heritage is secondary to one's bank balance. Elsewhere in the world Jews and Arabs may be in deadly conflict, but in Beverly Hills wealthy Arabs and wealthy Jews live as neighbors. Another change is that wealthy suburbs are no longer automatically communities of single-family homes. Luxury high-rise condominiums are increasingly found in newer suburbs for the well-to-do.

As a cautionary note, there is a tendency to equate the high costs of housing in an area with the affluence of the residents. This is generally the case, but it can be misleading insofar as it might suggest that counties with high housing costs, such as those in southern California, necessarily also have the highest percentages of affluent householders. In fact the 1990 census indicates that the counties having the most affluent householders are still concentrated on the east coast. Of the twenty counties having the greatest proportion of population with households earning $100,000 or more in 1989, fully half are found in the suburban ring of the New York Consolidated Metropolitan Area.[29] Leading the list is Westchester County, New York, with 18 percent of its households having incomes of $100,000 or more. Just behind are Morris County, New Jersey; Fairfield County, Connecticut; and Nassau County, New York. Another three counties: Montgomery County, Maryland; Fairfax County, Virginia;

---

[29] Judith Waldrop and Linda Jacobsen, "Affluent Americans," *American Demographics,* December, 1992, p. 38.

and Howard County, Maryland, are in the Washington, D.C.–Baltimore suburban ring. Only six counties among the top twenty are west of the Mississippi. Marin and San Mateo counties in the San Francisco metropolitan area were numbers 5 and 16, respectively. Santa Clara County (San Jose) was number 19, and Orange County in southern California just made the list as number 20.

Working-Class Suburbs

Before the mass suburbanization following the Second World War, working-class suburbs were older industrial or factory suburbs. An example is Cudahy south of Milwaukee, which was established when the Milwaukee city government refused to allow Patrick Cudahy to build a stockyard and slaughterhouse works within the city. Another example is the working-class suburb of Cicero west of Chicago. Cicero achieved national notoriety during the 1920s as the headquarters of Al Capone's operations when a short-lived reform administration in Chicago temporarily forced the mob to move its headquarters to the suburbs. Most prewar working-class suburbs, however, were simply factory towns. Plain, but generally well-kept, houses with small yards were the norm.

Following World War II, the previously mentioned GI loans allowed blue-collar workers as well as the traditional middle class to successfully apply for long-term mortgages. Growing prosperity also made it possible for working-class workers to purchase a family automobile. At the same time, new interstate and other road networks made new suburban locations a reasonable alternative for aging inner-city factories. As a result, both factories and labor forces decentralized. It is sometimes forgotten that the new postwar working-class suburbanites that followed the factories to the suburbs were not fleeing decaying city neighborhoods. More often than not, they were somewhat reluctantly leaving tight ethnic neighborhoods with high levels of social interaction.

Bennett Berger studied the life-style of some 100 blue-collar Ford assembly workers and their families who were forced to move from Richmond, California, to the suburb of Milpitas, California, in order to work at a new automobile plant.[30] He found that suburbanization had little or no effect on the workers' style of life. They didn't see the move in terms of social mobility; they had no great hopes of getting ahead in their jobs. They had no illusions of wealth; their wage level was dependent on the union contract. As a consequence of becoming suburbanites, they didn't change their political affiliation (81 percent Democrat), go to church more, or join community organizations. They participated only minimally in formal groups. What they did do is continue their traditional working-class pattern of tight informal socialization with long-term friends and neighbors. In brief, they lived life patterns quite similar to those workers living in blue-collar central-city neighborhoods. Their new suburban homes were not seen as a weigh station on the road to social mobility, but rather as a permanent place of residence.

Now many of these postwar blue-collar suburbs are experiencing the same downward economic pressures suffered by central cities. Declines in nearby heavy

---

[30] Bennett M. Berger, *Working Class Suburbs,* University of California Press, Berkeley, 1960.

industry and manufacturing jobs mean that those living in older inner-ring suburbs have long commutes to service jobs in outlying edge suburbs. The automobile factory that triggered the move Berger described was itself closed for being technologically out of date. Commercial tax bases are also eroding in working-class suburbs. Thus class divisions between suburbs are becoming sharper rather than blurring. Additionally, older working-class suburbs with their low-cost housing have been most likely to attract minority families escaping the city. The deterioration of job prospects for blue-collar workers in a postindustrial economy suggests that such workers may now find themselves trapped in declining working-class suburbs. These suburbs lack both the affluence of other suburbs and the basic amenities of the central city.

New Definitional Systems

Since defining a model-type suburbanite, or a model suburban life-style, is becoming less and less possible, one way out of the difficulty is not to even try. Rather than seeking overall similarities, business-oriented researchers now more often focus on the differences that will aid politicians and marketers to fine-tune their advertising campaigns to meet specific needs and markets. A marketing research firm named Claritas has developed a system that places every zip code area in the country into one of forty different types of communities on the basis of the dominant economic, family life cycle, and ethnic-racial characteristics of households, along with the physical characteristics of the areas in which they live.[31]

In effect, Claritas has tried to create homogeneous ethnographic areas, what Chicago school sociologists of the 1920s referred to as natural areas. Claritas has done this using statistical cluster analysis techniques to explain the relationship between physical space and social behavior. These areas have become a virtual Bible for market researchers, but thus far they have had less use by academics who are more concerned with the universality of standards.

The strength of the system is that it provides fairly detailed information on areas as small as zip codes, but the limitation is that some of this detail may be spurious. This is because postal zip codes are sometimes anything but homogeneous, and the cluster analysis technique gives the average characteristics for the area. Therefore, if population or housing characteristics are diverse within the area, there is a serious risk of committing the "ecological fallacy" of attempting to predict the behavior of individuals from the characteristics of an area. The more homogeneous the zip code, the greater the validity of the coding. Of the forty life-style communities Claritas identifies, a dozen have a suburban location. Roughly going from upper income to lower, these areas and their characteristics are:

Blue-Blood Estates—The wealthiest neighborhoods of largely suburban homes
Furs and Station Wagons—Newer-money metropolitan bedroom suburbs
Pools and Patios—Older upper-middle-class suburban communities
Gray Power—Upper-middle-class retirement suburbs

[31] Michael Weiss, *The Clustering of America*, Tilden Press, New York, 1988.

New Beginnings—Outer-city or suburban areas of single complexes, garden apartments, and well-kept bungalows (single or childless)
Two More Rungs—Comfortable multiethnic suburbs
Blue-Chip Blues—More affluent blue-collar suburbs
Young Suburbia—Outlying child-rearing suburbs
Young Homesteaders—Exurban boomtowns of younger midscale families
Levittown, U.S.A. —Aging postwar working-class tract suburbs
Rank and File—Older blue-collar industrial suburbs
Norma Rae-Ville—Older industrial suburbs and mill towns, primarily in the south

EXURBS

The term "exurb" refers to the type of upper-middle-class settlement that has taken place in outlying semirural suburbia, the area beyond the second ring of densely settled subdivisions. Fringe exurban areas have more widely separated homes, often with woods between, and the homes tend to be large and expensive. Sometimes exurbanites settle around old villages or small towns. Exurbanites as a rule are affluent, well-educated professionals. Sometimes these individuals work in fields such as communications, advertising, and publishing which allow them to work at home and avoid daily commuting, and instead use PCs with modems and fax machines. If their base is New York, they may live in Fairfield County, Connecticut, or northern New Jersey; if the office is in Philadelphia, then Bucks County, Pennsylvania; and if in San Francisco, then Marin County, California.

Unfortunately, the study of exurbia that gave the areas its name, *The Exurbanites,* presents a caricature of suburban life-styles.[32] Exurbanites were portrayed as hyperactive, upwardly mobile strivers who are desperately trying to find meaning in their lives by moving out of the city. Working in highly competitive industries where the standards for judging performance are subjective and fickle, they seek solace by escaping the city. Basically, exurbanites are displaced cosmopolites living in the twentieth-century version of what a century ago were called romantic suburbs. They are urbane seekers of the American dream who seek to reside in rustic settings. They want to move out of the city but not away from its advantages and services. According to the stereotype, living in exurbia also puts considerable pressures on wives, who find themselves locked into a schedule of maintaining the house and providing shuttle service for children and commuting husbands while attempting to maintain their own careers and interests.

If the above sounds familiar, it is, because this general outline has served as the plot for dozens of novels, television soaps, and movies. The problem is that it is often taken as a scientific reflection of reality rather than inventive fiction. Based on demographic characteristics, there is no support for the belief that exurbanites are significantly different from other same-status suburbanites. In fact, exurbs have a way of turning into reluctant suburbs as more and more people move into the same area, all seeking to escape urban life.

[32] A. C. Spectorsky. *The Exurbanites,* Berkeley, New York, 1957.

RURBAN AREAS

Harder to pin down are those places beyond the exurbs that are *not* oriented toward a major city. While definitionally these areas may still be within a metropolitan area, the orientation of residents may be more rural than urban. Housing in these in-between areas that are not truly rural, but are probably never destined to become suburban, is sometimes of marginal quality. Some of those living in such "rurban" areas are barely getting by economically in spite of low housing costs and taxes. It is not uncommon for rurban residents to commute long distances to work at low-income jobs. They are anything but affluent suburban commuters.

Adding to the confusion over what is suburban are places such as outlying college towns that the census has defined as metropolitan but are not really urban in character. One of these is Centre County, Pennsylvania, which is the home of Pennsylvania State University. Because of its population, Centre County is defined as a metropolitan area named State College, but it is clearly neither urban nor suburban. The county includes a widely dispersed and mixed population having a wide range of interests and occupations. There are 165 acres for every person in the metropolitan area.[33] The consequence is a metropolitan area that is known for its hiking trails, numerous lakes, trout streams, and mountains.

In practice, even residential suburbia, to say nothing of the outer cities discussed in Chapter 6, has become remarkably diverse—so diverse, in fact, that calling an area "suburban" doesn't really tell us much anymore. As suburbia has come to house and employ the largest segment of the American population, the characteristics that define a "typical suburb" and "typical suburbanites" have become even more difficult to define.

CHARACTERISTICS OF SUBURBANITES

Who, then, are the suburbanites, and does the popular image of suburbanites as white, middle-class homeowners with children fit the facts? To a degree it does. In terms of income the Census Bureau's figures show some 18 percent of central-city residents were below the poverty line, while this was true of only 8 percent of suburbanites.[34] More people live alone in the city. One-person households made up 35 percent of city households but only 23 percent of suburban households. During the 1980s suburbs showed a sharp drop in the number of children. As the baby-boom generation grew up and left home, the number of children aged seventeen and under has declined in suburbs in spite of total suburban population growth. In cities the higher birthrate of urban black and Hispanic populations has kept the number of city children from declining as rapidly.

The big difference, however, is not that there are fewer suburban than city children, but that suburban children are much more likely to live in two-parent

[33] John Herbers, *The New Heartland: America's Flight beyond the Suburbs and How It Is Changing Our Future*, Times Books, New York, 1986.
[34] U.S. Bureau of the Census, "Money, Income and Poverty in the United States: 1988," *Current Population Reports*, series P-20, no. 166, Washington, D.C., October, 1989, table A.

families. Twice as many city children as suburban children live in families headed by an unmarried, divorced, or widowed mother. This is in large part the reflection of the racial composition of cities, since over half of all central-city black families are headed by women.

Suburbanites also tend to be homeowners. Approximately three-quarters of suburban housing units are owner-occupied, as compared with half of those in the cities. Home ownership, of course, provides greater economic security, not to mention tax benefits.

However, the most pronounced difference between cities and suburbs is their racial composition. In spite of heavy black suburbanization during the 1970–1990 census periods, the percentage of blacks in suburbs was only 6.6 percent in 1990, half of what would be expected given random distribution. (Black suburbanization trends are discussed later in this chapter.)

THE MYTH OF SUBURBIA

Over the years the suburbs have become more than mere places of residence. Suburbia has become endowed with a long list of physical and even psychological attributes: ranch-style houses, neat lawns, station wagons and car pools, uptight parents, and togetherness. It is the place where one supposedly finds

> . . . a home of one's own, a small piece of real estate on which to practice yeoman's skills, good schools, plenty of land for recreation, clean and traffic free neighborhoods, a small town atmosphere, Christmas lights, a Fourth of July parade, a homogeneous community without social tensions.[35]

This caricature has been called by some sociologists the "myth of suburbia," the myth being the belief that there is, in fact, a uniquely suburban way of life.[36] According to the myth of suburbia, people living in suburbs are, or become, somehow different from those who remain in the city. Upon moving, noncommunicative people become friendly neighbors, Democrats become Republicans, and religious fundamentalists join main-line denominations.

The postwar stereotypes of suburbia were frequently less than complimentary. The suburban way of life was supposedly one of wide lawns and narrow minds in which family life is child-oriented rather than adult-oriented. Critics described the suburban family as surrendering all individuality and creativity.[37] The late Margaret Mead characterized suburban life as consisting of "a living room or recreation room which often resembles a giant playpen into which the parents have somewhat reluctantly climbed." Television shows such as *Ozzie and Harriet* and *Leave It to Beaver* stereotyped this view.

---

[35] Robert Lineberry and Ira Sharkansky, *Urban Politics and Public Policy,* Harper & Row, New York, 1971, p. 34.
[36] Bennet M. Berger, "The Myth of Suburbia," *Journal of Social Issues,* **17**:38–49, 1971; Herbert J. Gans, "Urbanism and Suburbanism as Ways of Life: A Re-evaluation of Definitions," in Arnold Rose (ed.), *Human Behavior,* Houghton Mifflin, Boston, 1962.
[37] David Riesman, "The Suburban Sadness," in W. Dobriner (ed.), *The Suburban Community,* Putnam, New York, 1958, pp. 375–408.

A generic suburban neighborhood that could be anywhere in the United States. This one is outside Wichita, Kansas. (Michael Dwyer/Stock, Boston.)

In terms of life-style, suburbanites—particularly those in the newer suburbs—were said to be gregarious. Numerous parties were interspersed with extensive informal visiting or neighboring. Togetherness was a way of life. Organizationally, suburbanites were said to be hyperactive joiners, with hobby groups, bridge clubs, neighborhood associations, and church-related social activities taking up several nights a week. On top of this, there was a proliferation of women's groups, scout troops, and kaffeeklatsches. Husbands were said to spend their weekends cutting grass, watching football games, picking up kids, going to parties, going to church, and watching more football games.

This myth of suburbia is now out of date. It has been replaced with a new myth that sees the compulsive group conformity of the 1950s and 1960s replaced by competitive self-advancement and manic self-fulfillment during the 1980s and 1990s. Status and money supposedly are the new suburban icons. The home is less a place to relax than a site for showcasing goods. Middle-class suburbia is said to have gone "from glorifying group bonding to glorifying individual happiness and achievement."[38]

While the myth of suburbia is something of a straw man, it is unfortunately true that suburbs have not received enough study. For all the talk, the number of scholars studying suburbs remains limited. During the 1960s, urban research came to be focused almost exclusively on the inner city. The vacuum left by the absence of hard research on suburban life-styles was filled with popular books and articles dealing with suburban conformity, adultery, alcoholism, divorce, and plain boredom. Even the best of the popular writing on suburban life (e.g., John Updike's short stories and novels) painted a highly selective, if not inaccurate, picture. The

[38] Nicholas Lemann, "Stressed Out in Suburbia," *The Atlantic,* November, 1989, p. 46.

Women's Housing Preferences

A fair amount has been written about the relative advantages for women of urban and suburban environments. One feminist writer refers to cities as being "masculine" and suburbs as being "feminine."[*] To Marxist-oriented feminists, suburban housing is a problem since "the dominance of the single-family detached dwelling, its separation from the workplace, and its decentralized urban location are as much the products of the patriarchal organization of household production as of the capitalist organization of wage work."[†] The suburban home thus is seen as handicapping the housewife through isolation, lack of variety, and lack of public life.[‡] The result is that suburban wives are seen as both isolated and restricted to traditional gender roles.[§]

Studies from the 1960s and 1970s tended to support the view of husbands being more satisfied with life in the suburbs than their wives. The Levittown study discussed elsewhere in this chapter, for example, found that only three out of ten husbands, but twice as many of their wives, would like to live in the city "if not for the children."[¶]

A major housing study in Toronto found that women living in urban residential areas had the greatest satisfaction with their neighborhoods.[**] Men, on the other hand, were said to prefer the relaxation and escape from urban pressures associated with the typical residential suburb.[††]

However, with most women now in the labor force, the image of the suburban homemaker isolated in her suburban house without access to either car or culture seems quaintly dated. Such images speak more to the 1950s and 1960s than to the 1990s. Contemporary suburban women, whether working outside the home or not, are not anywhere as physically or socially isolated as suggested by such writers. Today, two- and even three-car families are the norm, and even most women with young children are in the paid workforce. Having too

---

[*] Susan Saegert, "Masculine Cities and Feminine Suburbs: Polarized Ideas, Contradictory Realities," in C. Stimpson et al. (eds.), *Women and the American City*, University of Chicago Press, Chicago, 1980, pp. 93–108.
[†] Ann R. Markasen, "City Spatial Structure, Women's Household Work and National Urban Policy," *Signs*, **5**:31, 1980.
[‡] Dolores Hayden, *Redesigning the American Dream*, Norton, New York, 1984.
[§] Gerda Wekerle, "Women in the Urban Environment," in Stimpson, et al., *Women and the American City*, pp. 185–211.
[¶] Herbert J. Gans, *The Levittowners*, Vintage Books, New York, p. 272.
[**] William M. Michelson, "Environmental Choice," *Human Behavior and Residential Satisfaction*, Oxford University Press, New York, 1977.
[††] Susan Saegert and Gary Winkel, "The Home: A Critical Problem for Changing Sex Roles," in Gerda Wekerle, R. Peterson, and D. Morley (eds.), *New Space for Women*, Westview Press, Boulder, Colo., 1980, chap. 1.

much spare time at home is not one of the problems of women of the 1990s. Most suburbanites, male as well as female, would welcome having a few days alone at home.

Contemporary data on residential preferences do not fit easy gender stereotypes. Older ideas that women prefer cities because of the access to employment, public transportation, and child care and that suburbs are isolating no longer appear to apply.[*] In part, this may be, as Sylvia Fava has pointed out, because the majority of young adults today have grown up in suburban rather than central-city settings.[†] Thus, they are comfortable with the suburban settings that they know. Suburbs also have become considerably more diverse over the years.

Spain's analysis of the federal government's Annual Housing Survey data covering 32,000 households found that female householders as well as married couples actually expressed higher levels of satisfaction with suburban than central-city neighborhoods.[‡] Not only do both women and men share greater preferences for the suburbs, but they show little difference in the reason for moving to a particular neighborhood, with lower rent and ease in commuting being at the top of the list. Spain suggests that the urban advantages of access to shopping, public transit, and public schools are more than offset by the concerns over urban neighborhood crime, unsatisfactory police protection, and inadequate public schools. While some minor differences remain, research suggests gender is becoming less relevant as a predictor of residential preference.

One group of suburban women whose life-style and problems deserve more attention are women who head their households. What happens to a woman's life after divorce? Are female householders in suburbs particularly subject to problems of isolation and economics? Do female heads of households remain in suburbs, or do they sell their homes and relocate elsewhere?

[*] Sylvia F. Fava, "Residential Preferences in the New Suburban Era: A New Look?" Sociological Focus, 18:109–117, April, 1985.
[†] Ibid.
[‡] Daphne Spain, "An Examination of Residential Preferences in the Suburban Era," Sociological Focus, 21:1–8, January, 1988; and Daphne Spain, "The Effects of Changing Household Composition on Neighborhood Satisfaction," Urban Affairs Quarterly, 21:581–600, June, 1988.

best known of the early social works was William H. Whyte's influential book, *The Organization Man.*[39] Unfortunately, many of his imitators were not as careful.

Postwar suburban studies suffered from three liabilities. First, the postwar suburban studies were highly selective of one type of suburb. Attention was focused on the large subdevelopments for young families, while little attention was given to industrial suburbs, working-class suburbs, or even older established suburbs. The result was that the image of suburbia was loaded by an emphasis on middle-class subdivision suburbs. Second, it is likely that some of the communities chosen for study were selected precisely because they were in some respects atypical and thus presumably more interesting. Third, many of the observations were based on a single look at a suburb immediately after the first wave of settlement. It is highly likely that another look five or ten years later, after the community had matured, would show changes in the pace of life.[40]

AFRICAN-AMERICAN SUBURBANIZATION

After World War II, suburbs lost their social-class exclusiveness but not their racial exclusiveness. Blacks in suburbs were noticeable by their absence. Zoning laws mandating lot and dwelling sizes were used to keep out both the poor and minorities.[41] The general conclusion of researchers was that black suburbanization was increasing, but only marginally.[42] See Figure 9-1.

Population Changes

However, the last two decades have seen considerable change. While one still hears reference to "lily-white suburbs," and the media often give the impression that African Americans reside overwhelmingly in central-city neighborhoods, the reality is that with metropolitan areas for every two central-city residents there now is one suburban resident. Further, the 1990 census reported that overall 27 percent, or 8 million of the 30 million blacks in the United States, were suburbanites.[43] These suburbanites remain largely ignored in spite of the fact that there are some forty metropolitan areas in the country where the suburban African-American population exceeds 50,000.

Suburbs are now the major area of African-American growth. Three-quarters (73 percent) of all black population growth between 1986 and 1990 took place in suburbs. Generally blacks are following the same suburbanizing pattern set by

[39] William H. Whyte, *The Organization Man,* Doubleday (Anchor), Garden City, N.Y., 1956.
[40] On this point, see S. D. Clark, *The Suburban Society,* University of Toronto Press, Toronto, 1966.
[41] Michael N. Danielson, *The Politics of Exclusion,* Columbia University Press, New York, 1976.
[42] George Sternlieb and Robert W. Lake, "Aging Suburbs and Black Home-Ownership," *The Annals of the American Academy of Political and Social Science,* **422:**105–117, 1975; Karl E. Taeuber, "Racial Segregation: The Persisting Dilemma," *The Annals of the American Academy of Political and Social Science,* **422:**87–96, 1975; and Leo F. Schnore, Carolyn D. Andre, and Harry Sharp, "Black Suburbanization 1930–1970," in Barry Schwartz (ed.), *The Changing Face of the Suburbs,* University of Chicago Press, Chicago, 1976, pp. 69–94.
[43] U.S. Bureau of the Census "The Black Population of the United States: March 1990 and 1989," *Current Population Reports,* P-20, no. 448, Washington, D.C., 1991, table 15, p. 66.

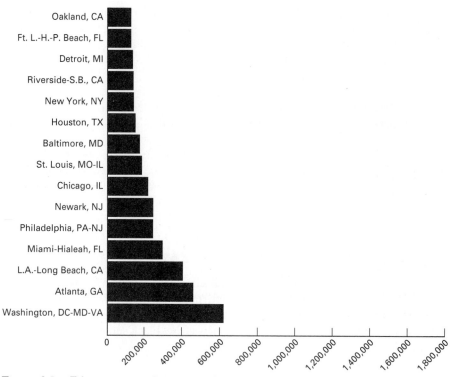

Figure 9-1. Fifteen metropolitan areas having the greatest number of Black suburbanites. Note that these metropolitan areas account for 45.4 percent of the total number of suburban Blacks in the United States.
Source: Compiled from 1990 census data.

whites after World War II.[44] Between 1970 and 1990 black rates of suburbanization exceeded white rates in all sections of the country. Older patterns of token suburban integration have been replaced by major population transfers. For example, between 1980 and 1990 Atlanta added 250,000 black suburbanites, Washington, D.C., added almost as many, and Miami added 100,000 black suburbanites.[45] As of 1990, Washington, D.C., had 620,000 black suburbanites, Atlanta 463,000, and Los Angeles 401,000. Chicago's metropolitan area showed only an insignificant 0.2 percent population increase between 1980 and 1990, but the black suburban population grew 65 percent.[46] Moreover, the major growth was not in the older inner-ring suburbs but rather in the newer suburbs on the suburban edge.

Blacks, who represent 13 percent of the national population, now represent 6.6 percent of all suburbanites. Blacks have not suburbanized at the rate one would expect based upon economics alone. Blacks (and to a lesser extent Hispanics, but not

[44] William H. Frey, "Mover Destination Selectivity and the Changing Suburbanization of Metropolitan Whites and Blacks," *Demography,* **22:**223–243, May, 1985.
[45] William O'Hare and William Frey, "Booming, Suburban, and Black," *American Demographics,* September, 1992, p. 33.
[46] Ibid., p. 36.

Three-quarters of African-American population growth is now occurring in the suburbs. (B. Bachmann/The Image Works.)

Asians) live in suburbs that have lower proportions of whites, and lower average income levels than would be predicted using socioeconomic characteristics alone.[47] Decades of racial segregation have ensured that suburbs remain predominately white. Also, suburbs are predominately white because whites constitute the overwhelming majority of the population. Thus, so long as whites continue their exodus to the suburbs, the suburbs will retain their white complexion.

As a result of black suburbanization, a decreasing proportion of the black population is living in central cities. Major cities such as Philadelphia, Washington, D.C., Cleveland, and St. Louis actually have had declines in their numbers of black residents. In Washington, D.C., for example, blacks left during the 1970–1990 decades at twice the rate of whites. Moreover, many of the departing blacks were people in their twenties and thirties with young children. Central cities have a higher proportion of blacks only because black birthrates are somewhat higher and because whites continue to leave the cities. Interestingly, the white population is increasingly dispersing to exurbia, small towns, and even rural areas, while a growing proportion of the black population is living in suburbs. In the future, white suburbanization may be at a less hectic pace. Most upper- and middle-class whites who want to move to suburbs have already done so. Increasingly, the remaining

---

[47] Richard Alba and John Logan, "Minority Proximity to Whites in Suburbs: An Individual Level Analysis of Segregation," *American Journal of Sociology*, **98:**1388–1427, 1993.

central-city whites, whether there by choice or economics, will remain city folk. The proportion of black suburbanites will continue to increase.

Integration or Resegregation?

The crucial question regarding black suburbanization is not whether it will increase, but rather whether increasing black suburbanization represents housing integration or merely the growth of suburban African-American enclaves. Research data prior to the 1980 census substantially showed a pattern of black spillover from central cities into older inner-ring suburbs.[48] Suburban blacks were more likely to live in suburban communities that had lower income, less adequate housing, and strained local finances.[49]

However, the 1980s and 1990s show less of the racial displacement of the invasion-succession model and more of the parallel growth of both racial groups. Overall, suburbs are becoming more diverse racially. Spillover is not today the pattern in the major metropolitan areas having the largest black populations. The reality is that rather than invasion-succession with one group supplanting another, stable multiracial suburbs are now more common.[50] The old model of the racial tipping point has less and less empirical validity.[51] However, the invasion-succession model of racial change retains acceptance and adherents in spite of its decreasing contemporary validity. Rather than spillover, the pattern now is more likely to be a "leapfrog" effect, with blacks "leaping" over older suburbs into newer subdivisions on the periphery.[52]

It also should be noted that not all suburban blacks necessarily want to live in racially integrated neighborhoods. To significant numbers, fair housing means nondiscrimination in housing purchases, not integration.[53] While research shows that blacks are generally more open to integrated housing than whites, some African Americans are making affirmative decisions to live in predominately black suburbs. Among these are affluent black suburbs such as Rolling Oaks in the Miami area, Brook Glen and Wyndham Park near Atlanta, and many of the newer outer subdivisions in Prince Georges County outside Washington. Black suburbanites in such areas often say they find it just more comfortable to live with black neighbors.[54]

The changes noted above suggest that while racial equality has not arrived, suburban middle-class blacks are becoming more similar to suburban middle-class whites. In metropolitan areas of a million or more, black suburban families have incomes 55 percent higher than the average for blacks living in the city. The 1990

[48] John M. Stahura, "Changing Patterns of Suburban Racial Composition," *Urban Affairs Quarterly*, 23:448–460, 1988.

[49] Mark Schneider and John R. Logan, "Racial Segregation and Black Access to Local Public Resources," *Social Science Quarterly*, 63:762–770, 1982.

[50] Barrett A. Lee and Peter B. Wood, "Is Neighborhood Racial Succession Place Specific?" *Demography*, 28:37, 1991.

[51] Nancy A. Denton and Douglas S. Massey, "Patterns of Neighborhood Transition and a Multiethnic World: U.S. Metropolitan Areas 1970–1980," *Demography*, 28:41–63, 1991.

[52] Morton D. Windsberg, "Flight from the Ghetto: The Migration of Middle Class and Highly Educated Blacks to White Neighborhoods," *American Journal of Economics and Sociology*, 44:411–421, 1985.

[53] Andrew Wiese, "Neighborhood Diversity: Social Change, Ambiguity, and Fair Housing since 1968," *Journal of Urban Affairs*, 17:107–129, 1995.

[54] David J. Dent, "The New Black Suburbs," *New York Times Magazine*, June 14, 1992, p. 23.

census indicates that in the suburbs outside Washington, D.C., black suburban incomes rose faster than white incomes during the previous decade, but black incomes were still only 82 to 88 percent of those of suburban whites. Both groups were well above the then national median household income of $34,210. The median black household income was $42,160 in Prince William County, $41,657 in Fairfax County, and $41,265 in Prince Georges County.[55] As of 1989, 47,000 black households in Prince Georges County, Maryland, had family incomes in excess of $50,000.[56] Today that figure has doubled.

The overall pattern offers both hope and discouragement. Old patterns of suburban racial segregation are increasingly becoming history. Suburban racial changeover is no longer automatically triggered by the presence of minority residents, but whites continue to exhibit reluctance to move into predominately minority areas. Racial steering by real estate agents, and discrimination against minorities by mortgage institutions, and insurance companies still continues.[57] Higher-income blacks still have significantly higher rates of home loan and home insurance rejections than do lower-income whites. However, in spite of all the obstacles, African–American suburbanization is the contemporary reality.

HISPANIC SUBURBANIZATION

Within a little over a decade the largest minority population in the United States will no longer be blacks, but rather Hispanics, or Latinos. The 1990 census reported 22.4 million Hispanics comprising 9 percent of the total population.[58] Approximately 43 percent of those Hispanics were suburbanites. Hispanics accounted for almost a quarter of all suburban growth between 1980 and 1990.[59] Latino suburban growth is greatest in the areas of the country showing the greatest economic growth. The eight metropolitan areas having the greatest number of Hispanic suburbanites are all in the sun belt—five in California, two in Texas, and one in Florida. The Los Angeles metropolitan area counts over 1.7 million suburban Hispanics, and during the 1980s the Latino population grew to more than 600,000.

For Hispanics suburban residence is closely associated with higher income levels.[60] Suburban residence is also associated with less spatial segregation, and more integration with non-Hispanic whites.[61] Currently, among the fastest-growing Hispanic suburbs are predominately Cuban growth areas in Florida, especially the areas surrounding Orlando. Future growth will disproportionately be found in Florida and in the states along the United States–Mexico border. (For further

[55] Palen, *The Suburbs,* p. 138.

[56] Judith Waldrop and Linda Jacobsen, "American Affluence," *American Demographics,* December, 1992, p. 34.

[57] Gregory D. Squires and William D. Velez, "Neighborhood Racial Composition and Mortgage Lending: City and Suburban Differences," *Journal of Urban Affairs,* **9:**217–232, 1987.

[58] U.S. Bureau of the Census, "The Hispanic Population of the United States: March 1990," *Current Population Reports,* P-20, no. 444, Washington, D.C., 1990.

[59] William H. Frey and William P. O'Hare, "Viano los Suburbinos!" *American Demographics,* April, 1993, p. 32.

[60] William Frey and Alden Speare, *Regional and Metropolitan Growth and Decline in the United States,* Russell Sage Foundation, New York, 1988, pp. 311–316.

[61] Douglas Massey and Nancy Denton, "Trends in Residential Segregation of Blacks, Hispanics, and Asians," *American Sociological Review,* **52:**802–825, 1987.

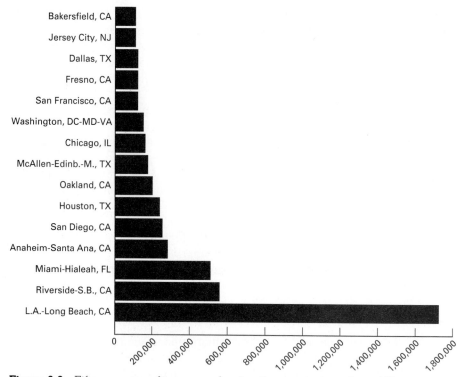

Figure 9-2 Fifteen metropolitan areas having the greatest number of Hispanic suburbanites. Note that these metropolitan areas account for 57.1 percent of the total number of suburban Hispanics in the United States.
Source: Compiled from 1990 census data.

details on Hispanic populations, see Chapter 10, Ethnic Diversity: Ethnics, African Americans, Hispanics, Asians, and Native Americans.)

ASIAN SUBURBS

Asians, who numbered 7.3 million in 1990, are the most suburban of the minority groups, with half (50.6 percent) living in suburbs. Unlike earlier immigrant groups who first settled in the city, almost half of all Asian immigrants are likely to bypass the city and go directly to the suburbs. In Washington, D.C., for example, there is no central-city Koreatown; only 800 of the 44,000 Koreans in the metro area actually live in the District.[62] Legal Asian immigrants having educational skills tend to move directly into those suburban neighborhoods where employment and schooling opportunities for children are greatest. This is particularly true in the west and southwest. The suburbs are where the best employment opportunities are found,

---

[62] "Area Koreans See No Need for Enclaves," *Washington Post,* Jan. 11, 1992, p. E1.

and a majority of the suburban-bound immigrants speak fluent English and hold advanced degrees. Asian Americans living in the suburbs have average household incomes 25 percent higher ($59,000 as of 1989) than Asian-American populations in the central city.[63] Those living in the central city are more likely to be less educated and also are more likely to be illegal immigrants.

Generally Asians live in suburbs that have an Asian presence but are not predominately Asian. An exception is the Los Angeles suburb of Monterey Park, which is the first Chinese suburb in America. Monterey Park, a suburb of 60,000 which is projected to be 80 percent Chinese in 2000, has experienced a series of growth and land-use controversies as it has been transformed from a low-density suburb to a more urban high-density "Little Taipei."[64] Part of the controversy reflects cultural differences in the use of land. Americans value open spaces around suburban houses, while Taiwanese and Hong Kong newcomers were accustomed to a more urban environment, and thus built more urban-looking buildings right up to the property line and paved over the front yard for auto parking. (For further discussion of Asian Americans see Chapter 10, Ethnic Diversity.)

THE FUTURE?

Over the decades suburbs have taken justified criticism as being all-white communities, but suburbs are becoming more multiracial and multiethnic. Ironically, the suburbs now have the opportunity to achieve what the cities have largely failed to accomplish—establishing stable, economically viable, and racially and ethnically integrated communities.

---

[63] William P. O'Hare, William H. Frey, and Dan Fost, "Asians in the Suburbs," *American Demographics*, May, 1994, p. 34.
[64] Timothy P. Fong, *The First Suburban Chinatown*, Temple University Press, Philadelphia, 1994.

Managed Integration: Oak Park

The suburban Chicago community of Oak Park is a working example of how older neighborhoods can be integrated and preserved. Once the home of Frank Lloyd Wright, and with many architecturally interesting homes, Oak Park by the late 1960s was a prime candidate for disinvestment and change. It is an old suburb of 60,000 with half its population in rental units. More important, it directly abuts Chicago's lower-class West Side ghetto. The adjacent Austin section of Chicago, a prime residential area twenty-five years ago, has experienced severe deterioration.

What makes Oak Park unique is that most of its residents, instead of picking up and fleeing, decided to face integration head-on. Their efforts have been so successful that Oak Park is currently a desirable housing area, particularly for young white home buyers. The reason for Oak Park's success is a tightly managed community. The community both quickly intervenes to halt building deterioration and encourages racial diversity. The community enforces housing codes and virtually controls all the activities of realtors. Being able to control its own institutions gives the community a major advantage.[*]

Ten percent of every apartment building's flats are inspected every year, and every apartment must be inspected and the building brought up to code before selling. A new shopping mall and village hall brighten up the community, while local lending institutions have been persuaded to keep open funds for mortgages and remodeling. Several million dollars has also gone into low-interest loans for upgrading of apartments. House-to-house solicitation by real estate companies and the posting of "For Sale" or "For Rent" signs are banned to prevent panic selling. After some pressure, all real estate companies now report all sales or rentals twice a week to the Oak Park Community Relations Department. To further discourage panic selling, the community initiated "moral homeowners' insurance." Homeowners who sign up for the insurance and stay in the community at least five years are guaranteed that they can sell their homes for 80 percent of the difference between the appraisal value and the selling price. The major reason for the homeowners' equity insurance is psychological rather than economic. It is meant to forestall any fears of declining housing values. Actually, the program, which went

---

[*] Carole Godwin, *The Oak Park Strategy*, University of Chicago Press, Chicago, 1979.

into operation in 1978, has had few takers, since property values in the suburb are appreciating.

Oak Park changed from 11 percent minority to 18 percent in 1990. Emphasizing diversity, the community actively welcomes minority residents and actively discourages all-white or all-black apartment buildings. To do this, Oak Park in 1985 began a unique plan to pay landlords to integrate their apartment buildings.* On a voluntary basis the landlord can enter into a five-year agreement to let the Oak Park Housing Center act as the landlord's rental agent. In return the landlord will be eligible for matching grants of up to $1,000 per unit to improve apartment interiors and larger grants for exterior renovations. The Housing Center will then actively seek black tenants for buildings that are now predominantly white and white tenants for buildings that are now predominantly black. If a suitable tenant cannot be found immediately, the apartment will stay off the market for up to ninety days, while the landlord receives 80 percent of the last rent received in the unit. The goal is to improve racial diversity and prevent resegregation while improving the basic housing stock and protecting landlords against vacant units. In spite of a small tax increase, the plan is supported by most local residents and real estate agents. The program has not been as successful as hoped since the census tracts nearest Chicago increased their proportion of minority residents to between 25 and 40 percent according to the 1990 census. It has been argued that as an invasion-succession pattern seems to be emerging, assumptions about Oak Park's remaining a stable integrated area may be premature.[†] Residents, though, tend to be far more optimistic.

It has to be kept in mind that Oak Park, with its middle-class to upper-middle-class residents, is not typical of many urban areas faced with rapid racial change. Nor do many communities exhibit such a strong sense of community involvement. There is no question that Oak Park manages its housing and rental market to an extent not found elsewhere. The community is integrated racially but not economically. Poor families are not desired.

Still, Oak Park's prosperity indicates that older areas—even when abutting a deteriorated, crime-ridden, lower-class ghetto— can both integrate racially and upgrade physically. Outside observers are sometimes critical of the extent of housing controls in the community, but for Oak Park, managed integration works.

* "Chicago Suburb to Pay Landlords to Integrate," New York Times, Nov. 11, 1984, p. 24.
† Richard A. Smith, "Creating Stable Racially Integrated Communities: A Review," Journal of Urban Affairs, 15:127–128, 1993.

CHAPTER

10

ETHNIC DIVERSITY
Ethnics, African Americans, Hispanics, Native Americans, and Asian Americans

The rich man in his castle,
The poor man at his gate,
God made them, high or lowly,
And order'd their estate.

From a Church of England hymn,
"All Things Bright and Beautiful"

INTRODUCTION: URBAN MINORITIES

In this chapter, attention is concentrated on ethnic and racial minorities whose futures are closely bound to the urban scene: white ethnics, African Americans, Hispanic Americans, Asian Americans, and Native Americans. These groups differ from one another in numerous respects; what they have in common is that, compared with other Americans, they are relatively recent newcomers to the urban scene, and most important, they are to various degrees deprived minorities encountering problems of acceptance and adjustment. White ethnics, African Americans, Hispanics, and Asians have different histories and cultures, but until very recently, all have been dismissed as unimportant or marginal to the mainstream of urban America. Minority status is a measure of social position and life chances, not necessarily numbers. However, by the middle of the twenty-first century blacks, Hispanics, and Asians will constitute half the national population.

Examination of contemporary trends in urbanization reveals a strong association between ethnicity and race and the patterns of urban residential segregation, patterns that are reinforced by socioeconomic differences. In the classic North American pattern of urban settlement described in Chapter 3, The Rise of Urban America, the point of entry for poor immigrants was the tenement district surrounding the core of the city. As their economic condition improved, the more established immigrants moved outward, leaving their tenements to be occupied by a wave of more recent immigrants such as blacks and Latinos. Americans tend to assume that this is the natural pattern of urban settlement, but it is not. For instance, in the preindustrial cities discussed in Chapter 2, Emergence of Cities, and in cities of the developing world as seen in Part Five, Worldwide Urbanization, newcomers first settle on the periphery of the urban area. Whether immigrants settle in the decaying core, as in North American cities, or on the least-developed periphery, as in the third world, there is one constant: The poor live in the least desirable location.

WHITE ETHNICS

Immigration

There is a story (probably apocryphal) that President Franklin Roosevelt enraged the Daughters of the American Revolution (DAR) during the 1930s by addressing them as "Fellow Immigrants." If so, he was only starting what is frequently forgotten. That is, all groups—including Indians—were once newcomers. The only difference is in time of arrival. Indians came perhaps 15,000 to 20,000 years ago, while Europeans first came in significant numbers less than 400 years ago. Substantial numbers of blacks have been here for three centuries, while many of the most recent arrivals have been Hispanics or Asians. Most of these are first- or second-generation newcomers. Thus, it is impossible to discuss American urban patterns and life without discussing the role played historically—and in the present day—by the newcomer to the American city (see Table 10-1).

It is a cliché to state that America is a nation of immigrants, but it is sometimes forgotten that American immigration was the largest mass migration in the history

TABLE 10-1
Largest Ten Ancestries of U.S.
Population Groups, 1990 Census

Reported ancestry	Percent of population*
German	23.3
Irish	15.6
English	13.1
African	9.6
Italian	5.9
American	5.0
Mexican	4.7
French	4.1
Polish	3.8
American Indian	3.5

* Source: Bureau of the Census, 1993.

of the world. Precise data are lacking, but some 30 million to 45 million immigrants arrived in the United States before the immigration laws of the 1920s. We will never know the exact number or distribution. In some cases overworked immigration officials automatically listed all newcomers on a ship as being of the same nationality. Thus, those on a ship from Hamburg were automatically German. First-class passengers usually were not even included in the immigration figures until this century.

Generally there is a loose pattern of association between higher social status of an ethnic group and the early arrival of ancestors on these shores. (The exception is the African American population, who in spite of their early arrival remained a separate caste excluded from mobility in American society.) So having colonial or Revolutionary War ancestors is considered preferable to being the son or daughter of recent immigrants. At the time of the Revolutionary War some nine-tenths of the new nation's white population traced their ancestry to the British Isles: English, Scotch, or Northern Irish (called Scotch-Irish to distinguish them from Catholic Irish).[1] Even cosmopolitan New York was dominated by English customs, laws, values, and mores. Protestantism in various forms was in effect the national religion.

The founding fathers strongly supported free and open migration. However, immigrants were not welcomed, without reservations. George Washington's views were that

> The bosom of America is open to receive not only the Opulent and Respectable Stranger, but the oppressed and persecuted of all Nations and Religions, whom we shall welcome to participation of all our rights and privileges, if by decency and propriety of conduct they appear to merit the enjoyment.[2]

Washington was more liberal in his admission criteria than many of his contemporaries (his successor, John Adams, lengthened the waiting period for citizenship),

[1] David Ellis et al., *A Short History of New York State,* Cornell University Press, Ithaca, N.Y., 1957, p. 64.
[2] Quoted in the President's Commission on Immigration and Naturalization, *Who Shall We Welcome?* U.S. Government Printing Office, Washington, D.C., 1953.

but even Washington's statement has a final clause that says in effect, "if we think they behave themselves."

First-Wave Immigrants

Major ethnic migrations began in the 1820s and sharply accelerated in the mid-1840s with the Irish fleeing the potato famine in Ireland. The famine caused over a million deaths by starvation in Ireland, and another million or so impoverished Irish peasants immigrated to America. The Irish were closely followed by the Germans and somewhat later the Scandinavians. These groups are collectively called the "old immigrants" to distinguish them from the early settlers—overwhelmingly of British origin.

The Germans, in spite of the fact that they played cards and insisted on drinking beer on Sunday—shocking some bluenoses—fared rather well. They earned a reputation for industriousness, thrift, and orderly living—although they rioted in Chicago in 1855 when the mayor banned the sale of beer on Sunday. Easing assimilation was the fact that the majority of Germans were Protestant.

The Irish had greater problems, for not only were they viewed as recalcitrant, papist rowdies, but they voted Democratic and were the poorest of the poor. The Irish, rather than slaves, were used in hard or hazardous work in the south. As it was explained by a New Orleans riverboat captain to a famous visitor, "The niggers are worth too much to be risked here; if the Paddies are knocked overboard or get their backs broke, nobody loses anything."[3] Irish labor built many of the nation's railroads, and a saying of the time was "An Irishman is buried under every tie." Confronted by discrimination—"No Irish Need Apply" was common in help-wanted ads—the Irish organized themselves. For the immigrant Irish, the route to social mobility was said to be through becoming one of the three P's, "priest, politician, or policeman"; and by the latter part of the nineteenth century, the Irish controlled the city halls in cities where they lived in significant numbers. Stereotypes also softened as more and more of the Irish became skilled workers. By the 1880s it was a common saying that "a good worker does as much as an Irishman."[4]

Second-Wave Immigrant Groups

While the ethnic groups of the first wave came from northern and western Europe, those of the second wave came largely from southern and eastern Europe (Figure 10-1). After 1880, increasing numbers of immigrants had a Slavic, Polish, Jewish, Italian, or Greek heritage. During the 1860s less than 2 percent of all immigrants came from southern or eastern Europe; by the 1890s those from southern and eastern Europe were a majority (52 percent) of all immigrants; and by the first decade of this century seven out of ten immigrants came from southern or eastern Europe. Today all European migration is much reduced, with only one out of nine coming from all of Europe. For an excellent account of the life of the newcomers, see Irving Howe's, *World of Our Fathers.*[5]

[3] Frederick Law Olmstead, *The Cotton Kingdom,* Modern Library, New York, 1969, p. 215.
[4] John Higham, *Strangers in the Land,* Atheneum, New York, 1977, p. 26.
[5] Howe, Touchstone, New York, 1976.

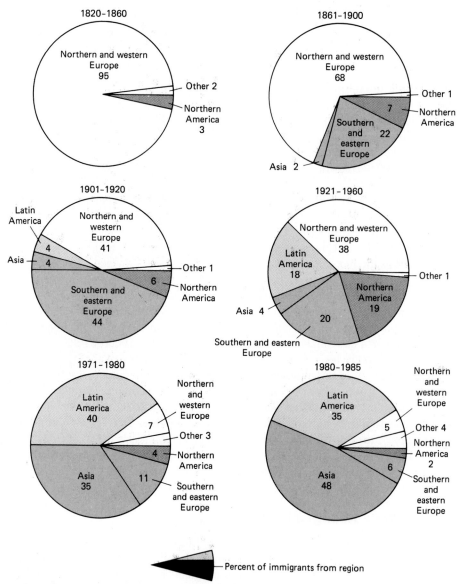

Figure 10-1. Immigrants to the United States by region of origin: 1820 through 1985.

Source: Population Reference Bureau, *Statistical Yearbook of the Immigration and Naturalization Service,* and author.

Immigrants traveling steerage had to undergo a complete physical examination on Ellis Island. No such requirements were imposed on first-class passengers. (Library of Congress.)

To ethnocentric WASP (white Anglo-Saxon Protestant) Americans, the new immigrants were alien races about to overwhelm American institutions and cities. First, they were coming from what were considered the most backward areas of Europe—regions that did not have self-government and thus by implication were incapable of self-government. Second, their customs and even food habits differed greatly from the Anglo-Saxon–Teutonic norm of earlier settlers. Third, their religions were different. They were more likely to be Catholic, Eastern Orthodox, or Jewish than Protestant. Finally, they came in large numbers, were concentrated in the cities, and thus were highly visible. (The technology of larger and faster steamships spurred immigration.)

By the time the second-wave immigrants arrived, the frontier had closed and the good farmlands were taken. Of necessity the new immigrants became industrial factory workers. Easy assimilation of the immigrants was retarded not only by their overwhelming numbers but also by their concentration in ethnic ghettos—in the inner-city zone of transition. Residence in central-city tenements reflected an economic necessity, but it also reflected the desires of the immigrants to have their own communities where they could follow traditional customs free from Anglo-Saxon hostility. The consequence was the development of ethnic neighborhoods which were isolated as far as possible from the larger city. The social organization of one such neighborhood, with its strong peer-group relationships, is described in William F. Whyte's *Street Corner Society.*[6]

Well into the twentieth century, the majority of the urban population was foreign-born or first-generation American. As of 1900, only half (51 percent) of the country's population was native white and of native parentage. In eastern seaboard cities such as New York and Boston, over three-quarters of the population was of foreign stock (foreign-born or second-generation American).

The negative reaction of WASP rural and small-town America to the nation's cities was closely linked to the perceived "foreignness" of the cities. Cities were considered cesspools of "rum, Romanism, and rebellion." Nineteenth-century writers and preachers such as Josiah Strong raised the clarion call against the menace of cities teeming with foreigners:

> The City has become a serious menace to our civilization. . . . It has a peculiar attraction for the immigrant. . . .
>
> While a little less than one-third of the population of the United States was foreign by birth or parentage, sixty-two percent of the population of Cincinnati was foreign, eighty-three percent of Cleveland, sixty-three percent of Boston, eighty percent of New York and ninety-one percent of Chicago. . . . Because our cities are so largely foreign, Romanism finds in them its chief strength. For the same reason the saloon, together with the intemperance and the liquor power which it represents, is multiplied in the city.[7]

As noted in Chapter 3, The Rise of Urban America, middle-class attempts to remove the bosses and reform the city generally meant removing power from the central-city immigrants. In the early twentieth century the city-manager system was seen as such an urban reform.

"Racial Inferiority" and Immigration

Before the turn of the century, arguments to restrict immigration were largely based upon (1) the ethnocentric assumption of the superiority of American ways and (2) the assumption that American industrial society represented a higher evolutionary form than the backward regions of Europe. Nonetheless, "the wretched refuse of your teeming shore" were felt to be convertible into the American mainstream. As the *Philadelphia Press* commented in 1888: "The strong stomach of American civilization may, and doubtless will, digest and assimilate ultimately this unsavory and repellent throng. . . . In time they catch the spirit of the country and form an element of decided worth."[8]

---

[6] William F. Whyte, *Street Corner Society,* University of Chicago Press, Chicago, 1943. See Chapter 7, City Life-Styles, for a review of material on inner-city communities.
[7] Josiah Strong, *Our Country,* rev. ed., Baker and Taylor, New York, 1891, chap. 11.
[8] Quoted in Higham, *Strangers in the Land,* p. 63.

However, around the turn of the century a new argument, that of racial inferiority, was added to the argument for exclusion. (The term "race" meant ethnicity or nationality rather than color, so that such terms as the "Polish race" and the "Italian race" were used. Various "experts" of the time agreed that the new immigrants were genetically inferior to the Anglo-Saxons who, combined with Germans, Scandinavians, and other first-wave immigrants, had formed the "American race." Discovering genetics, they jumped to the conclusion that not only hair color, size, and bone structure were genetically transferable, but also disposition, creativity, criminality, poverty, illiteracy, and all social behavior. Blood would tell—and what they believed it told was that Anglo-Saxon America was genetically committing suicide by allowing in unrestricted numbers of inferior races such as Poles, Italians, Slavs, and other eastern and southern Europeans. The conclusion seemed clear to opponents of immigration. "To admit the unchangeable differentiation of race in its modern scientific meaning is to admit inevitably the existence of superiority in one race and of inferiority in another."[9]

According to a leading sociologist of the time, even the appearance of the American population was likely to deteriorate: "It is unthinkable that so many persons with crooked faces, coarse mouths, bad noses, heavy jaws, and low foreheads can mingle their heredity with ours without making personal beauty yet more rare among us than it actually is."[10] While this sounds absurd today, the importance of the genetic argument cannot be overstressed. These genetic beliefs were held not by a lunatic fringe but by major scholars with national influence.

In the United States, the effect of the genetic argument was seen in the restrictive "racial"-based immigration laws of 1921 and 1924, the National Origins Act of 1929, and the McCarran-Walter Act of 1952. (President Truman vetoed the latter as discriminatory, but Congress passed it over his veto.) Southern and eastern Europeans were reduced from 45 percent of all immigrants under the already restrictive law of 1921 to 12 percent under the law of 1924. Northern and western Europeans were welcome—particularly if they were Protestant. About 85 percent of the quota went to northwest Europe, and roughly half the total quota went to three countries: England, Germany, and Ireland. Eastern and southern Europeans were given minimal quotas. While Great Britain's quota was 65,721 per year, that for Italy was only 5,802. Not until 1968 were the "racial" quotas eliminated.

New-Wave Immigrants

The days of mass European migration are past. Ellis Island is now a museum. In the cities of the east and midwest the majority of the white ethnic population now has been dispersed outward from segregated ethnic neighborhoods.[11] Ethnic neighborhoods, as described in Chapter 7, City Life-Styles, are viewed by some as

[9] Madison Grant, *The Passing of the Great Race,* Scribner, New York, 1921, p. XXVIII.
[10] E. A. Ross, *The Old World in the New,* Century, New York, 1914, p. 287.
[11] Stanley Lieberson, *Ethnic Patterns in American Cities,* Free Press, New York, 1963; and Avery M. Guest and James A. Weed, "Ethnic Residential Segregation: Patterns of Change," *American Journal of Sociology,* **81**:1088–1111, March, 1976.

simply historical remnants of bypassed ways of life.[12] However, ethnic neighborhoods are far from a thing of the past. The difference is that today immigrant groups, and immigrant neighborhoods, are most likely to be Hispanic or Asian. Also, large immigrant populations are now located in cities in Florida and the west. Four of five of the 880,000 legal immigrants now come from Asia and Latin America (primarily Mexico). Los Angeles is the immigrants' new Ellis Island. California absorbed half of all the 8 million immigrants that entered the United States during the 1980s, and it houses half those who enter illegally.

In addition to legal immigrants there are approximately 300,000 permanent illegal immigrants a year, for a net increase of 1.25 million persons a year.[13] Immigrants, and the children of immigrants, now account for over half the United States population growth. Thus, contrary to expectations of a generation back, immigrants are increasing rather than decreasing as a demographic force in American cities. In the case of Miami the largely immigrant Hispanic community has evolved into the dominant population group. Half of greater Miami's population is Hispanic, and 60 percent of that is Cuban. By contrast only 30 percent is non-Hispanic white. Miami has become a bilingual city that is economically and socially being shaped by Latin immigrants.[14] Later in the chapter we will discuss how Hispanic and Asian immigrants are changing western cities, especially those in California.

The revival of anti-immigrant sentiment in the mid-1990s reflects concern over the economic and social costs of illegal immigration, especially in California. As of 1994 over half the births in Los Angeles hospitals were to nondocumented mothers, and over half the city's public school children have illegal alien parents.

Melting Pot, Cultural Pluralism, Or?

Assimilation into American society through a "melting pot" was the model that guided the early studies of the Chicago school sociologists.[15] The melting pot model was implicit in the Burgess zonal hypothesis discussed in Chapter 4. The melting pot assumed that as populations moved toward the urban periphery, they would lose much of their ethnic identification. The children of the immigrants would leave the ethnic enclaves for the more "American" outer areas.

By the 1960s the melting pot metaphor had been largely replaced by that of "cultural pluralism." Cultural pluralism suggested that rather than merging, there continued to be separation of national-origin groups, so that the nation is really a mosaic of ethnic blocks. For instance, Glazer and Moynihan, in *Beyond the Melting Pot,* a study of ethnicity in New York City, found continuing cultural pluralism: "The point about the melting pot is that it did not happen. At least not in New York, and, mutatis mutandis, in those parts of America which resemble New York."[16]

---

[12] Melvin M. Webber, "The Post-City Age," in J. John Palen (ed.), *City Scenes,* Little, Brown, Boston, 1977, pp. 307–319.

[13] U.S. Bureau of the Census, "Population Projections of the United States by Age, Sex, Race, and Hispanic Origin 1993 to 2050," *Current Population Reports,* series P-25, no. 1104, Washington, D.C., 1993.

[14] Alejandro Portes and Alex Stepick, *City on the Edge: The Transformation of Miami,* University of California Press, Berkeley, 1993.

[15] For a review of literature on the melting pot, see Charles Hirschman, "America—Melting Pot Reconsidered," *Annual Review of Sociology,* **9,** Annual Reviews, Palo Alto, Calif., 1983, pp. 397–423.

[16] Nathan Glazer and Daniel Patrick Moynihan, *Beyond the Melting Pot,* MIT Press, Cambridge, Mass., 1963.

Note that the discussion of ethnic villagers in Chapter 6 assumes a degree of cultural pluralism.

In discussing assimilation, it helps to remember Milton Gordon's often-quoted distinctions between "cultural assimilation" and "structural assimilation." Cultural assimilation is said to occur when the newcomers adopt the dress, food habits, and cultural habits of the dominant group. Partially because of exposure through public schools and common media, cultural assimilation of new groups has been relatively rapid in America.

Structural assimilation is far more comprehensive, since it involves acceptance into the primary groups, cliques, and institutions of the dominant group. Structural assimilation is thus a more gradual process; ultimately it means intermarriage. "Once structural assimilation has occurred . . . all other types of assimilation will necessarily follow."[17] Alba's research, using a random sample of the national Catholic population, found that one measure of structural assimilation—intermarriage—had proceeded farther than had been commonly acknowledged.[18] Excepting the Hispanic and French Canadian populations, intermarriage was extensive, particularly in the English, Irish, and German populations.

Does ethnicity really make a difference in the attitudes, values, or life-style of second- and later-generation whites now living in the suburbs? Most social scientists say knowing one's social class is far more useful than knowing one's ethnicity. Scott Greer suggests that ethnicity has lost real meaning when increasing proportions of the population have mixed ancestry and thus can choose whether to identify themselves as, for example, Italian, Irish, or Polish. He believes that "the romantic idealization of the ethnic bond persists, despite the difficulty many Americans have in deciding which ethnic background is the right one."[19] He maintains that the melting pot was effective, and that the result is a common American culture. Research does indicate that the differences between the first-wave northern European immigrant groups and the second-wave southern and eastern European groups has largely disappeared.[20] Alba argues that differences between European ethnicities are fading and a new ethnic group is forming based on ancestry from anywhere in Europe.[21] African Americans, however, continue to remain outside the melting pot. For those residing in inner-city ghettos the most appropriate model is not the melting pot, or even cultural pluralism, but internal colonialism. The persisting inequality in inner cities suggests colonialism is a more appropriate paradigm than the melting pot or pluralism.

AFRICAN AMERICANS

The following pages review the past and present status of African Americans. Major white immigration to the industrializing cities occurred during the nineteenth

[17] Milton N. Gordon, *Assimilation in American Life,* Oxford University Press, New York, 1964, p. 81.
[18] Richard D. Alba, "Social Assimilation among American Catholic National-Origin Groups," *American Sociological Review,* **41:**1030–1046, December, 1976.
[19] Scott Greer, "The Faces of Ethnicity," in Palen, (ed.), *City Scenes,* pp. 147, 157.
[20] Stanley Lieberson and Mary C. Waters, *From Many Strands: Ethnic and Racial Groups in Contemporary America,* Russell Sage Foundation, New York, 1988.
[21] Richard D. Alba, *Ethnic Identity: The Transformation of White America,* Yale University Press, New Haven, Conn. 1990

TABLE 10-2
Black Population in the United States
by Number and Percent, 1790 to 1990

Year	Number	Percent of total population
1790	757,000	19.3
1800	1,002,000	18.9
1850	3,639,000	15.7
1900	8,834,000	11.6
1930	11,891,000	9.7
1940	12,866,000	9.8
1950	15,042,000	10.0
1960	18,860,000	10.6
1970	22,672,570	11.2
1980	25,969,000	11.8
1990	31,000,000	12.4

Source: U.S. Bureau of the Census. The 1990 figure
is corrected for census undercount.

and early twentieth century, when the number of unskilled jobs was expanding. Black immigration to urban areas, on the other hand, occurred somewhat later, mostly from World War I to 1960. Black blue-collar workers have been hit especially hard by the deindustrialization of the cities during the last decades.

White ethnics who suffered from discrimination or the imposition of quotas could, and often did, change their names as well as their life-styles, adopting the attitudes and customs of WASP America. But this choice is not open to most blacks and other nonwhites. Race is far more of a social than a biological construct. However, unlike ethnicity, color is a difference that is immediately visible as an identifier.

Table 10-2 shows the black population of the United States from 1790 to 1990. Blacks in the United States now number over 33 million—more than the total population of Canada. Due largely to higher birthrates the black population grew 13 percent in the decade 1980–1990, or double the 6 percent increase of whites.

Historical Patterns

The first blacks in the American colonies were not slaves but indentured servants. That meant that they had to serve for a given time—usually seven years—in bondage or indentureship before they became legally entitled to own property. However, this system—particularly in the south, where plantations required large labor forces—rapidly evolved into one of perpetual servitude. In 1661 Virginia passed a law allowing perpetual slavery, and two years later the Maryland colony declared that "all Negroes or other slaves within the province, to be hereafter imported, shall serve during life."

The fundamental conflict between America's social and political philosophy of freedom and equality on the one hand and the practice of social inequality on the other was aptly characterized by Gunnar Myrdal as the "American dilemma."[22] Two centuries earlier, Thomas Jefferson (who owned slaves while opposing slavery) had referred to it as justice in conflict with avarice and oppression.[23]

Population Changes

At the time of the first census in 1790, blacks made up one-fifth (19 percent) of the total population. In spite of a high rate of natural increase, the proportion of blacks in the population declined during the nineteenth century because of heavy European immigration. European immigration was restricted by the immigration laws of the 1920s' and since that time blacks have been increasing as a proportion of the population. African Americans currently constitute an eighth (12 percent) of the population.

The black population was—until this century—overwhelmingly rural and southern. Despite the Civil War and the extensive political and social upheavals of Reconstruction, there was but slight change in this pattern. As recently as 1910, nine out of ten blacks still lived in the south, and 73 percent of blacks were rural. Today only half (56 percent) live in the south, and 85 percent live in urban areas (compared with 71 percent of whites).

Slavery in Cities

Slavery was basically a rural institution, founded upon the plantation economy, but by 1820 about 20 percent of the people in the major southern cities were slaves.[24] Slavery in southern cities differed fundamentally from slavery on the plantations, so much so that plantation owners vigorously opposed the use of slaves in urban manufacturing, fearing that it would undermine the south's "peculiar institution." As a consequence, slavery drastically declined in the large cities by 1860. (Richmond's iron works were an exception.) The reason for the decline was not economic but social.

On the plantation, slaves were totally controlled by the overseer and could, if necessary, be controlled through fear of repression. Some might try to run away, but pursuit by specially trained tracking dogs and professional slave hunters made successful escapes difficult. In urban areas, on the other hand, slaveholders had far less mastery:

> While plantation slaves were typically field hands or house servants, urban slaves engaged in a wide variety of occupations, skilled as well as unskilled, in addition to those who worked as domestic servants for their owners. A very large number of slaves were hired out to work for others, the arrangement being made either by the slave owners or the slaves themselves.[25]

The system of slaves being hired out or hiring themselves to others and sharing the income with their owners meant that the slave was, in Frederick Douglass's words, "almost a free citizen."[26] In effect, the slave and owner entered into an informal

[22] Gunnar Myrdal, *An American Dilemma,* Harper & Row, New York, 1944.
[23] Ulrich B. Philips, *American Negro Slavery,* Louisiana State University Press, Baton Rouge, 1969, p. 122.
[24] Richard C. Wade, *Slavery in the Cities: The South 1820–1860,* Oxford University Press, New York, 1964.
[25] Thomas Sowell, *Race and Economics,* McKay, New York, 1975, p. 12.
[26] Wade, *Slavery in the Cities.*

contract in which the slave, through the sharing of his or her earnings, "purchased" some degree of freedom. Escaping from slavery was far easier and more common in the cities; therefore, to prevent the loss of large capital investments, urban slaveholders had to rule with a lighter hand.

The fact that urbanism undermined the traditional slave-master relationship did not escape plantation owners. Therefore, they were constantly making new restrictions and laws to govern urban slavery. Many nineteenth-century southerners saw city life as a direct threat to the southern way of life, and they were right.

"Free Persons of Color"

Nor were all blacks slaves. By the eve of the Civil War, roughly one out of eight blacks was a "free Negro," and most of these lived in cities—usually in border states. In Richmond, Virginia, the capital of the Confederacy, one-fifth of the city's black population were "free persons of color," and one-fourth of the city's blacks (including some slaves) owned their own homes. This growing population of "free persons of color" created serious problems for the slave states, for although most "free persons" did poorly in economic terms, they were still free men and women and thus a threat to the system. A handful of the southern antebellum free blacks were slave owners themselves. For example, William Ellison of South Carolina owned more slaves than all but the richest white southerners and lived in the former home of a governor of South Carolina.[27] However, such persons were anomalies. In Virginia as of 1830, census data indicate that at most some 1,000 free blacks were themselves slaveowners.[28]

Until the 1960s or so, the descendants of those who were free persons of color at the time of the Civil War dominated leadership roles in the black urban community. While Booker T. Washington was indeed "up from slavery," few other early leaders were. W. E. B. DuBois and most other founders of the NAACP, for example, had never been slaves.

Jim Crow Laws

Segregation of public facilities was not characteristic of the pre-Civil War urban south. Jim Crow laws, which established separate railway cars, streetcar seating, dining areas, rest rooms, and even doorways for blacks, were largely a product of the years between 1890 and 1910.[29] Segregation of facilities was most common in urban areas. Grandfather clauses (you could vote if your grandfather did, thus excluding blacks), literacy tests, and poll taxes disenfranchised blacks, while segregation laws were passed to separate the races in schools and public facilities. Crucial to segregation was the 1896 case of *Plessy v. Ferguson,* in which the

---

[27] Michael P. Johnson and James L. Roark, *Black Masters: A Free Family of Color in the Old South,* Norton, New York, 1984.

[28] Philip J. Schwarz, "Emancipators, Protectors, and Anomalities: Free Black Slaveholders in Virginia," *Virginia Magazine of History and Biography,* **95:**317–338, 1987.

[29] C. Van Woodward, *The Strange Career of Jim Crow,* Oxford University Press, New York, 1966.

Supreme Court, in effect, ruled that physical distance could be substituted for social distance. The pernicious doctrine of "separate but equal" was not finally eliminated until the famous 1954 case of *Brown v. Board of Education of Topeka,* in which the Supreme Court ruled that "separate educational facilities are inherently unequal."

"The Great Migration"

Significant migration of blacks out of the south began with World War I. When the war cut off the tide of European immigrant labor and flooded industries with war orders, a new source of labor had to be found. Soon labor recruiters were scouring the south, encouraging blacks to migrate north to "the promised land." In some cases, one-way railroad tickets were even provided. Recruiters "stirring up the negroes" were unwelcome guests in southern communities. A licensing regulation in Macon, Georgia, required each labor agent to pay a $25,000 fee and obtain recommendations from ten local ministers, ten manufacturers, and twenty-five merchants. Elsewhere, methods were more direct, and recruiters were shot or tarred and feathered.

The pull of northern industrial jobs, combined with the boll weevil's destruction of cotton and the mechanization of agriculture, encouraged what became known as "The Great Migration." Cotton production was shifting out of the old south to the west and southwest, and field-hand labor was no longer so necessary. Between 1910 and 1920 the five states of the deep south—South Carolina, Georgia, Alabama, Mississippi, and Louisiana—lost 400,000 blacks through out-migration. (Poor whites were also out-migrating at this time.)

There were three major migratory streams. The first was from the Carolinas, Georgia, and Florida up the east coast to key locations such as Washington, Philadelphia, New York, and Boston. The second was from Mississippi, Arkansas, and part of Alabama into the midwestern cities of St. Louis, Detroit, Chicago, and Milwaukee. The third stream was from Texas and part of Louisiana to Los Angeles and the west coast.

The depression of the 1930s cut off employment opportunities in the north and stemmed the flow of immigrants to the cities. But the resurgence of industry during World War II again accelerated the pace of migration, and it continued into the 1950s and 1960s. As a result of the great northern migration, Chicago houses more blacks than all of Mississippi, and the New York metropolitan area has more blacks than any state of the old south.[30]

This was an extremely substantial migration, but it should be kept in perspective. Between 1910 and 1960 somewhat under 5 million blacks left the south, largely for the big cities of the north. This is a great number of people but was fewer than the waves of European immigrants that inundated American shores during the first years of this century. For example, between 1900 and 1910 some 9 million foreign immigrants entered the United States.

---

[30] Thomas F. Pettigrew, *Racially Separate or Together?* McGraw-Hill, New York, 1971, p. 3.

Blacks were evicted from houses in white neighborhoods after the Chicago race riots of 1919. (Jun Fujita/Chicago Historical Society.)

End of Mass Migration

The period of mass migration from the south is now history. This movement contained the seeds of its own destruction, for as blacks moved to the cities, there were fewer persons left behind to become migrants in the future. Today most black movement is from one urban area to another. Increasingly, urban blacks are second- and third-generation urban residents. Today, while just over half of all blacks still live in the south, blacks are now one of the most urban segments of the total population. Since World War II most blacks have lived in urban areas. Blacks are more concentrated in the large cities and MSAs than whites. Over half of all blacks (55 percent) currently live in central cities of metropolitan areas (this is down from 59 percent in 1970), and as of 1995, 30 percernt of African Americans reside in the suburbs. One out of every three metro area blacks is a suburbanite.

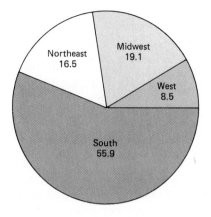

Figure 10-2.   Black population, by region. *Source:*   U.S. Bureau of the Census, "The Black Population in the United States: March, 1988," *Current Population Reports,* series P-20, no. 442, November, 1989.

Moving South

The great migration *from* the south has now been replaced by movement *to* the south. African Americans today are more likely to be moving into the south than migrating north. In this respect the movement of blacks parallels that of whites. Both are moving toward metropolitan areas in the south and west. Between the 1980 and 1990 censuses more than a million more blacks moved south than went north.[31] (See Figure 10-2.) As a consequence some 56 percent of blacks were living in the south in 1990 compared to 52 percent in 1980.[32] The same economic conditions that attract whites to the sunbelt are also drawing African Americans, particularly now that the racial climate in the south is perceived to be at least as good, and often better, than that in the north.[33]

The great bulk of the blacks moving north early in the 20th century were dirt poor, and they settled in the tenement slums of the inner city. By contrast, many of those moving south today are middle-class. Young college-educated blacks are now more likely to move south than north.[34] Rather than moving into crowded inner city slum neighborhoods today's migrants often are heading directly to the comfortable outer suburbs. These affluent suburban newcomers are sometimes called "buppies" or black urban professionals. They are moving south in substantial numbers for employment opportunities, more affordable housing, and a more congenial social atmosphere. Atlanta alone added a couple of hundred thousand new black suburbanites during the 1990s, and many of these suburbanites are newcomers from other metropolitan areas. To the beginning-of-the-twentieth-century image of the southern rural black sharecropper needs to be added the new-century image of the southern suburban black professional.

---

[31] U.S. Bureau of the Census, "The Black Population of the United States: March 1988," *Current Population Reports,* series P-20, no. 442, November, 1989.

[32] Ibid.

[33] Kenneth Weiss, "Migration by Blacks from South Turns Around," *New York Times,* June 11, 1989, p. 36.

[34] Reynolds Farley and Walter R. Allen, *The Color Line and the Quality of Life in America,* Russell Sage Foundation, New York, 1987, p. 128.

Urban Segregation Patterns

Extent of Segregation. Segregation of racial and ethnic groups into ghettos is not new to American life. Anti-immigrant and anti-Catholic political movements, from the Know-Nothing Party of the nineteenth century to the Ku Klux Klan of the 1920s, attempted to keep newcomers "in their place" socially and physically. Their "place" was the old and overcrowded housing in the central area near the factories. As members of ethnic groups prospered, they often moved out of the ghetto into outlying neighborhoods with better-quality housing, and so residential segregation decreased.[35] Blacks also started in the poorest central-city ghetto neighborhoods, but to a far greater degree than other groups, they remained restricted to such "black belts."[36] For blacks the pattern has been one of race overriding economics. African Americans who have increased their personal socioeconomic status do not live as far from the central-city ghetto as do comparable Hispanics.[37]

Major Studies. The landmark study of changing patterns of racial segregation was that of Karl and Alma Taeuber, in which they compared segregation indexes for American cities for 1940, 1950, and 1960 and found high incidences of segregation virtually universal.[38] They used what has become the best known of the segregation indexes, the index of dissimilarity which measures the degree to which groups are distributed evenly among city blocks or census tracts. A score of zero reflects complete integration, while a score of one indicates complete segregation. Later studies using the 1970 and 1980 censuses found decreasing, but still high, levels of segregation.[39] African Americans are less likely to live near similar-socioeconomic-status whites than are Hispanics, or especially Asians. A study of sixty metropolitan areas from 1970 to 1980 found that the index of segregation fell from 0.8 to 0.7 between blacks and whites.[40] (For Hispanics it was 0.4 in 1980, and for Asians it was 0.3.)

A major study by Farley and Frey examining trends in 232 metropolitan areas from 1980 to 1990 suggests that peak segregation levels occurred in the past and the trend now is for modest declines in segregation levels.[41] The largest decreases

[35] Lieberson, *Ethnic Patterns in American Cities;* and Guest and Weed, "Ethnic Residential Segregation."

[36] For an excellent study of ghetto life during the 1930s, see St. Clair Drake and Horace Cayton, *Black Metropolis,* Harcourt, Brace, New York, 1945.

[37] Douglas S. Massey and Brendan P. Mullan, "Processes of Hispanic and Black Spatial Assimilation," *American Journal of Sociology,* **89**:836–873, 1984.

[38] Karl E. Taeuber and Alma F. Taeuber, *Negroes in Cities: Residential Segregation and Neighborhood Change,* Aldine, Chicago, 1965.

[39] Annemette Sorenson, Karl E. Taeuber, and Leslie J. Hollingsworth, Jr., "Indexes of Racial Residential Segregation for 109 Cities in the United States, 1940 to 1970," *Sociological Focus,* April, 1975, pp. 125–142; Thomas Van Valey, Wade Clark Roof, and Jerome E. Witcox, "Trends in Residential Segregation: 1960–1970," *American Journal of Sociology,* **82**:826–844, 1977; Karl E. Taeuber, "Racial Residential Segregation in 28 Cities, 1970–1980," Center for Demography and Ecology, University of Wisconsin Working Paper 83–12, 1983; and Michael J. White, *American Neighborhoods and Residential Differentiation,* Russell Sage Foundation for the National Committee for Research on the 1980 Census, New York, 1988.

[40] Douglas Massey and Nancy Denton, "Trends in Residential Segregation of Blacks, Hispanics, and Asians, 1970–1980," *American Sociological Review,* **52**:802–825, 1987.

[41] Reynolds Farley and William H. Frey, "Changes in the Segregation of Whites from Blacks during the 1980s: Small Steps toward a More Integrated Society," *American Sociological Review,* **59**:23–45, 1994.

in segregation are occurring in young western and southern metropolitan areas having significant housing construction. As of 1990 some 30 percent of all blacks lived in all-black neighborhoods, a decrease from 34 percent in 1980.[42] Whites dropped from three-quarters living in all-white neighborhoods in 1980 to two-thirds in 1990. However, much of this change was due to Asians living in white neighborhoods. In spite of laws to the contrary, some realtors and financial institutions still employ discriminatory mechanisms to maintain dual markets for white and minority home buyers.[43]

Diversity and Inequality Today

The Middle Class. As Chapter 9, Changing Suburbanization Patterns, indicated, it no longer makes sense to speak of the African-American population as if all 33 million share similar characteristics. The numbers of middle-class and affluent blacks are increasing, while at the same time those at the bottom (frequently in female-headed families) are slipping ever further behind. These two black worlds have been slipping further and further apart. Black married-couple families have been increasing their earnings for a quarter of a century, and as of the 1990 census, their incomes were 82 percent those of whites.[44] Families headed by younger college-educated blacks had 92 percent income parity with whites. The median 1989 income for married-couple families where the head of household was age twenty-five to forty was $54,400 for blacks and $58,000 for whites. Over a million black familes (one out of seven black families compared with one out of three white) had an income of $50,000 or more. Within these affluent familes one-third (32 percent) are college graduates, three-quarters (77 percent) own their own homes, and four out of five are married (79 percent).

The Truly Disadvantaged. The black population at the other end of the spectrum is falling further behind. This is the large inner-city population referred to as the "underclass" or the "truly disadvantaged." By this it is meant that these are the poor who are essentially outside the system of social mobility—unskilled dropouts, drug addicts, and teenage mothers on welfare and their children. These groups are increasingly excluded from the economic growth that has benefited both the black and white middle class.[45] The overall poverty rate of blacks remains high, with one-third of blacks in poverty (compared with just over one-quarter of Hispanics and one-tenth of whites).[46] There is increasing feminization of poverty, and especially black poverty. While intact black families continue to move out of poverty, two-thirds (66 percent) of black families headed by divorced or never-married women

---

[42] Dan Gilmore and Stephen K. Doig, "Segregation Forever?" *American Demographics,* January, 1992, p. 49.

[43] Douglas Massey and Nancy Denton, *American Apartheid: Segregation and the Making of the Underclass,* Harvard University Press, Cambridge, Mass., 1993.

[44] William P. O'Hare et al., "African Americans in the 1990s," *Population Bulletin,* **46:**28, 1991.

[45] William Julius Wilson, *The Truly Disadvantaged: The Inner City, the Underclass, and Public Policy,* University of Chicago Press, Chicago, 1987.

[46] U.S. Bureau of the Census, "Population Profile of the United States: 1989," *Current Population Reports,* series P-23, no. 159, 1989, p. 34.

are now below the poverty level. Or to look at it another way, of all poor black families, seven out of ten are headed by women.

As jobs have left the inner city, the pool of marriageable—that is, reasonably economically secure—men has dropped sharply. As a consequence, marriage and illegitimacy rates have changed radically over the last three decades. In 1960 two-thirds (65 percent) of black women aged thirty to thirty-four were married. By 1990 this figure had dropped to 39 percent. The change in marital status has most affected the children. Black out-of-wedlock births have jumped from a quarter of all births in 1960 to 68 percent in 1994. Half of all black children under age eighteen now live only with their mother.

As William Julius Wilson, the major researcher in this area, has documented, the future for the truly disadvantaged is dim.[47] Over the last two decades the movement of reasonably paying blue-collar durable-goods manufacturing jobs to suburbia has eliminated a major source of employment for working-class males. Deindustrialization has led to rust belt cities of the north losing half their manufacturing workers since 1965. These losses have occurred most heavily among working-class males. As joblessness increased among blue-collar blacks, the number of marriageable men decreased, and divorce and illegitimacy have increased. Poverty has undermined family strength, and increased the number of female-headed families. As job opportunities have plummeted, joblessness in Chicago's poverty ghetto has resulted in adult unemployment rates of over 60 percent.[48] The absence of jobs is made even worse by the absence of adult working males who can provide both knowledge of available jobs and assistance in entry into the work force. People tend to learn about employment opportunities through employed relatives and friends, and those among the truly disadvantaged don't have this opportunity. Further, massive joblessness weakens the perception that there is a relationship between going to school and getting a job. This in turn decreases academic aspirations for young males who see no purpose in attending classes. The link between school and work has been broken.

Blacks, especially blue-collar blacks, were hit hard by the deindustrialization of the central cities since due to racial discrimination poor minorities are disproportionately concentrated in the inner city where the manufacturing plants have closed. The absence of traditional entry-level lower-skilled jobs means that it is increasingly difficult for those without skills to climb the socioeconomic ladder out of the ghetto.[49] As was discussed in Chapter 6, Metropolitan and Edge-City Growth, there is a major disjuncture between where people live and where employment opportunities exist. Children coming of age in inner-city ghettos (often in female-headed poverty families) are substantially worse off than those of earlier generations.

Moreover, as the middle class and successful working class move out of the ghettos, the inner city becomes increasingly associated with drugs, violent crime, commercial blight, family disruption, and educational failure. The once-viable so-

[47] Wilson, *The Truly Disadvantaged,* 1987.

[48] Loic J. D. Wacquant and William Julius Wilson, "The Cost of Racial and Class Exclusion in the Inner City," *The Annals,* **501**:17, 1989.

[49] John D. Kasarda, "Urban Industrial Transition and the Underclass," *The Annals,* **501**:26–47, 1989.

cial structure of the area collapses. William Julius Wilson and others argue that the crisis of the inner city is increasingly one of an economic underclass rather than one of race. Racism explains why working-class blacks were especially vulnerable, but the changes in the economy are the critical key to the problems of the underclass or truly disadvantaged. Most scholars now agree with Wilson's contention that the crisis has occurred not because a "welfare ethos" has suddenly taken over, but because the economic structure has collapsed, and the resulting economic exclusion has led to social collapse.[50] Thus, welfare reforms cannot work without providing the alternative of jobs. Reforms that fail to address the need for inner-city employment are doomed to failure. How to do this in a society that is increasingly information- rather than manufacturing-based is the major urban challenge of the new century.

HISPANIC POPULATION

Hispanic Americans are among the most rapidly growing segments of the urban population.[51] The nation's 27 million persons of Hispanic origin account for 10 percent of the national population, and this figure largely excludes the estimated 2.5 to 4 million undocumented aliens. Latin America accounted for 42 percent of new legal immigrants to the United States during the 1980s. It is projected that by 2010 the United States Hispanic population will number 39 million.

From 1980 to 1990 the Hispanic population increased by 53 percent (7.7 million persons).[52] This is much larger than the non-Hispanic increase of only 7 percent. About half the Hispanic growth is because of immigration, but there would be considerable growth even without immigration. This is because of the Hispanic population's young age structure (median age of twenty-six compared with thirty-three for non-Hispanics) and high birthrates (about 50 percent higher than the U.S. average).[53] Thus growth will occur even if immigration, legal and undocumented, ceases. It is projected that the Hispanic population will outnumber blacks within a score of years.

Hispanics are highly concentrated geographically (see Table 10-3). Half the Hispanic population of the United States is clustered in two states: California and Texas. Florida also has a growing Latino population. In California, Hispanics constitute a quarter (25.8 percent) of the population. In both California and Texas, the Hispanic population is overwhelmingly urban. There are over 3 million Hispanics in Los Angeles County alone. Hispanics in Houston will outnumber both blacks and whites by A.D. 2000. The Latino population is more concentrated in metropolitan areas than either the whites or blacks, with 84 percent living in such areas. Within

[50] Wilson, *The Truly Disadvantaged,* 1987
[51] There is no consensus on how the "Hispanic" population should be addressed. A 1995 Bureau of the Census Current Population Survey of Hispanic origin members indicated 58 percent preferred the term "Hispanic," and 12 percent each favored "Latino" or of "Spanish origin." Hispanic also is the term used in census and government documents.
[52] U.S. Bureau of the Census, "The Hispanic Population in the United States: March 1990," *Current Population Reports,* series P-20, no. 444, 1990.
[53] National Center for Health Statistics, "Advanced Report of Final Natality Statistics, 1986," *Vital Statistics Report,* **37**(3):9, July, 1988.

TABLE 10-3
States with Largest Hispanic Populations (in millions), 1980 and 1990, and Percentage of U.S. Population

	1980		1990	
	Number	Percent	Number	Percent
United States	14.6	100%	21.0	100%
California	4.5	31	7.7	34
Texas	2.3	20	4.3	20
New York	1.7	11	2.2	10
Florida	0.8	6	1.6	7
Illinois	0.6	4	0.9	4
Arizona	0.4	3	0.7	3
New Jersey	0.5	3	0.7	3
New Mexico	0.5	3	0.6	3
Colorado	0.3	2	0.4	2

Source: U.S. Bureau of the Census.

Spanish is more common than English in some East Los Angeles neighborhoods. (Spencer Grant/Stock, Boston.)

metropolitan areas the Spanish-speaking population is more evenly distributed than the black population. As noted in Chapter 9, Changing Suburbanization Patterns, some 43 percent of the Hispanic population reside in suburbs, and Hispanics accounted for a quarter of all suburban population gain between 1980 and 1990.[54]

Socioeconomic Position

Although Hispanics are very heterogeneous with regard to economic and social variables, overall Hispanic income levels are two-thirds that of other Americans. The Spanish-speaking population as a whole is better off than blacks, but below non-Hispanic whites. While one-third of blacks are below the poverty level, this is true of only one-quarter of Hispanics and 9.5 percent of non-Hispanic whites.[55] This general comparison, however, masks wide variations among those of different Spanish-speaking backgrounds. Puerto Ricans earn slightly less than blacks, Mexican Americans earn slightly more, and Cuban Americans—many of whom as refugees from Fidel Castro's rule left Cuba with marketable skills—earn considerably more.[56]

Overall, in spite of considerable diversity Hispanics tend to be concentrated in low-wage service jobs. Contributing to the low economic position of Latino Americans are generally low levels of education. Only half are high school graduates, and among young adults, only six in ten (62 percent) have completed high school and only 12 percent are college graduates.[57] (For non-Hispanics, 89 percent have completed high school, and 25 percent have completed college.) Since in the United States lack of a high school diploma means virtual exclusion from much of contemporary industrial life, many Hispanics are employed in the so-called secondary labor market of marginal jobs and illegal enterprises. While older immigrants, especially Cubans, sometimes came with skills, recent immigrants (especially Dominicans and Salvadorans) are largely unskilled and have especially low educational levels. Thus it is projected that they will have employment problems, have lower than average incomes, and spend more time on welfare.[58] However, keep in mind that the Spanish-speaking population is very diverse. Mexican Americans and Puerto Ricans—the two largest groups—are discussed below.

Mexican Americans

Today 63 percent of all Hispanics are Mexican Americans.[59] Hispanics living in California and Texas are overwhelmingly of Mexican or Central American in

[54] Willian H. Frey and William P. O'Hare, "Vivano los Suburbios!," *American Demographics*, April, 1993, p. 32.

[55] U.S. Bureau of the Census, "The Hispanic Population of the United States: March 1991," *Current Population Reports*, series P-20, no. 455, 1991.

[56] For data on initial Cuban-American economic adjustment, see Kenneth L. Wilson and Alejandro Portes, "Immigrant Enclaves: An Analysis of the Labor Market Experience of Cubans in Miami," *American Journal of Sociology*, 96(2):295–319, September, 1980.

[57] Rafael Valdivieso and Cary Davis, "U.S. Hispanics: Challenges and Issues for the 1990s," *Population Trends and Public Policy*, Population Reference Bureau, Washington, D.C., December, 1988.

[58] George J. Borjas, *Friends or Strangers: The Impact of Immigrants on the U.S. Economy*, Basic Books, New York, 1990.

[59] There is no generally accepted term used by Americans of Mexican ancestry to describe the ethnic group. "Mexican American," "Spanish American," and "Latino," are all used, and the preferred term differs from place to place. For convenience, we will generally use the term "Mexican American."

origin, while those living in Florida are heavily Cuban and those in New York are largely Puerto Rican. The stereotype of Mexican Americans as agricultural workers—an image strengthened by Cesar Chavez's successful struggle to organize California farm workers—is quite erroneous. While many Hispanic immigrants have rural roots, 90 percent of California's 8.7 million persons of Mexican descent are urban residents. Los Angeles today has over 3 million Latinos (most of whom are of Mexican background), without fully counting the undocumented aliens in the heavily Spanish-speaking East Los Angeles area. There are more Hispanics than blacks in Los Angeles. The city is 40 percent Hispanic, 37 percent Anglo, 13 percent African American, 9 percent Asian, and 1 percent Native American.

Education. Low educational levels are a major barrier to economic advancement, and overall Mexican Americans have the lowest educational level among Hispanic groups. Mexican Americans have lower median levels of education than blacks. Poorer academic performance is not simply the result of being handicapped by not knowing English since the Cuban population is the most likely to speak Spanish at home but has the highest educational levels. Frequent moving of families disrupts some children's education. The comparatively lower value placed on education in the traditional lower-class Mexican family is also a factor, particularly as regards the education of women. Some 45 percent have completed high school or more and 7 percent college or more.[60] As noted above, concerns over employment of immigrants is heightened by the fact that current immigrants from Mexico have lower educational levels than immigrants of earlier generations.

Urbanization. The problem of adequate schooling and other problems of adjusting to the larger Anglo society have become more acute with the rapid urbanization of the Mexican-American population. Traditional isolated towns and villages in New Mexico and other southwestern states have been losing population, while the Mexican-American population of cities such as Albuquerque, San Antonio, and Los Angeles has been increasing. South-Central Los Angeles where the 1992 riots resulted in 58 deaths, 2,400 injured, and 15,000 arrested was one of the areas in ethnic transition. Between 1980 and 1990, not only had South-Central lost many of its jobs, but 48,000 blacks departed and 146,000 Latinos moved in. Today Los Angeles has more people of Mexican ancestry than any other city in the Americas except Mexico City and Guadalajara. Clearly, the Mexican American's future is an urban future. The geographical movement out of the southwest is not only migration out of a region; it is a symbol of the inevitable change from rural to urban residence and rural to urban ways of life.

Despite dramatic growth, Mexican Americans as a group generally have attracted less attention than have other minorities such as blacks. The relative quiet of Mexican-American city dwellers can be partially attributed to the fact that despite low-level income, housing, and services, cities in the United States are still infinitely superior to the destitute *barrios* of the Mexican *municipios*. The United

---

[60] U.S. Bureau of the Census, "The Hispanic Population of the United States," 1991.

States offers relative opulence compared with the poverty of the suburban squatter *barrios* of the border region where many United States manufacturing plants have relocated in order to profit from wages that averaged a dollar an hour in 1995. Also, some of the relative quiet of the Mexican-American population in the United States is doubtlessly due to the fact that some are undocumented immigrants and thus do not seek attention in any way.

Housing and Other Patterns. The crowded *barrios* of California and Texas are where new arrivals are most likely to settle. Poverty is common in the urban *barrios,* or ghettos, and Chicano gangs remain a serious problem. Gang-related drug use and crime have become common in the *barrios.*[61] Los Angeles County is estimated to have 40,000 gang members, and yearly has in excess of 400 gang murders.

For Mexican Americans there are wide variations in patterns of physical segregation.[62] Outside of the border states, economics plays an increasing part in determining residential patterns. Segregation is increasing in cities, such as Los Angeles, that are experiencing heavy in-migration of newcomers.[63] However, although segregation and discrimination do occur, they are not institutionalized to the extent that they are in the relationships between blacks and whites. Middle-class Mexican Americans have heavily suburbanized.[64]

Fertility rates among Mexican Americans are still extremely high, with an average family of four children. Only American Indians, another poor minority, have larger families. Today the Mexican-American population is a young population due to high fertility rates and the large number of young immigrants. The median age of the Mexican-origin population is 25.5 years, well below the median age of 33.0 years for non-Hispanics. Increasing urbanization and urbanism, plus socioeconomic mobility, should bring fertility rates of Mexican Americans more in line with those of the larger society over the next decade.

Political Involvement. Mexican Americans are still underrepresented in the halls of political power, but signs point to increased political activity. Mexican Americans today are torn between viewing themselves as a distinct minority group or as individual Americans who share the speaking of Spanish. Chicanos often look to black groups as an example of how they should organize, while assimilated middle-class Mexican Americans resist the minority-group label. ("Chicano" is a contraction and corruption of "Mexicano"; it originally was a term of derision for one who was unsophisticated, but now means one who has soul.) Overall, political awareness is increasing and class division and rhetoric are more muted than a decade ago. While economically successful Mexican Americans are moving out of

---

[61] For a study of Chicano gangs and the role of drugs, see Joan W. Moore, *Homeboys: Gangs, Drugs and Prison in the Barrios of Los Angeles,* Temple University Press, Philadelphia, 1978.

[62] Frank D. Bean and Marta Tienda, *The Hispanic Population of the United States,* Russell Sage Foundation, New York, 1987, pp. 170–177.

[63] Ibid., p. 170.

[64] Frey and O'Hare, "Vivano los Suburbios!"

the *barrios,* their places are being taken by ever-more newcomers attracted by the promise of life in urban America.

Political differences among Hispanic groups are considerable. For example, while California Mexicans as a group voted Democratic in the 1992 elections, Florida, where Cubans dominate, voted overwhelmingly Republican. Compared with those in northern cities, Hispanics in the south are generally also more upscale in income and more likely to perceive themselves in the mainstream of American life.[65]

Immigration. Much of the early Mexican-American population came north because there was a lack of economic opportunities in the labor-heavy Mexican economy and a demand for temporary farm workers in the United States. Particularly after World War II, the economic boom in the United States, coupled with the inability of the Mexican industrial economy to absorb all of its workers, led both legal ("green-carders") and illegal immigrants northward to supply the shortage in American agricultural labor. Today the agribusiness enterprises in California and Texas are replacing human workers with machines, a process that is likely to accelerate. Economic difficulties in Mexico such as the 1995 financial crisis increase the influx of illegal immigrants to the United States, largely regardless of economic opportunities.

Currently, just about every aspect of the immigration question is embroiled in emotional dispute. The resurgence of anti-immigrant sentiment is evident in the 1994 passage in California of Proposition 187, which bans illegal immigrants from using government-supported welfare services and nonemergency health care. Much of the concern was economic driven since the state's 2 million nondocumented immigrants were costing the state over $3 billion a year, or 10 percent of the state budget. Polls indicate a split in the Mexican-American community over immigration, with a slight majority supporting reduced immigration.[66] As long as it is not an ethnic attack, middle-class Mexican Americans are in favor of tighter border controls. Immigration is not a major concern to all Hispanics. Mexican Americans are very concerned over immigration changes, but such concerns mean little to Puerto Ricans, all of whom are already citizens.[67]

Internal Diversity. It has to be remembered that the Mexican-American population is remarkably diverse. Traditionally, Mexicans (and Anglos) made a broad distinction between the upper-class "Spanish" of "pure blood" and the lower-class "Mexicans." Spanish ancestry has traditionally been considered more prestigious than Mexican ancestry, and Indian ancestry is at the bottom. This attitude is not just a reaction to the racial situation in the United States, but rather has roots deep in the early colonial history of Mexico under the Spanish crown. (The Spanish colonial social system is discussed further in Chapter 18, Urbanization in Latin America.)

The gracious Spanish grandee of his California rancho typifies the first stereotype. Mexicans, by contrast, were stereotyped as lazy and cowardly. The lesson of

---

[65] Cheryl Russell, "The News about Hispanics," *American Demographics,* March, 1983, p. 20.
[66] Peter Skerry, *Mexican Americans: The Ambivalent Minority,* Free Press, New York, 1993.
[67] William A. Diaz, *Hispanics: Challenges and Opportunities,* Ford Foundation, New York, 1984.

the Alamo was clear: "One Texan was worth ten Mexicans." Particularly disparaged are the most recent Mexican immigrants. Often residing in the country as undocumented aliens and serving in menial jobs, they constitute one of the poorest-educated and least-skilled segments of the population. This division into "Spanish" and "Mexican" serves the sociological function of allowing the former to be accepted into the businesses, homes, and even families of Anglo society, while discrimination and exploitation of lower-class Mexicans continues.

Puerto Ricans

General Characteristics and Conditions.   Puerto Ricans constitute the second-largest Hispanic minority in the United States. Puerto Ricans differ from other Spanish-speaking Americans in several significant respects. First, Puerto Ricans have been American citizens since 1917. Thus, there is no question regarding their legal right to live on the mainland. Second, many Puerto Ricans are first-generation migrants, the bulk of Puerto Rican migration having occurred since World War II. Third, Puerto Ricans are almost totally urban. Some 96 percent of mainland Puerto Ricans reside in metropolitan areas. Finally, as noted earlier, Puerto Rican family income is the lowest of that of Hispanic groups, with over a third (36.5 percent) of Puerto Rican families living in poverty.[68] Puerto Ricans, thus, are even more hard-pressed than blacks.

As with blacks, but not other Hispanics, there is a high proportion of female-headed families. Over four out of ten (43 percent) of all Puerto Rican families are headed by a woman without a husband present. Two-thirds of these female headed families are living in poverty.[69] Puerto Rican women are less likely to be in the labor force than other Hispanic women. The New York area houses approximately half (49 percent) of mainland Puerto Ricans. This is down from 64 percent in 1970.

Mainland Puerto Ricans have a young age structure, with a median age of twenty-seven. As of the 1970 census, only 2 percent had finished college.[70] In 1990, 11 percent had finished. Upgrading educational levels is essential if Puerto Ricans are to move ahead. New York's former deputy mayor, Herman Badillo, himself a Puerto Rican, is not optimistic about the schools' accomplishments with Puerto Rican youngsters. "We have plenty of jobs in skyscrapers of midtown Manhattan," he says. "The problem is that kids can't spell."[71]

Central cities such as New York have lost many of the entry-level blue-collar jobs filled by immigrants. Newcomer Puerto Ricans can't sell their muscles the way the earlier Germans and Italians—or even an earlier generation of Puerto Ricans—did. Today economic advancement strongly favors those having white-collar skills and levels of education.

---

[68] U.S. Bureau of the Census, "Hispanic Population in the United States," March, 1993, *Current Population Reports,* series P-20, no. 475, Washington, D.C., Table 2, 1994.
[69] Ibid.
[70] Jose Hernandez et al., *Social Factors in Educational Attainment among Puerto Ricans in U.S. Metropolitan Areas,* Aspira, New York, 1979, pp. 1–2.
[71] Quoted in *Time,* Oct. 16, 1978.

For Puerto Ricans, political involvement tends to be low compared with that of previous immigrant groups. In part, this is due to the availability of flights back to Puerto Rico. If things get difficult, it is sometimes easier just to return to the island.

The New Generation. The picture just sketched is heavily influenced by experiences of first-generation mainland Puerto Ricans.[72] Thus it may be unduly pessimistic for younger generations. The second generation is beginning to make its impact. Indications are that the educational and occupational levels of young Puerto Ricans will be far higher than those of their parents (although still below the average for all whites). Family patterns are also changing. First-generation Puerto Ricans have larger-sized families than the national average, while second-generation Puerto Ricans born in the United States in two parent families have fewer children than the national average. Thus, while the first generation is among the nation's poorest citizens, the fate of the mainland-born may be brighter. Increasingly, the major distinction is between two parent families and poor female-headed households.

NATIVE AMERICANS

By omission, we have in essence denied that the American Indian has a heritage other than that portrayed in old John Wayne movies on cable television.[73] Only in recent decades have there been popular books telling history from the Indian's side, such as *Bury My Heart at Wounded Knee*.[74] Such works have helped to restore our perspective, but valuable as they are, they do not confront one basic problem: our tendency always to refer to Indians in the past tense, as if they had disappeared with the buffalo and the frontier. They didn't disappear—they were simply ignored and forgotten.

Socioeconomic Status

As noted in Chapter 3, The Rise of Urban America, the first colonist saw Indians as part of the environment, to be mastered and tamed like the forests and wild animals. The Indians' antiurban orientation—they lived in nomadic bands or small villages—left them particularly vulnerable to exploitation. Indians were systematically exterminated by Indian wars, destruction of the buffalo, and epidemics of European diseases against which they had no immunity. By 1890, when the first federal census of Indians was taken, their population had been reduced to 250,000, most barely surviving on government reservations. The 1990 census showed that the number of Native Americans increased 38 percent to 1.9 million—seven-tenths

---

[72] U.S. Commission on Civil Rights, "Puerto Ricans in the United States: An Uncertain Future," Washington, D.C., 1976, p. 36.

[73] American Indians—from Algonquin to Cherokee to Lakota—are heterogeneous in patterns of social organization and in their world view. The only justification for subsuming such diversity under the generic term "Indian" is that the white society has consistently done this for several centuries and has responded similarly to all groups it has labeled "Indian." Recently intertribal and pan-Indian groups have begun to stress common Indian roots.

[74] Wounded Knee was the final episode of the Indian wars. Here 300 Lakota Sioux were massacred by the army in 1890. It was also the site of an unsuccessful militant political occupation by Indians in 1973. See Dee Alexander Brown, *Bury My Heart at Wounded Knee: An Indian History of the American West,* Holt, Rinehart and Winston, New York, 1971.

of a percent of the national population. The increase is not due so much to a baby boom as to more persons identifying themselves as Indian on census forms. Some 7 million persons claim some Indian ancestry.[75] What this doesn't tell is how many of these have a majority of Indian ancestry.

In spite of higher mortality, the extremely high birthrate of American Indians indicates that the "vanishing red man" is vanishing no more. A birthrate almost double that of the whole population ensures continued growth. Rural Indians have an average of four children per family—the highest fertility rate in the country.

Just under a quarter of Native Americans live in poverty. This is high, but it is a substantial improvement from the 1970s when a third of American Indians lived below the poverty level. Indians, who in the 1970s were the poorest group in the United States, have now moved ahead of blacks.[76] Only a few reservations are rich in natural resources, but other reservations have recently caught on to a new economic benefit, gambling casinos. Indian "sovereignty" under treaties means many state or federal laws do not apply on Indian territory. Gambling may be banned in the state, but not on reservations. Nor do reservations have sales or property taxes, so cigarettes and gas can be sold at discount prices. Within the last decade some previously poor tribes have become affluent from gambling and selling nontaxed items. Indian tourist items have also become quite popular.

The education levels also are rising, but a special Bureau of the Census survey showed only 61 percent of Indians being high school graduates.[77] At present almost all Indian children are attending school, but the quality of the education, particularly in reservation schools, remains suspect.

Movement to Cities

Native Americans are increasingly deserting the reservations for the cities, since most reservations offer only a future of illiteracy, poverty, and alcoholism, all too frequently terminated by an early death. The Bureau of Indian Affairs has been urging Indians to leave their reservations and resettle in urban areas. Today, under one-third of American Indians live on reservation lands.

Between 1930 and 1990, the minority group that experienced the greatest degree of urbanization was not, as is commonly thought, blacks, but rather Native Americans. As of 1930, only 10 percent of the Indian population lived in metropolitan areas, and as recently as 1960, seven out of ten Indians were estimated to be rural. Today, over half the Native American population is urban.[78] Indians have been moving to cities in general, rather than to any one city. A dozen cities in the country have more than 10,000 Indians each, but in no large city do Indians account for more than 5 percent of the population. The largest urban Indian populations are found in Los Angeles, Chicago, Minneapolis, Milwaukee, Phoenix, Albuquerque, and Oklahoma City.

[75] Dan Fost, "American Indians in the 1990s," *American Demographics,* December, 1991, p. 28.
[76] C. Matthew Snipp, *American Indians: The First of This Land,* Russell Sage, New York, 1989.
[77] U.S. Bureau of the Census, "Ancestry and Language in the United States," *Current Population Reports,* P-23, no. 16, Washington, D.C., 1982, p. 11.
[78] Ibid., p. 11.

The common pattern of shuttling between city and reservation hinders effective urban organization. Tribal differences and lack of stable urban Indian populations have worked against the creation of tight ethnic social communities such as those of European immigrants. Shuttling back and forth also interferes with holding stable city jobs. To some the reservation is still necessary, since it "functions as an outpost and haven from the urban scene where the adult battle for survival really takes place."[79]

Life in the city may not be grand, but it is superior to the cycle of acute poverty that is the lot of Indians on the reservation. While the earnings of urban Native Americans are less than urban whites', they are substantially more than what rural Native Americans earn.[80] Paradoxically, as noted above, some tribal groups have become relatively wealthy during the last decade due to the establishment of gambling casinos on Indian lands.

Urban Native Americans often live in poorer central-city neighborhoods, much as newer immigrant groups do. Persons whose ancestry is Indian but who have been assimilated into middle-class America may not identify themselves as Indians except under particular circumstances, such as the distribution of funds from selling tribal estates, or of profits from gambling enterprises. These people have Indian ancestry, but in their behavior, attitudes, and daily life, they are indistinguishable from their neighbors of European ancestry. These culturally assimilated Indians are sometimes referred to by other Indians as "apples"—"red on the outside and white on the inside." More than one-third of Indians now marry non-Indians, and in some tribes it is difficult to find pure-blood Native Americans.

Urban ways can produce a cultural bind for some Native Americans. Most (but not all) Indian cultures stress cooperation and noncompetitiveness over competition and personal achievement. Indian heritages are thus often at variance with the larger American culture. American Indians who want to remain Indian are caught in a dilemma: They want educational and employment opportunities, but they want to live according to Indian ways that may make it difficult to take advantage of such opportunities.[81]

The problem of being pulled between two cultures is, of course, not unique to groups new to the American city. The antiurban orientation of most Native American cultures, however, gives special sharpness to the issue of cultural separateness versus assimilation. Policymakers in Washington and Ottawa have also vacillated: They seem unable to decide whether Indians should be encouraged to remain tribal nations, with separate cultures, or whether Indians are better served by detribalization and urban relocation.

---

[79] Jeanne Guilhemin, *Urban Renegades,* Columbia University Press, New York, 1975, p. 150.

[80] C. Matthew Snipp and Gary D. Sandefur, "Earnings of American Indians and Alaskan Natives: The Effects of Residence and Migration," *Social Forces,* **66**(4):994–1008, 1988.

[81] Bruce Chadwick and Joseph Strauss, "The Assimilation of American Indians into Urban Society, The Seattle Case," paper presented at the meeting of the American Sociological Association, San Francisco, August, 1975, pp. 33–34.

ASIAN AMERICANS

A "Model Minority"?

Asian Americans are not the nation's largest minority, but they are the fastest-growing. The Asian population had a 108 percent increase from 3.5 million in 1980 to 7.3 million in 1990. This is projected to increase to 17.1 million in 2010 and 34.5 million by 2040.[82] With roughly half of all legal immigrants coming from Asia, Asian Americans now account for 4 percent of the nation's population. The Asian population is almost entirely metropolitan and highly concentrated on the West Coast, with four out of ten (39 percent) of all Asians living in California. The Asian population of metropolitan Los Angeles numbers a million. In spite of its concentration, the Asian population is ethnically diverse, with Chinese (32 percent) the largest group, followed by Filipinos (19 percent), Japanese (12 percent), and Koreans and Indians (11 percent each).

Urban Asian-American groups are also quite diverse culturally. Nonetheless, in many ways, they resemble each other more than they do other ethnic or racial minorities. High school completion rates outstrip other minorities but also are higher than those for whites. Asian Americans have twice the proportion graduating from college as do whites.[83] As a group Asian Americans have the highest average family income levels of any census group. The 1990 census indicated over a third (35 percent) of Asian Americans had 1989 family incomes of $50,000 or more compared with a quarter (26 percent) of white families.[84] Within the Asian population there is a great economic range, with Japanese Americans having the highest income levels and the more recently arrived Vietnamese the lowest. Some 14 percent fall below the poverty line (compared with 9.8 percent for whites).

The relative success of metropolitan-located Asian (and Cuban) immigrant groups has been linked to the availability of an ethnic enclave economy to give newcomers a start.[85] While it limits contacts with the larger economy, it provides an environment where non-English speakers can obtain employment. Asian newcomers also have high levels of human capital due to household composition. Most are located in intact families having several workers and close family ties. The role of extended households with multiple workers is very positive in raising household income.[86] One consequence of the relative success of Asians is that Asian Americans are now reporting encountering "glass ceiling" job discrimination. Ironically, much of this comes not because Asian Americans are perceived as a "problem" minority, but because they are seen as a "superminority."

[82] See J. John Palen, *The Suburbs,* McGraw-Hill, New York, 1995, p. 149.
[83] Robert Gardner, Bryant Robey, and Peter Smith, "Asian Americans: Growth, Change, and Diversity," *Population Bulletin,* **40**(4), October, 1985.
[84] Judith Waldrop and Linda Jacobsen, "American Affluence," *American Demographics,* December, 1992, p. 34.
[85] Min Zhou and John R. Logan, "Return on Human Capital in Ethnic Enclaves: New York City's Chinatown," *American Sociological Review,* **54**:809–820, 1989.
[86] Sharon M. Lee and Barry Edmonston, "The Socioeconomic Status and Integration of Asian Immigrants in the 1980s," in Barry Edmonston and Jeffrey Passel (eds.), *Immigration and Ethnicity: Integrating America's Newest Immigrants,* Urban Institute Press, Washington, D.C., forthcoming.

Changing Patterns

The first Asian immigrants were Chinese laborers brought to America to build the transcontinental railroad, but with the completion of the railroad further immigration was forbidden by the 1882 Chinese Exclusion Act. Within cities Chinese were restricted to living in Chinatowns, which were viewed as being a combination of mystery, vice, and inscrutable Oriental ways of life. By the 1930s Chinatowns began to have a still exotic, but more cosmopolitan, image, a "city within a city," but a city still plagued by low-prestige, low-paying jobs.[87] Following World War II, Chinatowns declined as populations aged and the upwardly mobile moved out.[88] Revival of immigration has brought new life to ethnic enclave economies, but most new poorer immigrants, although living in crowded housing, do not form traditional Chinatowns.[89] During recent decades immigrant groups—Asian, Hispanic, and others—have been instrumental in bringing indirect urban renewal and reversing blight in city neighborhoods. For example, small commercial strips have been revitalized by Korean grocery stores and Chinese restaurants. Pooling of capital, often through small revolving credit associations, has aided Asians in the establishment of small businesses.

Asian immigrants speaking English and holding academic degrees now largely bypass the cities and move directly to suburban residences. Of the 44,000 Koreans who live in the Washington, D.C., area, only 800 actually live in the District. Asians commonly live in suburbs that have a strong Asian presence but are predominately white. A major exception is the Los Angeles suburb of Monterey Park, which is the first Chinese suburb in America.[90]

A Note on Japanese Americans

Whenever one starts making generalizations about minorities, one is brought up short by the example of the Japanese Americans. Japanese Americans, who during World War II were our most hated minority, are now accepted, successful, and prosperous citizens. Japanese Americans have been notably successful in adapting to the values, behaviors, and expectations of the American system. Harry Kitano suggests that the statement "Scratch a Japanese American and find a white Anglo-Saxon Protestant" is generally accurate.[91] What makes this all the more remarkable is that Japanese Americans have had to overcome severe discrimination—discrimination that included being forcibly driven from their homes and businesses during World War II and being incarcerated behind barbed wire in "relocation camps."

---

[87] Chalsa M. Loo, *Chinatown: Most Time, Hard Time,* Praeger, New York, 1991.

[88] Rose Hum Lee, "The Decline of Chinatowns in the United States," *American Journal of Sociology,* **54:**422–432, 1949.

[89] Hsiang-Shui Chen, *Chinatown No More: Taiwan Immigrants in Contemporary New York,* Cornell University Press, Ithaca, N.Y., 1992.

[90] Timothy P. Fong, *The First Suburban Chinatown,* Temple University Press, Philadelphia, 1994.

[91] Harry H. L. Kitano, *Japanese Americans: The Evolution of a Subculture,* Prentice-Hall, Englewood Cliffs, N.J., 1976. p. 3.

Chinese residents doing 'Tai Chi in suburban Monterey Park, California. (Tony Freeman/Photo Edit.)

The Internment Camps

The entry of the United States into World War II on December 7, 1941, resulted in anti-Japanese hysteria. It was popularly believed that a Japanese fifth column existed, conducting sabotage on orders from Tokyo. Interestingly, considering their later political development, such well-known liberals as Earl Warren and Walter Lippmann were among the most vocal against the Japanese, while one of the few public officials to denounce the rumors of sabotage as "racist hysteria" was J. Edgar Hoover, the director of the FBI.

The public clamor for action was met in February 1942, when President Roosevelt, on the recommendation of advisors, signed Executive Order 9066. The order designated military areas from which military commanders could exclude persons because of national security. The order also authorized the construction of inland "relocation centers." It was quickly implemented. On March 2, 1942, General De Witt, commander of the Western Defense Area, ordered all persons of Japanese ancestry to be evacuated from the three western coastal states and part of Arizona. He summed up his feelings with the statement, "Once a Jap, always a Jap." The evacuation order included children with as little as one-eighth Japanese ancestry. Two-thirds of those ordered to leave their homes were citizens of the United States. They were each allowed to take one suitcase with them as they were herded by army troops into assembly centers and then shipped to one of ten inland

Japanese Americans from the West Coast were sent to internment camps during World War II. There they attempted to recreate normal life. This is the Owens Valley Alien Reception Center in California. (UPI/Bettmann.)

relocation camps. More than 110,000 of the 126,000 Japanese in this country were put in these camps—regardless of their citizenship.

No such action was taken against those of German and Italian ancestry on the east coast, nor was any action taken against the Japanese on the strategic islands of Hawaii, where the Japanese made up a full 37 percent of the population. Long after the war, it was officially admitted that no Japanese American had committed a single subversive act anywhere within the United States. But for as long as three years many Japanese Americans lived in dismal tar-paper shacks in deserted, inhospitable areas of California, Arizona, Idaho, Wyoming, Utah, and Arkansas, surrounded by barbed wire and machine guns. The inmates were let out only on "seasonal leaves"—which was a euphemistic way of saying that they were used as cheap labor on local farms. Jobs in the camps paid from $16 to $19 a month. In 1942 the Federal Reserve Bank of San Francisco estimated the Japanese Americans' financial loss—abandoned or cheaply sold stores, farms, and businesses—at $400 million. In 1986 the courts recognized the right of interned Japanese Americans to compensation.

Life in the camps radically changed the structure of Japanese-American society. The second generation, or Nisei, who spoke English and were citizens, quickly filled most of the local leadership positions, displacing the older, Issei, or first gen-eration. Ironically, the Nisei could fill a host of leadership positions which anti-Japanese discrimination on the west coast would have made unavailable to them on the outside. After the war many Nisei chose to move east, where their skills and abilities had a better chance of recognition, rather than back to the more ghettoized west coast.

One of the many paradoxes of this period was that the 442d Regimental Com-bat Team—the most-decorated American unit in World War II—was composed of Japanese Americans. More than 1,000 of the men in the 442d had enlisted directly from the internment camps to fight for the country that had forcibly removed them from their homes and livelihood. (A further irony was that the Japanese-American volunteers were sent to Camp Shelby in the racially segregated state of Mississippi. Since all public facilities were either "white" or "colored," the governor had to de-cide which the Japanese were. He decided that during their stay in Mississippi they were "white.") The 442d's war cry, "Go for Broke," is a part of American history. Less well known is the fact that the average IQ of the unit was the highest (119) for a combat group and that the 442d had more college graduates than any other com-parable unit in the armed forces. The Nisei earned, in blood, the grudging respect of other GIs. In action in Italy and France, the unit suffered 9,486 casualties—or over 300 percent of its original infantry strength. In 1988, the U.S. government is-sued an apology to those incarcerated in the camps and in 1990 began payment of $20,000 to each person so treated.

Japanese Americans Today

After the war and the internment camps, the second-generation Nisei had an un-paralleled record of upward mobility. The group is almost entirely metropolitan in residence. In 1940 over a quarter of all Japanese Americans were laborers; by the 1980s this figure was down to only an insignificant number. Among all nonwhite groups the Japanese rank first in income and education. The generations born since World War II have become almost totally acculturated.

Compared with other Americans, older Japanese Americans, particularly on the west coast, are more likely to live in ethnic communities with a strong sense of group responsibility and group "image." The sense of group identity is reflected in the low delinquency and crime rates—rates that are rising as "American" behavior patterns replace those of the once tightly bound ethnic community.

Soon after arrival, Japanese Americans stopped teaching their children the Japanese language, and over the years many Japanese customs have been aban-doned in favor of American models. Another sign of change has been the number of marriages outside the group. The breakdown of distinctive ways of life is a mixed blessing. On the positive side, Japanese Americans now participate fully in all aspects of national life. However, it would be sad and more than a little ironic if in an urban world that is seeking a sense of community the Japanese Americans, who prospered because of their strong community and their cohesive family sys-tem, would now allow their distinctive culture to be eroded or abandoned.

Southeast Asians: A Success Story

The "boat people" was the name given to the wave of refugees leaving southeast Asia in the late 1970s and early 1980s, following the U.S. pullout from Vietnam. Unlike earlier refugees from Vietnam, the boat people had little education and few resources or transferable skills. Most were farmers, fishermen, or laborers. Those picked up adrift at sea were packed into refugee camps. Most of those refugees reaching America arrived at a time of economic recession during the early 1980s. Few spoke any English. Their prognosis seemed one of long-term economic dependency and social problems.

The reality, however, has been one of remarkable progress against stiff odds. Research on 1,400 refugee households in Houston, Chicago, Boston, Seattle, and Orange County, California—major resettlement areas—found that the families were rapidly moving from bleak poverty to economic self-sufficiency. Most families were still below the federally defined poverty level, but according to the researcher Nathan Caplan, "a stunning proportion of these families are climbing out of deep poverty—largely through an impressive demonstration of hard work and initiative."*

The refugees had a long way to climb. Only one-quarter of the refugees had completed high school, and only one in a hundred spoke fluent English when arriving in America. Moreover, resettlement programs were of only limited use to the refugees. Sixty percent of those employed found jobs not through employment programs but exclusively through friends and relatives. Caplan found that three years after arrival, nine out of ten of the urban refugee households reported at least one family member employed, usually at a low-status, low-income job. Three-quarters of the refugees were taking classes in English.

In a separate, related study of 350 school-aged children it was found that the children were making even more remarkable progress. Although most spoke no English on arrival in the United States, after an average of just three years in the country they were outperforming their school-age peers in terms of grade point averages. They remained as of the late 1980s somewhat below the national average in English, but 27 percent scored in the ninetieth percentile on math achievement—almost three times the national average.** The

---

* Nathan Caplan, "Southeast Asian Refugees: Achieving Independence in America," *ISR Newsletter*, Institute for Social Research, University of Michigan, Spring/Summer, 1985, p. 7.
** Nathan Caplan, John Whitmore, and Marcella Choy, *The Boat People and Achievement in America*, University of Michigan, Ann Arbor, 1989.

highest-achieving children came from cohesive families with traditional Confucian values and a strong respect for education.

Overall, southeast Asian refugee families remain the poorest of the Asian populations, but in only a handful of years they have already made noticeable progress. For the southeast Asian boat people, the American dream of hard work and success appears to be an emerging reality. Their success also suggests that the possibility for urban social mobility still exists for immigrants coming to these shores.

CHAPTER
11

WOMEN IN METROPOLITAN LIFE

Christine Wright-Isak
Sylvia Fava

Women hold up half the sky.

Chinese Proverb

INTRODUCTION

Men's and women's spaces as well as places in society have differed. Of sociological interest is that *her* place has not been the same as *his* place. This social fact was overlooked in urban research at the beginning of the twentieth century because the focus of inquiry was directed at more general urban patterns such as the assimilation processes of ethnic immigrant groups. Research focused on the male experience because men were the legitimate occupants of the more visible public spaces of the city. Research on women tended to take place in terms of the woman's typical place, the family, and wasn't defined as urban sociology.[1]

The foundation work of urban sociology gives us three elements of community, namely its territorial area, the sense of belonging of its inhabitants, and "institutions, interactions, and shared perspectives within this area."[2] Early urban research emphasized the territorial and socially defined boundaries of the city's ethnic communities, their institutions, and the publicly visible interactions of their residents. Sociologists of the early Chicago school and other urban sociologists of that time shared national expectations of immigrants that led to research questions about social ethnic identities, characteristic social and physical labels, and the ways immigrant communities differed from the Anglo-Saxon culture of the nation. The research did not emphasize the dimensions of belonging within a community, most often taking that aspect as a fact of residence and shared ethnicity. Yet "belonging" is where the female influence on the structure and processes of community takes place in greatest richness. This, plus the less publicly visible traditional roles of women, tended to make women invisible in early urban research.

A look back at specific evidence about the different experiences of men and women reveals that existing assumptions about the urban experiences of each gender need revision. For example, common stereotypes that foster the idea that city life is dangerous to women and therefore that the suburbs are preferable places for them to be are not necessarily true. In addition, the historical pattern of change in the actual social places of both genders, but especially of women, has not been linear. It has been a roller coaster of legal, social, and political ups and downs rather than a steady advance from simple to complex. In particular, the social history of women in the city is one of ambiguity and paradox rather than steadily expanding opportunity and fulfillment. Finally, urban theory has tended to understate the continued complexity of roles and expectations of rural life compared with life in the city and of women compared with men in either setting.

In both urban and rural settings women cope with sets of conflicting demands on them to be, at the same time, individuals, personal emotion managers and nurturers for their husbands, and, increasingly, providers of economic support for their families. Historically women in the city have been powerfully bound by ascribed role and status expectations based on prevailing social beliefs about female gender.

---

[1] Lyn Lofland, "The 'Thereness' of Women: A Selective Review of Urban Sociology," in Marcia Millman and Rosabeth Moss Kanter (eds.), *Another Voice: Feminist Perspectives on Social Life and Social Science,* Anchor Books, New York, 1975.

[2] Lyn Lofland, "The Gendered War against Public Space: Consequences for Community," paper presented at the Annual Meetings of the American Sociological Association, 1995.

As we shall see, for women metropolitan life continues to be more of a patchwork quilt than a homogenous "city" way of living, due to their continuing greater responsibility for family and to variations in their class and social status.

Gender and Place

Class and ethnic aspects of location have had powerful social ramifications for women's changing social roles and identities. Many of the observations made about gender and place focus on the experience of middle-class, primarily white, women, but the experience of poor women (white and nonwhite), has been different. Women of color or ethnicity have often been researched as if their color or ethnicity were synonymous with poverty. Because of this, their experience has often been studied in relation to theories of deviance or social problems rather than as part of urban life. This sort of classification has had the unfortunate consequence of minimizing the contribution of their various experiences to understanding metropolitan diversity. Theory seeks to find order, and women in the city have represented sources of actual and theoretical disorder, especially when their differences add to accumulating observations that force new explanations.[3]

In general, urban research has addressed and described the experience visible in public spaces, which has until recently been the male experience.[4] Women have been invisible because they have been expected to be occupants of private space or domestic space, or have occupied "invisible classes" of workers, domestics, or deviants. Although women worked in factories and sweatshops, this was not part of their expected image, and thus was overlooked. However, as social change has expanded the roles and work opportunities for women, sociology has come to focus on the ways in which their experiences require us to modify or amplify our theories and research techniques regarding the city.

Looking at early community studies, we can tease out observations that inform us of the place, if not the experiences, of women in the city. More recently, many conscientious male participant observers have acknowledged their limits in recording the lives of women in the communities and urban neighborhoods they studied.[5] Some explicitly attempted to redress this imbalance in subsequent work by directing questions directly to female community experience.[6] We can also search existing urban community studies and infer the places of women when we read work like *Tally's Corner: A Study of Negro Streetcorner Men, The Social Order of the Slum,* or *The Urban Villagers.*[7] If we search, we can also find forgotten monographs by women social scientists. In this chapter we acquaint you with some of them and encourage you to discover others.

[3] Elizabeth Wilson, *The Sphinx in the City: Urban Life, Control of Disorder, and Women,* University of California Press, Berkeley, Calif., 1991.

[4] Lofland, "The Gendered War against Public Space."

[5] Herbert Gans, *The Urban Villagers,* Free Press, New York, 1962. Gerald D. Suttles, *The Social Order of the Slum,* University of Chicago Press, Chicago, 1968.

[6] Herbert Gans, *The Levittowners,* Vintage Books, New York, 1967.

[7] Elliot Liebow wrote *Tally's Corner* (Little, Brown, Boston, 1967) about the community of street-corner men in Washington, D.C. *The Social Order of the Slum* (University of Chicago, Chicago, 1968) by Gerald D. Suttles describes ethnic community life in two subcultures in a changing neighborhood of downtown Chicago. *The Urban Villagers* by Herbert Gans describes an Italian immigrant community in New York City in the late 1950s.

Evolving Ideas of Gendered Space

As gender roles evolved in the 1970s and 1980s, women social scientists began to approach urban studies with fresh perspectives.[8] Research on women and urbanism began to focus on describing fundamental social patterns that produced and perpetuated gender inequities. Two main ideas were brought out. One was the recognition that different places mean different knowledge and experiences of the social world for women and for men, and often mean different social worlds altogether. The other was the understanding that industrial urban life, contrary to the nineteenth-century image of the city as a deadly and dangerous place for women in both physical and moral or social respects, actually was associated with relatively more equality between the genders.

Finally, the expansion of women's roles in the urban public sphere has provided new subjects for research. On one hand, as women have gained public positions of power and influence, they have also become subjects of research as part of the city's visible social life. On the other, feminist perspectives on social research in the past fifteen years have focused attention on the importance of studying the informal and private areas of social life that have traditionally been underexamined and female.[9]

HISTORICAL PATTERNS: INVISIBLE WOMEN AND CONTRADICTORY IMAGES

Early Patterns

The changes in American life in the nineteenth century that transformed city and town were accompanied by changes in the lives of women. On the frontier, women's versatility and strength in providing such fundamentals of civilized life as soap, fabric, clothing, and meals made them necessary partners of their men. As industrialization took men from farms and placed them in factories, it also meant that women's labor changed too. Women increasingly remained at home with children, and domestic work occupied the women's energies. At least this "simple" domestic evolution was the popular conception. The reality was more complex. Many women worked as servants for wealthy households, supported their families by working in factories, or did piecework for long hours each day at home. Socially

---

[8] In 1975 Lofland contributed to a collection of feminist writings on sociology assembled by Marcia Millman and Rosabeth Kanter. The pieces, published in their book *Another Voice,* set forth for the first time an explicit woman's perspective of scholarly sociology. Lofland applied this perspective to urban studies in arguing that women historically were just "there" and not explicitly studied in their differences from male models of urban social dynamics. In the early 1980s three separate volumes of accumulated work were published on women and urban space. One was *New Space for Women,* edited by Gerda R. Wekerle, Rebecca Peterson, and David Morley (Westview Press, Boulder, Colo., 1980), and another was *Women and the American City,* edited by Catharine R. Stimpson, Elsa Dixler, Martha J. Nelson, and Kathryn B. Yatrakis (University of Chicago Press, Chicago, 1980). The third, on urban planning, was Suzanne Keller's *Building for Women* (Heath, Lexington, Mass., 1981).

[9] Judith N. DeSena, *Protecting One's Turf: Social Strategies for Maintaining Urban Neighborhoods,* University Press of America, Lanham, Md., 1990. Lofland, "The Gendered War against Public Space." Susan A. Ostrander, *Women of the Upper Class,* Temple University Press, Philadelphia, 1984.

constructed images of women were not accurate descriptions of their lives. Public rhetoric of the time, in defining as "respectable" only women who lived in a middle-class domestic ideal, tended to obscure the reality of working women and poor immigrant women.

Importantly, the *imagery* of women and their domestic value to society became more distinct and separate as their familial workday became separate from the *imagery* of men as husbands who went off to the city for the day to the competitive world of business. Berg[10] suggests the urban threat to America's farm-based society provoked a cultural need to preserve the image of the agricultural ideal about women and their place in society. As the economic and political rise of the city accompanied the nation's industrial development, longing for an imagined simpler agrarian life grew and became symbolically expressed as the ideal of the single-family home with its green yard. As one observer noted:

> During the 1820's and 1830's, gift books, periodicals, and novels exhibited a special form of writing, expressive of an attempt to harmonize the agricultural tradition with the urban experience. Avoiding tales of peaceful village life with its traditional churches, orderly schoolrooms, and virtuous farmers, a new agrarianism, an urban-agrarianism, developed. It focuses exclusively on descriptions of the home and its immediate environs. Invariably nested snugly amidst "a fine range of green, softly swelling hills" overlooking a "lovely valley through which a stream was gliding," the simple cottage home presented its quaint charms to urban readers.[11]

The Home

As the home became the physical place where the rural emotional and moral ideal of simplicity and purity could continue within urbanism, it also became the social location for the altruism and nurturance that were part of the rural myth. Within this emerging set of meanings, a redefined ideal of womanhood emerged.

> Emphasis upon woman's essential domesticity completed the transfer of the pastoral legend to the urban environment. The insistence that woman's sphere be limited to the home became a prevailing dogma of nineteenth-century faith.[12]

A woman's own location was expected to be the home, with the idea that in it she would find fulfillment by providing the human warmth so lacking in the daily urban business environment.

> Woman placed nature as the sole repository of goodness and ethicality. Absolving males from guilt that their unbridled pursuit of wealth might be injurious to the fabric of the nation, she emerged as a substitute for the allegedly democratic proclivities of yeoman farmers. In her domestic role, idealized and fantasized, woman embodied all the attributes of bountiful nature. Untainted by the corrupt world, she soothed, purified, and nurtured.[13]

---

[10] Barbara J. Berg, *The Remembered Gate: Origins of American Feminism,* Oxford University Press, New York, 1978.
[11] Ibid., p. 65.
[12] Ibid., p. 67.
[13] Ibid., p. 69.

In the 1870s young and old, male and female, all worked side-by-side on the family farm. (Library of Congress.)

This imagery grew and proliferated through the writings and lectures of a number of proponents of the "cult of domesticity." Prior to the Civil War and for decades afterward, Catharine Beecher, sister of Harriet Beecher Stowe of *Uncle Tom's Cabin* fame, wrote book after book encouraging women in the belief that although women were morally superior to men, their appropriate role was to be man's subordinate.[14] Catharine Beecher's books argued for "the physical and social separation of the population into the female-dominated sphere of home life, preferably suburban, and the male-dominated sphere of the business world, usually urban.[15] In Beecher's works and similar works by others of the time, the link was made between the domestic ideal of suburban family life and the ideal family of private women and public men. In reality it was an image that only applied to the middle "respectable" classes.

The theme of evil, dangerous, or sinful city versus safe, physically and morally pure life outside the city in America was carried out in popular and pulp fiction, in penny presses, and in other newspapers and magazines.[16] Embedded in these tales was a paradox of feminine nature as both good and evil depending on the woman's literal location in the urban terrain. The cautionary tale of respectable male travelers being seduced, drugged (usually with alcohol), and

[14] Kenneth T. Jackson, *Crabgrass Frontier: The Suburbanization of the United States,* Oxford University Press, New York, 1985, p. 62.
[15] Ibid., pp. 62–63.
[16] Lofland, "The Gendered War against Public Space," p. 8.

robbed by disreputable females was a recurrent theme. Respectable women were not featured in these stories. Their place was at home, especially a home in the suburbs, while "town women," or prostitutes, were present as part of the city's enticing sinful backdrop. The locus of problems, dangers, and misadventures was the public space of the city, not the private areas.[17] The emerging social expectations of women that they be private defenders of home virtue translated to concern over their presence in the public spaces of the city as unnatural and as an undesirable abandonment of hearth and home.[18] What moralists, both male and female, emphasized in the public spaces of the city was concern "not [about] the presence of women per se, but the presence of *respectable* women."[19]

To summarize, in nineteenth-century urbanizing America, respectable women acquired the paradoxical ascriptive elements of moral superiority and social subordination. This ascriptive status included expectations and social limitations about the spaces they would properly occupy if they were to be considered respectable, namely the household, the suburban or rural community, and especially the non-public spheres of each.

The city consisted of public diversity, strangers, and therefore physical and symbolic pollution. In nineteenth-century America, women were thought to be too weak to provide for their own safety from contamination in such settings, while men were expected to pass the tests of moral and physical survival. Middle-class "respectable" women who were in the "wrong" place (public space in the city) presented challenges to social order and were themselves construed as seductive dangers to male virtue.[20] This dual definition of potential victim and seductive threat was one of the more pervasive paradoxes of women's place in urban life. The other was the simultaneous existence in the city of poor and working-class women whose social illegitimacy was reinforced by their continued presence in "immoral" places.

THE "THERENESS" OF WOMEN: TAKING GENDER FOR GRANTED IN URBAN STUDIES

Early social research on the city reflected the intersection of place and gender imagery. Many of the early urban sociologists saw the city through the nineteenth-century cultural lens that put men and women in their separate spheres. In their focus on various urban phenomena, that lens was largely male, and their perceptions were imbued with the model of the American Protestant "missionary for democracy" among immigrant groups.[21] This early perspective has had consequences for our present-day understanding of fundamental social concepts like community, democracy, and social order.[22]

---

[17] Ibid.
[18] Berg, *The Remembered Gate*. Lofland, "The Gendered War against Public Space."
[19] Lofland, "The Gendered War against Public Space," p. 5.
[20] Berg, *The Remembered Gate*. Lofland, "The Gendered War against Public Space." Wilson, *The Sphinx in the City.*
[21] Stanford M. Lyman and Arthur J. Vidich, "Qualitative Methods: Their History in Sociology and Anthropology," in Norman K. Denzin and Yvonna S. Lincoln (eds.), *Handbook of Qualitative Research,* Sage Publications, Thousand Oaks, Calif., 1994.
[22] Lofland, "The Gendered War against Public Space."

Until recently most sociologists were men, and their experience and focus tended to be not only on men but also on male-defined institutions that did not recognize female social patterns as a subject for urban research. Our task in developing an understanding of women in the city now is to use ethnographics like *Tally's Corner* or *The Social Order of the Slum* and search within them for clues to the place and experiences of the women they sometimes refer to. In this way they can help us see more clearly woman's place in the city.[23] We can also search for other work done at the same time as these classic ethnographies that may offer more direct observations of the experiences of women.

URBAN POOR WOMEN

Women in the 1960's classic *Tally's Corner,* are a backdrop to the dramas of men. We see the men as having intermittent job opportunities and continual difficulties maintaining respectable masculinity among the inhabitants of Tally's corner in Washington, D.C. He also documents the emotional ramifications, attitudes, and behaviors that they developed to cope with repeated failures to sustain this model of working head of family. His descriptions and analyses reveal many of the socioenvironmental conditions in the city that contribute to their situations. His focus does not extend to the female side of these situations in any depth. If we are to understand the full picture, it helps to have accounts of both sides, which means finding the female complement to this urban poverty experience. Fortunately we have several sources of this "other side of the coin." Two are ethnographies conducted in Washington, D.C., at about the same time. Another comes from longitudinal survey work in New York City explicitly designed to address some of the hypotheses in *Tally's Corner* as they apply to women.[24]

Hard Living on Clay Street

Clay Street was the street in Washington, D.C., where Joseph Howell and his wife and child lived for a year. Howell's presence in the community with his wife and child enabled him to describe the situations of women in urban life more directly than other male participant observers.[25] His subjects are two poor white families living on Clay Street. One family is a poor working-class family. The husband is a skilled mechanic who has a stable work situation, and the wife manages by carefully distributing their resources and by limiting their family size to one child. Both parents were married before and have grown children from those unions. The other family is considerably more marginal. Greatly handicapping the family's efforts to

---

[23] Liebow in *Tally's Corner* and Suttles in *The Social Order of the Slum* both referenced the presence of women in the communities they studied, but their focus remained on the men. In rereading them we catch glimpses of women's lives in the city, but only by inference.

[24] Harriet Presser, "Sally's Corner: Coping with Unmarried Motherhood," in *Journal of Social Issues,* **36**(1):107–129, 1980.

[25] In recent times male participant observers have often relied on their own wives or female research partners to help provide gender perspective and balance to their observations. Benjamin D. Zablocki in *The Joyful Community* (University of Chicago Press, Chicago, 1980), a study of the Bruderhof communitarian society in 1970, explicitly credits his wife with gathering observations on the lives of the Bruderhof women that he would not have been able to make.

get by are the problems that the husband is an alcoholic and the wife's stepfather who lives with them has a physical illness. The family also has four children, which to a great extent limits the family's ability to find and keep housing.

What is clear in these two poor urban households is that in fulfilling traditional roles as best they can, the women do the social work of maintaining family cohesion and negotiating its connections to the larger society. They do so in ways that parallel their men's efforts at working and providing a living. Moreover, the efforts of the women are as important as those of the men for the urban social system when the men are working and even more important when the men are not.

Living Poor

The experiences of women within the situations suggested for them by *Tally's Corner* have been studied directly by a contemporary of Elliot Liebow, Camille Jeffers. She provides interesting new dimensions of urban life in her ethnography of the black women in a public housing project in Washington, D.C. It is a world that is more cohesive and socially knit than the world of corner men. Jeffers's study, which was published in 1967, under the title *Living Poor,* gives us a picture of a key transitional time in the history of public housing before the political rhetoric used stereotypes to condemn all public housing and its residents.

Even today Jeffers's work illustrates the need of the poor for help if their efforts to maintain family cohesion have any hope of succeeding. But perhaps the greatest contribution of *Living Poor* is its illustration of the persistence and even strength of social ties among women. These patterns of mutual advice, help, and instruction or social control are difficult to observe and record and are often left out of urban research because of their private and informal nature. One description illustrates the extent to which neighborly and friendship ties help counter the constraints of poverty:

> It was impressive to see how quickly some mothers could parcel out their children and just as impressive to see the way some neighbors would rise to the occasion when such demands were made. For example, when Mrs. Martin had to undergo emergency hospitalization for a few days, some friends of hers, who already had three children of their own, took in Mrs. Martin's children. The wife cared for them during the day and the husband slept in the apartment with the children at night.
>
> Sometimes an informal barter system developed when mothers did not require or could not reciprocate with the same service, but could render some other service for which there was a demand. For example, Mrs. Todd, who had skill as a hairdresser, would often set hair in exchange for baby-sitting services.[26]

In living in public housing and recording the nature of women's lives there, Jeffers reveals the initiatives and organizational capacities of poor black women. Jeffers's work shows us the alternative social fabric these women knit and use to cope with their situations. The community of women is called on for giving advice, for transmitting knowledge about child rearing, and also for managing the perplexing or annoying proclivities of their men. In gossiping, talking, interacting, and

---

[26] Camille Jeffers, *Living Poor,* Ann Arbor Publishers, Ann Arbor, Mich. 1967, p. 21.

helping each other with getting to the bank or to the doctor, these women renew and add to a local store of collective experience and knowledge that provides alternative solutions or coping strategies for the particular challenges they face.

Since the time that Howell's and Jeffers's studies were completed, we have seen the difficulties involved in bringing the strengths of that private caretaking sphere into the system of public housing and other programs that proliferated after the 1960s. We are currently undergoing much public debate about throwing this responsibility back into private laps. These ethnographies, which delineate in great detail the difficulties that poor women were able to manage, continue to be of value in displaying the complexity of urban life and the inseparability of private and public spheres.

Sally's Corner

In the 1970s Harriet Presser investigated hypotheses about first-time, poor mothers that she developed after reading Liebow's ethnography. She examined how these mothers accomplish the tasks of parenting and what roles the fathers of their children play in the mothers' and children's lives, in the context of their urban environment. Her findings amplify and develop many of the observations Jeffers made, although Presser seems not to have been acquainted with Jeffers's work. Presser's research consisted of a series of three interviews with each of 310 respondents conducted over three years' time. Her sample of respondents was drawn randomly from first-time mothers in New York City, so her findings add some generalizability to the participant observation research findings of earlier studies. The patterns Presser found were like the general patterns delineated in other research in this chapter: She found a woman's community of other mothers and friends to be a significant factor in fulfilling the tasks inherent in the role of motherhood and in the development of each woman's personal growth and success in her situation. Presser also found in her surveys that the mother's social attachment to the father of her children was a strong factor in the father's presence in their children's lives, but that formal institutions were not. She also found that paternal involvement did not necessarily mean monetary support.[27]

Summary

These examinations focused on mostly black poor women in the city neighborhoods of thirty years ago. Things have changed considerably with the advance of social-service bureaucracies and public housing. Moreover, we see from this comparison that the experiences of poor blacks should not be assumed to be the only experience of urban poverty. The experience of poor white women as well as poor black women described in these situations demonstrates how stereotyping by race or economic position oversimplifies the situations and abilities of poor urban women.

---

[27] Presser interviewed 408 mothers, (mostly black women) intending to follow each case with two more interviews. Attrition over the two-year interval between the first and third interview yielded a final sample size of 310. The unmarried portion of the sample consisted of 69 mothers, each of whom had three interviews over a two-year time span.

WEALTHY WOMEN

Susan Ostrander's work on women from very wealthy families, while describing very different conditions of life from those of poor women, reveals one pattern that both sets of women in the city share. They are equally constrained by social expectations ascribed to women's "natural" abilities in maintaining order in the emotional and social aspects of family life.

> The wives' tasks reflect not only the division of labor, or social differentiation, but also a clear subordination of the women to the men, a social stratification based on gender. This is particularly true of the expectations that the wives be accommodating, adaptive, available. This general mode makes it difficult, if not impossible, for the women to have life agenda independent of the men. This mode of subjugation seems inherent in all the tasks for which the women are responsible. They not only run the house, they do so in a way that shields their husbands from any concern over what goes on there; they do so even when he is away from home for extended periods of time. They not only make the social arrangements, they make them on short notice and at their husband's request.... They are not only available to listen to their husbands talk about business problems, they also learn, for the most part, to hold their tongues and not give any real advice.[28]

Thus wealthy women are just as invisible as women of poverty or color. The value of observing different kinds of women in the city is that when we find common patterns across social locations with similar consequences in each, we can be more certain that the dynamics of women's space and women's place are gender-based.

WOMEN IN ETHNIC URBAN LIFE: HONOR AND THE AMERICAN DREAM

Studies of ethnic enclaves are a staple of urban research. Searching work like Gans's *Urban Villagers* or Suttles's *Social Order of the Slum* provides a traditionalist view of women and their participation in male social worlds that is accurate but that offers only one point of view of a more complex phenomenon. It is one that leaves us wondering what the inner workings of the female aspects of ethnic worlds are like, and again there is an alternative perspective. Ruth Horowitz provides it in her account of how the conflicting demands placed on them as women coming of age affects their male counterparts, and the social system that organizes both genders.

Horowitz studied the urban life of one Latin gang, the Young Lions, in Chicago in the 1970s. In focusing not on the gang per se, but on two intersecting sets of values, she had a broad perspective that enabled her to include the unique aspects of female roles and behaviors within the gang world. She examined the traditional Latino concept of honor (personal and family) as it intersected with the American dream. In her work we find particular importance given to the dilemma of young women as they encounter the conflicting expectations of virginity, pas-

---

[28] Ostrander, *Women of the Upper Class*, p. 49.

sion, and marriage in coming of age. In this community, how the young women resolve the conflicting demands—by their young men for sex and love and by their
families to uphold personal and familial honor by remaining a virgin—has serious
ramifications for the expectations of the men in their lives, namely their fathers and
brothers as well as their lovers or potential husbands.

Young women are expected to stay virgins until they marry. But urban life
gives young women greater freedom than they had under old traditional rules of
chaperonage.

> Freedom from direct supervision is perceived as threatening to a young woman's chastity. It
> is the moral duty of the men in her family to protect the family honor by guarding her sex-
> ual purity. Since the men cannot live up to the responsibility, women inevitably must fail if
> they are not careful to avoid situations that might be tempting or appraised as tempting.[29]

A full understanding of the expectations inherent in family honor provides an
important context in which to understand other behaviors of the Latina women being studied. As members of the Latino community, young women share a belief in
the importance placed on family honor that both women and men are expected to
uphold. Recent feminist perspectives have addressed the social problems and needs
of women in the city that recognize the unique aspects of danger in urban environments and the continuing role realities that stem from the fact that child rearing
continues to be the responsibility of women. Such perspectives often focus on analyzing the nature of policies and services that might better address these problems
and needs. However, in not understanding the full meaning of Latino social beliefs
and customary behaviors, they tend to understate culture as a factor in contemporary behaviors.

For example, ten years after Horowitz's study, Santiago and Morash[30] found,
in the cities they studied, that of all poor urban women, the Latina women have the
lowest incidence of use of shelters for battered women, although they along with
black women suffer a higher incidence of spousal abuse than do majority women.
In fact, Latina use of crisis centers or shelters, is almost nonexistent. Santiago and
Morash acknowledge that because there is such a strong expectation that family
matters are to remain private, it is unlikely to expect Latina women to seek out shelters; instead they turn to family.

Horowitz's work tells us that the cultural significance of Latina reluctance
runs far deeper than simply needing to keep family problems private. In asking a
Latina woman to use a shelter we are asking her to change not only her reliance on
her family, but also her concept of femininity as accepting male initiatives. The use
of a shelter would also force her to challenge the concept of aggressive masculinity held not only by her and her partner, but also by her father, brothers, and other
significant males. Thus the urban social services being offered challenge fundamental aspects of identity of both genders in this community.

[29] Ruth Horowitz, *Honor and the American Dream: Culture and Identity in a Chicano Community,* Rutgers University Press,
New Brunswick, N.J., 1979, p. 117.
[30] Anne M. Santiago and Merry Morash, "Strategies for Serving Latina Battered Women," in Judith A. Garber and Robyn
S. Turner (eds.), *Gender in Urban Research,* Sage Publications, Thousand Oaks, Calif., 1995.

WORKING- AND MIDDLE-CLASS WOMEN: PROTECTING ONE'S TURF

If the patterns of informal social organization to manage urban life are observed among working- or middle-class women to resemble that of poor women, then we can say with more certainty that informal institutions and informal social cohesion developed in private spheres of metropolitan life are an intrinsic part of the city's organization and operation. Judy DeSena, in studying how Greenpoint, Brooklyn, maintains its local community by socially controlling which newcomers enter its local territory, shows another way in which the informal processes of women maintain urban community.[31] Whereas students of the wider metropolis tend to view local resistance to neighborhood change as a way to prevent real estate interests from simply taking them over, DeSena's focus is on the informal local social networks of women in Greenpoint. How they operate reveals ways in which women's networks of communication and information screen who will rent or buy in their neighborhood.

DeSena's work begins by spotlighting something commonly overlooked by researchers who themselves have been residentially mobile, namely that poor inner-city families are not the only ones whose mobility in choosing where to live is limited. As DeSena points out,

> The meaning of blue collar neighborhoods has changed along with the metropolis. Blue collar workers experience a reduction in residential choices. Many do not have the economic wherewithal to participate in the suburban movement. In addition, the pool of other blue collar neighborhoods to choose from as a place of residence has greatly diminished. Blue collar groups are not affluent, and cannot move to gentrified areas, and some find racially mixed areas unacceptable.[32]

When we consider this viewpoint, it is not surprising that some neighborhoods find successful ways to resist change. They have virtually no choice. DeSena found two kinds of resistance to change. One was a building-by-building reluctance to accept incoming occupants in the northern section of the neighborhood and the other a block-by-block strategy in the southern area.

> It is difficult to rent an apartment or purchase a house in Southern Greenpoint. Local realtors have said that "there isn't a one, two, or three family house available." The local newspaper lists only a few apartments and houses for sale, while the length of its "APTS. WANTED" and "HOUSES WANTED" columns increase. Residents are particularly cautious about renting their vacant apartments. Not only do they want to control rigidly the type of tenants they may get, but they also want to determine who will be informed about the availability of an apartment. All respondents in southern Greenpoint, regardless of ethnicity, claimed that available apartments are rented "by word of mouth."[33]

DeSena found that homeowners find new tenants by using an informal network through which they let their family, friends, and neighbors know an apartment

---

[31] DeSena, *Protecting One's Turf.*
[32] Ibid., p. 6.
[33] Ibid., p. 59.

is available. Newcomers must be "sponsored" by local residents who inform the owner that they know someone who might be a good tenant. As one of her respondents summed up the process, "It's like getting a job, it's who you know."[34] Home buying follows a similar process that sometimes takes quite a long time.

> It is common to hear anecdotes such as this one where homeowners select a buyer for their house before their house has actually gone up for sale. For example, homeowners may watch a family grow over the years and when they decide to sell their home, they may approach that family. As with apartments, this illustrates another way that the network operates.[35]

The network is mainly women, because they are more likely to be spending time in the supermarket or the local stores or in areas where the life of the community is discussed and such information is transmitted.

THE "OTHER" FORM OF METROPOLITAN COMMUNITY: SUBURBIA

The Levittowners[36]

The "other" metropolitan area phenomenon that provides different experiences for women and men is suburbia. As we have seen in earlier chapters, suburbia was the subject of great interest and research in the postwar decades. At that time, suburbia was popularly stereotyped as the location of the white, managerial, middle-class nuclear family's domestic life. Women in suburbia were evaluated through the lens of the traditional expectations of men's and women's role at the time. Herbert Gans, however, specifically asked residents about aspects of their experiences in this emerging form of community.[37] He asked about boredom and directly asked women about loneliness. He then compared data from the Levittown sample with data from a comparable Philadelphia neighborhood. He identified the adjustments women needed to make in this new setting, where there was no established community interactions—where community ties had to be formed "from scratch."

Contrary to what its critics feared, Gans found *in general* "that suburban life has produced more family cohesion and a significant boost in morale through the reduction of boredom and loneliness."[38] Improved morale centered on the satisfaction of owning a new home. The community aspect of life, however, was not uniformly satisfying. Dissatisfaction occurred primarily among Levittown's women. The new residents who reported a "worse disposition" since leaving the city tended to fit into one of the four groups. The first three were young women who became mothers in Levittown, "especially those who had worked before"; working-class women who found it difficult to cut ties to family and former neighbors; and

---

[34] Ibid., p. 62.
[35] Ibid., p. 62.
[36] This is not the familiar Levittown of Long Island. Gans studied the Levittown built on what had been the town of Willingboro, New Jersey, just outside Philadelphia, Pennsylvania. Ten years after Levitt's housing had been completed, residents of the community voted to restore the original name of Willingboro to the town.
[37] Gans, *The Levittowners*.
[38] Ibid., p. 220.

women who suffered from loneliness because they had poor marriages or husbands who were on the road a lot. The fourth group having difficulty adjusting were Jewish women, who pointed out that "here you meet people only through organizations, churches, and clubs, but we are not organizational types and I don't care for organizational life."[39]

Working-Class Suburb

Bennett Berger provided a clear counterpoint to the nature of suburbia that was becoming part of popular-press stereotypes in the 1960s.[40] However, his observations did not focus on the different experiences of women as much as on the fact that not all suburbs are middle-class. Neither the men nor the women in his blue-collar suburb have the involvement with social organizations that the Levittowners did, nor do they socialize as much or in the same nonfamilial ways. Women do tend to fulfill traditional female roles, and Berger did not dwell on differences in his experiences from those of men. Not surprisingly, he found that wives who had jobs were less likely to join social organizations. This became a widespread pattern twenty years later as women in the United States have centered and remained in the work force in great numbers.

> The memberships and activity of the women we've interviewed seem to be related only to whether or not they are employed outside the home. Of the wives, 34 percent had full-time, part-time, or seasonal (mostly in the canneries) jobs outside the home, but only 25 percent of the employed women were members of organizations. With the same figures rearranged another way, 23 percent of the employed women belonged to one or more organizations, but 39 percent of the women who do not have jobs outside the home belonged to one or more organizations.[41]

Although Berger only hinted at a different experience for women in suburbia, other sociologists directly addressed the overlooked and profound disadvantages of the suburban stereotype and its reality.

Women's Place in the New Suburbia

In the decades immediately after World War II, the disadvantages to women in suburbia stemmed from the isolating and time-limiting effects of lower residential density.

For example, Fava argued that:

> the chief environmental feature of suburbs that impinges differentially on women is low density. Furthermore, the demographic and labor force characteristics of suburban women are changing in ways that make low density more of a problem, yet suburbs themselves are being constructed at ever lower density levels![42]

[39] Ibid., p. 227.
[40] Bennett Berger's study *Working Class Suburb* is profiled earlier in this book in Chapter 9. Bennett M. Berger, *Working Class Suburb: A Study of Auto Workers in Suburbia,* University of California Press, Berkeley, Calif., 1960.
[41] Ibid., p. 62.
[42] Sylvia Fava, "Women's Place in the New Suburbia." pp. 125–149 in Wekerle, Peterson, and Morley (eds.), *New Space for Women,* p. 133.

Fava went on to describe how low density and "scatteration" of homes, work-places, children's schools, and shopping areas together placed a huge burden on the suburban woman's time needs, and coupled with the lack of mass transit (also due to low density) required her to own a car. These were serious constraints on women in traditional married-couple households. The problems were even worse for sin-gle-family household heads—whose numbers were rising at that time due to na-tionally rising divorce rates. Moreover, the number of working women was in-creasing, and they had to deal with the constraints brought about by their need to be able to return home for child emergencies or at day's end. Fava pointed out that "the friction of space weighs heavily on suburban women because they have less ability to overcome distance. . . ." At the time she first pointed this out, women had less access to cars than they do now, but the factors of greater responsibility than men for the daily needs of families and children remains a constraint on women's travel distances.[43]

American and Swedish Women in Suburbs

Support for Fava's analysis came from David Popenoe's comparison of suburbs in the United States, where lower density, as Fava described, had an impact on women's lives, and Sweden, where planning had taken some of these needs of women into account. In contrast to the U.S. suburb, he found that the Swedish sub-urb was one of moderately high density, was tied to the city by public transporta-tion, and contained relatively abundant day care and other services despite the fact that it was originally designed for the stay-at-home wife just as U.S. suburbs were.[44] Popenoe observed:

> One reason many Swedish women work is because the suburb is exceptionally well de-signed from the point of view of working women; it is highly congruent with their needs and behavior patterns. Swedish women have access to a large job market, easily reached by pub-lic transportation, and they have necessary public facilities, such as day-care centers, play parks, and youth centers. Moreover, they have a safe environment for their children, a low maintenance dwelling unit, and a husband who has a reasonably short journey to work and hence can be home more.[45]

The suburbs of the 1950s and 1960s were the "bedrooms" of the city. They were mainly residential and had little industry or other facilities. They were tied to the city by the commuters (mainly male) whose jobs were in the downtown areas. These postwar suburbs provided a good fit for only one female role, namely that of

[43] Earlier in this book, in Chapter 9, some of these changes are outlined, including the fact that there are a predominance of working women, that most two-income families are also two-car (or more) families, and that many employers have relo-cated in suburban areas in the past twenty years. All these changes have diminished the isolation of the suburban "house-wife" of earlier decades, but not her familial responsibilities. In addition, William Michaelson delineates the ways in which woman's role definitions translate into the complex demands of her daily life. William Michaelson, *From Sun to Sun: Daily Obligations and Community Structure in the Lives of Employed Women and Their Families,* Rowman and Allanheld Publishers, Totowa, N.J., 1985.

[44] David Popenoe's comparison of the United States with a different spatial configuration of homes, work, and trans-portation in Sweden demonstrates in yet another way how spatial location of women affects their social places. David Popenoe, "Women in the Suburban Environment: A U.S.-Sweden Comparison," in Wekerle, Peterson, and Morley (eds.), *New Space for Women,* p. 169.

[45] Ibid., p. 169.

the housewife-mother who had the benefit of her own home and yard. Women often felt trapped if they wanted to obtain further education or training, hold a job, or pursue a career or other activities outside the home.[46]

Suburbs grew rapidly as population, jobs, and services moved out from cities. The United States has become a suburban nation, with more people living in suburban locations than anywhere else. Even so, gender differences persist. The Louis Harris organization conducted a survey of a nationally representative sample of men's and women's residential preferences; the findings were that men and women did not necessarily live in the type of location they preferred. The men had a stronger preference for "rural" areas, which were mainly nonfarm residential areas of very low density far from a town or city. The women preferred suburban locations in towns and villages, where the amenities and services were closest to home, thus enabling the women to more easily coordinate their many roles.[47]

Women Made Visible in Urban Research

By the 1980s, then, critical masses of work that were shared among the community of urban researchers began to foster a climate where theory could be revised to address the question of women and their place in urban metropolitan social structures and processes. Theoretical work began to describe underlying urban spatial arrangements that could account for persistent gender inequities. As society across the nation changed, the images of women's social and spatial places also changed. The slow pace of women's emergence into public arenas of urban influence started to gain momentum. Research began to identify and describe the interaction of these social constructions with the new daily realities of women.

Close examination of different types of women in urban life reveals a common pattern of more complex role expansion and more equal status with men, compared with women living in rural areas. The informal and private networks of experience and information sharing as well as cooperative actions take place more easily in the more densely populated urban places. In addition, cities provide the critical masses of people necessary to support mass transportation that increases women's mobility in daily life. Early suburbs lacked this density and the resources it offers women, but as the suburbs have become increasingly populated with families and workplaces, and as two-income families are also multicar families, this is changing.

In the 1970s and 1980s women sociologists were reflecting societal change by bringing women's unique and changing experiences to bear directly on urban theory and research. In 1975 Lofland addressed the female perspective for urban research in a volume of feminist research by labeling women's invisibility.[48] In 1980, in a volume of sociology edited by Gerda Wekerle, Rebecca Peterson, and David Morley, aspects of women in urban life were explicitly examined. In this book,

---

[46] Betty Friedan's *The Feminine Mystique,* W.W. Norton, New York, 1963, was implicitly about the middle-class suburban woman of the 1950's and 1960's United States. Suburbs were fine for men but not supportive of women's diverse but integrated personal identities.

[47] Sylvia Fava, "Gender and Residential Preferences in the Suburban Era: A New Look?" *Sociological Focus,* **18:**109–117, April, 1985.

[48] Lofland, "The 'Thereness' of Women: A Selective Review of Urban Sociology," in Millman and Kanter (eds.), *Another Voice.*

A mother kisses her son good-bye as she leaves for work. (Spencer Grant/Stock, Boston.)

Sylvia Fava gave perspective to the emerging phenomenon of suburbia that challenged prevailing views.

WOMEN'S PLACE, WOMEN'S SPACE: GENDER GEOGRAPHY

Though we've examined some aspects of urbanism that occur when women have been socially assigned to home and men to the market, other approaches to understanding women in urban settings focus on how gender inequities are maintained in different spatial locations. First is within the home. Second is in more public institutions of society, namely access to and the character of colleges and universities. Third is in the workplace. The general idea is that separate places offer different kinds of learning to each gender. Typically "male" spaces have provided access to new knowledge that fosters expanded personal experience and greater individual confidence based on increasing familiarity with a wider range of situations. Simmel described the impact of city life on industrial sensibility as one of "intensification of nervous stimulation."[49] He maintained that if one does not succumb to anomie, the city can provide liberating alternatives to traditional life-styles and role definitions, each with its own risks and rewards. The city's relative freedom from social constraints historically was interpreted to mean it was a source of sin and temptation to stray from socially accepted paths. Another interpretation is that in the city there are a variety of alternatives that mean a greater likelihood of finding ways in which to modify traditional expectations to suit one's own personality. Under modern conditions of societal change, this can offer liberating potential for women who occupy urban settings.

Gendered Spaces

Daphne Spain explicitly addresses how different levels of spatial arrangements for men and women have the effect of reinforcing traditional gender definitions.[50] Her main thesis is that "Women and men are spatially segregated in ways that reduce women's access to knowledge and thereby reinforce women's lower status relative to men's. Gendered spaces separate women from knowledge used by men to predict and reproduce power and privilege."[51] She notes "both women and men create spatial segregation and stratification systems. Both sexes subscribe to the spatial arrangements that reinforce differential access to knowledge, resources and power: men because it serves their interests, and women because they may perceive no alternatives."[52] This is not always because there *are* no alternatives; often powerful belief systems foster shared conceptions of the reasons why the existing social order is good for everyone.

Architecture Shapes Lives

Perhaps the most important aspect of home design in the nineteenth and early twentieth century in America was the strong belief that architecture shaped lives. "Order within the household was expected to create order in society."[53] Rooms like the library, the smoking room, and many of the public rooms of the house were intended for exclusive male use at specified times of day, if not all the time. For example, the social custom that women were not to be found in a man's study since that was where business was conducted reinforced the social expectation that women should not be business managers. Domesticity as expounded on by Beecher and her contemporaries made this very clear.[54]

As the nineteenth century evolved, housing began to become more democratic, more egalitarian, keeping pace with the changes in the larger society. Changes

[49] Georg Simmel, "The Metropolis and Mental Life," in *The Sociology of Georg Simmel,* Kurt Wolff (trans. and ed.), Free Press, New York, 1950, p. 409.
[50] Daphne Spain describes how assignment of genders to certain areas of the home or certain places in the educational system or at work operates to maintain women's inequality because the male spaces contain the kinds of knowledge that determine who holds power. Daphne Spain, *Gendered Spaces,* University of North Carolina Press, Chapel Hill, 1992.
[51] Ibid., p. 3.
[52] Ibid., p. 18.
[53] Ibid., p. 123.
[54] Jackson, *Crabgrass Frontier.*

in home design and rationales for new interior arrangements paralleled changes in the status and "place" of women in American society.

> By the beginning of the twentieth century, American women could attend coeducational colleges, own property, and vote. Concomitantly the middle class ideal home was minimizing the segregation of women and men by combining previously single-purpose, gender-typed rooms into multipurpose, sexually integrated rooms.[55]

Public Spatial Arrangements: Educational Institutions

Like the evolution of the home in America, the evolution of educational places for women and men have also moved in the direction of greater equality, though not in linear fashion. In the last century, like those nonindustrial societies that have ceremonial secret knowledge huts for men, schools in the United States were places where men but not women were prepared for adult leadership roles in business, politics, and religion. Racially segregated schools placed a double limitation on women of color since for many years they were excluded from both male and white schools.[56]

Whereas in the city men gained occupational freedom and mobility, diversity of economic opportunity, and increased freedom from restrictive social roles with industrialization, compared with their situations in an earlier agrarian economy, women remained unidimensionally defined by their procreative and nurturing domestic functions. In fact, compared with colonial times, women's sphere had actually narrowed as the cult of domesticity advanced in the early part of the nineteenth century.[57]

Cultural images of both genders were used to legitimize the unequal access to knowledge of women in the education system, in the same way they had been used to exclude "respectable" women from the public areas of the city.[58] Fears about the dangers of such knowledge were voiced in the form of concern that women, "might forge their husband's signatures or neglect their household duties by reading cheap novels."[59] Girls who now could go to school could only go after the boys had had their day in class. Girls went for fewer hours and for fewer months of the year. Moreover, they were restricted in the nature of the knowledge they were permitted to share. At first they were only taught reading and writing, not arithmetic as the boys were.[60]

Social pressure to remind women of their proper place in the domestic sphere took the form of separate quarters, separate facilities, and often separate curricula. Lest we think the segregation by gender of higher educational institutions was only a nineteenth-century phenomenon, bear in mind that the University of Virginia was the last major state university to go coeducational, only admitting undergraduate women in 1972.[61]

---

[55] Spain, *Gendered Spaces*, p. 127.
[56] Ibid., p. 143.
[57] Berg, *The Remembered Gate.*
[58] Ibid. Jackson, *Crabgrass Frontier.*
[59] Newcomer quoted in Spain, *Gendered Spaces*, p. 147.
[60] Spain, *Gendered Spaces*, pp. 147–148.
[61] Ibid., p. 157.

Integrating the genders in the same space changes existing stratification systems and the distribution of power they represent. Even more important than integrating the formal curricula is the opportunity the presence of women in such space offers for learning an expanded repertoire of informal or unstated norms and customs linked to higher status, leadership, and power in the public institutions of society.

Social Constructions of Gender and Space in the Workplace

In her book *Gendered Spaces,* Spain illustrates the importance of knowledge gained through social sponsorship and participation by using an example described in Harry Levinson's 1980 book *Executive.* Levinson observed that managerial leadership is not learned by reading books. Instead his research uncovered a dynamic built on relationships of younger managers to older ones by which the younger ones are mentored and learn by example. Spain identifies the profound significance of this process, namely that for it to take place younger managers must share space with their mentors on a regular basis. Senior managers demonstrate how decisions are made and often provide the explicit rationales or explanations for their actions during informal moments in the course of doing business. Today, with more than half of the entering college freshmen being young women and with the proportion of women managers increasing as women remain in the workplace during child-rearing years, this dynamic is slowly extending such experiences to women managers.

Women's place at work is still not as egalitarian as her place in educational institutions. Although the twentieth century ends with a higher proportion of both white and black women at work outside their homes, gender segregation within the workplace has remained fairly stable.[62] The historical dynamics of gender-based occupational segregation are similar to those we saw in domestic and educational spheres: Spatial segregation in the workplace separates women from important streams of knowledge and experiences that provide status and power advantages to those who are part of them.

Social Disadvantages of Spatial Distance

In addition to social segregation within the workplace, residential location often inhibits women's opportunities to work, largely because of women's continuing role within the family as the primary child-care provider. Here too the imagery of a woman's nature and role within the family, and as manager of the home, operates to limit occupational entry and mobility. In their study of women and work in Worcester, Massachusetts, Hanson and Pratt[63] examine the commuting patterns of women and how the advantages and disadvantages of distance between home and workplace are different for men and women.

They point out two clear urban spatial dimensions that intersect with gender stratification to affect workplace patterns. One relates to child care. Of necessity as

---

[62] Ibid., p. 201.
[63] Susan Hanson and Geraldine Pratt, *Gender, Work, and Space,* Routledge, New York, 1995.

long as the traditional division of parenting roles persists, mothers must take jobs close enough to home to enable them to get there in emergency situations or in time to supervise children after school or after day care ends. The other relates to geographical location. Industrial employers are attracted to specific regions because of the nature of their work forces. The geography of gender is central to industrial relocation. Low-wage employers moving into declining heavy industry areas, for example, benefit from a reserve labor force of women who are inexperienced as organized wage labor and therefore have lower expectations. Employers in industrial parks located in suburban rings where there is a domestically "captive" daytime work force living nearby also benefit from low-cost female labor.

URBAN LOCATION AND FEMALE EQUALITY: CROSS-CULTURAL SIMILARITIES

Patterns of geography and equality are consistent with both knowledge and travel aspects of "differential access" hypotheses about women's equality. We would expect urban life to offer more opportunities for women than rural life, by virtue of the density and close proximity of individuals to a range of work and social alternatives. Within the United States, analysis of sex ratios reveals different proportions of genders in urban versus rural locales. Low-population western states like Nevada and Idaho have high sex ratios (more men than women), which may be a legacy of migration and their frontier history. Women typically are underrepresented in frontier situations and do not begin to approach the numbers of males until settlement has become established. On the other hand, Florida has a low sex ratio, with many more women than men. This is because the population skews older, consisting mainly of retirees, and women outlive men by several years. Blacks have low sex ratios (more women), and this affects the gender representation in states where they are concentrated, like Mississippi and Alabama. Major cities have low sex ratios, more women than men, because cities also have higher concentrations of black and poor citizens. Women single heads of households are more heavily represented in cities, contributing to the low sex ratio, because they are generally poorer than married-couple heads of households.[64] These spatial distributions reveal status distributions that support the hypothesis that urban life fosters greater status equality of women.

Perhaps the most interesting spatial location pattern is the pattern of equality found around the world. Women in urbanized countries have greater equality of rights and opportunities than women in less urbanized countries. Simmel's view of the city as potentially liberating due to its diversity of situation and relative freedom from individual constraint is borne out. Status for women is highest in western countries, where the women are socially permitted in the widest variety of human settings; and it is lowest in the middle east, Asia, and tropical Africa, where

---

[64] Mary Ellen Mazey and David R. Lee explore several hypotheses regarding different distributions of population by gender by comparing countries in different stages of economic and political development. Mary Ellen Mazey and David R. Lee, *Her Space, Her Place, A Geography of Women,* Association of American Geographers, Washington, D.C., 1983.

women are often formally excluded from the spheres of men.[65] The western nations are also the most urban. Associated with this pattern are similar urban-rural distinctions within the United States.

Mazey and Lee's work was done in the early 1980s, and so some aspects of social barriers they discuss are outdated. But a fundamental dynamic they describe—of how social change on an individual level happens—still holds. In explaining their observations they describe the individual's subjective world of self, home, houses of friends, distant towns, and the like to be an atlas of places of personal significance and meaning. The familiar places constitute a conscious "comfort zone" of social meaning for anyone living within them. Typically women's "comfort zones" have been more circumscribed than men's for the middle, working, and poorer classes. Unknown places are filled with strangers and uncertainty.

The experience for women of being in unfamiliar places is more anxiety-producing than for men because of several social barriers. They include shared cultural beliefs about women's lower likelihood of being able to handle transportation failures (especially car breakdowns) than men, greater likelihood of challenges or unwanted attention in places like hotels or restaurants if traveling alone, street hassling, and, in the extreme, rape. The sources of anxiety include persistent social definitions of women as intruders or "out of place" in these locations. These experiences are illustrative of the cultural idea that there are places where women are not entitled to be that is part of a dynamic described earlier in this chapter.[66] They contribute to women's "mental maps" of subjective spatial knowledge that affects their different experience of the city.

NEW DIRECTIONS: WOMEN IN URBAN PUBLIC SPACE

So far in this chapter we have learned how the dual imagery of women in the city has reinforced historically different places and experiences for them in metropolitan life. We've learned from early community studies about the constraints of poverty and how women collectively cope with them. We've seen the strength of women's personal communities of family members and neighbors in helping them lead city lives. How women are taking on public governing roles in city life reflect the persistent nature of how spatial arrangements and social statuses are interdependent and have tended to reinforce traditional role expectations of each gender.

Changing Realities of Gendered Space

We have seen the historical impact of good and bad stereotypes of women in the city which has limited women's social and geographic mobility in the past. Participant observers have revealed alternative and powerful female social processes that

---

[65] Ibid., p. 4.

[66] Berg, *The Remembered Gate*. Mazey and Lee, *Her Space, Her Place*. Spain, *Gendered Spaces*. Hanson and Pratt, *Gender, Work, and Space*.

contribute significantly to the fabric of city life. Research has also described how social institutions like education and business mark off territory as belonging to one or the other gender in ways that reinforce existing arrangements. However, in the past twenty years those social structures and processes have changed dramatically. We have seen how urban compared with nonurban environments tend to foster increasing equality of the genders. Despite the slow pace of social change, women now do have new social roles and places, and new expectations assigned to each.

Recent urban research is investigating the new places and experiences of women in the city by focusing on formal, public urban institutions like government as they shape women's place in the city via their management of land use, city services, and housing control. This work directly challenges the economic logic approach to understanding urban structures. The accumulated mass of research on women now enables theorists to argue that economic processes are no longer sufficient for understanding the dynamics of the city (if they ever were).[67] Garber and Turner reinforce the importance of the often overlooked strength of women's private social networks for urban analysis. They argue that urban analysis cannot choose to restrict itself only to the study of separate public spheres as if they were unattached to personal and private spheres. As they put it,

> Because gender relationships are not solely individual, the political and environmental manifestations of gender are not necessarily conscious or uncontradictory. The subtlety of relationships should be construed as evidence that they are woven into the fabric of the city and simply taken for granted, not proof that they are nonexistent.[68]

Recent approaches to studying women in the city recognize that women often do not (and have not) acted within gender roles as traditional imagery describes them. This may seem self-evident, but social theories of all kinds have until recently *not* managed to incorporate this insight. In addition, two decades of changing gender-role definitions have also changed the urban fabric. The majority of women today do *not* live adult lives solely as homemakers, nor can they expect to in the near future. The economics of middle-class life requires two-income households. As more and more women are better educated not only by schooling but also by work experiences, they are increasingly managing businesses and they are moving into positions in city government as their political participation increases.

Women in Urban Politics

The most recent research on women and urbanism examines the impact of women as they assume more and more public offices around the United States. The new findings are consistent with earlier work that showed that urban areas offer women more gender equality than rural areas or towns. Susan Abrams Beck has found that

---

[67] Garber and Turner explicitly assert that economic logic tends to cloud our view of the fact that the city is an entire social fabric and therefore that analyzing only its economic operation or its governance as if that would explain the metropolitan diversity of experience is inadequate. Judith A. Garber and Robyn Turner (eds.), *Gender in Urban Research,* Sage Publications, Thousand Oaks, Calif., 1995.

[68] Ibid., p. xi.

Women are increasingly involved in local politics.
(Grantpix/Monkmeyer.)

compared with state and federal arenas where women's issues have made greater strides in being addressed, local political processes offer political challenges for women's issues. Her analysis of five New Jersey communities concerning housing issues found that local communities resolve cleavages and respond to women's needs in housing only when faced with pressure from state agencies. Caroline Andrew's work in Canada has found that there is a persistent tendency for local politics to see women in traditional role definitions.

In examining the election of female mayors and council members around the country, Susan MacManus and Charles Bullock found that, in general, larger places are more favorable to women in public offices in a number of ways. Women are more likely to serve in cities with populations of 25,000 or more—in these cities women hold at least 22 percent of the council seats.[69] Other variables favorably associated with the election of women include "at-large" elections and larger council sizes (more than nine members). Both of these are features of larger (city rather than small local) governments. Length of term seems to have little association with one gender or another except in the case of very long terms (five years or longer), which then are associated with fewer women.

---

[69] Susan MacManus and Charles Bullock, "Electing Women to Public Office," in Judith A. Garber and Robyne S. Turner (eds.), *Gender in Urban Research*, Sage, Thousand Oaks, Calif., 1995, p. 162.

WOMEN IN METROPOLITAN AREAS IN THE TWENTY-FIRST CENTURY

We've seen change from the nineteenth century to the twentieth century in a variety of aspects of men's and women's lives. Three aspects of the situations of women in metropolitan life today are important to remember. All of them need further research. First, the changes in women's statuses, roles, and places in the social life of the metropolis are ongoing but uneven in their progression and their impact on society. Inequalities of opportunity for education, personal freedom, and domestic and caretaking expectations of women continue even as women are becoming familiar in the formerly male environments of work and government. Progress is especially uneven between the genders when you consider the persistent gaps in the provision of child care, public transportation, and provision for care of the elderly and/or the sick.

Second, all these are women's issues because women are still expected to be the caregivers and caretakers in their families. Thus women continue to carry an invisible burden of responsibility in addition to their increasing roles in public life that inhibits their ability to take advantage of the new equalities and freedoms open to them. Because these new opportunities have added to their existing responsibilities, women have a "second shift" of work in their lives. Although research has identified this second shift,[70] its effects on urban life have yet to be fully examined.

Finally, many subgroups of women have not been studied adequately, if at all. It will become more sociologically necessary to study older women, especially widows, as their numbers swell with the aging baby-boom generation. Similarly, the elder never-married group of women have not been studied. They too are a growing segment of the population. Women in religious orders, black women in suburbia, and Irish, Italian, and other second-generation immigrant women in a variety of ethnic groups (Latinas and Asians in particular) are all overlooked in research. The nonemployed traditional housewife is still another subcultural group whose needs and lives have been assumed on the basis of stereotyping rather than systematic research. We know very little about the lives of these women after young children go off to school all day. All these subgroups remain fruitful subjects needing systematic investigation. Our increasing knowledge of these women will also help us understand the metropolitan landscape in more comprehensive ways.

---

[70] Arlie Hochschild's research describes how this happens in great detail. Arlie Hochschild with Anne Machung, *The Second Shift*, Avon Books, New York, 1989.

PART 4

PROBLEMS, HOUSING, AND PLANNING

CHAPTER 12

THE QUESTION OF
URBAN CRISIS

*The decline of Rome was the natural and inevitable effect
of immoderate greatness—as soon as time or accidents had
removed the artificial supports, the stupendous fabric
yielded to the pressure of its own weight.*

Edward Gibbon, 1737–1794

INTRODUCTION

The Urban Crisis Thesis

As recently as 1930 a planner could describe Los Angeles as "a federation of communities coordinated into a metropolis of sunlight and air."[1] No one makes such claims today. A much discussed recent book on Los Angeles, *City of Quartz,* paints a far darker picture of the metropolis as a place of Dickensian extremes.[2] It is an accepted cliché that we live in an age of urban crisis. Crime, violence, pollution, ugliness, congestion, and alienation are all attributed in one degree or another to urban life. Certainly there is no lack of prophets to passionately catalog our urban ills. As stated by Lewis Mumford:

> Nobody can be satisfied with the form of the city today. Neither as a working mechanism, as a social medium, nor as a work of art does the city fulfill the high hopes that modern civilization has called forth—or even met our reasonable demands.[3]

Are cities, particularly large cities, doomed? During the 1970s voices were raised everywhere announcing the inevitable decline, if not death, of the city. A conference of large-city mayors in 1977 proclaimed that what was at stake was not only "the survival of our cities" but the survival of the American way of life as we have known it. The chairman of the New York Real Estate Board stated: "American cities are collapsing. This peril to the nation, and in consequence to over 200 years of experiment in democracy, is no overstatement."[4]

Philip Hauser contended that "the stark facts indicate that the worst still lies ahead. The urban crisis will grow worse before it grows better," while George Sternlieb pessimistically suggested that "the Newarks of America are forecasts of things to come, and if we want to understand the probable future that faces many of our older cities, then we will first have to get clear on what is happening—has happened—in places like Newark."[5] Sternlieb contended that the older cities lost their economic function, particularly as areas of entry for newcomers, and have become simply "sandboxes." People in the sandbox occasionally get new toys (federal programs), but these don't allow the underclass to move into the larger world—they just keep the people in the sandbox from being bothersome to the rest of society. As well-paying manufacturing jobs left the older cities, the cities no longer provided opportunities for upward mobility for unskilled African Americans and Hispanics. As we enter the new century, the rhetoric has hardly changed. For example, at a 1990 conference of big-city mayors, the mayor of Los Angeles warned, "If we do not save our cities we shall not save the nation."[6]

---

[1] R. M. Fogelson, *The Fragmented Metropolis: Los Angeles 1850–1930,* Harvard University Press, Cambridge, Mass., 1967, p. 163.
[2] Mike Davis, *City of Quartz,* Vintage, New York, 1992.
[3] Lewis Mumford, *The Urban Prospect,* Harcourt Brace Jovanovich, New York, 1968, p. 108.
[4] Seymour B. Durant, "Laetrile for the Urban Crisis: Planned Shrinkage and Other Dangerous Nostrums," *Journal of the Institute for Socioeconomic Studies,* **4**:68, Summer, 1979.
[5] Philip M. Hauser, "Chicago—Urban Crisis Exemplar," in J. John Palen (ed.), *City Scenes,* Little, Brown, Boston, 1977, pp. 15–25; George Sternlieb, "The City as Sandbox," *The Public Interest,* **4**(25):14, Fall, 1971.
[6] William Scheider, "The Suburban Century Begins," *Atlantic Monthly,* July, 1992, p. 34.

In the view of pessimists, cities are having their vital signs maintained by external life-support systems, with the federal government making the judgment about whether to pull the plug. Not surprisingly, such discussions regarding the future of urban areas have focused not on what will occur, but rather on questions of the degree and timing of the collapse.

URBAN REVIVAL: ANTITHESIS

If the 1970s was the decade of "urban crisis," the 1980s was the decade of "urban revival." Cities from Columbus to Memphis to Miami to Los Angeles rediscovered downtown and renovated selected older neighborhoods. In many cities the 1980s witnessed a rebirth of hope. The media discovered that the city was not only alive but healthy.[7] Suddenly the urban crisis was said to have left town and the slumming of the suburbs became the problem.[8] Meanwhile, the central cities experienced an urban renaissance. Revitalized downtowns showed economic vigor, while affluent whites rediscovered the city as a place of residence and rehabilitated inner-city areas. (This is discussed in detail in Chapter 13, Housing and the Community.) Some academics (perhaps prematurely) further echoed that the urban crisis was over because cities had put their fiscal affairs in order and were surprisingly resilient.[9]

[7] Horace Sutton, "America Falls in Love with Its Cities—Again," *Saturday Review,* August, 1978, pp. 16–21; and "A City Revival," *Newsweek,* Jan. 15, 1979.

[8] T. D. Allman, "The Urban Crisis Leaves Town," *Harper's,* December, 1978, p. 5.

[9] Mark Gottdiener, "Retrospect and Prospect in Urban Crisis," in Mark Gottdiener (ed.), *Cities in Stress: A New Look at the Urban Crisis,* Sage, Beverly Hills, Calif., 1986, pp, 277–292.

From a landscape of rubble and abandoned buildings, much of the South Bronx of New York is being rebuilt as new rowhouse and apartment developments. (UPI/Bettmann.) (Joe Tabacca/AP/Wide World Photos.)

CRISIS AGAIN?

The 1990s have seen the wheel turn once more, with crisis talk again in the air. This time the crisis is over both economics and public safety. Cities nationwide are confronting heavy use of heroin, crack cocaine, and other drugs, and high crime rates. As the decade opened, the Gallup poll for the first time saw drugs as the nation's number one problem, far outrunning nuclear weapons, AIDS, the economy, and homelessness.[10]

Some scholars who take a longer view would argue that drugs and crime are symptoms of the increasing economic isolation of those lacking the educational credentials to enter the legal job market. The crisis, thus, is a long-standing one of opportunity, rather than a short-term one of fiscal management.[11]

The 1990s have also witnessed the reemergence of urban riots or rebellions as an urban issue. The 1992 verdict in the Rodney King police beating case led to South-Central Los Angeles erupting in looting and burning. The toll was 58 deaths, almost 2,400 injured, 5,600 businesses suffering losses, and approximately 15,000 arrested.

What then is the status of the cities as the century turns? Readers understandably may be confused by the contradictory statements. This chapter attempts to evaluate the various claims and counterclaims; but as you read the material, keep in mind that these are the judgments of this author, and others might draw different conclusions.

A NEO-MARXIST APPROACH

One cannot discuss the urban crisis without the perspective provided by the political economy approach discussed in detail earlier in Chapter 5. Until the 1990s and the collapse of the Soviet Union and other socialist systems, much of the theoretical underpinings of this approach were neo-Marxist.[12] Neo-Marxist sociologists hold that cities cannot be examined separately from the political, historical, and, particularly, economic system of which they are a part. Manuel Castells argued, for example, that not only is the crisis of the cities real, but the decay of the central cities, their fiscal insolvency, and flight to the suburbs are inevitable and necessary consequences of a capitalistic economic system.[13] He says that the quest for ever-greater profits by large monopolistic companies led to government policies such as government-insured mortgages and subsidies for expressways. The corporations—and their wealthy managers—thus could move to the suburbs, where land costs and taxes were lower, while still maintaining the economic benefits of being near the central city. The fiscal crises of cities such as New York thus are not the consequence of excessive services, public-service jobs, and welfare, as the elites argue.

---

[10] "Public Lists Drugs as Number One Problem," *Washington Post,* Aug. 18, 1989, p. 1.
[11] Gregory R. Weihner, "Rumors of the Demise of the Urban Crisis Are Greatly Exaggerated," *Journal of Urban Affairs,* 11(3):225–242, 1989.
[12] See, for example, Manuel Castells, *The Urban Question: A Marxist Approach,* Alan Sheridan (trans.), MIT Press, Cambridge, Mass., 1977; and David Harvey, *Social Justice and the City,* Arnold, London, 1973.
[13] Manuel Castells, "The Wild City," *Kapital State,* 4–5:2–30, Summer, 1976.

Rather, the near "bankruptcy" of cities is the result of the corporations' rejection of increased taxes to pay for social services. The result is the abandonment and destruction of largely poor areas of the city, while corporations concentrate on issues important to themselves such as downtown redevelopment.[14] Social movements by the poor are either repressed or bought off. The consequence is said to be a future where the urban crisis is sharpened and mass repression and control become inevitable adjuncts of an exploitative metropolitan model.[15]

Similarly, neo-Marxists analyze gentrification not as a decision of individual home buyers, but as a conscious product of land-based interest groups able to control the real estate market.[16] According to this view, investment capital was systematically moved out of inner cities and into suburbs because suburban profit rates were higher. The subsequent deterioration of inner-city neighborhoods led to the development of a rent gap, which in turn made it possible for capital to return to the central city seeking profits. The ownership class benefits from these decisions, while the costs of gentrification fall upon the urban poor in the form of displacement. Advocates of a non-Marxian political economy approach similarly see gentrification as a conscious action by business groups that profit by maintaining an urban "growth machine."[17]

SOME PROBLEM AREAS

Central Business Districts

In evaluating what is occurring in cities, it is necessary to distinguish between what is occurring in the economic heart of the city—the central business district (CBD)—and what is happening in residential neighborhoods.

Discussions of the decline of downtowns often focus on the weakening position of the CBD as a center of retail trade. As suburban shopping malls have proliferated, downtown sales have been declining both in absolute terms and in terms of a percentage of metropolitan area sales. Aging downtown stores have not been able to compete effectively with suburban shopping malls.

On the other hand, the CBD has been far more successful in retaining business and government administrative offices. Economically, the downtowns of most large cities have experienced new business construction. New office towers and high-rise apartment buildings have sprouted on Manhattan streets; downtown Los Angeles has undergone a building boom; Chicago has seen new skyscrapers under construction.

[14] Scott Cummings (ed.), *Business Elites and Urban Development*, State University of New York, Albany, 1988.
[15] Castells, "The Wild City."
[16] Neil Smith and Michele LeFaivre, "A Class Analysis of Gentrification," in J. John Palen and Bruce London (eds.), *Gentrification, Displacement and Neighborhood Revitalization*, State University of New York Press, Albany, N.Y., 1984; and Neil Smith and Peter Williams (eds.), *Gentrification of the City,* Allen and Unwin, London, 1986.
[17] John Logan and Harvey Molotch, *Urban Fortunes: The Political Economy of Place,* University of California Press, Berkeley, 1987.

Seattle's Pike Place Market is an example of central-city vitality.
(David Danelski/Pike Place Market PDA, Seattle.)

Nationwide, downtowns have experienced a boom in high-rise construction mainly for office space. Offices concerned with processing knowledge and information find it easy to move vertically from floor to floor. Manufactured goods, on the other hand, move much easier horizontally. Thus, new manufacturing facilities seek outlying locations with plenty of horizontal space. Downtowns no longer process goods; rather, they process information.

Manhattan, apparently already full decades ago, is a classic example of the CBD building boom. Between 1960 and 1980 a remarkable 142 new buildings were completed in midtown Manhattan containing 77 million square feet of space. This is more than all the office space in Houston and Dallas together. Moreover, over fifty new buildings have been added since 1980. More office space was built in the last five years of the 1980s than during all of the 1970s. (One consequence of all this office building is high vacancy rates for office space.) Older buildings are also being rehabilitated and upgraded. Cities have actively promoted downtown office development and convention centers as an economic growth strategy.[18]

[18] Bernard J. Frieden and Lynne B. Sagalyn, "Downtown Mass and the City Agenda," *Society,* July–August, 1990, pp. 43–49.

The last decade has witnessed city after city building convention centers and encouraging downtown hotel construction in order to attract conventions and trade meetings. Middle-sized cities now attract meetings that once were held in a handful of the largest cities. Downtown shopping malls such as Harbor Place in Baltimore or Quincy Market in Boston are also drawing people. Throughout the country, new downtown convention facilities, cultural centers, hotels, and office buildings are sprouting. This is occurring in Atlanta, Denver, San Antonio, Portland, and a host of other cities. Cultural activities, art, music, and theater centers are also part of the urban development strategy.[19] The dominance will not return, but most cities' CBDs are in the process of stabilizing at a moderate but reasonable level of economic activity.

Overall, downtown stores will never again have the unchallenged control of retail trade they exhibited during the centralizing era of the streetcar and subway; but so long as the downtown is a major white-collar employment center, the CBD will be a profitable location for selected retail sales. Moreover, downtown remains the location of choice of insurance firms, financial and legal services, government, and administrative headquarters of all sorts. One visible consequence of the CBD's change from retail trade to office space is that the crowded CBD of working hours often becomes a virtual wasteland after 5 p.m., when offices close.

However, there is a catch to this development of the CBD. Central-city offices provide new jobs—but only for those possessing specific white-collar skills. Factories and manufacturing plants continue to move to the suburbs—or beyond. Cities have more blue-collar job seekers and white-collar job opportunities.[20] The result often is a mismatch between city people and central-city jobs. Stagnant or declining central-city manufacturing and factory sectors offer scant employment opportunities for those with limited educational backgrounds and job experience.

Entry-level jobs and jobs that required little education once attracted disadvantaged migrants to the cities. The availability of such jobs, however, has dropped precipitously in central cities. The cities experiencing the greatest loss of entry-level jobs over the past two decades have been those simultaneously experiencing the greatest increases in minority populations. The result is school dropout rates, welfare dependency, and unemployment rates higher than national averages, as blue-collar employment opportunities contract and white-collar opportunities expand. Thus, depending on the emphasis, one can make a case that job opportunities are substantial or getting much worse.

Fiscal Crisis and Declining Federal Support

During the 1970s numerous cities first experienced grave financial trouble. The fiscal crisis was due to the departure of tax-paying businesses from the city, as well as the exodus of the middle class with its tax dollars. At the same time, central-city expenses were skyrocketing. Particularly in the older industrial cities, declining

[19] J. Allen Whitt, "Mozart in the Metropolis: The Arts Coalition and the Urban Growth Machine," *Urban Affairs Quarterly,* **23:**15–36, September, 1987.
[20] John Kasarda, "Urban Change and Minority Opportunities," *The New Urban Reality,* in Paul Peterson (ed.), Brookings Institution, Washington, D.C., 1985, pp. 33–67.

populations meant greater costs to those who remained. As middle-class taxpayers left, municipal payrolls and public assistance expenditures commonly increased rather than declined. Growing numbers of poor residents needing services raised costs while depressing revenues. Cities are becoming polarized between affluent and poor. (As of 1990 the income of one in four New Yorkers was below the poverty line.) Aging city properties also require more fire and police protection, and older street, lighting, and sewer systems require more maintenance. Today cities vary dramatically in their fiscal health. The National League of Cities reported that as of the mid-1990s, after years of belt-tightening, cities were in their most solvent financial shape in years.[21]

Two major exceptions were New York and Los Angeles, which both suffered from weak regional economies during the first half of the 1990s. In addition, New York simply spent considerably more on city services than other communities. (New York City is twice the size of Los Angeles but spends six times as much.) In order to reduce expenditures, New York in the mid-1990s began to cut back its comparatively generous services to bring it closer to per capita costs in other cities. The city in by far the worst shape was Washington, D.C., which under home rule had run up huge deficits—$722 million in 1995—and was in defacto bankruptcy. Washington, however, is not typical of most cities. It is noted not only for the exceptional inefficiency of its city bureaucracy, but also for the size of its municipal work force—by far the largest municipal work force in the land. As of 1995, one out of every twelve residents of Washington, including children and the elderly, was on the city payroll. To put it in perspective, this gave Washington some 45,000 city employees compared with 41,000 in Chicago, which had a population five times as large.

The solvency of most cities owes little to federal assistance, for while "saving the cities" was a major emphasis twenty years ago, today municipalities are left to sink or swim on their own. Most of the city-oriented federal programs of the 1970s have disappeared. Until the mid-1980s, direct and indirect federal aid to the cities was a major source of revenue. However, in the Reagan era this aid was substantially cut back from about 16 percent of local budgets to 8 percent by 1995. As a consequence cities have become more dependent on state funding. The Republican Congress has drastically further slashed funding for urban programs. Excepting the area of crime, neither President Bush nor President Clinton gave urban-based programs or their funding much priority. Without any possibility of federal help, cities have cut back on programs to solve poverty and social problems. Municipalities increasingly just focus on the day-to-day delivery of core services. Some see this as a positive move insofar as it means the city is concentrating efforts on those things it can do well, and cutting back on those things it does less well such as solving social and personal problems.[22] Others see it as an abandonment of urban problems.

Increasingly, effective mayors, both Republican and Democrat, have been lowering government costs by privatizing city services. In the best cases this both

---

[21] Steven Holmes, "Budget Woes Ease for Cities in U.S. Analysts Report," *New York Times,* Jan. 8, 1995, p. A1.
[22] Nathan Glazer, "Fate of a World City," *City Journal,* Autumn, 1993.

improves services and saves money. For example, in Chicago Mayor Daley (the son of *the* Mayor Daley, who ran Chicago in the 1950s and 1960s) has privatized the towing of autos abandoned on city streets. Previously it cost the city $30 to tow each auto; now the city is paid $25 for each abandoned car private companies tow away.

Cutting services and costs, however, is not the only reason for municipal financial solvency. Local governments also have been raising tax levels. This, of course, makes lower-tax suburban business and residential locations look more attractive. Los Angeles, hit by riots in 1992 and earthquakes in 1994, found itself in difficult financial shape—in part because Proposition 13, passed in 1978, severely limits the ability of California municipalities to raise property taxes.

It should also be noted that the fact that cities can meet their payrolls does not mean that they are in financial health. Cities are still squeezed between growing expenditures and a slower-growing tax base. The larger the city, the greater the financial burden. Per capita debt is more than twice as high in cities of over 1 million as in smaller cities. City administrators are concerned that because of federal cutbacks, burdens will be shifted to the local level. They fear that cities will be stuck with higher tax burdens and unfunded mandates while their tax base grows smaller. Currently, of every dollar of taxes, 66 cents goes to the federal government, 20 cents goes to the states, and only the remaining 14 cents goes to local governments.[23]

With the federal debt at a critical level and with defense spending, entitlement, and debt service taking five-sixths of federal revenues, local governments cannot count on federal assistance. Successful local governments thus increasingly are those receiving community support (i.e., taxes) for necessary services.

Crumbling Infrastructure

Generally overlooked by most urban observers is the problem of infrastructure deterioration. In the late 1990s deterioration of the cities' physical infrastructure is a serious problem. Within cities, the most severe problem is often antiquated water and sewage systems. In New York, bursting water mains and collapsing streets have become commonplace, yet relatively little is being done to remedy this. At the present level of construction, it would take over 200 years to replace New York City's streets and water mains and 300 years to replace its sewers.[24] Nor is New York alone; Philadelphia's sewers are falling apart, while Boston and Houston are plagued with hemorrhaging water mains.

How and why is this occurring? The major reason for infrastructure decline is that it is relatively easy for politicians to ignore until the problems become massive. Local and state politicians claiming to cut taxes invariably raid infrastructure funds. This creates huge and expensive problems for the next generation but it is relatively safe politically, for it is only when infrastructure fails that it attracts attention. An example would be the 1989 steam pipe rupture under a street in New York City's fashionable East Side. The geyser of hot steam shot up over ten stories and killed three persons.

---

[23] William Tucker, *Insight,* Sept. 6, 1993, pp. 18–22.
[24] "City Fiscal Time Bomb—Decaying Facilities," *New York Times,* Jan. 29, 1989.

The cost of rebuilding the infrastructure is high. Since 1972 the federal government has invested $44 billion in sewage treatment. It, however, will take another $83.5 billion to meet the wastewater treatment mandates of the Clean Water Act by 2005 according to the Environmental Protection Agency.[25] Without major federal assistance, the problem of infrastructure deterioration cannot be addressed.

Quo Vadis?

The overall economic health of the cities remains clouded. On the positive side, cities have not defaulted. The state of the cities is fiscally and—perhaps equally important—psychologically healthier than a decade or two ago. Bright new office buildings and refurbished shopping malls are a sign of hope. There are also clear if limited signs of middle-class movement into older city neighborhoods.

On the debit side, the long-term indicators are still grim. There is still an outflow of tax dollars, older cities continue to lose manufacturing jobs, and the cost of services is rising. Drug usage and related violence fray the social fabric. Physically some neighborhoods are experiencing regeneration, but deterioration of the physical infrastructure (e.g., water mains and sewers) remains an expensive if often unseen problem. Meanwhile, the political climate does not favor new urban programs.

As a new century begins, it is clear that not all cities are going to experience similar situations. For example, declines in population may reflect deterioration, or may spur the development of new roles as cultural and service centers. Cities such as Newark may remain stagnant regardless of valiant efforts to reverse the process. On the other hand, old cities such as Boston, Baltimore, and even Cleveland have undergone some urban renaissance. Revival, however, is heaviest in central business areas. Other cities such as Denver, Dallas, Seattle, Los Angeles, and Phoenix show signs of increasing problems but also retain considerable vigor and attractiveness.

NEIGHBORHOOD REVIVAL

Although the purpose of the urban renewal programs of the 1950s and 1960s was to rebuild the cities' inner cores in order to encourage middle-class residency in such areas, the effort was largely unsuccessful. Talk of a "back-to-the-city" movement was not followed up by actual movement. As Chapter 9, Changing Suburbanization Patterns, documents, population movement has long been outbound rather than directed toward the central city. The assumption has been that those having the choice (i.e., middle-class home buyers) would shun the central city for the suburbs. As noted in Chapter 7, City Life-Styles, Gallup polls supported the view of suburban preference, with only 19 percent of those interviewed preferring city residence to residence in the suburbs or a small town.[26]

---

[25] "Our Crumbling Infrastructure," *Nation's Business,* August, 1989, p. 18.
[26] Gallup Organization, "Your Kind of Town," *New York Times,* Oct. 8, 1989.

There has been for a quarter of a century a limited but symbolic counter-movement toward residence in the central city. Ironically, the movement has not been to rebuilt urban renewal areas, but to older neighborhoods that are recycling from a period of decay. Middle-income and upper-middle-income whites (and some minorities) are buying and restoring old homes and new houses—a process commonly known as "neighborhood regeneration" or "gentrification."[27] Additionally, coalitions of local government and community action groups have been bringing abandoned buildings and neighborhoods back to life. First we will discuss gentrification and then new inner-city neighborhoods for the poor.

Gentrification is not occurring in all city neighborhoods, but is thus far limited largely to areas having substantial residences with historic or architectural merit. While the homes in these neighborhoods may be in disrepair when purchased by the "urban pioneer," they were originally constructed to standards generally unavailable in new suburban houses. Revitalizing areas are also generally well located in terms of accessibility, transportation routes, and overall physical location. Neighborhoods such as the East Village in New York, Lincoln Park in Chicago, or Haight-Ashbury in San Francisco are examples.

Middle-class in-movement to older central-city neighborhoods challenges traditional theories of growth. According to the classical Burgess model (discussed in Chapter 6, Metropolitan and Edge-City Growth) or the filtered-down economic model, this in-movement should not be occurring. Rather, older central-city residences should be abandoned to the economically marginal. Also, according to the original Burgess model, central-city residential property is vacated for commercial or industrial usage. Today, the pattern is more often the reverse; in some cities, formerly commercial buildings such as warehouses are being rehabilitated as residences. The SoHo section of New York, for instance, contains numerous older commercial structures that have been transformed into homes.[28] Other cities provide

---

[27] J. John Palen and Bruce London (eds.), *Gentrification, Displacement and Neighborhood Revitalization,* State University of New York Press, Albany, 1984.

[28] James R. Hudson, "SoHo, A Study of Residential Invasion of a Commercial and Industrial Area," *Urban Affairs Quarterly,* **20**:46–63, September, 1984.

DOONESBURY   **by Garry Trudeau**

similar examples. Commercial-to-residential transformations may become more common during the next decade, but most of the regeneration is occurring in older residential neighborhoods. Neighborhoods such as Ansley Park in Atlanta, the Fan in Richmond, New Town in Chicago, Five Points in Denver, Montrose in Houston, the Mission District in San Francisco, and Capitol Hill in Washington, D.C., are physically more robust than they were a decade ago.

Often overlooked in discussions of neighborhood revitalization is the regeneration of working-class neighborhoods. Even the term "gentrification" suggests that newcomers are young professionals of higher income and status than existing residents. This is not always the case. Upgrading of working-class neighborhoods is often less dramatic since newcomers, while often younger, are not that different from existing residents in terms of ethnic or social-class characteristics.[29] Physical improvements may be slow to show in city data since working-class residents are more likely to make home improvements without getting building permits. The important point is that local residents have accomplished neighborhood improvement without middle-class influx, and without the displacement of existing residents.

Role of Government

In the 1950s the federal government sponsored urban clearance and renewal, and since the 1960s, government has been involved with federally supported "redevelopment authorities" concerned with rebuilding the economic and physical structure of the central city.[30] However, to date, urban gentrification has been funded almost entirely by the private sector. Nonetheless, government, particularly municipal government, has played a role in urban gentrification—a role different from what one might imagine. During the 1970s and early 1980s municipal governments unintentionally served as a catalyst to bring neighbors together. Whether it was failure to enforce building codes, inadequate police protection, poor garbage collection and sanitation, nonmaintenance of parks, streets, and sidewalks, or just general neglect of the area, residents often were brought together in opposition to city hall. The common cry was, "They can't do that to us." It will be interesting to see whether communities can maintain the same level of commitment now that neighborhood revitalization has become popular at city hall.

Who Is Moving In?

Descriptive accounts suggesting that renovators are disillusioned suburbanites returning to the city from the suburbs are simply in error. Although one commonly hears the phrase "return to the city," most in-movers actually come from other areas of the city.[31] In fact, research by Spain indicates that the best predictor of an

---

[29] J. John Palen and Chava Nachmias, "Revitalization in a Working-Class Neighborhood," in Palen and London (eds.), *Gentrification, Displacement and Neighborhood Revitalization.*

[30] Scott Cummings (ed.), *Business Elites and Urban Development,* State University of New York Press, Albany, 1988; Gregory D. Squires (ed.), *Unequal Partnerships: The Political Economy of Urban Redevelopment in Postwar America,* Rutgers University Press, New Brunswick, N.J., 1989.

[31] Dennis Gale, *Neighborhood Revitalization and the Postindustrial City,* Lexington Books, Lexington, Mass., 1984.

Hoboken Gentrifies

In the 1980s Hoboken, New Jersey, just across the Hudson River from New York City, underwent a rapid gentrification and influx of yuppies from New York, locally called "Yorkies." The following are four of the hundreds of letters to the editor published in the *Hoboken Reporter*.*

Dear Editor:

Based on some very elementary research, I am pleased to announce the search is over, and "Yorkies" identifiable. They have certain characteristics in common but place of birth is not one of them; probably none are from the "sidewalks of New York." The type migrates to New York and brings with them these characteristics which are so endearing.

They work in New York and live in Hoboken.

They are generally "flunkies" by New York standards.

They feel that the local provincials will be overwhelmed by a display of undistilled sophistication.

They confuse a patronizing manner with charm.

They would engulf our public institutions as cultural saviors.

They seek special attention. Even in our small public library they suggest certain books be stocked and reserved just for them.

They cause stoppages in shopping lines while they hold court.

They have been a disappointment to many of their greedy landlords.

And finally, Dorothy might fulfill her wish to meet a "Yorkie" by consulting a mirror.

Dear Editor:

Regarding [the] amusing letter of October 3 warning Hobokenites to identify the villians properly when looking for a scapegoat, I'd like to point out that being a New Yorker isn't really a geographical classification. Many insufferable New Yorkers come from places like Delaware, California, Minnesota, Hawaii, (especially) Massachusetts, and East Jabib for that matter. Even "natives" grasp such obvious truths.

Being a New Yorker is, after all, a state of mind, something akin to senility or permanent, rutting adolescence—a near incurable malady which manifests itself most notably in an ill-justified sense of superiority and in an inability to distinguish reality from sham. Witness the horde of Yuppies and Radical Chic Yahoos rushing to the fore in the recent banning of Nukes from the confines of the Mile Square Miracle. Holy Mackerel, imagine the military industrial complex conspiring to erect nuclear silos on the ruins of places like the Max-well House factory, O'Niel's tavern, or Biggies Clam Bar! (Admittedly, the loss of an institution like Biggies genuinely smacks of tragedy. What clams!)

As for friendliness, if one wanted to bathe in the welcome wagon scene, perhaps he or she should have settled nearer the mythical environs of "Father Knows Best", or "The Brady Bunch." Besides, any denizen of

* From Joseph Barry and John Derevlany (eds.), *Yuppies Invade My House at Dinnertime*, Big River Publishing, Hoboken, N.J., 1987.

Hudson County should realize Hobokenites often express affection best in terms of abuse. Felix Unger would understand.

Dear Editor:

As a New Yorker, I would like to put in a good word for gentrification. It has made an amazing improvement in a stagnant and dying Hoboken. When I first came here, in 1963, Hoboken was a slum, choked by welfare recipients the way algae kills a lake. Nostalgiacs pretend to lament the change, as if they really preferred to see a bunch of winos in front of the American Hotel and on every downtown corner, instead of pretty young women funneling from all over Hoboken into the neck of the PATH station. What really worries the nostalgiacs, however, is not that the town is becoming less hospitable to the bums and slums, but to them. They're afraid of losing their cheap apartments, but won't admit this. Instead, they shake their heads and mutter sanctimoniously about Hoboken losing its character. Where were they a few years ago, when nobody gave a damn about Hoboken or its character? Everybody expected it to go down the tubes any day. All the B&Rs (Hoboken born and raised) who owned houses were desperate to sell them. Talk about character: where were they when, in an orgy of destruction, three blocks of River Street and three blocks of Hudson Street (the most traditional area in Hoboken, with old waterfront bars and sleazy hotels) were demolished to make way for ugly highrises and parking lots? The B&Rs who were there didn't lift a finger to stop the mayor and his cronies. The only thing they were concerned about, naturally, was how that big money pie cooked up by all the wholesale demolition and construction was going to be divided: yummy, all those contracts and bribes and kickbacks.

No, Hoboken's renaissance, begun in the seventies, was not the work of its B&Rs, but of outsiders. Its native sons and daughters were too busy bad-mouthing Hoboken and trying to sell out and move away to the suburbs to see its potential until it was too late; then they bad-mouthed the successful "Noo Yawkuhs" who bought and renovated the unwanted houses and made the rebirth possible.

Now the B&Rs with the loudest and most self-pitying voices ("I been heah all my life, and I can't affowd a house because the Noo Yawkuhs are coming ovah and pushing prices up"), those who had missed the boat, in other words, boiled with resentment against those who hadn't. It wasn't as if the Boat of Opportunity slipped in at night and sailed at dawn; no, it was tied up at the pier for years, in plain sight of everybody, the subject of endless conversation, and when it did cast off its ropes it was in a kind of reluctant slow-motion, with many a warning blast of its whistle. Only the village idiots missed it.

Dear Editor:

I'm sure that many longtime Hoboken residents were deeply insulted by the [last] letter. The condemnation of those of us who are concerned about the extraordinary amount of development, displacement of the poor and other problems facing this city is filled with arrogance (some may say not surprising coming from a New Yorker) and ignorance.

I can only assure your readers that [he] is "talking out of his hat." I grew up on 10th and Willow during the 60's and 70's in a neighborhood that still has many of the people and stores that were there when I was a child.

The audacity of this buffoon to say that many of the hard-working families that have lived in Hoboken for generations were bad-mouthing the city and dividing big money pies. Most of the bad-mouthing of Hoboken usually came from big mouths like this character who is more interested in "boats of opportunity" than human beings.

Hoboken, like most cities, faced economic hardship during the late '60s and early '70s (I'm sure New Yorkers can recall the problems across the river). The city did have a much larger segment of the population that was poor. Of course, there is little room on [his] boat for the less fortunate, let alone, "welfare recipients."

To say that Hoboken was just a city of crooks, slums, winos and bums is absurd. This is a city that is changing, some of it is good and some not so good. And people who think like [him] should get on their "boat of opportunity" and set sail for other shores.

affluent in-mover is someone who already lives in a central-city location.[32] Thus, gentrifiers are perhaps better described as "urban stayers" than as "urban in-movers."

While it is a misconception to suggest that those moving into or staying in the city are largely childless professionals, it is true that young adults have been in the vanguard of the return to older neighborhoods. Newcomers are generally young, childless, married adults, white, urban-bred, well-educated, employed in professional or managerial positions, and earning middle-class to upper-middle-class incomes. Studies also support the view of renovators being relatively affluent.[33] Newcomers also are portrayed as socially active, with an intense commitment to "their" neighborhood, although some research suggests that older community residents may be better integrated into neighborhood social networks and have higher levels of community participation.[34]

WHY IS GENTRIFICATION OR REVITALIZATION TAKING PLACE?

Changes in three areas help to explain the surge of urban revitalization. Revitalization is a consequence of major changes in the demographic, economic, and lifestyle factors impacting on the U.S. population.

Demographic Changes

Probably the most predictable indicators are the demographic variables. Compared with their counterparts in earlier decades, young adults are more often living independently, and there are high rates of separation and divorce. Where in the past there would be one household of several people, today there is often a fragmentation into several households, each containing fewer people. The Bureau of the Census has clearly documented the decline in marriage, later age at marriage, increases in unmarried couples, and declines in the number of young children per family.[35] This changing population composition of urban households, with more of adults living alone, means increasing housing demands. Between 1980 and 1987 population increased 7 percent and households 11 percent.

Among well-documented recent demographic changes are the rising age at first marriage, declining fertility rates, nontraditional living arrangements, later birth of the first child, increasing entry of both single and married women into the labor force, and the rising number of dual-wage-earner families. Not only are these factors reciprocally related, but taken together, they represent a decline of the sort of "familism" that played such an important part in the postwar flight to the suburbs. The post–World War II American ideal of a suburban home, your own

[32] Daphne Spain, "Why Higher Income Households Move to Central Cities," *Journal of Urban Affairs,* **11**:283–299, 1989.

[33] Daphne Spain and Shirley Laska, "Renovators Two Years Later: New Orleans," in Palen and London (eds.), *Gentrification, Displacement and Neighborhood Revitalization, p. 108.*

[34] Chava Frankfort-Nachmias and J. John Palen, "Neighborhood Revitalization and the Community Question," *Journal of the Community Development Society,* **24**:1–14, 1993.

[35] U.S. Bureau of the Census, "Marital Status and Living Arrangements," *Current Population Reports,* series P-20, no. 478, Washington, D.C., 1993.

backyard, good schools, and so on, neatly met the needs of many new families with children. However, this option has far less appeal for contemporary two-career families without children.

Some relatively affluent, young, child-free couples, not having to worry about the quality of inner-city schools and the shortage of urban play space, are more likely than their parents' generation to choose to live in the city, close to places of work and recreation. To the extent that aggregate demographic changes are producing more nontraditional family units of this type than ever before, we have another partial explanation of urban revitalization of central-city neighborhoods.

Economic Changes

Economic factors also favor increased gentrification. Economic considerations, particularly for single persons or two-income households, are more likely to encourage central-city location than in the past. For most of the years following World War II, both the cost of new housing and the availability of mortgage money clearly favored the suburbs. It was easiest for new homeowners to obtain minimum-down-payment, low-interest loans on suburban housing. In spite of critics of suburbia, suburban housing met the needs of families with young children (see Chapter 9, Changing Suburbanization Patterns). And if a suburban move necessitated a long commute to work, the cost of gasoline was minimal.

Today the situation is altered. Commuting costs, in terms of time as well as money, can be high when both partners work. If one or both work downtown, commuting time can be cut substantially, and public transit often can be used, saving extra auto and parking fees. Suburban home heating and cooling expenses also can be expensive. Couples are rediscovering what their grandparents knew: Heating and/or cooling a two-story townhouse with buildings on either side is more efficient than heating and/or cooling a single-story, freestanding ranch-style home. Higher energy and maintenance costs are particularly onerous when both partners work, leaving the home empty during large portions of the workweek.

Revitalizing existing city housing is often less expensive than buying a new house on the suburban periphery. This is especially the case if the new urban homeowners are willing to put in sweat equity by doing rehabilitation and upgrading work themselves. Most important, mortgage funds for city properties are now available. Changes in government loan policies mean government-insured mortgages are now available in the city. Lending institutions are also increasingly realizing that revitalizing areas are good investment risks.

Life-Style Changes

Gentrifiers espouse an urban life-style that emphasizes urbanity, historical preservation, architectural designs, and good community restaurants. Many of the new central-city households are not "typical," two-children families. Young couples are postponing, and sometimes sidestepping, matrimony. Childbearing, likewise, is being postponed in favor of dual incomes and freer life-styles. Inner-city living tends to have a disproportionate appeal to such nontraditional households. The potential quality of the housing units, the greater convenience to central-city work, and the availability of adult amenities associated with the central city dovetail well with the needs of the increasingly numerous, smaller-sized, adult-oriented households.

One of the most serious liabilities of central-city neighborhoods—the low quality of city schools—does not weigh as heavily on such urbanites. The availability of cultural and social activities and shorter commuter time are more important. This is particularly the case for urban subpopulations such as the gay community. Establishments and activities that low-density suburban areas tend to ban, such as late-night bars, restaurants, and grocery stores, are just the things that give high-density urban areas their vitality. A growing number of middle-class urbanites are in effect voting for sticking with their image of good city life.

There also has been some change in aesthetic values. After postwar decades in which newer homes were more or less automatically judged better, there is a reversal of values among some buyers. Older restorable houses are often considered more desirable. Residences in regenerating neighborhoods frequently have design and construction features that appeal to young, upwardly mobile adults, a group whose tastes outrun their pocketbooks. Where else but in older U.S. neighborhoods can one obtain a first home possessing hardwood floors and trim, fireplaces built with tile or marble, lath-and-plaster walls, leaded glass windows, and oak doors with solid brass trim? True, much of this charm may be under several coats of paint at the time the house is purchased, but the basic quality is present. To central-city aficionados, the ones to be pitied are those suburbanites who remain trapped in outlying postwar suburban housing developments.

DISPLACEMENT OF THE POOR

Finally, let us discuss the question of displacement, since physical regeneration can have social costs. While there is widespread agreement that it is desirable for neighborhoods to improve and upgrade themselves, there is less agreement on how to evaluate this change if it also causes displacement of incumbent residents. Are the poor becoming urban nomads, priced or pushed out of their neighborhoods?

There are very real problems of displacement, particularly for lower-income and elderly households.[36] Displacement, however, has to be put in perspective. The impression is sometimes given that prior to the onset of revitalization both the neighborhood and its population were stable and secure. The implied suggestion is that, were it not for revitalization, the area would again return to stability. Both these assumptions are usually inaccurate. While displacement of long-term residents does occur, the portrait of typical potential displaced residents having lived in the area for years is usually inaccurate.[37]

---

[36] Barrett Lee and David Hodge, "Social Differentials and Metropolitan Residential Displacement," and Jeffrey Henig, "Gentrification and Displacement of the Elderly," in Palen and London (eds.), *Gentrification, Displacement and Neighborhood Revitalization,* pp. 140–169 and 170–184.

[37] There are, however, cases in which the stereotype fits. For an example of what gentrification means to long-term residents of Hoboken, New Jersey, see the collection of letters in this chapter sent by readers to the *Hoboken Reporter,* in Joseph Barry and John Derevlany (eds.), *Yuppies Invade My House at Dinnertime,* Big River Publishing Co., 1987, Hoboken, N.J., 1987.

Residents most likely to be displaced are most often poorer renters, and poorer renters as a group have high mobility. For example, according to census data nearly 40 percent of all renters move at least once a year. For the poor, who rent from month to month rather than under long-term leases, the moves are far more frequent. Areas undergoing revitalization thus are likely to have had high levels of residential mobility prior to renewal activity. Such areas frequently also have high levels of displacement due to eviction and building abandonment.

Fortunately, research indicates displacement may not be as serious a problem as originally thought.[38] While displacement has high emotional costs for some who are displaced, others find moving has long-term benefits. Research findings (as opposed to public statements) usually indicate that the majority of people who are displaced move to nearby housing of comparable or better quality, but they pay more after moving.[39]

Hand-wringing over too-rapid upgrading has a bit of an "Alice in Wonderland" quality to it. Many of the people who are most vocal about the negative consequences of middle-class return to the city have also been the most eager to condemn middle-class flight from the city. It seems ironic that some now are complaining that too many middle-class buyers are moving in, housing is being upgraded, and the property tax base is being augmented too fast. The conflict of varied political-interest groups creates a situation in which someone is always unhappy.

Gentrification as yet encompasses only a few neighborhoods in any one city. Its importance lies not so much in its size but in its reversal of long-term patterns and in its potential for shaping future housing trends.

REVITALIZATION OF INNER CITIES

When the federal government, during the 1980s, withdrew from its role as the prime builder of low-income housing in New York City, the local government stepped in to build homes for low-income working-class populations. Working with community groups, by 1995 the city had worked a quiet revolution, building some 50,000 new residences in what had been the the most devastated areas of the city.[40] In the early 1980s, areas of the South Bronx, Harlem, and Brooklyn were littered with the burned-out hulks of some 5,000 abandoned buildings. Rather than just trying one program, the city tried a number of approaches to revitalize abandoned buildings and vacant land that the city had come to own through foreclosures. Some of the vacant shells of building were given over to private developers for rehabilitation, some were given to churches and nonprofit community groups, and some re-

---

[38] George Grier and Eunice Grier, "Urban Displacement: A Reconnaissance," in Shirley Laska and Daphne Spain (eds.), *Back to the City,* Pergamon, New York, 1980, pp. 252–268; and Michael H. Schill and Richard P. Nathan, *Revitalizing America's Cities: Neighborhood Reinvestment and Displacement,* State University of New York Press, Albany, 1983.

[39] U.S. Department of Housing and Urban Development, "Residential Displacement: An Update," Office of Policy Management and Research, Washington, D.C., 1981; and Schill and Nathan, *Revitalizing America's Cities.*

[40] Alan Finder, "New York Pledge to House Poor Works a Rare, Quiet Revolution," *New York Times,* Apr. 30, 1995, pp. 1 and 40.

habilitation was done by city-hired large construction companies. It turned out that the top-of-the-line city-hired companies had major cost overruns and that smaller firms with rehabilitation experience were more effective. Private rehabilitation with government subsidies was more effective, but by far the best results have been obtained by the locally run community action groups. Overall some 3,000 abandoned apartment houses have been rebuilt with some 39,000 new apartment units. Additionally some 12,000 one-, two-, and three-family houses have been constructed on vacant city-owned land and sold to working families.

There have been some problems. Initially, much against the wishes of community organizers the city filled buildings with homeless families. Local organizers argued that it was foolhardy to put so many poor and troubled families together. As the level of experience with revitalization of inner-city areas has grown, the city has learned from its mistakes. For example, now more working families are being intermixed. More effort is also being concentrated on scattered site infilling of littered vacant lots. The overall result of New York's efforts though has been a true inner-city success story. In the mid-1980s anyone taking Interstate 95 through New York on the Cross-Bronx Expressway saw acres of abandoned apartment buildings upon which the city had painted shutters and flowerpots on the blocked-over windows facing the expressway. Today some of these now-restored buildings have been brought back to full occupancy, and what was vacant wasteland now houses rows of single-family homes. New York City, which is often verbally trashed for its urban problems, has in effect reinvented abandoned neighborhoods by building over 50,000 housing units. The major concern now is that federal and state cutbacks to housing will endanger the long-term stability of the rebuilt areas. It would be a tragedy to undermine what has been one of the major urban success stories of the 1990s.

CHAPTER

13

HOUSING AND THE COMMUNITY

You can see how pleasantly our city is situated, but the water is polluted and the country is troubled with miscarriages.

The people of Jericho to Elisha
Second Kings 2:19

STATUS AS THE CENTURY ENDS

Changes in Housing

The goal of owning one's own home is one of the central aspirations of Americans. However, throughout most of the nation's history, it has been only a dream. Until the post–World War II era, most householders had been renters. Not until about 1950 were half of all husband-wife families homeowners.

Let us look at the current situation. There has been a dramatic increase in housing units. Between 1975 and 1995 the housing stock increased at a rate over twice as fast as the population. There are now over 100 million units.[1] Just the ten-year growth in U.S. units represents more than the entire housing stocks of Canada, the United Kingdom, or France.

Some two-thirds of the housing increase of the last two decades occurred in the sun belt, with the three states of California, Florida, and Texas accounting for over 6 million additional units. Eight out of ten new homes are located in the suburbs or in nonmetropolitan territory.

One-quarter of all the dwelling units in the United States have been built in the last fifteen years. The median age (half older, half younger) of houses in the United States is twenty-three years, and the median overall quality is relatively high. The 1940 census reported only half of all homes having full plumbing facilities. Ninety-seven percent of year-round homes now have complete private plumbing. Living space has also increased, with 97 percent of the units having less than one person per room. This is a great improvement over the more crowded post–World War II era. Over one-fifth of all homes have seven or more rooms. Living space has increased 20 percent since 1960. Almost 98 percent of all housing units have complete kitchens, and 93 percent have telephones. Virtually all homes have TVs.

As of the 1990 census some four-fifths (78 percent) of married couples were homeowners—up from 70 percent in 1970. Renters now constitute only one-third (36 percent) of all households, and—significantly—about 40 percent of all rental units have a female head of household. Two-thirds (68 percent) of all white households live in their own homes, but only 44 percent of blacks and Hispanics do so. For blacks and whites, but not Hispanics, this represents a 3 percent increase since 1970.

Also, contrary to what many people think, we are becoming more residentially stable, and not becoming more mobile. About 20 percent of the population moved in the 1960s. The rate then fell to a low of 16.6 percent in 1983 and now is 18 percent.[2] Whether it is due to greater home ownership, widening commuter distances, an aging population, or greater female participation in the labor force, the result is the dampening of mobility rates.

[1] U.S. Bureau of the Census, "Housing in America, 1985/86," *Current Housing Report,* series H-121, no. 19, Washington, D.C., 1989, p. 1.

[2] U.S. Bureau of the Census, "Geographical Mobility: March 1986 to March 1990," *Current Population Reports,* series P-20, no. 456, Washington, D.C., 1991, p. 2.

Housing Costs

The positive news that the number of housing units has increased is accompanied by some far more negative changes. Simply put, the cost of becoming a homeowner has been going up. A way to show the changes in costs while controlling for inflation is to examine the portion of a worker's pay required to buy the average home. In the mid-1950s, the average thirty-year-old male worker could carry a mortgage on a median-priced home for 14 percent of his gross earnings.[3] Thirty years later it took a full 44 percent of his gross earnings to make the monthly payment on a median-priced home. The consequence of the above is that members of the current generation seeking housing carry a much heavier housing cost burden than did their parents' generation. As a result, today both husband and wife must work to purchase the average house, a house that in the 1950s could be purchased with one income. Today, the question of whether or not a wife with children works outside the home is determined not so much by choice as by economic necessity.

During the 1980s there was a decline in the proportion of young adults becoming homeowners.[4] Generally lower interest rates during the 1990s increased the number of new home buyers. It is possible that the coming decade will show only slow increases or stability in the cost of housing. This would be good news to new home buyers—and bad news to those expecting the value of their homes to dramatically increase. The relative price stability may come because of weakening demand due to demographic changes. Simply put, there are smaller numbers of persons in the generation X age groups (the twenties) just behind the baby-boomers. As these "baby-bust" cohorts reach home-buying ages, the demand for homes should slacken, thus affecting prices. Those who bought during the inflated prices of the late 1980s might be worse off because they bought houses at baby-boomer prices and will be selling in what might be a weakening market due to fewer new young buyers. On the other hand, older baby boomers, who are now in their forties and early fifties, are at the prime ages for purchasing vacation homes, so that market should be solid.

Changing Households

There were somewhat over 95 million households in the United States as of 1995. The Census Bureau recognizes two types of households: family (a householder and one or more other persons related by blood, marriage, or adoption) and nonfamily [a householder living alone (84 percent) or with persons not related]. Household arrangements are continuing to change from what many think of as the traditional family. Some seven out of ten households are family households, well down from the 82 percent of twenty years ago. Family size at 2.6 persons per household has been level since 1980, but well down from the 3.2 persons of the 1960s. Married-couple families have dropped from 87 percent of all family households in 1970 to

---

[3] Frank Levy, *Dollars and Dreams: The Changing American Income Distribution,* Russell Sage, New York, 1987.
[4] U.S. Bureau of the Census, "Housing in America 1985/86"; and "Real Estate Report—Residential Property," *New York Times,* Sept. 10, 1989, pp. 4–5.

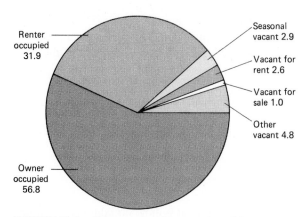

Renter
occupied
31.9

Seasonal
vacant 2.9

Vacant for
rent 2.6

Vacant for
sale 1.0

Other
vacant 4.8

Owner
occupied
56.8

FIGURE 13-1. Percent distribution of total housing
inventory.
Source: U.S. Bureau of the Census, "Special Studies,"
Current Population Reports, series P-23, no. 164,
January, 1990, P. 4.

just over three-quarters today. The number of families maintained by a woman
without a husband present doubled during that period. A quarter of all white children under eighteen and two-thirds of all black children are currently living with
one parent. Beginning in the late 1980s, for the first time there were more families
without children at home than with children.[5]

About one in eight adults lives alone, and six in ten of these are women. More
elderly women than elderly men live alone, reflecting the higher mortality rates for
men. Among young adults there are six unmarried couples for every one hundred
married couples. In 1970 the figure was only one unmarried couple for every one
hundred married. Of particular interest to many college students is that the number
of "return nesters" is increasing. The proportion of young adults aged eighteen to
twenty-four years of age living at home with their parents includes 61 percent of all
males and 48 percent of all females (women marry at younger ages and, thus, are
less likely to be living with parents).[6]

CHANGING FEDERAL ROLE

With many in Congress proposing to abolish not only all federal housing programs, but also the Department of Housing and Urban Development (HUD), it is
difficult to say much about current programs that is unlikely to be made out of
date by further developments. What is certain is that federal housing programs are

---

[5] U.S. Bureau of the Census, "Households, Families, Marital Status, and Living Arrangements: March 1993," *Current Population Reports,* series P-20, no. 487, Washington, D.C., 1994.
[6] U.S. Bureau of the Census, "Marital Status and Living Arrangements: March, 1988," *Current Population Reports,* series
P-20, no. 433, Washington, D.C., 1989, p. 1.

in flux, with even the secretary of housing recommending in 1995 that HUD get out of the business of managing public housing. The U.S. government's official housing policy was formulated in 1949. It stated that it was the aim of the government to:

1. Eliminate substandard and other inadequate housing through clearance of slums and blighted areas.
2. Stimulate housing production and community developments sufficient to remedy the housing shortage.
3. Realize the goal of a decent home and a suitable living environment for every American family.[7]

However, in the decades that this has been official policy, no administration has taken these aims to be guidelines for clear and decisive action; rather, they have been viewed as goals or objectives to be sought. Today, as when the policy was written into law, safe, decent, and sanitary housing at affordable prices within a suitable living environment remains but a dream for all too many Americans.

Housing in America has traditionally been considered a private rather than a public concern, and the whole concept of involvement by the U.S. government in the housing of its citizens is fairly recent. The concept of government support for housing is far from universally accepted in the United States—a situation unlike that in European countries, for example. Republicans in Congress are attempting to eliminate existing federal housing programs.

It took the massive economic collapse of the great depression of the 1930s to involve the government in the question of housing. During the depression, residential construction dropped by 90 percent and downtown skyscrapers stood vacant. Even the prestigious Empire State Building in New York City was unable to fill its many offices. Franklin D. Roosevelt's administration came into office committed to reviving the economy through federal intervention, a new and radical approach at that date. In order to get a sick housing industry on its feet and encourage "builders to build and lenders to lend," the government engaged in extensive "pump priming" in the housing area.

The Housing Act of 1937, for example, established a slum-clearance program and created the United States Housing Authority, which built some 114,000 low-rent public housing units before the program was ended during World War II. However, it was never clear whether the goal of the programs of the 1930s was to put people to work or to provide new housing for those lacking "standard" dwellings. Whatever the purpose, the result was that several deteriorating slums were cleared, and every substandard unit of housing that was cleared was replaced with a standard unit.

The program of the 1930s differed from later efforts in at least two respects: First, only public housing was built on the cleared land, not shopping centers or of-

[7] Martin Anderson, *The Federal Bulldozer,* M.I.T Press, Cambridge, MA, 1964, p. 4.

fice buildings; second, the housing projects were by and large successful—many of them are still well maintained today. Their success can be attributed both to their design (few were over four stories high, giving the buildings the atmosphere of family apartment buildings where people knew each other) and to the fact that residents initially were largely workers and artisans on WPA or other jobs. Projects at this time did not house the very poor on welfare.

FEDERAL HOUSING ADMINISTRATION SUBSIDIES

In order to get bankers to invest in mortgages during the depression, the government, through the Housing Act of 1934, created the Federal Housing Administration (FHA) to insure home loans. After World War II, the Veterans Administration also made loans (VA loans) guaranteed by the government to veterans. Under such schemes, banks and lending institutions still decide who will get loans, and the FHA or VA in effect insures the bank against loss if the buyer defaults. The theory is that this system encourages lending institutions to make loans to buyers whom they would otherwise reject.

After World War II, the FHA and the VA became active in issuing mortgages to working-class and lower middle-class families who wanted to buy homes. The consequence was the urban exodus to the new subdivisions discussed in Chapter 9, Changing Suburbanization Patterns. During the 1950s these government subsidies meant that a young couple could move into a new suburban home with a $500 down payment. The FHA program encouraged and subsidized white suburbanization. As recently as the 1980s about half the outstanding mortgage debt on single-family homes was insured by either the FHA or the VA. As of 1995 the FHA had insured some 22 million home purchases. Most of the balance is financed through banks whose deposits are insured. At the same time, the urban renewal program, which will be discussed presently, was designed to hold these same middle-class white families in the central city. The government was thus simultaneously trying to hold the middle class in cities while subsidizing them to leave. As this is being written, legislation is being debated that would turn the FHA into a semigovernment corporation in order to speed up loan decision making.

Government housing policies also encouraged racial segregation. After World War II, suburbs (with FHA encouragement) used restrictive covenants to exclude blacks and other "undesirables" who might lower property values and threaten the FHA's investment. Until 1950, FHA regulations expressly forbade issuing loans that would permit or encourage racial integration.

From 1935 to 1950, the federal government insisted upon discriminatory practices as a prerequisite to government housing aid. The Federal Housing Administration's official manuals cautioned against "infiltration of inharmonious racial and national groups," "a lower class of inhabitants," or "the presence of incompatible racial elements" in the new neighborhood. . . . Zoning was advocated as a device for exclusion, and the use was urged of a racial covenant (prepared by FHA itself) with a space left blank for the prohibited races and religions, to be filled in by the builder as occasion required.[8]

Not until 1968 were racial convenants outlawed. Restrictive racial covenants were declared illegal by the 1968 Fair Housing Act. Redlining, a practice in which lending institutions refuse to make loans in minority or mixed-race areas, has also been declared illegal. However, insurance redlining, a practice in which insurance companies make it more difficult or expensive to obtain insurance coverage in minority areas, still persists.[9]

UPPER- AND MIDDLE-CLASS HOUSING SUBSIDIES

In the United States today we have anything but a laissez-faire housing policy. Almost all financing for new houses or apartments involves the federal government in one way or another. The largest, but least discussed, subsidy is the middle- and upper-class tax break of the mortgage interest deduction on federal taxes. As of 1993 the mortgage interest deduction benefit amounted to an entitlement of $41.6 billion.[10] No such government middle-class housing entitlement is available in Canada. Additionally, property taxes paid by homeowners (but not renters) can be deducted from federal taxes. The direct and indirect consequence of these subsidies

[8] Charles Abrams, *The City Is the Frontier,* Harper & Row, New York, 1965, p. 61.
[9] Gregory D. Squires and William Velez, "Insurance Redlining and the Transformation of an Urban Metropolis,"*Urban Affairs Quarterly,* **23:**63–83, September, 1987.
[10] Vicki Kemper, "Home Inequity," *Common Cause Magazine,* Summer, 1994, p. 15.

The freestanding suburban home on its own lot has become an American cliché. (Alexander Lowry/Photo Researchers.)

plus depreciation write-offs costs the U.S. Treasury more than $81 billion a year.[11] These subsidies may help many people to purchase homes, and they certainly prop up the housing industry, but whether a good idea or not they are clearly a major government subsidy.

URBAN REDEVELOPMENT

Since World War II, a variety of programs have been implemented to upgrade cities in general and improve housing stock in particular. After the war, it was widely recognized that cities were headed for trouble if the federal government didn't intervene. Housing was in poor shape, and downtowns were showing age and wear. Problems were particularly acute on the deteriorating fringe areas of CBDs. Downtown business leaders were concerned that the expense of buying, tearing down, and rebuilding in the inner city was not economically feasible for private developers.

Liberals and conservatives in Congress had radically different ideas of what government should do. The eventual result was a classic American compromise, the Housing Act of 1949. The act contained both a public housing section, which the liberals had lobbied for, and an urban development section, which conservatives and businesspeople had sought.

Commercial and financial interests in the central cities supported urban renewal because they saw the renewal areas as providing the downtown area with a buffer, or *cordon sanitaire,* against encroachment by slums. Moreover, the occupants of the urban renewal housing were expected to be families with substantial purchasing power and thus able to help stimulate retail trade. Urban renewal was seen as being both good for business and good for the city. The purpose of urban renewal was not to rebuild the area for the old residents but rather to change land-use patterns.

The urban redevelopment section of the Urban Renewal Act was a radical break with past housing policies in that it provided for the use of public funds to buy, clear, and improve the renewal site, after which the ownership of the land would revert to the private sector. When the renewal area was approved, the authorities were given the power to buy properties at market prices and, in cases where the owner refused to sell, to have the property condemned and compensation paid through the government's right of eminent domain.

Once the city acquired all the land in the renewal area, the existing buildings were destroyed (or rehabilitated under later modifications of the act) and the land was cleared. New streets, lights, and public facilities were then installed, and finally the land was sold to a private developer who agreed to build in accordance with an approved development plan.

The developer paid about 30 percent of what it had cost the local government to purchase, clear, and improve the land. This so-called write-down was the difference between what the land had cost the public and what it was sold for to the private developer. Two-thirds of the city's loss was made up in a direct subsidy from

[11] Ibid., p. 14.

the federal government. Thus, the control of the program was basically local, while most of the funds were federal.

Since the purpose of urban redevelopment was to change patterns of land use for the benefit of the city as a whole, there is no requirement that housing which is destroyed has to be replaced with housing for people with a similar income level. In fact once the dwelling units within the renewal area were demolished and cleared, the land could be used for a shopping center, a park, or an office building. When urban renewal essentially ended in the 1970s, over one-third of the federal funds were being used largely for nonresidential projects.

Relocation and New Housing

The most glaring weakness of urban renewal programs was the displacement of large numbers of low-income families without adequate provision for their relocation. Until criticism built up to a point where it could no longer be ignored, little was done to rehouse those who were forced to move from a renewal area. It is generally agreed that during the first years of the urban renewal program, residents were dispossessed and ejected from their homes in a fashion that can only be characterized as ruthless. The residents of the West End of Boston, for example, found themselves bulldozed out of their old Italian community virtually before they knew what was happening. Far from being encouraged to participate in planning for the area, local residents were actively discouraged, since it had already been decided that the existing low-rent area would be far more valuable to the city as an area of expensive high-rise apartments.[12] The result was essentially similar when removal was for the purpose of construction of expressways.

Critique

Scott Greer contends that much of the confusion and downright contradiction in urban renewal programs were a result of the mixture of three different goals. These were increasing low-cost housing while eliminating slums, revitalizing the central city, and creating planned cities through community renewal programs.[13] As Greer put it: "At a cost of three billion dollars the Urban Renewal Agency (URA) has succeeded in materially reducing the supply of low-cost housing in American cities."[14]

Finally, it is only fair to say that the urban renewal program had some notable successes, such as the comprehensive renewal effort in New Haven, the Southwest Project in Washington, D.C., the Western Addition in San Francisco, and Society Hill in Philadelphia. Also, very few of the renewal sites were originally attractive communities; the majority were blighted, dilapidated, filthy slums that no one wants to bring back. Even critics of urban renewal concede that the grossest mistakes were made by the earliest projects and that as the program matured, it profited from earlier errors.

---

[12] Herbert J. Gans, *The Urban Villagers,* Free Press, New York, 1962.
[13] Scott Greer, *Urban Renewal and American Cities,* Bobbs-Merrill, Indianapolis, 1965, p. 165.
[14] Ibid., p. 3.

Public Housing

About 3.4 million persons are currently living in 1.2 million public housing units (this is roughly 1.5 percent of the nation's housing stock). Public housing was originally designed to provide standard-quality housing for those who could not afford decent, safe housing on the private market. One of the basic unwritten assumptions of the program was that by changing a family's residence you could also change the way they lived and the way they behaved.

Advocates of social planning originally supported public housing as a means of social uplift and betterment. Tearing down slum housing was seen as a way of destroying the crime, delinquency, drunkenness, and lax morals that were considered to be associated with slum housing. Once again, technology was going to solve social problems—a naive belief of long-standing in America. This can be characterized as a "salvation by bricks and mortar" or an "architectural determinism" approach.

Public housing erected during the 1930s was built as much to give workers jobs as to eliminate slums. Projects were filled mainly with lower-middle-class families who were there because, owing to the depression, family heads could not get regular work and could not find adequate housing elsewhere. After World War II, with other housing becoming more plentiful, those who were working their way into the middle class sought new housing. As these families moved out, the projects gradually lost their sound working-class image.

By the 1960s public housing was beset by massive problems. Families living in projects were often minority, female-headed, on welfare, and without any reasonable expectation of moving into the middle class. The lack of education and training of the newer project residents, coupled with regulations that placed low limits on how much a family could earn and still qualify for public housing, meant that those who could be upwardly mobile moved on, while those who were not mobile stayed. The policy of evicting the successful also has meant that in the largest projects successful adult role models are virtually nonexistent. This has had disastrous results for children, who have few images of successful adults who are not dealing in drugs, gambling, or prostitution.

Inner-city projects have today become the residence of last resort for the permanently poor. The public has become disillusioned with the whole concept of public housing, since it obviously isn't remaking the present-day poor into middle-class citizens. Once professionals thought that if they could get problem families out of the slums, then fathers would stop drinking, mothers would stop fooling around, and kids would stop doping and stealing. It didn't work; as caustically expressed by one professional in urban affairs, "they're the same bunch of bastards they always were."[15]

Public housing construction and finance costs are paid by the federal government. Originally, local housing authorities provided operating and maintenance costs out of tenant rents. However, by the 1960s, operating costs were escalating.

[15] Michael Stegman, "The New Mythology of Housing," *Trans-Action,* 7:55, January, 1970.

Thus, Congress put a cap of 25 percent of tenant income (raised to 30 percent in the Reagan years) and began providing operating subsidies to the local housing authorities.[16] The subsidies have never covered the needs. Particularly during the Reagan years of 1980–1988, the payments were not sufficient to cover major repairs and replacements. Thus, the 3,000 local public housing agencies that administer the projects saw public housing deteriorate to the point where many units became unlivable.

The cost of repairing and restoring the nation's 1.2 million public housing units to a safe and healthy condition would be high. A three-year study ordered by Congress reported in 1987 that $21.5 billion would be needed.[17] This money is unlikely

[16] Allen Hays, "Housing Subsidy Strategies in the United States: A Typology," in Elizabeth Huttman and Willem van Vliet, *Handbook of Housing and the Built Environment in the United States,* Greenwood Press, New York, 1988, p. 184.
[17] "H.U.D. Disputes Cost of Fixing Public Housing," *Washington Post,* Aug. 4, 1988.

The notorious Cabrini-Green housing projects in Chicago were among the country's worst. They are now being demolished, and some residents are being resettled in a mixed low-income and working-class low-rise development. (Beth A. Keiser/AP/Wide World Photos.)

ever to be allocated. The replacement value of the nation's public housing stock is $70 billion, and some argue that the investment should be protected. Most, however, argue that public housing programs should be phased out and the existing projects sold. In Chicago the massive, and notorious, Cabrini-Green project has been torn down, and the city plans to develop the very valuable land on which it sits.

Certainly, public housing has few friends. Republicans want to eliminate all public housing. The Democratic Leadership Conference has proposed putting a two-year limit on living in public housing, phasing out rent subsidies, and using the saved subsidy money to build low-cost homes in poor areas.[18] Even the liberal Secretary of Housing has recommended getting the federal government out of the business of financing and running public housing. Instead persons needing assistance would simply receive payment vouchers that they could use to pay for any housing. This system is already widely in use (see the next section). The major concern is whether the private market has enough low-income housing available. The consensus seems to be that vouchers are better as social policy than as housing policy. Vouchers do little to encourage the construction of new low-income housing. Nonetheless, with public housing for the poor generally viewed as a failed policy, rent vouchers are becoming more common. The debate over public housing is largely over. Public housing is being eliminated.

Section 8

In 1974 subsidy programs other than public housing were largely replaced by the Section 8 Program. This allows tenants to shop for a private-market unit. The landlord enters into a subsidy contract with the government, and the tenant pays 30 percent of his or her income as rent, with the rent subsidy making up the balance.

The Section 8 Program has been very popular with landlords, and particularly with developers building under Section 8 New Construction. During the Reagan years (1980–1988), subsidies for low-income housing were slashed from $34.2 billion to $14.9 billion. During the same period, massive mismanagement and fraud in the Department of Housing and Urban Development led to losses of $8 billion. One influential Republican, former Interior Secretary James Watts, received $420,000 for providing access to top HUD officials to get approval for grants and subsidies for building questionable projects.[19] He pleaded guilty in 1995. The influence peddlers wasted and stole billions meant to house needy families.

ABANDONMENT OF BUILDINGS

Nationally, 150,000 housing units are abandoned a year. In New York City, during the early 1980s, abandonments reached 40,000 units a year.[20] How is it that usable

---

[18] "Democratic Centrists Offer Alternative," *Richmond Times-Dispatch,* Dec. 6, 1994, p. A11.

[19] "The HUD Ripoff," *Newsweek,* Aug. 7, 1989, p. 16.

[20] Some conservative scholars have argued that abandonments occurred because there is a housing surplus in some cities. For example, see William Gorham and Nathan Glazer, *The Urban Predicament,* The Urban Institute, Washington, D.C., 1976, pp. 129–130.

buildings are being abandoned? The answer lies in the economics of the private housing market. Being a slumlord traditionally was a lucrative business, but by the 1970s things had begun to change. Tenants, often urged on by community organizers, began militantly to demand improvements in their buildings. Sometimes these demands were accompanied by rent strikes. At about the same time, some cities began to actually enforce housing codes and even order that illegally converted units be returned to original occupancy (that is, increase the number of rooms per apartment and decrease the number of paying renters). The interest of absentee landlords declined dramatically with the urban riots of the late 1960s (increasing vandalism) and with the rapidly escalating heating costs of the 1970s. Slumlords simply found that housing the poor was no longer a paying proposition, particularly in cities with rent controls. The cost of owning buildings was rising faster than rental income.

When landlords saw no long-term economic potential in their property, improvements and even necessary maintenance were allowed to slip. As a last type of profit taking, the landlord invariably stopped paying property taxes. (Cities traditionally did not begin foreclosure action until there were three years of tax arrears. Some states such as New York have now shortened the period to one year.) An area with a sharp spurt in tax delinquencies is almost always on the verge of abandonment.

Finally, when landlords see no more economic potential, they default on their mortgages and simply abandon their buildings. Under the law, action can be taken by the city to take possession of the property, but no action can be brought against the slumlords themselves. Once the landlord abandons a building, services are cut off and the tenants move to other housing. Vandals and professional looters strip the building of anything of value. They pull up with trucks and rip out plumbing and heating systems and whatever else can be sold. Fires set by vandals or others are common in such abandoned buildings.

BURNING FOR PROFIT

Arson for profit is a problem in the cores of older central cities. Exact figures are difficult to determine, partially because a good arsonist destroys the evidence and partially because there are an inadequate number of fire investigators to officially categorize suspicious blazes as arson. In the United States as a whole, it is estimated that the arson rate is over 15,000 cases annually. Detroit has had more than 400 cases of arson on "devil's night," the night before Halloween, for over a decade. The chief of operations of the New York City Fire Department estimates that 25 to 40 percent of the building fires in that city are deliberately set.

Many of these fires are set by slumlords or businesspeople who burn their buildings for the insurance money. Some are entrepreneurs who buy decrepit buildings in order to set profitable fires. Others are "building strippers" who "torch" old buildings in order to gain access and strip the building of plumbing and other items that can be sold for scrap. In New York, slum residents have been known to ignite their own apartments to get the relocation allowance of up to $2,000. Those who are burned out also obtain a high priority for public housing vacancies. There are also youngsters who, even if they are not paid to torch a building by the owner, will do it for the sheer excitement.

New York State is trying to take some of the profit out of arson by permitting the city to deduct unpaid taxes and other payments from landlords' insurance settlements. There also have been sporadic attempts in New York and elsewhere to indict persons for arson fraud, but so long as urban decay and building abandonments continue in inner cities, arson will also be an urban problem.

URBAN HOMESTEADING

One of the more innovative and imaginative housing programs is urban homesteading. Homesteading programs turn over abandoned and foreclosed homes to those who agree to stay for a period of years (at least three) and bring the homes up to code standards within two years. Urban homesteading programs conjure up the image of the hardy pioneers, who, under the Homestead Act signed by President Lincoln, were given 160 acres of western land if they could stick it out for five years. Urban homesteaders, on the other hand, are not supposed to build on the land but to rebuild inner-city neighborhoods.[21] The first urban homesteading program (and still one of the most active) began in Wilmington, Delaware, in 1973. As expressed by Wilmington's mayor, who pushed the program, "We are not trying to provide housing for people. We are trying to provide people for (abandoned) housing."[22] Offering homes at nominal fees such as $100, urban homesteading programs implicitly recognize that by definition there is no market for abandoned property. Thus it is given away to those who agree to improve and use it. The Housing and Community Development Act of 1974 got the federal government into the business of transferring residential properties to local governments for homesteading.

So far, the record of urban homesteading has been mixed. While the concept sounds ideal, there are some major limitations.

First, it involves a limited number of homes. The programs to date are only a drop in the bucket, with 70,000 homes having been rehabilitated by the homesteading mechanism. (By comparison, 150,000 inner-city homes and apartments are abandoned annually.) Baltimore, for example, has rehabilitated 600 homes through homesteading, but has 40,000 families on the waiting list for public housing.[23] Homesteading has had only a minor impact on our complex housing problems.

Second, by the time government action is taken, most abandoned properties are beyond the point of economic rehabilitation. As noted earlier, professional and amateur looters strip homes to the shell, and vandals deface what isn't taken. Fires

[21] Ann Clark and Zelma Rivin, *Homesteading in Urban U.S.A.*, Praeger, New York, 1977.
[22] Quoted in Wiltram G. Conway, "People Fire in the Ghetto Ashes," *Saturday Review,* July 23, 1977, p. 15.
[23] Mittie Olion Chandler, *Urban Homesteading: Programs and Policies,* Greenwood Press, New York, 1988, p. 147.

Urban homesteading oftern demands "sweat equity" from those rehabilitating the property. (Courtesy of the Baltimore Department of Housing and Community Development.)

are also common, and no one wants to rehabilitate a burned-out hulk. Unlike gentrification, urban homesteading often occurs in less desirable areas without historic distinction.

Third, there is the cost factor. Title to the property may come cheap, but rehabilitation costs big money. Even when owners use "sweat equity" (i.e., their own labor), rehabilitation loans commonly run from $35,000 to $100,000. Thus urban homesteading is definitely not the answer for the urban poor.

Fourth, as a home rehabilitation program, urban homesteading does not affect multifamily apartments, where the bulk of the poor are housed.

Fifth, for loans, of course, lenders are necessary, and thus far financial institutions have been reluctant to invest in rehabilitating abandoned slum properties.

Thus low-interest municipal loans or loans guaranteed by the municipality appear to be essential. Also necessary are changes in municipal tax policies. While cities invariably say that they are in favor of urban homesteading, most are unwilling to change policies that raise taxes when improvements are made. Without some form of tax moratorium, those who upgrade abandoned buildings are rewarded by the municipality with higher taxes.

Finally, there is no point in rehabilitation of one home if the remainder of the neighborhood consists of vandalized burned-out buildings. There has to be an over-all change in the neighborhood, with a substantial number of homes being simulta-neously redone and reasonable public services and police protection provided. Homesteading, therefore, is likely to be most successful in areas where only a few homes have been abandoned.

Nonetheless, urban homesteading has had a psychological as well as physical impact on cities ranging from Baltimore to Pittsburgh to Denver to Oakland. It is not the answer to most urban housing problems, but the success of homesteading has provided a psychological lift. An additional "nonlegal" form of homesteading is "walk-in homesteading," or urban squatting. This is a politically important movement in European countries such as Holland, Germany, and Sweden.

TAX CREDITS

In order to encourage the private rehabilitation of older central-city areas, the Reagan administration encouraged Congress to pass a rehabilitation tax credit pro-gram in 1981. Under the program, investors who renovate old structures can qual-ify for tax credits. The amount of the credit depends on the age and the historical or architectural significance of the structure. This program has been a boon to older cities. Under the program, central-city office buildings have been restored, hotels revitalized to their nineteenth-century glory, and factories converted into rental apartments or commercial space. The 1986 revision of the tax code allowed reno-vation of a historic structure to qualify for a 20 percent tax credit.

THE USE OF SPACE

As noted in Chapter 7, City Life-Styles, and Chapter 8, Social Environment of the City, physical space often has different meanings to different groups. Understand-ing the symbolic uses of space can certainly be of practical use to architects and planners who want to use sociological information to increase the adequacy of their designs.

Public housing projects in particular can be designed to minimize rather than maximize feelings of deprivation and isolation from the community at large. Tra-ditional high-rise projects too often are designed to be not only dull and monoto-nous but also dangerous to the inhabitants. Large open areas outside the projects frequently become "no-man's-lands" after dark, while within the buildings the cor-ridors, washing rooms, and even elevators are unsafe. Residents are helpless to prevent muggings and rapes and feel that the only area they can control, and thus feel safe in, is the space within their own apartments.

Architectural design can increase the security and livability of projects.

One of the simplest changes is to build low-rise buildings (six stories at most) where no more than a dozen families share the same stairwell and thus know who should or should not be present. Oscar Newman suggests some other elements that can help in providing security:

1. The territorial definition of space in developments reflecting the areas of influence of the inhabitants. This works by subdividing the residential environment into zones toward which adjacent residents easily adopt proprietary attitudes.
2. The positioning of apartment windows to allow residents to naturally survey the exterior and interior public areas of their living environment.
3. The option of building forms that avoid the stigma of peculiarity that allows others to perceive the vulnerability and isolation of the inhabitants.
4. The enhancement of safety by locating residential developments in functionally sympathetic urban areas immediately adjacent to activities that do not provide continued threat.[24]

The effect of proper planning can be seen in a comparison of the Brownsville and Van Dyke housing projects in New York, which are separated only by a street. The low-rise Brownsville buildings, although older, have significantly fewer problems of crime and maintenance than the high-rise Van Dyke buildings. This is in spite of the fact that the average density per acre of the two projects is virtually identical. The difference appears to be that the Brownsville projects, with their six-story buildings and three-story wings, are humanly manageable and controllable to a far greater degree than the thirteen- and fourteen-story Van Dyke projects across the street. Architectural design alone, however, does not prevent crime. Few social relationships among residents, fear, and a sense of futility may result in residents not becoming involved in helping one another.[25] The best way to augment safety is to have areas visible to residents, and have design barriers such as corner street narrowing that discourage entry to those who don't belong.[26] Fuller discussion of how design can help promote safe neighborhoods is provided in the next chapter.

Finally, it is well to keep in mind that even the best-designed cities and housing cannot solve social and economic problems. Unemployment, high dropout rates from school, drug usage, and crime cannot be expected to vanish simply because of redesigned buildings. Making cities more attractive and livable is a noble goal in and of itself.

[24] Oscar Newman, *Defensible Space,* Macmillan, New York, 1972, p. 9.
[25] Sally Merry, "Defensible Space Undefended: Social Factors in Crime Control through Urban Design," *Urban Affairs Quarterly,* **16:**397–422, 1981.
[26] Timothy D. Crowe and Diane L. Zahm, "Crime Prevention through Environmental Design," *Land Development,* Fall, 1994, pp. 22–23.

Death of Poletown

Today, the razing of central-city neighborhoods for public purposes, expressways, or urban renewal projects is largely history. Public outcry over the destruction of residential neighborhoods and changing program priorities have stopped the bulldozers. However, the new threat to older neighborhoods in some cities is that homes will be taken by eminent domain, not so that the land can be put to public use, but so that it can be turned over to a private company. This is what happened to the Poletown neighborhood in Detroit, a long-standing neighborhood that involuntarily vanished in less than a year. During 1981 the entire neighborhood of Poletown—1,362 homes and apartments, 143 businesses and stores, 16 churches, 2 schools, and 1 hospital—was torn down.

The land, which was condemned and razed at a cost of over $200 million in local, state, and federal tax money, was then sold to General Motors at a price of $8 million. The reason that all of this took place was economics and employment. Mayor Coleman Young had seen many industries leave Detroit, and felt that everything had to be done to keep the new GM plant and its promised 6,000 jobs in the city. It was felt downtown that Detroit needed the jobs more than it needed an aging neighborhood. It was also believed that GM, by building a new-generation assembly plant in the city, would give a much-needed psychological lift to a city that had lost 800,000 people and much of its economic energy since its heyday in the 1950s. The sharp bitterness and anger of those Poletown residents who saw their homes, businesses, and churches torn down was felt to be the unfortunate price an industrial heartland city with an aging infrastructure and tax base had to pay in order to keep GM in Detroit.

Poletown was leveled because GM made it clear that it would build its new assembly plant outside Detroit unless the city cleared and gave the corporation the 465.5-acre area. The world's third-largest corporation also demanded and received a 50 percent tax concession from the city administration as the price for not leaving the city. What is more, the United Auto Workers Union, the city council, the Archdiocese of Detroit, and both the Carter and Reagan administrations supported the deal. Even the Michigan Supreme Court, in a controversial decision, ruled that Detroit had the right to condemn and clear Poletown and sell the site to General Motors.* Almost everyone was in favor of the new plant except the residents of Poletown, who saw their homes and businesses leveled. A decade and a half later all that remains is the bitterness.

* "Legal Report,"*Planning,*June, 1982, p. 10.

CHAPTER 14

PLANNING IN THE UNITED STATES AND ELSEWHERE

*Let there be one man who has a city obedient to his will,
and he might bring into existence the ideal polity about
which the world is so incredulous.*

Plato, *The Republic*

INTRODUCTION: HISTORICAL BACKGROUND

The Bible, in Genesis 11:4, tells of one of the earliest attempts at urban planning:

> It came to pass as they journeyed to the East that they found a plain in the land of Shinar and they dwelt there. . . . And they said, "Come let us build us a city, and the tower the top of which may reach unto heaven; and let us make ourselves a name, lest we be scattered upon the face of the whole earth. . . .

As we all know, the Tower of Babel was not noticeably successful as a form of urban planning in spite of the fact that it did have full citizen participation. The hope is that some of our more modest attempts will be more successful.

Ancient Greece and Rome

Ancient cities, as was indicated in Chapter 2, Emergence of Cities, were rarely based on a plan or even a general concept of what the city should be. The Greeks, who appreciated organization and structure in other aspects of their lives, gave little attention to the physical arrangement of the communities in which they lived. In classical Greek cities the main thoroughfares were generally planned as processional avenues, but residential development was undisciplined and chaotic. Rhodes, with its avenues radiating from a center, was something of an exception. What planning did take place was limited to the central municipal area, containing the principal monuments, temples, and stately edifices.

Aristotle tells us that Hippodamus of Miletus, who lived in the fifth century B.C., was an early city planner. According to Aristotle,

> Hippodamus, son of Euryphon, a native of Miletus, invented the art of planning and laid out the street plan of Piraeus. . . . He planned a city with a population of 10,000 divided into three parts, one of the skilled workers, one of farmers, and one to defend the state. The land was divided into three parts: sacred, public, and private supporting in turn the worship of the gods, the defense of the state, and the farm owners. . . .[1]

Note that provision was made for farming within the city walls, a most necessary consideration during periods when the city was under siege.

The Romans were somewhat more successful than the Greeks at planning their towns. As noted in Chapter 2, Rome itself showed limited evidence of planning, but provincial Roman towns, with their central square and gridiron pattern of residences, established a model that can be seen in most American communities today. The provincial cities of western Europe were modeled after the pattern of encampment developed by the Roman legions. Civilian buildings simply followed the pattern of the military outpost, particularly since much of the planning was done by military engineers.

It has been said that these outpost towns were so similar that if a Roman centurion was dropped in the middle of any one of them, he could not tell which town he was in. The largest of the planned Roman cities was Constantinople, the "Rome of the East," which the emperor Constantine built to glorify his reign and escape the fate of previous emperors at the hands of the Roman Senate and street mobs.

[1] Aristotle, *Politics,* Book VII, ii, 8, B. Jowett (trans.), 1932 ed.

Renaissance and Later Developments

The fall of the Roman Empire in the west meant the death of western urban planning for virtually a millennium. However, even during the Middle Ages, when gradual organic growth was most likely to be the rule, some of the newly reviving towns built by French, Italian, and German princes followed the planned pattern of the earlier Roman colonial settlements—a grid layout and a central square with a market.[2]

The Renaissance revived cities and thinking about cities, but few of the planners' conceptions for total communities ever became more than academic exercises. Since these conceptions were rather fanciful and artificial, and bore virtually no relationship to the haphazard but vital cities then in existence, it is perhaps just as well that they were rarely executed. Star-shaped cities were especially popular; Vicenzo Scamozzi designed a utopian city shaped as a twelve-pointed star and actually built a small city, Palma Nova, in the shape of a nine-pointed star in 1593. The star shape was not entirely fanciful, however, since in the age of cannons and gunpowder the points of a star could serve as bastions for directing the defenders' enfilading fire.

[2] Howard Saalman, *Medieval Cities,* Braziller, New York, 1968, p. 114.

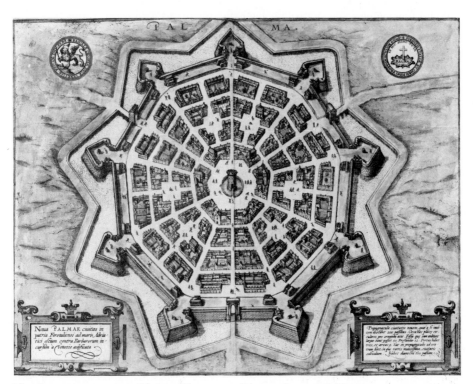

The Renaissance city of Palma Nova was designed to resemble a nine-pointed star. The points were military defense positions. (British Library.)

Planners often designed unrealistic static communities that completely ignored the needs of the inhabitants, as well as basic considerations such as topography. Stylized form rather than naturalness was the goal. The epitome of the insistence on symmetrical perfection was Versailles, the magnificent home of the French kings, whose gardens, palaces, and town were planned as a unit.[3]

The English also made their own attempts, largely unsuccessfully, at town planning. In 1580 Queen Elizabeth proclaimed restrictions on London's growth that were designed to give the city a green belt of open land and thus prevent crowding and poverty.[4] This policy—which foreshadowed the twentieth-century green belt towns discussed later in this chapter—failed, although it was backed by royal statute. Probably the most noteworthy master plan was that designed by Christopher Wren for the rebuilding of London after the disastrous fire of 1666. His plan was, unfortunately, not adopted in the rush to rebuild the city.

During the nineteenth century, the changes in the physical organization of Paris must be listed among the more successful attempts at planning. Contemporary Paris, with its broad avenues and magnificent squares, is the result of seventeen years of rebuilding directed by Baron Haussmann under the sponsorship of Napoleon III (1852–1870). The beauty of Paris today is not accidental but the result of Haussmann's genius. Boulevards were cut through festering slums, and the city was planned for separate industrial and residential areas. However, the rationale for the changes was not solely aesthetic; the broad boulevards provided excellent fields of fire for cannon and divided the city into districts that could be more easily controlled and isolated in times of civil insurrection.

AMERICAN PLANNING

Within the next thirty years the United States' population is projected to grow by 30 million. That is the equivalent of constructing 60 new cities of 500,000. Would we prefer these places be planned or unplanned? City planning in the United States is usually regarded as a twentieth-century development, but as early as 1672 Lord Ashley Cooper instructed that Charles Town be laid out "into regular streets for be the buildings never so mean and thin at first, yet as the town increases in riches and people, the void places will be filled up and the buildings will grow more beautiful." The town was designed to form a narrow trapezoid four squares long by two squares wide, fronting on the Cooper River. Philadelphia was also laid out according to the gridiron pattern. Today, the area surrounding Independence Hall once again shows the original pattern as William Penn intended. North American colonial cities as disparate as Quebec in the north and James Oglethorpe's Savannah in the south began their existence as planned enterprises.

However, as is indicated in Chapter 18, Urbanization in Latin America, planning was developed furthest in the Spanish colonies. The sixteenth-century Laws of the Indies, promulgated by the Spanish crown, clearly specified how the con-

---

[3] Ralph Tomlinson, *Urban Structure*, Random House, New York, 1969, p. 250.
[4] Daniel R. Mendelker, *Green Belts and Urban Growth*, University of Wisconsin Press, Madison, 1962, p. 27.

quistadors should construct their cities. Every new town was to have a wide central plaza (the *plaza mayor*) bordered by the major religious and administrative buildings, which were to radiate outward from the *plaza mayor* according to a gridiron plan. Better residences were located near the center of the city; the poor lived on the periphery. The effect of the Spanish town planning can be seen to this day in Latin America. The patterns are almost the reverse of Burgess's pattern, which was by and large typical in the development and growth of North American cities.

Washington, D.C.

There is little that can be said for North American town planning during the eighteenth and nineteenth centuries. Pierre L'Enfant's plan for Washington, D.C., is one of the few bright spots in the picture of urban planning after the Revolutionary War. L'Enfant's original design, produced in 1791, called for broad, sweeping diagonal boulevards overlying a basic gridiron pattern with major avenues. Economic realities soon forced the effective abandonment of L'Enfant's overall plan, and L'Enfant himself was removed in 1792, after numerous disputes. His contention that his plan was "most unmercifully spoiled and altered" is largely accurate. For example, he planned a broad boulevard along the river to be lined with gardens; these have never been seen except on his own detailed maps. He even had a plan to divert the river, making it flow toward the Capitol, whence it would be routed over a 40-foot waterfall and then back to its original course.[5] It was probably fortunate, however, that this particular feature was never constructed.

For much of the nineteenth century, Washington remained, in Charles Dickens's words, "a city of magnificent intentions." Washington's oppressively hot, unhealthful summers did not encourage year-round residence. At the time that Lincoln assumed the presidency, Washington was still a half-finished quagmire, packed with members of Congress, lobbyists, job seekers, prostitutes, gamblers, and hangers-on while Congress was in session, and deserted when it was not. Only near the end of the century did a revival of interest in L'Enfant's original plans give us the neoclassical style of government buildings found in the capital today. Railway lines actually ran across the Mall in front of the Capitol until the lines were put underground a hundred years ago.

One of the city's most notable legacies from L'Enfant is the numerous traffic circles. Any tourist who has ever had the folly of driving into the city is not likely to forget the traffic circles, which disorient even the most experienced drivers.

Nineteenth-Century American Towns

During the nineteenth century little creative energy went into the design of the rapidly multiplying new towns. New western settlements merely replicated older urban traditions. Communities were built as if God had intended that streets be laid out in a grid, at right angles to each other. This was in fact a fairly useful model in the midwest and on the prairie, but it was applied even when it was inappropriate.

---

[5] Charles N. Glaab and A. Theodore Brown, *A History of Urban America,* Macmillan, New York, 1967, p. 253.

If hills got in the way, for example, as in San Francisco, streets were simply cut up one side and down the other rather than following the natural contour of the land.

The gridiron pattern, in which plots could easily be divided, was well suited to the feverish speculation that accompanied the nation's early growth; most promoters of sites were speculators whose major interest in the new communities was quick profit. The Federal Land Ordinance of 1785 also encouraged the gridiron pattern, since it divided all lands west of the Appalachians in the public domain into units of one square mile to facilitate their sale to settlers.[6] A gridiron pattern was also good for fire protection.

Roads and the way they divide land are another strong influence on the pattern of development of a city. A circular pattern, with roads leading from the center like the spokes of a wheel, focuses attention on the center of the city. It is a system "beloved by chieftains, emperors, priests, and popes."[7] Washington, D.C., and Detroit, Michigan, were both designed on modified circular patterns. The gridiron system, with its square lots, has always facilitated subdivision and thus is the model used in industrial and other economically oriented cities in the United States and elsewhere (Johannesburg is an example outside the United States). "The open lot and speculation have always gone hand in hand."[8] This was certainly true of the development of North American cities.

It is interesting to note that by the early twentieth century the rectangular grid, although also used for newer additions to European cities, had come to be identified with the American city.

> It is in America that the persistence of uniform right-angled streets has been most marked. Here the universality of the plan's adoption, and the rigidity of adherence to it, has been such that Europeans, forgetting the long history of rectangular street planning refer to it now as the American method.[9]

In the new frontier towns, housing was as predictable as the pattern of streets. The same American businesspeople who prided themselves on their originality and inventiveness in business, created towns that were dull and repetitive. Every town had its Main Street, Oak Street, and Elm Street.

Planned Communities

Totally planned communities fared little better. Lowell, Massachusetts, for all its early promise as an idealistic, paternalistic community, quickly deteriorated into just another New England mill town. Pullman, Illinois, was designed in the 1880s as an experiment in both well-managed labor relations and town planning. In the words of its founder and sole owner, George Pullman, "With such surroundings and such human regard for the needs of the body as well as the soul the disturbing conditions of strikes and other troubles that periodically convulse the world of labor would not be found here." George Pullman proved to be a poor prophet. Pullman

---

[6] Edmund K. Faltermayor, *Redoing America,* Harper & Row, New York, 1968, p. 17.
[7] Christopher Tunnard, *The City of Man,* Scribner, New York, 1953, p. 121.
[8] Ibid., p. 77.
[9] C. M. Robinson, *City Planning,* Putnam, New York, 1916, p. 16.

Salt Lake City streets were designed to be wide enough for a team of oxen to be turned around. Such wide streets were a major advantage when automobiles came on the scene. (Library of Congress.)

is today best known because of a bitter strike that took place there in 1894 and was finally put down by the National Guard.[10] Today the Pullman community is legally part of the city of Chicago and is undergoing urban revitalization efforts.

Planned urban communities tended quickly to become satellites and then suburbs of the nearest central city, since, on their own, they lacked both the economic and social diversity necessary to keep them viable. Of the new communities organized around religious or political-philosophical doctrines—New Harmony and Oneida, for example—only Salt Lake City has grown and prospered, possibly because it had, under Brigham Young, a very tight social organization, plus an excellent environmental location along the trail to the California gold fields. An early twentieth-century attempt to create a feminist planned community was Alice Austin's "Socialist City" of Llano del Rio in southern California.[11] The homes were built without kitchens and backed up on a communal eating area. This latter feature was to relieve housewives of the drudgery of cooking.[12] Some homes were built, but the planned community, like most utopian communities, was underfinanced and went bankrupt in 1917. As a sidelight, it might be noted that such early feminist plans often had a distinctly middle-class orientation. Middle-class women would be relieved of cooking and heavy cleaning, with that work to be done by lower-class women servants.

Parks

One of the brightest aspects in the rather discouraging story of nineteenth century urban planning is the work of Frederick Law Olmstead. In 1857, after much controversy, he began the building of Central Park on 843 acres of wasteland on the outskirts of New York City. The site was hardly promising, for, as Olmstead described it, much of it was a swamp "seeped in the overflow and mush of pigsties, slaughterhouses, and boneboiling works, and the stench was sickening." Not only

[10] Stanley Buder, *Pullman,* Oxford University Press, New York, 1967, p. vii.
[11] Dolores Hayden, *The Grand Domestic Revolution: A History of Feminist Designs for American Homes, Neighborhoods and Cities,* MIT Press, Cambridge, Mass., 1981.
[12] Dolores Hayden, "Two Utopian Feminists and Their Campaigns for Kitchenless Houses," *Signs,* **4:**283–286, Winter, 1978.

did Central Park serve the function of providing "lungs" for the city, but it inspired other cities to copy New York's successful plan. Parks were built across the country, and some of them, such as the park systems of Kansas City, Milwaukee, Chicago, Philadelphia, and San Francisco, have become invaluable assets of their cities. There also was a pronounced profit motive in creating parks since adjacent property greatly increased in value. Thus, major real estate developers favored the construction of parks and parkways. Private interests favored public facilities that increased property values.

The City Beautiful Movement

The movement that had the most pronounced effect on the design of American cities was the "city beautiful" movement that more or less emerged from the Chicago Columbian World Exhibition of 1893. The Columbian exhibition gave Chicago a chance to show the world that it was no longer a ramshackle town surrounding stockyards, but a booming modern metropolis; and the city leaders were determined to make a good impression.

Daniel Burnham was placed in charge of assembling the nation's leading architects and landscape designers to create for the exposition the famous White City. In order to produce an impression of magnificence, a uniform cornice line was set. All the buildings—with the exception of the Transportation Building, designed by the great architect Louis Sullivan—were classical in style. The classical buildings of White City, combined with harmoniously planned lagoons and grounds, created an overwhelming impact even to the architecturally sophisticated.

The World Columbian Exhibition of 1893 impressed all who saw it. Its emphasis on monumental grandeur influenced American public architecture for decades. (Library of Congress.)

The classical ancestry and majestic size of such buildings neatly meshed with the optimistic and expansionist mood of the country at the turn of the century. Strong, powerful buildings were a way of expressing the fever of imperialism and material success then sweeping the land. The United States in 1898 easily humiliated Spain in a short war and was (it believed) blessed by God with a "manifest destiny" to rule.

White City, with its magnificence and grandeur, started a trend; it became customary to design all government buildings in neoclassical or pseudoclassical style. As a result of the city beautiful movement, there is not a city in the nation without at least one building—a city hall, court, or library—designed to resemble a Greek temple. Cleveland, St. Louis, Detroit, Los Angeles, San Francisco, and especially Washington, D.C., were strongly affected by the city beautiful movement.

The influence of this movement on the architecture of the federal government has been pronounced. For fifty years after the Colombian exposition, almost every large post office was designed as a Greco-Roman temple. Many of these buildings were poor imitations of the classical style, but among the better products of the neoclassical revival are the famous civic center in San Francisco and the Benjamin Franklin Parkway in Philadelphia. The latter terminates at a majestic neoclassical art museum. It must be pointed out that the city beautiful movement paid attention almost exclusively to city centers; there was little concern for housing or neighborhoods.

Parks, which have already been discussed briefly, were related to—though not an integral part of—the city beautiful movement. A number of elaborate park systems, tied together by attractive boulevards, were developed to further beautify the city. The excellent parks of Chicago, Kansas City, and Washington are largely a result of the early-twentieth-century trend for planned public, if not yet private, development.

The model for the ideal city beautiful plan was Daniel Burnham's Chicago Plan. At the request of Chicago's businesspeople, Daniel Burnham drew up in 1909 a master plan for that city which included a massive civic building program; a central feature of this plan was an extensive network of city parks tied together by a system of grand, tree-shaded boulevards. It is noteworthy that pressure for planning came from business and civic leaders rather than city hall. Burnham captured the mood of the age when he ordered his staff to "make no little plans." The nation's capital also profited from the new emphasis on planning. L'Enfant's long-neglected design for Washington, D.C., was revived, and the appearance of the Capitol was greatly improved by the removal of the Pennsylvania Railroad tracks from the Mall in front of it. Burnham and other architects prepared plans for the beautification of Washington from which have been developed the present-day "federal triangle" group of government buildings and the Mall between the Capitol and the Lincoln Memorial.

The city beautiful movement may of course be criticized on aesthetic grounds, but it did have a concept of the city as an integrated whole and a vision of what it could be. The city beautiful movement was a solid, conscious, and sincere attempt to improve the urban environment. Perhaps the greatest weakness of the city beautiful movement was that it almost totally ignored the problem of housing, particularly that of the slums.

Tenement Reform

The early twentieth century saw a movement by social reformers such as Jane Addams to improve the quality of life in inner-city slums. (Also influenced were the slightly later Chicago school of urban scholars.) Among other things, social reformers were concerned with protecting immigrant populations by passing model tenement laws to correct some of the worst abuses of the design and construction of older tenements. To reformers such as Jacob Riis, the slum was the enemy of the home and of basic American virtues. To quote Riis:

> Put it this way: You cannot let men live like pigs when you need their votes as freemen; it is not safe. You cannot rob a child of its childhood, of its home, its play, its freedom from toil and care, and expect to appeal to the grown-up voter's manhood. The children are our to-morrow, and as we mould them to-day so will they deal with us then. Therefore that is not safe. . . . The slum is the enemy of the home. Because of this the chief city of our land [New York] came long ago to be called "The Homeless City." When this people comes to be truly called a nation without homes there will no longer be any nation.[13]

The answer at that time appeared clear: Destroy the slum and you will destroy the breeding ground of social problems. Symptoms of social disorganization such as alcoholism, delinquency, divorce, desertion, and mental illness were to be cured, or at least greatly reduced, through the provision of better housing and more open spaces for the young. This belief in salvation by bricks and mortar fit in neatly with the American belief in the unlimited potential of technology. Note the following 1905 assertion:

> Bad housing is tremendously expensive to a community. It explains much that is mysterious in relation to drunkenness, immorality, poverty, crime and all forms of physical and social decline. Improved dwellings are the best guarantee of civilization. They help conserve the family institution, which is the underlying basis to society. In great cities especially there is no more important phase of civic welfare.[14]

Many greatly needed improvements in housing were made as a result of the campaigns of the reformers; but crime, violence, and alcoholism were not banished as a result. The relationship between housing and social behavior is complex and unfortunately not amenable to simple technological solutions.

TWENTIETH-CENTURY PATTERNS

The City Efficient

The golden age of concern with, and reform of, urban social life, aesthetics, and politics died with the entry of the United States into World War I. Holistic visions of

[13] Jacob Riis, *The Children of the Poor,* Scribner, New York, 1892.
[14] *Model Homes,* City and Suburban Homes Company, New York, 1905, p. 5.

the city's future such as had been provided by the city beautiful movement did not fare well during the war or in the postwar laissez-faire atmosphere of the 1920s. As a result, the emphasis was gradually shifted from the city beautiful to the city efficient, and urban planning was replaced by city engineering. During the 1920s, the city was viewed as an engineering problem, and planners became technicians concerned with traffic patterns, traffic lights, and sewer systems. The city was viewed as a machine, and the goal was to keep the machine running smoothly. To this end, planning and land-use regulation became accepted functions of local government.

Zoning

The concept of the city as an evolving organic unit was also overshadowed by the development of a new planning tool, zoning. Zoning, which became a force in the United States with the New York City Zoning Resolution of 1916, was originally seen as a device to "lessen congestion in the streets" and to "prevent the intrusion of improper uses into homogeneous areas."[15] "Improper" use of land meant not only industrial and commercial establishments, but also lower-class housing. It was an attempt, largely successful, to segregate land use and freeze "noncompatible" uses out of upper-middle-class neighborhoods. What made zoning significant was that now land usages could be controlled by law.

The effect of the first weak zoning laws was mainly negative—that is, to keep unwanted types of buildings from being constructed. Zoning laws had little retroactive effect. (Zone boundaries in many cases recognized the existence of "natural areas" described by the early human ecologists, and then went a step farther and tried to prevent further change in these areas.) The 1921 Standard State Zoning Enabling Act, which was issued by the federal government, advised state legislatures to grant the following power to the cities:

> For the purpose of promoting health, safety, morals, and the general welfare of the community, the legislative body of cities and incorporated villages is hereby empowered to regulate and restrict the height, number of stories, and size of the buildings, and other structures, the percentage of the lot that may be occupied, the size of the yards, courts, and other open spaces, the density of the population, and the location and use of buildings, structures, and land for trade, industry, residence, or other purpose.[16]

In practice, zoning was often used for social purposes of racial, social, and economic exclusivity. In the south, zoning was used during the period before the Fair Housing Act of 1968 as a means of enforcing racial segregation.[17] Even when used to control land use, the results often were unfortunate (see the box on Jane Jacobs in this section). For example, by overzoning for commercial usage, cities unintentionally often pushed new residential developments to the suburbs. After World War II, subdivision regulations often became the main control device in new suburban areas.

---

[15] Dennis O'Harow, "Zoning, What's the Good of It?" in Wentworth Eldridge (ed.), *Taming Megalopolis,* Doubleday (Anchor), Garden City, N.Y., 1967, p. 762.

[16] Newman F. Baker, *Legal Aspects of Zoning,* University of Chicago Press, Chicago, 1927, p. 24.

[17] Christopher Silver and John V. Moeser, *The Separate City: Black Communities in the Urban South, 1940–1968,* University Press of Kentucky, Lexington, 1995.

Today Houston, Texas, is the only major city in the country without zoning laws. Houston does not look noticeably different from other cities because the market mechanism allocates the downtown land to business and commercial usage while outlying land is used for residential purposes. It is not economically feasible to deviate from the normative pattern of land use. Deed restrictions on land use are a de facto functional equivalent of zoning in many cases. More than 10,000 deed restrictions cover over two-thirds of the city although they are most often enforced in wealthy neighborhoods along Memorial Drive and in River Oaks.[18] Despite outrage in some neighborhoods that homes were being converted into bars and car-repair businesses, Houston in 1993 again voted against zoning. Houston remains the only large city without land-use rules.

From Master Plans to Equity Planning

The idea of the city efficient was also evidenced in the general or master plans for city development that became the hallmarks of the city-planning agencies from the 1920s to the 1970s. The purpose of the master plan was to coordinate and regulate all phases of city development; but in practice the preparation of the plan frequently became an end in itself, since the planners rarely had any real authority over the nature and direction of urban development. The plan, even if formally adopted by the city council, was not legally binding unless backed up by specific zoning and other laws.

In defining neighborhoods, physical criteria were used almost exclusively. In the words of Herbert Gans:

> The ends underlying the planners' physical approach reflected their Protestant middle-class view of city life. As a result, the master plan tried to eliminate as "blighting influences" many of the land uses and institutions of lower class and ethnic groups. Most of the plans either made no provision of tenements, rooming houses, second hand stores, and marginal loft industry, or located them in catchall zones of "nuisance uses," in which all land uses were permitted. Popular facilities that they considered morally or culturally undesirable were also excluded.[19]

However, in reality planners often made their recommendations on the basis of arbitrary considerations without fully examining or understanding the consequences. The death blow for many a general plan was the upsurge of urban renewal and other development plans after World War II. These development schemes were frequently put forward by interest groups in business or government that had no concern for the general plan as such. Conflicts between the static general plan and specific development proposals with available funding were almost always resolved in favor of the specific proposals.

The social upheavals of the 1960s and 1970s, plus advocacy planning, have led to more socially responsive planning.[20] Today most planners question the util-

---

[18] Richard F. Babcock, "Houston: Unzoned, Unfettered, and Mostly Unrepentent," *Planning,* **48:**21–23, March, 1982.

[19] Herbert J. Gans, "Planning, Social: II, Regional and Urban Planning," in David Sills (ed.), *International Encyclopedia of the Social Sciences,* vol. 2, Crowell Collier and Macmillan, New York, 1968, p. 130.

[20] Allan Heskin, "Crisis and Response: A Historical View on Advocacy Planning," *Journal of the American Planning Association,* **46:**50–63, January, 1980.

ity of creating citywide plans, unless the plans are directly related to, and can have influence on the future development of, the city. Neighborhood-level plans are often more useful. Not infrequently neighborhood-level plans are used by neighborhood groups to block unwanted changes such as institutional expansion, or to redirect city resources to the neighborhood level.

Planners have become directly involved in the policymaking and the political process. So-called equity planners consciously try to change the bureaucracy to move power and decision making away from elites and to mobilize low-income and working-class residents to demand that their needs be met. The work of equity planners focuses on the short-term rather than long-range comprehensive planning. Advocates of equity planning tend to see it as another form of politics.[21]

Empowerment or Enterprise Zones

One of the few community development programs to garner both Republican and Democratic support is that of empowerment zones, called enterprise zones during the 1980s. The programs define economically depressed areas in which employers who invest in businesses within the enterprise zone get tax breaks and wage credits for employing local residents. The idea is to provide economic activity in poor areas. Chambers of commerce like the idea because it seems a practical alternative to "big-government" programs administered by Washington, while inner-city community groups like the idea because it suggests inner-city areas have strengths and it provides resources coming into the area. Politicians like the idea because it makes them look like they are bringing something to the area. It is the rare inner-city program most everyone can agree upon. The only catch is that all but the most ardent empowerment zone supporters do not really believe it will work.[22]

The major reason is that empowerment zones are going against the economic tide. Inner-city neighborhoods, as the Burgess hypothesis of the 1920s documented, have long been transitional rather than stable areas. The idea of holding employed residents in these inner-city areas goes against the history of poor people moving out as soon as they get enough money. Local residents who get jobs in empowerment zones are likely to move out once they have a steady paycheck just as earlier generations did. Also inner-city ghettos are simply not good business locations. Other business costs outweigh the tax advantages. The tax benefits and wage supplements paid to employers rarely compensate for the much higher operating costs of running a business with unskilled workers without work experience in a high-crime area without an economic infrastructure. These "taxes" means that even with the subsidies it is cheaper for most businesses to locate where the work force is already available, be that in the suburbs or abroad. As a result, businesses that do locate in empowerment zones tend to be marginal firms and tend not to make long-term contributions to the community. Commonly they are highly mobile operations that use the subsidies to employ locals at minimal wages and provide minimal job

---

[21] "Perspective: Listening to Equity Planners," *Urban Affairs,* Autumn, 1994, p. 4.
[22] Nicholas Lemann, "The Myth of Community Development," *New York Times Magazine,* Jan. 9, 1994, pp. 27–31, 50, 54.

training. When the subsidies are gone, they are gone. Empowerment zones sound good, but what they best provide is an expensive government business subsidy. They do little for inner-city residents.

Growth Policies

One of the newer planning concerns in rapidly growing communities is the question of limiting growth. For years it was part of the American creed that bigger is better. City boosters, as a matter of course, bragged that their town or city was growing faster than neighboring places. Now that is changing, and rapidly growing communities from St. Petersburg, Florida, to Boulder, Colorado, to San Diego are seeking ways of limiting growth. In growing areas suburban residents have concerns about future growth. Studying responses of citizens in Orange County, California, Baldassare found that over half his sample cites environmental concerns such as traffic congestion and environmental deterioration while a third cites economic worries such as maintaining property values and keeping down government costs and taxes.[23]

Those groups favoring control, such as the Sierra Club, generally argue that uncontrolled sprawl has destroyed the physical and cultural environment, and believe that indiscriminate gobbling up of land by developers has to be controlled. Opponents of control, such as the National Association of Home Builders and the National Association for the Advancement of Colored People, on the other hand, say that the real question is whether those already in the area can infringe on what they see as a constitutional right to settle where one chooses. They deplore a "pull up the gangplank" approach on the part of established communities that resist change in their way of life or level of amenities. Not all opponents have similar reasons for opposition. The homebuilding industry is concerned about the effect of building restrictions on the profits of developers; the NAACP, on the other hand, is concerned that setting minimum lot sizes and imposing environmental protections (e.g., requirements for municipal sewers and water hookups rather than septic systems and wells) will drive up prices and exclude blacks. Zoning for fewer people can be used to exclude low-income minorities.[24]

While the debate goes on, the legal issue has been resolved for the moment by a case involving the farming center of Petaluma, a city of some 35,000 roughly 35 miles north of San Francisco. To control runaway growth the city developed a plan limiting development to 500 new dwelling units a year. Developers and builders challenged the limits in court. In 1976, the Supreme Court let stand the decision by the court of appeals that the traditional responsibility of local communities for public welfare was sufficiently broad to allow Petaluma to preserve its small-town character and open spaces. The court rejected the developers' argument that limits to growth unconstitutionally restricted people's right to travel and live where they please.

Now Petaluma and other communities have dealt developers another blow. Communities are charging developers a fee to pay for the public services needed

[23] Mark Baldassare, *Trouble in Paradise,* Columbia University Press, New York, 1986.
[24] Michael Danielson, *The Politics of Exclusion,* Columbia University Press, New York, 1976.

by new homes. The fees, called "proffers," are largely passed on to home buyers. The idea is that new residences not be a financial burden to existing taxpayers.

To date, only a limited number of communities, usually in areas in the south and west which are environmentally attractive, have actually tried to put lids on growth. However, decisions by the courts seem to indicate that while a town can't simply ban all growth, it can try to control its future. This is what most citizens also favor. Research in southern California shows strong suburban support for slow growth, but little support for no growth.[25] Charging fees for new homes using local road, sewer, water, and school services is becoming a more common practice.

However, new research indicates that municipal zoning and other techniques to control growth have only a modest effect. Stating goals and accomplishing them are not the same thing.[26]

Crime Prevention through Design

As noted in the box, the work of Jane Jacobs alerted planners to think about how a mix of land usages, shorter blocks, and twenty-four-hour activity contribute to lower crime levels. Earlier in the text, we examined how physical space often has different symbolic meanings to different groups. That is, the physical environment is not neutral, but can be used to increase or decrease various behaviors. As noted in Chapter 13, contemporary concern with this question dates to the 1972 publication of Oscar Newman's book *Defensible Space*.[27] He used sociological knowledge to emphasize design factors that would contribute to a sense of having control over one's environment.

In recent years there has been a revival of interest in *crime prevention through environmental design* (CPTED). City or suburban neighborhoods can use design to augment safety by using natural access control—for example, house fences and shrubs—as well as physical design elements to discourage entry except by those who belong there.[28] Natural surveillance can be increased by the placing of windows so that open areas can be observed. Lighting and landscaping can also be used to promote unobstructed views. Finally, territorial behavior can be encouraged by using sidewalks, porches, and landscaping to define the boundaries between what is public space and what are private areas. The goal is to increase surveillance and human activity in order to decrease the opportunity for crime.

Even street design can play a role since criminals prefer locations with high traffic that permit anonymity and easy escape. Streets that are well maintained and landscaped, and especially those that slow down traffic and discourage pass-through traffic, discourage criminal activity. Sometimes something as simple as blocking off a street at one end can produce noticeable improvements. Importantly, none of the above requires walling off a community or adding police. They are attempts to produce safe and livable communities without resorting to gates or guards.

[25] Mark Baldassare, "Suburban Support for No-Growth Policies," *Journal of Urban Affairs,* **12:**197–206, 1990.

[26] John Logan and Min Zhou, "Do Suburban Growth Controls Control Growth?" *American Sociological Review,* **54:**461–471, June, 1989.

[27] Oscar Newman, *Defensible Space,* Macmillan, New York, 1972.

[28] Timothy D. Crowe and Diane L. Zahm, "Crime Prevention through Environmental Design," *Land Development,* Fall, 1994, pp. 22–23.

The Approach of Jane Jacobs

Among the critics of urban planning practices, Jane Jacobs is the best known. More than three decades after publication, *The Death and Life of Great American Cities* remains the classic critique of zoning and other planning tools as commonly applied.*

Using as an example her own beloved area of Greenwich Village in New York City (she now lives in Toronto), Jacobs argued that the mixed housing and commercial usages and the resulting congestion—factors that orthodox planners are said to deplore—are the very reason why the area has retained its buoyancy and unique character over time. Cities, she suggested, are natural economic generators of diversity and incubators of new enterprises, and attempts by planners to zone various activities into distinct areas only work toward dullness and eventual stagnation both economically and socially.†

Jacobs said that four conditions are indispensable if diversity and liveliness are to be generated in a city:

1. The district, and indeed as many of its internal parts as possible, must serve more than one primary function; preferably more than two. These must ensure the presence of people who go outdoors on different schedules and are in the place for different reasons.
2. Most blocks should be short; that is, streets and opportunities to turn corners must be frequent.
3. The district must mingle buildings that vary in age and condition, including a good proportion of old ones so that they vary in the economic yield they must produce. This mingling must be fairly close-grained.
4. There must be a sufficiently dense concentration of people, for whatever purposes they may be there. This includes dense concentration in the case of people who are there because of residence.‡

Thus she saw the physical environment of the city directly affecting city life, and argued for a mix of social activities and a heterogeneous population to increase neighborhood vitality. By advocating mixed populations and land usages she directly challenged one of the basic tenets of city planning. Jacobs argued that providing a mixture of functions—residence, work, place of entertainment—ensures that eyes are constantly on the

---

* For a retrospective analysis of Jacobs's views, see Harvey M. Choldin, "Retrospective Review Essay: Neighborhood Life and Urban Environment," *American Journal of Sociology,* **48:**457–463, September, 1978.
† Jane Jacobs, *The Death and Life of Great American Cities,* Random House, New York, 1961.
‡ Ibid., pp. 150–151.

streets, maintaining safety. Research appears to support the view that such diversity does contribute to lower crime rates.* This diversity of use further means that uniquely urban specialty shops can operate profitably, since there is considerable traffic past their doors. Short city blocks provide for alternative routes and use of different streets—with the result that a cross section of the public passes the doors of the smaller specialty operations. Old buildings are needed, since, as Jacobs puts it, "Old ideas can sometimes use new buildings. New ideas must use old buildings." New buildings are limited to enterprises that can support the high costs of construction and rent. Old buildings not only provide space for new enterprises; they also break the visual monotony, and they can house cozy stores that provide gossip and a place to leave your keys as well as merely selling goods. Finally, the dense concentration of people in an area contributes to its vitality and liveliness. Jacobs suggests that it is not accidental that the district in San Francisco with the highest dwelling density is the popular North Beach–Telegraph Hill section. High building density does not, of course, necessarily mean crowding. Medium-density areas fail to provide liveliness and safety, and they have none of the advantages of low-density, semisuburban areas.

In Jacobs's view, the population and environmental characteristics of a neighborhood shape its social character:

> Great cities are not like towns, only larger. They are not like suburbs, only denser. They differ from towns and suburbs in basic ways, and one of those is that cities are, by definition full of strangers. . . . Even residents who live near each other are strangers, and must be, because of the sheer number of people in small geographical compass. The bedrock attribute of a successful city district is that a person must feel safe and secure among all these strangers. He must not feel automatically menaced by them. A city district that fails in this respect also does badly in other ways and lays up for itself, and for its city at large, mountains on mountains of trouble.†

A criticism of Jacobs is that her preoccupation with street safety makes her oblivious to other urban problems and values. She views the city as a place where people will do violence to one another unless restrained. One of her most knowledgeable critics, Louis Mumford, suggested that Jacobs puts so much emphasis on the necessity for continued street life because her ideal city is mainly an organization for the prevention of crime.

* E. P. Fowler, "Street Management and City Design," Social Forces, **66**:365–389, December, 1987.
† Jacobs, The Death and Life of Great American Cities, p. 300.

Mumford pointed out that according to Jacobs's view, "the best way to overcome criminal violence is to create a mixture of economic and social activities such that at every hour of the day the streets will never be empty of pedestrians and that each shopkeeper, each householder, compelled to find both his main occupations and his recreations on the street, will serve as watchman and policeman, each knowing who is to be trusted and who not. . . ."* Mumford pointed out that London of the eighteenth century, violent and crime-ridden, met these prescriptions. Furthermore, the benefits of high-density, pedestrian-filled streets, cross-lines of circulation, and a mixture of primary economic activities can be found in Harlem—where they do not reduce street or other crime. On the other hand, a dispassionate observer would have to concede that whatever else Harlem is, it is certainly not dull.

Mumford also argued that the emphasis on safety blinds Jacobs to other values in an urban environment. Convenience, beauty, the absence of the noise of trucks crowding the street, the minimizing of the effects of pollution—all these factors are made subservient to safety.

Jacobs can also be criticized for not dealing with the question of racial change in the city. Nonetheless, the importance of her work should not be underemphasized. Partially because of her influence, the planners of today are far more conscious of the social impact of design and planning decisions. The message that cities are for people is finally affecting urban policies.

* Lewis Mumford, "Home Remedies for Urban Cancer," in Louis K. Loewenstein (ed.), *Urban Studies*, Free Press, New York, 1971, pp. 392–393.

URBAN PLANNING IN EUROPE

Europe has a tradition of urban planning for the community welfare that goes back many years. Europeans, lacking the land resources of the United States, have been more concerned with conserving their resources and preventing unlimited growth. The tendency toward compactness and public ownership also means that the desires of the individual builder are more subject to the criteria of the public welfare.

The United States, by contrast, has yet to formulate a national or even regional land-use policy. In the United States, plans concentrate on the local level. (Ironically, those who most oppose national land-use controls as "socialistic" are often the strongest supporters of stringent local controls in their suburbs. Some opponents of a national land-use policy live in suburbs that regulate in detail matters such as lot sizes, home sizes, placement and height of fences, colors that houses can be painted, and even whether residents can park a trailer in the driveway.)

Control of Land

One advantage enjoyed by some European communities is control over their own municipal lands. Stockholm began buying land in 1904 outside the city limits, with the goal of providing both green space and room for future garden suburbs. Most of this land has since been annexed to the city, so that Stockholm is now in the position of owning about 75 percent of the land within its administrative boundaries. The city rarely sells its land; instead, it leases the land on sixty-year renewable leases to both public and private developers. The money earned from the leases pays off the cost of the loan used to buy the land; and the municipality has the additional advantage of profiting directly from increases in land values. The public, rather than private land speculators, thus profits from the increased value of the land. If the city wants the land after the sixty-year lease is up, it must go to court and prove that the land is needed for the public interest, and then pay the leaseholder the value of any buildings on the property. Such a system would clearly not be politically or economically acceptable in the United States, with its value of private profit making.

Students should keep in mind that land-use systems are not socially neutral. The U.S. system of laissez-faire land purchase and use tends to further the gap between rich and poor, which, in turn, contributes to instability and social problems.

There is a tradition of urban planning in Europe. Since World War II, the city-owned land in Stockholm has been used to develop a system of subcenters, or "mini-cities," built one after another along rapid transit lines extending in five directions from the old city center. Each subcenter contains between 10,000 and 20,000 inhabitants and is served by its own community services, schools, and shops. Unlike the British new towns, these subcenters emphasize easy access to the center city. Blocks of flats, frequently high-rises, are built 550 yards from the transit station; detached and terrace-style housing is built beyond up to about 1,000 yards from the station. Cars are routed through green areas surrounding the living areas.

Along each string of subcenters, "main centers" are built at appropriate intervals. Each main center, with a large shopping mall, theaters, and a major transit station, has a supporting population of between 50,000 and 100,000 persons within ten minutes by automobile or public transit.

Housing Priorities

The post–World War II western European housing shortage largely came to an end by the 1980s. Attention has thus been shifting from massive building programs to the quality of the urban environment. During the postwar period there was heavy emphasis on clearance of slums and war-damaged central areas, and on the building of new towns on the urban periphery. Outside of England, these new towns were often high-rise in nature. A welfare-state approach also led to the construction of largely rent-controlled and rent-subsidized units.[29] In Great Britain, council housing—that is, public housing—accounted for a third of the entire housing stock, before the conservative government under Mrs. Thatcher (1979–1990) began selling council houses to their clients. In Sweden only 35 percent of all housing built since World War II has been constructed by the private sector.

Greater affluence and interest in upgrading older central-city housing is leading to more owner-occupied housing and to the rehabilitation and revitalization of

[29] Wynn Martin (ed.), *Housing in Europe,* St. Martin's Press, New York, 1984.

Geneva, Switzerland, provides an example of a humane urban habitat. (Peter Menzel/Stock, Boston.)

older inner-city housing stock. Middle-class populations have less interest in massive high-rise housing projects of twenty years ago and greater interest in gentrification of older neighborhoods. More conservative governments have led to greater emphasis on private-market housing, although this "private market" is often subsidized to an extent unknown in the United States.

Most new residential building in Europe remains subsidized in one way or another in order to hold down costs and maintain quality. Germany and the Netherlands have elaborate programs for loans to nonprofit housing organizations, Great Britain has rent rebates, and Sweden has an annual housing allowance for all families with two or more children, plus other housing subsidies.

Housing costs in most western European countries take approximately 20 percent of family income because of subsidies. This is excellent by American standards. In the Netherlands and Germany, subsidized rents often do not exceed 15 percent of family income. The trade-off is that taxes are higher.

Transportation

Cars are relied on extensively in comparatively low-density American cities, with their commitment to housing patterns of dispersed single-family houses on private land. On the other hand, in more densely populated European cities, where most people reside in apartment buildings (typically of three or four stories), public transit is the norm. Even in affluent Sweden, which has a higher per capita income than the United States, only 7 percent of the households have two cars; and 45 percent do not own an auto.[30] Sixty percent of the trips to or from work in Stockholm are made by public transit and 20 percent by foot. In spite of their high auto taxes Swedes can afford automobiles. Many do not buy cars because they do not need them; there is excellent, public government-subsidized subway and ground transportation.

In many European cities with narrow streets and few garages, the convenience of driving is outweighed by the problem of where to park the car. In cities such as Rome or Paris, cars are often parked on sidewalks as well as streets. Also, even though an average European city may have only half the autos of its American counterpart, these cars can cause immense congestion (in addition to parking problems), as an American tourist driving there can attest. Fortunately, mass transit in London, Paris, or anywhere in Holland, Germany, or Scandinavia is remarkably fast and efficient.

Urban Growth Policies

While the United States does not have a national land-use or growth policy, several European countries have explicit growth policies. Great Britain, France, Italy, the Netherlands, Sweden, and the Soviet Union are all seeking to disperse national population and stem migration to the largest centers. While the measures haven't been entirely successful, they have slowed the movement from smaller to larger places.

[30] David Popenoe, *Private Pleasure, Public Plight,* Transaction, New Brunswick, N.J., 1985, p. 43.

In Britain, the goal has been to stem the so-called drift to the south—out of Scotland and Wales and into the area centering on London. In France, the goal has been to lessen the domination of Paris; in Italy, to develop the economy of the depressed south, or Mezzogiorno; in the Netherlands, to save the remaining green areas; and in Sweden, to halt the flow out of more northern areas into Stockholm and the south.

The basic tool has been to provide manufacturers with economic incentives to invest in depressed areas needing growth. Subsidies in terms of capital grants are provided by the national government. In addition, controls are increasingly imposed upon adding factories or offices to places where growth isn't wanted. For example, to build a factory or office building in the London area, the developer must show that the enterprise cannot be developed elsewhere. The Netherlands also puts higher taxes on buildings in the cities of Amsterdam, Rotterdam, and The Hague. Another policy is to relocate government offices to areas where growth is desired. Sweden is relocating one-quarter of its government offices outside of Stockholm—a policy that definitely does not appeal to the government bureaucrats who have to move.

It is difficult to see any urban growth and redistribution policy being implemented in the United States. There is no clamor for a program administered out of Washington, and programs by individual states are unlikely to be effective. If one state imposed sanctions, a company could—and probably would—simply up and move to another state that did not. Thus, while European programs for dispersion of growth have been somewhat successful, they are unlikely to be copied in North America, with our stronger opposition to decision making by the central government. Our decentralized system also has a flexibility lacking elsewhere. The economic and housing growth in some sun belt states reflects a de facto decentralization of people and power from established northern and eastern cities.

The Dutch Approach

Americans who fear that certain regions of the United States are turning into unrelenting megalopolises should find it instructive to see how the Dutch are coping with similar problems. The Netherlands is a small country with a population of 15 million and a population density of over 1,030 persons per square mile. If the United States had this population density, it would have a population of over 3.7 billion instead of 165 million. The problem in the Netherlands is aggravated by the fact that the majority of the Dutch population is found in a megalopolis about 100 miles in diameter, including Amsterdam, Rotterdam, and The Hague. This conurbation is known as the *randstad,* or "rim city." Thus, because of necessity the Dutch have had to make planning choices not addressed by the land-abundant United States.

Nonetheless, it is possible to reach the open countryside in half an hour's time from the center of any of the cities in the *randstad.* In spite of considerable population growth and a housing shortage following World War II, the Dutch lead remarkably uncluttered lives. Urban sprawl such as that found in the United States is virtually unknown. The line between town and country is sharply drawn. When a city such as Amsterdam stops, it stops abruptly. It is quite common at the city's edge to see massive blocks of high-rise apartments overlooking cows peacefully grazing in totally open fields. By building upward rather than outward, the Dutch have kept their towns compact; and valuable woods, lakes, and fields are kept as a reserve for the use of all.

The Dutch have been able to save much of their environment, and at the same time provide for an ever-expanding demand for housing, by building tall, multiple-unit residential buildings. The use of high-rises is dictated by the shortage of land and the necessity to keep down costs of land. Single-family houses are usually built in rows. Many families in the Netherlands, particularly those with small children, prefer free-standing single-family houses; and the privately financed dwellings now being built are substantially of this type. However, only the more affluent segment of the population can afford the high building costs. During the 1960s and 1970s, Amsterdam, Rotterdam, and The Hague lost a quarter of their populations to suburbs. Now, however, the exodus has been stemmed. The 1980s and 1990s have seen old residential areas being renovated and gentrified. To date, the social problems that come with young, dual-income families displacing other groups have not been prevalent.[31] This is partially because the numbers seeking inner-city housing are limited.

The government in the Netherlands subsidizes both rents and building costs for those not able to carry the full cost. The Dutch feel that every family, regardless of income level, is entitled to reasonable housing. As a result, rents are low by comparison with those in the United States. After deduction for taxes and social insurance, the average Dutch family pays about 15 percent of its income for rent. This is a result of the government's policy of rental subsidies and loans for building new dwellings. The average rent of a new dwelling financed with a state loan is under 20 percent of the average gross income of an industrial worker. (This is bit more than half paid by a U.S. worker.) Subsidies and rent supplements are periodically readjusted so that the poor and the working classes will not be priced out of the housing market. All this requires high taxes, but the government has chosen this over lower human services.

The Dutch also believe in public ownership of urban land; about 70 percent of Amsterdam is now owned by the city. In The Hague the policy is somewhat different: Only about 20 percent of the land is owned by the city, but it is strategically located so that it can be used to set the pattern of real estate prices for the city. The third major city of the Netherlands, Rotterdam, saw its downtown area reduced to rubble by Nazi dive bombers in 1940. Rotterdam began to reconstruct after the war, with the core of the city as a commercial, cultural, and administrative center. Dutch officials now concede that it was a mistake to rigidly segregate commercial and residential areas. The Lijnbaan, the downtown shopping mall that has received much praise, contains fine shops, sidewalk cafes, and several apartment buildings without vacancies. Rotterdam's land policy is somewhere between that of Sweden and

[31] Jan von Weesep and Ronald van Kempen, "Dual Incomes and Residential Preferences; The Changing Population Profile of Large Dutch Cities," paper presented at the Conference on Social Theory and the Built Environment in Cross-National Perspectives, Noszvaj, Hungary, June 24–27, 1989.

that of the United States. The city retains ownership of industrial and commercial land, with the land being leased and rents reviewed every three to five years. Land to be used for housing, on the other hand, is sold outright after it has been determined that the land use is in conformity with the overall development plan for the city.

Rotterdam also has what is credited to be the most successful housing revitalization program in Europe, a program that allows low-income residents to remain in their neighborhoods.[32] The city has avoided the problem of other European and American cities where gentrification has meant the displacement of existing residents. Neighborhood project groups of residents are used to involve existing residents in the whole range of local decisions. Public monies are used for acquisition and upgrading of existing structures, whether small-scale or wall-to-wall renovations. Only when the local project group can agree on what should be done is the matter referred to the Town Urban Renewal Committee for resolution.

Throughout Holland a system of local, regional, and—finally—national controls prevents unwanted urban sprawl. New buildings cannot be constructed unless they conform to the detailed development plan prepared by each municipality. Plans for development are drawn up by the city, but they must be approved by provincial authorities, who have certain limited powers of review and veto. If a local development is in conflict with the regional plan and if the differences cannot be resolved at that level, the question then goes to the national level for a decision. There is no national plan as such; rather there are national guidelines that influence the regional plans and the detailed city development plans. An attempt is made to avoid rigidity, and plans are constantly being modified—within the national guidelines—to meet new situations and needs. Without some controls, the remaining green space between The Hague, Rotterdam, and Amsterdam would soon be filled, and a megalopolis would become inevitable.

NEW TOWNS

Throughout the centuries, humans have had visions of creating new towns free from the fads and foibles of older cities. The term "utopia" originated as the title of a book (1516) by Thomas More which gave his version of how a new land of towns should be organized. Here the emphasis is on new towns that have actually been built, beginning with the world-renowned English new towns program and then discussing other European alternatives.

British New Towns

The British new town movement owes its origins to Ebenezer Howard (1850–1928), an English court stenographer who proposed the building of whole new communities. His idea appeared in a book called *To-morrow, A Peaceful Path to Real Reform* (1898), which was soon reissued under the title *Garden Cities of To-*

[32] J. van der Ploeg, "The Rotterdam Model: Renewal without Gentrification," *Urban Innovation Abroad*, 6:4, April, 1982.

morrow (1902).[33] Howard's new towns, which were called "garden cities," were not to be simply another version of suburbs. Rather, they were to be self-contained communities of 30,000 inhabitants which would have within their boundaries ample opportunities not only for residence but also for employment, education, and recreation. The towns were to be completely planned, with all land held in public ownership to prevent speculation.

Howard's garden cities were essentially a reaction against the urban abuses of the industrial revolution in England. His new towns were not to be extensions of the morally and socially polluted city but self-sufficient towns with all the necessary amenities, where one could enjoy the benefits of a healthful country life. In Howard's words:

> There are in reality not only, as is so constantly assumed, two alternatives—town life and country life—but a third alternative in which all the advantages of the most energetic and active town life, with all the beauty and delight of the country, may be secured in perfect combination.[34]

[33] Ebenezer Howard, *Garden Cities of To-morrow,* Faber and Faber, London, 1902.
[34] Ibid., pp. 45–46.

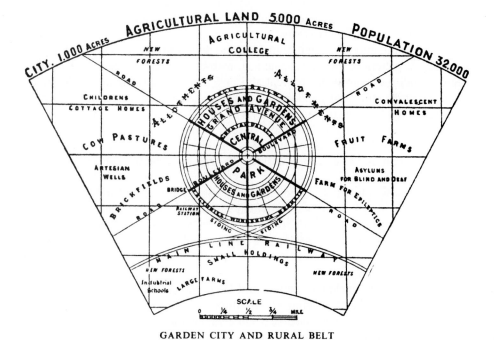

GARDEN CITY AND RURAL BELT

Figure 14-1. Howard's garden cities were designed to be self-sufficient and self-contained communities. Note that the railroads were not to enter the city proper, but would remain within the manufacturing belt on the town periphery.

This combination would in turn spur "the spontaneous movement of the people from our crowded cities to the bosom of our kindly mother earth, at once the source of life, of happiness, of wealth, and of power." Thus the garden city was fundamentally antiurban in its basic conception. It was to solve the problem of the great cities largely by abandoning them and starting over with a fresh environment.

Frederick Osborn, one of the major proponents of new towns, described them as follows:

> Howard's Garden City is to be industrial and commercial with a balanced mixture of all social groups and levels of income. Areas are worked out for the zones: public buildings and places of entertainment are placed centrally, shops intermediately, factories on the edge with the railway and sidings. Houses are of different sizes, but all have gardens and all are within easy range of factories, shops, schools, cultural centers, and the open country. Of special interest is the central park and the inner Green Belt or Ring Park, 420 feet wide, containing the main schools with large playgrounds and such buildings as churches.[35]

However, the most distinctive feature of the garden cities was that beyond the city itself there was an encircling "green belt" of natural fields and woodlands which were owned by the town and could never be sold. This green belt could not be encroached upon for housing, business, industry, or even farming—although it could be used for pasturage. Because of this feature, garden cities are also known as green belt cities. The green belt not only was to provide a way for the residents to enjoy nature; it also was intended to prevent the city from growing beyond its planned limit of 30,000 inhabitants.

Nor was the internal design of the garden city left to chance. The whole town, including its pattern of roads, was planned, with both the quality and the basic design of buildings controlled. The central 5 or 6 acres were to contain civic buildings, a library, lecture halls, and theaters. Stores and shops were nearby. This core was surrounded by rings of houses, each with its own yard. Neighborhood schools and churches were scattered throughout the city, and small parks connected the various neighborhoods. The outermost ring of the city was to contain industries and warehouses with direct access to rail lines. The rail lines did not penetrate the center of the city proper.

The town was totally planned, and strict zoning was central to Howard's basic scheme. The residential city was divided into five neighborhoods or wards, each with approximately 5,000 residents. Each was to have its own centrally located school and community subcenter, and every attempt was to be made to keep all houses within walking distance of factories, schools, churches, shops, and, of course, the open country.[36]

The whole site, including agricultural land, was to be under quasi-public or trust ownership to ensure planning control through leasehold covenants. When the population outgrew the prescribed size and area, another new town was to be created with its own sacrosanct green belt. As with the ancient Greeks, problems of

---

[35] Frederick J. Osborn, *Green-Belt Cities,* Schocken, New York, 1969, p. 28.

[36] For a detailed discussion of the community's organization, see Osborn, *Green-Belt Cities.* For a detailed description of the history of new towns, see E. R. Scoffham, *The Shape of British Housing,* Godwin, London, 1984.

growth were to be handled by colonization rather than by extending city boundaries.

First Towns. The concept of garden cities would have gone the way of other utopian plans had Howard not been an activist as well as a visionary. In 1902, with the aid of the newly formed Garden City Association, he established the first garden city at Letchworth, some 30 miles north of London.[37] This initial venture was plagued by many difficulties, the principal one being that the site selected was poor. Another problem was the difficulty of finding investors for a project that limited dividends to a maximum of 5 percent per year. In fact, it was twenty years before the shareholders received any dividends at all.[38] The understandable reluctance of industry to move out to the new town meant that residents became commuters to London—a situation directly opposed to Howard's conception of a town that would provide its own employment. Howard was emphatically against the green belt towns becoming commuter suburbs.

Despite these problems, while the first garden city was still not out of the financial woods, land for a second, Welwyn Garden City, was secured in 1920. Howard did this without consulting his board of directors since he knew they would not approve. Welwyn Garden City suffered financial crises for many years, but it eventually surmounted them. Today it is a pleasant and prosperous community of 44,000 residents about twenty-five minutes by rail from London.

Government Involvement. Were it not for World War II, Howard's garden cities would probably have remained a quaint experiment. However, World War II, with its extensive destruction in the heart of London, led Patrick Abercrombie to publish a Greater London Plan of 1944, with decentralization as one of its major aims.

The new towns were to be one part of a four-part policy. The policy included (1) a green belt around London to halt continuous metropolitan growth, (2) new towns to house the expanding urban population, (3) redevelopment of inner-city areas, conforming to higher standards than had existed previously, and (4) an attempt to control the location of employment and to prevent everyone from building in London.[39]

The British government became directly involved in the building of new towns through the New Towns Act of 1946. Advocates of new towns had long argued that they would provide a healthier, cleaner, safer, and more democratic environment. In the back of everyone's mind was also the fact that London had suffered grievously from bombing during the war and that new towns would disperse both population and industry at numerous smaller nodes rather than create one massive target in London. Furthermore, it was considered undesirable to rebuild badly damaged areas of London, such as the East End, at the old unsatisfactory population

---

[37] Frank Schaffer, *The New Town Story,* MacGibbon and Kee, London, 1970, p. 4.
[38] Lloyd Rodwin, *The British New Towns Policy,* Harvard University Press, Cambridge, Mass., 1956, pp. 12–13.
[39] Wyndham Thomas, "Implementation: New Towns," in Derek Senior (ed.), *The Regional City,* Aldine, Chicago, 1966, pp. 19–20.

densities; new towns would help to absorb the surplus population. Government involvement in new towns meant that building on a grand scale was now possible, as a result of government financing. Compulsory purchase of land from private owners for building the town was also possible.

The involvement of the British government, however, meant that the new towns would differ in significant ways from Howard's original scheme. First, the development corporation was appointed by and answerable to the central government, not to the town. Second, the population size was pushed upward—first to 60,000; and some towns plan for ultimate populations of up to 250,000 in cluster cities. This is far from Howard's limit of 30,000. Third, no provision was made for nearby land to be used only for agriculture. "As far as access to the countryside is concerned the new towns do not differ from most other settlements in Britain."[40] Finally, the concept of a city providing all its own employment was also abandoned, in practice if not in theory, although the new towns are certainly not designed to be commuter suburbs. They are basically manufacturing centers, with approximately half the population in industry and the other half in trade, the services, and the professions.

The first of the English government-sponsored new towns, Stevenage, was begun in 1947. Among other innovations, it had the first pedestrian shopping mall in Britain and neighborhoods designed to separate pedestrian walkways from contact with automobile and truck traffic. Today Stevenage is a pleasant and economically self-supporting community of approximately 70,000.

Houses and apartments built by the local new towns development corporations were not distributed on a first-come, first-served basis. Rather, priority was determined by a number of criteria, including employment by local or incoming industries and previous residence in one of the more crowded inner-city areas of London. Originally, following Howard's plan, almost all dwellings were rented, but successive British governments have been moving toward increasing the number of owner-occupied homes. As a means of encouraging home ownership, the Conservative government offered renters the option of purchasing the property in which they lived for 20 percent below the market value.

While the new towns have been successful economically, they have not significantly altered social behavior. New town residents have no fewer class prejudices and social problems than their counterparts not living in new towns.[41] The early expectation that planned communities could determine people's behavior has not been met. What the new towns do provide is a decent and economically viable community.

Some thirty-four new towns have been completed in Great Britain, with a total investment of over $5 billion. It should be pointed out that only 5 percent of Britain's housing construction after World War II has taken place in new towns. Still, the British are well pleased with their new towns program and have some 4 million persons in new towns.

[40] Ray Thomas and Peter Cresswell, *The New Town Idea,* Open University Press, London, England, 1973, p. 24.

[41] William Michelson, "Planning and Amelioration of Urban Problems," in Kent P. Schwirian et al. (eds.), *Contemporary Topics in Urban Sociology,* General Learning Press, Morristown, N.J., 1977, pp. 562–640.

New Towns in Europe

Not only England but other European countries, including Sweden, Finland, the Netherlands, and Russia, built new towns after World War II. The Russian development of new towns has been generally explained as part of broad schemes for national development and the decentralization of industry. Many of the earlier new towns in Russia were connected with hydroelectric power projects and then expanded into manufacturing centers.[42]

In Russia, as in England, the new towns were planned to be separate from existing urban centers although related to them. Local industry was to provide sufficient employment so that few, if any, residents would be required to commute to the large city. Generally, these communities were originally designed to house a maximum of 60,000 to 100,000 people. These new communities were not a consequence of the garden city concept, as were the British new towns. Rather, they were closer to company towns. The goal was not to build more humane environments but to provide housing for the workers in the factories.

In Sweden and the Netherlands, the new communities were designed to be closely tied to the central city, and to serve as residential—not employment—areas. Scandinavian new towns such as Vallingby, Farsta, and Taby are basically residential and shopping areas. Unlike the British new towns, they are constructed along rapid transit lines so that they will be an integral part of the city's life; they are not designed to be independent and self-contained employment units. It is expected that most residents will work in the central city; consequently, rapid transit to the core of the central city is a basic feature of the design of these towns. Zoetermeer, a Dutch new town of 100,000 inhabitants 7 miles from The Hague, speeds its residents to the center of The Hague in less than twenty minutes. Such new towns are really extensions of the older city into the countryside rather than attempts to create new rural or suburban utopian communities.

All European new towns have in common the fact that they were initiated, planned, and financed by the government. While there has occasionally been some financing from cooperatives, unions, or even private sources, the land and the facilities built on it have been owned either directly by the local government or indirectly by the government through quasi-public corporations chartered by the national government to build and administer the town. Since much of the land for new towns was drained from marshes, Dutch planners also have the advantage of planning for land over which there is little dispute about how it is to be used.

Throughout Europe high-rise apartment buildings are generally used, not only to make economical use of the land because land costs are high but also to avoid suburban sprawl and to provide open spaces for recreation and enjoyment of the natural environment. In Sweden, Finland, and the Netherlands over 80 percent of the units are in blocks of flats. English new towns, on the other hand, built over 80 percent single-family homes.[43]

[42] J. Clapp, *New Towns and Urban Policy—Planning Metropolitan Growth,* Dunellen, New York, 1971, p. 28.
[43] Pierre Merlin, *New Towns,* Methuen, London, 1971, p. 250.

Some of the concentration of high-rise units in Sweden has less to do with planning ideology than with economic considerations. Owners of large stores in the main towns demanded a high density of residents in close proximity to the shopping malls as a condition for opening department stores or supermarkets.

Everywhere automobiles remain a problem. Britain, for example, has proportionately only half the autos of the United States but higher densities, fewer garages, and narrow streets in older cities, creating considerable congestion.[44] Every attempt is made to put parking lots underground or otherwise out of sight to constantly outrun the planners' ideas about where to put them all. Generally there is satisfaction with the new towns, although they lack the excitement of the central city. Residents of Vallingby, a suburb of Stockholm, report that both sexes have more time to devote to recreation and other leisure activities than do American suburbanites. This is because residents of Vallingby as apartment dwellers do not have to spend weekends on home maintenance and repair.[45]

Although Swedish new towns such as Vallingby and Farsta were constructed in the 1950s to deliberately high densities (only 8 percent of the former and 13 percent of the latter are single-family homes), the communities have an openness and closeness to nature that residents find appealing. While there are no private yards as in the North American model, there are many walkways, trees, and common open spaces.

More recently built Swedish new towns have a far more negative image among Swedes. The brick-sided walk-up apartments characteristic of Vallingby have been largely replaced with six- to eight-story concrete-slab buildings—many more than a block long. Such slab cities have been criticized as "inhuman environments" and social disaster areas. Built in parallel rows, they present a very sterile and uninviting appearance. Only the color of the buildings distinguishes one group from another. (After dark all the colors look alike, a fact I once discovered when I got lost trying to locate the building where I was staying.)

The relative lack of popularity of such buildings has resulted in their having a high concentration of younger persons with lower incomes and being identified in the popular mind with social problems—drug addiction, alcoholism, and crime. Some of the newest housing areas also have high concentration (25 percent or more) of foreign workers such as Turks—groups often poorly integrated into Swedish society. German new towns have had similar problems, and as a result Germany no longer builds new towns. High-rise towns on the outskirts of Paris also house a high concentration of immigrants, from North Africa and elsewhere. In the eyes of many French these high-rise areas are havens of crime, drugs, and Islamic political subversion. In Europe the outer city is often viewed the way many Americans view the inner city.

Social problems associated with new towns—and the high cost of building them—resulted in European nations' ending or drastically curtailing new town building during the 1980s. There has been little pressure to revive new town growth

---

[44] Popenoe, *Private Pleasure, Public Plight,* p. 51.
[45] David Popenoe, *The Suburban Environment,* University of Chicago Press, Chicago, 1977, especially chap. 9.

during the 1990s. Having largely overcome their housing shortages, western European nations direct their attention to quality-of-life issues. Only in eastern Europe, and especially Russia, is housing itself still a major problem. According to Russian researchers at least 45 percent of all urban households share their apartment with another nonrelated family.[46]

AMERICAN NEW TOWNS

Government-Built New Towns

Today, when European governments have directly taken the responsibility for planning and financing new towns, it is almost forgotten that during the 1920s Radburn, New Jersey, was the archetype of the planned community. Also, during the 1930s the United States government designed, financed, built, and for a decade managed three of the world's first planned new "green belt" towns surrounded by areas of open land. Like Howard's garden cities, the green belt towns were an attempt to create an idealized less-urban past. The building of these towns reflected specific measures that were being taken to combat the depression of the 1930s. The government had three main objectives in building new towns:

1. To demonstrate a new kind of suburban community planning which would combine the advantages of city and country life.
2. To provide good housing at reasonable rents for moderate-income families.
3. To give jobs to thousands of unemployed workers which would result in lasting economic and social benefits to the community in which the work was undertaken.

The three American green belt towns were Greenbelt, Maryland, outside of Washington, D.C.; Green Hills, Ohio, near Cincinnati; and Greendale, Wisconsin, just south of Milwaukee. They were basically experimental or demonstration projects. (An interesting sidelight is that bureaucrats in Washington somehow mixed up the blueprints so the homes with basements designed for wintery Wisconsin were authorized for Cincinnati, while the cement-slab homes designed for Cincinnati were built outside Milwaukee.)

Plans called for the towns to be composed of neighborhood units and to have their own industry, as in the British model. But first a shortage of funds and then World War II kept them basically commuter suburbs. After World War II, the private housing industry was able to convince Congress that having the government involved in the building and renting of low-rent homes was socialistic and dangerous to the free-enterprise system. As a result of Public Law 65 of 1949, all the homes built by the government were sold. The green belts surrounding the towns—which with the expansion of the central cities had become valuable land—were

---

[46] N. V. Kalinina and G. Rodkin, "Housing Ownership, Control, Distribution," paper published by the Soviet Academy of Sciences, 1989. (The estimate was provided by Dr. N. B. Kosareva.)

converted to other uses. Much of Greendale's green belt, for example, is now occupied by privately developed housing tracts and a large shopping center.

Federal Support and Withdrawal

Enthusiastic about the idea of new communities free from urban blight or suburban
sprawl, Congress during 1968 and 1970 passed legislation to spur the development
of new towns. The legislation offered federal funds and technical aid to developers
and—most important—guaranteed up to $50 million worth of each developer's
bonds plus the interest on the bonds. This was done because a new town is an inherently risky financial venture and requires front-end outlays for land purchase and infrastructure well before the first house is built or sold. The Nixon administration,
however, opposed the program and withheld all funds for planning grants and technical assistance. The processing of applications was deliberately ensnared in red tape.

By 1974, twelve projects had issued bonds for a total of $252 million in fed-
erally guaranteed debentures. At this critical point the program was hit with the energy crisis and a depressed housing market, and developers found themselves
caught between expensive front-end costs (one developer spent the equivalent of
$40,000 a day in 1990 dollars just for interest and taxes) and no customers. While
established towns such as Reston and Columbia were able to weather the crisis,
brand-new towns still in the infrastructure-building stage were not. At that point
(1975) the Ford administration announced that the new towns would be cut loose
to sink or swim. They didn't make it. The last to go under was Soul City, North Carolina, the dream of civil rights activist Floyd McKissick. The Department of Housing and Urban Development assumed ownership of Soul City in 1980.

The federal government acquired all but one of the new towns by foreclosure
and sold the assets at a total loss of $570 million. The one exception was Wood-
lands, 30 miles north of Houston, which held on because its developer had extensive natural gas holdings. Critics charge that much of this loss was the government's own doing, since it deliberately underfunded the towns and then pulled back
at a critical juncture. By contrast, the British do not anticipate that their government-built new towns will be self-supporting for the first decade and a half. There
is at present no sign that the United States government is willing to make such a
commitment. Economically, new towns, except for the affluent, cannot be expected
to stand alone financially in their early years. With existing domestic programs suffering cutbacks, it is not likely there will be any United States government new
towns programs in the foreseeable future.

Privately Built New Towns

Privately built new towns were a phenomenon of the years after World War II.
Among the best known and most successful of the American new towns are Reston,
Virginia, just west of Washington, D.C., Columbia, Maryland, near Baltimore on
the way to Washington, D.C., and Irvine in southern California. All were financed
privately rather than by the government. Irvine, however, differs from the other two
insofar as while it was built on new town principles, it never had a commitment or

A more urban section of the successful privately
built new town of Reston, Virginia. (Ken
Heinen/NYT Pictures.)

interest in economic or racial diversity.[47] It was designed to be an elitist and upper-class community.

Reston, which was the brainchild of developer Robert E. Simon, was taken over by the Gulf Oil Corporation in 1967 and later by Mobil because the town was not returning a profit. Economically, the town of 57,000 is now healthy and has a large number of corporate offices and other "clean" industries. Reston, like other privately financed new towns, and unlike the earlier ventures by the government, has from the first had a distinctly upper-middle-class character. Studies revealed that the average buyer in Reston was between thirty and forty years old, was the head of a family with two children, and had an annual income over one-third higher than the national average. Reston, however, does have several hundred units of federally subsidized housing. One of six Reston residents is a minority member. Architecturally, Reston represents some of the best in contemporary design.

[47] Martin J. Schiesl, " Designing the Model Community: The Irvine Company and Suburban Development, 1950–1988," in Robert Kling, Spencer Olin, and Mark Posner (eds.), *Posturban California: The Transformation of Orange County since World War II,* University of California Press, Berkeley, 1991, pp. 55–91.

Although Robert Simon had attempted to integrate the community economically by placing middle-income and more expensive houses side by side, this was abandoned as not being economically sound. Mixed-income housing is desirable for social reasons, but it is a drain on profits, and Reston is a profit-making enterprise.

Columbia, Maryland, the second new town, 20 miles from Washington, D.C., was developed by James Rouse, perhaps the nation's most respected builder. Architecturally, Columbia is generally judged less successful than Reston. Columbia more resembles an ideal supersuburb. It covers 15,600 acres and will eventually house 110,000 people. As of 1995, it had some 79,000 residents living in nine "villages." It represents an investment of over $2.5 billion. Builders of Columbia's various sections were given a relatively free hand and built a mixture of their best-selling models. For example, a buyer could choose a standard interior and then decide whether the facade was to be Cape Cod, Nordic, or Georgian colonial. Columbia is, however, a pleasant and well-planned community. Wooded areas and pathways run throughout the town. Like most new towns, it is organized into neighborhoods. Each neighborhood has some 900 houses, and each has its own elementary school and recreational facilities, including a swimming pool, a neighborhood center, and a convenience store. Four neighborhoods are combined to form a "village" of about 3,500 units, which has an intermediate or middle school, a meeting hall, and larger and more varied shops plus a supermarket. These are all designed to cluster around a small plaza with benches and a fountain. There is also a larger shopping center for the whole community in the downtown city center, which contains office buildings and larger department stores. Other innovations include a community college and a comprehensive full-care medical program in conjunction with the Johns Hopkins Medical School.

Socially, Columbia has made a conscious effort to be a racially integrated community: One-third of the residents are black. Income integration has generally not been as successful. Subsidized units have not been as clustered as in Reston, but are spread over five different sites to avoid the creation of a low-income ghetto. Nonetheless, when an expensive bicycle is stolen, it is the low-income residents who are usually blamed. Within the community, use of automobiles was to be discouraged by providing walkways and bicycle paths that are both more direct and not in physical contact with the highways. Nonetheless, cars are as numerous as in other suburbs, the parking lots of the shopping centers are filled, and the corporation has had to discontinue the minibus service within the city because it did not attract enough customers.

All in all, residents seem pleased with new towns, although they are not significantly more satisfied than residents of other suburban communities. Raymond Burby and Shirley Weiss compared responses of 7,000 residents in fifteen new towns and fifteen conventional suburbs of similar location, age, size, and income level.[48] Ninety percent of the respondents from the new towns thought their community a good place to live—but then so did 86 percent of those in conventional suburbs. New towns per se had little effect on social behavior or perceptions.

[48] Richard J. Burby III et al., *New Communities U.S.A.*, Lexington Books, Lexington, Mass., 1976.

Office and Research Parks

One newer form of planned community is business-oriented office parks located on the periphery of cities. Perhaps the most famous of these, the Research Triangle, was founded over three decades ago on a 6,700-acre tract in the Raleigh–Durham–Chapel Hill area of North Carolina. The Research Triangle is run by a state-created foundation that owns and operates the research park.

The Research Triangle has come to be an exclusive address. Today, the campuslike park is home to more than fifty high-technology companies with more than 30,000 employees, at least a quarter of whom must be directly engaged in research. To get into the Research Triangle a company must buy at least 8 acres of parkland, and its building cannot be high-rise, has to meet architectural standards, and can cover no more than 15 percent of the property. The nearby communities try to replicate the atmosphere of the Research Triangle Park by establishing construction restrictions on everything from the size of buildings to that of McDonald's arches (the latter are largely banned).

Communities seek office and research parks because they bring nonpolluting, high-tech, high-paying employment to the area. There are, however, real limits to the number of such enterprises possible in a region.

Back to the Future?

A limited number of private new town developers and planners are turning away from the community development practices of recent decades and are returning to the nineteenth-century town as a model. This means building deliberately "old-fashioned"-style homes on narrow-grid streets that encourage walking, and keeping shopping on the intimate scale of a small town.[49] The goal is to move away from subdivisions to the more personal scale of a walking small town.[50] These neotraditional towns, designed with a nineteenth-century flavor and scale, include Seaside on the Florida Panhandle and Mashpee on Cape Cod. An excellent example of one of the traditionalist communities designed to combat sprawl and produce a sense of community through the purposeful design of compact neighborhoods is the 352 acre community of Kentlands in Gaithersburg, Maryland. A more contemporary styled example is RiverPlace in downtown Portland, Oregon.

Roads in such communities are deliberately kept narrow to discourage auto usage, and sidewalks are encouraged. Homes in Seaside even are required to have front porches. Rather than the typical subdivision zoning that segregates housing from commercial activities, the neotraditional communities are designed to encourage a mixture of people and activities in order to create lively streets.[51] Neotraditional towns project a strong user-friendly mood. The goal of neotraditional communities is to provide an inviting, livable, and walkable public environment as

---

[49] For a full discussion of these ideas, see Philip Langdon, *A Better Place to Live: Reshaping the American Suburb,* University of Massachusetts Press, Amherst, 1994.

[50] Edward J. Blaely and David L. Ames, "Changing Places: American Planning Policy for the 1990s," *Journal of Urban Affairs,* **14:**433, 1992.

[51] Andres Duany and Elizabeth Plater-Zberk, "The Second Coming of the American Small Town," *Wilson Quarterly,* Winter, 1992, pp. 19–48.

Kentland, in Gaithersburg, Maryland, successfully applies traditional neighborhood concepts to create a highly livable community. (John Humble/Newsweek.)

well as secure private-home environments. As such, the neotraditionalists derive inspiration from the ideas of Jane Jacobs (see pp. 350–352 of this chapter). Neotraditionalists are strongly opposed to today's pattern of segregating housing and shopping into separate pods. They also oppose curvilinear streets, which discourage walking, and favor feeding all of a subdivision's traffic into an access road.

Critics question whether suburbanites are willing to give up their wide lots for higher-density small towns. There is also the question of whether businesses in the downtown sections of neotraditional towns can compete economically with the Wal-Mart down the road. Nineteenth-century small-town residents had to shop locally. They couldn't hop in the car. The critics point out that Seaside for all its charm is still more of a weekend retreat than a full-time community. Underlying all this is the question of how much community design can affect behavior.

PART FIVE

WORLDWIDE
URBANIZATION

CHAPTER
15
LESS-DEVELOPED COUNTRIES

*He that will not apply new remedies must expect new evils;
for time is the greatest innovator.*

Sir Francis Bacon

THE URBAN EXPLOSION

While city growth in developed countries is virtually stagnant, large cities in less-developed countries (LDCs) are growing by a million people a week. As the century turns, there will be twice as many people in LDC cities as in the cities of developed nations. Each year the world's population increases by 86 million persons, and 90 percent of these newcomers to the globe are born in LDCs. Three-quarters of this growth is concentrated in cities in LDCs. Within a decade over half the world's population will be living in urban places. According to the World Bank a quarter of the world's urban population lives in poverty, and urban shantytowns are doubling in size every five to seven years.

According to United Nations' estimates, every year some 7.8 million children worldwide die from what they eat, drink, and breathe, but even meeting basic health needs is a challenge in LDCs, where only 40 percent of all dwellings are connected to sewers. For those that are connected to sewers over 90 percent of the sewage and wastewater is untreated. Rapid economic development is not an unmixed blessing. Air pollution with heavy lead and other contaminants is a major concern in cities such as Bangkok where autos have no emission controls and are stalled in traffic an average of 44 days a year. Mexico City schoolchildren are not allowed outside during much of the winter due to some of the most polluted air on the globe. When this author was in Taiwan on a Senior Fulbright grant in 1992, he lived on a college campus outside of the city of Taichung, but due to pollution the city could rarely even be seen from the campus.

As recently as 1950, only two cities in developing countries had populations of over 5 million. Today twenty-six cities have over 10 million population, and twenty-one of these mega-cities are in LDCs. Bombay, for example, is adding 500,000 people a year and will have 18 million by 2000. What this means is that the so-called population explosion is in actuality an urban population explosion. By the year 2000, the United Nations projects there will be 284 LDC cities of a million or more.[1] How many of us could name more than a score or two of these cities?

Thus, by the turn of the century, not only will the world for the first time in history be more urban than rural, but most of the growth will be in third world mega-cities.[2] Mexico City, which reached 1 million population only in 1930, is projected to have 26 million people by 2000. And it will not be alone. Using low estimates, Sao Paulo is projected at 24 million, Calcutta may reach 16–17 million, and Seoul and Jakarta are expected to reach 14 million each. To ignore or give only glancing attention to these major urban developments would be the height of ethnocentrism.

It is difficult to keep up either mentally or emotionally with the spectacular nature of these changes, and while this text devotes far more attention than others do to third world urban changes, we obviously cannot look at every city. What this and the following chapters can do is give the reader some feeling and understanding of the patterns of urban change.

[1] United Nations Population Division, "IDCP Programme of Action," United Nations, New York, 1994.
[2] J. John Palen, *Cities and the Future: The Urban Explosion,* United Nations Fund for Population Activities Report, New York, 1985.

Plan of Organization

The chapters in Part Five, because of limited space, necessarily focus on what is common to third world cities rather than on their unique differences. Readers should keep in mind, though, that particular cities may differ from the general pattern.

Common or Divergent Paths?

Large-scale urbanization in Europe and North America was a process that spanned more than a century and involved massive economic and social change. Industrialization spurred in-migration from rural hinterlands. As documented in Chapter 2, Emergence of Cities, urban places in Europe and America, even with their high death rates, were able to grow only because of massive inflows of rural population. The question is whether LDCs are converging on the western pattern or whether they are following a different path. The ecology-modernization approach implies that there is a general pattern and LDC cities will in time follow the western model. As Chapter 5, Urban Political Economy, indicates, those taking a neo-Marxist political economy approach often see differences among cities reflecting differences between capitalist and socialist economic systems.[3] A world-systems perspective sees LDCs remaining in a "dependent" or "peripheral" position as suppliers of raw material and labor to the developed capitalist states.[4] Each of these positions involves ideological assumptions.

Contemporary urbanization in less-developed countries differs from that of North America and western Europe in several respects. First, the *extent—and rapidity*—of the urban increase in LDCs is outpacing anything that occurred in the west. Between 1920 and 1980 the population in LDC cities of over 1 million increased fiftyfold. While western cities grew rapidly during the nineteenth and even the twentieth centuries, the absolute numbers of urbanites were not anywhere as large as the numbers found today in Cairo, Manila, or Sao Paulo.

The pace of change also has accelerated. As Table 15-1 indicates, New York and London were the two largest cities in 1950. It took them each nearly 150 years to reach 8 million residents. By contrast, the two largest cities in 2000, Mexico City and Sao Paulo, will each add 8 million people to their populations in the next fifteen years.[5]

Second, industrialization, rather than providing a spur for urbanization, often trails *behind* the rate of urban growth. In the nineteenth century the western industrializing cities needed workers. Often the jobs were low-paying, physically exhausting, and emotionally unsatisfying, but they were available. The cities of the industrial revolution were magnets drawing peasants off the land. Today by contrast, people flood into the cities in spite of high urban unemployment because of a push from overpopulated rural areas. Without employment in rural areas, migration

[3] Michael Timberlake (ed.), *Urbanization in the World-Economy*, Academic Press, New York, 1985. For an ecological overview and critique of political economy models, see John D. Kasarda and Edward M. Crenshaw, "Third World Urbanization: Dimensions, Theories, Determinants," *Annual Review of Sociology*, **17**:467–501, 1991.

[4] Immanuel Wallerstein, *The Modern World System*, vols. 1–3, Academic Press, New York, 1979, 1980, 1989.

[5] W. Parker Frisbie and John D. Kasarda, "Spatial Processes," in Neil J. Smelser (ed.), *Handbook of Modern Sociology*, Sage, Beverly Hills, Calif., 1988, p. 654.

TABLE 15-1
Ten Largest Cities in the World, 1950, 1985, 2000

Population in 1950 (in millions)		Population in 1985 (in millions)		Population in 2000 (in millions)	
1. New York–N.E. New Jersey	12.3	1. Mexico City	18.1	1. Mexico City	26.3
2. London	10.4	2. Tokyo-Yokohama	17.2	2. Sao Paulo	24.0
3. Rhine-Ruhr	6.9	3. Sao Paulo	15.9	3. Tokyo-Yokohama	17.1
4. Tokyo-Yokohama	6.7	4. New York–N.E. New Jersey	15.3	4. Calcutta	16.6
5. Shanghai	5.8	5. Shanghai	11.8	5. Greater Bombay	16.0
6. Paris	5.5	6. Calcutta	11.0	6. New York–N.E. New Jersey	15.5
7. Greater Buenos Aires	5.3	7. Greater Buenos Aires	10.9	7. Seoul	13.5
8. Chicago–N.W. Indiana	4.9	8. Rio de Janeiro	10.4	8. Shanghai	13.5
9. Moscow	4.8	9. Seoul	10.2	9. Rio de Janeiro	13.3
10. Calcutta	4.6	10. Greater Bombay	10.1	10. Delhi	13.3

Source: United Nations, Department of International Economic and Social Affairs, 1985.

becomes the only mechanism to relieve rural population pressures. In India today, for example, there is only one acre of arable land for each peasant farmer. With 15 million Indians being added each year it is almost inevitable that surplus population gravitates toward the cities.

Third, cities in LDCs differ from the western model in having continued high rates of growth by *natural increase* (births) as well as in-migration. Until a century or so ago, western cities lost more inhabitants through disease and illness than they gained through births. By contrast, rural-to-urban migration accounted for a little over half of third world city growth between 1975 and 1995. Even if in-migration ceased tomorrow, LDC cities would continue to grow. Modern public health and vaccination programs mean that contemporary third world cities are not the "graveyards of countrymen" as developing western cities were. Cities in developing countries may appear unhealthful by contemporary western standards, but they are, nonetheless, comparatively healthy places. Certainly public health programs mean they are often more healthful than the rural alternatives. The consequence often is dramatic urban growth.

Fourth, LDC cities of today are part of the *legacy of colonialism*. While colonialism is now history, poorer LDCs remain beholden to trading patterns that exploit their natural resources. As is detailed in the next chapters, LDC cities were often founded not as a consequence of internal economic development but rather because of the colonial powers' need for trade and administrative centers. Their industrial and economic bases, or lack of same (see Chapter 16), thus reflect colonial patterns of economic exploitation.

LDC INCREASES

Amount of Growth

By the year 2000 almost two-thirds of the world's urban population of 3.1 billion will live in developing countries. The United Nations estimates that two-thirds of the world's cities of over 5 million will be in less-developed regions. The impact of this urban explosion on cities of the developing world is difficult to overexaggerate. As previously noted, some cities in less-developed countries already top 10 million; with current growth rates, they will double their population in a decade (London or Tokyo, by contrast, will grow less than 1 percent). While each city is in some ways unique, the cities generally share problems of unemployment, poverty, crowding in slums and squatter settlements, inadequate transportation systems, and heavy pollution.

Recently, publicity has been given to the fact that the worldwide rate of population increase has begun to show declines. Today's growth rate of 1.8 percent may continue to fall. This, however, emphatically does not mean that world population will be declining, since today's growth rates are being applied to a base population of 5.7 billion. This translates into 235,000 persons being added to the world's population each day; and even with declines in fertility a billion people will be added during the 1990s. The United Nations as of 1994 projected that the world population twenty years hence would be between 7.2 and 7.9 billion people.[6] The difference between these two projections may not seem like much until you realize the difference is the size of the entire population of Africa today.

Problems of Growth

Increases of this magnitude are certain to create almost unbearable pressures for food, better living conditions, more education, and more employment. Total fertility rates, that is, the number of children born per woman, range from a low of 1.3 children per woman in Italy to a high of 8.3 children per woman in Rwanda. Zero population growth may be a reality in Europe, Japan, and the European heritage populations of the United States and Canada; but it is still only a slogan in the developing world, where the combined population of the various countries is currently increasing by 86 million a year. This means an additional 86 million persons a year who must be fed, clothed, housed, and otherwise provided for before the developing countries can even begin to improve the quality of life for those already present.

Much of the present population explosion, with yearly national population increases of 2.5 and even 3.5 percent (2 percent doubles a population in only thirty-five years; 3.5 percent, in less than twenty years), can be traced to the importation of modern sanitation, public health services, and medicine. Following World War II, death rates in LDCs were reduced drastically and at little cost, but were often only slowly accompanied by other changes in the social or economic fabric of the

---

[6] United Nations Population Division.

societies. Malaria, for example, was largely eradicated in Sri Lanka (Ceylon) by the decision of a handful of officials in government ministries to spray DDT from airplanes. This achieved a decline in the death rates of 40 percent in one year—a decline that took half a century in the west. The result was a population explosion. In contrast to reducing death rates, the decision to restrict the number of births must be made by millions of individual couples. Even when a society favors small families, there is a time lag in implementation.

The resulting population increases greatly exacerbate already serious problems, including problems of economic development. Funds that should be devoted to economic development are instead consumed in providing minimal subsistence and service to an ever-increasing number of people. Rather than investing capital, some developing nations are forced to spend it in order to meet, even marginally, the needs of their growing populations. Less-developed countries have 35 to 50 percent of their population under age fifteen, as contrasted with a maximum of 25 percent in the industrialized countries. The consequence is that the cities of LDCs are filled with dependent children and young people who must be fed, clothed, housed, educated, and otherwise provided for. The problem is not just that there are more people, but that LDCs have an age structure in which much of the population consists of dependents who have yet to make any contribution to the economic well-being of their families or nation.

In addition to the economic demands put on developing countries by new mouths to feed, there are also increasing demands from those already present. This "revolution of rising expectations" occurs because increasing numbers of people in developing countries—and particularly in the cities—became aware that their condition of poverty is not the immutable natural order of life everywhere. Developments in communication technology—radio and television—have exposed the urban underclasses to the existence of higher standards of living. The urban populations, with their greater exposure to alternatives and their greater awareness of nontraditional ways of life, have expectations for themselves and their children; and governments that ignore these expectations do so at their own risk.

RICH COUNTRIES AND POOR COUNTRIES: SOME DEFINITIONS AND EXPLANATIONS

Less-developed countries vary in their rates of development, but they all suffer in varying degrees from common problems such as low industrial output, low rates of savings, inadequate housing, poor roads and communication, a high proportion of the labor force engaged in agriculture, insufficient medical services, inadequate school systems, high rates of illiteracy, poor diets, and sometimes malnutrition. The developing countries contain two out of three of the world's people, but they account for only one-sixth of the world's income, one-third of the food production, and one-tenth of the industrial output.

It is thus quite clear that the term "developing country" is a euphemism. Various other terms, such as "modernizing country" and "third world country," have been used, and they sometimes reflect ideological differences, but essentially they are all polite ways of saying "poor country." The current preferred term is "less-developed countries," or LDCs. While the differences between the developed and the underdeveloped countries is usually phrased less harshly, the major distinction is that one category includes the "haves" and the other the "have-nots."

This rich-poor classification cuts across conflicting ideological systems and geographical regions. Developed nations, whether in Europe, Asia, or the western hemisphere, all have urban-industrial economies. Less-developed countries are so named because of their relationship to the economic power of the developed countries, which are used as the standard of comparison. "Development" is thus a relative rather than an absolute state. Newly developing countries are underdeveloped in the context of an economic comparison with Europe, the United States, or Japan. Whether the indigenous economic organization of a developing country is simple or complex—and in many cases it is extremely complex—it is invariably not a modern industrialized urban economy.

Economically, the poorest LDCs of Asia, Africa, and Latin America find themselves locked into a system where prices for the raw products they produce remain relatively stable while the cost of imported goods skyrockets. Such nations are seeking to achieve industrial development while the marketplace in which they must operate is largely controlled by the developed nations.

Those taking a world-systems approach argue that underdevelopment of third world countries, then, is due not to traditionalism or internal problems, but to a worldwide system of structural dependency and unequal exchange. Data indicate that for many developing nations the status of "underdevelopment" may become relatively permanent; while the poorest nations are not getting poorer—as a whole—the rich nations are certainly getting richer.

On the other hand, data now show that LDC status is not necessarily permanent since some former LDC nations are rapidly developing economically. The 1980s and 1990s saw some LDCs such as Indonesia make major strides. A new category, "newly industrialized country" (NIC), refers to countries that already have made major movement toward economic development. Today many of the NICs are in Asia, with countries such as Singapore, Taiwan, Korea, Malaysia, Thailand, and Indonesia in this category. Newly industrialized countries invariably show not only economic development but also sharply declining birthrates. All less-developed countries have high birthrates, while all developed countries have low birthrates.

CHARACTERISTICS OF POORER THIRD WORLD CITIES

Youthful Age Structure

While each city, like each person, is distinct and in some ways unique, certain characteristics are more or less general to cities of the developing world. The first of these is a youthful population age structure. An almost certain comment of tourists upon first encountering third world cities is that "children and young people are everywhere." This is not an illusion but an observation of demographic reality. It is estimated that as of 1995, some 35 percent of the inhabitants of LDCs were under fifteen years of age—this compared with 20 percent under age fifteen in economically developed nations.[7]

Thus, compared with the developed nations, the poorer countries have age structures that are heavily loaded with dependent young people. This dependency is particularly so in cities, where often almost half of all city residents are youngsters. LDC cities, thus, not only have more people vis-à-vis resources than do the richer cities, but, as noted earlier, also have far more persons who are dependent—young people who have yet to make any contribution to the cities' economies or well-being. One does not have to be an expert to figure out that these large numbers of dependent young are a heavy drain on limited resources. Even if more schools are built and new jobs created, there is no gain if these advances merely keep pace with the growth of young people.

Differences by region underline the problem: Africa has 45 percent of its population under the age of fifteen, and Asia has 33 percent. By comparison, the percentage of dependent young is at most only half as high in developed nations. Western Europe has only 20 percent of its population under the age of fifteen.[8] For North America the figure is 22 percent.

The consequence of these differences is that the cities of LDCs are getting hit twice. First, they have less resources. Second, the lower resource base must be stretched to cover double the proportion of young dependents. Of course, it goes without saying that this leaves precious little for either personal or national investment purposes. The old saying that "the poor get children" is definitely the case for LDCs.

Employment

Of all the common problems faced by the cities in developing countries, the problem of providing employment is, next to that of population growth, the most severe. According to the United Nations, LDC nations already have 500 million unemployed or underemployed workers. Moreover, some 30 million new workers enter the job market every year. This situation is quite different from that faced by the economically advanced western countries during their earlier periods of urban-industrial expansion. In the era of western industrialization during the nineteenth century, farmers and peasants were drawn to the city because of the economic opportunities it offered. Entry-level jobs, both in manufacturing and in services, were generally available; and there was a solid demand for unskilled, if low-paid, workers. This was true both in Europe and in North America.

The experience of the developing countries has been quite different. There is no need today for armies of industrial workers. Instead of being labor-intensive, contemporary industrial and postindustrial economies depend on capital and technology.

[7] "1995 World Population Data Sheet," Population Reference Bureau, Washington, D.C., 1995.
[8] Ibid.

Thus in LDCs workers flood into the cities not because of the availability of jobs but because of the lack of opportunity in the rural areas and small villages. Stagnating rural economies simply cannot absorb more workers. For years it has been recognized that high agricultural density and plantation-type agriculture spur urbanization regardless of the rate of economic development.[9] The consequence is "subsistence urbanization," in which the ordinary citizen has only the bare necessities for urban survival. Urban unemployment rates commonly exceed one-quarter of the work force.

Despite these problems, cities offer more economic hope than rural areas. Cities also offer access to health facilities and schools. For women, the city can also provide some relief from traditional patterns of male domination. Cities also have public amusements and more consumer goods. In-migration may bring more costs than benefits to the city; but for the migrant, the benefits of moving to the city far outweigh those of staying in the countryside.

However, within the cities public works do not necessarily benefit those most in need. Public funds may be invested in projects such as airports or multilane highways for the automobiles of the rich and universities for their offspring, while slums still have mud roads and the poor receive only minimal schooling.

Informal-Sector Economy

Much of the economic activity in less-developed countries does not take place in formal business settings. A third to perhaps half of all urban workers in less-developed countries are employed in the informal sector of the economy.[10] The informal sector comprises small enterprises without access to credit, banks, or formally trained personnel.[11] Often these are family-run businesses. They may involve everything from small manufacturers to street-stall vendors. The informal sector commonly provides most of the consumable food products and much of the services, trade, transportation, and construction.[12] Informal-sector businesses are usually small and operate on minimal capital. The old picture was of the marginality of informal businesses and workers, but more recent evidence indicates that the informal sector is quite productive. It is also very mixed. Street vendors are indeed very poor, but some informal-sector economic activities are a major source of entrepreneurial activity, and many of these activities pay as well as formal-sector activities. However, informal-sector businesses largely operate outside the law in that they are not registered and rarely pay taxes.[13] In fact, the less

[9] Glenn Firebaugh, "Structural Determinants of Urbanization in Asia and Latin America, 1950–1970," *American Sociological Review,* **44:**195–215, April, 1979.

[10] S. V. Sethuraman, *The Urban Informal Sector in Developing Countries: Employment, Poverty and Environment,* International Labour Organization, Geneva, 1981.

[11] Warwick Armstrong and T. G. McGee, *Theatres of Accumulation: Studies in Asian and Latin American Urbanization,* Methuen, London, 1985; and Lisa Peattie, "An Idea of a Good Currency and How It Grew: The Informal Sector," *World Development,* **15:**851–860, 1987.

[12] S. V. Sethuraman, "The Informal Urban Sector in Developing Countries: Some Policy Implications," in Alfred de Souza (ed.), *The Indian City,* South Asia Books, New Delhi, India, 1978, pp. 1–15; and Johannes F. Linn, *Cities in the Developing World,* World Book Publications, Oxford University Press, New York. 1983. For one of the most famous studies of informal-sector street vendors, see Lea Jellinek, "The Life of a Jakarta Street Trader," in Janet Abu-Lughod and Richard Hay (eds.), *Third World Urbanization,* Maaroufa Press, Chicago, 1977, pp. 244–256.

[13] For a good textbook-oriented overview of the informal sector, see Ivan Light, *Cities in World Perspective,* Macmillan, New York, 1983, pp.367–378.

the business depends on formal sources of working capital such as banks, and the less it complies with government regulations and tax codes, the more "informal" the business.[14] Government statistics on economic activity in third world countries often exclude those not in the wage economy, and thus grossly understate actual economic activity. Unemployment figures that do not count the informal economy also are likely to be in error.

Squatter Settlements

The population growth of virtually all cities in LDCs has outrun the capacity of municipalities to house them. Much of the growing population is housed in illegal subdivisions filled with non-standard poor-quality housing. These squatter settlements house one-third of the entire urban population in most LDC nations. The present squatter population of Mexico City exceeds 4 million, and squatters in both Seoul and Calcutta number over 2 million. With shantytowns mushrooming at 15 percent a year (doubling their size in six years), the squatter population of poorer cities is certain to increase.[15]

---

[14] S. Kannappan, "Urban Employment and the Labor Market in Developing Countries," *Economic Development and Cultural Change,* **33:**699–730, 1985.
[15] Estimate by the United Nations.

Shantytown dwellers living on the hills around Caracas, Venezuela, at least have a magnificent view of the city. (UPI/Bettmann.)

Squatter and peripheral settlements are called *barriedas, favelas, bustees, kampongs,* or *bidonvilles* in various countries; but everywhere their function is the same—to house those who have the least resources and nowhere else to go. In the squatter settlements, shanties and shacks initially are built in random fashion out of whatever refuse material the builder can salvage. Old packing crates, loose lumber, and odd pieces of metal are somehow patched together to provide a shelter. Since shantytowns almost by definition are "illegally" occupying the land on which they are built, they cannot demand city services. Streets, police, fire protection, and—most important—sanitary services are usually nonexistent. Water almost always has to be carried from the nearest public tap. Schools are rare. Electricity is the most commonly found utility, since wires can easily be strung from shack to shack.

Public services such as running water and schools are first provided to those with economic clout. Shanty dwellers in Lima, for instance, pay ten times as much for water carried on private trucks as the middle class pays for plumbing in its homes. Health problems are exacerbated by the crowding, by the lack of proper disposal for sewage and refuse, and by the fact that the settlements are frequently built on the least desirable terrain, such as city dumps, marshlands, or hillsides. However, as we will discuss in Chapter 18, Urbanization in Latin America, many of these squatter settlements are not places of defeat, but organized if poor communities.

Attempts by the government to remove squatters are invariably unsuccessful: If one slum is destroyed, another is built overnight with the refuse from the earlier settlement. When no other city housing is available, there is little alternative. As one authority confesses, "We have learned that we cannot hope to provide 'standard' housing for all, or even most of the urban poor in the developing countries in this century, almost no matter how one defines 'standard.'"[16]

Demolishing settlements and relocating the urban poor in new fringe settlements is often disastrous for the poor. It often impoverishes families who not only lose what they have invested in the demolished squatter shack, but also are faced with increased transportation costs. Women in particular tend to become unemployed because of the increased distance to their traditional places of work. Most countries thus have stopped bulldozing squatter settlements. One exception is Sudan, where in 1992 the military government razed thirty-two shantytowns around Khartoum. The resettlement area chosen by the government is 25 miles from the capital, and had only a handful of hand-operated water pumps. Since there was no transport to the capital, those moved were essentially dumped to die without food or water in a closed camp. Even when countries better provide for outlying resettlement areas, they are rarely successful since for the very poor a location near work is much more important than the quality of shelter. The same was true of the nineteenth-century American poor, who crowded into tenements near central-city factories.

---

[16] Maurice Kilbridge, "Some Generalizations on Urbanization and Housing in Developing Countries," *Urban Planning, Policy Analysis, and Administration,* Policy Note P. 76-1, Harvard University Press, Cambridge, Mass., 1976, p. 13.

Primate Cities

A characteristic common to most developing countries is the so-called primate city. A primate city is a principal city overwhelmingly large in comparison with all other cities in the country. In many countries, the primate city is frequently the only city of note.[17] Commonly, within developing countries there is no hierarchy of cities of various sizes such as that found in developed nations. Ethiopia, for example, is 95 percent rural and has few towns; but its capital city, Addis Ababa, has over 1.5 million inhabitants. Bangkok, with approximately 7 million people, is the most extreme case. Twenty years ago, Bangkok had half its current population.[18] Today, Bangkok is over thirty times larger than Thailand's second largest city, Chang Mai.

Most primate cities owe their origin and development to European colonialism. Cities such as Accra, Nairobi, Saigon, Hanoi, Singapore, and Hong Kong do not have long histories as urban places but rather were created consciously by colonial powers in order to establish bases from which they could exercise administrative and commercial control. They were established as little "Europes-in-Asia" or "Europes-in-Africa." Thus, they were usually located along the coasts in order to facilitate communication with, and transportation of raw material to, the mother country. From the very first, the orientation of the primate city was toward other cities in the developed countries rather than toward its own hinterland, and this pattern of commerce and culture coming from the outside has largely endured to this day. Government elites, particularly in Africa and Asia, may also be more oriented to the outside than to their own hinterland or "bush."

The concentration of population and economic activity in primate cities presents some typical features throughout the developing world:

1. In the earlier stages, the economies of such cities were primarily export-oriented, and the cities also specialized in political and administrative activities. Today, manufacturing and services are the primary economic activities.
2. Economic advantages result from the concentration of industry. Thus, income from peripheral areas finds its way to the metropolitan area. The higher rate of return attracts more capital; and this in turn leads to more enterprises, particularly services.
3. The concentration of industrial activities—and above all the accompanying services—increases employment. Skilled workers are attracted from peripheral locations. Thus, the city represents an advantage in terms of quality as well as quantity.
4. Concentration of population and economic activities goes hand in hand with the centralization of administrative activity. The decision-making power of the primate city increases, while that of outlying cities and towns decreases. The center thus receives the lion's share of the available investment funds.
5. The basic infrastructure of the nation is heavily determined by the requirements of the major city. This in turn encourages further concentration.[19]

[17] Mark Jefferson, "The Law of the Primate Cities," *Geography Review,* **29:**226–232, April, 1939.
[18] Ralph Thomlinson, "Bangkok: Beau Ideal of a Primate City," *Population Review,* **16:**32–38, January–December, 1972.
[19] Based on information in "Some Regional Development Problems in Latin America Linked to Metropolitanization," *Economic Bulletin for Latin America,* United Nations, New York, **17:**58–62, 1972.

The rate of growth of large LDC primate cities invariably outpaces that of the country as a whole. The largest city grows the fastest. This is often in spite of government policies to encourage more regional growth. The cities of Mexico City, Bogotá, and Santiago continue to grow faster than their national populations even though the governments of Mexico, Colombia, and Chile all seek a more balanced growth. Latin America has one-fifth (21 percent) of its urban population in very large cities of over 5 million persons.

Primate cities dominate the rest of the nation economically, educationally, politically, and socially. They control the lion's share of the manufacturing, administrative, investment, and service activities of the country. Government, education, and commerce all are concentrated in the primate city, and skilled workers are attracted from outlying regions. The city thus has a qualitative as well as a quantitative advantage. Growth and concentration, as noted above, lead to further concentration of resources, which, in turn, leads to greater growth. The decision-making power of the city increases while that of outlying towns decreases. Urban-bred civil servants, teachers, and employees are, perhaps understandably, most reluctant to give up the activity and excitement of city life for the underdevelopment of the more backward hinterland.

However, given the above, it does not necessarily follow that such places are parasitic on the countryside. In fact primate cities contribute more than their share to national economies. Mexico City provides a third of Mexico's gross national product. Similarly, Bangkok holds a tenth of Thailand's population, but provides 86 percent of the gross national product.[20] While regional balance is a desirable goal of planners, many smaller developing nations simply cannot support more than one major city at this point. In time, intermediate-sized cities may emerge, but meanwhile there frequently is no realistic alternative to the primate city.

Whatever their faults, primate cities grew in part because the residents were—and still are—open to economic and social change. Most of the movements for independence were nurtured in the cities, and those who currently set policy and govern are invariably urban dwellers. The city remains an incubator of change.

Overurbanization

Closely related to the concept of primate cities is the concept of overurbanization. The term "overurbanization" is in many ways a loaded one insofar as it suggests that there is too large a proportion of the nation's population residing in cities for the nation's level of economic development. Overurbanization is defined as "a level of urbanization higher than that which can 'normally' be attained given the level of industrialization."[21] Given the level of national economic development, the term suggests there are too many urban residents for the available jobs, housing, schooling, and other services. Egypt, for instance, is far more urbanized than its degree of economic development would lead one to expect: Indeed, it is more urbanized than

---

[20] Kasarda and Crenshaw, "Third World Urbanization," p. 473.
[21] Manuel Castells, *The Urban Question,* Alan Sheridan (trans.), MIT Press, Cambridge, Mass., 1977, pp. 41–43.

Traffic in Bangkok, Thailand, has the distinction of being considered by many to be the worst in the world. Without any pollution controls, vehicle fumes cloud the air. (Koji Sasahara/AP/Wide World Photos.)

France or Sweden, both industrial nations. Some urbanists, for example, refer to Egypt with 45 percent of its population in cities as being overurbanized.

While there has been some attempt to keep the term "overurbanization" free of any connotation of values, the concept invariably has negative connotations: It suggests that overurbanization is both artificial and harmful to economic growth. However, the whole picture is not as glum as the term suggests, for it has been true for decades that the productivity of the rural in-migrants is higher in the city than in the rural areas, and per capita incomes of rural immigrants to cities are almost universally higher than in rural areas.[22] If the concept of overurbanization is meant to suggest the undesirability of rapid urbanization in developing countries,

---

[22] N. V. Sovani, "The Analysis of Over-Urbanization," *Economic Development and Cultural Change,* **12:**113–122, January, 1964.

the argument is difficult to prove. Certainly the data do not support the belief that rapid urbanization necessarily slows or impedes economic development.

It can be argued that the rapid growth of cities is a positive sign of the social and economic development of an area.[23] The city not only is the first area to reflect change, but also is a source of change. City growth is correlated with the change from agriculturalism to industrialism, with economic rationality, with lower birthrates and death rates, with increased literacy and education—in short, with the whole process of modernization. Insofar as urbanization is associated with the development of a modernized mode of life, the problem in much of the developing world, one could argue, is not overurbanization but underurbanization. Many argue that, on balance, the positive aspects of urban growth continue to outweigh the negative. For example, Lagos provides 50 percent of Nigeria's manufacturing.[24]

Some see the above arguments as an urban bias. It has been argued, for example, that a developed agricultural sector is a necessary precondition for industrialization.[25] It has also been argued that the burden of new urban dwellers on existing urban infrastructures far outweighs the cost of absorbing new persons in rural areas.[26] However, what is good for the nation and what is good for individual immigrants may differ. For the newcomer, life may be difficult in the city, but is almost always better than life in the countryside. Thus peasants invariably vote with their feet for urban life. In the city there is, at least, always hope of something better.

THE FUTURE

This chapter concludes with a number of observations regarding the most likely patterns to extend into the next century. The reader should keep in mind, though, that what follows are this author's views; the opinion of others may differ.

First, cities in the developing world are going to continue to grow, and to grow at a rapid rate. Growth will occur in spite of government policies to the contrary. For example, Jakarta was unsuccessful in becoming a "closed city." Between 1980 and 1986 the Indonesian government sent 2 million persons from Java to less populated islands, and an equal number migrated on their own. Nonetheless, massive Jakarta still continues to grow. India's new policies of directing growth to smaller places will be equally unsuccessful. Natural increase as well as in-migration will spur city growth.

Second, given such growth, squatter settlements, which currently hold one-third of the urban population, are unavoidable. Official disapproval will not make

---

[23] Not all scholars agree that overurbanization and primate cities are not a problem. See, for example, Anthony J. LaGreca, "Urbanization: A Worldwide Perspective," in Kent P. Schwirian (ed.), *Contemporary Topics in Urban Sociology,* General Learning Press, Morristown, N.J., 1977. For further discussion of the questions, see Kasarda and Crenshaw, "Third World Urbanization."

[24] For further information on specific cities, see Matteri Dogan and John D. Kasarda (eds.), *Mega-Cities: The Metropolis Era,* vol. 2, Sage, Beverly Hills, Calif., 1988.

[25] Michael Lipton, *Why Poor People Stay Poor: Urban Bias in World Development,* Harvard University Press, Cambridge, Mass., 1977.

[26] Joseph Gugler, "Overurbanization Reconsidered," *Economic Development and Cultural Change,* **31:**173--189, October, 1982.

them go away. Thus, it is best to accept and legalize them and provide at least minimal community services. Squatter settlements are going to be a part of LDC cities for the indefinite future. Increasingly the response is to support self-help housing.

Third, urban infrastructure will inevitably remain inadequate. For example, attempts to provide "standard housing" are probably doomed to failure, though countries experiencing new wealth (as from oil), or highly organized states such as Singapore, will be an exception. Western-style industrialization will lag behind population growth and thus will not provide necessary urban jobs. A secondary informal labor market and high unemployment will remain a fact of life.

Fourth, the factors just noted suggest that political instability may be a serious problem in some countries. Rising expectations, widespread needs, and the availability of mass media will enable charismatic leaders to exploit anger and frustrations. Throughout LDCs, unprecedented urban growth and urban industrialization are transforming traditional societies, and are upsetting traditional attitudes, beliefs, customs, and behaviors. Scholars and politicians can debate whether these changes are for the better, but it is certain that urban-industrial growth means change—a great deal of change.

The whole city is arranged in squares just like a chessboard, and disposed in a manner so perfect and masterly that it is impossible to give a description that should do it justice.

Marco Polo, writing on Beijing

ASIAN CITIES

Of all the world's regions, it is Asia about which one must be most careful when attempting to make generalizations. Patterns of urbanization in China, Japan, India, and southeast Asia all have different historical roots and have developed in dissimilar cultures. These areas do, of course, have some things in common; but generalizations must be applied with some care to individual cities.

What can be said is that Asia has a great tradition of city life and numerous cities whose histories go back many centuries. In fact, until 200 years ago Asia contained more city dwellers than the rest of the world combined.[1] And if present demographic trends continue, by the year 2000 Asia will again have more city dwellers than any other continent. Asia's population is projected to jump 40 percent to 3.64 billion by the century's end. By that time Asia will contain 58 percent of the world's population. And of this number, perhaps half will reside in urban areas. Already, Asia has more large cities and a larger number of people—but not a larger *percentage* of people—in cities than either Europe or America.

Despite this, the majority of Asia's population still consists of village-based agrarians; only a minority live in true urban places. Overall, some 33 percent of the population of Asia is urban.[2] This low level of overall urbanization places Asia just above Africa in the percentage of the population that is urbanized. However, while Asia overall is still predominantly rural, it has many of the world's largest cities. Tokyo has between 9 million and 23 million people, depending upon whether one uses the most restrictive definition of the historic twenty-three wards of the city or the broad definition of the Tokyo agglomeration. The Asian cities of Shanghai, Beijing (Peking), Calcutta, and Bombay also number among the world's largest. (See Figure 16-1.)

It has been suggested that less-developed Asian nations are in the position of being "overurbanized" while at the same time their momentum of urbanization is increasing. "Overurbanization," however as suggested in Chapter 15, Less-Developed Countries is a loaded term.

Indigenous Cities

Asian cities other than those founded and developed by westerners display a spatial organization having much in common with the preindustrial city (discussed in Chapter 2, Emergence of Cities). Indigenous Asian cities of the past were predominantly political and cultural centers and only secondarily economic centers. The function of these traditional capital cities was to serve as a symbol of the authority, legitimacy, and power of the national government. Administrative functions were everywhere more important than commercial or industrial functions.

Such cities were located inland, near the centers of their empires, except in Japan and parts of southeast Asia, where this was not practical. Such inland cities were centers physically as well as socially and were also far safer from attack than coastal cities. Beijing, Old Delhi, and Ankor are classic examples: They served as

[1] Rhoads Murphey, "Urbanization in Asia," *Ekistics,* 21:8, January, 1966.
[2] "1995 World Population Data Sheet," Population Reference Bureau, Washington, D.C., 1995.

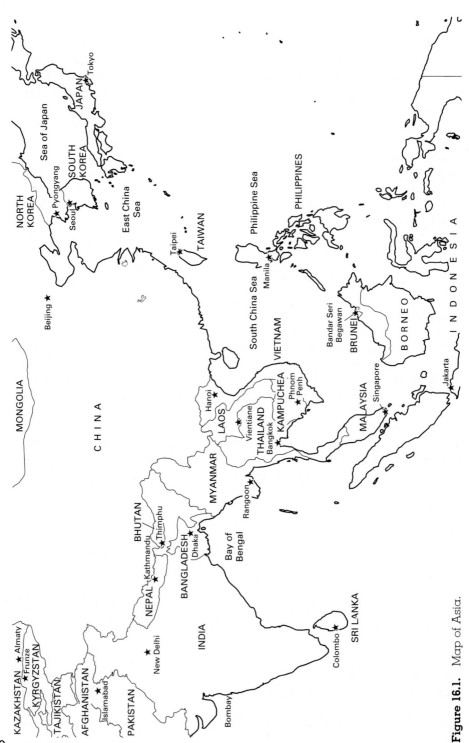

Figure 16.1. Map of Asia.

symbols of legitimate authority and were planned with monumental architecture, such as temples and palaces, that would emphasize this role. Beijing is famous for its Forbidden City Palace, Old Delhi for its magnificent Red Fort, and Ankor, until their recent destruction, for its many fine temples. In China and sometimes in India the city was walled; in southeast Asia it usually was not; and in Japan walls rarely existed.

Colonial Cities

The history of western-type cities is quite different from that of indigenous cities. Western-type cities were imported to the east by Europeans seeking trade. These cities, in contrast to the traditional preindustrial cities, were primarily oriented toward exportation and commerce and thus were located along seacoasts in order to facilitate trade and communication with the mother country. Originally small trading sites, perhaps with a small fort for protection, these cities are now among the largest in the world. Hong Kong, Singapore, Shanghai, Calcutta, and Bombay all developed as foreign-dominated port cities.

INDIA

India is only 26 percent urban, but that accounts for 235 million city dwellers, more than the population of all but the most populous countries. India has a history of cities going back to 2,000 B.C., but the modern period began with European colonial rule during the eighteenth century.[3] The Indian colonial city was the location of the rich and powerful. As such, it not only reflected western organization and values, but also housed the upper-class "sahibs." Industrialization played only a limited role in the growth of Indian cities.[4] British "civil lines" contained civil administrative headquarters and the homes of the British in the Indian civil service, while "cantonments"—military reservations—graciously housed the British officers (the troops themselves fared far worse).

In contrast to the model typical in the United States, the military reservations occupied central land rather than being peripherally located. Much of the city of Poona, for instance, is still occupied by military cantonments, reflecting that city's heritage as a headquarters for the British and then the Indian army. Even within New Delhi, military bases continue to occupy much prime land. Attempts to persuade the military to move to outlying areas have been notably unsuccessful.

The spacious houses of the colonial city, graciously separated by large lawns and trees, to a lesser degree also reflect the nineteenth century's lack of knowledge about causes of disease. Malaria was thought to be caused by bad air *(mala aria),* and so the British constructed their residential areas with ample space for circulation of air between homes.

Old Delhi, with its stores and homes right on the edges of its always crowded streets and lanes, is a world apart from New Delhi, with its lawns and boulevards.

---

[3] Hans Nagpaul, "India's Giant Cities," in Mattei Dogan and John D. Kasarda (eds.), *The Metropolis Era,* vol. 1, Sage, Newbury Park, Calif., 1988, p. 253.
[4] Ibid., p. 254.

Density figures clearly document the difference between the old and new areas, varying from 13.2 persons per acre in New Delhi to 213.3 in Old Delhi.[5] The high figure for Old Delhi, moreover, is not for an area of apartment buildings but for an area of one- and two-story buildings. (In parts of Old Delhi the density rises to 600–700 persons per acre, while in Calcutta the average density is 45,000 people per square kilometer.)[6] Old Delhi is also a remarkably lively and interesting place. Its largely Muslim population successfully fought plans to raze some of the area and resettle its inhabitants elsewhere. It is important to keep in mind that even when indigenous cities lack modern amenities, this may be more than compensated for in the eyes of residents by the areas' vitality and activity.

In the following pages we will focus on India's two largest cities—the economically dominant city of Bombay and the more economically stagnant city of Calcutta. In reading the following text, keep in mind that India has been going through a dramatic transformation since it abandoned its controlled economy for free markets in 1992. For example, prior to the 1990s, India had only one brand of TV, one brand of refrigerator, and no washing machines. Now there is considerable domestic and foreign competition. As of 1995, India was second only to the United States in exporting computer software.

Bombay

Bombay, India's traditional gateway to the west, is the nation's most dynamic city.[7] It is the heart of India's financial and industrial life and the center of the nation's large and colorful film industry. India's abandonment of its controlled economy for a more capitalistic system in the early 1990s dramatically accelerated Bombay's boom. Greater Bombay, with over 13 million residents, provides a full third of India's income taxes and 30 percent of India's gross national product. During the 1990s Bombay experienced a major building boom accompanied by skyrocketing land prices. The cost of prime commercial property in Bombay is four times that in the heart of New York City.[8]

Bombay has far more growth than it can handle and is showing signs of coming apart at the seams. The city is built on a peninsula and can extend only northward along a narrow corridor of two rail lines; but it contains more people than it can reasonably service—and the situation is getting worse. Bombay gains 10,000 residents every day, and few cities anywhere could keep up with such an influx. Most come seeking not better employment, but any employment. Sewage systems, housing, educational systems, and transportation systems are overwhelmed. For example, only one-fifth of the sewage now receives treatment, and the once-beautiful beaches along the bay are badly polluted. Likewise, the air is seriously polluted.

Many of the poor commute by rail from the suburbs on the once-excellent but now alarmingly overused and overextended commuter railroads. Not only are the

---

[5] Gerald Breese, *Urbanization in Newly Developing Countries,* Prentice-Hall, Englewood Cliffs, N.J., 1966, p. 62.

[6] Alfred de Souza (ed.), *The Indian City,* South Asia Books, Bombay, India, 1978, p. xiv.

[7] This section is partially based upon discussions with officials of the Bombay Metropolitan Region Development Authority and the City of Bombay Industrial Development Corporation. The opinions are, of course, the author's.

[8] Molly Moore, "Bombay's Boom Widens Gap between City's Richest and Poorest," *Washington Post,* Feb. 3, 1995, p. A21.

Entire families of "pavement people" living on the street are a
common feature of contemporary Bombay, India. (Gehangir
Gazdar/Woodfin Camp & Associates.)

rail cars full, but riders hang onto the exterior of windows and even crowd the
roofs. Not surprisingly, there are frequent accidents and approximately a dozen
deaths on the commuter lines each day.[9] Inside the city, overloaded derelict trucks,
crowded buses, cars, and bicycles all congest the jammed streets.

[9] *Poona Herald,* Feb. 23, 1979, p. 2.

Bombay's social fabric threatens to unravel. Greater Bombay has over 13 million residents and, like other great cities, has always had its wealthy and its poor. However, the gap between the super rich and the super poor is becoming more sharp and painful. The national average per capita income is $290 per year, and already some 5.5 million poor live in Bombay's 35 slum districts. Now even some of these are being taken from the poor and gentrified as neighborhoods for the new rich. The poor are being forced out. There is an immense and growing gap between the rich residing in the high-rise apartments lining the bay and the desperately poor "pathway dwellers" or "pavement people" who must sleep, eat, work, and raise their families while living in hovels on the edges of the roads. Perhaps a quarter million people sleep in the streets while another million people in Bombay live in ramshackle shanties.[10] For the middle class, Bombay is a city of opportunity; for Bombay's pavement people, the city streets are not paved with gold. Rather, they are the last refuge of a swelling tide of humanity.

To stress the point made earlier, Bombay is better off than many LDC cities. Bombay is also fortunate to have a trained civil service to administer the city. However, planners and city administrators openly concede they are losing the battle. Those who love the city admit sadly that it has physically declined over the last two decades. Given Bombay's population growth, overall urban decline is likely to continue. Equally important, the gap between the increasingly affluent upper and middle class and the desperately poor is growing greater.

Bombay is a city that could handle 5 million people reasonably well and, possibly, even cope with 8 million—but it has 13 million. And the 13 million are straining the municipality beyond its limits. Officials keep reassuring everyone that Bombay is not another Calcutta. The fear now increasingly expressed is whether, with a projected population of 16 million in under a decade, Bombay will still be able to make such a claim.

Calcutta

Calcutta, on the eastern side of India, is opposite from Bombay both geographically and emotionally. If Bombay is entrepreneurial, Calcutta is fatalistic. Until 1912 Calcutta was the proud seat of the British raj and a major financial center, landscaped with Victorian parks and monuments. Today, Calcutta's international image is one of decay, misery, and disaster; Calcutta's very name suggests the nadir of urban life. As of 1990 more than 70 percent of Calcutta's population lived below the poverty level, which is calculated at a low $8 a month.

Calcutta's overall metropolitan area population of 12 million is not growing as rapidly as that of Bombay or New Delhi, but neither is its aging industrial economy. Calcutta is losing its economic base. The once-active machine-shop industry, for example, is now too antiquated to compete with more advanced operations elsewhere in India. The important jute industry is also affected by a fluctuating market and obsolescence.[11] The Hooghly River running through the city received half of India's

---

[10] Nagpaul, "India's Giant Cities," p. 256.
[11] Harold Cubell, *Urban Development and Employment: The Prospects for Calcutta,* International Labour Office, Geneva, 1974.

Until 1911 Calcutta was the colonial capital of British India. (Mary Evans Picture Library.)

imports at the end of World War II; today the port is virtually closed with silt.[12] Nor has the national government been eager to invest its interest and funds in Calcutta.

The city also has problems with a unique land-tenure system that promotes nonmaintenance of slum properties. In Calcutta, virtually all slums are privately owned. In the *bustee,* or slum, one person owns the land, another then builds a hut upon it, and a third serves as a tenant, paying a monthly rent without any claim to either the land or the hut. Under this land-tenure system no one has any incentive to maintain the property. *Bustee* residents technically are not squatters but tenants. Since landlords can't legally raise the rent without the tenants' permission, buildings are literally left to rot until they tumble into the street.

Attempts by the Municipal Development Authority to upgrade the slums, and by the Municipal Corporation to maintain them (a major problem), are hampered by lack of funds. Meanwhile, people and the sacred cattle coexist in the *bustees.* As a form of recycling, cattle dung is collected by women and children and formed into circular patties that serve as fuel when dried.

Physically, there is no question that Calcutta is in an advanced state of decay. Forty percent of the city's buildings are more than eighty years old. Twenty percent of the buildings are classified as unsafe. Less than 10 percent of households have bathrooms and other basic amenities.[13] A series of development plans to arrest further deterioration have not been successful in reversing the damage done by

[12] "Gritty Calcutta a Fragile Balance of Wealth, Misery," Associated Press, Dec. 9, 1990.
[13] Nagpaul, "India's Giant Cities," p. 270.

decades of infrastructure collapse. For instance, drainage and sewer networks, all of which were laid in the central city prior to 1910, are in a serious state of disrepair. The last main sewer was laid in 1896. Currently, most of the sewer system is either inoperative or badly clogged. However, this is not the only problem, for were the sewers cleared, the old treatment plant would be overwhelmed. All this is of little consequence to the majority of residents living in *bustees* or in outlying squatter settlements since most of their dwellings are without private toilets or sewers.

Water, electricity, and telephone systems are also overloaded and in need of both major repairs and extensive upgrading. Power blackouts are a regular evening feature, and telephones often do not work. All Calcutta residents go without city-supplied electricity at least two hours every day. Water supplies are, however, getting better, with two-thirds of Calcutta's residents now having some access to piped drinking water—frequently from a street standpipe. In Calcutta physical labor often is substituted for technology. Some 40,000 barefoot rickshaw pullers still transport goods and people, earning under $1.00 a day. Calcutta is the last city on earth where people still pull rickshaws.

Within the city, groups occupy geographical wards largely on the basis of religion (Hindu or Muslim), caste, and ethnic region of origin.[14] Occupations are also ethnically segregated. For example, Bengalis traditionally prefer white-collar jobs and avoid heavy labor, while the rickshaw pullers are mostly Bihari. Taxi drivers used to be largely Punjabi but now also include Bengalis.

Three-quarters of the population of Calcutta is housed in crowded tenements and *bustee* huts.[15] These *bustee* dwellers are in some ways fortunate, for between half a million and 1 million pathway dwellers—no one knows the exact figure— have no housing of any type. They work, eat, sleep, breed, and die on the streets without the benefit of any shelter.

Nonetheless, Calcutta, even with all its social and physical problems, remains one of the world's more vital cities. It is the active center of Bengali poetry and theater, and most Bengalis would not trade the city's excitement for all the fine neighborhoods and homes of New Delhi.

Calcutta is also remarkably free of street crime. Residents fatalistically may accept power outages, poor housing, malaria, cholera, antiquated transportation, and constant strikes that close down municipal services, but they do not tolerate street crime against women. Any violator risks the wrath of the ever-present street crowds. Indian women in Calcutta can walk even at night with a degree of safety unknown in New Delhi, London, or New York. Physically the city is in decay; socially it retains a vigor of life and pride that other cities might envy.

Programs to alleviate Calcutta's problems have been proposed by the United Nations, the Ford Foundation, and the Indian government. Unfortunately, the aid that Calcutta has received has not always met its real needs. For example, to solve the city's transportation problems, the national government built Calcutta an ex-

---

[14] Nirmal Kumar Bose, *Calcutta 1964: A Social Survey,* Larani, Bombay, India, 1968. See also Brian J. Berry and John D. Kasarda, *Contemporary Urban Ecology,* Macmillan, New York, 1977, pp. 134–157.

[15] K. C. Sivaramakrishnan, "The Slum Improvement Program in Calcutta: The Role of the CMDA," in de Souza (ed.), *The Indian City,* p. 134.

pensive subway system. The new system is in a city where all buses are ancient and constantly in disrepair, where into the 1980s the last new streetcar was purchased before World War II, and where rickshaw pullers still provide transportation for people and goods.

In a perverse fashion the very excesses of Calcutta's problems are acting to slow the city's growth. Such problems are accomplishing what urban planning and policy could not. The shrinking industrial base and difficult living conditions have made the city less attractive to rural in-migrants. Improvements in rural living have also reduced the pressures to abandon the countryside for Calcutta. Calcutta thus may be going through a self-correction cycle.

Prognosis

Overshadowing all other Indian problems is that of how to cope with population growth. India's population is now 930 million people and its population will top 1 billion by the year 2000. To put it in more understandable terms, each year India is adding 17 million persons, or the total population of Australia.

The eradication of smallpox, the partial eradication of malaria, and the control of cholera have reduced infant mortality drastically. As a consequence, 36 percent of the population is under fifteen years of age. When these young people come of age, it will be difficult to provide the necessary educational opportunities, jobs, and housing. India for decades has had various birth control programs, and birth rates are declining. However, the population is already so large that even a moderate growth rate has a tremendous numerical impact. India, with a 1.9 percent yearly increase, will double its population in thirty-six years. India feeds itself, and there are also very substantial nonagricultural resources. India has been undergoing an economic boom during the 1990s. Economic growth, though, benefits the elite and the middle class more than the masses. (Nationally, half of the urban families must survive on monthly incomes of under $100.) Also, as a result of continual population growth, development is distorted: Attention must be constantly focused on meeting the basic needs of an ever-larger population. Other problems such as improving education and housing necessarily receive lower priority. Questions of improving the quality of life and saving the environment thus far have received much less attention.

CHINA

The 1995 Chinese population was 1.2 billion. To put China's population in terms most westerners would understand: China *alone* is roughly equal to the combined populations of all the twenty-one nations of western Europe, all the thirty-six nations of Latin America and the Caribbean, plus the populations of the United States and Canada.

Yearly, China adds 17 million persons to its population. This is in spite of China as of 1995 dropping its rate of natural increase to 1.1 percent, half the 2.2 percent of other LDCs. China's goal was to hold its population to 1.2 billion by the end of the century, a number it hit in 1995.

Everything, including a car with driver, can be transported by rickshaw in Bangladesh. (UN/DPI Photo 151867.)

China's billion-plus population is still three-quarters rural, but the urban population is already the world's largest population of urban dwellers. Moreover, this has not been primarily due to rural-to-urban movement. Two-thirds of the urban growth since 1949 has come from natural increase of urban births over deaths.[16]

The People's Republic of China has an area of about 3.8 million square miles, with 96 percent of the population living on 40 percent of the land area. The population of China is concentrated in the southern and eastern sections of the country. The greatest density is found in the Yangtze valley, where there are 2,000 to 2,500 persons per square mile.

Background

The first modern manufacturing and industrial cities of China were the western-dominated treaty ports. During the nineteenth and twentieth centuries the ports of Chinese coastal cities were at various times physically controlled and occupied by European, and later Japanese, administrators and troops.

The European powers forced the weak and ineffectual Manchu, or Qing, dynasty to give foreigners substantial control over the economic life of the major Chinese cities. Europeans lived in separate, newer sections of the cities. The foreign

---

[16] H. Yuan Tien, "China: Demographic Billionaire," *Population Bulletin,* Population Reference Bureau, Washington, D.C., April, 1983, p. 29.

concessions of Shanghai were even policed by European troops; nor could foreigners be tried for crimes in Chinese courts. In Shanghai, the largest and most prosperous of the treaty ports, the park along the "Bund," or riverfront, according to legend had signs stating "No Dogs or Chinese Allowed." Even the capital of Peking (now known as Beijing) had its "legation quarter" for foreigners, near the central Imperial City. However, the number of foreign residents was never particularly large. In Canton, China's major southern city, foreigners at their most numerous were only 894 out of a city population of over 1 million.[17]

The Nationalist government, which replaced the Qing dynasty in 1911, was made up of an urban military and upper-class elite which continued the traditional practices of taxing and coercing the peasants to support the urban-based government. Landowners, many of whom lived in the cities, had little sympathy for the declining quality of life in rural China. The government continued to serve the landowners and disregard the plight of the peasants; land reform was ignored.

The communists also initially ignored the peasants and attempted to organize in the cities, but having failed at that, Mao Tse-tung redirected attention to the peasants. After decades of internal struggle and the civil war of 1947–1949, the communists achieved national dominance.

Urbanization Policies

China currently has an urban population of over 300 million, or 26 percent of its total population.[18] Figures published by the State Statistical Bureau indicate that China's proportion of urban population doubled from 21 percent in 1982 to 41 percent four years later in 1986.[19] This is because the latter figure includes counties under municipal jurisdiction even if they are not truly urban. Today one-fourth of the population as the urban figure is closer to the "true" urban population. This means that China—although three-quarters rural—still has the world's largest population of urban dwellers.

China's policy under Mao was resolutely antiurban. This was in part a reaction to the treaty port cities being seen (correctly) as the centers of western thought and influence. "The foreign presence (in China) was almost exclusively urban."[20] (Inland cities such as Tsinan were more successful in resisting foreign intervention.[21]) The initial failures of the communist cause in the cities further separated the cities from the original communist leadership. However, in spite of the discouraging of urban growth, between 1949 and 1956 some 20 million Chinese migrated from rural areas into the cities.

Rustication. In 1963, following the economic crisis brought on by the failure of the "great leap forward" campaign, the government decided to stabilize the urban

[17] Ezra Vogel, *Canton under Communism,* Harvard University Press, Cambridge, Mass., 1969.
[18] H. Yuan Tien, "The New Census of China," *Population Today,* January, 1991, p. 6.
[19] State Statistical Bureau, *Statistical Yearbook of China,* State Publishing House, Beijing, 1982, p. 89.
[20] Rhoads Murphey, "The Treaty Ports and China's Modernization," in Mark Eivin and G. William Skinner (eds.), *The Chinese City between Two Worlds,* Stanford University Press, Stanford, Calif., 1974, p. 67.
[21] David D. Buck, *Urban Change in China,* University of Wisconsin Press, Madison, 1978.

population at 110 million, which was considered a manageable figure.[22] During the "cultural revolution" of 1966–1976, the government tried to reverse the flow to the cities and send surplus urban population, and especially young school graduates, into the countryside. A combination of social coercion and ideological conviction was used to persuade at least 15 million urban Chinese youths to "volunteer" to resettle permanently in rural villages.[23] Some estimates suggest that as many as 25 million urban young adults were resettled in this manner. Most of these migrants made a poor adjustment to their new surroundings.

Following the bloody repressions at Tienanmen Square in 1989, there briefly was some return to the practice of sending students to the countryside for a period before starting college. The job assignment system in which graduates are permanently assigned to jobs also was reasserted. However, neither of these survived for long under what is increasingly a capitalistic economy in practice if not name. Four decades of antiurban ideology emphasizing the reduction of urban growth have run up against economic reality.

Displaced Workers

China is making a major effort to relocate industries to outlying areas in order to stem the potential flood of rural-to-urban migrants. The Labor Ministry in 1994 estimated that as many as 214 million workers (a quarter of the labor force) were out of work and migrating, seeking employment. Chinese officials estimate that at least a quarter of the rural labor force is unemployed or underemployed. Moreover, Chinese demographers estimate that mechanization of farming will eventually displace a total of 300 million to 500 million peasants, of whom 100 million will be displaced between 1980 and the turn of the century.[24] Planners hope to relocate displaced peasants in small cities and towns scattered across the countryside. Medium- and small-sized cities are rapidly expanding.[25] Government plans call for increasing the number of cities from 622 in 1994 to 1,003 in 2010. However, contrary to government claims, such cities do not provide a better quality of life than large cities.[26] In the past, rural-to-urban migration was held in check by a very strictly enforced policy of household registration which does not legally permit those without urban jobs to remain in the cities. However, while nominally still in force, such regulations are now commonly ignored. Technically, there were no unemployed persons, only those working or those temporarily awaiting assignment. An indirect consequence of this policy of job and housing control was the proliferation of marginal jobs outside the formal structure, such as free-enterprise markets and food stalls—places where those not supposed to be in the city sometimes can find work. In the Special Economic Zones of the south none of the government mobility controls have any force.

[22] Pi-chao Chen, "Overurbanization, Rustication of Urban-Educated Youths, and Politics of Rural Transformation," *Comparative Politics,* April, 1972, p. 374.

[23] Ibid., p. 235.

[24] Yuan Tien, "China: Demographic Billionaire."

[25] Gu Daochong and Jiang Meiqiu, "The Impact of Urbanization on Environment in China," paper published by the Department of Sociology, Beijing University, 1988, pp. 6–7.

[26] York Bradshaw and Elvis Fraser, "City Size, Economic Development, and Quality of Life in China: New Empirical Evidence," *American Sociological Review,* **54:**986–1003, December, 1989.

Special Economic Zones

The economic reforms of the last decade and a half have first occurred not in the established cities of Beijing and Shanghai, but in the Special Economic Zones in the south. Southern Guandong province with its new factories and cities has catapulted far ahead of the north. In spite of the political hostility between the mainland and Taiwan, many of the factories in the Special Economic Zones are actually financed and managed by Taiwanese businessmen who have invested over $20 billion in the region. (Hong Kong still provides the majority of investors.) It is an open secret that some goods labeled "Made in Taiwan" are actually assembled in mainland factories. The result of the economic boom is that the southern zones now boast considerable prosperity, a prosperity that is easily seen in the new superhighways and neighborhoods of spacious garden apartments. Southern provinces also tend to increasingly ignore decrees from Beijing that interfere with local business or convenience. Thus, for example, government bans on satellite dishes are totally ignored. The south tends to follow the ancient Chinese saying that "the mountains are high, and the Emperor is far away."

Shanghai

Shanghai, China's largest city, grew as a treaty port built on western commercial enterprise. It was largely imposed upon the existing civilization.[27] Within a decade of its opening to foreign trade in 1843, Shanghai's manufacturing sector had become a physical and economic embodiment of nineteenth-century European thought. In nineteenth-century Shanghai, with its extraterritoriality laws (foreigners had their own laws, police, and courts), foreign concessions, and foreign gunboats, the modern industrial world of European rationality came face to face with the traditional seclusionist ways of the Chinese Empire.

Today Shanghai, with a city and suburban population of over 13 million, is one of the world's largest cities. For Chinese planners, the physical development of Shanghai has been complicated by several factors.

Following the communist takeover in 1949, the city was allowed to deteriorate. Political leaders in Beijing distrusted Shanghai's independence and still drain tax monies from the city. Only now are Shanghai's needs being seriously addressed. Shanghai also had to overcome the effects of the previous pattern of mixed foreign domination. Each of the foreign settlements had not only its own administration and police but also its own pattern and width of streets, water pipes, and sewers. Developing a uniform citywide street pattern has required widening existing streets as well as extending others by tearing down buildings and houses. Now old Shanghai is rapidly being dismantled and a new city built in its place. Since 1989, across the Hangpu River, a vast industrial, commercial, and residential zone called Pudong has been constructed.[28]

---

[27] For a description of Shanghai before communism, see Rhoads Murphey, *Shanghai—Key to Modern China,* Harvard University Press, Cambridge, Mass., 1953.

[28] Ian Buruma, "The 21st Century Starts Here," *New York Times Magazine,* Feb. 18, 1996, p. 31.

In an attempt to catch up to the Special Economic Zones in the south, the city now has set up its own special economic zones. Shanghai also has one of only two stock markets in the country, and has a new 9.2-mile subway. A tunnel will soon connect the old colonial business district of the riverfront Bund with the east bank of the Huangpu River and the new Pudong New Area project, and a new bridge is also planned. A water filtration system is also being installed, as is a new telephone system. Many of these projects are being financed with loans from Japan, the United States, and Europe.

With the mass of industrial activity still located within the city proper, there is considerable pollution and transportation congestion. Most of the city's factories and utilities burn heavily polluting soft coal for energy. The pollution and congestion from automobiles is rapidly growing as automobile ownership increases. However, in order to get to work the populace still uses a crowded bus system and bicycles. There are at least 6 million bicycles in the city.

Housing is still recovering from the ravages of the 1966–1976 cultural revolution. (The cultural revolution virtually stopped all development for a decade. For example, the prestigious Singapore Conservatory of Music saw not only its once-fine buildings decay but most of its instruments destroyed and historically invaluable sheet music sold as scrap paper.) During the decade of the cultural revolution virtually no new urban building, repairs, or even painting was done anywhere in China. The official policy was "Production first. Livelihood second. Construction where there is room." Housing was considered part of the "nonproductive" sector.

Now housing is being repaired and new buildings are being constructed. Still, some 14 percent of city residents are so crowded that they must fit all their household belongings into the per capita housing space of a king-size bed.[29] In the past, one's place of work usually not only provided a job, but also managed the housing where one lived. Serious crowding was a problem, but the rent was low; the average working family paid only 4 to 8 percent of its income for monthly rent. Now housing is moving toward a market rent system. Today the bulk of homes still lack hot water, but virtually every family has a color TV set.

Beijing

Beijing was first made the capital of China in the Yuan dynasty in 1292. The old walled city was expanded during the Ming and Qing dynasties into the political and cultural center of the nation. The Forbidden City which housed the imperial court and bureaucracy is now a museum, and the historic city walls were torn down by the Maoist government and replaced with a road. At the time of the 1990 census the municipality had 10.8 million residents.[30] This is not an accurate reflection of the actual metro population, for the Beijing municipality covers a huge, 16,800-square-kilometer territory (roughly four-fifths the size of New Jersey), and 3.4 million of the inhabitants of the municipality are rural residents.[31] These agricultural workers

[29] Lena H. Sun, "Crowded Shanghai Tries to Catch Up with Booming Economic Free Zones," *Washington Post*, Sept. 24, 1992, p. A21.
[30] Carl Haub, "World's Largest Head Count Ever," *Population Today*, January, 1991, p. 3.
[31] David Buck, "New Municipal Plan for Beijing," *Urbanism Past and Present*, 8:14, Summer/Fall, 1983; and Haub, "World's Largest Head Count Ever," p. 3.

Car traffic is increasing but bicycles remain a major form of transportation for those living in Chinese cities. (Charles Kennard/Stock, Boston.)

worked collectively prior to the abolishment of communes in 1984. Now, under the free-enterprise-type "responsibility system," they represent a highly prosperous category of largely independent farmers who help feed the capital city. Independent farmers' markets are found throughout the city. Beijing's urban residents are the most economically favored in China. The average annual salary of a Beijing worker is over four times that of the national average, which according to the World Bank was $490 as of 1993. This reflects Beijing's role as the home of China's political leaders and top bureaucrats. It is the chief center of political, administrative, industrial, educational, and cultural activity.

During the 1950s, when Soviet influence was still important, the city was divided into functional zones for different activities following the Moscow model. Factory sectors were concentrated in the eastern and southern suburbs, while the northwest sector was primarily for higher education and research. Since the prevailing winds are from the northwest, this also helps to keep down pollution levels.

Beijing has very serious pollution problems, particularly in the winter, when 20 million tons of soft coal is used by virtually all businesses and families for heating.[32] On some cloudless days the sun is not visible until afternoon because of the heavy pollution. Contributing to the problem of windblown particulate matter is Beijing's location on an almost treeless plain south of the Gobi Desert. Also, during the cultural revolution, it was decreed for health reasons that all cats and dogs

---

[32] Daochong and Meiqiu, "The Impact of Urbanization on Environment in China," p. 12.

be killed. This led to a proliferation of nuisance birds, who were then ordered killed. This led to a proliferation of insects, so the municipal government then decreed that all grass be torn up. This was done, with the result of substantially increased dust in the air. This is an interesting example of how social organization policy decisions can negatively impact the environment.

In 1983 an overall plan for the future development of Beijing envisioned placing the entire former central Imperial City under special protection to preserve historic buildings and prohibit any more houses taller than two stories in that area.[33] Older neighborhoods are to be renovated, polluting factories are to be moved away from the city, parks and woodlands are to be greatly expanded, and streets are to be improved. However, shutting down major industrial polluters has proved to be a difficult task, and little of the plan has been implemented.

All of this comes none too soon since, while Beijing still has under a million motor vehicles, it now has over 6 million bicycles, and their number is increasing by 9 percent a year. Beijing's comparatively empty streets of 1980 are now curb-to-curb bicycles, motor scooters, and increasingly cars every morning and evening rush hour.

In spite of considerable building of high-rise flats, crowded housing still remains a major problem in the capital. The cultural revolution did not cause the physical suffering in Beijing that was found in other cities, but there was a gap in housing construction which will take current programs many years to fill. Still, Beijing was clearly moving forward until the 1989 bloody repression of students and suppression of the pro-democracy movement. Beijing, tied as it is to the old political order, has shown less rapid economic development than have the more free-wheeling south coastal provinces. If it implements its modernization plans, it will indeed become a first-rank metropolis early in the twenty-first century.

A Note on Hong Kong

The British Crown Colony of Hong Kong, although on the Chinese mainland, was most noted for its extremely laissez-faire economic structure. Hong Kong, including the New Territories, reverted to mainland Chinese ownership in 1997. Much of Hong Kong's 402 square miles are so steep and mountainous as to be incapable of development or are on scattered islands where development would be uneconomical. This, plus the strong desire of newcomers to remain in the city proper, means that Hong Kong's population is heavily concentrated in a narrow ring around the harbor. As a consequence, densities in Hong Kong reach 6,500 persons *per acre,* the highest in the world.[34] The continued influx of refugees into this already overcrowded environment further strains the city's resources.

In an attempt to provide public housing for all who need it, Hong Kong has developed several new towns. Tsuen Won, which was begun in 1973, already

---

[33] "Beijing to Be Turned into a Metropolis," *Hong Kong Standard,* Aug. 3, 1983.
[34] Murray MacLehose, "Modern Urban Development in Hong Kong," paper delivered by the Governor to the Commonwealth Society, Hong Kong, Nov. 28, 1977.

Hong Kong intensively uses all space. Even the streetcars are double-deckers. (Bernard Pierre Wolff/Photo Researchers.)

holds over 800,000 persons and eventually will have over 1 million. (Obviously the new towns are far larger than Ebenezer Howard's vision of self-contained communities of only 30,000.) Hong Kong's new towns (or cities) are being developed as self-sufficient entities, but in fact cannot yet fully meet their own educational, retail trade, and entertainment needs, nor provide their own employment base.

Hong Kong is noted for its vitality and for having produced an economic miracle. What it has not produced is a means of equitably sharing that miracle. One reason new towns can be constructed rapidly is that construction workers labor ten hours a day, seven days a week. The only break in the workers' routine occurs at the Chinese New Year holidays. Nonetheless, for its residents, Hong Kong represents living standards and opportunities unavailable on the mainland. The city now boasts a substantial middle class. This population is particularly nervous about the consequences of Hong Kong's transfer from British to mainland Chinese control in 1997. Although the Chinese government has promised not to change the economic system in Hong Kong for fifty years, there is uncertainty about whether this assurance will be honored. The Chinese government has indicated that its guarantees are not absolute but are dependent upon Hong Kong dropping its limited elected self-government and following the mainland's political line.

Density and Economic Development

It should be noted that there is no clear relationship between population density per se and the level or rate of economic development. High agricultural density is usually seen as a sign of underdevelopment, but high urban densities may or may not be desirable, depending on the level of economic development.

High densities of rural, and particularly agricultural, labor indicate inefficient agricultural production and a surplus of personnel which is either unemployed or underemployed. In closed extractive economies—such as farming, lumbering, and mining—the employment of a high proportion of the labor force in such pursuits means smaller average holdings. India, for example, employs about 70 percent of its labor force in agriculture, with an average holding of about 2 acres for every person of working age (fifteen to sixty-five years of age). In Asia over 83 percent of the available acreage is already under cultivation; thus increases in rural population will necessarily mean less land per person. Rural out-migration thus will continue to be a major force into the foreseeable future.

In developed countries, where nonextractive industries dominate and a large volume of trade is possible, density is frequently an advantage rather than a liability. The industrial ring cities of the Netherlands and the Rhine River urban complex of Germany both have extremely high densities and high standards of living. Hong Kong provides an even more extreme example. Hong Kong has a population of 5 million crowded on a land area of 402 square miles: This comes out to over 14,000 persons per square mile. Nonetheless, Hong Kong has for years managed to increase its GNP at a rate far in excess of the rest of the world. Hong Kong has practically no natural resources, but it is blessed with a literate, energetic, and trained labor force. Its extremely high population density has not prevented Hong Kong from achieving one of the highest levels of per capita income in Asia, although much exploitation of workers remains.

This in no way suggests, of course, that high densities automatically result in high income levels and economic expansion. However, high density can be an advantage to a highly organized and heavily industrialized economy. The city concentrates large numbers of people in one place and thus minimizes what has been called "the friction of space." Production can be concentrated in one place; the city itself is a massive factory. Technological breakthroughs in transportation and communication also are means of overcoming the friction of space, and allow the city to export both to its rural hinterland and to other urban areas.

In the noneconomic sphere, population concentration also permits and encourages specialized educational, cultural, and scientific organizations. Accumulations of personal and capital resources necessary for the emergence of such organizations can be found only in the city. The requirements of urban living also produce new problems, such as housing, sanitation, and the prevention of crime; and the necessity of dealing with these problems can lead to an emphasis on innovation and rational problem solving.

The requirements of contemporary urban life and those of industrialization complement one another. Both emphasize the importance of adapting to changing conditions. Urbanization and industrialization are not the same thing, but it is not surprising that industrialism in the third world is directly associated with the growth of urban areas and the spread of urban ideas.

JAPAN

Any discussion of Asian urban patterns must include Japan, the region's most urbanized large nation. Japan is not an urban newcomer; it has an urban tradition even longer than that of India as regards the role of the city in regional and national life. Japan's urban tradition goes back at least to the fifteenth century. The so-called castletowns formed a basic urban stratum upon which later cities were built. Edo, as Tokyo was then called, may have had 1 million people in 1700, while Osaka, the great trade center, and Kyoto, the ancient capital, both had several hundred thousand inhabitants.[35]

Extent of Urbanization

The forced opening of Japan to western influences in the nineteenth century led to a boom in city building. Cities such as Tokyo, Nagoya, and Osaka grew, first as trading centers and later as manufacturing and commercial cities. Industrialization and urbanization took place so completely that today Japan equals and in some cases surpasses western levels in these two areas. Today Japan is three-quarters urban (77 percent), a figure that is essentially the same as that for the United States.[36] Moreover, the urban population of Japan is remarkably concentrated, with an overall national density of over 300 persons per square kilometer and 45 percent of the total population occupying only 1 percent of the land area. Unlike the United States, Japan does not have a Jeffersonian tradition of idealizing rural areas and distrusting cities. Almost all the people want their activities to be located in Tokyo.

Current Patterns

In discussing contemporary Japanese urbanization it is important to remember that while Japan is an Asian country, its levels of urbanization and industrialization are similar to those of Europe and North America rather than to those of the rest of Asia. The strengths and problems of Japanese cities are largely those of developed western metropolises. Japan, along with the small enclaves of Hong Kong and Singapore, has both a level and a pattern of urbanization atypical of Asia in general.

Many current urban problems in Japan are a result of the decision of the Japanese after World War II to concentrate all their efforts on industrial production for export. Only minimal attention and resources were devoted to "social overhead" such as sewage systems, water systems, pollution control, and urban transportation. The result is that today Japan has a massive backlog of demands for urban services. Japan spends *less* on urban infrastructure than other industrial nations. Housing has had a particularly low priority.

While Japan has large problems, it also has great resources. Japan has the technology, the skilled personnel, and the financial resources to rebuild and remake its cities. What it now requires is the will to make the commitment. The problem is one of social policy rather than technology or resources.

---

[35] Edwin O. Reishauer, *The Japanese,* Belknap Press, Cambridge, Mass., 1978, p. 25.
[36] 1995 "World Population Data Sheet," Population Reference Bureau, Washington, D.C., 1995.

Tokyo

Tokyo-Yokohama, the world's most populous city at 17 million persons (or second largest after Mexico City, depending on definition), is to the western observer a series of contradictions. Signs of prosperity are everywhere, from the streets clogged with new automobiles to futuristic new office buildings to luxury department stores unmatched in Paris, London, or New York. A shabbily dressed person is difficult to find. Few would disagree with the statement made by the president of Tokyo University to this author that Japanese women are, as a group, better and more expensively dressed than women anywhere in Europe or the United States.

Yet Japan, in spite of its affluence, has not been able or willing to house its population properly and provide urban amenities taken for granted in other developed countries. Japan's cities reflect the emphasis on production for export rather than an attempt to upgrade the urban infrastructure. For example, housing conditions are extremely cramped and excessively expensive by American standards. Single-family homes within a 45-minute commute of Tokyo average $500,000.[37] This means that a small home within commuting distance that would cost the average American worker 3.4 times his or her yearly income costs the average Tokyo resident 8.7 times his or her annual income.[38] Moreover, the Japanese would be purchasing a 900-square-foot home, compared with 1,200 square feet in the United States. Young people, therefore, spend money on consumer goods and holidays since, without parental assistance, they are unable to purchase homes.

Housing. Exorbitant land costs have also resulted in structures being built wall to wall up to the lot lines. Unfortunately, within the Tokyo-Yokohama agglomeration, the traditional Japanese gardens exist only in memory or on the estates of the wealthy. There is little parkland. Tokyo has half the parkland of Washington, D.C., and one-tenth that of London. Zoning regulations are minimal, and even they are frequently flouted. This absence of control over construction is notable in such a structured society.

There is also a lack of public services. Within the area of the Tokyo metropolitan government (the old city of twenty-three wards and the immediate surrounding suburbs with a population of 11.5 million), as of the 1990s only 85 percent of the population have flush toilets.[39] Nationally, less than half the homes are connected to sewage systems. At the same time, 98 percent of the homes have color television.

The Japanese economic miracle has thus far failed to provide the average family with a standard of housing commensurate with the nation's wealth. Three-quarters (77 percent) of those in Japan's urban areas live in homes or apartments of less than 60 square yards of floor space. Central-city housing is prohibitively expensive, and as a result most Japanese are forced to commute long distances between their offices and cheaper residential accommodations in satellite towns on

---

[37] Robert J. Samuelson, "Japan's Other Face," *Washington Post,* Feb. 8, 1989, p. A27.
[38] T. R. Reid, "Japan's Housing: Pricey, Chilly and Toilet Poor," *Washington Post,* Mar. 4, 1991, p. A9.
[39] Ibid.

the outskirts of Tokyo. Even the homes of well-paid white-collar "salarymen" are minuscule by world standards.[40] Fewer than a fifth of Japanese houses had central heating as of 1995. Given the high housing costs, construction quality is not always the best. The devastating 1995 Kobe earthquake demonstrated the danger of putting heavy tile roofs on weakly supported walls. Government policies, unlike the United States F.H.A. and V.A. subsidy programs that help home purchasers, tend to push up real estate prices and thus hamper new construction of housing. Therefore, Japanese savings have been invested in export industries or foreign stocks and properties rather than local housing.

Transportation. Tokyo-Yokohama is not only the world's largest metropolitan area; it is also among the world's most congested. Roadways are vast bottlenecks during rush hours, so most workers take public transport. Tokyo has a remarkably clean and efficient subway system, but during rush hours it and commuter rail lines must employ an army of 700 pushers whose job it is to force additional passengers into the overcrowded cars. The Yamanote Line which rings central Tokyo commonly operates at 250 percent of capacity during rush hours.[41] Above ground, the roads are continually packed with curb-to-curb vehicles. Because space is at a premium, express roads are usually built above existing roadways, but they also are commonly clogged. The system is simply not adequate for a city half Tokyo's size.

For many Japanese the bicycle, not the auto, is the most efficient means of transportation. The nation has some 55 million bicycles, and at least 5.6 million of these are in Tokyo.[42] Since a third of all Tokyo office workers spend between two and four hours a day commuting, a bicycle stored during the day at the suburban railway station may help people cut ten or fifteen minutes off this total in the morning and evening. It also leads to unbelievable seas of bicycles outside railway stations and stores. Periodically, police confiscate illegally parked bicycles (200,000 in Tokyo each year), but it seems to have little impact.

Crime

Japan has one of the world's lowest crime rates. Comparisons with the United States put Japanese achievements in perspective. The United States has twice the population of Japan, but over 10 times as many murders, 45 times as many rapes, and 270 times as many robberies. Japanese newpapers speak of the country having a crime wave, but by this they mean that the entire nation of 125 million people had 38 murders in 1994. By 1995 the figure had dropped back to the more normal half that number.

Why the huge differences in crime? Experts cite several factors. First, Japan has a unified culture and racial population with fewer of the sharp differences between wealthy and poor found in the United States. Second, the Japanese have a strong sense of the group and the individual's subservient position. Criminal be-

---

[40] James Sterngold, "Life in a Box: Japanese Question Fruits of Success," *New York Times,* Jan. 2, 1994, pp. A1 and A6.
[41] Ibid., p. A6.
[42] Clyde Haberman, "For Cramped Japan, 55 Million Bicycles Is a Glut," *New York Times,* Mar. 4, 1985.

Commuter lines servicing Tokyo employ
uniformed pushers to shove additional people into
already overcrowded cars. (Niroko Okahasi/The
Picture Cube.)

havior shames one's group. Third, Japan has had strict gun control for 400 years. Only those in law enforcement can possess handguns. Finally, Japan relies on some 15,000 small neighborhood police stations known as *koban*. In suburban and rural areas, the policeman and his family actually live in the *koban*. In the cities as well as small localities, police make local rounds by foot or bicycle, knocking on doors to inquire about neighborhood concerns. They are an integral part of the neighborhood, spending far more time providing neighborhood services than solving crimes. Thus, even in Tokyo, the *koban* provides the local neighborhood with small-town services and atmosphere.

Planning. During the final years of World War II, much of Tokyo was leveled— the city lost 56 percent of its housing stock—and Tokyo had the opportunity to rebuild itself with widened streets, open spaces, parks, and reasonable lot sizes. The fact that this was not even seriously considered is still seen as more of a tragedy by outsiders than by the business elites of Tokyo. These elites continue Japan's extremely successful emphasis on foreign exports and trade surpluses, while strongly resisting any meaningful national or municipal government spending on infrastructure. Tokyo residents have only one-eighth the parkland of New York City residents.[43] Thus far, urban planning and development have taken a distinct back seat to export-oriented economic growth.

Planned Towns

There are, of course, some exceptions. For example, Suma New Town, near Kobe, currently with a population exceeding 100,000, was built on reclaimed land. To provide land the tops of hills were literally blasted and bulldozed off, and the rock was then carried underground for miles to the sea on huge conveyer belts. The fill was then used to construct the artificial port and Rokko Islands in Kobe harbor. The inland project, which was officially dedicated in 1980, is estimated to have cost $2.5 billion. The 1995 Kobe earthquake, unfortunately, demonstrated that filled-in land can become virtually liquid in a major earthquake.

Public housing, in new towns or elsewhere, is built for middle-class rather than low-income groups. The public Japan Housing Corporation, for example, is required by law to break even financially on the projects it constructs, and so rents are usually far more than the poor can afford. Limited public housing for low-income groups is built by the Metropolitan Housing Supply Corporation.

Suburbanization

Suburbanization has been a factor in Japan ever since the massive earthquake of 1923, which first encouraged decentralization. The Japanese have a tradition of city living; and before World War II, the poor lived outside the municipal boundaries, particularly in marshy areas. A long commute to work in that era was a penalty of poverty rather than a prerogative of affluence as in the United States.

More recently, high land costs have resulted in heavy middle-class and even upper-class suburbanization. Since commuting to and from suburbs is done largely by rail, the greatest suburban development has been along the very profitable suburban rail lines. The average commuter travels a remarkable 1.5 hours each way. (The U.S. average is 22 minutes each way.) It is estimated that the average salaryman commuter spends three and a half years of his life commuting. As land prices rise, the center of Tokyo is more and more given over to shops and commercial and business activities. The resident central-city population can be expected to decline further while suburban growth—some of it quite distant—accelerates.

SOUTHEAST ASIA

General Patterns

Most cities of southeast Asia—except in Thailand—are a product of European colonial expansion, Chinese enterprise, or a combination of the two.[44] This is some-

---

[43] Sterngold, "Life in a Box," p. A6.

[44] Norton S. Ginsburg, "Urban Geography and 'Non-Western' Areas," in Philip M. Hauser and Leo F. Schnore (eds.), *The Study of Urbanization,* Wiley, New York, 1965, p. 332.

what of an exaggeration, but generally the pattern holds true. Cities in southeast Asia are relatively new. Few date back more than a century or so. Primate cities, particularly ports, are common. Most of the cities originally were clearly divided into western and nonwestern districts. Ho Chi Minh City, formerly Saigon, provides an example.

Saigon's urban history began in 1859, when the French captured a village of native huts, none of them permanent structures. On this site the French built Saigon as an administrative capital, laying out the streets in the grid pattern. The Chinese quarter and marketplace, known as Cholon, developed simultaneously with Saigon. Thus Saigon became the French colonial capital for Cochin China, later named Vietnam, while Cholon was the Chinese city. Early growth in Saigon was orderly, while Cholon grew haphazardly. The two areas were merged by the French in 1932 for administrative purposes.

Before World War II, the largest population group in Saigon-Cholon was Chinese.[45] Roughly 60 percent of Cholon, and 30 percent of the entire city, was Chinese at this time. Following the Vietnam War, the government of Vietnam expelled the Chinese, fearing that they would dominate the economy and constitute a potential "fifth column" loyal to China. The majority of the early so-called Vietnamese boat people fleeing Vietnam during the 1970s and early 1980s were in fact ethnic Chinese.

Singapore

The modern island Republic of Singapore is highly atypical of southeast Asia.[46] Whether this is good or bad depends on the perspective of the observer. Economically there is no question that, in spite of the total absence of natural resources (Singapore even has to import sand for building), the country is prosperous. Singapore has some 2.7 million persons in an area of only 225 square miles (584 square kilometers), making it one of the most densely crowded areas on the globe. Singapore has roughly ten times the density of Holland, which is the most densely populated western country. Officially, Singapore is 100 percent urban, although some semi-rural areas remain.

One of the things that makes Singapore unique is its strategy for control and development. Since independence in 1965, the government has been involved in an ambitious program to replace virtually all of Singapore's previous housing with high-rise apartment buildings. Slums and squatter settlements have been eradicated, sometimes by the use of draconian measures. The old Chinese neighborhoods of street vendors and dilapidated overcrowded buildings, so dear to the hearts of travelers, and the Malay *kampongs* (villages) have been replaced almost entirely by government-sponsored high-rise estates and new office buildings and hotels. Currently, over four-fifths of the population reside in government-built high-rise housing estates. By 1995 some 85 percent of the population lived in

[45] Norton S. Ginsburg, "The Great City in Southeast Asia," *American Journal of Sociology,* **60:**459, March, 1955.
[46] See J. John Palen, "Singapore," in Willem van Vliet (ed.), *International Handbook of Housing,* Greenwood Press, Westport, Conn., 1989, chap. 20.

government-built housing. Singapore is also rapidly building several new towns—also of high-rises—the largest of which is Woodlands New Town, with a population of 290,000.

The rapid transformation of Singapore into an ultramodern city, however, is not without its critics. Some charge that too much of the traditional culture has been sacrificed to the god of efficiency. For example, once government planners decide to rebuild a district, the land is compulsorily acquired; and although compensation is paid, neither litigation by owners nor public protests by residents will stop redevelopment. If an ancient temple sits on land desired for redevelopment, the temple is either moved or rebuilt elsewhere.

Singapore's sharp break with the past has both advantages and disadvantages. While the high-rise structures are not as effective as the old *kampongs* and squatter settlements in fostering community ties and close human relationships, they do provide better housing and living facilities for the majority of the population.[47] Compared with high-rise housing projects in the United States, the buildings are well maintained. Perhaps this is because, as a result of government policy, more residents own than rent their flats.

Under the government's "home ownership for the people" scheme, residents can draw upon their mandatory social security payments for the down payment and even monthly payments for their flats. Four-fifths of those living in government-built housing estates are engaged in purchasing their apartments. Over three-quarters of these are using their social security payments for down payments and mortgage payments. Most apartments are still relatively small, but it is not uncommon for a family to spend a considerable amount of money upgrading and redecorating its flat. The Housing and Development Board has "thinned out" some of the earlier projects by tearing down every second building. At the same time it is phasing out one-room flats by converting them to two-room units. Singapore is thus in the unique position of having solved in two decades its physical housing problems, insofar as government-built housing of standard quality is available to most residents.

Whether the high-rise projects can meet the social and community needs of the populace remains to be seen. Singaporeans enjoy one of the highest standards of living in Asia, with a per capita income second only to that of Japan.[48] Economic prosperity has resulted in so many automobiles that to control congestion and pollution, cars not having an expensive entry permit are banned from the center of the city during working hours. The city is also engaged in a major program of beautification by planting trees and bushes along the roadways. (Because Singapore is near the equator, newly planted trees grow rapidly along the streets and around the housing projects.)

Overall, Singaporeans live in a tightly controlled society where efficiency ranks well ahead of participation by citizens in making decisions. Regulations, even on littering (a $225 fine), are enforced. Today Singapore is a modern com-

[47] Peter S. J. Chen and Tai Ching Ling, *Social Ecology of Singapore,* Federal Publications, Singapore, 1977.
[48] Thai-Ker Lin, "Housing Policies and Life Style," paper presented at the High Rise, High Density Housing Conference, Singapore, Sept. 5–9, 1983.

mercial city. If it isn't as quaint, colorful, and interesting as in the old days, that is a price most residents seem willing to pay.

Other Cities

Other southeast Asian cities that merit discussion, if space permitted, include Jakarta, the booming capital of Indonesia; Bangkok, the capital and principal city of Thailand; Kuala Lumpur, the dominant center of Malaysia; Seoul, the capital of South Korea; and Taipei, the major city of Taiwan. Sprawling and booming Jakarta already has 9 million people and may well have half again as many by the turn of the century. The main priority of the government is to attract new jobs and industry. Jakarta, which as of 1980 had only a handful of high-rise buildings, now has a skyline filled with high-rises, and as well has some of the world's worst traffic jams. Today it has the excitement and the chaos of a boomtown.

Bangkok, with 8 million persons, is one of the most dynamic and most chaotic cities in Asia. While crowding and pollution grow ever worse, the city is an economic, educational, and cultural magnet not only for Thais, but for other Asians. Bangkok is reputed to have the world's worst traffic jams, and they will be much worse for the next several years as major streets lose two lanes in order to build the Tanayong elevated railway system.

Kuala Lumpur, once a mining town, now the national capital, is growing with more speed than beauty. Kuala Lumpur is currently building two high-rise towers that will be the tallest buildings in the world, some 23 feet taller than the Sears Tower in Chicago. Surrounding Kuala Lumpur is suburban congestion that is spreading ever further over what were once agricultural estates.

Seoul is also a very modern city. Seoul largely was destroyed in the Korean war (1950–1953), and is now a city of modern skyscrapers. Little of the historic city remains.

In Taiwan the Taipei metropolitan area holds some 6 million persons, and is not considered to be well designed or environmentally attractive by its residents. Because it is located in a natural basin, air pollution remains a serious problem; but after decades of neglect, environmental problems are now being addressed. Clogged Taipei as of the mid-1990s even has cleared a central area for a new park.

OVERVIEW

Everywhere in Asia physical urbanization and social urbanism are both increasing spectacularly. Even in China, where government policies strongly encourage population control, the cities are inevitably going to grow, since industrial development and trade are attracting migrants into the cities.

Within Asia, individual cities are frequently immense, but the overall level of urbanization at 33 percent is still relatively low. This is certain to change. Looking at Asia as a whole, it is clear that dramatic urban growth will be the pattern for the first decades of the twenty-first century. Increasingly the great cities of the world will be Asian cities.

Generalizing beyond this point for the entire Asian region is impossible, since the outstanding characteristic of the area is its diversity. Many of the urban problems may be similar, but the solutions to date have differed widely in both content and degree of success.

Japan is by far the most urbanized of the large nations of Asia and has the greatest resources, both technical and economic, that can be brought to bear on specific problems such as housing, sanitation, and transportation. China has immense human resources but a more limited technological base. For decades it managed potential urban problems by controlling urban population growth—something it is unlikely to be able to do in the future. Indian cities, for years, came closest to the old "teeming masses of Asia" stereotype, but moving to a more capitalistic system in the 1990s has revitalized the economic system. It has also further exacerbated the divisions between the prosperous and the poor. Rapid population growth has severely strained the physical capabilities of cities such as Bombay and Calcutta to house, educate, and employ their residents. Indian cities, though, possess vitality, color, and even safety that other nations might envy.

It is important not to try to transfer American ideas about declining cities to cities elsewhere. In Asia cities are booming, not declining. In Asia the cities, even with all their very real problems, are not places of defeat, abandonment, and despair but of growth, hope, life, and optimism. American clichés such as the "decline of the city" have little meaning in the Asian context.

CHAPTER

17

AFRICAN AND MIDDLE EASTERN URBANIZATION

There is always something new out of Africa.
Pliny the Younger (A.D. 62–113)

AFRICA

Africa is currently the least urbanized of the continents. (See Figure 17-1.) As of 1995, 31 percent of its inhabitants lived in urban places.[1] At the same time, however, Africa is the continent with the highest rate of increase in urban population. In 1950 only two African cities had populations greater than a million. By 2000, there will be thirty-seven such cities.[2] The population of the continent as a whole is estimated to be 720 million. Birthrates are collectively the world's highest at 41

---

[1] "1995 World Population Data Sheet," Population Reference Bureau, Washington, D.C., 1995.
[2] Dennis Rondinelli, "Giant and Secondary City Developments in Africa," in M. Dogan and J. D. Kasarda (eds.), *The Metropolis Era: A World of Giant Cities,* Sage, Beverly Hills, Calif., 1988.

Figure 17-1. Map of Africa.

per 1,000. As of the mid-1990s the average number of births per woman in sub-Saharan Africa was 6. Rwanda has the world's highest birthrates at 8.5 children per woman. Sub-Saharan death rates average 14 per 1,000. (Comparable U.S. birthrates and death rates are 15 and 9.) Life expectancy in sub-Saharan Africa is only fifty-five years, well below that of any other world area.[3] Africa's rate of natural increase is by far the highest in the world. If current rates continue, nearly thirty African countries will double their populations in the next twenty-three years. Sub-Saharan cities are growing by an average of almost 6 percent a year— a rate that doubles their populations every twelve years. Sub-Saharan Africa's population is projected to more than triple to 1.4 billion by 2030. Some mid-1990s lower projections are not due so much to population control as to the AIDS epidemic that is ravaging the continent. Of the 14 million persons worldwide who were infected with the HIV virus in 1994, some 9 million lived in sub-Saharan Africa.

Problems

Everyone acknowledges that Africa has serious problems. Population control has only recently been recognized by most governments as a major factor in economic development. Indeed, a few African nations still have official policies encouraging more rapid population growth. Nonmarket economic policies had by the 1990s driven most economies below their level of twenty years earlier. According to the World Bank, as of 1992 more than one in three Africans live in "absolute poverty."[4] The combination of war, government policies, drought, and desert encroachment resulted in per capita food production as of 1990 being 20 percent lower than it was in 1970. The trend continued into the 1990s. Although nearly self-sufficient in food in 1970, today sub-Saharan Africa has to import one-fifth of its grain requirements. As a consequence, when drought strikes, its effects are far more severe than might otherwise be the case. As of the mid-1990s, some 150 million people in twenty-two countries faced hunger and malnourishment. Per capita income in sub-Saharan Africa actually dropped during the 1970s and 1980s.[5] It continued to decline in much of sub-Saharan Africa into the 1990s.

Reform?

Nonetheless, there also are signs that the future may be brighter. Politically, South Africa is now a stable multiracial nation. Population control is spreading, and economically many African nations are undergoing reform. Across the continent, governments have taken tough economic steps to reduce government deficits, making exchange rates reflect reality through devaluations, ending price controls, and tightening the monetary supply. Inefficient and corrupt state industries are being sold

[3] "1995 World Population Data Sheet."

[4] John Darnton, "Africa: Spreading Misery as Living Standards Fall," *International Herald Tribune,* June 20, 1994, p. 7.

[5] "Toward Development in Sub-Saharan Africa: A Joint Program of Action," World Bank, Washington, D.C., 1984, p.1.

off, and farmers, who make up 80 percent of most societies, are being permitted to sell at market prices. World Bank studies show that the countries that instituted the most extensive reform policies are enjoying the strongest resurgence in economic performance.[6] The downside is that freeing up domestic markets is creating major disparities within countries. More advanced regions with education and infrastructure are doing much better than more backward regions.

Regional Variations

Africa has some fifty-four separate nations, and African cities vary greatly; the major regional distinction is between the cities of north Africa and those of sub-Saharan Africa. North Africa is the most urbanized of the African regions. All the countries bordering the Mediterranean Sea have between two-fifths and three-fifths of their population in places of 20,000 or more inhabitants. This is not at all surprising when one considers the great civilizations this region has produced and its superior location for the development of trade centers. Also, away from the coast much of the land of north Africa is either mountainous or arid desert and hardly suited for urban growth (the Nile Valley being the obvious exception). Thus the population is highly concentrated in a limited area.

West and central Africa lie in the middle range of African urbanization—ranging from 15 percent in Burkino Faso to 44 percent in Cape Verde.[7] The larger cities are located along, or within easy access to, the coast. Their founding and development can almost always be tied to their role as colonial entrepôt cities. Of the west African countries, oil-rich Nigeria, with 115 million inhabitants, is the largest and has by far the most cities. The World Bank projects that Nigeria's population, currently 101 million, could increase to 618 million within a century.[8]

East Africa has long been the least urbanized part of the continent.[9] It does not have a tradition of cities. Zambia is the most urban at 44 percent, while Rwanda is only 5 percent urban. Kenya is fairly typical, having 27 percent of its population in cities.

It should be noted that virtually none of what can be said regarding the rest of sub-Saharan Africa applies to South Africa. The Republic of South Africa is by far the most industrialized nation on the continent, with almost two-thirds (63 percent) of its population in urban places. In terms of economic position, South Africa, with its gold reserves and industrial base, is, in spite of economic difficulties, a world economic power. South Africa now is a multiracial society with a black president, and it has put its former policy of *apartheid,* or forced racial segregation, behind it. Still, within South Africa the economy is 85 percent controlled by whites, and except for wealthy blacks, neighborhoods remain largely racially segregated.

---

[6] Thomas Friedman, "Africa's Economies: Reforms Pay Off," *New York Times International,* Mar. 13, 1994, p. 18.
[7] "1995 World Population Data Sheet."
[8] Thomas J. Goliber, "Sub-Saharan Africa: Population Pressures and Development," *Population Bulletin,* **40(1)**:3, 1985.
[9] Edward Soja, "Spatial Inequality in Africa," *Comparative Urbanization Studies,* University of California School of Architecture and Urban Planning, Los Angeles, 1976.

CITY DEVELOPMENT

Until a score of years ago, a reading of the literature gave the impression that there were few, if any, indigenous African cities south of the Sahara. This was due partially to a colonial mentality that did not admit the possibility that "backward natives" were capable of building cities and partially to a lack of serious research on African history.

Scholars studying Muslim traditions in Africa also have been prone to minimize the contributions of black Africa. For instance, one writer suggests that "historic [or ancient] capitals are confined to Arab Africa" and "Native" [or medieval] capitals are in fact a transition between the historical and colonial capitals. . . . "Culturally, they are universally associated in one way or another with intrusive, alien influences, mainly Arab and generally Asian."[10]

More recently, the pendulum swung in the opposite direction. Trading centers such as Timbuktu (whose current population is under 10,000 poverty-stricken inhabitants) were elevated to the status of major metropolises, a position they occupied for only relatively short periods of time. Nonetheless, the region did produce substantial cities, some of which had considerable importance, especially during the Ghana, Mali, and Songhay empires of west Africa (roughly the eleventh to late sixteenth centuries).

Of all African cities, those of north Africa have the longest urban traditions. Alexandria was founded by its namesake, Alexander the Great, in 332 B.C., but settlements on that location go back at least another 1,000 years. The north African city of Carthage, until it was utterly destroyed, was the greatest rival of Rome. During the height of the Roman Empire, north Africa was dotted with many important cities, some of which may have contained as much as 25 percent of the population of their regions.[11] With the decline of the Roman Empire these cities suffered the same fate as Roman cities in Europe. Over time, most of them disappeared—although, again as in Europe, newer cities now sometimes sit over the ancient ruins.

Elsewhere in Africa, many cities were first built during the peak of Muslim power. The revival of trade in the tenth century benefited not only north African cities such as Fez and Algiers but also sub-Saharan towns, including Kano in northern Nigeria. The Yoruba towns of southwest Nigeria also emerged at about this time, as did caravan centers such as Timbuktu. During the following centuries a number of west African kingdoms created capitals, but most of these capitals had short histories. Segou in Mali, Labe in Guinea, Zinder in Niger, and Kumasi in Ghana all rose and fell. These cities served their kingdoms primarily as market and trade centers.

Then, as now, east African cities were less numerous, with only a few towns, found generally along the coast of the Indian Ocean. Present cities such as Mog-

[10] G. Hamdan, "Capitals of the New Africa," *Economic Geography,* **40:**239–241, July, 1964.
[11] William A. Hance, *Population, Migration, and Urbanization in Africa,* Columbia University Press, New York, 1970, p. 211.

adishu in Somalia and Mombasa in Kenya prospered as trading centers. These towns served almost until the present century as centers for the trading in goods, and slaves from the interior, for shipment to Arabia.

The Colonial Period

European Influence. During the sixteenth century, the Portuguese founded the first European settlements. These were little more than fortified trading posts where goods from the interior could be collected and stored for shipment to Europe. Attempts by the Portuguese to extend their influence inland were unsuccessful. Their early successes in Ethiopia, for example, were short-lived, and Portuguese missionaries and traders were later expelled from that country.

Until the late nineteenth century, Europeans showed little interest in colonization. Cape Town in the Republic of South Africa, for example, was established by the Dutch East India Company only as a station to provide meat, fresh produce, and water to the Dutch ships on the way to the Indies.[12] The seizure of land in black Africa by Europeans rapidly accelerated during the last quarter of the nineteenth century. Britain, France, Germany, Belgium, and Portugal all rushed in to carve up the continent into colonies. Important African cities of the present are largely the products of this colonialism, since each colony had to have

[12] H. M. Robertson, *South Africa*, Cambridge University Press, London, 1957, pp. 3–4.

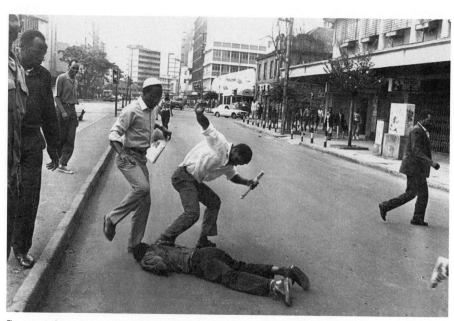

Street violence is not unique to American cities. Nairobi is noted for its high crime rate, but citizens quickly respond when witnessing crime. (Nation Newspapers Ltd, Nairobi, Kenya.)

an administrative capital. Major cities, founded during the colonial period, with the dates of their founding, are Accra, Ghana (1876); Abidjan, Ivory Coast (1903); Port Harcourt, Nigeria (1912); Brazzaville, Congo (1883); Kinshasa, Zaire (formerly Leopoldville, Belgian Congo) (1881); Yaoundé, Cameroon (1889); Kampala, Uganda (1890); Nairobi, Kenya (1899); and Johannesburg, South Africa (1886). Of the major new towns founded during this period, only Addis Ababa in Ethiopia (1886) and Omdurman in Sudan (1885) were indigenous rather than colonial creations.

Most of the cities of Africa are in actuality far newer than the dates mentioned above would indicate, for rapid increases in the populations of sub-Saharan African cities did not begin until somewhere around forty years ago. Until the 1950s, most African cities were relatively small. Nairobi, for most of this century one of the most pleasant of all African cities, had a population of only 33,000 in 1930. The population jumped to 200,000 in the 1950s, and today it is well in excess of 1 million. The pattern is similar, and in many cases even more spectacular, in other African cities. Kinshasa, for example, has tripled its population in the last two decades. In spite of these increases, Africa still remains—as has been noted—the least urbanized of the world's major regions.

Colonial-Period Cities. The colonial cities founded by Europeans a century ago did not grow out of the local culture. Rather, the layout of the city, its social and political organization, and even its architectural styles came from Europe. The government housing in Accra, Ghana, with its wide lawns and large single-family houses, looks like nothing so much as Victorian England. The centers of colonial cities were for the use and residence of Europeans. Nighttime curfews frequently prevented the entry of Africans into the European sections and the entry of Europeans into the African sections.

The colonial city was organized around the central district, which in addition to stores and other business offices also included the administrative offices of the colonial government. Streets were usually wide and crossed at right angles in a grid pattern. A description of Stanleyville (now Kisangani) is typical:

> The physical layout of the town could be seen as both an expression and a symbol of the relations between Africans and Europeans. European residential areas were situated close to, and tended to run into, the area of administrative offices, hotels, shops, and other service establishments, while African residential areas were strictly demarcated and well removed from the town centre.[13]

Spatial location thus reflected social power within colonial society.[14] Without significant industrialization, central residence was preferred. Africans who worked in the European center were in effect commuters from suburban locations—although, in this case, the suburbs were high-density indigenous communities. This is, of course, the complete reverse of the pattern in American industrial cities where the poorest lived in the inner city.

---

[13] V. G. Pons, cited by A. L. Epstein, "Urbanization and Social Change in Africa," *Current Anthropology,* **8:**(4)277, 1967.
[14] Geoffrey K. Payne, *Urban Housing in the Third World,* Routledge & Kegan Paul, Boston, 1977, p. 53.

Indigenous Cities. Indigenous cities often were located next to colonial developments, but in other cases they were almost completely separate developments. In west Africa the most noted cities of strictly African origin are the Yoruba cities of Nigeria. Many of these cities had large populations, although for years there has been scholarly debate about whether these were true cities or extremely large agglomerations of basically agricultural villages. These are referred to in the literature as "rural cities," "city villages," or "agrotowns." In any case, the Yoruba cities had the largest populations in sub-Saharan Africa before the colonial period. Ibidan as of 1850 had roughly 70,000 inhabitants. In east Africa many of the functions of towns, such as markets, took place at permanent sites—although residence was not one of the functions.[15]

Ecologically, indigenous cities were not as sharply differentiated as western cities. In the indigenous city the main focus was and is the central market, which is commonly quite large and frequently out of doors rather than housed in buildings. Nearby were the quarters of the chief or ruling prince. The main mosque is also centrally located in Muslim cities. Historically, surrounding this central core were the quarters of the lesser chiefs and nobles. These areas contained not only the nobles but also their retainers, soldiers, followers, and servants. Each quarter was a self-contained area within the larger city. Much of this legacy persists today in cities such as Addis Ababa.

Frequently, quarters were divided on the basis of tribal or religious affiliation—not by social class as in America. Walls and gates sometimes separated the quarters from one another. Within a quarter, there was no overall plan or scheme. Streets wound in an irregular pattern and were suitable only for walking or animal traffic, since the lanes were narrow and buildings came right up to the passageway. Structures were rarely more than two stories high and were constructed of local materials. Congestion was common.

As these indigenous towns came under the control of colonial powers, a new administrative area on the European style was frequently appended to the periphery of the old city, and a major road or two would be cut through the old city to connect its center with the offices of the colonial administrators. Rarely did the indigenous city and the colonial city blend. Each was a separate entity; and though existing side by side, they frequently even followed different laws, with western legal systems applying only in the European quarters. In time, the European quarters expanded to include modern commercial and business districts. In a few cases, the modern city came completely to surround the old city. The Casbah in Algiers, for example, has long been completely enclosed by a modern city created during the first half of this century by French colonial occupation.

Contemporary Patterns

Primate Cities. The term "primate city" is clearly appropriate to the pattern of urbanization found in most of the nations of sub-Saharan Africa. For example, as of

---

[15] D. R. F. Taylor, "The Concept of Invisible Towns and Spatial Organization in East Africa," *Comparative Urban Research,* **5**:44–70, 1978.

1980, 57 percent of Kenya's urban population was found in Nairobi; 83 percent of Mozambique's, in Maputo; half of Tanzania's, in Dar es Salaam; and half of Zimbabwe's, in Harare. Moreover, the importance of the primate city is increasing.

Cities—and most particularly the capital cities—are the dominant economic force, the seats of government, the cultural centers, and the hubs of transportation and communication networks. The primate city is the manufacturing center, the break-of-bulk transportation node, the major market, and the financial center.

The dominance of the primate cities is easy to document. Dakar, for example, as of early 1980 had only 16 percent of the population of Senegal, but consumed 95 percent of all the electricity in the country and accounted for three-quarters of its commercial and manufacturing workers and over half of its employees in transportation, administration, and other services.

The importance of the primate cities is heightened by the economic separation of the major city from the surrounding countryside. Africa even today is noted for a break between the modernizing city and the tribal "bush." Urban influences are concentrated in the cities themselves. There is little of the American pattern, in which the city gradually tapers off and becomes the countryside. Going a few miles into the bush can take someone not only away from built-up areas but also away from the major influence of the city.

The physical size and structure of the primate city is the most visible sign of its dominance, but its social role as the breaker of the cake of custom is even more significant. It is in the primate cities that a major restructuring of African society as a whole is taking place. Just how deep into the countryside major restructuring has penetrated is, of course, open to some dispute. But that change is taking place in the cities is accepted by all.

The association between the growth of cities and the rise of African independence movements has been commented upon by many observers. In Africa the city is the incubator of social change. It was in the urban townships rather than the countryside where Nelson Mandella's ANC gained its strength. More than on any other continent, the African city not only towers over the countryside but controls it economically, educationally, politically, and socially.

Squatter Slums. Shantytowns, or squatter settlements, are a standard part of the "suburban" landscape of every growing African city. They house up to one-third of the total urban population. The rapid population growth of recent years, along with the push from the land, has resulted in an explosive expansion of the urban population—without a proportionate increase in the city housing.

As a result, squatter settlements are a fact of city life, from Casablanca in the north to Lusaka in the south. Most governments simply do not have the resources to engage in massive housing programs. Moreover, some argue that improvements are counterproductive since improvements act as magnets drawing ever-more rural newcomers.

Compounding the problem is the inability of the increasing urban population to pay even the minimal rents that standard-built housing would require. Food and clothing generally absorb from two-thirds to nine-tenths of a newcomer's income.

That doesn't leave much for extras such as decent housing. Shantytowns with hovels of packing crates, scrap metal, or mud and wattle thus will be part of the urban scene for years to come. Needs such as education for children and medical care are often unmet in shantytowns. Unfortunately, education and health needs often are being poorer met in 1995 than they were in 1975. Africa is the only continent where the poor are getting poorer and education and health services are not improving.

Lagos: An Example of Urban Growing Pains. Lagos, the capital of Nigeria, provides an example of the difficulties facing even relatively affluent metropolises. Lagos has grown from a city of just over a million residents in 1963 to a metropolis of over 4.5 million today. Because of oil revenues, Lagos is far better off than many growing cities, but it is nonetheless unable to keep up with its need for roadways, sewers, housing, and efficient government.

Some of the problems stem from the city's location. Lagos was originally founded on a narrow island close to the coast. This made considerable sense when the concern was defending a trading post; but today the island is the crowded center of the city, and the lagoon separating it from the mainland is a foul-smelling, polluted sewer. At peak traffic hours, it can take forty-five minutes just to get over the bridges from the island to the mainland. Urban problems apparently can be exported to developing countries more rapidly than urban solutions.

Population growth by in-migration is about 10 percent per annum, and the many local, state, and federal governments and agencies often seem to work at cross-purposes.[16] At the time of this writing (1995), Nigeria is being governed by military leaders who both refuse to acknowledge election results and are viewed by most Nigerians as incompetent at anything but staying in power. As in every LDC, there are many urban contradictions. For example, new, expensive, high-rise buildings were constructed in Lagos during the last decade; yet, the open street drains continue to overflow, refuse collection is erratic, and big, overloaded trucks continue to tear up colonial-era roads.

While comparatively economically affluent cities such as a Lagos in Nigeria are having economic difficulties, the problems of poorer countries are far more severe. Dar es Salaam in Tanzania, for instance, is quite visibly decaying. The rundown buildings emphasize the country's status as one of the world's twenty-five poorest. Unlike other countries, Tanzania for a quarter of a century had a socialist government that virtually ignored its capital while emphasizing the total resettlement of the agricultural population in new communal agricultural villages which were agricultural failures. Today Tanzania has made major macroeconomic changes and since 1990 has brought its amounts of goods and services produced from a negative to a positive level.[17]

---

[16] Rasheed Gbadamosi, "Growing Pains in Lagos," *Draper World Population Fund Report,* Spring, 1976, pp. 15–17.
[17] Friedman, "Africa's Economies," p. 18.

One Indigenous City: Addis Ababa

Indigenous cities are most common in north and west Africa. In east Africa the most notable indigenous city is Addis Ababa, Ethiopia. Although founded in 1886 at the height of European colonial expansion, the city was an authentically African creation.*

Addis Ababa (the name means "new flower") was not originally intended to be a permanent city. Rather, it was founded by Emperor Menelik II as a temporary capital. Having no urban tradition, the Ethiopian emperors moved their capital from time to time as military factors, weather, or exhaustion of local resources (food and firewood) dictated. Addis Ababa—which was Menelik's eighth capital—was laid out as an armed camp. The emperor chose for his *guebi*, or palace, a hill above the northern thermal springs and then allotted various surrounding quarters, known as *sefers*, to his leading nobles. Social organization was strongly feudalistic. Each *sefer*—literally, "camp"—included the residence of an important noble plus all the noble's warriors, troops, retainers, and slaves and their families. No distinctly upper- or lower-class areas were initially developed, as was the case in cities founded by Europeans. The effect of this original organization as an armed camp can still be clearly seen in the city's social, economic, and ethnic arrangements.

Early visitors to Addis Ababa universally commented that it resembled a large straggling village more than a city.† Further contributing to this impression of a large floating camp were fluctuations in the city's population. The normal population around 1910 was roughly 60,000; during the rainy season, it sometimes dropped to as low as 40,000.‡ When important chiefs came to the capital, they brought their entire armies and households with them. There are reports of chiefs who brought 100,000 to 150,000 people with them, and even as late as 1915 it was not unusual for a governor to bring 30,000 to 50,000 people along as a personal guarantee of safety.

As the city grew, its eastern side surrounding the palace gradually developed into the administrative center, while the western zone surrounding the old marketplace, or *mercado*,

* John Palen, "Urbanization and Migration in an Indigenous City: The Case of Addis Ababa," in Anthony Richmond and Daniel Kubat (eds.), *International Migration*, Sage Publications, London, 1976.
† Docteur Merab, *Impressions d'Ethiopie*, vol. 2, Leroux, Paris, 1921–1923, p. 11.
‡ Richard Pankhurst, "Notes on the Demographic History of Ethiopian Towns and Villages," *The Ethiopian Observer*, 9:71, 1965.

became the commercial center. Because the ruling Amhara tribe despised any type of commercial activity or trade, business activities were relegated to subordinate tribes. The Amhara concentrated their attentions on ruling, farming, and mounting expeditions to the south to capture more slaves.

Haile Selassie I ruled the country, first as regent and then as emperor, from 1916 to 1973. (The Italians occupied Ethiopia from 1936 to 1941. They envisioned Addis Ababa as the capital of their sub-Saharan African empire.) From 1973 to 1991 Ethiopia was a totalitarian Marxist police state and was involved in continual war with its northern provinces. Today it has an elected government, and it is trying to rebuild after decades of stagnation.

The southern end of the city, which is somewhat lower in altitude and thus warmer, was set aside in the 1930s as the Italian residential area, and a southward movement has been characteristic of the city since that time. Most of the newer housing and high-rise apartments are in the southern area.

Today the radius of the city is about 6 miles, with the most heavily built-up area roughly in the center. Although its present population is over 1.5 million, Addis Ababa still retains much of its nonurban character. Fewer than 10 percent of the homes have running water or bathrooms.* Many housing units are still constructed of *chica*—a mixture of earth, straw, and water plastered around eucalyptus poles. The ever-present and fast-growing eucalyptus trees also serve to give the city a small-town appearance by masking the houses. The trees do a yeoman service, since they provide firewood for all heating and cooking, lumber for building, and wood for furniture. Even the leaves are used in baking the Ethiopian bread, called *injera*.

The rural feeling of the city is also partially due to the fact that Addis Ababa is a city of rural migrants. Three-quarters of the inhabitants were not born in the city, and warfare during the 1970s and 1980s with the Eritrean and Tigrean Liberation Fronts encouraged greater movement to the city, as did the famines of 1984, 1985, and 1988–1989.

In terms of its functional base, Addis Ababa is still primarily a political and administrative center. All major Ethiopian government agencies, all foreign embassies, the United Nations Economic Commission for Africa, and the Organization of African Unity are located in the capital. Recently there have been noticeable increases in several sectors: transportation,

---

* J. T. Marlin, I. Ness, and S. T. Collins, *Book of World City Rankings*, Free Press, New York, 1986, p. 354.

communications, manufacturing, and education. Industrialization is growing but is still, relatively speaking, in its infancy, with most capital goods being imported. Retail trade is also growing but is oriented largely to Addis Ababa itself. Transportation to and from the city is still primitive, particularly for goods. A sole narrow-gauge railroad connects Addis Ababa and the port of Djibouti. Each day firewood and produce are brought into the city from surrounding areas on large, overloaded trucks.

Addis Ababa at the end of the century remains both a traditional city and a modern city. It is both an overgrown village and the headquarters of the United Nations Economic Commission for Africa. It has high-rise apartments, but still no sanitary sewers. Addis Ababa is a vibrant place whose contradictions mirror the continent.

The Economic Future

Colonialism may be dead, but the economic effects of exploitation linger on. Overdependence on a single crop or mineral resource leaves many countries vulnerable to fluctuations in world market prices. Ghana was set back by two decades of depressed cocoa prices; Ethiopia is affected by fluctuations in the price of coffee; Liberia, in addition to suffering the problems brought on by civil war, is subject to fluctuations in the price of crude rubber; Zambia depends for its export income on the price of copper. It is difficult to plan a development budget under such circumstances.

Economically, sub-Saharan Africa remains in serious trouble. Over two dozen countries as of the mid-1990s have a negative rate of economic growth, while their total foreign debt mounts alarmingly. The Organization of African Unity (OAU) in 1985 adopted a declaration that most of the continent's countries were near "economic collapse."[18] The infrastructure of roads, buildings, and sewers had been allowed to deteriorate, and poor planning, political instability, and widespread corruption contributed to the deteriorating economic picture. However, the 1990s showed the first signs of improvement in two decades. As a result of the imposition of stiff World Bank economic reforms and the freeing up of domestic economies, Ghana, Tanzania, Gambia, Burkina Faso, Nigeria, and Zimbabwe are showing some economic resurgence.[19] Multinational corporations, which have been criticized for their exploitation of Latin American and Asian nations, generally play but a small, and diminishing, role in sub-Sahara Africa. With the partial exception of South Africa, multinationals for a decade have been pulling out of, rather than increasing investment in, the continent.

Agriculture. Problems also remain severe in the crucial agricultural sector. The UN Food and Agriculture Organization reported in the 1980s that nineteen sub-Saharan countries containing 190 million people required massive food aid to avoid famine.[20] The immediate cause was drought, but the long-range cause was twenty-five years of declining per capita food production.[21] During the 1980s, food production in Africa fell 11 percent.[22] The result, as mentioned earlier, is that while sub-Saharan Africa was agriculturally self-sufficient in 1960, it now imports one-fifth of its grain needs.

Stagnation in this crucial area is generally attributed to inefficient methods of farming and, most important, government policies that have deliberately depressed and controlled agricultural prices to benefit urban dwellers at the farmers' expense. As a result, nations whose economies are based on agriculture find themselves in the unfortunate position of having to import foodstuffs.

---

[18] "Africa near 'Economic Collapse,' OAU Says," *New York Times,* July 21, 1985.
[19] Friedman, "Africa's Economies," p.18.
[20] "Brief on the 1984–85 Cereal Import and Food Aid Needs for 21 African Countries," UN Food and Agriculture Organization, Rome, Dec. 5, 1984.
[21] "Toward Development in Sub-Saharan Africa."
[22] "A Continent in Crisis: Building a Future for Africa in the 21st Century," The Population Institute, Washington, D.C., 1988, no. 8, p. 3.

Proposed solutions stress freeing marketplaces from government controls. Also suggested are the avoidance of the "narrow nationalism" that hinders regional development, and the establishment of an African common market to pool strength and avoid uneconomic duplication. However, given the political and economic realities, these latter are not likely developments. While it would be pleasant to predict a better future for all the developing African countries, the economic facts of life indicate that while some countries are clearly moving toward self-sufficiency, others are getting poorer. Answers will have to come largely from within since the pattern and rate of western investment and aid are unlikely to be increased.

Urban Growth. Regardless of the extent of economic growth, continued urban growth is clearly the pattern for as far into the future as anyone cares to project. There really is little alternative. Many semiarid agricultural and grazing areas are already overused. Remaining in the area of one's birth, and further raising the density of the area, is not a reasonable alternative for those who hope to better their way of life. The opening up to farming of lands not previously used for settlement requires costs far out of proportion to the possible returns. The cost of providing necessary services—water, roads, schools, housing—would be extremely high. In east Africa it would also involve a political decision to destroy many of the remaining game parks and wildlife refuges, since there is little other land that is not already being used. Finding employment for the masses in the cities is an increasingly serious problem. Urbanization is clearly the wave of the African future, but whether it will mean economic development is still problematic. Another pressing problem in African cities is housing. Kenya, for example, will require 3 million new housing units to accommodate the projected increase in urban dwellers by 2010.[23]

Some west African governments have tried to stem the migrant tide by passing legislation providing for the repatriation of unwanted new workers back to their villages and setting stiff prison terms for those who return to the city. Repatriation has not proved successful: Workers either drift back to the city or are replaced by others. Other governments have tried to increase the attractiveness of rural villages and to settle unemployed urban populations in new, self-contained communal villages. Both of these approaches are expensive, and as a result seldom move beyond the planning or pilot-project stage. Such schemes have difficulty competing for scarce governmental funds. Moreover, the pressures driving younger people to the cities are social as well as economic and are not likely to be solved by such government programs as can be presently implemented.

The construction of low-cost houses or flats cannot come near to meeting the need for new housing. As a result, governments are coming more and more to accept the idea of aiding in the construction of reasonably planned slums which at least have minimal urban amenities such as an available water supply, roads, and group sanitary facilities for the disposal of human waste.

Zambia adopted a "site and service" scheme, by which a township is laid out and a prospective builder is given a plot and a loan of $50 to buy necessary building

[23] Goliber, "Sub-Saharan Africa."

materials, such as cement for the floor or a corrugated iron roof. After that, the builders are for all intents and purposes on their own. The rationale underlying this approach is that the goal of the government should not be to build housing but to raise the standard of living. Slum dwellers don't need more prodding to improve their living conditions; what they need is more money. As shanty dwellers get decent jobs and begin to make some money, they begin to improve their housing on their own.

Social Composition of Contemporary African Cities. The recent explosive growth of urban areas means that the majority of the adults in the cities were not born there but are in-migrants. The African city is a city of newcomers. In Abidjan, only 7 percent of those over twenty years of age were actually born in the city. Research by the author shows that over three-quarters of the inhabitants of Addis Ababa over fifteen years of age were born outside the city and are thus in-migrants.

Sociologist Louis Wirth's view of the city as a place where social relations are dominated by the labor market and contacts with others are superficial, impersonal, and transitory is only partially accurate as a description of African urbanism. There is no question that some of the disorganizing aspects of urbanism posited by Wirth can be found in any large African city. Family life sometimes breaks down, and prostitution is common. In Africa where most AIDS transmission is heterosexual, prostitution contributes to the rapid spread of the disease. Urban sex ratios are typified by disproportionate numbers of males. The situation is reasonable in west Africa, where in the cities there is a ratio of roughly 95 females to every 100 males. However, in middle Africa there are only about 85 females per 100 males, and in parts of east Africa there are only 55 to 75 females per 100 urban males. The absence of family situations encourages drunkenness, gambling, prostitution, and violent crime. The situation is not unlike that found in the towns of the American west before the arrival of the homesteaders with their families.

Problems of psychological maladjustment to city life appear as a rule to be far rarer than Wirth's thesis would suggest. The town may be a new experience, but since a major proportion of the townspeople were once migrants themselves, almost all newcomers know someone in the city who will take them in and who will help them adjust to urban life. Family ties and wider kinship ties are surprisingly strong and resilient to urban pressures. Relatives are expected to take the newcomers in and provide for their basic needs until they can get on their feet. A migrant who does get a job is then expected to contribute to providing for the family.

In the cities, tradition and modern ways often blend. An example of such blending is the use of both courts and traditional agents to resolve conflicts.[24] Outside observers are struck by the ebullience, gusto, and camaraderie found in African towns, particularly in west Africa. A description of Dar es Salaam fits other African cities equally well:

> It would be difficult to find a single African who arrived in Dar-es-Salaam knowing not a soul. . . . Almost every African who decides to come comes to a known address, where lives

---

[24] Michael J. Lowy, "Me Ko Court: The Impact of Urbanization on Conflict Resolution in a Ghanaian Town," in George Foster and Robert Kemper (eds.), *Anthropologists in Cities,* Little, Brown, Boston, 1974, pp. 153–177.

a known relation; this relation will meet him, take him in and feed him and show him the ropes, help him seek a job . . . until he considers himself able to launch out for himself and take a room of his own.[25]

It is well to keep in mind that the pull of the town is not uniform for all groups. The Masai of Kenya, although pressured by the Kenyan government to improve their agriculture and adopt modern ways, have consistently rejected town life in favor of their traditional rural culture. The Ila of Zambia have also rejected urbanization and modernization. Both tribes seem to be an embarrassment to their national governments because they don't want to "modernize." The Kenyan government plans to divide up the Masai communal lands and give each family individual plots. A similar program was tried by the United States government to modernize the American Indians, with the result that many Indians lost their lands. There are indications that the same fate awaits the Masai. It is quite possible that for the next generation the self-reliant virtues and warrior strengths of the Masai will be praised in every local Kenyan schoolbook, but that by then the independent Masai culture may have been effectively destroyed.

Tribal and Ethnic Bonds. Urbanization is supposed to weaken traditional bonds, but it can be argued that urbanization in Africa has strengthened rather than weakened tribal identification.[26] The immigrant, rather than being "detribalized," is "supertribalized" as a result of coming into contact, for perhaps the first time, with people from other cultures. Tribal origin usually replaces kinship as a symbol of belonging. This is an expansion of identity from the parochial to the more general.

The role played by cultural or tribal subsystems in modernizing societies is analogous to that played by immigrant enclaves in the American city of several decades ago. Cultural, ethnic, tribal, class, or occupational groupings perform a number of functions not only for the newcomer but for the society at large. First, the tribal, ethnic, or other group introduces newcomers to others in the city and indoctrinates them into the ways of the city. Information on such matters as where to live, how to get a job, and how to avoid the police is transmitted to migrants in order to aid their adaptation to the city. Second, the subgroup, being originally itself a part of the rural culture, maintains within the city many rural customs and traditions. While learning the new ways, migrants will still have some contact with their past. Third, because migrants return to rural areas for periods of time, and because there is a pattern of visiting between rural villages and the city, the customs and ways of the city (urbanism) are spread to villages—so that patterns of urbanism are gradually being diffused throughout rural areas.[27]

[25] J. A. K. Leslie, *A Social Survey of Dar es Salaam,* Oxford University Press–The East African Institute, London, 1963, p. 33.

[26] William John Hanna and Judith Lynne Hanna, *Urban Dynamics in Black Africa,* Aldine-Atherton, Chicago, 1971, p. 107; and J. Clyde Mitchell, *Cities, Society, and Social Perception: A Central African Perspective,* Clarendon Press, Oxford, 1987.

[27] Gideon Sjoberg, "Cities in Developing and in Industrial Societies: A Cross-Cultural Analysis," in Philip M. Hauser and Leo F. Schnore (eds.), *The Study of Urbanization,* Wiley, New York, 1965, pp. 226–227.

Kinship and tribal affiliation provide bridges by which the migrant crosses into the urban arena. Being a member of a tribe gives a newcomer an immediate identification that is recognized by everyone. It tells the newcomer how to behave, and it provides a more or less ready-made group of associates, friends, and even drinking partners. While tribalism may have negative effects in a country seeking to develop national rather than tribal loyalties, on the individual level one's tribal membership eases the adjustment of city life. A far less positive use of tribalism is national leaders' deliberate manipulation of ethnic differences in order to stay in power. President Moi of Kenya was widely accused of instigating tribal bloodshed as part of a "divide and rule" strategy.[28]

Status of Women. It is difficult to make generalizations about the position of women in Africa, since this varies from country to country and from one tribal and cultural group to another. Still, several overall statements can be made. It is generally safe to say that norms, attitudes, and values in Africa have a long history of strongly favoring male dominance. It is also clear that, regardless of other factors, cities are far more egalitarian in practice than the countryside. Urban populations are young, newer to urban life, and more flexible than their rural counterparts.

Women often are part of the informal self-employed sector. For many it is the only viable alternative to marriage.[29] Men immigrants do not have to choose between marriage and economic independence as do many women.

In Ghana "mammy wagons" (small buses) dominate local transportation. Ghanaian women are noted throughout the continent for their organizing skills. Ninety percent of the retailing of food and other goods is controlled and operated by women. Even in north African Muslim cultures, where the status of females traditionally has been inferior, changes are taking place in the education of women and participation by women in national life—Libya, with its strongly traditionalist internal policies, being the major exception.

Nonetheless, while the overall situation is improving, women have yet to attain equal status with men. Among the elites, western ideology—particularly Christian missions, with their doctrine of equality of marriage partners and schools open to both sexes—generally fostered equality.[30] However, no African nation at the time of this writing has a woman head of government or any women in the very top policymaking positions. Women are also underrepresented in the education system—in most countries, there are roughly two boys at school for every girl.[31]

In rural villages, the position of women is set by custom; but in the city, with its new occupations and skills, the occupational structure is more flexible. Urban occupations such as computer operator may be so new that they are not yet sex-defined. Skills and professional training of all sorts are usually in short supply, so that the

---

[28] Kenneth Richburg, "Kenya's Ethnic Conflict Drives Farmers off Land," *Washington Post,* Mar. 17, 1994, p. A36.

[29] Vici Nelson, "How Women and Men Get By: The Sexual Division of Labor in the Informal Sector of a Nairobi Squatter Settlement," in Joseph Gugler (ed.), *The Urbanization of the Third World,* Oxford University Press, Oxford, 1988, p. 201.

[30] Ester Boserup, *Women's Role in Economic Development,* St. Martin's Press, New York, 1970.

[31] "Draft of United Nations ICPD Programme of Action," 1994 Cairo United Nations World Population Conference, 1994, p. 8.

Women play a major role in the market economy of west Africa. (Owen Franken/Stock, Boston.)

woman who has had the benefit of education and training can generally use her training. On the other hand, women (or men, for that matter) without specific skills or abilities are likely to remain locked into poverty. While it is true that trained women participate in the social and economic life of the city to an extent unknown in the countryside, it is also true that for lower-class women without husbands there frequently is little alternative to prostitution and other marginal economic enterprises.

Differences from the Western Pattern. The geographer William Hance has assembled a number of characteristics differentiating between urban growth in Africa and urban growth in the west during the nineteenth century. These differences highlight certain aspects of African urbanization that differ from the western experience. The points of difference Hance notes are as follows:

1. The rates of growth, particularly of the major cities, are much more rapid in Africa. Some have achieved their present position in one-fifth to one-tenth the time required in western Europe.

2. There is less correlation—association—between the cities' rate of growth and the measures of economic growth in their countries.

3. The growth of urbanization is often not paralleled by a comparable revolution in the rural areas.

4. A less favorable ratio of population to resources in rural areas means that the push factor is more important than it was in Europe. That is, people pour into the cities not because the city needs workers, but because the countryside is overpopulated.

5. The linkage of some cities with their domestic hinterlands is less developed, while the ties of these cities to the outside world and their dependence on it remain striking.

6. There is relatively less specialization in the African cities. The division of labor is less developed.

7. There are generally higher rates of unemployment. Here the European cities had the advantage of being able to drain off large numbers of people who might have become redundant to the new world. The African cities have no such convenient safety valve.

8. Differences in outlook and values may slow the adjustment to the city and reduce the tempo of its economic life, as, for example, the reliance on the extended family for support and the absence of the Protestant ethic with its emphasis on hard work, achievement, and success.

9. There is a dual tribal and western structure in many African cities.

10. Migrants to the town differ in several important respects: almost all are unskilled, their level of educational achievement is relatively lower though above average as far as the source areas are concerned, and almost all arrive without capital resources.

11. Heavier responsibility is placed on governments, local and national, to provide for the urban residents. In the west, private enterprise normally met the needs for new housing, while local governments had a tax base adequate to provide the public services. Not so in Africa, where the demands on government are far more onerous, and almost none are capable of meeting them.[32]

The reference to a "dual structure" in point 9 has to do with the simultaneous existence of tribal customs and westernized ways of life. Generally, western ways tend to dominate in the economic sphere, while in the social and family sphere traditional customs retain their old strength. For instance, a man who has graduated from college may choose his job, but his family may strongly influence his choice of a wife.

The Future

Discouraging overall figures regarding population growth, rural poverty, and economic stagnation must be applied with discretion. While urban growth is occurring virtually everywhere, some nations are coping with the transformation more adequately than others. In sub-Saharan Africa, the nations of Ghana, Nigeria, Kenya, and Tanzania appear to be on the road to national economic development, while other nations just as clearly appear to be mired in internal strife and economic regression. As we enter the new century, Africa will remain the world's least urbanized continent even while its major cities continue to mushroom.

[32] Hance, *Population, Migration, and Urbanization in Africa,* pp. 293–294.

THE MIDDLE EAST

The middle east is in many respects more a political than a geographical concept. Technically, most of what we call the "middle east" is in Asia Minor, with some overlap into north Africa (for example, Egypt—see Figure 17-2). However, in terms of history, culture, and development, the middle east is a relatively distinct area.

The middle east is sometimes referred to as the "cradle of civilizations." This is not entirely an exaggeration, for the great ancient civilizations of Mesopotamia, Egypt, and the Levant all developed in this relatively small geographical area. The early development of this area was discussed briefly in Chapter 2, Emergence of Cities. In this chapter, the emphasis is on the cities of the middle east from the Islamic period to the present, for the social and spatial organization of present cities in the area is directly related to their preindustrial past. In terms of economic development as well as geography, the middle east occupies a position somewhere between the countries of western Europe and those of Asia and Africa, with some OPEC nations developing as economic forces.

Figure 17-2. Map of the Middle East.

Scholars agree that Islamic civilization has been predominantly an urban civilization.[33] In the words of one, "From the beginning of recorded history Middle Eastern cities and civilization have been one and the same."[34] The city was the center of political, social, and cultural activities. This was true in spite of the fact that many of the countries still are not unified and tribal factors are important.

Middle eastern cities differed in significant respects from the medieval corporate city and the autonomous city-state of the classical world. The medieval European city with which we are most familiar grew out of a feudal, land-based system; its charter defined its rights vis-à-vis the rural manors that were the real centers of power. European medieval cities initially were only on the fringes of power and were forced to develop their own political structure because they did not fit into the dominant, agriculturally based system. They had to evolve their own laws and customs, often in opposition to those of the countryside.

Islamic cities, by contrast, did not have the distinct legal privileges of a charter—criteria that Max Weber, using the legally autonomous European model, has suggested were necessary for a true city.[35] Under Islamic law all believers, whether in the city or the countryside, were equal. The laws of the city were those of the entire territory. Since laws were written in the cities, there was no need for autonomous laws and regulations for cities—and thus no independent group that could legally challenge the caliphate as the western middle class challenged its rulers by developing constitutional law. The caliphs, like the earlier Roman emperors, lived in the cities, not the countryside with its fortified rural castles. The city was not viewed as a rival of the hinterland: The city was superior and dominant. City authorities enforced the laws and collected the taxes. Thus there was no need for independent municipal governments of the type developed in western Europe. Rather, the middle eastern cities resembled Asian cities in that they lacked independent formal organizations.[36]

In the middle east, the peasants—many of whom actually lived within the protection of the city walls and cultivated adjacent lands—needed the technical skills, such as the canalizing and storing of water, and the military security, particularly from roaming nomads, provided by an urban population. Some cities, like Damascus, had agriculturalists living within the city and working the fields outside.[37] This is directly opposite to the American pattern of people living outside the city and working within it.

Traditional Islamic Cities

Roughly four-fifths of the middle east is either desert or arid mountains, and this basic environmental fact greatly influenced the location of cities. In addition to the limitations of the environment, political and military considerations influenced the

[33] S. M. Stern, "The Constitution of the Islamic City," in A. H. Hourani and S. M. Stern (eds.), *The Islamic City,* Cassirer, Oxford, 1970, p. 25.

[34] Ira M. Lapidus, *Middle Eastern Cities,* University of California Press, Berkeley, 1969, p. v.

[35] Max Weber, *The City,* D. Martindale and G. Neuwirth (trans.), Free Press, New York, 1959, p. 88.

[36] J. Gernet, "Note sur les villes chinoises au moment de l'apogee islamique," in Hourani and Stern (eds.), *The Islamic City,* pp. 77–85.

[37] Charles Issawi, *The Economic History of the Middle East,* University of Chicago Press, Chicago, 1966, p. 216.

location of Islamic cities. During the Roman Empire and earlier, the great cities were almost always seaports—Alexandria, Antioch, and Carthage are examples. The Muslims did not follow this ancient pattern: They shunned the sea and instead built an inland empire. This was partly from choice—the origins of Islam were in the interior rather than on the more sophisticated coast—but also partly from military necessity. Arab armies were successful on land, but the Mediterranean Sea was controlled by others—first by the hostile Byzantine Empire and later by the equally dangerous Italian city-states.

As a result, the Muslims built an interior empire, and previously great cities such as Alexandria shrank to the status of frontier outposts. The great Muslim cities, such as Damascus, Baghdad, Cairo, Tehran, Jerusalem, Mecca, and Medina, were all inland. Some, such as Kairouan and Fustat, were originally Arab camps at the edge of the desert; others, such as Damascus and Yazd, had been handling desert traffic for centuries; still others, such as Samarra, Baghdad, and Cairo, had once served as royal cities; and a few, such as Jerusalem and Mecca, were religious centers.

The holy city of Mecca in Saudi Arabia illustrates how social organization can sometimes override environmental conditions. Mecca is 40 miles from the Red Sea along a series of *wadis,* or gullies, flanked by steep granite hills. Summer temperatures reach 105-degrees Fahrenheit, and there is an almost total lack of greenery and cultivation. Nonetheless, as the focus of prayer and pilgrimage for Muslims throughout the world—non-Muslims are forbidden to enter the holy city—Mecca has prospered.

The traditional Islamic cities had a number of physical features in common. First, located in the most dominant natural defense position within the city would be the citadel. This was the military heart of the city, the place where, if necessary, a last-stand defense could be made.

Second, all cities had a central mosque that served as the focus of urban life. Around the mosque—which contained the religious school—could generally be found the main religious, civic, social, cultural, and even economic activities.

Third, there was the palace of the local ruler. Sometimes this was located in the very heart of the city, and sometimes on virgin land; but wherever it was placed, it invariably grew and absorbed surrounding properties. Not only did the compound contain the palace, treasury, and other directly related operations; it also was the center for all administrative offices. In addition, there were barracks for the house guards and personal troops whose loyalty could be counted on in times of revolt or attempted coup. Today major international hotels are often the dominant feature.

Finally, there was the central market area or bazaar. The citadel and palace are now tourist sights, but the grand bazaars continue to serve an important commercial function. Various sections of the bazaar are devoted to specific goods or products; all the spice markets are found in one section, another section specializes in shoes, another in clothing, and another in copper or brass metalwork. Silversmiths and goldsmiths also have their own special locations. The fabled Khanel Khalili bazaar of Cairo covers over a square mile of the city center.

Internally, Islamic cities have traditionally been divided into quarters that resemble village communities. Damascus in the sixteenth century had some seventy quarters.[38] Most of one's daily life would be lived within a quarter; there were relatively few institutional ties cutting across district lines to bind various quarters together. Guilds, merchant associations, and professional organizations, which were so important in medieval European cities, were all extremely weak.[39] What little organization that did cross the boundaries of quarters was created by the *ulma,* the learned religious elite that later came to exercise political and social power as well. The schools of law of the *ulma* were socially, religiously, and physically central.

Within the various quarters there were wide differences in social, economic, and political power. There were no specifically upper-class districts. Residence in quarters was based on adherence to particular religious or political positions. Ethnic minorities, specialized crafts workers, and even foreign merchants might have their own quarters. Some of the more suburban quarters were composed largely of people of recent village or nomadic origin—again, a contrast to the North American pattern.

Today the various quarters are far more mixed, in both usage and habitation. They still, however, maintain some of the characteristics of distinct neighborhoods. Social-class factors, rather than a particular trade or occupation, are far more important today in distinguishing quarters.

Contemporary Urban Trends

Urbanization in middle eastern countries today is so diverse that common generalizations are no longer realistic.[40] Most cities are growing at a rapid rate, with many doubling their population in a decade. Accurate figures occasionally are difficult to come by, since censuses are often viewed as political instruments. Saudi Arabia, for instance, will probably never release the results of its last census because it would document that 18 million Saudis and foreign workers live in an oil-rich country three times the size of Texas.[41] Rich countries do not like to be thought of as underpopulated, as it implies the inability to people their own armed forces. In Lebanon, there are only 3.7 million people, but a census would undoubtedly demonstrate that Muslims far outnumber Christians, further undermining Beirut's marginal political system. Thus Lebanon deliberately avoids taking a census.

In smaller oil-wealthy OPEC countries such as Kuwait (a million inhabitants), even before the 1990 invasion and destruction by Iraq old sections of the city had been virtually obliterated by new building. Air-conditioned steel, cement, and glass office buildings tower over streets clogged with automobile traffic. Residential neighborhoods are filled with new villas and apartments, while garages are filled with Mercedes automobiles. Elsewhere on the Arabian peninsula, traces of the previous traditional—and often poverty-stricken—cities remain.

---

[38] Ira M. Lapidus, *Muslim Cities in the Later Middle Ages,* Harvard University Press, Cambridge, Mass., 1967, p. 86.

[39] Lapidus, *Middle Eastern Cities,* p. v.

[40] Janet Abu-Lughod, "Culture, Modes of Production, and the Changing Nature of Cities in the Arab World," in J. Agnew, J. Mercer, and D. Sopher (eds.), *The City in Cultural Context,* Allen and Unwin, Boston, 1984.

[41] According to a story that is probably apocryphal, former King Saud commissioned a national sample during World War II. In making his report to the king, the western demographer confidently said that the monarch had some 3 million subjects. The king, with some upset, replied that he had at least 7 million subjects. The expert countered that there might be 4 million. The king demanded 6 million; the expert said that perhaps there might be 5 million. "So be it," the king declared.

In the Middle East, coffee shops have long served males as both business settings and social clubs. This shop is in Cairo. (UN/DPI Photo 148805.)

The premier mideastern city remains Cairo. The world city of Cairo is a place of extremes. Over the past three decades Cairo's population has grown from 2.5 million to over 8 million. Another 6 million are massed in the greater metropolitan area. For twenty-five years there has been virtually no meaningful maintenance or repair of the city's streets, sewers, telephones, or housing. Even today building codes are not enforced. The city is notorious for its power outages, and out-of-commission telephones. Egyptian residents, with endless patience and tolerance, respond with an Arabic expression: *Molish* ("Never mind").

The housing crisis is so severe that landlords can charge $4,000 a month for an unheated apartment where the water may or may not run. On the other hand, rent control means wealthy tenants who don't move pay the same rent they paid twenty-five years ago. The poor among Cairo's residents fare much worse. Building space is so scarce that several hundred thousand Cairo residents live in rooftop shanty shacks where residents raise food and even goats, as well as children. Another unique response is that half a million people live in the mausoleums of Cairo's cemetery, the famous City of the Dead. Squatters have returned the City of the Dead to life. Another group, the Zebaleen, live off, and in, Cairo's massive city dump. Such living may seem intolerable to westerners, but it is actually an improvement over the impoverishment of rural life. With all its problems, Cairo has a magic allure for newcomers and remains one of the world's great cities.

There is no pattern of economic and social change common to all middle eastern cities. Tel Aviv, for example, differs enormously from Baghdad, Damascus, or even Jerusalem. The development of Tel Aviv as a primate city can be explained in great part by the emergence of Israel as a nation-state. Founded in 1909 as a Jewish "garden city" separated from the Arab city of Jaffa, Tel Aviv grew rapidly, particularly after World War II. Its reservoir of trained professional and managerial talent aided its transformation into a major industrial commercial center. Tel Aviv has expanded its metropolitan area until now it encompasses numerous formerly independent surrounding towns. After Jerusalem came under Israeli administration as a result of the Six-Day War in 1967, Tel Aviv was no longer the only Israeli city, but its economic primacy remains.

Comparisons and Conclusions

In making comparisons with other regions of the world, and particularly with North America, certain differences should be remembered. First, middle eastern cities are not industrialized centers in the western sense. The cities are commercially oriented. Many have substantial middle classes. However, the way of life remains less bureaucratic than in industrial states. Contacts count for more than formal rules. For example, *baksheesh* (the giving of gifts or bribes) is an accepted way of doing business in the middle east.

Second, theories of urban ecological organization developed in America have little relevance to the middle east. If one looks at the ecology of Cairo, it is apparent that Burgess's concentric-zone theory has little utility there.[42] Contrary to the American pattern, in Cairo the areas of high social status are centrally located, and close to both the old and the new central business districts. Housing patterns still largely follow the traditional preindustrial model rather than the industrial model. This is partially because heavy industries were never located in the central part of the city, as in the North American model.

Third, because they are in-migrants, many city dwellers exhibit characteristics and behavior patterns that reflect their rural or village background. Family ties, kinship, ethnic groups, and primary groups still have a great deal to do with determining the nature of the life one will lead. In Cairo more than one-third of the residents were born outside the city. Migrants do not simply pick up urban ways; they also, in effect, ruralize the cities. Many city dwellers are still tied to rural customs and culture, and migrants shape the city as much as the city shapes them. Overall, evidence indicates that migrants do not suffer from social disorientation on the scale experienced by America's immigrants.[43]

Fourth, formal institutions, such as civic associations, labor unions, and charitable organizations, rarely play more than a minor role in adjusting the migrant to the city. Informal organizations or subsystems based on tribal, cultural, or ethnic identification are far more important. For instance, the role of the coffee shop is often central. Men still conduct social and business transactions from the coffee shop. Frequently it is a place where news of the village can be exchanged and assistance can be given to newcomers. As such, the coffee shop is more of a social than an economic institution.[44]

---

[42] See, for example, S. S. Hassan, "The Ecology and Characteristics of Employed Females in Cairo City," paper presented at the Seminar on Demographic Factors in Manpower Planning in Arab Countries held at the Cairo Demographic Center, November, 1971; and Janet Abu-Lughod, "Testing the Theory of Social Area Analysis: The Ecology of Cairo, Egypt," *American Sociological Review,* **34**:198–212, April, 1969.

[43] V. V. Costello, *Urbanization in the Middle East,* Cambridge University Press, Cambridge, 1977, chap. 5.

[44] For a description of this pattern in Cairo, see Janet Abu-Lughod, "Migrant Adjustment to City Life: The Egyptian Case," *American Journal,* **67**:22–32, July, 1961.

Fifth, the existence of large cities should in no way be confused with the domination of a secular urban culture. Secular ways have not always replaced traditional ways, even within the oil-rich cities that are physically most modern. External signs of western influence such as high-rise buildings, western automobiles, and western clothing styles do not signify abandonment of traditional beliefs. Even in supposedly secular states the statements of traditional Islamic religious leaders can produce civil disorder and even bring down governments. The power of religious leaders in expressly religiously oriented states such as Saudi Arabia and Iran is even greater. The urbanites of the middle east often remain more traditional than those of Asia, Europe, or the Americas.

Finally, in spite of the wealth of some middle eastern nations, the region does not fully control its own destiny. The world economy, particularly oil prices, will in substantial part determine the future of middle eastern cities.

CHAPTER 18

URBANIZATION IN LATIN AMERICA

Gazing on such wonderful sights, we did not know what to say or whether what appeared before us was real, for on one side in the land there were great cities and in the lake ever so many more, and the lake itself was crowded with canoes, and in the causeway there were many bridges at intervals, and in front of us stood the great City of Mexico, and we . . . we did not even number four hundred soldiers.

Bernal Díaz del Castillo, The True History
of the Conquest of New Spain, 1568

AN URBAN CONTINENT

News media discussions of Latin America focus heavily on drugs, violence, and national economic problems, while advertisements, such as those for Colombian coffee, portray an image of peasants with donkeys. Many think of Latin America as an overwhelmingly rural continent. The facts are otherwise. According to the World Bank, Latin America (including Mexico) is 76 percent urban—or about as urban as the United States. Of the world's ten largest urban places, three are in Latin America: Mexico City, Sao Paulo, and Rio de Janeiro. Buenos Aires at 10 million is just behind. (See Figure 18-1.) Latin American cities are growing at a remarkable rate of 4 percent a year and suffer from the maladies of growing places. Urban problems such as violent crime and infrastructure deterioration are especially severe. Sao Paulo, for example, with its 15 million inhabitants has about twice as many people as New York, but its annual operating budget is one-tenth as large.[1]

SPANISH COLONIAL CITIES

Latin American cities, unlike most of those of Asia and Africa, are not a consequence of European colonial expansion during the late nineteenth century. Latin America already had grand cities at the time the Pilgrims were beginning to learn from the Indians how to raise corn. In fact, all the Latin American metropolitan areas that had more than 1 million inhabitants in 1960—except Montevideo—were founded in the sixteenth century.[2] However, while many of the cities have ancient roots, the bulk of their growth is very recent, a product of the last half century.

The Spanish designed their colonial cities to be remarkably similar in both ecological plan and functional purpose. Growth and development over the centuries have blunted many of the original similarities, but elements of the first cities still remain. The purpose of the cities was to serve as administrative centers and garrison posts for the Spanish military forces.

Spanish colonial cities did not enjoy the virtual independence of most of the early English towns in North America. Administrative decrees were promulgated from Spain. The city was the center from which the mining or agricultural hinterland was to be controlled and the funnel through which wealth was to flow to the mother country. The Spanish crown discouraged commercial and manufacturing activities that would make the colonial city any less dependent on Spain.

Socially and commercially, the early cities looked toward Spain rather than toward their own hinterland. Cities were placed on the land; they did not grow out of it. Unlike the North American colonies, the Latin American cities did not develop into commercial or manufacturing centers. The limited manufacturing and processing that did exist, such as the production of syrup and molasses and the spinning

---

[1] Kevin Noblet, "Troubled Continent," *Richmond-Times Dispatch,* July 9, 1993, p. E1. For national data see "1995 World Population Data Sheet," Population Reference Bureau, Washington, D.C., 1995.
[2] Jorge E. Hardoy, *Urbanization in Latin America: Approaches and Issues,* Doubleday (Anchor), Garden City, N.Y., 1975, p. viii.

Figure 18-1. Map of Latin America.

and weaving of cotton and woolen cloth, took place on the *haciendas* and other large landed estates.

The decrees governing the colonies were written in Spain by the Council of the Indies; home rule was unknown. These policies had two objectives: "(1) to make the colonies into producers of gold, silver, and precious stones; and (2) to limit their consumption of manufactured goods strictly to those produced in Spain, shipped in convoys from Spanish ports, and destined for a few strongly fortified seaports, of which the principal ones were Vera Cruz, Cartagena, and Callao."[3] The effect of all this was a throttling of trade and commerce as a basis for urban life in Latin American cities under Spanish domination. The merchant, who enjoyed such a prominent position in the social structure of New England, did not have influence in the Spanish colonies. Spanish colonies lacked the middle-class base of English colonies. The seaports were heavily fortified entrepôts designed for receiving the manufactures of Spain in the annual convoys and assembling the treasure that was to be shipped to Spain on the return voyage. The impact of this pattern can be seen today; few metropolitan areas are found other than on the coastline. The planned city of Brasilia is one exception to this rule.

Physical Structure

Regulations of Charles V (1519–1556) and Philip II (1556–1598), eventually codified into the famous Laws of the Indies, specified how cities were to be organized. For example, cities were to follow a rectangular plan and be founded near rivers in a manner permitting expansion. However, as Hardoy points out, "legislation only formalized a situation already perfectly defined in practice."[4] The existence of indigenous cities, of course, modified the plans, as did various practical considerations such as topography.

Nonetheless, most Spanish settlements adhered to the classical model of a central *plaza mayor.* Around the central plaza were the cathedral and the major government buildings. The *solares,* or house lots, were of uniform shape, and the city was laid out in a grid with intersections at right angles. Houses and grounds were to be surrounded by walls, and because of this the early cities frequently appeared to be more heavily inhabited than was actually the case. Since the cities were to serve as fortified strong points performing administrative functions for the surrounding hinterland, they were not always ideally located from the standpoint of transportation; Mexico City, founded by the Aztecs and conquered by the Spanish in 1521, was located on an island in the middle of a lake. Political rather than economic considerations often weighed heavily in the location of cities. Even the legal rank of a city was a matter decided in Spain rather than in the new world.

The Spanish colonial government did everything possible to retain a rigid class system. One edict even reserved all the top administrative, religious, and political positions for *peninsulares,* or those born in Spain. Those born in the colonies, regardless of their wealth or family position, were relegated to a secondary status— one factor that directly motivated local leaders to instigate the early nineteenth-century rebellions against Spain.

Fortunately, the grid layout of the cities offered considerable flexibility; the boundaries could be expanded as more room was needed. Additional grids were easily added by extending the straight streets and adding more identical blocks. The

---

[3] T. Lynn Smith, "The Changing Functions of Latin American Cities," *The Americas,* **25**:74, 1968.
[4] Hardoy, *Urbanization in Latin America,* p. 30.

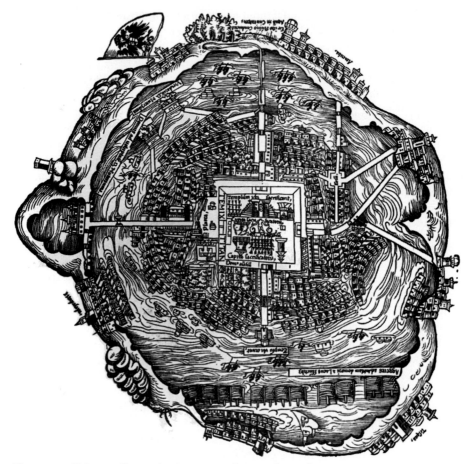

This map of Mexico City is the first printed map of any American city. It is from a 1524 volume on the discoveries of Hernando Cortéz. (Map Division/New York Public Library.)

focus on the central plaza meant that there were no markets, walls, or storehouses at the periphery of the city to impede expansion.[5] The large lots (which the law required be enclosed by walls) initially resulted in a relatively low population density. Later, subdivision of lots occurred, and this—and the cutting of new streets midway between existing streets—allowed the city to increase its density with relative ease.

Brazilian cities differed from the model just described in that they were not built to any standard plan such as that provided by the Laws of the Indies. Cities in Brazil were few and with little influence, since the Portuguese, unlike the

[5] Ralph A. Gakenheimer, "The Peruvian City of the Sixteenth Century," in Glen H. Beyer (ed.), *The Urban Explosion in Latin America,* Cornell University Press, Ithaca, N.Y., 1967, p. 50.

Spaniards, preferred to live a semifeudal existence on their estates in the country. Portuguese policy also kept towns such as Santos, Bahia, and Recife relatively small. Their splendid natural ports were open only to ships from Portugal, and this trade was not sufficient to turn these towns into real cities. By the nineteenth century Rio de Janeiro was the undisputed political, economic, and cultural center of Brazil.

Policy and Traditions

The differences in ecological patterns between the North American and South American cities are frequently attributed to Spanish colonial policy as typified by the Laws of the Indies.[6] However, factors more powerful than "Iberian values" were at work: "The fact of the matter is that the traditional Latin American pattern could be observed in cities of the New World prior to the Spanish conquest."[7] Both historical and archeological evidence suggest that among the pre-Columbian Aztec and Maya civilizations the elites tended to live in the centers of the great cities. The pattern is confirmed by Bishop Landa's account, first published in 1566:

> Before the Spaniards had conquered that country, the natives lived together in towns in a very civilized fashion. . . . In the middle of the towns were their temples with beautiful plazas, and all around the temples stood the houses of the lords and the priests, and those of the most important people. Thus came the houses of the richest and of those who were held in the highest estimation next to these, and at the outskirts of the town were the houses of the lower class.[8]

Thus, the pattern of spatial distribution by social class was set well before the Spaniards arrived. The pattern conforms to that suggested by Gideon Sjoberg for preindustrial cities.[9] (See Chapter 2, Emergence of Cities.)

EVOLVING PATTERNS

Before the introduction of modern transportation technology, and before industrialization contaminated central areas with its noise, noxious fumes, and congestion, the central area of the city was the most pleasant and the most convenient area. This is where the elite built their homes, frequently with extensive grounds and almost always behind high walls that effectively isolated the home from the confusion of the streets and markets outside.

[6] See, for example, George A. Theodorson (ed.), *Studies in Human Ecology,* Row, Peterson, Evanston, Ill., 1961, pp. 326–327.
[7] Leo F. Schnore, "On the Spatial Structure of Cities in the Two Americas," in Philip Hauser and Leo Schnore (eds.), *The Study of Urbanization,* Wiley, New York, 1965, p. 369.
[8] Edwin M. Shook and Tatiana Proskouriakoff, "Settlement Patterns in Meso-America and the Sequency in the Guatemalan Highlands," in Gordon R. Wiley (ed.), *Prehistoric Settlement Patterns in the New World,* Wenner-Gren Foundation for Anthropological Research, New York, 1956, pp. 93–100.
[9] Gideon Sjoberg, *The Preindustrial City: Past and Present,* Free Press, New York, 1960, pp. 96–98.

The pattern of high socioeconomic status in the center has also been found in North American cities before industrialization, particularly in the less industrial cities of the old south. According to Leo Schnore, the data suggest that the residential structure of cities evolves in a predictable direction and that this pattern is observable both in North America and, more recently, in Latin America:

> Given growth and expansion of the center, and given appropriate improvements in transportation and communication, the upper strata might be expected to shift from central to peripheral residence, and the lower classes might increasingly take up occupancy in the central area abandoned by the elite. Despite mounting land values occasioned by the competition of alternative (nonresidential) land uses, the lower strata may occupy valuable central land in tenements, subdivided dwellings originally intended for single families, and other high-density "slum" housing arrangements.[10]

POET

The earlier discussed ecological complex of *population, organization, environment,* and *technology* (POET) helps us understand these changes. Technology has done much in recent times to change the configuration of cities. As was indicated earlier, railroads and steam power did much to produce the nineteenth-century American city. Since the 1920s, the automobile has permitted a form of population dispersion that was impossible earlier. The telephone and advances in communication technology such as e-mail and fax have meant that interrelated functions can be spatially separated without loss of contact and control. In preindustrial Latin American cities, the elite preempted the more central areas for their residences, since these were the most accessible sites in an era of primitive transportation technology. Technological changes—automobiles, good roads, extension of power and sewage lines—have drastically reduced the attractiveness of the central city as a place of residence. Upper-class and middle-class suburbanization is now found in Latin America on the pattern of North America.

Early Social and Economic Structure

As previously noted, in colonial Latin America the pattern was one of creating deliberate dependency. Political independence from Spain and Portugal in the early nineteenth century did not end economic dependency. Independence, if anything, increased the dependence of the new republics upon European powers and the United States.[11] Cities remained tied to external markets while virtually ignoring their hinterlands. Until this century, geography also set limits on penetration of the interior and fostered a pattern of external dependence.

The absence of a substantial entrepreneurial middle class also stunted the economic growth of the cities. Merchants and businesspeople were looked down upon socially; for membership in the elite, one's income was expected to come from landholdings rather than manufacture or trade. As a result, the Latin American

---

[10] Schnore, "On the Spatial Structure of Cities in the Two Americas," pp. 373–374.
[11] Hardoy, *Urbanization in Latin America,* p. viii.

city—in contrast to cities in North America—was a political rather than an economic or manufacturing center.[12]

The growth of the middle class in the nineteenth century, when it did occur, was due in large part to the technological changes in transportation and to immigration. The railroad and later the highway opened up new territories—territories that could be developed with the newly emerging agricultural technology. Also, in the latter years of the nineteenth century, waves of European immigrants brought about the formation of new urban institutions. Simultaneously, a new professional middle class and an urban bureaucracy began to develop.

However, this middle class, the most important group in economic growth and industrial development, usually weakened its possible influence by allying itself with the upper classes and against the urban proletariat. Upper-middle-class professional groups often became so involved with the establishment that they ceased to be a force for political change. The urban middle class, which so dominates political life in North America and Europe, has a growing but still limited influence on national policy in many Latin American nations.

RECENT DEVELOPMENTS

Urban Growth

The Latin American cities of today are far from the sleepy towns of the turn of the century. Urbanization in Latin America is currently proceeding at a phenomenal rate. As recently as 1950 only 39 percent of the population lived in places of 20,000 or more. Currently South America is three-quarters urban.[13]

As noted in the opening, the world's largest and second-largest urban places (Mexico City and Sao Paulo), as well as the 10 million-plus cities of Rio de Janeiro and greater Buenos Aires, are all found in Latin America. By contrast, among the ten largest urban places there are no European cities, and only one North American city: New York (sixth).[14]

Latin America is growing rapidly. As of 1950, the North American and Latin American populations were of equal size. As of 1990, Latin America was over $1\frac{1}{2}$ times larger (447 million versus 278 million). By 2025, United Nations projections foresee a Latin American population over twice as large as that of North America. To put it another way, in 1930 Latin America had only one city of over 1 million persons (Mexico City). In 2000 the number will be over fifty. The greatest growth has been in the very largest cities. Latin America is a continent of primate cities, with over half of its population in cities of over 100,000 inhabitants.[15]

[12] James Scobie, quoted in Glenn H. Beyer (ed.), *The Urban Explosion in Latin America,* Cornell University Press, Ithaca, N.Y., 1967.

[13] "1995 World Population Data Sheet."

[14] United Nations, Department of International Economic and Social Affairs, 1990.

[15] Philip M. Hauser and Robert W. Gardiner, "Urban Future: Trends and Prospects," in Philip Hauser et al. (eds.), *Population and the Urban Future,* State University of New York Press, Albany, 1982, Table 1.6.

Mexico City now has the dubious distinction of being the largest city in the world. And it is still growing. (Owen Franken/Stock, Boston.)

Within the period of a lifetime, Latin America has been transformed from a rural, agriculturally oriented continent to one that is predominantly urbanized and urban-oriented. The process of urbanization, which took over a century in North America, was compressed into decades.

Figures for the entire continent, of course, cloud variations among nations. The range of urbanization in Latin American countries is great. Haiti has only 31 percent of its population in urban places, while Argentina (87 percent), Chile (85 percent), Venezuela (84 percent), and Uruguay (90 percent) are more urban than the United States and among the most urbanized nations in the world. Half of Uruguay's population lives in the capital city of Montevideo.

Taken as a whole, Latin America is one of the world's more urbanized regions. It is far more urbanized than Asia or Africa. Latin American cities, and particularly the largest primate cities, are growing at a rate that outpaces their ability to provide urban services and employment.

During the twenty-first century, Latin America's city growth will increasingly come not from in-migration but from the natural increase of births over deaths.

Latin American cities already generally have low death rates owing to reasonably adequate programs of public health, vaccination, and sanitation. Birthrates, on the other hand, are two and sometimes three times as high as European levels. The inevitable consequence of such a high rate of natural increase is an urban population explosion.

Twenty-five years ago the annual increase in the rural populations of Latin America was such that each year jobs on the land had to be created for over half a million new workers.[16] Today that figure has doubled. The chance of finding employment for so many workers in the already overloaded agricultural sector is, however, minimal, for there is a surplus in the rural labor force.[17] One of the few economic growth sectors has been tourism in coastal areas. In order to increase income from tourism, Mexico (and others) has established resort cities where villages once stood (i.e., Cancun).

Economic Change

While agriculture needs to be made more productive, it probably makes little economic sense to try to hold the farmers in the country or in small towns. It is sometimes argued that if rural life can be made more attractive, people will be less likely to abandon rural areas for the opportunities and advantages of the city. However, the costs of modernizing the rural sector are high, particularly when the cities also need modernization. Rural electrification, for example, is far more expensive than providing electricity for urban slum dwellers. The same amount of money often can do more for more people if it is spent in the city than if it is spent in the country. In Sao Paulo, for instance, the only source of water for 400,000 shanty dwellers is contaminated with human waste. Because funds are limited, "community development" often is more effectively directed toward urban populations, who by their very presence in the city have already indicated a willingness to make changes.

For the majority of ruralites, the move to the city is a wise decision. Even low urban standards are likely to represent an improvement in quality of life. On the other hand, what is good for them personally is often a disaster for the city itself when viewed from a national perspective. The in-migration of ever-more peasants simply compounds already severe urban problems.[18]

Characteristics of Urban Inhabitants

In Latin America, migration to cities for years has been more permanent and less seasonal than in other developing regions.[19] The city-bound migrants, like those elsewhere in the world, tend to be mostly young adults. Older people are less prone to leave villages or rural areas for the opportunities and bright lights of the city.

---

[16] *Estudio Económico para América Latina,* ECLA, United Nations, 1966, pp. 41–51.
[17] Solon L. Barraclough, "Rural Development and Employment Prospects in Latin America," in Arthur J. Field (ed.), *City and Country in the Third World,* Schenkman, Cambridge, Mass., 1970, p. 106.
[18] Aprodicio A. Laquian, "Issues and Instruments in Metropolitan Planning," in Hauser, et al. (eds.), *Population and the Urban Future,* p. 68.
[19] "Some Regional Development Problems in Latin America Linked to Metropolitanization," *Economic Bulletin for Latin America,* United Nations, New York, 1972, p. 70.

Migration of young persons, plus the population explosion—which, of course, adds only young people to the population—means that there are proportionately few people of working age in the urban population. The impression of outsiders that "everyone seems so young" is borne out by the empirical data: Some 34 percent of the Latin American population is under fifteen years of age. (The figure for North America is 21 percent.)

The cities of most developing countries have more males than females; cities in Latin America, on the contrary, have more females than males. In this respect, Latin America is more similar to economically developed western areas. While there is general agreement that there are more females, there is no agreement about why this is the case. Perhaps the greater degree of urbanization and economic development in Latin America, compared with developing countries elsewhere in the world, accounts for the difference.

Shantytowns

In addition to central-core slums, squatter settlements ring all the great cities of Latin America, but there is no universally accepted view of this phenomenon. Some observers emphasize the squalor and disorganization of the squatter settlements; some argue that these shantytown settlements are in effect evolving into reasonable low-income suburban housing areas. Frequently, it seems that what a

These children in the squatter settlements of Rio de Janeiro live a life far removed from that seen by tourists at the beach. (Annie Sager/Photo Researchers.)

The World's Largest City

Urban change can be grasped more easily by looking at its impact on an individual city. Mexico City had one-quarter of New York's metro population in 1950 (2.9 million compared with 12.3 million). Currently, greater Mexico City has 18 million inhabitants, and United Nations estimates project Mexico's population in the year 2000 at 26 million (probably an overestimate). Mexico City already has the world's largest urban population, and it receives 1,000 new immigrants every day.

Mexico City is an extreme case, but the pattern and problems it represents are, unfortunately, not unique. Mexico City, even after the deadly 1985 earthquake that killed 10,000 persons, still attracts newcomers seeking employment in its 300,000 factories. These factories, plus 4 million motor vehicles without pollution controls, result in 6,000 tons of gas and soot pollution falling on the city daily. Since Mexico City is geographically located in a basin, thermal inversions seriously exacerbate an already major smog problem. The thin air is fouled by 5.5 million tons of contaminants a year.[*] In practical terms this works out to a pound and a half of pollutants a day for every man, woman, and child in the city. Or to put it another way, every resident regardless of age receives the equivalent health damage of smoking two packs of cigarettes a day. Lead quantities, according to a Harvard Medical School researcher, are at a level that causes severe retardation in infants.[†]

One out of every five Mexicans lives in the Mexico City area, making garbage disposal an impossible problem. Each day Mexico City produces 14,000 tons of garbage but can dispose of only 8,000 tons. Another 2,000 to 3,000 tons goes into landfills, and the rest sits in open dumps which are the breeding ground of some 115 million rats.[‡] The dumps also are a source of income for poor scavengers who sift the refuse in search of recyclable or salable items.

Poor newcomers to the city settle in the sprawling and congested shantytowns such as "Neza" (Netzahualcoyotl), which already houses over 3 million persons. Whether or not greater Mexico City will hold 26 million persons at the beginning of the twenty-first century or only 20 million, it is a sure bet that the populations of Mexico City and other LDC

[*] William Branigin, "Bracing for Pollution Disaster," *Washington Post*, Nov. 28, 1988, p. 14-A.
[†] Ibid.
[‡] David De Voss, "Mexico City's Limits," in Andrew Maguire and Janel Welsh Brown (eds.), *Bordering on Trouble*, Adler and Adler, Bethesda, Md., 1986, p. 21.

metropolitan areas are going to continue to increase for the next several decades. To a resident of Mexico City, it is probably academic whether the urban area will soon have 26 million or slightly fewer persons.

No matter what the figure is, the infrastructure is not up to handling even the present population. Even without natural disasters such as earthquakes, the city's grossly overloaded transportation system, sewers, and schools will not be able to cope. Already 2 million Mexico City children do not have access to a school. Unless a miracle occurs, there is no way that services such as garbage collection, schooling, and medical services can be adequately provided for 26 million people. Badly strained systems simply cannot handle double the present load—not in Mexico City, and not elsewhere.

writer describes is not shaped as much by what he or she sees as by the writer's philosophy and political beliefs. There is no unanimity, as the next pages show.

What is agreed upon is that the peripheral slums grow like mushrooms (in Chile they are called *poblaciones callampas,* which means "mushroom towns"). They grow because of the population explosion and the migration of peasants from the countryside in search of a better life. For instance, the number of squatters in Sao Paulo is estimated to be between 500,000 and 1.5 million. One-quarter of Lima's population lives in *barriadas.* In Caracas, the capital of Venezuela, over 35 percent of the total metropolitan population is living in squatter settlements, while in Bogotà, Colombia, more than half the population lives in neighborhoods still considered illegal by officials. (In Bogotà, unlike elsewhere, the illegal occupants are not really squatters since they technically own the land upon which their illegal "pirate developments" have been built.) Over one-third of Mexico City's inhabitants live in slums and squatter settlements, where it is not uncommon for entire families to live in one room.[20] Many live in the aptly named "lost cities" surrounding Mexico City. Mexico City's Neza (Netzahualcoyotl) houses over 3 million persons. Twenty-five years ago it was a dry lake bed. Today it is a city of homes made of cinder blocks, crates, corrugated metal, and plastic sheets.

Half of Mexico's work force, and most of the shanty dwellers, are in the informal economy. Virtually everyone over twelve contributes to family incomes.[21] Adults work in construction, in-home manufacturing, vending, domestic service, or one-person businesses such as repairing shoes. The average wage is about $3 a day. Children peddle cigarettes, gum, newspapers, or trinkets on the street. Everyone works because every peso is necessary for survival.

Some of the fastest-growing shantytowns are just south of the United States border where American firms have set up *maquiladoras,* or assembly plants, to cheaply produce goods for the United States market. Sometimes this involves working with toxic substances that require expensive precautions and cleanup in the United States. Since *maquila* workers cannot live on the average wage of $1 per hour, they must moonlight in the informal economy in order to survive. Most live in makeshift shanty housing. Water, sewage, and health problems are so severe that Mexican health and welfare officials have refused to visit them.[22]

It is clear that shantytown squatter settlements will be part of the Latin American urban scene for the foreseeable future. As long as the urban population continues to increase because of high birthrates and migration to the cities, the cities will continue to add more people than they can house. The Peruvian government has been more candid than most in admitting that it is unable to reduce the urban housing deficit because public investment must be directed toward developing national objectives, but the situation elsewhere is similar. Mexico has to pay 60 percent of its income for debt payment.

Social upheavals and group violence may become more common in marginal settlements. Clashes between squatters and police often occur in places such as

[20] Bart McDowell, "Mexico City: An Alarming Giant," *National Geographic,* **166:**139–144, 1984.
[21] Robert J. Stout, "Making It Day to Day in Netzahualcoyotl," *Notre Dame Magazine,* Spring, 1993, p. 23.
[22] Ibid., p. 26.

Mexico City when landlords, as land prices escalate, attempt to evict squatters who previously were ignored. Activist attempts to organize the vast but largely still silent urban proletariat have had limited success.

On the other hand, Castells has argued that establishment governments may, in fact, support land invasions by squatters in return for political support from the poor. In effect, the establishment makes a political deal with the squatters.[23]

Settlements as Squalor. A description of daily life in squatter shantytowns is provided by the supposed diary of a dweller in a *favela* outside Sao Paulo, Brazil. The following are excerpts from her diary for one day in July:

> July 16 I got up. . . . I went to get the water. I made coffee. I told the children that I didn't have any bread, that they would have to drink their coffee plain and eat meat with *farina*. I was feeling ill and decided to cure myself. I stuck my finger down my throat twice, vomited, and knew I was under the evil eye. The upset feeling left and I went to Senor Manuel, carrying some cans to sell. Everything that I find in the garbage I sell. He gave me 13 cruzeiros. I kept thinking that I had to buy bread, soap, and milk for Vera Eunice. The 13 cruzeiros wouldn't make it. I returned home, or rather to my shack, nervous and exhausted. I thought of the worrisome life that I led. Carrying paper, washing clothes for the children, staying in the street all day long. Yet I'm always lacking things.[24]

The picture conjured up by such accounts is one of fecund, festering slums filled with dirty shacks and having no sanitary facilities, no garbage collection, and no hope of improvement. Typically, squatter settlements are built without planning or organization on undesirable land such as hillsides, marsh lands, or even dumps. Building materials are often whatever the squatter can salvage. One graphic account describes the notorious *barriadas* of Lima as:

> . . . so bestial, so filthy, so congested, so empty of light, fun, color, health, or comfort, so littered with excrement and garbage, so swarming with barefoot children, so reeking of pitiful squalor that just the breath of it makes you retch.[25]

A former official of the United Nations has described squatter settlements as a "spreading malady" and "plague" of "excessive squalor, filth, and poverty, fostering mounting social disorder and tension."[26]

Squatter Settlements as Transitional Settlements. On the other hand, others suggest that while there is some truth in the conventional image, and while some inhabitants of squatter settlements are indeed wretchedly poor, there are "many squatter settlements that are socially developing and physically self-improving suburbs rather than slums.[27] William Mangin's description of the same

---

[23] Manuel Castells, "Squatters and the State in Latin America," in Joseph Gugler (ed.), *The Urbanization of the Third World*, Oxford University Press, Oxford, 1988, pp. 338–366.

[24] From the book *Child of the Dark: The Diary of Carolina Maria de Jesús*, David St. Clair (trans.), p. 18. Copyright 1962 by E. P. Dutton & Co., Inc. and Souvenir Press, Ltd. Published by E. P. Dutton & Co., Inc., and used with their permission. There is some question about the diary's authenticity.

[25] James Morris, *Cities*, Harcourt Brace Jovanovich, New York, 1964, p. 227.

[26] Morris Juppenlaty, *Cities in Transformation: The Urban Squatter Problem in the Developing World*, University of Queensland Press, Australia, 1970.

[27] John F. C. Turner, "Squatter Settlements in Developing Countries," in Daniel P. Moynihan (ed.), *Toward a National Urban Policy*, Basic Books, New York, 1970, pp. 256–257.

areas surrounding Lima, described above as "bestial" and "filthy," is far more optimistic:

> At worst a *barriada* is a crowded, helter-skelter hodge-podge of inadequate straw houses with no water supply and no provision for sewage disposal; parts of many are like this. Most do have a rough plan, and most inhabitants convert their original houses to more substantial structures as soon as they can. Construction activity usually involving family, neighbors, and friends is a constant feature of *barriada* life and, although water and sewage usually remain critical problems, a livable situation is reached with respect to them.[28]

For most of the migrants the *barriada* represents a definite improvement in terms of housing and general income, and Lima represents an improvement over the semi-feudal life of the Indian, *cholo,* or lower-class mestizo.

One of the better squatter settlements is Villa El Salvadore, an hour's drive from central Lima. In 1971, a bloody confrontation between landless peasants and police led to the Peruvian government offering the squatters a large tract of desert land then used by the army. Rather than allowing chaotic growth, the government together with squatter leaders laid out a city plan with equal-size lots.

Today, Villa El Salvadore has over 300,000 residents and is the fifth largest city in Peru. More importantly, residents pitched in not only to build their own homes but also to build the city's water and electric systems. They constructed thirty-two of the thirty-four schools and five of the nine health clinics.[29] Elected neighborhood residential groups have improved educational opportunities to the extent that 98 percent of school-age children graduate from primary school and 51 percent from high school; both statistics are well above the national average.[30] Women's groups have set up milk and vaccination projects, and have helped set up some 250 communal kitchens in which twenty to thirty women pool their money to buy food and take turns cooking.

In generalizing, it has to be remembered that squatter settlements differ markedly not only in their physical appearance and services available but in the social composition of the groups inhabiting them. Usually, the newest settlements are most disorganized and ramshackle; others that have existed longer are highly organized "slums of hope." Some squatter settlements have well-built homes.

Contrary to conventional assumptions, not all squatters own their own houses. As areas become more settled, the proportion of squatter renters often increases. There are several distinct squatter types.[31]

1. *Owner squatters* are the "typical" squatters who own their own shack, but not the land on which it stands.
2. *Squatter tenants* are new in-migrants who pay rent to another squatter. Landlords' profits are often considerable, since landlords pay no taxes or upkeep.

---

[28] William P. Mangin, "Mental Health and Migration to Cities: A Peruvian Case," *Annals of New York Academy of Sciences,* **84:**911–917, 1960.

[29] Tyler Bridges, "Shanty Dwellers of Peru Turn Desert Tract into Young Town," *Washington Post,* May 21, 1987, pp. E1–E2.

[30] Ibid.

[31] Charles Abrams, "Squatting and Squatters," in Janet Abu-Lughod and Richard Hay, Jr. (eds.), *Third World Urbanization,* Maaroufa Press, Chicago, 1977, pp. 297–298.

3. *Speculator squatters* are holding property as a way to make a profit. They view squatting as a sound business venture, expecting eventually to obtain title to the land.
4. *Store or business squatters* open businesses, catering to the needs of other squatters. They often live on the premises. Most are marginal operators; but some, in the absence of rents or taxes, make substantial profits.
5. *Semisquatters* build their huts on private land but eventually come to some sort of terms with the owner. Strictly speaking, semisquatters are perhaps better classified as tenants.

A casual observer, however, is unlikely to be conscious of these differences. While most settlements are terribly poor and without municipal amenities, it has to be remembered that they differ in condition, services, and social composition. Some are self-upgrading communities; some are horrendous.

The Myth of Marginality. Authorities differ when discussing the lives lived by the inhabitants of shantytowns. One view is that these inhabitants are set apart from the other city residents not only by their poverty but by their marginality and traditional rural orientation.[32] Their rural backgrounds and continued rural ties mean that they remain essentially peasants, but peasants who by force of circumstance live in what is defined as an "urban" area. They are *in* but not *of* the city. The implicit, if not explicit, assumption here is that the problem is how to integrate these nonurban people into a complex modern economic system.

The view of the city as a disorganizing force is part of an intellectual tradition going back to the Chicago school of sociology and its concern with problems of assimilating immigrants into the inner-city slums of North America. Louis Wirth—as you recall from Chapter 7, City Life-Styles—defines "urbanism" as the mode of life of people who live in cities and are subject to their influences. These influences, it is said, act to destroy primary groups, weaken family ties, loosen the bonds of kinship, and lessen neighborliness. The result was said to be impersonality, superficiality, anonymity in personal relations, and the substitution of large secondary organizations for the declining role played by kith and kin. Disruption of family life, rejection of traditional religion, delinquency and alienation among the young, and a generally fragmented social world were some of the consequences associated with life in the slums of North American industrial cities.

A second position is that the rural character of the immigrants is considerably overemphasized, and that problems of adjustment are far less severe than is commonly supposed. Data tend to support this view. For example, the largest study of an LDC city—sponsored by the World Bank and called The City Study—covers 3,000 householders in Bogotà. It indicates that the behavior of in-migrant and nonmigrant city dwellers in both developed and developing countries is much more similar than was once believed.[33] In-migrants to Bogotà, for example, are not worse

---

[32] Oscar Lewis, *The Children of Sanchez,* Random House, New York, 1961; and *La Vida,* Random House, New York, 1966.
[33] R. Mohan and N. Hartline, "The Poor of Bogotá: Who They Are, What They Do, and Where They Live," World Bank Staff Working Paper no. 635, 1984.

Planned Capitals: Brasilia

Twentieth-century planned capital cities have been mixtures of success and failure. Canberra, Australia, which was begun in 1918, is pleasing to the eye; but it is difficult to go anywhere in Canberra without using a car, owing to the strict segregation of the city into governmental, residential, and commercial areas. The economic base of Canberra is almost completely dependent on government, middle-class employment. The population is widely dispersed in single-family homes, which makes it difficult to develop a sense of community. Canberra is sometimes referred to as the world's most inconvenient suburb.

Like Canberra, Brasilia is a planned capital city. Inaugurated as the capital of Brazil in 1957, Brasilia is located 700 miles inland from Rio de Janeiro; it was deliberately located far inland in order to economically develop the interior.

Brasilia was designed from the ground up, primarily by Lucio Costa. The city was designed to reflect contemporary times, and it is characterized by massive superblocks of concrete and glass. While the design is unquestionably bold and creative, it is also somewhat stark and abstract—and the visitor finds it hard to escape the feeling that Brasilia is not really meant to be lived in.

The city was conceived in the shape of an airplane, with government offices, commerce, and recreation occupying the central axis and residences located along the wings (creating monumental twice-daily traffic jams).

Brasilia was designed to house 2 million persons by the year 2000 and currently has surpassed that level. Fears are that its population will swell to 4 million in a decade—a population that the current city cannot reasonably support. Without any rivers or springs, Brasilia has a serious water problem, and water is rationed during the dry season.

An unanticipated problem has been the continuing influx of poor workers into the so-called satellite cities and the *favelas* (unplanned peripheral slums) at a rate of over 10 percent a year. The superblocks of the central city—known as the *plano piloto* (pilot plan)—house the upper and middle classes, while the slum settlements are mostly hidden from view miles from the center of the city. The shantytown *favelas* and squatter shacks now house more people than the apartment superblocks.

Too much may have been expected of the utopian city. As the designer Costa replies to critics:

> Things are done differently here. You have to accept the country for what it is. Of course, half the people in Brasilia live in favelas. Brasilia was not designed to solve the problems of Brazil, it was bound to reflect them.[*]

Although Brasilia encouraged the economic development of the center of the country, much of this development has been an ecological disaster. Nor has Brasilia been successful in generating that perhaps indefinable human response we experience in the great cities of the world. Brasilia lacks Rio's human warmth and livability. The city is a remarkable monument, but monuments are not always comfortable places in which to live. Perhaps the Brazilian spirit will, with the passage of time, convert Brasilia, if not into another Rio, at least into a more comfortable and livable city.

[*] "Brazil's Dream City Has Flaws," United Press International, Aug. 19, 1973.

off than the rest of the population. In fact, they earn higher wages than nonmigrants in all income categories.[34] Moreover, informal-sector jobs, such as domestic service, showed wage rates as high as or higher than formal-sector factory worker jobs. There was, however, great disparity in income levels between the well off and the poor, with the lowest 40 percent of the population earning less than 12 percent of total income.[35]

The most important finding of The City Study was that even the very poor newcomers to the city showed economic rationality.[36] There was little support for the widely held belief that the poor had a distinctly short-term orientation or culture of poverty that made them unable to defer gratification or plan for the future.[37] The City Study showed the poor, like others, act to maximize utility. That the poor are rational does not, however, necessarily mean that they will be economically successful. In spite of their best efforts, they remain trapped by their poverty in circumstances in which it takes all their energy simply to feed their families.

Another empirical study has also tended to discredit the so-called marginality of newcomers.[38] The widespread belief that squatter settlers have behaviors and attitudes supposedly associated with marginal groups has little empirical support. What sets squatters apart is not their different values or aspirations, but their lack of opportunity.

There is little question that the move from the country to the city has a considerable impact upon the migrant's way of life. However, what strikes many observers is not the difficulty of the adjustment to urban life, but rather the speed and facility with which the rural migrant becomes a city slicker. It is easy to forget that the urban dwellers with whom we are comparing the new migrant were quite likely migrants themselves. Half the population of many Latin American cities were originally migrants. Within a few months of his or her arrival, it is often very difficult to tell the migrant from someone who has spent years in the city.

An unanswered question is how the squatter or slum dweller, after the initial period of adjustment, will respond to his or her relative deprivation, compared with affluent city dwellers. Will the slum dweller accept semipermanent poverty? News reports from El Salvador, Nicaragua, Brazil, and Mexico suggest not.

A SUCCESS STORY

Discussions of LDC cities in Latin America often have a depressing sameness. Thus, it is useful to look at an out-and-out success. Curitiba, Brazil, a city of 1.6 million, shares many of the problems of the continent: It has increased elevenfold in the past fifty years, and it has an average family income of less than $100 a week. Nonetheless, Curitiba is a green, clean, and very livable city.[39] It began twenty-five

[34] Ibid.
[35] World Bank, "Anatomy of a Third World City," *Urban Edge,* **8**(8):4, 1984.
[36] Ibid., p. 3.
[37] See, for example, Oscar Lewis, "The Culture of Poverty," *Scientific American,* **215**(4):19–25, 1966.
[38] Janice E. Perlman, *The Myth of Marginality,* University of California Press, Berkeley and Los Angeles, 1976.
[39] James Brooke, "Brazilian Mayor Built Third World Showplace by Keeping It Simple," *International Herald-Tribune,* May 29, 1992, p. 3.

years ago when the mayor, rather than building highway overpasses and shopping centers as was occurring elsewhere in Brazil, instead advocated pedestrian malls and recycled buildings. Today the center of the city is the *calcadao,* or big sidewalk, which provides forty-nine blocks of pedestrian streets clogged with shoppers and strollers. A block-long arcade, opened in 1992, boasts of eighty shops open twenty-four hours a day. Crime is minimal. People come into the center on a system of express buses running in separate high-speed bus lanes.

To help rural migrants adjust and learn new trades, old city buses have been converted into mobile vocational classrooms. Street children can enter an apprentice program where they work half-time in return for schooling, food, and a living stipend. Since garbage trucks can't get to those living in the hilly shantytowns, the poor are encouraged to bring their garbage to the trucks. Twenty-pound bags of garbage can be exchanged for surplus eggs, butter, rice, and beans.[40]

Curitiba isn't a miracle, but it does show that even without substantial funding, ingenuity and common sense can do a great deal to turn around urban problems. There is hope.

IMPORTANCE TO THE UNITED STATES

Latin America is a highly urbanized continent, and it holds some of the largest cities in the world. Large cities are plagued by decaying infrastructures, crime, congestion, pollution, lack of decent jobs, and poor education. Nonetheless, the cities with all their problems remain locations of hope for newcomers.

What happens in Latin America is important to North Americans for practical as well as moral and ethical reasons. Questions of land reform and urban poverty in Asia or Africa are literally oceans away. Latin America, however, is a neighbor with whom we share a land border. Also, Hispanics are by far the fastest-growing population in the United States. By choice or necessity, what occurs in Latin America is increasingly important to North America.

---

[40] Ibid.

PART SIX

CONCLUSION

CHAPTER
19
TOWARD THE
URBAN FUTURE

We will ever strive for the ideals and sacred things of the city, both alone and with many; we will unceasingly seek to quicken the sense of public duty; we will revere and obey the city's laws; we will transmit this city not only not less, but greater, better and more beautiful than it was transmitted to us.

Oath of the Athenian city-state

RECAPITULATION

This book—through its examination of the concept of the interaction of population, organization, environment, and technology (POET)—has illustrated the evolution of the first cities. Such initial urban places were severely limited in size by the environment and the limited agricultural technology. As the nineteenth century began, only 3 percent of the world's population lived in places of 5,000 people or more. Then, spurred by inventions in agriculture, manufacturing, and transportation, nineteenth-century city populations in Europe and North America began to mushroom. A classic example is Chicago. The city that had only 4,100 people when incorporated in 1833 had some 2 million residents only three-quarters of a century later. The development of railway technology in the mid-nineteenth century made it possible to locate commercial and industrial cities inland.

Early Concentration

The nineteenth century and early twentieth century fostered a period of concentration. From the Civil War (1865) to World War II (1945), population, power, manufacturing, finance, and fashion concentrated in urban areas. Technological developments in transportation and communication during the first half of this century both reinforced the importance of the core and extended its dominance to the end of the paved road and telephone lines. As Part Five, Worldwide Urbanization, demonstrated, urban economic, political, and population concentration remains the dominant third world pattern.

Contemporary Deconcentration

Now, however, communication and—to a lesser degree—transportation technologies no longer automatically favor centralization. Urban deconcentration has increasingly become the western European as well as the American pattern.[1] Technology has overcome spatial barriers. Today, goods as well as information can move from one coast to another with unprecedented speed. Many companies guarantee overnight delivery of packages, while e-mail and fax provide worldwide instantaneous communication.

  The degree to which technology can become a substitute for propinquity is still not fully grasped. We are only beginning to understand, for example, that the Nissan and General Motors automobile manufacturing plants built in semirural Tennessee reflect more than a desire to escape Detroit's unions and wage scales. While the late-nineteenth-century industrial city demanded concentration, the late-twentieth-century city does not. Changed transportation and communication technologies have outmoded the necessity to locate factories in urban centers. Today, the once-proud, industrial-based, railway-built cities of the industrial midwest either are economically depressed or have totally reoriented themselves to the

[1] Daniel R. Vining et al., "Population Dispersal from Core Regions: A Description and Tentative Explanations of Patterns in 21 Countries," in Donald A. Hicks and Norman J. Glickman (eds.), *Transition to the 21st Century,* JAI Press, Greenwich, Conn., 1983, pp. 81–111.

postindustrial economy. Pittsburgh, once the grimy center of the steel industry, now has a gleaming center and a service-based economy.

Easy accessibility and propinquity are no longer linked. Technological advances have reduced the friction of space. (For two decades, we have been able to directly telephone all over the world—from Singapore to Atlanta, Georgia.) Now we can fax, send e-mail, and even shop at home on the shopping channel and on the Internet. Spatial uncoupling from the metropolitan area by moving out to exurbia no longer means leaving behind urbanism as a way of life.

Socially, the urban and rural behavioral characteristics that played such an important part in the late-nineteenth- and early-twentieth-century social theories discussed in the first three chapters have largely lost their explanatory force. At the end of World War II, substantive distinctions could still be made between metropolitan and nonmetropolitan ways of life. Today with the nation having 350 metropolitan areas, and with the boundaries of existing areas progressively expanding, it becomes increasingly difficult to distinguish between metropolitan and nonmetropolitan areas. Satellite TV dishes, cable hookups, PCs, and fax are today an integral part of nonmetropolitan growth. Increasingly, urban-nonurban differences are differences that have ceased to make a difference. Still, personal interaction with neighbors in rural or small-town areas continues to have an expectation of permanence that distinguishes such areas from metropolitan areas.[2]

One of the more interesting developments is that of decentralization to fringe developments that are neither urban nor suburban (see Chapter 9, Changing Suburbanization Patterns). Rather than wanting to be an extension of the city, these rural suburbanites are often anticity. These new, very dispersed, rurban areas don't easily fit into the existing urban, suburban, or rural classification scheme. It has been suggested that the state of North Carolina, with its policy of dispersed economic activity, could be a prototype of a more spatially dispersed residential pattern.[3] In terms of business, suburban locations have become the norm.

None of this should be taken as suggesting that America's existing urban places are in danger of becoming ghost towns. They aren't. The "death of the city" clichés of the last decades have turned out to be poor prophecy. Within many older cities both central business districts (CBDs) and residential neighborhoods have arrested the pattern of decline and are showing evidence of stability or even growth. What is clear is that American urban places and patterns are undergoing profound changes. It appears that the future will be both more complex and more interesting than previously projected.

MAJOR ISSUES AND QUESTIONS

Urban Funding

Until the Reagan administration of the 1980s, the major disputes in Washington, D.C., over urban programs were where to target the money and how much to bud-

---

[2] I am indebted to Thomas Drabek of the University of Denver for making this point.
[3] John Herbers, *The New Heartland,* Times Books, New York, 1986.

get. There was a consensus among both Democrats and Republicans that programs and funding were needed; the lawmakers fought over specific programs. A Republican, President Nixon, it should be recalled, initiated the program of federal revenue sharing.

The broad consensus regarding at least partial responsibility for urban places now has been shattered. The 1995 Republican "Contract with America" envisioned not just the trimming back, but the total elimination, of virtually all federal aid to cities. Excepting "enterprise zones," there is little federal interest in urban problems.

Nor did President Clinton do anything to put urban funding back on the national agenda. As a result, cities have been increasingly thrown back upon state and local funding. The consequences and amounts of such revenue patterns differ widely. Some central cities are slipping toward insolvency, while others are managing quite well. The loss of federal funds is further widening, rather than decreasing, the gap between the have and have-not localities.

People versus Places

Beyond the question of amount of funds is whether limited urban funds should be spent on people or places. Should the federal government continue efforts to revitalize the economies of older central cities? The orthodox response for the five decades since the Housing Act of 1949 has been to funnel funds into the renewal and rebuilding of the economic and housing bases of the neediest older cities.

Harbor Place, Baltimore, is an example of how a derelict harbor area can be revitalized. (Tom Bross/Stock, Boston.)

Although there has been a mishmash of various programs, policies designed during the 1950s, 1960s, and 1970s had at least the implicit goal of halting or at least slowing the middle-class exodus to the suburbs. More recently this implied goal has been enlarged to include arresting the drift of jobs and population from older frost belt cities to the sun belt.

However, some urban sociologists and other urbanologists argue that trying to restore older industrial cities is a mistake.[4] Those holding this position say that such policies place the needs of places ahead of those of people. They maintain that rather than propping up obsolete industries or declining places, urban policies should be redesigned to help the poor and the unemployed to migrate to places where job opportunities are expanding. The current focus on saving the cities, they argue, results simply in warehousing the poor in cities, to no one's advantage.

According to a proponent of this view, John Kasarda, "It would be an expensive mistake to attempt to draw (by tax incentives or other means) larger production facilities back to the metropolitan cores or continuously to prop up declining urban industries that are no longer nationally or internationally competitive."[5] Obsolete areas should be allowed to shrink to a size where they are economically viable.

In practice this would mean, for example, that the declining steel-manufacturing city of Gary, Indiana, which received one of the nation's highest per capita infusions of federal money during the 1970s, should not have received such massive urban renewal, redevelopment, and retraining funds. Rather than pumping in funds in a futile attempt to save a dying industrial city, the federal government should have encouraged and aided Gary's residents to move from an area with a minimal future to regions where jobs were available. Not surprisingly, central-city mayors take strong exception to this view. They say that not attempting to save older cities seriously undermines both the places and the people who live in them. They remind us that cities are not simply to be written off, and people are not simply cargo or items of furniture to be moved from place to place.

On the other hand, North America's history is one of immigrants who came—and are still coming—far distances from other countries in search of opportunity. Should not residents of depressed areas be encouraged by economic incentives to also move toward opportunities?

Changing Population Distribution

For almost 200 years after the American Revolution, American cities had a growth rate far in excess of that of the countryside. This was a combination of heavy migration from abroad and internal movement from farm to city. Now that period has ended.

---

[4] See John D. Kasarda, "The Implications of Contemporary Redistribution Trends for National Urban Policy," *Social Science Quarterly,* **61:**373–400, 1980; and Gerald D. Suttles, "Changing Priorities for the Urban Heartland," in J. John Palen (ed.), *City Scenes: Problems and Prospects,* Little, Brown, Boston, 1981.

[5] Kasarda, "The Implications of Contemporary Redistribution Trends for National Urban Policy," p. 395.

Without substantial numbers of new arrivals, central-city populations generally can be expected to remain fairly stable for the next decade. The exceptions to this pattern are the growing cities of the sun belt, particularly those of the southwest, Texas, California, and Florida. These latter three states account for roughly half the total U.S. population growth between 1980 and 1995. All three experienced substantial in-migration from other states plus immigration of Spanish-speaking people. California has also experienced substantial Asian immigration. Population losses have been most severe in the old industrial cities, and rural heartland, although California is now experiencing out-movement of working-class whites.[6] This shift also means a shift of political power from the industrial cities and farm belt to the growing areas of the south and west. After reapportionment based on the last two censuses, the midwest and northeast lost thirty-six seats in the House of Representatives (seventeen in 1980 and nineteen more in 1990). In both reapportionments, suburban areas were the big winners.

However, the hemorrhaging population losses that affected older U.S. cities during the 1970s and 1980s appear to have ended. The sharp population declines during the 1970s that cost New York and Chicago 10 percent of their residents have moderated. As of the 1990s, Detroit, Cleveland, Baltimore, Philadelphia, Boston, and Milwaukee were still losing population, but at a declining rate. Elsewhere urban populations generally were remaining stable or even showing minor increases.

Migration in North America today is increasingly between one metropolitan area and another. Poorer migrants most commonly go from central city to central city. The more affluent and the middle class move from the suburbs of one metropolitan area to the suburbs of another metropolitan area without touching the cities themselves. Aggregate movement in the United States is toward the south and the west, particularly the southwest. The effects of population concentration are already all too visible in parts of California and Florida.

If continued suburban sprawl is to be constrained, it will be not by government fiat or planning, but by escalating costs. For some new young home buyers, a housing alternative may be purchasing a home in a revitalizing, gentrifying central-city neighborhood. Changing life-styles and priorities combined with commuting costs (time and money) have made residence in peripheral locations less attractive for some young adults. For young urban professionals and perhaps even the elderly, the option of living in a restored central-city neighborhood may well become increasingly attractive. However, as indicated in Chapter 13, Housing and the Community, such a location does not appeal to all householders. Most internal metropolitan area movement is still toward the periphery rather than toward the central city.

Suburban Development

Suburbanism is destined to be the American way of life for the early twenty-first century. As noted in Chapter 9, Changing Suburbanization Patterns, survey after survey indicates that suburban living is a life-style that appeals to most Americans.

[6] William Frey, "The New White Flight," *American Demographics,* April, 1994, pp. 40–88.

Suburbia is no longer just families with children living in free-standing homes. (Mimi Forsyth/Monkmeyer.)

Equally important, an immense investment has already been made in existing suburban homes, office parks, shopping centers, and industrial complexes. Since most suburbanites not only live but also work in suburban areas, these suburbanites have little incentive to move back to the city for reasons of employment. Moreover, there is a tendency to exaggerate the distance people commute to work. The median distance from home to work, according to Bureau of the Census data, is 7.6 miles.[7] Even in the Los Angeles area, where one hears stories of 75-mile commuter trips, the average distance is under 9 miles.

Racially, suburban areas continue to maintain an image as all-white enclaves, but black suburbanization—particularly black middle-class suburbanization—is rapidly accelerating. Currently one out of every three metro area blacks lives in a suburb, and three-quarters of all African-American population growth is in the suburbs. Atlanta, for instance, added 250,000 black suburbanites between 1980 and 1990. Hispanic-American suburbanization is also a major trend, while Asian Americans are more suburban than the white population.

However, regardless of the amount of minority-group migration to suburbs, as long as whites constitute over five-sixths of the population, and whites continue to remain in the suburbs, it is demographically impossible for suburbia as a whole to be anything but predominately white.

[7] U.S. Bureau of the Census, "Selected Characteristics of Travel to Work in 20 Metropolitan Areas: 1976," *Current Population Reports,* series P-23, no. 72, Washington, D.C., 1978.

Technology and Nonmetropolitan Health Care

To illustrate how technology can become a substitute for propinquity, let us briefly examine what is occurring with health care. In mid-century the family physician bringing health care directly to the home was replaced by the large-scale hospital medical center or clinic. Treatment, particularly specialized diagnosis and treatment, increasingly became the prerogative of urban-based and urban-organized health care systems.* Those living in nonurban areas journeyed to the city for medical care.

Attempts to decentralize medical and health services have not been very successful. Arguments that what is wrong with contemporary health care is that there are too many specialists, too much technology, too much treatment, and too much surgery have not had noticeable success in changing health care delivery.† In spite of the emphasis on general practice, practitioners still choose to specialize in the city with its research hospitals and extensive medical community.

However, the future may well see the current pattern of urban concentration of health services supplanted by a more dispersed pattern. Where subsidies and exhortations failed to break the metropolitan areas' near monopoly of medical services, a radical expansion and transformation of our communication capabilities may do so. Advances in interactive communication technology can now make the most complex medical diagnostic procedures, and even treatment, available to geographically remote areas of the country.

As an example, the state of Georgia as of 1995 had built 59 Telamedicine rooms onto rural health clinics. The rooms are wired by interactive two-way TV so that rural patients can be seen and examined by urban medical center specialists without having to journey to the city. Today distant diagnosticians see and speak with the patient. Within a few years an already existent wired glove that the physician puts on at the medical center will allow the specialist to actually touch the patient with a similar wired glove at the rural clinic. Although its capabilities have yet to be fully grasped, technology has once again made it possible for the physician to come to the patient

---

* J. John Palen and Daniel M. Johnson, "Urbanization and Health Status," in Ann L. Greer and Scott Greer (eds.), *Cities and Sickness*, Sage, Beverly Hills, Calif., 1983, pp. 25–54.
† Ann L. Greer, "Health Care Policy: Disillusion and Confusion," in J. Blair and D. Nachmias (eds.), *Urban Policies in Transition*, Sage, Beverly Hills, Calif., 1979.

rather than requiring the patient to come to the physician.

The crucial questions today regarding the adoption of these options are not technological but social. Militating against rapid adoption is the well-documented fact that older physicians are noted for their conservative social and political orientation. Will nonurban physicians be interested in plugging into high-tech medical access systems?

The evidence of the past decade suggests that it will be difficult for health professionals—whatever their personal desires—to avoid the consequences of living in what is increasingly becoming a "wired" society. Nor will health professionals be able to ignore the fact that after two centuries of concentration the nation is now dispersing its residents, industries, and services. With this diminishing need for propinquity, and the resulting dispersal of population, will come a dispersal of health and medical services—both physically and through communication technology. It is reasonable to predict that the general practitioner's famous black bag will increasingly be supplanted by the health practitioner's interactive computer black box.

Of course, huge central-city medical complexes will not suddenly fade away; downtown department stores did not close once widespread auto ownership made outlying shopping more convenient. Downtown medical complexes, like downtown department stores, will continue to have a substantial clientele. This is especially true of hospitals associated with medical schools. However, the master trend for medicine, similar to other specialties, will be dispersal rather than central city concentration.

PLANNING FOR THE FUTURE CITY

To many people, urban planning almost automatically means physical planning: But physical planning is never free from social implications—the two are always intertwined. Moreover, our view of the future influences our contemporary behavior. As Scott Greer expressed it:

> It is my assumption that images of the future determine present actions. They may or may not determine the nature of the future—that depends on a much more complex set of circumstances. But willy-nilly much of our behavior is postulated upon images of a possible and/or desirable future.[8]

Planned Utopias

Ebenezer Howard's "garden cities" have already been discussed in Chapter 14, Planning in the United States and Elsewhere. Howard advocated a system of compact, self-contained cities of limited size that were designed to attract residents away from large cities such as London. Other planners have had different visions of utopia. Frank Lloyd Wright's model (1934) of a decentralized garden city called "Broadacre City" was more explicitly antiurban and decentralized than Howard's. In Wright's proposed model for Broadacre City there are no large buildings or high-rises.[9] Moreover, each individual would be allotted at least one acre, which that individual would be expected to farm. Significantly, his book *The Living City* ends with material excerpted from Ralph Waldo Emerson's "Essay on Farming."[10]

A different type of "city of tomorrow," and one that has had far more influence on American planners, is Le Corbusier's "Radiant City." Le Corbusier's ideal city was to be composed of a center of towering skyscrapers surrounded by parks and open spaces. Residences, similarly, would be tall, thin apartment superblocks surrounded by greenery.[11] Much of the high-rise urban renewal of the 1960s was affected by Le Corbusier's vision of the city of the future.

Similarly, the functional, Spartan, glass-box design of Mies van der Rohe now dominates the downtown architecture of major American cities. This modernist architecture has been sharply criticized as unlivable and unlovely by social critics such as Tom Wolfe.[12]

Brasilia, the new-city capital of Brazil, although not designed by Le Corbusier, followed his general plan: It has a unified high-rise center and residential superblocks united by a radial system of freeways. However, as was indicated earlier, Brasilia, while striking, is too uncomfortable and monumental for most people, who prefer the chaos of a Rio de Janeiro.

---

[8] Scott Greer, *The Urbane View,* Oxford University Press, New York, 1972, p. 322.

[9] For a contemporary view supporting Wright's Broadacre City, see Robert Fishman, "Megalopolis Unbound," *Wilson Quarterly,* Winter, 1990, pp. 25–45.

[10] Frank Lloyd Wright, *The Living City,* Mentor-Horizon, New York, 1958.

[11] Le Corbusier, *The Radiant City,* part I, Pamela Knight (trans.), parts II and VI, Eleanor Levieux (trans.), parts III, IV, V, VII, and VIII, Derek Coltman (trans.), Grossman-Orion, New York, 1967; this is a translation of the French version, *La Ville Radieuse,* 1933.

[12] Tom Wolfe, *From Bauhaus to Our House,* Farrar Straus Giroux, New York, 1981.

Sometimes physical planning for the future takes on a fanciful, "brave new world" character. The science fiction vision of Buckminster Fuller is an example: It cuts our ties to the physical earth and to mundane things such as water mains and sewers by means of recycling packs that we could wear on our backs like the astronauts' life-support systems. The urban architectural critic Wolf von Eckardt has a more earthbound view of such a future:

> The box regenerates our wastes and water and even reconditions our air and provides us with light and heat. If only we strap those little boxes to our backs, he says, we can all disperse over the world's mountains and deserts, telecommunicate with each other, and dispense with crowded settlements. Fuller, needless to say, did not acquire his astounding, sophisticated knowledge from video screens on lonely mountaintops. He acquired it in the lively bustle, the intellectual interchange, and the accumulation of wisdom that crowded human settlements stand for.[13]

The prescription of visionary and planner Constantinos Doxiadis for planning an organized community likewise is radically removed from the situation in contemporary cities. Doxiadis proposed a city of 2 million, organized into communi-

---

[13] Wolf von Eckardt, "Urban Design," in Daniel P. Moynihan (ed.), *Toward a National Urban Policy,* Basic Books, New York, 1970, chap. 9, p. 113.

This Japanese version of a pyramid-shaped city known as TRY 2004 would rise almost a mile and a half into the air and contain office buildings, homes, cultural facilities, hanging gardens, and parks. It would house a million people. (Courtesy of the Shimizu Corporation, Japan.)

ties of 30,000 to 50,000—each within an area of 2,000 yards by 2,000 yards. Services, schools, stores, businesses, and parks would all be organized so that residents could walk to them; public transit and highways would be around the communities. Movement from community to community within the city would be by means of "deepways"—underground highways.[14]

Another fanciful model for future cities was architect Paolo Soleri's "arcology," a compact three-dimensional city. Soleri placed heavy emphasis on building a city vertically, or layer on layer, and on using "miniaturization," or a more compact form, which he believed was the rule of evolutionary development.[15] Instead of urban sprawl, Soleri would have cities confined to a few square miles, with buildings 300 stories high. Soleri and volunteers attempted to build in Arizona a 3,000-person, twenty-five-story prototype of the future named Acrosanti. It would draw energy from the sun and food from greenhouses. There would be no need for automobiles. However, by the late 1980s work on Acrosanti had been virtually abandoned. Today Acrosanti contains only eight low-rise auxiliary buildings, some in a half-completed state. Acrosanti at this point resembles a ghost town more than a visionary city. Existing staff and students largely work fashioning ceramic and brass bells for revenue.

Dantzig and Saatz take this idea of vertical compactness a step further and propose a compact vertical city in one building that makes round-the-clock use of all facilities.[16] Such a city, though, would require constant services. Strikes by municipal workers would paralyze such a compact high-rise city, and thus would have to be prohibited. It is possible to foresee such a city turning into a tightly monitored totalitarian state.

Planned utopias may challenge the imagination, but they also frequently appear rather sterile and lifeless. They often seem better suited to guided tours than day-in, day-out habitation. To theorize about the future is one thing; to want to live in it is another. For example, plastic domes, similar to that covering the Houston Astrodome, can now be constructed, permitting a controlled climate and environment. Cities covered by domes could theoretically be built in otherwise hostile environments such as desert regions or even the smog-filled Los Angeles basin. Inside the domes, artificial light, controlled heating and cooling, and even grass could be provided. The question is whether we really want to live inside bubbles. Government regulations inside the domes would of necessity be more intrusive than those in current cities.

On the other hand, viewing the future as a lineal multiplication of the past is not only far less interesting but over the long run almost certain to be inaccurate. It would be rather depressing if our only dream for the future of the metropolitan area was of an endless growth of subdivisions and shopping malls. The choice for the future is not between planning and no planning—we will plan, even if it is only low-level planning of individual pieces of property or individual buildings. The

---

[14] C. A. Doxiadis, *Ekistics,* Hutchinson, London, 1968.

[15] Paolo Soleri, *Arcology, The City in the Image of Man,* MIT Press, Cambridge, Mass., 1969.

[16] George B. Dantzig and Thomas L. Saatz, *Compact City: A Plan for a Livable Urban Environment,* Freeman, San Francisco, 1973.

question thus is not whether planning should be done, but rather on what level it should be done.

Planning for People

Planners and social critics often seem caught in all-or-nothing approaches by which we exercise our imaginations either in grand fantasies or not at all. The trick is to find the line between speculative fancy and unimaginative extension of the past. This is another of those things that are far simpler in theory than in practice, for novel and innovative schemes are all too often considered unrealistic and dismissed out of hand. As Machiavelli accurately observed centuries ago, "There is nothing more difficult to carry out, nor more doubtful of success, nor more dangerous to handle than a new order of things."[17]

It is crucial to remember that whatever our formal plans for the city of the future, much of what will actually happen is the result of untold numbers of diverse decisions made by different individuals. As stated by Jane Jacobs:

> Most city diversity is the creation of incredible numbers of different people and different private organizations with vastly differing ideas and purposes, planning and contributing outside the formal framework of public action. The main responsibility of city planning and design should be to develop—insofar as public policy and action can do so—cities that are congenial places for this great range of unofficial plans, ideas and opportunities to flourish, along with the flourishing of the public enterprises.[18]

We need far more ideas and schemes of the middle range. An interesting architectural innovation in housing design, for example, was Moshe Safdie's Habitat, erected in Montreal. Safdie's design of modular boxes piled irregularly upon one another was originally hailed by some observers as the answer to the urban housing problem. The modular units were prefabricated and shipped to the construction site; the irregular placement of the units provided not only for variety but also for balconies and private space. The result was a rare combination of both privacy and a sense of community. Unlike most modern apartment buildings, Habitat gave the immediate impression of being concerned with human needs and designing buildings to meet these needs rather than simply stuffing people into space. Unfortunately, buildings like Habitat have turned out to be both more expensive and less practical than was hoped. In addition to the financial difficulties, there is also a less clearly expressed but nevertheless deep reluctance to try anything as different from conventional apartment buildings as Habitat. Thirty years after its construction, it still remains a "radical" idea.

One transportation alternative proposed by the author—and having virtually no chance of widespread adoption—is his "borrow a bike" plan. This plan actually has been implemented experimentally in Scandinavia and most recently in Portland, Oregon. (Although the author of this book first proposed this idea two decades ago, he makes no claim to having influenced either usage. Good ideas periodically

---

[17] Niccolo Machiavelli, *The Prince,* W. K. Marriot (trans.), Dent, London, 1958, p. 29.
[18] Jane Jacobs, *The Death and Life of Great American Cities,* Vintage–Random House, New York, 1961, p. 241.

After an area is cleared, but before new construction takes place,
Ann Arbor, Michigan, puts in "A Little Park for a Little While."
(Joseph Palen.)

independently reappear.) The idea is quite simple: The city would put up numerous
clearly marked municipal bicycle racks and fill them with city-owned bicycles.
Anyone could use any bike from any rack, the only requirement being that he or
she eventually return it to one of the racks. The bikes would be simple, straightfor-
ward, one-speed models painted a distinctive common color (yellow in Portland).
There would be little point in stealing the bikes, since in any event they would be
freely available as transportation to anyone who wanted them. Some people would
undoubtedly lock their "own" bikes, but if enough bikes were available, this would
not be an important problem. Certainly some riders would move on to purchase
their own more elaborate models, so that the scheme would probably increase
rather than decrease sales by private dealers—just as Henry Ford's cheap Model T
spurred the purchase of more elaborate automobiles. Bicycles could be manufactured and assembled at little cost by the city itself, employing persons on public assistance who want jobs but have only minimal skills.

Such a scheme would reduce pollution, reduce gasoline consumption, ease
traffic, and increase the physical—and probably emotional—health of the population. Increasing public awareness of the importance of regular exercise should contribute to the plan's success. The concept would have even greater appeal in certain
types of communities, such as university towns and sun belt retirement villages.
The possible disadvantages would be the initial cost of the bicycles (although lower

costs of repairing streets would far more than compensate for this) and the fact that in some cities the bikes would probably not be used much through the winter months. Also, even if the plan saved the city money, some residents would no doubt complain that it was socialistic nonsense and that government had no business giving people bicycles. In fact in Portland, partially because of liability concerns, the bikes are not provided by the city but by a nonprofit group. The "borrow a bike" plan is simply one example of how, without massive rebuilding or expense, we can make our cities more healthy and livable. Planning does not always have to be massive or formal. Some of the best planning is that which simply focuses on improving people's lives.

Planning Metropolitan Political Systems

Organizationally, metropolitan areas appear in a state of confusion and disorganization. Present home rule provides for local control at a substantial price. The political system itself becomes a major obstacle to effective planning. A multiplicity of city, suburban, county, township, regional, state, and federal bureaucracies all must intermesh if the metropolitan area is to be serviced effectively and at minimum cost, and this rarely works as well in practice as in theory. The interminable squabbling between city mayors and suburban political officials is one index of the ineffectiveness of the present system. The New York conurbation (admittedly an extreme example) includes people from three different states and some 1,400 different jurisdictions of one sort or another.

One alternative would be to abandon most local jurisdictions and move in the direction of a single metropolitan area government such as that found in Dade County, Florida (Miami), or Nashville, Tennessee. However, in spite of the generally favorable reports on these consolidations, there is little real agitation or political pressure in major American urban areas for adoption of this system. A recent book, *Cities without Suburbs,* has again stirred up interest among planners in a single metropolitan government.[19] The difficulty is that there is little political support for such a move. Suburban areas generally do not want to associate themselves politically with cities in economic or social trouble. In the past, cities could offer suburban areas higher levels of services as an inducement to consolidation; today suburbs often offer the higher level of services. Additionally, elected city officials increasingly represent minority populations that were previously excluded from city decision making. Most of these city officials oppose consolidation, fearing that if the city became part of a larger political unit, there would be a dilution of their influence and power. Thus, the majority of both suburban and city elected officials overtly or covertly oppose metropolitan consolidation. It is a good idea without a solid political base. Generally, dissatisfaction with current political divisions has yet to create sufficient pressures for change. For the immediate future we can only hope that voluntary cooperation among the various governmental units within metropolitan areas will increase.

---

[19] David Rusk, *Cities without Suburbs,* Johns Hopkins University Press, Baltimore, 1993.

Another, and perhaps more feasible, approach, is a two-level system that would move certain decision-making powers and organization to the level of a county or MSA while other functions would be handled by dividing the entire area—including the central city—into political units the size of suburbs, which would deal with local problems. Toronto, Canada, is a successful example of the two-tiered approach.

Under the larger metropolitan unit would be placed functions common to the urban system as a whole, such as water supply, waste disposal, expressways and streets, control of air and water pollution, museums, public hospitals, and major recreational facilities. On the other hand, local matters such as education, enforcement of housing codes, and recreation would be left to the local community. As for education, there is no reason why local central-city areas should not have their own school boards and school policies, just as suburbs currently do.

Police departments could also be organized on a local basis—with a common radio network and other specialized facilities—while fire protection could move to a metropolitan basis. It makes little sense for suburban fire departments to duplicate expensive equipment; furthermore, the area that a fire station services should be determined by the needs of a population for fast arrival rather than by political boundaries. Police officers, on the other hand, have a day-to-day contact with the community that firefighters do not. Small, locally administered departments such as those found in suburbs today are most likely to provide a setting in which the police and the community can come to know and respect one another. Large bureaucratic departments in which police are shifted from district to district seldom are able to establish rapport with citizens. This is especially true of many black inner-city areas, where the police are objects of overt hostility and are viewed by the residents as an occupying army. In such a situation, the police generally respond in kind. What would happen to the extremely high crime rates in these areas if locally controlled police forces replaced the present system? A new system would certainly be worth trying in selected cities as a closely monitored experiment.

Emergency management of disasters such as hurricanes, tornadoes, or earthquakes also has to be carried out on a metropolitan rather than a local basis.[20] However, areawide plans and approaches need to be accepted by local areas. The 1989 San Francisco–Oakland earthquake demonstrated the need for a regional response, as did the 1994 Los Angeles earthquake.

A Working City

Amid all the discussions of urban problems it is worthwhile to keep in mind that not all urban places are in crisis; some are working quite well. Portland, Oregon, home to 450,000 people in the city and 1.4 million in the area, is one of these places. Thirty years ago Portland had a beautiful location on the Willamette River, but its industries were closing, the bus system was bankrupt, and the downtown

---

[20] Thomas E. Drabek, *The Professional Emergency Manager,* Institute of Behavioral Science, University of Colorado, Boulder, 1987; and Michael T. Charles and John Choon Kim (eds.), *Crisis Management: A Casebook,* Thomas, Springfield, Ill., 1988.

showed increasing signs of store closing and decline. Today the warehouses and riverfront expressway have been replaced with a waterfront park that opens the city to the river; the downtown gleams with not only a new Nordstrom's and Saks Fifth Avenue, but also some 1,100 smaller stores. Moreover, the number of people working downtown has gone from 59,000 to 94,000, and nearly 40 percent of them ride downtown on the three county transit authority systems known as Tri-Met or on MAX, Portland's light-rail system.[21] Downtown Portland is filled with trees, small parks, and business-district fountains that, along with the heavy use of brick walkways, act to soften the downtown and make it people friendly. To make the city physically more attractive, a small percentage (1.33 percent) of the construction costs for state buildings, and a voluntary deduction from state income tax refunds, goes toward supporting public outdoor art. Downtown Portland is pedestrian friendly, so even on weekends one finds people downtown shopping, rummaging in bookstores, or enjoying themselves in coffeehouses and restaurants. Neighborhoods remain active and vital, and there are none of the zones of industrial or residential abandonment that blight other cities.[22]

All this didn't just happen. Major credit is given both to Portlanders' moral and civic culture, which is deeply concerned with the common good and quality-of-life issues, and to the implementation in 1972 of an excellent downtown development plan. Fortunately, nineteenth-century Portland was designed with small square blocks of the type advocated by Jane Jacobs (see Chapter 14, Planning in the United States and Elsewhere). In order to make the area more attractive, new buildings, including garages, must be friendly at ground level. Blank walls are prohibited. This means that every public building must have stores or eating places on ground level. It also means that buildings are built so dumpsters are placed inside, rather than outside, the buildings. To encourage use of public transit, Portland limited, rather than expanded, the number of parking places in the core. In contrast to what is happening elsewhere, locally adopted planning policy calls for a 20 percent *reduction* in vehicle miles traveled per capita over the next twenty years.[23] To encourage less auto traffic the 300-block downtown area has free public transit. As long as you travel within the downtown zone, there is no fare. Additionally, bike racks have been installed on the front of public buses so you can combine bus and bike travel.

Portlanders are deathly afraid of becoming another sprawl city like Los Angeles, and for twenty years the state has required that growth take place within a 362-square-mile metro area. All the communities in the area have been required to follow plans that allow half of new housing to be multifamily or apartment construction. This has the dual purpose of keeping housing costs affordable while preserving open land. Portlanders' greatest fear today is that their highly civil way of life is going to be swamped by the in-migration of ever-more Californians. Oregon residents tend to view southern California in particular as a disastrous example of what they do not want to become.

---

[21] Philip Langdon, "How Portland Does It," *Atlantic,* November, 1992, p. 136.
[22] Carl Abbott, "Portland: People, Places, and Politics," *Urban Affairs,* Winter, 1995, p. 3.
[23] Ibid., p. 4.

Social Planning

Three Approaches to Social Planning. Theoretical approaches to social planning and problem solving range from the use of existing social mechanisms in conventional ways to attempts to radically restructure the entire system. Three general assumptions regarding problem solving and the resulting approaches to planning can be delineated: (1) conventional approaches, which assume that problems can be solved by existing mechanisms, (2) reformist approaches, which assume that the system needs some major modification, and (3) radical approaches, which assume that problems cannot be solved by the existing social system (see Table 19-1).

Conventional approaches to planning and problem solving assume that the system itself is not in question. Inadequacies are attributed to the failings of individuals. The appropriate traditional response thus is to replace the offending personnel with new faces. Reassessment of priorities is also an essentially conventional response. Here, the emphasis is upon the allocation of resources and weighing of priorities within the system rather than upon structural modification of the system itself.

Reformist responses, as outlined in Table 19-1, are characterized by ideological commitment to the goals and ideals of the society but not by attempts to achieve them through conventional means, Reformers are more likely to see the system itself as the source of the problem and to have little faith in correcting it by traditional means. They accept quasi-legal methods falling outside the traditional system, as did some members of the civil rights movement and the environmental movement. Legislation such as the Clean Air Act reflects reformist pressure.

TABLE 19-1
Strategies for Planning and Problem Solving

Assumptions regarding problem solving	General approach to planning	Resulting action taken
Most, if not all, problems can be solved by existing mechanisms	Conventional approaches (System needs minor modifications, fine tuning, or both)	New leadership, better administration, shift in priorities, new legislation
Some problems cannot be solved by existing mechanisms	Reformist approaches (System needs some major modification; likely to see system itself as source of problems)	Mobilization of power bases outside existing party structures, quasi-legal protests, civil disobedience
Most, if not all, problems cannot be solved by existing mechanisms	Radical approaches (System needs major revision or replacement)	Rejection of societal goals, extreme countercultural movement, revolution, planned violence

Source: Based on J. John Palen and Karl H. Flaming, *Urban America,* Holt, Rinehart and Winston, New York, 1972, p. 335.

Radical approaches differ from the conventional and reformist positions by rejecting, at least implicitly, the traditional goals of the society as well as the means used to implement them. The existing system is judged to be so corrupt and repressive that the response is to destroy it and start over. Radical responses (Marxist approaches on the left or citizen militia approaches on the right, for example) are almost always overtly ideological in their vision of the new utopia.

Social Planning and Technology. One point upon which urbanists, including conservatives, generally agree is that the core problems of the city are social problems. The difficulty is that we are frequently unwilling to admit the existence of social problems until they reach serious proportions, and even then we seek solutions through other than social reforms in the naive belief that "technology saves." Public housing projects and freeways are perhaps the two best-known examples of how we have, with disastrous results for the cities, attempted to provide engineering solutions for social problems. For example, the technology exists for building mile-high apartment buildings. The real question should not be "Is it possible?" but rather "Is it desirable?" Still, faith in the ultimate technical solution has a long American history. As Jeb Magruder, an official of the Nixon administration, expressed it:

> The cities have no place else to turn except to technical solutions. There is no political or social solution to providing more adequate energy, or waste disposal, or drug abuse. I want to see something better and technology can do it if we work at it.[24]

The answers even to questions about energy usage or pollution are, of course, far more social and political than technical. Technical "solutions" often do little more than shift the strain to elsewhere in the system. It should be kept in mind that America's social orientation toward automobiles, its values concerning the environment, and even its political policies toward the oil monopolies determine whether the nation has an "energy crisis" far more than technology alone. The decision of an oil company not to build a refinery that produces less polluting products may be an economic or a political decision, or both, but it is not a technological decision. Of course, if one expects technology to solve all problems, even including drug abuse, there really isn't any need to even consider modifying or changing the social, economic, or political system.

THE "POSTCITY" AGE

Superterritoriality

Some futurists see us as inevitably moving toward immensely larger metropolises. Doxiadis, for example, viewed population increases resulting in a world where urban settlements covered an area not just seven to ten times larger than they now do, but

---

[24] *New York Times*, July 29, 1972.

as much as thirty, forty, or even fifty times as large. Moreover, he predicted that it is probable that all settlements will become interconnected to form a continuous system covering the inhabitable earth. In Doxiadis's opinion, there is no possibility of halting or changing the growth of this ultimate megalopolis he calls "Ecumenopolis." He felt that stopping the trend toward Ecumenopolis is impossible for two reasons:

1. These are trends of population growth determined by many biological and social forces which we do not even understand properly, let alone dare countermand.
2. The great forces shaping the Ecumenopolis—economic, commercial, social, political, technological, and cultural—are already being deployed, and it is too late to reverse them.[25]

Fortunately, this prediction has little contact with empirical reality. Population growth is far from inevitable; and biological and social forces do not operate in response to mysterious and mystical "forces" beyond our knowledge. Whatever our urban areas become, they will be the result of our present and future actions—wise or unwise—not the result of unchangeable forces.

Nonterritoriality

Others see the traditional city as passing away. In recent years, we have come to think less in terms of the city versus the country and more in terms of a larger urban-dominated community that often includes rural sectors. This new unit, commonly called the "metropolitan community," has evolved rapidly in the United States during the past half century. Now some scholars believe that we are moving from metropolitan communities to a new "postcity" age. As Melvin Webber states this position, "We are passing through a revolution that is unhitching the social processes of urbanization from the locationally fixed city and region."[26] Webber maintains:

A new kind of large-scale urban society is emerging that is increasingly independent of the city. In turn, the problems of the city place generated by early industrialization are being supplanted by a new array different in kind. With but a few remaining exceptions (the new air pollution is a notable one), the recent difficulties are not place-type problems at all. Rather, they are the transitional problems of a rapidly developing society-economy-and-polity whose turf is the nation. Paradoxically, just at the time in history when policy-makers and the world press are discovering the city, "the age of the city seems to be at an end."[27]

He suggests that we have failed to draw up a simple conceptual definition distinguishing between the spatially defined urban area and the social systems that are localized there. Because our cities have historically been spatially structured, we don't have the concepts or language to deal with the new situation. The resulting problems, Webber says, are serious ones, for we seek local solutions to problems

[25] Doxiadis, *Ekistics*, p. 430.
[26] Melvin M. Webber, "The Postcity Age," *Daedalus*, **97**:1092, Fall, 1968.
[27] Ibid., pp. 1092–1093. Reprinted by permission of *Daedalus*, Journal of the American Academy of Arts and Sciences, Boston, MA, Fall, 1968, *The Conscience of the City*.

that transcend local boundaries and are not susceptible to municipal treatment. Problems of poverty, crime, unemployment, and even transportation transcend any city or even cities in general.

Webber suggests that the future pattern can be discerned in the life-styles of the new cosmopolites who through frequent use of airlines and telephones have established new spatially dispersed networks of specialized knowledge. These cosmopolites are the producers of the information and new ideas that are transforming societies.

Like much of the Chicago school of sociology of half a century earlier, Webber assumes that movement from localized primary-group relationships to territorially unbounded secondary-group relationships is inevitable and irreversible. He states:

> At one extreme are the intellectual and business elites, whose habitat is the planet; at the other are the lower-class residents of city and farm who live in spatially and cognitively constrained worlds. Most of the rest of us, who comprise the large middle class, lie somewhere in-between, but in some facets of our lives we all seem to be moving from our ancestral localism toward the unbounded realms of the cosmopolites.[28]

This is far from certain. It *may* be true for segments of the upper middle class; but as we have seen in earlier chapters, upper-middle-class professionals tend to consistently underrate both the strength and the utility of territorially bounded urban life-styles.

Into the Future

As noted earlier in the chapter, deconcentration of population into developments on the periphery of metropolitan areas appears to be a trend as we enter the twenty-first century. Such population dispersal does not necessarily mean movement from important activities. With activities dispersed, moving "closer to the action" may mean moving away from rather than toward the urban center.[29]

There also are those such as John Seeley who argue that the western city has reached its highest point of development and that "there is something tragicomic about sitting around 'planning' to secure, extend, and improve what is about to be swept away."[30] So far, though, they have proved to be poor prophets. Telecommunication advances, while exposing us to international economic and social changes, have yet to eliminate the need for a spatial city. The "electronic city" has not eliminated the need for the physical city and the specialized managerial, residential, and leisure areas it nurtures.

Most urban sociologists are dubious about whether prophecies of the passage of the city will come to be. To paraphrase Mark Twain's famous remark on being told that he had been reported dead, the reports of the death of the city have been greatly exaggerated. What is certain is that as the twenty-first century begins urbanism has become *the* way of life not only in North America, but around the globe.

---

[28] Ibid., p. 1095. Reprinted by permission of *Daedalus,* Journal of the American Academy of Arts and Sciences, Boston, MA, Fall, 1968, *The Conscience of the City.*

[29] Barry Edmonston and Thomas M. Guterbock, "Is Suburbanization Slowing Down?" *Social Forces,* **62:**923, 1984.

[30] John Seeley, "Remaking the Urban Scene: New Youth in an Old Environment," *Daedalus,* **97:**1125, 1968.

BIBLIOGRAPHY

CHAPTER 1

Abu-Lughod, Janet L: "Migrant Adjustment to City Life: The Egyptian Case," *American Journal of Sociology,* **67:**22–32, July, 1961.

Aristotle; *Politics,* Book VII, B. Jowett (trans.), Modern Library, New York, 1932.

Berry, Brian J.: "The Counterurbanization Process: Urban America since 1970," in *Urbanization and Counterurbanization,* Vol. II, *Urban Affairs Annual Reviews,* Sage, Beverly Hills, Calif., 1976.

Chandler, Tertius, and Gerald Fox: *3000 Years of Urban Growth,* Academic Press, New York, 1974.

Demographic Handbook for Africa, United Nations Economic Commission for Africa, Addis Ababa, 1968.

Dreiser, Theodore: *Sister Carrie,* Doubleday, Page, New York, 1900.

Durkheim, Emile: *The Division of Labor in Society,* George Simpson (trans.), Free Press, Glencoe, Ill., 1960.

Eldridge, Hope Tisdale: "The Process of Urbanization," in J. J. Spengler and O. D. Duncan (eds.), *Demographic Analysis,* Free Press, Glencoe, Ill., 1956.

Fischer, Claude S.: "Urban Malaise," *Social Forces,* **52**(2):221, December, 1973.

Gerth, Hans Heinrich, and C. Wright Mills (trans. and ed.): *Max Weber: Essays in Sociology,* Oxford University Press, New York, 1966.

Hauser, Philip, and Robert Gardiner: "Urban Future: Trends and Prospects," in Philip Hauser et al., *Population and the Urban Future,* U.N. Fund for Population Activities, SUNY Press, Albany, N.Y., 1982.

—— and Leo Schnore: *The Study of Urbanization,* Wiley, New York, 1965.

Hawley, Amos H.: *Human Ecology: A Theory of Community Structure,* Ronald Press, New York, 1950.

International Urban Research: *The World's Metropolitan Areas,* University of California Press, Berkeley, 1959.

Lofland, Lyn H.: "Understanding Urban Life: The Chicago Legacy," *Urban Life,* **11:**491–511, 1983.

Macura, Milos: "The Influence of the Definition of Urban Place on the Size of Urban Population," in Jack Gibbs (ed.), *Urban Research Methods,* Van Nostrand, New York, 1961.

Marx, Karl, and Friedrich Engels: *The German Ideology,* R. Pascal (trans.), International Publishers, New York, 1947.

Meadows, Paul, and Ephraim Mizruchi (eds.): *Urbanism, Urbanization, and Change: Comparative Perspectives,* Addison Wesley, Reading, Mass., 1969.

Palen, J. John, and Daniel Johnson: "Urbanization and Health Status," in Ann Greer and Scott Greer (eds.), *Cities and Sickness,* Sage, Beverly Hills, Calif., 1983.

Park, Robert E.: "The City: Suggestions for the Investigation of Human Behavior in the Urban Environment," in Robert E. Park, E. W. Burgess, and Roderick D. McKenzie (eds.), *The City,* University of Chicago Press, Chicago, 1925.

Redfield, Robert: "The Folk Society," *American Journal of Sociology,* **52:**53–73, 1947.

Schnore, Leo: "Urbanization and Economic Development: The Demographic Contribution," *American Journal of Economics and Sociology,* **23:**37–48, 1964.

Shaw, Clifford R.: *The Jack Roller,* University of Chicago Press, Chicago, 1930.

Simmel, Georg: "The Metropolis and Mental Life," in Kurt Wolff (trans.), *The Sociology of Georg Simmel,* Free Press, New York, 1964.

Sinclair, Upton: *The Jungle,* published by Upton Sinclair, 1906.

Smith, Michael P.: *The City and Social Theory,* St. Martin's Press, New York, 1979.

Smith, Neil, and Michele Le Faivre: "A Class Analysis of Gentrification," in J. John Palen and Bruce London (eds.), *Gentrification, Displacement and Neighborhood Revitalization,* SUNY Press, Albany, N.Y., 1984.

Srole, Leo: "Mental Health in New York," *The Sciences,* **20:**16–29, 1980.

Stein, Maurice R.: *The Eclipse of Community,* Princeton University Press, Princeton, N.J., 1961.

Thomas, William I., and Florian Zaniecki: *The Polish Peasant in Europe and America,* 5 vols., University of Chicago Press, Chicago, 1918–1920.

Tönnies, Ferdinand: *Community and Society,* Charles P. Loomis (trans.), Harper & Row, New York, 1963.

United Nations: *Urbanization in the Second United Nations Development Decade,* New York, 1970.

Vidich, Arthur, and Joseph Bensman: *Small Town in Mass Society,* Princeton University Press, Princeton, N.J., 1958.

Weber, Adna Ferrin: *The Growth of Cities in the Nineteenth Century,* Cornell University Press, Ithaca, N.Y., 1899.

Wirth, Louis: *The Ghetto,* University of Chicago Press, Chicago, 1928.

————: "Urbanism as a Way of Life," *American Journal of Sociology,* **44:**1–24, July, 1938.

Zorbaugh, Harvey W.: *The Gold Coast and the Slum,* University of Chicago Press, Chicago, 1929.

CHAPTER 2

Adams, Robert M.: "The Origins of Cities," *Scientific American,* September, 1960.

Aristotle: *Politics,* Book VII, B. Jowett (trans.), Modern Library, New York, 1932.

Braidwood, Robert J.: "The Agricultural Revolution," *Scientific American,* September, 1960.

Braudel, Ferdinand: *The Mediterranean and the Mediterranean World in the Age of Phillip II,* E. O. Lorimer and Sian Reynolds (trans.), Harper & Row, New York, 1973.

Carcopino, Jerome: *Daily Life in Ancient Rome,* E. O. Lorimer (trans.), Yale University Press, New Haven, Conn., 1940.

Castells, Manuel: *The Urban Question: A Marxist Approach,* Alan Sheridan (trans.), MIT Press, Cambridge, Mass., 1977.

Chandler, Tertius, and Gerald Fox: *3000 Years of Urban Growth,* Academic Press, New York, 1974.

Childe, V. Gordon: "The Urban Revolution," *Town Planning Review,* **21:**4–7, 1950.

————: *What Happened in History,* Penguin Books, London, 1964.

Creel, H. G.: *The Birth of China: A Study of the Formative Period of Chinese Civilization,* Reynal and Hitchcock, New York, 1937.

Curwen, E. Cecil, and Gudmund Hatt: *Plough and Pasture: The Early History of Farming,* Collier Books, New York, 1961.

Davis, Kingsley: "The Origin and Growth of Urbanization in the World," *American Journal of Sociology,* **60**:430, March, 1955.

Deauz, George: *The Black Death,* Weybright and Talley, New York, 1969.

de Coulanges, Numa Denis Fustel: *The Ancient City: A Study on the Religion, Laws and Institutions of Greece and Rome,* Doubleday, Garden City, N.Y., 1956 (1865).

de Vries, Jan: *European Urbanization 1500–1800,* Harvard University Press, Cambridge, Mass., 1984.

Dice, Lee Raymond: *Man's Nature and Nature's Man: The Ecology of Human Communities,* University of Michigan Press, Ann Arbor, 1955.

Duncan, Otis Dudley: "From Social System to Ecosystem," *Sociological Inquiry,* **31**:140–149, 1961.

Eisenstadt, Shmuel Noah, and A. Shachar: *Society, Culture and Urbanization,* Sage, Newbury Park, Calif., 1987.

Engels, Friedrich: *The Condition of the Working Class in England in 1844* (1845), Progress Publishers, Moscow, 1973.

Feagin, Joe, and Robert Parker: *Building American Cities: The Real Estate Game,* Prentice-Hall, Englewood Cliffs, N.J., 1990.

Flannery, Kent J.: "The Origins of Agriculture," *Annual Review of Anthropology,* **2**:271–310, 1973.

George, Mary Dorothy: *London Life in the Eighteenth Century,* Harper Torchbooks, New York, 1964.

Gibbon, Edward: *The Decline and Fall of the Roman Empire,* Dell, New York, 1879 (first published 1776).

Glotz, Gustave: *Ancient Greece at Work,* M. R. Dobie (trans.), Norton, New York, 1967.

Gottdiener, Mark, and Joe Feagin: "The Paradigm Shift in Urban Sociology," *Urban Affairs Quarterly,* **24**:174, 1988.

Hammond, Mason: *The City in Ancient World,* Harvard University Press, Cambridge, Mass., 1972.

Hawley, Amos H.: *Urban Society,* Ronald Press, New York, 1971.

Hiorns, Frederick: *Town Building in History,* Harap, London, 1956.

Hohenberg, Paul M., and Lynn Hollen Lees: *The Making of Urban Europe 1000–1950,* Harvard University Press, Cambridge, Mass., 1985.

Jacobs, Jane: *The Economy of Cities,* Random House, New York, 1969.

July, Robert W.: *A History of the African People,* Scribner's, New York, 1970.

Kenyon, Kathleen Mary: *Archeology in the Holy Land,* Praeger, New York, 1970.

Lampara, Eric: "The Urbanizing World," In H. J. Dyds and Michael Wolfe (eds.), *The Victorian World,* Routledge and Kegan Paul, London, 1976.

Langer, William L.: "The Black Death," in *Scientific American's Cities: The Origin, Growth, and Human Impact,* Freeman, San Francisco, 1973.

Lenski, Gerhard: *Human Societies,* McGraw-Hill, New York, 1970.

——— and Jean Lenski: *Human Society: An Introduction to Macrosociology,* McGraw-Hill, New York, 1987.

Mumford, Lewis: *The City in History: Its Origins, Its Transformations and Its Prospects,* Harcourt, Brace and World, New York, 1961.

Mundy, John H., and Peter Riesenberg: *The Medieval Town,* Van Nostrand, New York, 1958.

Petersen, William: *Population,* Macmillan, New York, 1969.

Piggot, Stuart: "The Role of the City in Ancient Civilization," in R. M. Fisher (ed.), *The Metropolis and Modern Life,* Russel and Russel, New York, 1955.

Pirenne, Henri: *Medieval Cities: Their Origins and the Revival of Trade,* Frank D. Halsey (trans.), Princeton University Press, Princeton, N.J., 1939.

————: *Economic and Social History of Medieval Europe,* I. E. Clegg (trans.), Harcourt, New York, 1956.

Plato: *The Laws,* Book V, B. Jowett (trans.), Modern Library, New York, 1926.

Rörig, Fritz: *The Medieval Town,* University of California Press, Berkeley, 1967.

Saalman, Howard: *Medieval Cities,* Braziller, New York, 1968.

Siegfried, Andre: *Routes of Contagion,* Harcourt, Brace and World, New York, 1965.

Sjoberg, Gideon: *The Preindustrial City: Past and Present,* Free Press, New York, 1960.

Trigger, Bruce: "Determinants of Urban Growth in Pre-industrial Societies," in Peter Ucko, Ruth Tringham, and G. W. Dimbleby (eds.), *Man, Settlement, and Urbanism,* Schenkman, Cambridge, Mass., 1972.

Weber, Max: *The City,* D. Martendale and G. Neuwirth (trans.), Free Press, New York, 1958.

Wirth, Louis: "Urbanism as a Way of Life," *American Journal of Sociology,* **44:**1–24, July, 1938.

CHAPTER 3

Blake, Nelson M.: *A History of American Life and Thought,* McGraw-Hill, New York, 1963.

Bogue, Donald J.: *The Population of the United States,* Free Press, Glencoe, Ill., 1969, p. 178.

Bridenbaugh, Carl: *Cities in the Wilderness,* Capricorn Books, New York, 1964.

Brown, Andrew Theodore, and Lyle W. Dorset: *K.C.: A History of Kansas City, Missouri,* Pruett, Boulder, Colo., 1978.

Cassedy, James H.: *Demography in Early America,* Harvard University Press, Cambridge, Mass., 1969.

Chudacoff, Howard P.: *The Evolution of American Urban Society,* Prentice-Hall, Englewood Cliffs, N.J., 1975.

Cressey, Paul F.: "Population Succession in Chicago: 1898–1930," *American Journal of Sociology,* **44:**59, 1938.

Davis, William R. (ed.): *Bradford's History of Plymouth Plantation,* Scribner, New York, 1908.

Ford, P. L.: *The Works of Thomas Jefferson,* Putnam, New York, 1904.

Frame, Richard: "A Short Description of Pennsylvania in 1692," in Albert Cook Myers (ed.), *Narratives of Early Pennsylvania, West New Jersey, and Delaware,* Scribner, New York, 1912. Reprinted in Ruth E. Sutter, *The Next Place You Come: A Historical Introduction to Communities in North America,* Prentice-Hall, Englewood Cliffs, N.J., 1973.

Glaab, Charles N. (ed.): *The American City: A Documentary History,* Dorsey Press, Homewood, Ill., 1963.

———— and A. Theodore Brown: *A History of Urban America,* Macmillan, New York, 1967.

Green, Constance McLaughlin: *The Rise of Urban America,* Harper & Row, New York, 1965.

Harris, Marshall Dees: *The Origin of the Land Tenure System in the United States,* Iowa State University, Ames, 1953.

Hofstadter, Richard: *The Age of Reform: From Bryan to FDR,* Knopf, New York, 1955.

Hurd, Richard: *Principles of City Land Values,* Record and Guide, New York, 4th ed., 1924.

Jackson, Kenneth T., *Crabgrass Frontier,* Oxford University Press, New York, 1985.

————, and Stanley K. Schutty (eds.): *Cities in American History,* Knopf, New York, 1972.

Lipscomb, Andrew A., and Albert E. Bergh (eds.): *The Writings of Thomas Jefferson,* Vol. X, Thomas Jefferson Memorial Association, Washington, D.C., 1904.

McKelvey, Blake: *The Urbanization of America, 1860–1915,* Rutgers University Press, New Brunswick, N.J., 1963.

Merton, Robert K.: *Social Theory and Social Structure,* Free Press, Glencoe, Ill., 1957.

Mumford, Lewis: *Sticks and Stones: A Study of American Architecture and Civilization,* Liveright, New York, 1924.

Palen, J. John: *The Suburbs,* McGraw-Hill, New York, 1995.

Perlman, Janice: "Mega Cities and New Technologies," paper presented at XI World Congress of Sociology, New Delhi, July, 1986.

Petersen, William: *Population,* Macmillan, New York, 1961.

Riis, Jacob A.: *How the Other Half Lives,* Scribner, New York, 1890.

Robey, Bryant: "Two Hundred Years and Counting: The 1990 Census," *Population Bulletin,* **44:**1, April, 1989.

Sandberg, Carl: *Chicago Poems,* Holt, New York, 1916.

Schlesinger, Arthur M.: "The City in American History," *Mississippi Valley Historical Review,* **27:**43–66, June, 1940.

———: *Paths to the Present,* Macmillan, New York, 1949.

Smith, David A.: "Dependent Urbanization in Colonial America: The Case of Charleston, South Carolina," *Social Forces,* **66:**1–28, September, 1987.

Smith, John: *The General Historie of Virginia, New England, and the Summer Isles,* University Microfilms, Ann Arbor, Mich., 1966. (First published in London, 1624.)

Steffens, Lincoln: *The Autobiography of Lincoln Steffens,* Harcourt Brace, New York, 1931.

Strong, Josiah: *Our Country: Its Possible Future and Its Present Crisis,* Baker and Taylor, New York, 1885.

Tocqueville, Alexis de: *Democracy in America,* Henry Reeve (trans.), New York, 1839.

Tunnard, Christopher, and Henry Hope Reed: *American Skyline: The Growth and Form of Our Cities and Towns,* New American Library, New York, 1956.

U.S. Census of Population: "Residents of Farms and Rural Areas: 1990," *Current Population Reports,* series P-20 no. 57, 1992.

Warner, Sam Bass, Jr.: *Streetcar Suburbs,* Harvard University Press and MIT Press, Cambridge, Mass., 1962.

———: *The Private City: Philadelphia in Three Periods of Its Growth,* University of Pennsylvania Press, Philadelphia, 1968.

———: *The Urban Wilderness,* Harper & Row, New York, 1972.

White, Morton, and Lucia White: *The Intellectual versus the City,* MIT Press and Harvard University Press, Cambridge, Mass., 1962.

Zink, Harold: *City Bosses in the United States,* Duke University Press, Durham, N.C., 1930.

CHAPTER 4

Abbott, Walter F: "Moscow in 1897 as a Preindustrial City: A Test of the Inverse Burgess Zonal Hypothesis," *American Sociological Review,* **39:**542–550, August, 1974.

Alihan, Milla A.: *Social Ecology,* Columbia University Press, New York, 1938.

Alonso, William: "A Theory of Urban Land Market," in Larry Bourne (ed.), *Internal Structure of the City,* Oxford University Press, New York, 1971, pp. 154–159.

Burgess, Ernest W.: "The Growth of the City: An Introduction to a Research Project," *Publications of the American Sociology Society,* **18:**85–97, 1924.

———: "Residential Segregation in American Cities," *The Annals of the American Academy of Political and Social Science,* **140:**108, November, 1928.

Caplow, Theodore: "The Social Ecology of Guatemala City," *Social Forces,* **128:**113–135, 1949.

Changon, Stanley A., et al.: *Summary of Metromex,* Vol. 1: *Weather Anomalies and Impacts,* Illinois State Water Survey, Urbana, 1977.

Duncan, Otis Dudley, and Beverly Duncan: "Residential Distribution and Occupational Stratification," *American Journal of Sociology,* **60:**493–503, March, 1955.

Eachman, Donald, and Melvin Marcus: "The Geologic and Topographic Setting of Cities," in Thomas Detwyler and Melvin Marcus (eds.), *Urbanization and Environment,* Duxbury Press, Belmont, Calif., 1972.

Firey, Walter: "Sentiment and Symbolism as Ecological Variables," *American Sociological Review,* **10:**140–148, 1945.

Friedrichs, Jurgen, and Allen C. Goodman: *The Changing Downtown: A Comparative Study of Baltimore and Hamburg,* de Gruyter, New York, 1987.

Gettys, Warner E.: "Human Ecology and Social Theory," in George A. Theodorson (ed.), *Studies in Human Ecology,* Harper & Row, New York, 1961.

Gist, Noel: "The Ecology of Bangalore, India," *Social Forces,* **35:**356–365, May, 1957.

Gottdiener, Mark: *The Social Production of Urban Space,* University of Texas, Austin, 1985.

Haggerty, Lee J.: "Another Look at the Burgess Hypothesis: Time as an Important Variable," *American Journal of Sociology,* **76:**1084–1093, May, 1971.

Harris, Chauncy, and Edward Ullman: "The Nature of Cities," *The Annals of the American Academy of Political and Social Science,* **252:**7–17, 1945.

Hauser, Francis L.: "Ecological Patterns of European Cities," in Sylvia F. Fava (ed.), *Urbanism in World Perspective,* Crowell, New York, 1968.

Hawley, Amos Henry: *Urban Society: An Ecological Approach,* Wiley, New York, 1981.

——— and Otis Dudley Duncan: "Social Area Analysis: A Critical Appraisal," *Land Economics,* **33:**337–345, November, 1957.

Hoyt, Homer: "The Structure and Growth of Residential Neighborhoods in American Cities," U.S. Federal Housing Administration, Government Printing Office, Washington, D.C., 1939.

Kates, Robert, Ian Burton, and Gilbert F. White: *The Environment as Hazard,* Oxford University Press, New York, 1978.

London, Bruce, and William G. Flanagan: "Comparative Urban Ecology: A Summary of the Field," in John Walton and Louis H. Masotti (eds.), *The City in Comparative Perspective: Cross-National Research and New Directions in Theory,* Sage, Beverly Hills, Calif., 1976, pp. 41–66.

McKenzie, Roderick: *The Metropolitan Community,* McGraw-Hill, New York and London, 1933.

Michelson, William H.: *Man and His Urban Environment,* Addison-Wesley, Reading, Mass., 1970.

Palen, J. John: *The Suburbs,* McGraw-Hill, New York, 1995.

——— and Leo F. Schnore: "Color Composition and City-Suburban Status Differences," *Land Economics,* **41:**87–91, February, 1965.

Park, Robert: *Human Communities: The City and Human Ecology,* Free Press, New York, 1952.

Schnore, Leo: "The Myth of Human Ecology," *Sociological Inquiry,* **31:**139, 1961.

——— and Joy K. O. Jones: "The Evolution of City-Suburban Types in the Course of a Decade," *Urban Affairs Quarterly,* **4:**421–422, June, 1969.

Schwirian, Kent P.: *Comparative Urban Structure: Studies in the Ecology of Cities,* Heath, Lexington, Mass., 1974.

———, F. Martin Hanks, and Carol A. Ventresca: "The Residential Decentralization of Social Status Groups in American Metropolitan Communities, 1950–1980," *Social Forces,* **68:**1143–1163, June, 1990.

———— and Marc D. Matre: "The Ecological Structure of Canadian Cities," in Kent P. Schwirian (ed.), *Comparative Urban Structure,* Heath, Lexington, Mass., 1974.

Simkus, Albert: "Residential Segregation by Occupation and Race in Ten Urbanized Areas, 1950–1970," *American Sociological Review,* **43:**81–93, February, 1978.

Sjoberg, Gideon: *The Preindustrial City,* Free Press, New York, 1960.

————: "Cities in Developing and in Industrial Societies: A Cross-Cultural Analysis," in Philip M. Hauser and Leo F. Schnore (eds.), *The Study of Urbanization,* Wiley, New York, 1965.

Smith, Joel: "Another Look at Socioeconomic Status Distributions in Urbanized Areas," *Urban Affairs Quarterly,* **5:**423–453, June, 1970.

Thomlinson, Ralph: *Urban Structure,* Random House, New York, 1969.

Wirth, Louis: *The Ghetto,* University of Chicago Press, Chicago, 1928.

————: "Urbanism as a Way of Life," *American Journal of Sociology,* **44:**18–19, July, 1938.

Zorbaugh, Harvey W.: *The Gold Coast and the Slum,* University of Chicago Press, Chicago, 1929.

CHAPTER 5

Barff, R., and K. Austen: "'It's Gotta Be da Shoes': Domestic Manufacturing, Internal Subcontracting, and the Production of Athletic Footwear," *Environment and Planning,* **A:**25, 1993.

Birkbeck, Chris: "Garbage, Industry, and the 'Vultures' of Cali, Columbia," in R. Bromley and C. Gerry (eds.), *Casual Work and Third World Cities,* Wiley, New York, 1978.

Bluestone, Borg, and Bennett Morrison: *The Deindustrialization of America,* Basic Books, New York, 1982.

Castells, Manual: *The Urban Question: A Marxist Approach,* MIT Press, Cambridge, 1977.

Chase-Dunn, Christopher: "Urbanization in the World-System: New Directions for Research," in Michael P. Smith (ed.), *Cities in Transformation,* Sage, Beverly Hills, Calif., 1984.

Feagin, Joe R.: "Extractive Regions in Developed Countries: A Comparative Analysis of the 'Oil Capitals,' Houston and Aberdeen," *Urban Affairs Quarterly,* **25**(4).

———— and Robert Parker: *Building American Cities: The Real Estate Game,* Prentice-Hall, Englewood Cliffs, N.J., 1990.

Friedman, John: "Where We Stand: A Decade of World City Research," in Paul Knox and Peter Taylor (eds.), *World Cities in a World-System,* Cambridge University Press, New York, 1995.

Garfinkel, I., and S. McLanahan: "The Feminization of Poverty, Nature, Causes and a Partial Cure," Institute for Poverty Discussion Paper no. 776-85, University of Wisconsin, Madison, 1985.

Gerry, Christopher: "Petty Production and Capitalist Production in Dakar," *World Development,* **6:**9/10, 1978.

Glasberg, David: *The Power of Collective Purse Strings: The Effects of Bank Hegemony on Corporations and the State,* University of California Press, Berkeley, 1989.

Gottdiener, Mark: *Planned Sprawl: Private and Public Interests in Suburbia,* Sage, Beverly Hills, Calif., 1977.

————, and Joe Feagin: "The Paradigm Shift in Urban Sociology," *Urban Affairs Quarterly,* **24**(2), 1988.

Gugler, Joseph, and William Flanagan: "On the Political Economy of Urbanization in the Third World: The Case of West Africa," *International Journal of Urban and Regional Research,* 1977.

Harvey, David: *Social Justice in the City,* Arnold, London, 1973.

Hutchinson, Ray: "The Crisis in Urban Sociology," in Ray Hutchinson (ed.), *Research in Urban Sociology,* Vol. 3, JAI Press, Greenwich, Conn., 1993.

Logan, John, and Harvey Molotch: *Urban Fortunes: The Political Economy of Place,* University of California Press, Berkeley, 1987.

McGee, T. G.: *The Southeast Asian City,* Praeger, New York, 1969.

———: "Peasants in the Cities," *Human Organization,* **32**:135–142, 1973.

Sassen, Saskia: *The Global City: New York, London, Tokyo,* Princeton University Press, N.J., 1991.

Sassen-Koob, Saskia: "Growth and Information at the Core: A Preliminary Report on New York City," in Michael Smith and Joe Feagin (eds.), *The Capitalist City,* Robert Russ and Kent Tracthe, *Global Capitalism: The New Leviathan,* State University of New York, Albany, 1990.

———: "Capital Mobility and Labor Migration," in Michael Timberlake (ed.), *Urbanization in the World Economy,* Academic Press, New York, 1985.

Smith, David A.: "The New Urban Sociology Meets the Old: Rereading Some Classical Human Ecology," *Urban Affairs Review,* **30**(3), 1995.

———: *Third World Cities in Global Perspective: The Political Economy of Uneven Urbanization,* Westview Press, Boulder, Colo., 1995.

——— and Michael Timberlake: "Conceptualizing and Mapping the World-System's City System," *Urban Studies,* **32**(2), 1995.

Smith, Michael, and Joe Feagin: *The Capitalist City,* Blackwell, New York, 1987.

Soja, Edward: "Restructuring and the Internationalization of the Los Angeles Region," in Michael P. Smith and Joe Feagin (eds.), *The Capitalist City: Global Restructuring and Community Politics,* Blackwell, New York, 1987.

Solinger, Dorothy: "Child's Urban Transients in the Transition from Socialism and the Collapse of the 'Urban Public Goods Regime,'" *Comparative Politics,* **27**(2), 1993.

Sternlieb, George, and James Hughes: "New York City," in Mattei Dogan and John Kasarda (eds.), *The Metropolis,* Vol. 2: *Mega-Cities,* Sage, Beverly Hills, Calif., 1987.

Suthuraman, S.: "The Urban Informal Sector in Africa," *International Labor Review,* **116**(3), 1977.

Wallerstein, Immanuel: *The Capitalist World-Economy,* Cambridge University Press, New York, 1979.

Walloon, John: "From Cities to Systems: Recent Research in Latin American Urbanization," *Latin American Research Review,* **14**(1), 1979.

Walton, John: "Urban Sociology: The Contributions and Limits of Political Economy," *Annual Review of Sociology,* 1993.

———: "The International Economy and Peripheral Urbanization," in N. Einstein and S. Einstein (eds.), *Urban Policy under Capitalism,* Sage, Beverly Hills, Calif., 1982.

Whyte, Martin, and William Parrish: *Urban Life in Contemporary China,* University of Chicago Press, Chicago, 1995.

Williams, Bruce: *Black Workers in an Industrial Suburb: The Struggle against Discrimination,* Rutgers, New Brunswick, N.J., 1984.

Williams, G., and E. Tumusiime-Muteble: "Capitalist and Petty Commodity Production in Nigeria: A Note," *World Development,* **6,** 1978.

Wilson, William: *The Truly Disadvantaged,* University of Chicago, Chicago, 1987.

CHAPTER 6

Beale, Calvin Lunsford, and Glen V. Fuguitt: "The New Pattern of Non-metropolitan Population Change," Center for Demography and Ecology, University of Wisconsin, Madison, Center Paper 75-22, 1975.

Bernard, Richard M., and Bradley R. Rice (eds.): *Sunbelt Cities: Politics and Growth since World War II,* University of Texas Press, Austin, 1983.

Berry, Brian Joe Lobley, and John D. Kasarda: *Contemporary Urban Ecology,* Macmillan, New York, 1977.

Duncan, Beverly: "Factors in Work-Residence Separation: Wages and Salary Workers, 1951," *American Sociological Review,* **21:**48–56, 1956.

Duncan, Otis Dudley, "Community Size and the Rural-Urban Continuum," in Paul K. Hatt and Albert J. Reiss (eds.), *Cities and Society: The Revised Reader in Urban Sociology,* Free Press, New York, 1957.

Feagin, Joe R.: *Free Enterprise City: Houston in Political-Economic Perspective,* Rutgers University Press, New Brunswick, N.J., 1989.

———: "Tallying the Social Costs of Urban Growth under Capitalism: The Case of Houston," in Scott Cummings (ed.), *Business Elites and Urban Development,* SUNY Press, Albany, N.Y., 1989.

Frey, William H.: "Migration and Metropolitan Decline in Developed Countries," *Population and Development Review,* **14:**595–628, December, 1988.

Frieden, Bernard, and Lynne B. Sagglyn: *Downtown, Inc.: How America Rebuilds Cities,* MIT Press, Cambridge, Mass., 1989.

Friedman, Judith: "Suburban Variations within Highly Urbanized Regions: The Case of New Jersey," *Research in Community Sociology,* **4:**97–132, 1994.

Frisbie, W. Parker, and John D. Kasarda: "Spatial Processes," in Neil J. Smelser (ed.), *Handbook of Sociology,* Sage, Beverly Hills, Calif., 1988.

Garreau, Joel: *Edge City: Life on the New Frontier,* Doubleday, New York, 1991.

Graham, Dawn: "Going to the Mall: A Leisure Activity for Urban Elderly People," *Canadian Journal of Aging,* **10:**345–358, 1991.

Gras, Norman Scott Brien: *Introduction to Economic History,* Harper, New York, 1922.

Guterbock, Thomas A.: "Suburbanization of American Cities of the Twentieth Century: A New Index and Another Look," paper presented at the meeting of the American Sociological Association, Toronto, 1982.

Herbers, John: *The New Heartland: America's Flight beyond the Suburbs and How It Is Changing Our Future,* Times Books, New York, 1986.

Holmes, Steven: "Budget Woes Ease for Cities in U.S., Analysts Report," *New York Times,* Jan. 8, 1995.

Jackson, Kenneth: *Crabgrass Frontier,* Oxford, New York, 1985.

Kasarda, John D.: quoted in "Social Scientists Examine Common Challenge Facing Industrial Cities," *Chronicle of Higher Education,* July 11, 1990.

Kling, Rob, Spencer Olin, and Mark Poster (eds.): *Posturban California: The Transformation of Orange County since World War II,* University of California Press, Berkeley, 1991.

LaGory, Mark, and James Nelson: "An Ecological Analysis of Growth between 1900 and 1940," *Sociological Quarterly,* **19:**590–603, 1978.

Lockwood, Charles, and Christopher Lernberger: "Los Angeles Comes of Age," *The Atlantic,* January, 1988.

Long, Harry H.: "Population Redistribution in the U.S.: Issues for the 1980's," *Population Reference Bureau,* Washington, D.C., 1983.

——— and Diana DeAre: "US Population Redistribution: A Perspective on the Nonmetropolitan Turnaround," *Population and Development Review,* **14:**433–450, 1988.

Manners, Gerald: "The Office in the Metropolis: An Opportunity for Shaping Metropolitan America," *Economic Geographic,* **50:**93–119, 1974.

McKenzie, Roderick: *The Metropolitan Community,* McGraw-Hill, New York, 1933.

Mollenkopf, John H.: *The Contested City,* Princeton University Press, Princeton, N.J., 1983.

O'Malley, Sharon: "The Rural Rebound," *American Demographics,* May, 1994.

Palen, J. John: *The Suburbs,* McGraw-Hill, New York, 1995.

Perry, David C., and Alfred J. Watkins (eds.): *The Rise of the Sunbelt Cities,* Sage, Beverly Hills, Calif., 1977.

Sale, Kirkpatrick: *Power Shift: The Rise of the Southern Rim and Its Challenge to the Eastern Establishment,* Random House, New York, 1975.

Sawyers, Larry, and William K. Tabb (eds.): *Sunbelt/Snowbelt: Urban Development and Regional Restructuring,* Oxford University Press, New York, 1984.

Schneider, Mark, and Fabio Fernandez: "The Emerging Service Economy; Changing Patterns of Employment," *Urban Affairs Quarterly,* **24:**537–555, 1989.

U.S. Bureau and the Census, U.S. Department of Commerce: "Population Profile of the U.S.: 1981," *Current Population Reports,* series P-20, no. 374, Washington, D.C., September, 1982.

Ward, Sally K.: "Trends in the Location of Corporate Headquarters, 1969–1989," *Urban Affairs Quarterly,* **29:**468–478, 1994.

Wetrogen, Signe: "Projections of the Population of States by Age, Sex, and Race, 1988 to 2010," *Current Population Reports,* 1017, October, 1988.

Zuiches, James: "Residential Preferences and Rural Population Growth," paper presented for Farmers Home Administration, U.S. Department of Agriculture, Washington, D.C., 1980.

CHAPTER 7

Anderson, Elojah: *Streetwise: Race, Class and Change in an Urban Community,* University of Chicago Press, Chicago, 1990.

Bell, Wendell: "The City, the Suburb, and a Theory of Social Choice," in Scott Greer et al. (eds.), *The New Urbanization,* St. Martin's Press, New York, 1969.

Bott, Elizabeth: *Family and Social Network,* Tavistock, London, 1959.

Boulding, Kenneth E.: "The Death of the City: A Frightened Look at Postcivilization," in Gino Germani (ed.), *Modernization, Urbanization, and the Urban Crisis,* Little, Brown, Boston, 1973.

Conforti, Joseph M.: "Newark: Ghetto or City," *Society,* **9:**20–32, September–October, 1972.

D'Emilio, John: *Sexual Politics, Sexual Communities: The Making of a Homosexual Minority in the United States 1940–1970,* University of Chicago Press, Chicago, 1983.

Drabeck, Thomas: "The Impact of Disaster on Kin Relationships," *Journal of Marriage and Family,* **37**(3):481–484, August, 1975.

——— and William Key: *Conquering Disaster: Family Recovery and Long Term Consequences,* Irvington Publishers, New York, 1984.

Duneier, Mitchell: *Slim's Table: Race, Responsibility, and Masculinity,* University of Chicago Press, Chicago, 1992.

Fischer, Claude: "Toward a Subcultural Theory of Urbanism," *American Journal of Sociology,* **80:**1319–1341, 1975.

———: *To Dwell among Friends: Personal Networks in Town and City,* University of Chicago Press, Chicago, 1982.

———: *The Urban Experience,* Harcourt Brace Jovanovich, San Diego, Calif., 1984.

Freudenburg, William R.: "The Density of Acquaintanceship: An Overlooked Variable in Community Research?" *American Journal of Sociology,* **29:**27–63, July, 1986.

Gans, Herbert J.: *The Urban Villagers,* Free Press, Glencoe, Ill., 1962.

———: "Urbanism and Suburbanism as Ways of Life: A Re-evaluation of Definitions," in J. John Palen and Karl H. Flaming (eds.), *Urban America,* Holt, Rinehart and Winston, New York, 1972.

Kornblum, William: *Blue Collar Community,* University of Chicago Press, Chicago, 1974.

LeMasters, E. E.: *Blue Collar Aristocrats,* University of Wisconsin Press, Madison, 1975.

Levine, Robert: "The Pace of Life," *Psychology Today,* October, 1989.

Milgram, Stanley: "The Experience of Living in Cities," *Science,* **167:**1461–1468, Mar. 13, 1970.

Munro, William B.: "City," *Encyclopedia of the Social Sciences,* Macmillan, New York, 1930.

Poplin, Dennis E.: *Communities,* 2d ed., Macmillan, New York, 1979.

Rainwater, Lee: "Fear and the House-as-Haven in the Lower Class," in J. John Palen and Karl H. Flaming (eds.), *Urban America,* Holt, Rinehart and Winston, New York, 1972.

Simmel, Georg: "The Metropolis and Mental Life," *The Sociology of Georg Simmel,* Kurt H. Wolff (trans.), Free Press, Glencoe, Ill., 1950.

————: *The Sociology of Georg Simmel,* Kurt H. Wolff (trans.), Free Press, Glencoe, Ill., 1950.

Srole, Leo: "Comments," in Tim Hacker, "The Big City Has No Corner on Mental Illness," *New York Times Magazine,* Dec. 16, 1979.

Suttles, Gerald D.: *The Social Order of the Slum: Ethnicity and Territory in the Inner City,* University of Chicago Press, Chicago, 1968.

Terkel, Studs: *Division Street: America,* Pantheon Books (Avon ed.), New York, 1967.

Thomas, William Isaac, and Florian Znaniecki: *The Polish Peasant in Europe and America,* 5 vols., University of Chicago Press, Chicago, 1918–1920.

Toffler, Alvin: *Future Shock,* Random House, New York, 1970.

U.S. Bureau of the Census: "Income, Poverty, and Wealth in the United States: A Chart Book," *Current Population Reports,* series P-60, no. 179, 1992.

Wacquant, Loic J. D., and William Wilson: "The Cost of Racial and Class Exclusion in the Inner City," *Annals of the American Academy of Political and Social Science,* **50:**8–25, 1989.

Webber, Melvin M.: "The Post-city Age," in J. John Palen (ed.), *City Scenes,* Little, Brown, Boston, 1977.

Whyte, William F.: *Street Corner Society: The Social Order of an Italian Slum,* University of Chicago, Chicago, 1943.

Wilson, Thomas C.: "Urbanism and Tolerance: A Test of Some Hypotheses Down from Wirth and Stouffer," *American Sociological Review,* **50**(1):117–123, 1985.

Wilson, William Julius: *The Truly Disadvantaged: The Inner City, the Underclass, and Public Policy,* University of Chicago Press, Chicago, 1987.

Wirth, Louis: *The Ghetto,* University of Chicago Press, Chicago, 1928.

————: "Urbanism as a Way of Life," *American Journal of Sociology,* **44**(10):8, July, 1938.

Young, Michael Dunlop, and Peter Willmott: *Family and Kinship in East London,* rev. ed., Penguin Books, Baltimore, 1962.

Zorbaugh, Harvey Warren: *The Gold Coast and the Slum: A Sociological Study of Chicago's Near North Side,* University of Chicago Press, Chicago, 1929.

CHAPTER 8

Alba, Richard, John Logan, and Paul Bellair: "Living with Crime: The Implications of Racial/Ethnic Differences in Suburban Location," *Social Forces,* **73,** 1994.

Anderson, Elijah: *Streetwise, Race, Class, and Change in an Urban Community,* University of Chicago, Chicago, 1990.

Battlefield, Fox: "Many Cities in the U.S. Show Sharp Drop in Homicide Rate," *New York Times,* Aug. 13, 1995.

Biderman, A. D., M. Louria, and J. Bacchus: *Historical Incidents of Extreme Overcrowding,* Bureau of Social Science Research, Washington, D.C., 1963.

Bogue, Donald J.: *Skid Row in American Cities,* University of Chicago, Community and Family Study Center, Chicago, 1963.

Calhoun, John B.: "Population Density and Social Pathology," *Scientific American,* **206:**139–148, February, 1960.

Caplow, Theodore, Howard Bahr, Bruce Chadwick, Reuben Hill, and Margaret Holmes Williamson: *Middletown Families: Fifty Years of Change and Continuity,* University of Minnesota Press, Minneapolis, 1982.

Choldin, Harvey M., and Dennis Rancek: "Density, Population Potential and Pathology: A Block Level Analysis," *Public Data Use,* **4:**19–30, July, 1974.

Cohen, Carl I., and Jay Sokolovsky: *Old Men of the Bowery: Strategies for Survival among the Homeless,* Guilford Press, New York, 1989.

Dear, Michael J., and Jennifer R. Wolch: *Landscapes of Despair: From Deinstitutionalization to Homelessness,* Polity Press, Oxford, 1987.

Dickens, Charles: *The Adventures of Oliver Twist,* Chapman S. Hall, Ltd., London, 1841.

Erikson, Jon, and Charles Wilhelm (eds.): *Housing the Homeless,* Center for Urban Policy Research, New Brunswick, N.J., 1986.

Erikson, Kai: *Everything in Its Path: Destruction of Community in the Buffalo Creek Flood,* Simon and Schuster, New York, 1976.

Fischer, Claude S.: *The Urban Experience,* Harcourt Brace Jovanovich, New York, 1976.

———: *The Urban Experience,* 2d ed., Harcourt Brace Jovanovich, New York, 1984.

———, Mark Baldassare, and Richard Ofshe: "Crowding Studies and Urban Life: A Critical Review," *Journal of the American Institute of Planners,* **41:**406–418, November, 1975.

Freedman, Jonathan: *Crowding and Behavior,* Viking, New York, 1975.

Gans, Herbert J.: *The Urban Villagers: Group and Class in the Life of Italian Americans,* Free Press, Glencoe, Ill., 1962.

Greer, Scott A.: *The Emerging City: Myth and Reality,* Free Press, New York, 1962.

Gusfield, Joseph R.: *Community: A Critical Response,* Harper & Row, New York, 1975.

Hall, Stephen S.: "The Disorganization Man, William H. Whyte: Standing on Those Corners, Watching All the Folks Go By," *Smithsonian,* February, 1989.

Hartley, Shirley Foster: *Population Quantity vs. Quality,* Prentice-Hall, Englewood Cliffs, N.J., 1972.

Hillery, G. A.: "Definitions of Community: Areas of Agreement," *Rural Sociology,* **20:**111–123, 1955.

Hunter, Albert J.: *Symbolic Communities: Persistence and Change in Chicago's Local Communities,* University of Chicago Press, Chicago, 1974.

Jankowski, Martin Sanchez: *Islands in the Street: Gangs and American Urban Society,* University of California Press, Berkeley, 1991.

Janowitz, Morris: *The Community Press in an Urban Setting,* University of Chicago Press, Chicago, 1952.

Jencks, Christopher: *The Homeless,* Harvard University Press, Cambridge, Mass., 1994.

Kasarda, John D., and Morris Janowitz: "Community Attachment in Mass Society," *American Sociological Review,* **39:**328–339, June, 1974.

Keller, Suzanne: *The Urban Neighborhood,* Random House, New York, 1968.

———: "The American Dream of Community: An Unfinished Agenda," *Sociological Forum,* **3:**167–183, Spring, 1988.

Latane, B., and J. M. Darley: *The Unresponsive Bystander: Why Doesn't He Help?* Appleton-Century-Crofts, New York, 1970.

Lee, Barret A.: "Homelessness in Tennessee," in J. A. Momenti (ed.), *Homelessness in the United States,* Greenwood Press, New York, 1989.

Lofland, Lyn: *A World of Strangers,* Basic Books, New York, 1973.

Lupo, Alan, Frank Colcord, and Edmond P. Fowler: *Rites of Way,* Little, Brown, Boston, 1971.

Lynd, Robert, and Helen Merrell Lynd: *Middletown,* Harcourt, Brace, New York, 1929.

———: *Middletown in Transition,* Harcourt, Brace, New York, 1937.

Momenti, Jamshid A. (ed.): *Homelessness in the United States,* Vol. 1: *State Surveys,* Greenwood Press, New York, 1989.

Rossi, Peter Henry: *Down and Out in America: The Origins of Homelessness,* University of Chicago Press, Chicago, 1989.

——— and James D. Wright: "The Urban Homelessness: A Portrait of Urban Dislocation," *The Annals,* **105:**137, January, 1989.

Shaw, Clifford R., and Henry McKay: *Juvenile Delinquency in Urban Areas,* University of Chicago Press, Chicago, 1942.

Siegel, Fred: "Reclaiming Our Public Spaces," *City Journal,* Spring, 1992.

Silverman, Carol J.: "Neighboring and Urbanism: Commonality versus Friendship," *Urban Affairs Quarterly,* **22:**312–328, December, 1986.

Stahura, John M., and John J. Sloane III: "Urban Stratification of Places, Routine Activities, and Suburban Crime Rates," *Social Forces,* **66**(4):1102–1118, 1988.

Suttles, Gerald: *The Social Construction of Communities,* University of Chicago Press, Chicago, 1978.

———: *The Social Order of the Slum: Ethnicity and Territory in the Inner City,* University of Chicago Press, Chicago, 1978.

Swan, James A.: "Public Responses to Air Pollution," in Joachim F. Wohlwill and Daniel H. Carson, *Environment and the Social Sciences,* American Psychological Association, Washington, D.C., 1972.

Wagner, David: *Checkerboard Square: Culture and Resistance in a Homeless Community,* Westview Press, Boulder, Colo., 1993.

Warren, Roland L.: *New Perspectives on the American Community,* Rand McNally, Chicago, 1977.

Wellman, Barry: "The Community Question: The Intimate Networks of East Yorkers," *American Sociological Review,* **84:**1201–1231, March, 1979.

Whyte, William H.: *City: Rediscovering Its Center,* Doubleday, New York, 1989.

Wilson, James: "The Urban Unease," *Public Interest,* **12:**25–39, 1968.

Wilson, William Julius: *The Truly Disadvantaged: The Inner City, the Underclass, and Public Policy,* University of Chicago Press, Chicago, 1987.

Wright, James D.: *Address Unknown: The Homeless in America,* de Gruyter, Hawthorne, N.Y., 1989.

Yanaggishita, Maciko, and F. Lands MacKeller: "Homicide in the U.S.: Who's at Risk?" *Population Today,* **23:**2, 1995.

Young, Michael, and Peter Willmott: *Family and Kinship in East London,* Penguin Books, Baltimore, 1962.

CHAPTER 9

Alba, Richard, and John Logan: "Minority Proximity to Whites in Suburbs: An Individual Level of Segregation," *American Journal of Sociology,* **98:**1388–1417, 1993.

Berger, Bennett M.: *Working Class Suburbs,* University of California Press, Berkeley, 1960.

———: "The Myth of Suburbia," *Journal of Social Issues,* **17:**38–49, 1971.

Burgess, Ernest: "The Growth of the City," in Robert Part, Ernest Burgess, and Roderick McKenzie (eds.), *The City,* University of Chicago Press, Chicago, 1925.

Choldin, Harvey, Claudine Hanson, and Robert Bohrer: "Suburban Status Instability," *American Sociological Review,* **45:**972–983, 1980.

Clark, S. D.: *The Suburban Society,* University of Toronto Press, Toronto, 1966.

Danielson, Michael N.: *The Politics of Exclusion,* Columbia University Press, New York, 1976.

Dent, David J.: "The New Black Suburbs," *New York Times Magazine,* June 14, 1992.

Denton, Nancy A., and Douglas S. Massey: "Patterns of Neighborhood Transition and a Multiethnic World: U.S. Metropolitan Areas 1970–1980," *Demography,* **28:**41–63, 1991.

Edmonston, Barry, and Thomas Guterbock: "Is Suburbanization Slowing Down? Recent Trends in Population Deconcentration in U.S. Metropolitan Areas," *Social Forces,* **66:**905–925, 1984.

Fishman, Robert: *Bourgeois Utopias: The Rise and Fall of Suburbia,* Basic Books, New York, 1987.

Fong, Timothy P.: *The First Suburban Chinatown,* Temple University Press, Philadelphia, 1994.

Frey, William H.: "Mover Destination Selectivity and the Changing Suburbanization of Metropolitan Whites and Blacks," *Demography,* **22:**223–243, May, 1985.

——— and William P. O'Hare: "Viano los Suburbinos!" *American Demographics,* April, 1993.

——— and Alden Speare: *Regional and Metropolitan Growth and Decline in the United States,* Russell Sage Foundation, New York, 1988.

Gans, Herbert J.: "Urbanism and Suburbanism as Ways of Life: A Re-evaluation of Definitions," in Arnold Rose (ed.), *Human Behavior,* Houghton Mifflin, Boston, 1962.

———: *The Levittowners,* Vintage Books, New York, 1967.

Glaab, Charles N.: "North Chicago: Its Advantages, Resources and Probable Future," reprinted in *The American City,* Dorsey, Homewood, Ill., 1963.

Godwin, Carole: *The Oak Park Strategy,* University of Chicago Press, Chicago, 1979.

Hawley, Amos H., and Basil Zimmer: *The Metropolitan Community: Its People and Government,* Sage, Beverly Hills, Calif., 1970.

Hayden, Dolores: *Redesigning the American Dream,* Norton, New York, 1984.

Herbers, John: *The New Heartland: America's Flight beyond the Suburbs and How It Is Changing Our Future,* Times Books, New York, 1986.

Jackson, Kenneth T.: *Crabgrass Frontier: The Suburbanization of the United States,* Oxford, New York, 1985.

Kasarda, John D., and George Redfearn: "Differential Patterns of Urban and Suburban Growth in the United States," *Journal of Urban History,* **2:**43–66, 1975.

Lee, Barrett A., and Peter B. Wood: "Is Neighborhood Racial Succession Place Specific?" *Demography,* **28:**37, 1991.

Leinberger, Christopher, and Charles Lockwood: "How Business is Shaping America," *Atlantic Monthly,* October, 1986.

Lemann, Nicholas: "Stressed Out in Suburbia," *The Atlantic,* November, 1989.

Lineberry, Robert L.: "Suburbia and Metropolitan Turf," *The Annals of the American Academy of Political and Social Science,* **422:**1–9, 1975.

——— and Ira Sharkansky: *Urban Politics and Public Policy,* Harper & Row, New York, 1971.

Logan, John R., "Racial Change and Racial Segregation in American Suburbs, 1970–1980," *American Journal of Sociology,* **89:**874–888, 1984.

———, and Mark Schneider: "Stratification of Metropolitan Suburbs, 1960–1970," *American Sociological Review,* **46:**175–186, 1981.

Long, Larry, and Diana De Are: "The Suburbanization of Blacks," *American Demographics,* **3:**16–21, 44, September, 1981.

Markasen, Ann R.: "City Spatial Structure, Women's Household Work and National Urban Policy," *Signs,* **5:**31, 1980.

Massen, Douglas, and Nancy Denton: "Trends in Residential Segregation of Blacks, Hispanics, and Asians," *American Sociological Review,* **52:**802–825, 1987.

Michelson, William M.: *Environmental Choice, Human Behavior, and Residential Satisfaction,* Oxford University Press, New York, 1977.

O'Hare, William, and William Frey: "Booming, Suburban, and Black," *American Demographics,* September, 1992.

——, ——, and Dan Fust: "Asians in the Suburbs," *American Demographics,* May, 1994.

Palen, J. John: *The Suburbs,* McGraw-Hill, New York, 1995.

Popenoe, David: *The Suburban Environment: Sweden and the United States,* University of Chicago Press, Chicago, 1977.

Reutter, Mark: "The Lost Promise of the American Railroad," *Wilson Quarterly,* Winter, 1994.

Riesman, David: "The Suburban Sadness," in William Mann Dobriner (ed.), *The Suburban Community,* Putnam, New York, 1958.

Saegert, Susan: "Masculine Cities and Feminine Suburbs: Polarized Ideas, Contradictory Realities," in C. Stimpson et al. (eds.), *Women and the American City,* University of Chicago Press, Chicago, 1980.

—— and Gary Winkel: "The Home: A Critical Problem for Changing Sex Roles," in Gerda Wekerle, R. Peterson, and D. Morley (eds.), *New Space for Women,* Westview Press, Boulder, Colo., 1980.

Saltman, Juliet: *A Fragile Movement: The Struggle for Neighborhood Stabilization,* Greenwood Press, New York, 1990.

Schneider, Mark, and John R. Logan: "Racial Segregation and Black Access to Local Public Resources," *Social Science Quarterly,* **63:**762–770, 1982.

Schneider, William: "The Suburban Century Begins," *Atlantic Monthly,* July, 1992.

Schnore, Leo Francis: "The Social and Economic Characteristics of American Suburbs," *Sociological Quarterly,* **4:**122–134, 1963.

——, Carolyn D. Andre, and Harry Sharp: "Black Suburbanization, 1930–1970," in Barry Schwartz (ed.), *The Changing Face of the Suburbs,* University of Chicago Press, Chicago, 1976.

Smith, Richard A.: "Creating Stable Racially Integrated Communities: A Review," *Journal of Urban Affairs,* **15:**127–128, 1993.

Spain, Daphne: "Examination of Residential Preferences in the Suburban Era," *Sociological Focus,* **21:**1–8, January, 1988.

——: "The Effects of Changing Household Composition on Neighborhood Satisfaction," *Urban Affairs Quarterly,* **21:**581–600, June, 1988.

Spectorsky, A. C.: *The Exurbanites,* Berkley, New York, 1957.

Squires, Gregory D., and William D. Velez: "Neighborhood Racial Composition and Mortgage Lending: City and Suburban Differences," *Journal of Urban Affairs,* **19:**217–231, 1987.

Stahura, John M.: "Suburban Socioeconomic Status Change: A Comparison of Models, 1950–1980," *American Sociological Review,* **52:**268–277, 1987.

——: "Changing Patterns of Suburban Racial Composition," *Urban Affairs Quarterly,* **23:**448–460, 1988.

Sternlieb, George, and Robert W. Lake: "Aging Suburbs and Black Homeownership," *The Annals of the American Academy of Political and Social Science,* **422:**105–117, 1975.

Taeuber, Karl E.: "Racial Segregation: The Persisting Dilemma," *The Annals of the American Academy of Political and Social Science,* **422:**87–96, 1975.

U.S. Bureau of the Census, Department of Commerce: "Black Movers to the Suburbs: Are They Moving to White Neighborhoods?" Special Demographic Analyses, CDS-80.4, Washington, D.C., December, 1981.

——: "Population Profile of the United States, 1981," *Current Population Reports,* series P-20, no. 374, Washington, D.C., September, 1982, table 3-6.

——: "Patterns of Metropolitan Areas and County Population Growth," *Current Population Reports,* series P-25, no. 976, Washington, D.C., September, 1989.

————: "Money, Income, and Poverty in the United States: 1988," *Current Population Reports,* series P-20, no. 166, Washington, D.C., October, 1989, table A.

Waldrop, Judith, and Linda Jacobsen: "Affluent Americans," *American Demographics,* December, 1992.

Ward, Sally: "Trends in the Location of Corporate Headquarters, 1969–1989" *Urban Affairs Quarterly,* **23:**468–478, 1994.

Warner, Sam B., Jr.: *Streetcar Suburbs,* Harvard University Press and MIT Press, Cambridge, Mass., 1962.

Weber, Adna Ferrin: *The Growth of Cities in the Nineteenth Century,* Macmillan, New York, 1899.

Weiss, Michael: *The Clustering of America,* Tilden Press, New York, 1988.

Wekerle, Gerda: "Women in the Urban Environment," in C. Stimpson et al. (eds.), *Women and the American City,* University of Chicago Press, Chicago, 1980.

Whyte, William H.: *The Organization Man,* Doubleday (Anchor), Garden City, N.Y., 1956.

Wiese, Andrew: "Neighborhood Diversity: Social Change, Ambiguity, and Fair Housing since 1968," *Journal of Urban Affairs,* **17:**107–129, 1995.

Windsberg, Morton D.: "Flight from the Ghetto: The Migration of Middle Class and Highly Educated Blacks to White Neighborhoods," *American Journal of Economics and Sociology,* **44:**411–421, 1985.

CHAPTER 10

Alba, Richard D.: "Social Assimilation among American Catholic National-Origin Groups," *American Sociological Review,* **41:**1030–1046, December, 1976.

————: "Ethnic Identity: The Transformation of White America," Yale University Press, New Haven, Conn., 1990.

Bean, Frank D., and Marta Tienda: *The Hispanic Population of the United States,* Russell Sage Foundation, New York, 1987.

Borias, George J.: *Friends or Strangers: The Impact of Immigration on the U.S. Economy,* Basic Books, New York, 1990.

Caplan, Nathan: "Southeast Asian Refugees: Achieving Independence in America," *ISR Newsletter,* Institute for Social Research, University of Michigan, Spring/Summer, 1985.

————, John Whitmore, and Marcella Chay: *The Beat People and Achievement in America,* University of Michigan, Ann Arbor, 1989.

Chadwick, Bruce, and Joseph Strauss: "The Assimilation of American Indians into Urban Society, The Seattle Case," paper presented at the meeting of the American Sociological Association, San Francisco, August, 1975.

Chen, Hsiang-Shui: *Chinatown No More: Taiwan Immigrants in Contemporary New York,* Cornell University Press, Ithaca, N.Y., 1992.

Diaz, William W.: *Hispanics: Challenges and Opportunities,* Ford Foundation, New York, 1984.

Drake, St. Clair, and Horace Cayton: *Black Metropolis,* Harcourt Brace, New York, 1945.

Ellis, David, et al.: *A Short History of New York State,* Cornell University Press, Ithaca, N.Y., 1957.

Farley, Reynolds, and William Frey, "Segregation of Whites from Blacks during the 1980's: Small Steps toward a More Integrated Society," *American Sociological Review,* **59:**23–45, 1994.

Fong, Timothy P.: *The First Suburban Chinatown,* Temple University Press, Philadelphia, 1994.

Fost, David: "American Indians in the 1990's," *American Demographics,* December, 1991.

Frey, William, and William P. O'Hare: "Viviano Los Suburbios!" *American Demographics,* April, 1993.

Gilmore, Dan, and Stephen K. Doig: "Segregation Forever?" *American Demographics,* January, 1992.

Glazer, Nathan, and Daniel Patrick Moynihan: *Beyond the Melting Pot,* MIT Press, Cambridge, Mass., 1963.

Gordon, Milton N.: *Assimilation in American Life,* Oxford University Press, New York, 1964.

Grant, Madison: *The Passing of the Great Race,* Scribner, New York, 1921.

Greer, Scott: "The Faces of Ethnicity," in J. John Palen (ed.), *City Scenes,* Little, Brown, Boston, 1977.

Guest, Avery M., and James A. Wead: "Ethnic Residential Segregation: Patterns of Change," *American Journal of Sociology,* **81:**1088–1111, March, 1976.

Guilhemin, Jeanne: *Urban Renegades,* Columbia University Press, New York, 1975.

Hernandez, Jose, et al.: *Social Factors in Educational Attainment among Puerto Ricans in U.S. Metropolitan Areas,* Aspira, New York, 1979.

Higham, John: *Strangers in the Land,* Atheneum, New York, 1977.

Hirschman, Charles: "America—Melting Pot Reconsidered," *Annual Review of Sociology,* 9.

Johnson, Michael P., and James L. Roark: *Black Masters: A Free Family of Color in the Old South,* Norton, New York, 1984.

Kasarda, John D.: "Urban Industrial Transition and the Underclass," *The Annals,* **501:**26–47, 1989.

Kitano, Harry H. L.: *Japanese Americans: The Evolution of a Subculture,* Prentice-Hall, Englewood Cliffs, N.J., 1976.

Lee, Rose Hum: "The Decline of Chinatowns in the United States," *American Journal of Sociology,* **54:**422–432, 1949.

Lee, Sharon M., and Barry Edmonston: "The Socioeconomic Status and Integration of Asian Immigrants in the 1980's," in Barry Edmonston and Jeffrey Passel (eds.), *Immigration and Ethnicity: Integrating America's Newest Immigrants,* Urban Institute Press, Washington, D.C., forthcoming.

Lieberson, Stanley: *Ethnic Patterns in American Cities,* Free Press, New York, 1963.

——— and Mary C. Waters: *From Many Strands: Ethnic and Racial Groups in Contemporary America,* Russell Sage Foundation, New York, 1988.

Loo, Chalsa M.: *Chinatown: Most Time, Hard Time,* Praeger, New York, 1991.

Massey, Douglas S., and Nancy Denton: *American Apartheid: Segregation and the Making of the Underclass,* Harvard University Press, Cambridge, Mass., 1993.

——— and Brenda P. Mullan: "Processes of Hispanic and Black Spatial Assimilation," *American Journal of Sociology,* **89:**836–873, 1984.

Moore, Joan W.: *Homeboys: Gangs, Drugs, and Prison in the Barrios of Los Angeles,* Temple University Press, Philadelphia, 1978.

Myrdal, Gunnar: *An American Dilemma,* Harper & Row, New York, 1944.

National Center for Health Statistics: "Advanced Report of Final Natality Statistics, 1986," *Vital Statistics Report,* **37**(3):9, July, 1988.

Olmstead, Frederick Law: *The Cotton Kingdom,* Modern Library, New York, 1969.

Palen, J. John: *The Suburbs,* McGraw-Hill, New York, 1995.

——— and Leo F. Schnore: "Color Composition and City Suburban Status Differences," *Land Economics,* **41:**87–91, February, 1965.

Pettigrew, Thomas F.: *Racially Separate or Together?* McGraw-Hill, New York, 1971.

Phillips, Ulrich B.: *American Negro Slavery,* Louisiana State University Press, Baton Rouge, 1969.

Portes, Alejandro, and Alex Stepick: *City on the Edge: The Transformation of Miami,* University of California Press, Berkeley, 1993.

President's Commission on Immigration and Naturalization: *Who Shall We Overcome?* U.S. Government Printing Office, Washington, D.C., 1953.

Ross, E. A.: *The Old World in the New Century,* New York, 1941.

Russell, Cheryl: "The News about Hispanics," *American Demographics,* March, 1983.

Schwarz, Philip J.: "Emancipators, Protectors, and Anomalies: Free Black Slaveholders in Virginia," *Virginia Magazine of History and Biography,* **95:**317–338, 1987.

Shipp, C. Matthew: *American Indians: The First of This Land,* Russell Sage, New York, 1989.

———— and Gary D. Sandefur: "Earnings of American Indians and Alaskan Natives: The Effects of Residence and Migration," *Social Forces,* **66**(4):994–1008, 1988.

Skerry, Peter: *Mexican Americans: The Ambivalent Minority,* Free Press, New York, 1984.

Sorenson, Annemette, Karl E. Taeuber, and Leslie J. Hollingsworth, Jr.: "Indexes of Racial Residential Segregation for 109 Cities in the United States, 1940 to 1970," *Sociological Focus,* April, 1975.

Sowell, Thomas: *Race and Economics,* McKay, New York, 1975.

Strong, Josiah: *Our Country,* rev. ed., Baker and Taylor, New York, 1891.

Taeuber, Karl E.: "Racial Residential Segregation in 28 Cities, 1970–1980," Center for Demography and Ecology, University of Wisconsin, Working Paper 83-12, 1983.

———— and Alma F. Taeuber: *Negroes in Cities: Residential Segregation and Neighborhood Change,* Aldine, Chicago, 1965.

U.S. Bureau of the Census: "Persons of Spanish Origin in the U.S.," *Current Population Reports,* series P-20, no. 329, Washington, D.C., 1978.

————: "The Black Population of the United States: March 1998," *Current Population Reports,* series P-20, no. 442, November, 1989.

————: "Population Profile of the United States, 1989," *Current Population Reports,* series P-23, no. 159, 1989.

————: "The Hispanic Population in the United States: March 1990," *Current Population Reports,* series P-20, no. 444, 1990.

————: "The Hispanic Population of the United States: March 1991," *Current Population Reports,* series P-20, no. 445, 1991.

————: "Population Projection of the United States by Age, Sex, Race, and Hispanic Origin 1993 to 2050," *Current Population Reports,* series P-25, no. 1104, Washington, D.C., 1993.

U.S. Commission on Civil Rights: "Puerto Ricans in the United States: An Uncertain Future," Washington, D.C., 1976.

U.S. Department of Health, Education, and Welfare: *Indian Health Trends and Services,* Program Analysis and Statistics Branch of the Indian Health Services, Washington, D.C., 1969.

Valdivieso, Rafael, and Cary Davis: "U.S. Hispanics: Challenges and Issues for the 1990's," *Population Trends and Public Policy,* Population Reference Bureau, Washington, D.C., December, 1988.

Van Valey, Thomas, Wade Clark Roof, and Jerome E. Wilcox: "Trends in Residential Segregation: 1960–1970," *American Journal of Sociology,* **82:**826–844, January, 1977.

Wacquant, Loic J. D., and William Julius Wilson: "The Cost of Racial and Class Exclusion in the Inner City," *The Annals,* **501:**17, 1989.

Wade, Richard C.: *Slavery in the Cities: The South, 1820–1860,* Oxford University Press, New York, 1964.

Waldrup, Judith, and Linda Jacobsen: "American Affluence," *American Demographics,* December, 1992.

Webber, Melvin M.: "The Post-city Age," in J. John Palen (ed.), *City Scenes,* Little, Brown, Boston, 1977.

White, Michael J.: *American Neighborhoods and Residential Differentiation,* Russell Sage Foundation for the National Committee for Research on the 1980 Census, New York, 1987.

Whyte, William F.: *Street Corner Society: The Social Order of an Italian Slum,* University of Chicago Press, Chicago, 1943.

Wilson, Kenneth L., and Alejandro Portes: "Immigrant Enclaves: An Analysis of the Labor Market Experiences of Cubans in Miami," *American Journal of Sociology,* **96:**(2):295–319, September, 1980.

Wilson, William Julius: *The Truly Disadvantaged: The Inner City, the Underclass, and Public Policy,* University of Chicago Press, Chicago, 1987.

Woodward, C. Vann.: *The Strange Career of Jim Crow,* Oxford University Press, New York, 1966.

Wurdock, Bud: "The Role of White Flight in Neighborhood Racial Transition," paper delivered at the April meeting of the Midwest Sociological Society, 1978.

Zhou, Min, and John R. Logan: "Return on Human Capital in Ethnic Enclaves: New York City's Chinatown," *American Sociological Review,* **54:**809–820, 1989.

CHAPTER 11

Berg, Barbara: *The Remembered Gate: Origins of American Feminism,* Oxford University Press, New York, 1978.

Berger, Bennett M.: *Working Class Suburb: A Study of Auto Workers in Suburbia,* University of California Press, Berkeley, 1960.

DeSena, Judith: *Protecting One's Turf: Social Strategies for Maintaining Urban Neighborhoods,* University Press of America, Lanham, Md., 1990.

Fava, Sylvia: "Women's Place in the New Suburbia," in Gerda Wekerle, Rebecca Peterson, and David Morley (eds.), *New Space for Women,* Westview Press, Boulder, Colo., 1980.

———: "Gender and Residential Preferences in the Suburban Era: A New Look?" *Sociological Focus,* **18,** April, 1980.

Gans, Herbert: *The Urban Villagers,* Free Press, New York, 1962.

———: *The Levittowners,* Vintage Books, New York, 1967.

Garber, Judith A., and Robyn Turner (eds.): *Gender in Urban Research,* Sage, Thousand Oaks, Calif., 1995.

Hanson, Susan, and Geraldine Pratt: *Gender, Work and Space,* Routledge, New York, 1995.

Hochschild, Arlie, and Anne Machung: *The Second Shift,* Avon Books, New York, 1989.

Horowitz, Ruth: *Honor and the American Dream: Culture and Identity in a Chicano Community,* Rutgers University Press, New Brunswick, N.J., 1979.

Jackson, Kenneth T.: *Crabgrass Frontier: The Suburbanization of the United States,* Oxford University Press, New York, 1985.

Jeffers, Camille: *Living Poor,* Ann Arbor Publishers, Ann Arbor, Mich., 1967.

Keller, Suzanne (ed.): *Building for Women,* Heath, Washington, D.C., 1981.

Liebow, Elliot: *Talley's Corner: A Study of Negro Street Corner Men,* Little, Brown, Boston, 1967.

Lofland, Lyn: "The 'Thereness' of Women: A Selective Review of Urban Sociology," in Marcia Millman and Rosabeth Moss Kanter (eds.), *Another Voice: Feminist Perspectives on Social Life and Social Science,* Anchor Books, New York, 1975.

———: "The Gendered War against Public Space: Consequences for Community," paper presented at Annual Meetings of the American Sociological Association, 1995.

Lyman, M. Stanford, and Arthur J. Vidich: "Qualitative Methods: Their History in Sociology and Anthropology," in Norman K. Denzin and Yvonna S. Lincoln (eds). *Handbook of Qualitative Research,* Sage, Thousand Oaks, Calif., 1994.

Mazey, Mary Ellen, and David R. Lee: *Her Space, Her Place: A Geography of Women,* Association of American Geographers, Washington, D.C., 1983.

Michaelson, William: *From Sun to Sun: Daily Obligations and Community Structure in the Lives of Employed Women and Their Families,* Rowman and Allanheld Publishers, Totowa, N.J., 1985.

Popenoe, David: "Women in the Suburban Environment: A U.S.-Sweden Comparison," in Gerda R. Wekerle, Rebecca Peterson, and David Morley (eds.), *New Space for Women,* Westview Press, Boulder, Colo., 1980.

Presser, Harriet: "Sally's Corner: Coping with Unmarried Motherhood," *Journal of Social Issues,* **36**(1), 1980.

Santiago, Anne M., and Merry Morash: "Strategies for Serving Latino Battered Women," in Judith A. Garber and Robyn S. Turner (eds.), *Gender in Urban Research,* Sage, Thousand Oaks, Calif., 1995.

Simmel, Georg: "The Metropolis and Mental Life," in *The Sociology of Georg Simmel,* Kurt Wolff (ed. and trans.), Free Press, New York, 1950.

Spain, Daphne: *Gendered Spaces,* University of North Carolina Press, Chapel Hill, 1992.

Suttles, Gerald D.: *The Social Order of the Slum,* University of Chicago Press, Chicago, 1968.

Wilson, Elizabeth: *The Sphinx in the City: Urban Life, Control of Disorder, and Women,* University of California Press, Berkeley, 1991.

CHAPTER 12

Allman, T. D.: "The Urban Crisis Leaves Town," *Harper's,* December, 1978.

Barry, Joseph, and John Derulany (eds.): *Yuppies Invade My House at Dinnertime,* Big River Publishing, Hoboken, N.J., 1987.

Castells, Manuel: "The Wild City," *Kapital State,* **4:**2–30, Summer, 1976.

———: *The Urban Question: A Marxist Approach,* Alan Sheridan (trans.), MIT Press, Cambridge, Mass., 1977.

Cummings, Scott (ed.): *Business Elites and Urban Development,* State University of New York, Albany, 1988.

Davis, Mike: *City of Quartz,* Vintage, New York, 1992.

Durant, Seymour B.: "Laetrile for the Urban Crisis: Planned Shrinkage and Other Dangerous Nostrums," *Journal of the Institute for Socioeconomic Studies,* **4:**68, Summer, 1979.

Fogelson, R. M.: *The Fragmented Metropolis: Los Angeles, 1850–1930,* Harvard University Press, Cambridge, Mass., 1967.

Friedan, Bernard J., and Lynn B. Sagalyn: "Downtown Mass and the City Agenda," *Society,* July–August, 1990.

Gale, Dennis: "The Back to the City Movement Revisited: A Survey of Recent Homebuyers in the Capitol Hill Neighborhood of Washington, D.C.," George Washington University, Department of Urban and Regional Planning, 1977.

———: *Neighborhood Revitalization and the Postindustrial City,* Lexington Books, Lexington, Mass., 1984.

Glazer, Nathan: "Fate of a World City," *City Journal,* Autumn, 1993.

Gottdiener, Mark: "Retrospect and Prospect in Urban Crisis," in M. Gottdiener (ed.), *Cities in Stress: A New Look at the Urban Crisis,* Sage, Beverly Hills, Calif., 1986.

Grier, George, and Eunice Grier: "Urban Displacement: A Reconnaissance," in Shirley Laska and Daphne Spain (eds.), *Back to the City,* Pergamon, New York, 1980.

Harvey, David: *Social Justice and the City,* Arnold, London, 1973.

Hauser, Philip M.: "Chicago—Urban Crisis Exemplar," in J. John Palen (ed.), *City Scenes,* Little, Brown, Boston, 1977.

Hudson, James R.: "SoHo, A Study of Residential Invasion of a Commercial and Industrial Area," *Urban Affairs Quarterly,* **20:**46–63, September, 1984.

Kasarda, John: "Urban Change and Minority Opportunities," in Paul E. Peterson (ed.), *The New Urban Reality,* Brookings Institution, Washington, D.C., 1985.

Lee, Barrett, and David Hodge: "Social Differentials and Metropolitan Residential Displacement," in J. John Palen and Bruce London (eds.), *Gentrification, Displacement, and Neighborhood Revitalization,* SUNY Press, Albany, N.Y., 1984.

Mumford, Lewis: *The Urban Prospect,* Harcourt Brace Jovanovich, New York, 1968.

National Urban Coalition: *Displacement: City Neighborhoods in Transition,* Washington, D.C., 1978.

Palen, J. John, and Bruce London (eds.): *Gentrification, Displacement, and Neighborhood Revitalization,* SUNY Press, Albany, N.Y., 1984.

——— and Chava Nachmias: "Revitalization in a Working-Class Neighborhood," in J. John Palen and Bruce London (eds.), *Gentrification, Displacement, and Neighborhood Revitalization,* SUNY Press, Albany, N.Y., 1984.

Scheider, William: "The Suburban Century Begins," *Atlantic Monthly,* July, 1992.

Schill, Michael H., and Richard P. Nathan: *Revitalizing America's Cities: Neighborhood Reinvestment and Displacement,* SUNY Press, Albany, N.Y., 1983.

Smith, Neil, and Michele Le Faivre: "A Class Analysis of Gentrification," in J. John Palen and Bruce London (eds.), *Gentrification, Displacement, and Neighborhood Revitalization,* SUNY Press, Albany, N.Y., 1984.

Spain, Daphne: "Why Higher Income Households Move to Central Cities," *Journal of Urban Affairs,* **11**(3):283–299, 1989.

——— and Shirley Laska: "Renovations Two Years Later: New Orleans," in J. John Palen and Bruce London (eds.), *Gentrification, Displacement, and Neighborhood Revitalization,* SUNY Press, Albany, N.Y., 1984.

Sternlieb, George: "The City as Sandbox," *The Public Interest,* **4**(25):14, Fall, 1971.

Tucker, William: *Insight,* Sept. 6, 1993.

U.S. Bureau of the Census: "Marital Status and Living Arrangements," *Current Population Reports,* series P-20, no. 478, Washington, D.C., 1993.

U.S. Department of Housing and Urban Development, "Residential Displacement: An Update," Office of Policy Management and Research, Washington, D.C., 1981.

Weihner, Gregory R.: "Rumors of the Demise of the Urban Crisis Are Greatly Exaggerated," *Journal of Urban Affairs,* **11**(3):225–242, 1989.

Whitt, J. Allen: "Mozart in the Metropolis: The Arts Coalition and the Urban Growth Machine," *Urban Affairs Quarterly,* **23:**15–36, September, 1987.

CHAPTER 13

Abrams, Charles: *The City Is the Frontier,* Harper & Row, New York, 1965.

Chandler, Mittie Olion: *Urban Homesteading: Programs and Policies,* Greenwood Press, New York, 1988.

Clark, Ann, and Zelma Rivin: *Homesteading in Urban U.S.A.,* Praeger, New York, 1977.

Crowe, Timothy D., and Diane L. Zuhn: "Crime Prevention through Environmental Design," *Land Development,* Fall, 1994.

Gans, Herbert J.: *The Urban Villagers,* Free Press, New York, 1962.

Gorham, William, and Nathan Glazer: *The Urban Predicament,* The Urban Institute, Washington, D.C., 1976.

Greer, Scott: *Urban Renewal and American Cities,* Bobbs-Merrill, Indianapolis, Ind., 1965.

Kemper, Vicki: "Home Equity," *Common Cause Magazine,* Summer, 1994.

Levy, Frank: *Dollars and Dreams: The Changing of American Distribution,* Russell Sage, New York, 1987.

Merry, Sally: "Defensible Space Undefended: Social Factors in Crime Control through Urban Design," *Urban Affairs Quarterly,* **16:**397–422, 1981.

Palen, J. John: *The Suburbs,* McGraw-Hill, New York, 1995.

Squires, Gregory D., and William Velez: "Insurance Redlining and the Transformation of an Urban Metropolis," *Urban Affairs Quarterly,* **23:**63–83, September, 1987.

Stegman, Michael: "The New Mythology of Housing," *Trans-Action,* **7:**55, January, 1970.

U.S. Bureau of the Census: "Households, Families, Marital Status and Living Arrangements: March, 1988," *Current Population Reports,* series P-20, no. 432, Washington, D.C., 1989.

———: "Housing in America, 1985/86," *Current Housing Report,* series H-121, no. 19, Washington, D.C., 1989.

———: "Marital Status and Living Arrangements: March, 1988," *Current Population Reports,* series P-20, no. 433, Washington, D.C., 1989.

———: "Geographical Mobility: March 1986 to March 1990," *Current Population Reports,* series P-20, no. 456, Washington, D.C., 1991.

CHAPTER 14

Aristotle: *Politics,* Book VII, B. Jowett (trans.), Modern Library, New York, 1932.

Babcock, Richard F.: "Houston: Unzoned, Unfettered, and Mostly Unrepentant," *Planning,* **48:**21–23, March, 1982.

Baker, Newman F.: *Legal Aspects of Zoning,* University of Chicago Press, Chicago, 1977.

Baldassare, Mark: *Trouble in Paradise,* Columbia University Press, New York, 1986.

———: "Suburban Support for No-Growth Policies," *Journal of Urban Affairs,* **12:**197–206, 1990.

Blazly, Edward J., and David L. Ames: "Changing Places: American Planning Policy for the 1990's," *Journal of Urban Affairs,* **14:**433, 1992.

Buder, Stanley: *Pullman,* Oxford University Press, New York, 1967.

Burby, Richard J. III, et al.: *New Community, U.S.A.,* Lexington Books, Lexington, Mass., 1976.

Choldin, Harvey M.: "Retrospective Review Essay: Neighborhood Life and Urban Environment," *American Journal of Sociology,* **48:**457–463, September, 1978.

Clapp, J.: *New Towns and Urban Policy—Planning Metropolitan Growth,* Dunellen, New York, 1971.

Crowe, Timothy, and Diane L. Zahm: "Crime Prevention through Environmental Design," *Land Development,* Fall, 1994.

Csefalvay, Zoltan, and Istvan Pomazi: "Some Problems of Inner City Revitalization: A Case Study of Budapest," paper presented at Conference on Social Theory and the Built Environment in Cross-National Perspective, Noszvaj, Hungary, June 24–27, 1989.

Danielson, Michael: *The Politics of Exclusion,* Columbia University Press, New York, 1976.

DuAny, Andres, and Elizabeth Plater-Zberk: "The Second Coming of the American Small Town," *Wilson Quarterly,* Winter, 1992.

Fallermayor, Edmund K.: *Redoing America,* Harper & Row, New York, 1968.

Fowler, E. P.: "Street Management and City Design," *Social Forces,* **66:**365–389, December, 1987.

Gans, Herbert J.: "Planning, Social: II, Regional and Urban Planning," in David Sills (ed.), *International Encyclopedia of the Social Sciences,* Crowell Collier and Macmillan, New York, 1968.

Glaab, Charles N., and A. Theodore Brown: *A History of Urban America,* Macmillan, New York, 1967.

Hayden, Dolores: *The Grand Domestic Revolution: A History of Feminist Designs for American Homes, Neighborhoods and Cities,* M.I.T. Press, Cambridge, Mass., 1981.

Heskin, Allan: "Crisis and Response: A Historical View on Advocacy Planning," *Journal of the American Planning Association,* **46:**50–63, January, 1980.

Howard, Ebenezer: *Garden Cities of Tomorrow,* Faber and Faber, London, 1902.

Jacobs, James: *The Death and Life of Great American Cities,* Random House, New York, 1961.

———— and G. Ronkin: "Housing Ownership, Control, Distribution," paper published by Soviet Academy of Sciences, 1989.

Langdon, Philip: *A Better Place to Live: Reshaping the American Suburb,* University of Massachusetts Press, Amherst, 1994.

Lemann, Nicholas: "The Myth of Community Development," *New York Times Magazine,* Jan. 9, 1994.

Martin, Wynn (ed.): *Housing in Europe,* St. Martin's Press, New York, 1984.

Mendelker, Daniel R.: *Green Belts and Urban Growth,* University of Wisconsin Press, Madison, 1962.

Merlin, Pierre: *New Towns,* Methuen, London, 1971.

Michelson, William: "Planning and Amelioration of Urban Problems," in Kent P. Schwirian et al. (eds.), *Contemporary Topics in Urban Sociology,* General Learning Press, Morristown, N.J., 1977.

Mumford, Lewis: "Home Remedies for Urban Cancer," in Louis K. Loewenstein (ed.), *Urban Studies,* Free Press, New York, 1971.

Newman, Oscar: *Defensible Space,* Macmillan, New York, 1972.

O'Marron, Dennis: "Zoning, What Is the Good of It?" in Eldridge Wentworth (ed.), *Taming Megalopolis,* Doubleday (Anchor), Garden City, N.Y., 1967.

Osborn, Frederick J.: *Green Belt Cities,* Schocken, New York, 1969.

Popenoe, David: *The Suburban Environment,* University of Chicago Press, Chicago, 1977.

————: *Private Pleasure, Public Right,* Transaction, New Brunswick, N.J., 1985.

Riis, Jacob: *The Children of the Poor,* Scribner, New York, 1892.

Robinson, C. M.: *City Planning,* Putnam, New York, 1916.

Rodwin, Lloyd: *The British New Towns Policy,* Harvard University Press, Cambridge, Mass., 1956.

Saalman, Howard: *Medieval Cities,* Braziller, New York, 1968.

Schaffer, Frank: *The New Town Story,* MacGibbon and Kee, London, 1970.

Schiesj, Martin J.: "Designing the Model Community: The Irving Company and Suburban Development, 1950–1988," in Robert Kling, Spencer Olin, and Mark Posner (eds.), *Posturban California: The Transformation of Orange County since World War II,* University of California Press, Berkeley, 1991.

Scoffham, E. R.: *The Shape of British Housing,* Godwin, London, 1984.

Silver, Christopher, and John V. Mozser: *The Separate City: Black Communities in the Urban South, 1940–1968,* University Press of Kentucky, Lexington, 1995.

Thomas, Ray, and Peter Cresswell: *The New Town Idea,* University Press, England, 1973.

Thomas, Wyndham: "Implementation: New Towns," in Derek Senior (ed.), *The Regional City,* Aldine, Chicago, 1966.

Thomlinson, Ralph: *Urban Structure,* Random House, New York, 1969.

Tunnard, Christopher: *The City of Man,* Scribner, New York, 1953.

van der Ploeg, J.: "The Rotterdam Model: Renewal without Gentrification," *Urban Innovation Abroad,* **6:**4, April, 1982.

Von Weesep, Jan, and Ronald van Kempen: "Dual Incomes and Residential Preferences: The Changing Population Profile of Large Dutch Cities," paper presented at the Conference on Social Theory and the Built Environment in Cross-National Perspective, Noszvaj, Hungary, June 24–27, 1989.

CHAPTER 15

Armstrong, Warwick, and T. G. McGee: *Theatres of Accumulation; Studies in Asian and Latin American Urbanization,* Methuen, London, 1985.

Castells, Manuel: *The Urban Question,* Alan Sheridan (trans.), MIT Press, Cambridge, Mass., 1977.

Crenshaw, Edward M: "Third World Urbanization: Dimensions, Theories, Determinants," *Annual Review of Sociology,* **11:**467–501, 1991.

Dogan, Matteri, and John D. Kasarda (eds.): *Mega-Cities: The Metropolis Era,* Vol. 2, Sage, Beverly Hills, Calif., 1988.

Firebaugh, Glenn: "Structural Determinants of Urbanization in Asia and Latin America, 1950–1970," *American Sociological Review,* **44:**195–215, April, 1979.

Frisbie, W. Parker, and John D. Kasarda: "Spatial Processes," in Neil J. Smelser (ed.), *Handbook of Sociology,* Sage, Beverly Hills, Calif., 1988, p. 654.

Gugler, Joseph: "Overurbanization Reconsidered," *Economic Development and Cultural Change,* **31:**173–189, October, 1982.

Jefferson, Mark: "The Law of the Primate Cities," *Geographical Review,* **29:**226–232, April, 1939.

Jellinek, Lea: "The Life of a Jakarta Street Trader," in Janet Abu-Lughod and Richard Hay (eds.), *Third World Urbanization,* Maaroufa Press, Chicago, 1977.

Kannappan, S.: "Urban Employment and the Labor Market in Developing Countries," *Economic Development and Cultural Change,* **33:**699–730, 1985.

Kilbridge, Maurice: "Some Generalizations on Urbanization and Housing in Developing Countries," *Urban Planning, Policy Analysis and Administration,* Harvard University Press, Cambridge, Mass., 1976.

LaGreca, Anthony J.: "Urbanization: A Worldwide Perspective," in Kent P. Schwirian (ed.), *Contemporary Topics in Urban Sociology,* General Learning Press, Morristown, N.J., 1977.

Light, Ivan: *Cities in World Perspective,* Macmillan, New York, 1983.

Linn, Johannes F.: *Cities in the Developing World,* World Book Publications, Oxford University Press, New York, 1983.

Lipton, Michael: *Why Poor People Stay Poor: Urban Bias in World Development,* Harvard University Press, Cambridge, Mass., 1977.

Myrdal, Gunnar: *Asian Drama,* Vol. 2, Pantheon, New York, 1968.

Palen, J. John: *Cities and the Future: The Urban Explosion,* United Nations, New York, 1985.

Payne, Geoffrey K.: *Urban Housing in the Third World,* Routledge and Kegan Paul, Boston, 1977.

Peattie, Lisa: "An Idea of a Good Currency and How It Grew: The Informal Sector," *World Development,* **15:**851–860, 1987.

Population Reference Bureau: "1990 World Population Data Sheet," Washington, D.C., 1990.

"Some Regional Development Problems in Latin America Linked to Metropolitanization," *Economic Bulletin Latin America,* United Nations, **17:**58–62, 1972.

Sovani, N. V.: "The Analysis of Over-urbanization," *Economic Development and Cultural Change,* **12:**113–122, January, 1964.

Thomlinson, Ralph: "Bangkok; Beau Ideal of a Primate City," *Population Review,* **16:**32–38, January–December, 1972.

United Nations Population Division: "IDCP Programme of Action," United Nations, New York, 1994.

Wallerstein, Immanuel: *The Modern World System,* Vols. 1–3, Academic Press, New York, 1979, 1980, 1989.

CHAPTER 16

Berry, Brian J. H., and John D. Kasarda: *Contemporary Urban Ecology,* Macmillan, New York, 1977.

Bose, Nirmal Kumar: *Calcutta 1964: A Social Survey,* Lakuani, Bombay, 1968.

Bradshaw, York, and Elvis Fraser: "City Size, Economic Development, and Quality of Life in China: New Empirical Evidence," *American Sociological Review,* **54:**986–1003, December, 1989.

Breese, Gerald: *Urbanization in Newly Developing Countries,* Prentice-Hall, Englewood Cliffs, N.J., 1966.

Buck, David D.: *Urban Change in China,* University of Wisconsin Press, Madison, 1978.

———: "New Municipal Plan for Beijing," *Urbanism Past and Present,* **8:**14, Summer/Fall, 1983.

Chen, Peter S. J., and Tai Ching Ling: *Social Ecology of Singapore,* Federal Publications, Singapore, 1977.

Chen, Pi-chao: "Overurbanization, Rustication of Urban-Educated Youths, and Politics of Rural Transformation," *Comparative Politics,* April, 1972.

Cubell, Harold: *Urban Development and Employment: The Prospects for Calcutta,* International Labour Office, Geneva, 1974.

Daochong, Gu, and Jiang Meiqiu: "The Impact of Urbanization on Environment in China," paper published by Department of Sociology, Peking University, Peking, 1988.

de Souza, Alfred (ed.): *The Indian City,* South Asia Books, Columbia, Mo., 1978.

Ginsburg, Norton S.: "The Great City in Southeast Asia," *American Journal of Sociology,* **60:**459, March, 1955.

———: "Urban Geography and 'Non-Western' Areas," in Philip M. Hauser and Leo F. Schnore, *The Study of Urbanization,* Wiley, New York, 1965.

Haub, Carl: "World's Largest Head Count Ever," *Population Today,* January, 1991.

Lin, Thai-Ker: "Housing Policies and Life Style," paper presented at High Rise, High Density Housing Conference, Singapore, Sept. 5–9, 1983.

MacLehose, Murray: "Modern Urban Development in Hong Kong," a paper by the Governor to the Commonwealth Society, Hong Kong, Nov. 28, 1977.

Murphey, Rhoads: *Shanghai—Key to Modern China,* Harvard University Press, Cambridge, Mass., 1953.

————: "Urbanization in Asia," *Ekistics,* **21:**8, January, 1966.

————: "The Treaty Ports and China's Modernization," in Mark Eivin and G. William Skinner (eds.), *The Chinese City between Two Worlds,* Stanford University Press, Stanford, Calif., 1974.

Nagpaul, Hans: "India's Giant Cities," in Mattei Dogan and John D. Kasarda (eds.), *The Metropolis Era,* Vol. 1, Sage, Newbury Park, Calif., 1988.

Palen, J. John: "Singapore," Chap. 20 in William van Vliet (ed.), *International Handbook of Housing,* Greenwood Press, Westport, Conn., 1990, pp. 626–640.

Population Reference Bureau: "1990 World Population Data Sheet," Washington, D.C., 1990.

Ramachandran, P.: *Pavement Dwellers in Bombay City,* Tata Institute of Social Sciences, Bombay, 1972.

Reishauer, Edwin O.: *The Japanese,* Belknap Press of Harvard, Cambridge, Mass., 1978.

Sivaramakrishnan, K. C.: "The Slum Improvement Programme in Calcutta: The Role of the CMDA," in Alfred de Sousa (ed.), *The Indian City,* South Asia Books, Columbia, Mo., 1978.

State Statistical Bureau: *Statistical Yearbook of China,* State Publishing House, Beijing, 1982.

Tien, H. Yuan: "China: Demographic Billionaire," *Population Bulletin,* Population Reference Bureau, Washington, D.C., April, 1983.

————: "The New Census of China," *Population Today,* Jan. 1, 1991.

Vogel, Ezra: *Canton under Communism,* Harvard University Press, Cambridge, Mass., 1969.

CHAPTER 17

Abu-Lughod, Janet: "Culture, Modes of Production, and the Changing Nature of Cities in the Arab World," in J. Agnew, J. Mercer, and D. Sopher (eds.), *The City in Cultural Context,* Allen and Unwin, Boston, 1984.

————: "Migrant Adjustment to City Life: The Egyptian Case," *American Journal of Sociology,* **67:**22–32, July, 1961.

————: "Testing the Theory of Social Area Analysis: The Ecology of Cairo, Egypt," *American Sociological Review,* **34:**198–212, April, 1969.

Bienen, Henry: *Tanzania: Party Transformation and Economic Development,* Princeton University Press, Princeton, N.J., 1970.

Boserup, Ester: *Women's Role in Economic Development,* St. Martin's Press, New York, 1979.

Costello, V. V.: *Urbanization in the Middle East,* Cambridge University Press, Cambridge, Mass., 1977.

Draft United Nations ICPD Programme of Action, 1994 Cairo United Nations World Population Conference, 1994.

Gbadamosi, Rasheed: "Growing Pains in Lagos," *Draper World Population Fund Report,* Spring, 1976, pp. 15–17.

Gernet, J.: "Notes sur les villes chinoises au moment de l'apogée islamique," in A. Hourani and S. M. Stern (eds.), *The Islamic City,* Bruno Cassirer, Oxford, 1970.

Goliber, Thomas J.: "Sub-Saharan Africa: Population Pressures and Development," *Population Bulletin,* **40**(1):3, 1985.

Hamdan, G.: "Capitals of the New Africa," *Economic Geography,* **40:**239–241, July, 1984.

Hance, William A.: *Population Migration and Urbanization in Africa,* Columbia University Press, New York, 1970.

Hanna, William John, and Judith Lynne Hanna: *Urban Dynamics in Black Africa,* Aldine-Atherton, Chicago, 1971.

Hassan, S. S.: "The Ecology and Characteristics of Employed Females in Cairo City," a paper presented at the Seminar on Demographic Factors in Manpower Planning in Arab Countries held at the Cairo Demographic Center, November, 1971.

Issawi, Charles: *The Economic History of the Middle East,* University of Chicago Press, Chicago, 1966.

Lapidus, Ira M.: *Muslim Cities in the Later Middle Ages,* Harvard University Press, Cambridge, Mass., 1967.

————: *Middle Eastern Cities,* University of California Press, Berkeley, 1969.

Leslie, J. A. K.: *A Social Survey of dar es Salaam,* Oxford University Press, Cambridge, Mass., 1967.

Levasseur, Alain A.: "The Modernization of Law in Africa with Particular Reference to Family Law in the Ivory Coast," in Philip Foster and Aristide R. Zolberg (eds.), *Ghana and the Ivory Coast: Perspectives on Modernization,* University of Chicago Press, Chicago, 1971, pp. 151–168.

Lowy, Michael J.: "Me Ko Court: The Impact of Urbanization on Conflict Resolution in a Ghanaian Town," in George Foster and Robert Kemper (eds.), *Anthropologists in Cities,* Little, Brown, Boston, 1974, pp. 153–177.

Marlin, John T., Immanuel Ness, and Stephen R. Collins: *Book of World City Rankings,* Free Press, New York, 1986.

Merab, Docteru: *Impressions d'Ethiopie,* Vol. 2, Leroux, Paris, 1921–1923.

Mitchell, J. Clyde: *Cities, Society, and Social Perception: A Central African Perspective,* Clarendon Press, New York, 1987.

Nelson, Vici: "How Women and Men Get By: The Sexual Division of Labour in the Informal Sector of a Nairobi Squatter Settlement," in Josef Gugler (ed.), *The Urbanization of the Third World,* Oxford University Press, Oxford, 1988, pp. 183–203.

Palen, J. John: "Urbanization and Migration in an Indigenous City: The Case of Addis Ababa," in Anthony Richmond and Donial Kubat (eds.), *International Migration,* Sage, London, 1976.

Pankhurst, Richard: "Notes on the Demographic History of Ethiopian Towns and Villages," *The Ethiopian Observer,* **9**:71, 1965.

Payne, Geoffrey K.: *Urban Housing in the Third World,* Routledge & Kegan Paul, Boston, 1977.

Pons, V. G., as cited by A. L. Epstein: "Urbanization and Social Change in Africa," *Current Anthropology,* **8**(4):277, 1967.

Population Institute: "A Continent in Crisis: Building a Future for Africa in the 21st Century," no. 8, Washington, D.C., 1983.

Population Reference Bureau: "The Food Crisis in Sub-Saharan Africa," *Interchange,* **14**:2, March, 1985.

————: "1990 World Population Data Sheet," Washington, D.C., 1990.

Robertson, H.: *South Africa,* Cambridge University Press, London, 1957.

Rondinelli, Dennis: "Giant and Secondary City Developments in Africa," in Mattei Dogan and John D. Kasarda (eds.), *The Metropolis Era: A World of Giant Cities,* Sage, Newbury Park, Calif., 1988.

Sjoberg, Gideon: "Cities in Developing and in Industrial Societies: A Cross-Cultural Analysis," in Philip M. Hauser and Leo F. Schnore, *The Study of Urbanization,* Wiley, New York, 1965.

Soja, Edward: "Spatial Inequality in Africa," *Comparative Urbanization Studies,* University of California School of Architecture and Urban Planning, Los Angeles, 1976.

Stern, S. M.: "The Constitution of the Islamic City," in A. H. Hourani and S. M. Stern (eds.), *Islamic City,* Bruno Cassirer, Oxford, 1970.

Taylor, D. R. F.: "The Concept of Invisible Towns and Spatial Organization in East Africa," *Comparative Urban Research,* **5**:44–70, 1978.

United Nations Food and Agriculture Organization: "Brief on the 1984–85 Cereal Import and Food Aid Needs for 21 African Countries," Rome, Dec. 5, 1984.

Weber, Max: *The City,* D. Martindale and G. Neuwirth (trans.), Free Press, New York, 1958.

CHAPTER 18

Abrams, Charles: "Squatting and Squatters," in Janet Abu-Lughod and Richard Hay, Jr. (eds.), *Third World Urbanization,* Maaroufa Press, Chicago, 1977.

Barraclough, Solon L.:"Rural Development and Employment Prospects in Latin America," in Arthur J. Field (ed.), *City and Country in the Third World,* Schenkman, Cambridge, Mass., 1970.

Castells, Manuel: "Squatters and the State in Latin America," in Josef Gugler (ed.), *The Urbanization of the Third World,* Oxford University Press, New York, 1988, pp. 338–366.

del Castillo, Bernal Diaz: *The True History of the Conquest of New Spain (1568),* Maurice Keatings (trans.), McBride, New York, 1927.

De Voss, David: "Mexico City's Limits," in Andrew Maguire and Janet Welsh Brown (eds.), *Bordering on Trouble,* Adler and Adler, Bethesda, Md., 1986.

Dogan, Matteri and John D. Kasarda (eds.): *Mega-Cities: The Metropolis Era,* Vol. 2, Sage, Beverly Hills, Calif., 1988.

ECLA: *Estudia Econòmico par América Latina,* United Nations, 1966.

Gakenheimer, Ralph A.: "The Peruvian City of the Sixteenth Century," in Glenn H. Beyer (ed.), *The Urban Explosion in Latin America,* Cornell University Press, Ithaca, N.Y., 1967.

Hardoy, Jorge E.: *Urbanization in Latin America: Approaches and Issues,* Doubleday (Anchor), Garden City, N.Y., 1975.

Hauser, Philip, and Robert Gardiner: "Urban Future: Trends and Prospects," in Philip Hauser et al. (eds.), *Population and the Urban Future,* SUNY Press, Albany, N.Y., 1982.

Juppenalty, Morris: *Cities in Transformation: The Urban Squatter Problem in the Developing World,* University of Queensland Press, Australia, 1970.

Laquian, Aprodicio A.: "Issues and Instruments in Metropolitan Planning," in Philip M. Hauser, *Population and the Urban Future,* SUNY Press, Albany, N.Y., 1982.

Lewis, Oscar: *The Children of Sanchez: Autobiography of a Mexican Family,* Random House, New York, 1961.

Mangin, William P.: "Mental Health and Migration to Cities: A Peruvian Case," *The Annals of New York Academy of Sciences,* **84:**911–917, 1960.

McDowell, Bart: "Mexico City: An Alarming Giant," *National Geographic,* **166:**139–144.

Mohan, R., and N. Hartline: "The Poor of Bogotá: Who They Are, What They Do, and Where They Live," World Bank Staff Working Paper no. 635, 1984.

Morris, James: *Cities,* Harcourt Brace Jovanovich, New York, 1964.

Perlman, Janice E.: *The Myth of Marginality,* University of California Press, Berkeley, 1976.

Population Reference Bureau: "1995 World Population Data Sheet," Washington, D.C., 1995.

Schnore, Leo F.: "On the Spatial Structure of Cities in Two Americas," in Philip Hauser and Leo Schnore (eds.), *The Study of Urbanization,* Wiley, New York, 1965.

Scobie, James, quoted in Glenn H. Beyer (ed.): *The Urban Explosion in Latin America,* Cornell University Press, Ithaca, N.Y., 1967.

Shook, Edwin M., and Tatiana Proskouriakoff: "Settlement Patterns in Meso-America and the Sequency in the Guatemalan Highlands," in Gordon R. Willey (ed.), *Prehistoric Settlement Patterns in the New World,* Wenner-Gren Foundation for Anthropological Research, New York, 1956, pp. 93–100.

Sjoberg, Gideon: *The Preindustrial City: Past and Present,* Free Press, Glencoe, Ill., 1960.

Smith, T. Lynn: "The Changing Functions of Latin American Cities," *The Americans,* **25:**74, July, 1968.

"Some Regional Development Problems in Latin America Linked to Metropolitanization," *Economic Bulletin for Latin America,* United Nations, New York, 1972.

St. Clair, David (trans.): *Child of the Dark: The Diary of Carolina Mariá de Jesùs,* Dutton, New York, 1962.

Theodorson, George A. (ed.): *Studies in Human Ecology,* Row Peterson, Evanston, Ill., 1961.

Turner, John F. C.: "Squatter Settlements in Developing Countries," in Daniel P. Moynihan (ed.), *Toward a National Urban Policy,* Basic Books, New York, 1970.

World Bank: "Anatomy of a Third World City," *Urban Edge,* **8**(8):4, 1984.

CHAPTER 19

Abbott, Carl: "Portland: People, Places, and Politics," *Urban Affairs,* Winter, 1995.

Charles, Michael T., and John Choon Kim (eds.): *Crisis Management: A Casebook,* Thomas, Springfield, Ill., 1988.

Danzig, George B., and Thomas L. Saatz: *Compact City: A Plan for a Livable Urban Environment,* Freeman, San Francisco, 1973.

Doxiadis, C. A.: *Ekistics:* Hutchinson, London, 1968.

Drabek, Thomas E.: *The Professional Emergency Manager,* Institute of Behavioral Science, University of Colorado, Boulder, 1987.

Edmonston, Barry, and Thomas W. Guterbock: "Is Suburbanization Slowing Down?" *Social Forces,* **62:**923, 1984.

Frey, William: "The New White Flight," *American Demographics,* April, 1994.

Greer, Ann L.: "Health Care Policy: Disillusion and Confusion," in J. Blair and D. Nachmias (eds.), *Urban Policies in Transition,* Sage, Beverly Hills, Calif., 1979.

Greer, Scott: *The Urbane View,* Oxford University Press, New York, 1972.

Herbers, John: *The New Heartland: America's Flight beyond the Suburbs and How It's Changing Our Future,* Times Books, New York, 1986.

Jacobs, Jane: *The Death and Life of Great American Cities,* Vintage–Random House, New York, 1961.

Kasarda, John D.: "The Implications of Contemporary Redistribution Trends for National Urban Policy," *Social Science Quarterly,* **69:**373–400, 1980.

Langdon, Philip: "How Portland Does It," *Atlantic,* November, 1992.

Le Corbusier: *The Radiant City,* Grossman-Orion, New York, 1967 (1933).

Machiavelli, Niccolo: *The Prince,* Dent, London, 1958.

Palen, J. John, and Daniel M. Johnson: "Urbanization and Health Status," in Ann L. Greer and Scott Greer (eds.), *Cities and Sickness,* Sage, Beverly Hills, Calif., 1983, pp. 25–29.

Rusk, David: *Cities without Suburbs,* Johns Hopkins University Press, Baltimore, 1993.

Schmandt, Henry J.: "Solutions for the City as a Social Crisis," in J. John Palen and Karl H. Flaming (eds.), *Urban America,* Holt, Rinehart and Winston, New York, 1972.

Seeley, John: "Remaking the Urban Scene: New Youth in an Old Environment," *Daedalus,* **97:**1125, 1968.

Soleri, Paolo: *Arcology, The City in the Image of Man,* MIT Press, Cambridge, Mass., 1969.

Suttles, Gerald D.: "Changing Priorities for the Urban Heartland," in J. John Palen (ed.), *City Scenes: Problems and Prospects,* Little, Brown, Boston, 1981.

U.S. Bureau of the Census: "Selected Characteristics of Travel to Work in 20 Metropolitan Areas, 1976," *Current Population Reports,* series P-23, no. 72, Washington, D.C., 1978.

Vining, Daniel R., et al.: Population Dispersal from Core Regions: A Description and Tentative Explanation of Patterns in 21 Countries," in Donald A. Hicks and Norman J. Glickman (eds.), *Transition to the 21st Century,* JAI Press, Greenwich, Conn., 1983, pp. 81–111.

Von Eckardt, Wolf: "Urban Design," in Daniel P. Moynihan (ed), *Toward a National Urban Policy,* Basic Books, New York, 1970.

Webber, Melvin W.: "The Post-city Age," *Daedalus,* **97**(4):1092, 1968.

Wolfe, Tom: *From Bauhaus to Our House,* Farrar Straus Giroux, New York, 1981.

Wright, Frank Lloyd: *The Living City,* Mentor-Horizon, New York, 1958.

NAME INDEX

SUBJECT INDEX